HANDBOOK FOR
GEORGIA MAYORS AND COUNCILMEMBERS

Fourth Edition

HANDBOOK FOR
GEORGIA MAYORS AND COUNCILMEMBERS

Edited by Betty J. Hudson and Paul T. Hardy
Published in cooperation with the
Georgia Municipal Association

Carl Vinson | Institute of Government

Photo Credits

Cover. Athens–Clarke County, City of Dahlonega, City of Fitzgerald, City of Savannah, Columbia County, Ed Jackson, Georgia Department of Economic Development, Georgia Municipal Association, Mary Stakes. *Part 1.* Athens City Hall, Georgia Municipal Association; *Part 2.* Media coverage, City of Savannah; *Part 3.* Athens–Clarke County GIS, Reid McCallister; *Part 4.* Suaawee Playscape, Georgia Municipal Association; *Part 5.* City budget books, Reid McCallister; *Part 6.* Water treatment plant, Columbia County.

Carl Vinson Institute of Government
University of Georgia
© 1974, 1984, 1993, 2005 by the Carl Vinson Institute of Government
All rights reserved. First edition 1974
Fourth edition 2005
Printed in the United States of America
10 09 08 07 06 05   1 2 3 4 5

ISBN 0-89854-220-0

Library of Congress Cataloging-in-Publication Data

Handbook for Georgia mayors and councilmembers / edited by Betty J.
    Hudson and Paul T. Hardy.—4th ed.
        p. cm.

    ISBN 0-89854-220-0
    1. Municipal government—Georgia—Handbooks, manuals, etc. I. Hudson, Betty J., 1955- II. Hardy, Paul T., 1953- III. Carl Vinson Institute of Government.

    JS451.G45H36 2005
    352.14'09758—dc22   2004063222

Contents

Foreword xv

Preface xix

Part 1 | Structure of Municipal Government

Chapter 1. Effective Relations: Roles of Mayors, Councilmembers, and Appointed Officials 3
Larry H. Hanson and James A. Calvin

Understanding and Acceptance of Roles 4

Trust and Confidence 5

Teamwork 6

Communication 7

Planning 8

Operating as a Business 8

Conclusion 9

Chapter 2. Municipal Government Structure 11
Perry Hiott, Richard W. Campbell, and David N. Ammons

Roles of Municipal Officials 11

Forms of Municipal Government 12

Professional Management in Municipal Government 20

Changing a City's Form of Government 22

Chapter 3. Municipalities: Sources and Limits of Power 25
Susan M. Pruett and J. Devereux Weeks

Georgia Constitution and State Statutes 26

Ordinances and Resolutions   32

Municipal Taxation and Spending   35

Federal Limitations   36

Chapter 4. Mayors and Councilmembers: Powers, Duties, and Relationships   41
Becky Taylor

Powers and Duties of the Mayor and Councilmembers   41

Powers and Duties of the Governing Body as a Whole   43

Relationship of the Mayor and Council to Other Municipal Boards, Commissions, and Authorities   46

Municipal Appointed Boards, Commissions, and Advisory Groups   47

Parks and Recreation Boards   47

Planning Commission and Zoning Board of Appeals   48

Municipal Authorities   50

Chapter 5. Municipal Courts   63
Ted Baggett

Procedure   63

Jurisdiction   64

Court Personnel   65

Chapter 6. Liability of Public Officials and the City   69
Susan M. Pruett

State Law   69

Federal Law   71

Indemnification, Insurance, and Risk Management   73

Chapter 7. Ethics, Conflict of Interest, and Abuse of Office   77
Susan M. Pruett and W. Edwin Sumner

Common Law– or Court-Established Standards   78

Statutory Restrictions   78

Ethics Provisions in Charters and Ordinances   85

Federal Laws   86

Suspension and Removal of Elected Officials   88

Part 2 | Public Access and Media Relations

Chapter 8. Open Meetings and Open Records   95
Kelly J. L. Pridgen

Open Meetings   95

Open Records   103

Chapter 9. Meetings Procedure, Organization, and Public Participation   117
Walt McBride and Scot Wrighton

Meetings   117

Preparing for Meetings   119

Rules of Procedure   120

Participating in Meetings   124

Public Participation   126

Chapter 10. Public Relations   131
Audrey T. Griffies and Amy Henderson

Day-by-Day Public Relations   132

Working with the Media   135

Reporting to the Public   138

Role of PR in Disaster Preparedness   142

Role of the Public Information Officer   143

Chapter 11. Conflict Resolution   145
Margaret S. Herrman

The Function of Conflict   146

Responding to Conflict: Choosing the Correct Response   147

Summing Up   157

Part 3 | Management of Municipal Government

Chapter 12. Personnel Management 161
Stephen E. Condrey and Paul T. Hardy

Employer and Employee Duties and Rights 161

Human Resource Administration 173

Chapter 13. Contracting, Purchasing, and Sale of Municipal Property 185
Perry Hiott and Paul T. Hardy

Conflict of Interest 186

Types of Contracts 187

Purchasing 195

Sale of Municipal Property 197

Chapter 14. Planning 201
Stuart H. Dorfman

Comprehensive Planning 202

The Georgia Planning Act 204

Land-Use Controls 214

Participants in the Planning Process 219

Citizen Participation 222

Planning Activities 223

Intergovernmental Coordination 227

Sources of Help 228

Chapter 15. Annexation 231
Ted Baggett

Purpose 231

Methods 232

Relationship with Counties and Service Delivery 234

Chapter 16. Environmental Management 237
James E. Kundell, Tom Gehl, and Terry A. DeMeo

Local Governments and the Environment 237

Land Use 240

Water Quality and Quantity 246

Air Quality 253

Energy Use and Conservation 254

Solid and Hazardous Waste Management 255

Conclusion 260

Chapter 17. Geographic Information Systems 265
Jan Coyne, William C. Bell, and Mary Maureen Brown

What is GIS? 266

Local Government Applications 269

Benefits and Costs of Implementing GIS 271

Part 4 | Municipal Services

Chapter 18. Electronic Government, Infrastructure, and Governance 279
John A. O'Looney

Electronic Government 279

Electronic Infrastructure 282

Electronic Governance 283

Looking Toward the Future 287

Chapter 19. Public Works and Public Utilities 291
Tom Berry, Ron Kuisis, Bill Thornton, and Charles B. Tyson

Engineering 292

Streets and Traffic Control 293

Flood Control 296

Water 298

Sewerage 300

Solid Waste 300

Electricity and Natural Gas 302

Telecommunications and Cable Television 303

Rates, Reserves, and Transfer Policies 305

Chapter 20. Building Codes and Code Enforcement   307
Mike Gleaton and Jerry A. Singer

Construction Codes and the Progressive Community   307

Uniform Codes Act   309

State Minimum Standard Codes   309

Chapter 21. Recreation and Parks   317
Daniel Hope III

Why Should Municipal Governments Provide Recreation and Park Services?   318

What Does State Law Allow a Municipality to Do?   319

What Makes Up a Recreation and Park System?   320

Who Is Responsible for Operating the Recreation and Park System?   322

What Recreation and Park Services Should Be Offered?   324

Summary   327

Chapter 22. Public Safety   329
William F. Bruton, Bobby D. Moody, Jackie T. Gibbs, Charles R. Swanson Jr., Mike Sherberger, and J. Devereux Weeks

Police Services   329

Accreditation of Law Enforcement Agencies   333

Municipal Jails   334

Fire Protection   335

Emergency Management   339

Animal Control   341

Chapter 23. The Role of Elected Officials in Economic and Downtown Development   345
Jim Finch, Billy Parrish, and Paul D. Radford

The Strategy   345

Special Knowledge   346

Economic Development Is a Process, Not an Event   347

Other Services Available from the Office of Downtown Development   354

Partners in Downtown Development across Georgia   355

Part 5 | Financing and Revenues

Chapter 24. Understanding City Finance   361
Paul E. Glick and Sabrina Wiley Cape

Financial Reporting   361

Types of Statements   362

Municipal versus Business Finances   362

Independent Audits   364

Types of Audits   365

The Uniform Chart of Accounts   366

Fund Accounting   367

Financial Reporting Following GASB Statement 34   370

Basis of Accounting   371

Chapter 25. Financial Policies   377
Sabrina Wiley Cape and Paul E. Glick

What Are Financial Policies?   377

Adopting Financial Policies: Considerations   380

How to Develop Financial Policies   381

Summary   382

Chapter 26. Municipal Revenues   385
Betty J. Hudson, Gwin Copeland, Richard W. Campbell, and J. Devereux Weeks

Revenue Patterns   385

Tax Revenue   386

Nontax Revenue   398

Evaluative Criteria   403

Chapter 27. Operations Budgeting 409
Paul E. Glick, Sabrina Wiley Cape, and Richard W. Campbell

State Legal Requirements 410

Stages of the Municipal Budgetary Process 412

Budget Values and Budget Formats 420

Budget-Related Policies 423

Chapter 28. Capital Improvements Planning 429
Sabrina Wiley Cape, Paul E. Glick, and Richard W. Campbell

Capital Improvements Plan 430

The CIP Process 432

Chapter 29. Municipal Indebtedness 441
Paul T. Hardy

Economic Considerations 441

Types of Debt Instruments 441

Fundamental Legal Restraints and Exceptions 442

Marketing Municipal Bonds 446

Part 6 | Intergovernmental Relations

Chapter 30. Service Delivery Strategies, Merger of Governmental Functions, and Consolidation of Governments 451
Harry W. Hayes, Betty J. Hudson, and Paul T. Hardy

Extraterritorial Powers 451

Service Delivery Strategies 452

Merger of Governmental Functions 460

Consolidation of Governments 460

Chapter 31. City Officials and Their Role in Georgia's Intergovernmental Relations Network 469
Gwin Copeland and Paul D. Radford

Relations with City and County Governments 469

State and Federal Advocacy 474

Relations with State Government   476
Relations with the Federal Government   482
Conclusion   485

Foreword

For more than 75 years, the Carl Vinson Institute of Government of the University of Georgia has worked to make the resources of the university available to state and local public officials. Through training, research, policy analysis, technical assistance, and other educational programs, the Vinson Institute has brought the latest techniques, practices, and legal requirements to the attention of Georgia public officials. These efforts have also provided Vinson Institute faculty and staff with the opportunity to learn the practical problems facing municipal officials across the state.

The *Handbook for Georgia Mayors and Councilmembers*, the first edition of which appeared in 1974, is published in cooperation with the Georgia Municipal Association (GMA), which provided excellent advice and suggestions toward production of the book. The handbook consolidates the experiences of Vinson Institute personnel, municipal officials, GMA staff, and others, bringing together in one volume the fundamental principles of municipal government in Georgia.

Recognizing the increasing complexity and scope of providing and funding municipal government services and the advances in technology that affect municipal governments, the editors have expanded this fourth edition of the handbook by seven chapters. This edition includes chapters on municipal courts, annexation, service delivery strategies, electronic government, state and federal relations, conflict resolution, the role of elected officials in downtown and economic development, and building codes and code enforcement. Several of the existing chapters expand and enhance the discussion of geographic information systems, capital improvements planning, environmental management, and public access and media relations.

The *Handbook for Georgia Mayors and Councilmembers* is directed toward the practical problems faced by mayors and councilmembers in their work. However, other citizens who desire a greater understanding of city government will also find this book useful.

Credit for this publication is due to many people, including—most important—the elected and appointed municipal officials in Georgia who have invited Vinson Institute staff to their communities and have shared with them their knowledge and understanding of local government.

Ms. Betty J. Hudson and Mr. Paul T. Hardy are the editors of this volume. Ms. Hudson, who made major contributions as an author, is a public service associate in the Governmental Services Division of the Vinson Institute. Mr. Hardy, who also made major contributions to the publication as an author, is a senior public service associate with the Community and Regional Development Division of the Vinson Institute.

Other Vinson Institute faculty and staff members who wrote all or portions of chapters are

> Ms. Sabrina Wiley Cape, public service assistant,
> Governmental Training, Education, and Development Division;
>
> Dr. Stephen E. Condrey, senior public service associate,
> Governmental Services Division;
>
> Ms. Jan Coyne, public service assistant,
> Community and Regional Development Division;
>
> Ms. Terry A. DeMeo, project coordinator,
> Research and Policy Analysis Division;
>
> Mr. Harry W. Hayes, public service associate,
> Governmental Services Division;
>
> Dr. Margaret S. Herrman, senior public service associate,
> Governmental Services Division;
>
> Dr. James E. Kundell, senior public service associate,
> Research and Policy Analysis Division;
>
> Mr. Walt McBride, public service assistant,
> Governmental Training, Education, and Development Division;
>
> Dr. John A. O'Looney, senior public service associate,
> Governmental Services Division; and
>
> Mr. Scot Wrighton, management development associate,
> Governmental Training, Education, and Development Division.

Others who wrote all or portions of chapters are

> Mr. Ted Baggett, associate general counsel,
> Georgia Municipal Association;
>
> Mr. Tom Berry, former city manager, City of Thomasville, Georgia;

Mr. Bill Bruton, city manager, City of Marietta, Georgia;

Ms. Gwin Copeland, associate general counsel,
Georgia Municipal Association;

Mr. Stuart H. Dorfman, senior planner, Office of Coordinated
Planning, Georgia Department of Community Affairs;

Mr. James D. Finch, assistant director, External Affairs,
Georgia Department of Community Affairs;

Mr. Tom Gehl, senior legislative associate,
Georgia Municipal Association;

Mr. Jacki Gibbs, fire chief, City of Marietta, Georgia

Mr. Mike Gleaton, assistant director, Planning and Environmental
Division, Georgia Department of Community Affairs;

Mr. Paul E. Glick, principal, Glick Consulting Group,
Orange Lake, Florida;

Mr. Tom Hall, city manager, City of LaGrange, Georgia;

Mr. Larry Hanson, city manager, City of Valdosta, Georgia;

Ms. Amy Henderson, public information manager,
Georgia Municipal Association;

Mr. Perry Hiott, director, Research and Development Services,
Georgia Municipal Association;

Dr. Dan Hope, senior public service associate,
College of Environment and Design, University of Georgia;

Mr. Ron Kuisis, telecommunication franchise coordinator;
Georgia Municipal Association;

Mr. Bobby Moody, police chief, City of Marietta, Georgia;

Mr. Billy Parrish, director, Downtown Development Office,
Georgia Department of Community Affairs;

Ms. Kelly J. L. Pridgen, Douglas County staff attorney,
former assistant general counsel,
Association County Commissioners of Georgia;

Ms. Susan Pruett, general counsel, Georgia Municipal Association;

Mr. Paul D. Radford, deputy commissioner,
External Affairs, Georgia Municipal Association;

Ms. Becky Taylor, manager, Research and Outreach Services,
Georgia Municipal Association; and

Mr. Bill Thornton, deputy director, Division of Internal Affairs,
Georgia Municipal Association.

Sincere appreciation is expressed to the staff of GMA and others who reviewed the drafts of chapters and provided valuable advice and information during the book's preparation. Among them were Mr. Jason M. Fleury, educational program specialist, Governmental Services Division, Vinson Institute; and Ms. Mycla Palmer, intern, Community and Regional Development Division, Vinson Institute.

We hope this volume contributes to a better understanding of municipal government in Georgia.

> James G. Ledbetter
> Director
> Carl Vinson Institute of Government

January 2005

Preface

This handbook is designed primarily for new or first-term Georgia mayors and councilmembers needing an introduction to municipal government.

It is also for the experienced mayor or councilmember who

- desires to refresh or enlarge his or her concept of municipal government,
- wants a brief summary of current state and federal law pertaining to cities, or
- needs a concise description of new ways to solve city problems.

The book can be useful as well to other city officials and employees and to citizens and students desiring a greater understanding of Georgia municipal government and its relationship to the state and other local governments.

Because of the tremendous diversity in city population, structure, and services, this handbook is general in nature. Moreover, it concentrates on subjects that are of interest to officials in the largest number of cities. In determining which subjects to include and the amount of coverage they should receive, the editors aimed to develop a general work of manageable length that would adequately cover the major aspects of municipal government in Georgia.

While planning and producing this book, the editors and writers were constantly reminded of the complexity of present-day municipal government. Greater demands for services, considerable federal and state regulation, the need for additional city revenues, and the rapid influx of numerous technological innovations have made governing a city far more difficult than in past years.

Therefore, as never before, Georgia mayors and councilmembers need solid grounding in the fundamentals of municipal government, the numerous and diverse services it does or can provide, and the various state and federal mandates under which cities must operate today. Moreover, city officials must be knowledgeable about a broad range of subjects and be able to converse intelligently with and question specialists who help them solve city problems. This book is intended to assist in meeting these needs.

PART 1
Structure of Municipal Government

1

Larry H. Hanson and James A. Calvin*

Effective Relations: Roles of Mayors, Councilmembers, and Appointed Officials

One of the most important aspects of effective government is defining, understanding, and accepting the appropriate roles of elected and appointed officials. In local governments today, there are three primary forms of government: the council-manager, mayor-council, and commission forms of government. Nearly half of all governments in the United States today utilize the council-manager form of government. Newly elected officials often find that their preconceived ideas about roles and responsibilities are inconsistent with their form of government. Following the excitement of a campaign and the formality of the oath of office, they find that the process of governing is not nearly as simple as it may have seemed from the outside. Questions arise as to the role of the mayor or councilmember in relation to the city manager, administrator, or clerk. It is quickly discovered that to achieve success, it is imperative that the elected officials and staff work together successfully. This recognition, in turn, creates an atmosphere of trust and respect that leads to a well-run organization that can focus on its primary mission of providing efficient, effective, and responsive public services.

Being an effective elected official is not easy. It can be exciting, challenging, and rewarding, but it can also be painful, frustrating, and controversial. Elected leadership can successfully bring a community together or it can divide a community. Newly elected officials are also challenged by unfamiliar processes, laws and mandates, and public scrutiny. They quickly learn the challenge of governing while dealing with mandatory open meetings requirements, passionate differences of opinion from individuals and organizations about what is best for the community, and

---

* This chapter includes significant material developed by Jim Calvin, former city manager and executive director of the Georgia Municipal Association.

constant attention and scrutiny from the news media. Persons previously looked upon as community leaders may be viewed with skepticism. In this most difficult environment, it is imperative to understand and clearly define the proper roles of elected officials and staff.

Experience has shown that successful cities, leaders, and model local governments generally share a common set of characteristics:

1. Elected and appointed officials share a mutual understanding and acceptance of their respective roles.
2. Trust and respect is shared between the appointed and elected officials.
3. Teamwork is demonstrated in all actions and both elected officials and appointed staff understand that success is achieved through partnership.
4. Communications are open, honest, and consistent with expectations and outcomes clearly understood.
5. Planning is a part of the organizational culture and includes visioning, goal setting, and short- and long-range planning.
6. The city is operated in a businesslike manner.

UNDERSTANDING AND ACCEPTANCE OF ROLES

In a municipal organization, it is important that elected officials and appointed staff clearly understand and agree on their respective roles as defined by their form of government, the city charter, and the code of ordinances. As a general rule, the governing body is the legislative body, and its members are the community's decision makers. Power is centralized in the elected body, which sets policy, approves a budget, and determines the tax rate. The elected body also focuses on the community's goals, major projects, and long-term considerations such as community growth, land-use development, capital improvement plans, capital financing, and strategic planning. The elected body frequently hires a professional manager to carry out the administrative responsibilities, and it supervises the manager's performance. In addition, the mayor typically presides at meetings, serves as a community spokesperson, facilitates communication and understanding between elected and appointed officials, assists the elected body in setting goals, and serves as a promoter and defender of the community. In addition, the mayor serves as a key representative in intergovernmental relations. The elected body, the mayor, and the manager constitute a policy development and management team.

The appointed official or manager is hired to serve the elected body and the community and to bring to the local government the benefits of education, training, and experience in administering local government operations and management. The manager prepares a budget for consideration; recruits, hires, and supervises government staff; serves as the elected body's chief advisor; develops and makes recommendations on various policies, procedures, and ordinances; develops capital plans; and carries out the policies as set by the governing body. Elected officials and citizens count on the manager to provide complete and objective information, present alternatives, and explain the short- and long-term consequences of proposed actions or inactions.

The art of effective government begins with a clear understanding and acceptance of clearly defined roles. It is true that there is some flexibility based upon the skills, talents, and abilities of the members, but in most cases, roles are clearly defined. It is often best to begin with a review of the city charter and code of ordinances. These documents clearly distinguish between the role of elected officials in policy development and the creation of legislation and the staff's responsibility of administration and day-to-day operation and management. In its purest form, elected officials establish policy and enact laws, and administrators carry out those policies and laws. In this sense, the government works much like a major corporation in that the board of directors sets policy and provides oversight, and the CEO carries out that policy and provides professional oversight to achieve the corporation's goals and objectives. There are times when the distinction between roles is not completely clear or when elected officials wish to exercise more influence over day-to-day operations. These problems generally lead to organizational ineffectiveness or conflict among the parties. They can also create confusion among staff members and the public at large as to who is in charge of what.

The most effective elected officials direct their time and energies to legislation, policy development, and operational oversight. Oversight can best be carried out by ensuring that the city has professional and competent staff that is responsive, resourceful, efficient, and effective. Managers and administrators need broad oversight to manage the difficult organizational, legal, personnel, financial, and other administrative matters that occur on a regular basis. Elected officials should empower their manager but hold them accountable through regular updates and performance reviews.

TRUST AND CONFIDENCE

For any local government to be successful there must be trust and confidence between the elected body and the appointed official. The manager must respect the fact that citizens have elected these representatives and that they have certain responsibilities to both the public at large as well as their oath of office. Likewise, elected officials must have respect for the form of government citizens have chosen and confidence in their manager to carry out the responsibilities of the position. Both parties share common goals to improve the quality of life, create jobs, protect the public, and provide efficient and effective services. Trust and confidence grow in an environment in which common goals and objectives are established, such goals are monitored and measured, and parties work together to achieve those goals. Elected officials can cultivate trust and foster confidence by expressing their opinions in a constructive manner when policy is being formulated, rather than after the fact or in a surprise manner at the time of implementation. Managers prefer guidance while developing policy, and such a process usually leads to an outcome satisfactory to all. A good manager will make the life of an elected official easier and more successful, while a poor manager will make the job more difficult, less rewarding, and less successful.

There are instances in which elected officials do not have confidence and trust in the manager. In such cases, it is best that the relationship be terminated. Lack of trust, conflict between staff and elected officials, and lack of confidence create an environment that has negative consequences for all parties involved.

Trust and respect also include how disagreements are handled. Both parties should first discuss issues in private and one on one. If such issues cannot be resolved, it is often best to seek the involvement of an independent third party. Regardless, disagreements or differences of opinion can and should be handled with dignity and respect.

TEAMWORK

Any team or organization is only as strong as the sum of its parts. Teams combine the strengths and efforts of all members over those of an individual member. Successful teams generally accomplish more than successful individuals. Becoming an effective team member is not always easy and often takes a great deal of effort. The following suggestions may help:

- Each person on the team has a view that is important to them and deserves to be heard.
- Some of the best ideas come from listening rather than speaking.
- Debate is healthy and can lead to a better outcome. Once debate is finished and a decision is reached, the decision of the team should be supported.

- Policy should be developed with the input and advice of staff. Likewise, staff should involve and include elected officials in policy development.
- Teams function best with a clear understanding of roles and hierarchy. Particularly, an elected official should not consult with employees other than those who report directly to the elected body.
- Effective team players never worry about credit. They focus on outcomes. They work to build consensus and "sell" their vision. By doing so, others join in. Those who focus on the end result and the outcome rather than the credit consistently achieve the most success. Effective team players also give and share credit, when appropriate.

COMMUNICATION

Successful relations between elected and appointed officials always require open, consistent, and continuous communication. Information must flow in both directions. A primary responsibility of a manager is to keep elected officials informed in a variety of ways, including the following:

- one-on-one conversations between the manager and each elected official, as needed;
- monthly reports on each department's activities, finances, capital projects, etc.;
- recommendations with justifications on issues considered by the elected body;
- special reports on politically sensitive topics or those that are of major interest and concern to residents;
- annual reports, particularly in summary form;
- minutes of meetings of boards, authorities, and commissions; and
- notifications of emergencies either in written form or by telephone.

Opportunities should be provided for regular, informal conversations and dialogue. For instance, some agendas have a designated place for a manager's report and council comments. Such opportunities should be used for constructive, open communication and can build camaraderie for all involved.

PLANNING

Businesses and organizations are successful because they utilize planning as a management tool and a guide for the future. Cities should establish a mission, a vision, and a set of organizational values. These guides can be the foundation for the development of goals and short- and long-range planning. An effective tool for short-term goal setting and planning is a planning retreat. Away from the normal distractions and focused on a common objective, individuals often respond with their best ideas. Use of a facilitator often can help with the process by focusing on the task at hand, being objective and neutral, and sharing insight based on professional experiences as well as successes and failures of other communities. Short-term goals should establish implementation steps and timelines. They should be measurable. Those that involve funding should be included in an appropriate budget or capital improvement program.

Long-range plans are often the most difficult to develop. Citizens may be shocked by long-term growth plans or future land-use patterns. However, it is necessary for local governments to work effectively, maximize use of resources, and comply with ever more challenging permit and regulatory requirements to meet the needs of future long-range planning efforts. Long-range planning is a necessity, not a luxury. Too often, attention is diverted to potholes, property taxes, and a "how-will-this-affect-me" attitude among citizens. Elected officials must stay focused on the big picture and plan if a successful future is to be achieved. In addition to patience and compromise, effective long-range planning takes time, perseverance, and fortitude. It is important that there be a planning process that does not hurry to create a failure but is patient to create a success.

OPERATING AS A BUSINESS

One of the harsh realities of local government is that it must be operated as a business. In the past, many local governments knew that they were the only provider of many services and that citizens therefore had little choice but to tolerate poor customer service. This attitude is not the case in most cities today. Elected officials should treat citizens as customers and make conscientious efforts to resolve issues. However, it must also be understood that it is beyond the financial resources and, at times, the role of the local government to solve every problem. Local governments must understand the expectations of citizens, govern and budget accordingly to meet those expectations, and avoid the trap of political expediency by trying to solve every problem by spending more money. Elected officials should also work to treat all constituents fairly and equitably and to understand that at times it is necessary to say "no."

CONCLUSION

Effective government is a partnership between elected and appointed officials. It begins with identifying and establishing the roles of all parties based on legal instruments such as the city charter and its code of ordinances and resolutions and the city's type of government. The most successful elected officials direct their talents, skills, and abilities to legislation, policy development, and operational oversight. They set clearly defined and achievable goals and objectives and make sure that appointed staff understands what will constitute success. Effective local government requires trust and confidence. Efforts must be made to develop mutual trust and respect between elected officials and staff.

Most successful organizations work as a team. It is important to appreciate the views of others, balance listening with speaking, and support the decision of the team once it is made. Remember, employees look to the elected body for leadership and direction. A divisive elected body will lead to a fractured staff and, ultimately, failure. It is important to respect the democratic process more than any single point of view. Elected officials should vote on the content of the question and not on how other members are voting, nor should they worry about the credit but focus on the desired outcome.

Elected and appointed officials must communicate with one another. Information flow, regular reports, and knowledge of problems as well as successes are critical to a well-run organization. Communication must be open, candid, and honest. Likewise, proper planning, both short range and long range, is essential for success. Successful cities operate in a fiscally responsible, businesslike manner. They focus on core initiatives that are consistent with the mission and vision of the organization and guide their progress through goals, objectives, and measurement of outcomes. Successful leaders influence outcomes and have the ability to get others not to follow them but to join them.

2

Perry Hiott, Richard W. Campbell,* and David N. Ammons*

Municipal Government Structure

A municipal government's structure, also known as its form of government, assigns formal authority among the city's key officials, both elected and appointed. To this end, municipal government structure determines the primary policy-making and executive responsibilities among municipal officials.

This chapter examines the policy-making and executive roles in the principal forms of government found in Georgia's municipalities, the trend in support of professional management in municipal government, and the process for changing a municipality's form of government in Georgia.

ROLES OF MUNICIPAL OFFICIALS

A municipality's elected officials act in a policy-making role when they pass ordinances, resolutions, and formally adopted motions. Examples of the policy-making roles include the adoption of the municipality's annual budget, its personnel policy, and its land-use plan. Such examples represent the legislative responsibility of the municipality.

The executive role typically refers to administrative responsibilities, particularly with regard to the day-to-day operations of the municipality. Examples of executive responsibility include implementation of council policies, service delivery, and personnel management.

In some municipalities, these roles—policy making and executive—are combined, whereas in other municipalities there is a clear division of these roles to provide for a separation of powers.

---

* Parts of the chapter contain or are based on work by these authors from earlier editions of the *Handbook for Georgia Mayors and Councilmembers*.

FORMS OF MUNICIPAL GOVERNMENT

In Georgia, most municipalities utilize one of three forms of government: the mayor-council "strong" mayor form, the mayor-council "weak" mayor form, and the council-manager form.[1] Additionally, several cities in Georgia refer to their legislative bodies as commissions. However, most, if not all, of these cities actually operate under another form of government and not the commission form in its purest sense.

These forms of government divide executive and policy-making roles and responsibilities between the municipality's elected officials (i.e., the mayor and council) and appointive staff. While there are distinct differences between these forms of government, there are many variations in structure and policy roles, depending on the provisions of the municipality's charter and the philosophy of the municipality.

Mayor-Council Form ("Strong" Mayor)

Under this form of government, the city council provides the primary policy role, while the mayor provides the primary executive role. This form provides for a distinguishable separation of powers between the city's executive branch (the mayor) and its legislative branch (the city council). In this regard, the separation of powers contained in the strong mayor form is similar to those found in the national and state governments, with the office of mayor being similar to the president of the United States or a governor of a state. Likewise, the council acts as a legislative body similar to the Congress of the United States or a state legislature.

Under this form, the mayor serves as the city's chief executive officer and has full responsibility for the city's daily operations. Accordingly, the mayor normally possesses the power to hire and fire department heads and other city staff, prepare and administer the city's budget, and execute contracts. The mayor may also have the authority to appoint council committees, veto legislation passed by the city council, and appoint members to city advisory boards. In some cities, particularly larger ones, the mayor may appoint a professional administrator (e.g., chief administrative officer, city administrator, etc.) to assist in carrying out the daily operations of the city.

The city council is responsible for enacting the city's policies through the adoption of ordinances and/or resolutions. While the mayor may possess the authority to veto actions of the city council, the council may possess authority to override the mayor's veto.

Mayor-Council Form ("Weak" Mayor)

Under this form of government, the mayor and city council normally share the primary policy-making role, while the mayor provides the primary executive role. However, in many cities with the weak mayor form of government, the mayor's role is primarily ceremonial, with the mayor possessing few, if any, executive powers. For example, the mayor may not have the authority to appoint council committees, develop the city's budget, or veto actions of the city council. Also, the mayor may have limited authority to appoint department heads, subject to confirmation by the city council, but may not possess the authority to fire those department heads.

In some cities, particularly larger ones, the mayor and/or city council may appoint a professional administrator (e.g., chief administrative officer, city administrator, etc.) to assist in carrying out the daily operations of the city.

In its purest sense, the weak mayor form may include one or more independently elected positions such as the city attorney, city treasurer, or even the police chief. (In Georgia, these positions are similar to the constitutional offices at the county level.) However, this practice is not common in Georgia.

Council-Manager Form

Under this form of government, the city council provides the primary policy-making role, and an appointed city manager provides the primary executive role. It combines the strong political leadership of the elected mayor and council with the strong managerial experience of an appointed local government manager.[2]

The council-manager form of government has been in existence for almost 100 years. In 1908, Staunton, Virginia, adopted an ordinance creating the first position resembling what is known today as the city manager. In 1912, Sumter, South Carolina, became the first city to adopt a charter incorporating the council-manager form of government. In Georgia, the City of Cartersville became the first municipality to adopt the council-manager form of government in 1917.[3]

The council-manager form of government was developed in the early 1900s by reformers who envisioned a more businesslike approach to municipal government. Thus, the structure of a municipality operating under the council-manager form of government is similar to the structure of a corporation. To this end, the municipality's citizens are treated as shareholders that elect a city council to serve as their board of directors. The city council establishes the city's policies, while a professional city manager, hired by the city council, is charged with implementing the council's policies. In this capacity, the city manager functions similarly to a corporation's chief executive officer, or CEO.[4]

Primary Features of the Council-Manager Form of Government

Generally, the council-manager form of government deviates from the traditional separation of powers structure that exists at the national and state levels of government (as well as in many cities and counties throughout the United States). Instead of having an elected chief executive (such as the president or governor), the council-manager form of government gives formal governmental authority to an elected city council. The city council then hires a professional city manager to oversee all administrative and executive functions.

The city manager serves at the pleasure of the city council. Accordingly, if a majority of the city council is displeased with the manager's performance, the manager can be fired, subject to applicable laws and ordinances, as well as the terms of the manager's employment agreement with the city council, if any.

In summary, the council-manager form of government combines the strong political leadership of elected officials (mayor and council) with the strong managerial experience of an appointed local government manager. Under this form of government, responsiveness to citizens is enhanced because administrative accountability is centralized in one individual, the city manager. Additionally, because political power is concentrated in the entire city council rather than in one elected official, the council-manager form may provide citizens with greater opportunities to serve their community and to influence the future of their community.

Responsibilities of the City Council

The council is the city's legislative and policy-making body. Its members are the community's decision makers. As such, the city council is responsible for enacting policies, approving the city's annual budget, setting the city's tax rate, and focusing on major projects and issues such as land-use planning, capital financing, and strategic planning. The council is also responsible for hiring the city manager, supervising the manager, and evaluating the manager's performance.

By its very nature, the council-manager form of government is designed to free the city's governing body from the administration of daily operations, allowing councilmembers to instead devote attention to policy-making responsibilities.

Responsibilities of the Mayor

In the purest sense of the council-manager form, the mayor is a member of the city council and is usually chosen from among the councilmembers on a rotation basis (similar to many county commission chairs). Under this scenario, the mayor presides at council meetings, signs official documents (e.g., ordinances, resolutions, proclamations, etc.) and serves as the city's official spokesperson. In this sense, the mayor in a council-manager city is similar to a corporation's chairman of the board.

In actual practice, however, numerous cities, including many in Georgia, now elect the mayor citywide by the voters. In these cities, the mayor may possess expanded powers, including the power to veto legislation, appoint council committees and citizen advisory boards, and/or prepare an annual report ("state of the city") to the council and the community. However, the mayor normally does not possess any day-to-day administrative responsibilities.

In summary, in the council-manager form of government, the mayor normally assumes a significant and symbolic role as a key political leader and policy developer.

Responsibilities of the City Manager

The city manager is hired by the city council to carry out the policies established by the city council and to oversee the city's daily operations. The manager should be hired solely on the basis of relevant education and professional experience.

Typically, the city manager is responsible for the following: implementing policies and programs of the city council, hiring (normally subject to council approval) and supervising the city's department heads and administrative staff, developing a proposed budget for the council's consideration, administration and enforcement all city contracts, and serving as the mayor and council's chief advisor. The city manager may also serve as the mayor and council's liaison to the city's department heads.

While the reformers who created the council-manager form of government originally sought to separate the politics of local government from its administration, this separation is now mostly symbolic. Today, most city councils desire and expect their managers to make policy recommendations that provide accurate and detailed information, possible alternatives, and any long-term impacts. The city council can then adopt, modify, or reject the manager's recommendations.

While city managers are typically hired by the city council and serve at the council's pleasure, most managers, particularly those in medium-sized and large cities, now operate under the terms of an employment agreement. Such agreements normally outline the terms and conditions of employment and separation, along with providing clear guidelines for evaluating the manager's performance.

Popularity of the Council-Manager Plan

According to the International City/County Management Association (ICMA),

- 63 percent of U.S. cities with populations of 25,000 or more have adopted the council-manager form.
- 57 percent of U.S. cities with populations of 10,000 or more have adopted the council-manager form.
- 53 percent of U.S. cities with populations of 5,000 or more have adopted the council-manager form.[5]

The council-manager form is flexible enough to address the challenges of both small cities and large ones. In Georgia, this form of government exists in cities of all sizes, including small cities such as Adel (population 5,307) and Morrow (population 4,882), medium-sized cities such as Alpharetta (population 34,854) and Valdosta (population 43,724), and large cities such as Columbus (population 178,681) and Savannah (population 131,510).

The council-manager form of government can work effectively in cities that have either large or small councils. Additionally, this form can work in cities in which councilmembers are elected at-large, by single-member districts, or by a combination of the two (see Table 2-1).

Commission Form of Government

Another form of municipal government, although it is not common in Georgia, is the commission form. Under this form of government, the councilmembers (commissioners) are typically elected at large. A chair is normally selected from among the commissioners to preside at their meetings and to serve as the ceremonial head of the commission. The chairmanship may be rotated on an annual basis. The commission form of government is unique because each elected commissioner oversees one or more departments (e.g., police, recreation, water/sewer). Thus, this form of government combines legislative and executive responsibilities.

While the commission form is used by approximately one-third of the county governments in Georgia, few, if any, municipalities in Georgia use the commission form in its purest sense. A small number of cities in Georgia, including Cedartown, Cordele, Decatur, Rome, and Toccoa, refer to their legislative body as "city commissions" rather than as "city councils." However, each of these cities operates under the council-manager form of government, and each has an appointed city manager (see Table 2-2 and Figure 2-1).

Table 2-1. *Council-Manager Form of Government*

Pro	Con
As city government has become more complex, it stresses professionalism, with administrators chosen on the basis of competence.	An appointive city manager is less responsive. Most large American cities with a population of over one million have a politically elective chief executive.
Municipal administration is segregated from city politics.	Policy rarely can be separated from its implementation and management.
The city manager gives expert advice to council, resulting in maximum efficiency and economy.	The council still has ties to the municipal bureaucracy, and potential political liabilities may outweigh the savings in cost recommended by the manager.
The city manager, as an appointed expert, can provide more impartial judgment than can the council.	The manager may lack political sensitivity, and if there is an elected mayor, the roles of the manager and mayor may be ambiguous.

Source: David L. Martin, *Running City Hall: Municipal Administration in America,* 2nd ed. Tuscaloosa: University of Alabama Press, 1990), 72.

Table 2-2. *Form of Government Comparison*

Form of Government	Primary Policymaking Role	Primary Executive Role
Mayor-council "strong" mayor	Shared by city council and mayor	Mayor (perhaps with the assistance of an appointed administrator)
Mayor-council "weak" mayor	Shared by city council and mayor	Mayor, although executive authority is sharply limited by requirement of council concurrence for various administrative actions and by the long ballot*
Council-manager	City council	Appointed manager is held accountable for executive functions by city council. In pure form, manager reports to full council rather than primarily to the mayor.

* In the "weak" mayor form, the typical existence of several separately elected administrative officers, who often operate beyond effective control of the mayor or city council, generally dilutes policy-making and executive authority.

Figure 2-1. *The Four Forms of Georgia Municipal Government (Hypothetical Organization Charts)*

Mayor-Council

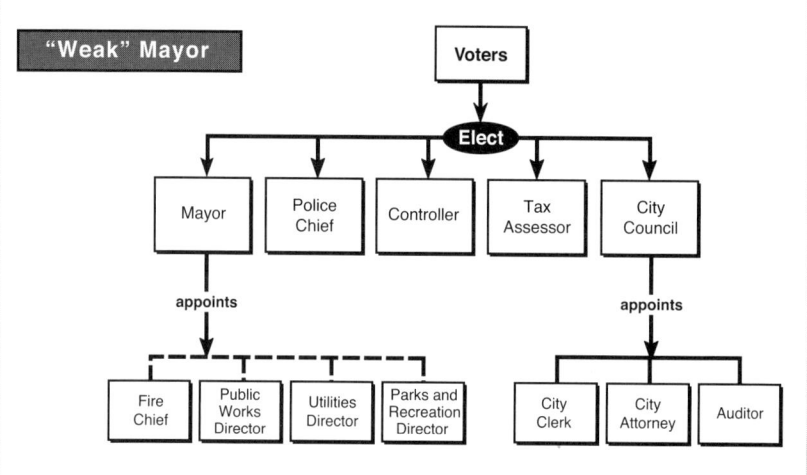

"Weak" Mayor

Voters **Elect**:
- Mayor — appoints → Fire Chief, Public Works Director, Utilities Director, Parks and Recreation Director
- Police Chief
- Controller
- Tax Assessor
- City Council — appoints → City Clerk, City Attorney, Auditor

– – – Council concurrence required for appointment of heads

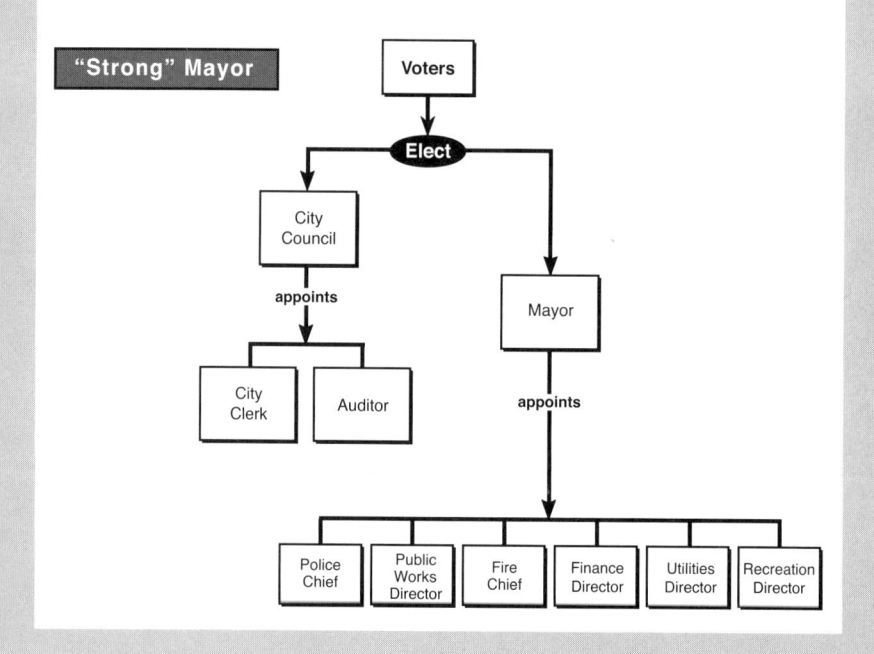

"Strong" Mayor

Voters **Elect**:
- City Council — appoints → City Clerk, Auditor
- Mayor — appoints → Police Chief, Public Works Director, Fire Chief, Finance Director, Utilities Director, Recreation Director

Commission

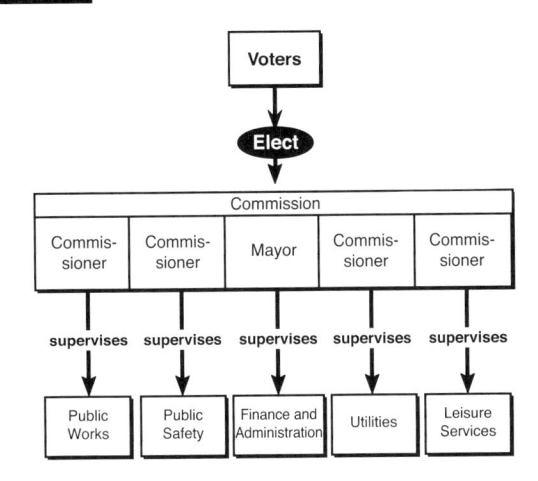

```
                        Voters
                          |
                        Elect
                          ↓
┌─────────────────────────────────────────────────────┐
│                    Commission                        │
│ Commis-  │ Commis-  │  Mayor  │ Commis-  │ Commis-  │
│ sioner   │ sioner   │         │ sioner   │ sioner   │
└─────────────────────────────────────────────────────┘
     ↓          ↓          ↓          ↓          ↓
 supervises supervises supervises supervises supervises

  Public     Public    Finance and  Utilities   Leisure
  Works      Safety    Administration          Services
```

Council-Manager

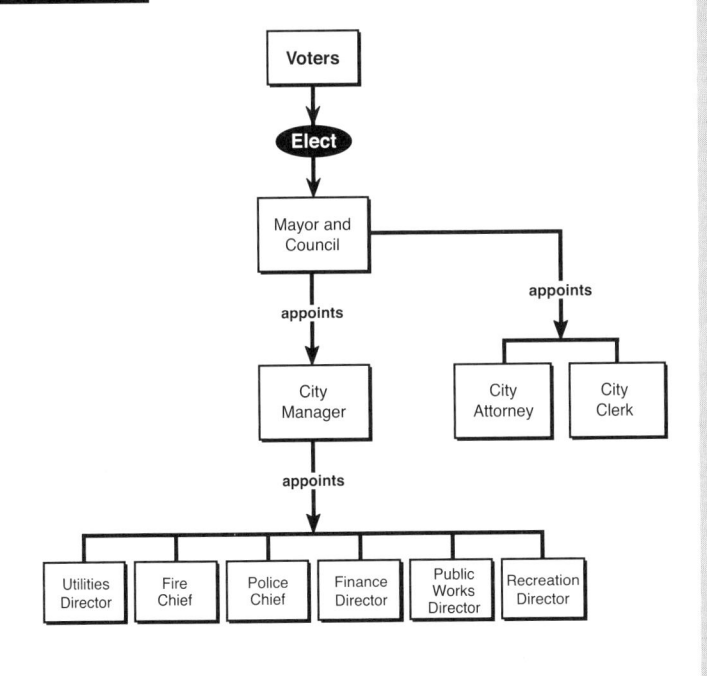

```
                   Voters
                     |
                   Elect
                     ↓
               Mayor and Council ──────────┐
                     |                  appoints
                  appoints                  ↓
                     ↓                 ┌────┴────┐
                City Manager          City      City
                     |              Attorney   Clerk
                  appoints
                     ↓
   ┌─────────┬─────────┬─────────┬─────────┬─────────┐
 Utilities  Fire    Police   Finance   Public    Recreation
 Director  Chief    Chief    Director   Works     Director
                                       Director
```

PROFESSIONAL MANAGEMENT IN MUNICIPAL GOVERNMENT

What determines whether a municipality is professionally managed? Many municipal governments claim to be professionally managed, while many others aspire to be managed in a professional manner. However, it is difficult to determine not only what constitutes professionalism, but also whether or not a municipality is actually managed in a professional manner.

A city's form of government is not an effective indicator of the city's professionalism. Professional management can exist in any of the forms of government found in Georgia. However, a municipality operating under the council-manager form of government has clearly chosen to alter fundamentally its form of government in order to instill professional management considerations in daily operations and the provision of service delivery.

The decision to employ a professional manager to serve as the municipality's chief executive is generally regarded as the ultimate desire for professionalism in municipal government. The form of government that best embraces this desire—the council-manager form—has been endorsed by the National Civic League since 1915.[6]

One theory of professional management requires the appointment of a professional manager who is granted by charter or ordinance certain executive responsibilities including, but not limited to, the following:

1. authority to appoint and remove department heads,
2. authority to develop the city's proposed annual budget for consideration by the city council, and
3. a direct reporting relationship to the full council rather than to a single elected official.

The authority of a professional manager to appoint and remove department heads is essential for effective executive control. When the mayor or city council has authority for such personnel actions, such decisions—and many resulting operational decisions—often remain political.

The manager's authority to develop the city's annual budget is necessary to increase the likelihood that management factors will be injected and considered during the preparation of the budget.

Finally, the manager should possess a direct reporting relationship with the city council. This allows the manager or administrator to provide his or her professional advice to the full governing body rather than to a single political official.

ICMA Recognition

The ICMA compiles a list of cities recognized as having professional local government management. The recognition process identifies municipalities that have established positions of professional authority by ordinance, charter amendment, or other legal means. ICMA's recognition process contains two categories: council-manager and general management. The criteria for the council-manager category requires that the city manager:

1. be appointed by a majority of the council,
2. have a direct role in both policy formulation and policy implementation,
3. have responsibility for preparation and implementation of the annual budget, and
4. have authority for the appointment and removal of at least most department heads.[7]

Among Georgia cities, 62 have been recognized as having council-manager government, while 30 cities have been recognized as being a general management government (see Tables 2-3 and 2-4).[8]

Table 2-3. *Cities in Georgia Operating under a Recognized Council-Manager Form of Government*

Adel	Columbus	Gainesville	Rockmart
Albany	Commerce	Griffin	Rome
Alma	Conyers	Hawkinsville	Savannah
Alpharetta	Cordele	Hogansville	Social Circle
Avondale Estates	Cornelia	Jesup	Statesboro
Bainbridge	Covington	LaFayette	Sylvania
Barnesville	Dallas	LaGrange	Thomaston
Baxley	Dawson	Manchester	Thomasville
Brunswick	Decatur	Marietta	Tifton
Buford	Douglas	Morrow	Toccoa
Camilla	Douglasville	Moultrie	Valdosta
Canton	Dublin	Newnan	Vildalia
Carrollton	East Point	Powder Springs	Waycross
Cartersville	Eastman	Quitman	Woodstock
Cedartown	Elberton	Rincon	
College Park	Forest Park	Riverdale	

Table 2-4. *Cities in Georgia Having a Recognized General Management Position*

Acworth	Fayetteville	Pelham
Americus	Fitzgerald	Roswell
Athens-Clarke County	Fort Oglethorpe	Smyrna
Atlanta	Garden City	St. Marys
Augusta-Richmond County	Helen	Stone Mountain
Austell	Hinesville	Sugar Hill
Blakely	Kingsland	Thunderbolt
Bowdon	Macon	Union City
Cairo	Monroe	Villa Rica
Fairburn	Peachtree City	Woodbine

CHANGING A CITY'S FORM OF GOVERNMENT

A municipality may change its form of government by amending its municipal charter through a local act of the Georgia General Assembly. The charter amendment should specify the duties and responsibilities of the city manager, the manager's relationship to the city council, and other associated requirements that involve this form of government.

Georgia law requires a local act of the General Assembly to take "(a)ction affecting the composition and form of the municipal governing authority. . . ."[9] Additionally, the Georgia Supreme Court has held that fundamental and substantive changes in city government cannot be made by a municipality under general home rule laws.[10]

Of course, a city council can establish the position of city administrator or city manager simply through the passage of an ordinance creating such a position. Such an ordinance could be abolished at any time by a subsequent city council. However, the ordinance cannot fundamentally alter the city's form of government without the city running afoul of the limitation on home rule powers contained under state law.[11]

NOTES

1. *See generally* Georgia Municipal Association, *Model Municipal Charter*, 3rd ed. (Atlanta: Georgia Municipal Association, 1994).
2. International City/County Management Association (ICMA), http://icma.org.
3. Ibid.
4. David L. Martin, *Running City Hall: Municipal Administration in America*, 2nd ed. Tuscaloosa: University of Alabama Press, 1990), 71.
5. http://icma.org.

6. National Civic League, *Model City Charter*, 8th ed. (Denver, CO: National Civic League, 2003)
7. http://icma.org.
8. Ibid.
9. OFFICIAL CODE OF GEORGIA ANNOTATED (O.C.G.A.) §36-35-6.
10. *See* Jackson v. Inman, 232 Ga. 566, 207 S.E.2d 475 (1974).
11. O.C.G.A. §36-35-6.

3

*Susan M. Pruett and J. Devereux Weeks**

Municipalities: Sources and Limits of Power

It has been stated on numerous occasions that Georgia is a Dillon's Rule state, meaning that the power of municipal corporations is limited to powers expressly granted, powers implied in or incidental to express powers, or powers "essential to the accomplishment of the declared objects and purposes of the corporation—not simply convenient, but indispensable."[1] Such rule also mandates that "[a]ny fair, reasonable, substantial doubt concerning the existence of power is resolved by the courts against the corporation, and the power is denied."[2] However, with the amendment to the Georgia Constitution in 1954 authorizing the General Assembly to allow municipal self-government and the enactment of the Home Rule Acts of 1962 and 1965, it may be more accurate to state that Georgia has a mixed system characterized by judicial attempts to determine the extent to which home rule serves as a source of power for local governments.

Georgia municipal corporations derive their power from a number of sources including the Georgia Constitution, state statutes, and local legislation. The municipal charter is a type of local legislation. Additionally, municipalities may be granted power by federal laws enacted by Congress. The U.S. Constitution, federal laws, the Georgia Constitution, state statutes, and local legislation also can limit the power of a city or direct that it act in a particular fashion. Finally, Georgia cities enact ordinances and resolutions to guide their own actions and the actions of those within the city limits.

---

* Parts of the chapter contain or are based on work by this author from earlier editions of the *Handbook for Georgia Mayors and Councilmembers*.

GEORGIA CONSTITUTION AND STATE STATUTES

The highest level of state law governing municipal corporations is the Georgia Constitution of 1983 and its amendments. It is supreme to all general and local acts of the General Assembly as well as to city ordinances and resolutions. Any legislation inconsistent with the constitution is void from the time of enactment.[3]

With respect to the sources of power for municipal corporations, some of the more significant provisions of the Georgia Constitution are the Home Rule provision, the Supplementary Powers provision, the Planning and Zoning provisions, the Eminent Domain clause, the Intergovernmental Contracts provision, the Special District clause, and the Gratuities clauses.

Home Rule

Home rule is a doctrine under which municipalities and counties are delegated the autonomy to act with respect to their own affairs and without the need for specific legislative authorization. Additionally, home rule limits the state's power to enact laws regarding matters falling within the home rule grant. The basic authority for municipal home rule in Georgia is found in the following constitutional provision: "The General Assembly may provide by law for the self-government of municipalities and to that end is expressly given the authority to delegate its power so that matters pertaining to municipalities may be dealt with without the necessity of action by the General Assembly."[4]

Acting upon this authority, the Georgia General Assembly passed specific enumerations of powers in 1962, now codified at Title 36, Chapter 34 of the Georgia Code, and it later passed the Municipal Home Rule Act in 1965. Under this statute, the governing authority of a municipal corporation has the power to adopt clearly reasonable ordinances, resolutions, or regulations relating to its property, affairs, and local government for which no provision has been made by general law and that are not inconsistent with the state constitution or any applicable charter provision.[5] General powers granted by state statute also include, among others, the power to hire employees; set duties and compensation; establish departments; authorize municipal employees and agents to serve any process or summons in the city for activity in the city that violates a law or ordinance; establish retirement, merit and insurance systems for employees; contract with other governmental agencies or political subdivisions; and grant franchises to public utilities for use and occupancy of the streets.[6]

State law allows the governing authority to set the compensation and benefits of its municipal employees and elected officials. Increases to the compensation of elected members of the governing authority cannot become effective until after the next election and cannot be adopted from qualifying date to inauguration date. Notice of intent to enact the increase must be published in the municipality's legal organ for three consecutive weeks immediately preceding its enactment.[7]

The Municipal Home Rule Act also permits amendment of the municipal charter by ordinance without the necessity of action by the legislature. Furthermore, the General Assembly cannot pass any local law to repeal, modify, or supersede any action taken by a municipal governing authority under this statute except with respect to matters reserved exclusively to the General Assembly.[8] Municipal charters may be changed by ordinance or by initiative and referendum.[9] Changes by ordinance require adoption of the ordinance at two regular consecutive meetings not less than 7 nor more than 60 days apart. Publication is also required for 3 weeks within a period of 60 days immediately before final adoption. There are limitations on changing provisions in the charter by referendum.[10] Charter amendments adopted pursuant to the Municipal Home Rule Act are not effective until a copy of the amendment and an affidavit from the municipality's legal organ attesting to publication of the notice have been filed with the secretary of state and the clerk of superior court.[11]

Subject to certain conditions and limitations, the home rule statute authorizes municipal governing authorities to reapportion the election districts from which their members are elected. Reapportionment may occur after each decennial census and is required if the annexation of additional territory to the city has the effect of denying voters residing in that territory the right to vote for members of the governing authority on substantially the same basis as other municipal electors.[12]

As previously mentioned, certain matters are reserved exclusively to the General Assembly and cannot be dealt with by ordinance. Municipal corporations cannot enact charter amendments or ordinances that do any of the following:

1. affect the composition and form of the municipal governing authority, the procedure for election or appointment to the governing authority, and the continuance or limitations on continuance in office;
2. define any criminal offense that is also an offense under Georgia law, provide for confinement in excess of 6 months, or provide for fines or forfeitures in excess of $1,000;

3. adopt a form of taxation beyond that authorized by the state constitution and laws;
4. affect the exercise of eminent domain;
5. expand regulation over business activities regulated by the Public Service Commission beyond that authorized by charter, general law, or the state constitution;
6. affect the jurisdiction of any court; or
7. change charter provisions relating to the establishment and operation of an independent school system.[13]

Another important constitutional provision granting specific powers to cities is the Supplementary Powers provision, also known as Amendment 19 for its position on the ballot in 1972 when ratified by the voters as an amendment to the Georgia Constitution. This provision spells out supplementary powers that municipalities and counties may exercise in addition to and supplementary to powers possessed by virtue of their charter or other local legislation. Specifically mentioned and included are the powers to provide police and fire services, solid waste collection and disposal, public health facilities and services, street and road construction and maintenance, parks and recreational programs and facilities, storm water and sewage collection and disposal systems, water treatment and distribution, public housing, public transportation, and libraries.[14] This provision also states that, unless otherwise provided by law, no county may provide services within a municipality except by contract with the municipality. Likewise, unless otherwise provided by law, no municipality may provide services outside its boundaries except by contract with the affected county or municipality.[15]

Notably, municipal charter provisions are laws recognized by the courts as empowering municipalities to act pursuant to those provisions even in the absence of a contract with the county.[16] However, intergovernmental agreements between cities and counties may limit the ability of municipalities to provide extraterritorial services, depending on the terms of the agreement.

The Supplementary Powers provision also states that while the General Assembly may enact general laws on the subject matters addressed by the provision and can regulate, restrict, or limit the exercise of such powers, the General Assembly may not withdraw any such powers.[17]

Zoning

One of the most controversial duties undertaken by local governing authorities is zoning. The Georgia Constitution authorizes cities to adopt plans and exercise the power of zoning, but it allows the General Assembly to enact general laws establishing procedures for the exercise of that power, which the General Assembly has done (see Chapter 14).[18] In addition, the General Assembly reserves the power to provide by law for "[r]estrictions upon land use in order to protect and preserve the natural resources, environment, and vital areas of this state. . . ."[19]

Eminent Domain

Although sometimes unpopular, eminent domain or condemnation is an important power of local governments. "The governing authority of each county and of each municipality may exercise the power of eminent domain for any public purpose."[20] Landfills, sewer lines, and jails are just a few of the public services provided by local governments that people rarely want located near them. However, both the U.S. Constitution and the Georgia Constitution require the payment of just and adequate compensation for the taking of private property for public purposes.[21] Thus, the exercise of eminent domain contains three basic requirements: the finding of a public purpose; the provision of just and adequate compensation to the property owner; and compliance with the statutory notice and requirements for how to proceed.[22]

Intergovernmental Contracts

The Georgia Constitution authorizes the state, cities, counties, and other political subdivisions to enter into intergovernmental agreements with one another or public agencies, corporations, or authorities for a period not exceeding 50 years.[23] Such contracts must deal with activities, services, or facilities that the contracting parties are authorized by law to undertake or provide. Intergovernmental contracts are frequently used to facilitate financing deals in conjunction with downtown development authorities, urban redevelopment authorities, or other types of authorities.[24] In addition, intergovernmental contracts are utilized by cities and counties to provide services and facilities jointly, to provide services within the jurisdiction of another local government, and to act on a regional basis.

Special Districts

The constitutional provision on special districts authorizes the creation of special districts for the provision of local government services within such special districts, and fees, taxes, and assessments may be levied and collected within such districts to pay for such services and to construct and maintain facilities for such services.[25] Special districts can be established by a general state law that directly creates the district, by a general law requiring the creation of districts under conditions specified by general law, or by a municipal or county ordinance or resolution. An example of a special district created by general state law is the local option sales tax (LOST) statute that establishes 159 special districts in Georgia for the purpose of levying the LOST.[26] Although the tax is a local option activated by local referendum, the special district is established by general state law, and the boundaries of the special districts in this instance are the same as the boundaries of Georgia's 159 counties. As another example, the excise tax on hotel and motel rooms is also a special district tax established by general state law.[27] However, for the purpose of this tax, the boundary of each special district is the corporate limits of the municipality when the tax is levied by a municipality and only the unincorporated area when the tax is levied by a county. An example of a special district created by local ordinance is a city business improvement district[28] or a tax allocation district.[29] Special service districts also are sometimes used by counties to provide services exclusively to or primarily for the benefit of residents of the unincorporated area.[30]

Typically, the services or facilities provided in a special service district are funded by special taxes, fees, or assessments levied within the special service district. To facilitate the financing of improvements within a special service district, the Georgia Constitution authorizes municipalities to incur debt on behalf of a special service district when the municipality, at the time of or prior to incurring the debt, provides for the assessment and collection of an annual tax within the special service district in an amount sufficient to pay the principal and interest within 30 years.[31] However, the amount of debt incurred, when taken together with all other outstanding debt of the municipality, cannot exceed 10 percent of the assessed value of all taxable property within the municipality, and a referendum must be held in which the qualified voters of the special district consent to incurring debt for the special district.[32]

Gratuities

Two important constitutional provisions limit the power of cities to make contributions of public funds or property. The first one states that "the General Assembly shall not have the power to grant any donation or gratuity or to forgive any debt or obligation owing to the public."[33] The Georgia Supreme Court has held that this section applies to municipalities[34] and that its purpose is to prevent the "extravagant outlay" of municipal funds.[35]

In a case involving a county contract with a private company for fire protection services, the court applied this provision. It held that local governments may furnish fire stations and firefighting equipment for a private company's use in providing fire protection. The court reasoned that no gratuity or donation is involved when the local government receives substantial benefits in return for the use of its property.[36]

Other decisions have acknowledged the principle that whether a municipality makes a donation or gratuity depends upon the benefits received by the city. A municipality cannot make a gift that conveys government property to a private party. For example, local government donations to a chamber of commerce, freight bureau, and a convention and tourist bureau have been held to violate this constitutional provision. In these cases, the local governments had not entered into a contract to receive benefits from the other party.[37]

It has likewise been suggested that it is impermissible to expend public funds for the purpose of conducting a straw poll or public opinion referendum without statutory authority.[38] The basis for this opinion is the constitutional provision that authorizes cities and counties to expend public funds to perform public services or functions authorized by the state constitution or by law.[39] Because the expenditure of city or county funds must be authorized by some legislative act or constitutional provision, the expenditure of funds for a referendum is proper only if it is authorized such as in the case of certain annexations[40] or to allow sales of distilled spirits.[41]

The constitutional provision prohibiting gratuities by municipal corporations provides that "[t]he General Assembly shall not authorize any county, municipality, or other political subdivision of this state, through taxation, contribution, or otherwise, to appropriate money for or to lend its credit to any person or to any nonpublic corporation or association except for purely charitable purposes."[42] Although this provision contains an exception allowing the expenditure of money for purely charitable purposes, the authority to make charitable contributions must be specifically authorized by the General Assembly in a general statute or in local legislation. The authority to spend for general welfare purposes is not enough.

Cities and counties are also prohibited from directly or indirectly making contributions or engaging in any activity to influence the outcome of an election or referendum. This prohibition extends to those acting on behalf of the city or county.[43]

Other Georgia Constitutional Provisions

The 1945 and the 1976 Georgia Constitutions recognized two types of constitutional amendments: general constitutional amendments submitted to the people of the entire state and local constitutional amendments submitted only to the people of the political subdivisions directly affected.[44] When the 1983 constitution was being drafted, the decision was made to prohibit future local constitutional amendments but to provide a mechanism for continuing those already in existence.[45] If no action was taken to continue a local constitutional amendment, it stood repealed no later than July 1, 1987. Local constitutional amendments continued in force may be repealed but may not be amended.[46] All local constitutional amendments that have been continued are recognized by the courts as having constitutional status.[47]

Population acts are laws that classify and apply to political subdivisions based on population and are generally prohibited by the Georgia Constitution.[48] However, legislation that repeals a population act or that amends a population act to allow it to continue covering political subdivisions already covered by such act is not considered an impermissible "population act" and is allowed.[49]

General law takes precedence over a local act.[50] A general law is one having general application or at least applying to all municipalities and/or all counties. A local act is one that deals only with a particular city or county. Municipal charters are an example of local legislation. Provisions in municipal charters may be more restrictive of the city's power than general law but may not be more expansive.

Local Legislation

Municipalities in Georgia—whether called a "city," "town," "municipality," or "village"—are creatures of state law. They are created by the General Assembly when it adopts a municipal charter. The municipal charter sets forth certain information such as the name and corporate limits of the municipality. It also enumerates the type of government the city will have and sets forth certain powers of the city governing body and elected officials. The charter may also address administrative affairs of the city, municipal finances, the municipal court, and a variety of other topics.

Although the municipal charter is originally adopted by the General Assembly, municipalities may, pursuant to the Municipal Home Rule Act, amend their charter as previously discussed.

ORDINANCES AND RESOLUTIONS

Enacting ordinances and resolutions is a major responsibility of mayors and councilmembers. Equally important, however, is ensuring that members of the public have access to the enactments of the governing body.

Codification

Georgia law requires that each municipality provide for the general codification of all of the ordinances and resolutions of the municipality having the force and effect of law.[51] The codification, and each ordinance and amendment to the general codification, is to be adopted by the local governing authority, published promptly, and made available to the public at a reasonable price fixed by the local governing authority. The codification is to be made available by posting it on the Internet or by furnishing a copy to the state law library. Additionally, in counties that have established a county law library, a copy must be furnished to the county law library. Cities having a population of 5,000 or less according to the most recent decennial census have the option of having their ordinances and resolutions compiled rather than codified. Such a compilation must include, at a minimum, the ordinances and resolutions arranged in a logical manner, such as by date, and preferably should include an index or other finding aids.

An important reason to codify a city's ordinances is that Georgia statutory law allows courts to take judicial notice of a certified copy of any ordinance or resolution included within the codification required by Section 36-80-19 of the *Official Code of Georgia Annotated*. Any such certified copy is considered self-authenticating and is admissible as proof of any such ordinance or resolution before any court or administrative body.[52]

Format

For the most part, Georgia statutory law does not define the types of legislation that mayors and councils may enact, nor does it stipulate subjects to be treated by a particular type of legislation. Therefore, guidance regarding enactments must be obtained from reviewing a municipality's charter and from court decisions.

An early case stated that "[t]he distinction between an ordinance and resolution is usually considered to be that, while a resolution deals with matters of special or temporary character, an ordinance prescribes some permanent rule of government."[53] A later case, providing a rather extensive discussion of municipal legislative enactments, asserted that "[l]egislation by a municipal corporation must be put in the form of an ordinance, and acts that are done in a ministerial capacity and for temporary purposes may be in the form of a resolution."[54]

A municipal enactment may at times be called something other than an ordinance or resolution (e.g., an order or motion). However, it should be noted that the name given an enactment does not appear to be overly important to the courts and is certainly not conclusive in determining its status.[55]

However, in striving to define these terms, the courts have reached certain important conclusions regarding municipal ordinances. Generally, ordinances based on legislative authority are laws within the meaning of the Georgia Constitution. They have the same effect as local laws, such as city charter provisions, enacted by the General Assembly. Because they are considered local or special acts, they are void in any case for which provision has been made by an existing general law.[56]

Although state law does not dictate a required format for a municipal ordinance, it is important to review a city's charter and previously adopted ordinances for provisions that may have requirements that need to be included in a municipal ordinance or resolution. However, there are some basic elements to a well-drafted ordinance that may allow a municipality to avoid challenges to the validity and meaning of its enactments, such as the following:

1. The title provides an identifying name for the ordinance or resolution.
2. The preamble briefly explains the purpose of the ordinance and the objectives sought to be accomplished by it. The preamble may be quite lengthy and include findings of fact for certain types of ordinances such as those regulating adult entertainment.
3. The enactment clause formally declares the passing or adoption of an ordinance and identifies the enacting legislative body (i.e., the city council).
4. The definition section defines any words or phrases that have special meaning in the ordinance.
5. The body is the basic act itself, organized and divided into identifiable sections.
6. The severability clause stipulates that if any portion of the ordinance is held invalid, the remaining provisions shall continue in full force and effect.
7. The repealer clause abolishes previous ordinances that the municipal governing authority no longer wishes to be operative. A repealer clause that specifically identifies provisions to be abolished is far preferable to a general clause simply stating that "all conflicting enactments are hereby repealed." The latter type can lead to confusion concerning which ordinances, or parts thereof, have been repealed. Additionally, an equal dignity rule govern-

ing the repeal or amendment of municipal ordinances exists in Georgia. That is, an ordinance must be repealed or amended by no less than another ordinance.[57]

8. The effective date specifies the date on which the ordinance becomes effective.

Adoption of Documents and Maps

Documents and maps may, in the absence of charter or other statutory provisions to the contrary, be adopted by reference, provided they are formally adopted, can be sufficiently identified "so there is no uncertainty as to what was adopted," are made public records, and are "accessible to members of the public who are or may be affected" by them. Moreover, the adopting ordinance should give notice of such accessibility.[58]

Note that one such instance when a map must accompany an ordinance and not merely be referenced is in the context of zoning. The courts have held that the zoning map is an indispensable part of a zoning ordinance.[59] Without a valid map, the zoning ordinance is void: "It is essential in order to enact the maps as a valid part of the ordinance that they be formally adopted and treated in each step of the legislative process with all of the solemnity required for the text."[60]

Procedural Requirements

Ordinances may be enacted that prescribe procedures for passing ordinances. However, the courts generally view procedural requirements in municipal ordinances differently from those found in the city charter or other statutory law. In three cases in which procedural requirements spelled out in an ordinance were not complied with, the court refused to invalidate subsequent ordinances that were not enacted in accordance with these procedures.[61] In a recent case, the Georgia Supreme Court held that a rezoning of property had been validly adopted even though the city did not comply with the provisions in the city's charter regarding the adoption of ordinances. The court found that compliance with state law, the Zoning Procedures Law, was sufficient.[62]

MUNICIPAL TAXATION AND SPENDING

The Georgia Constitution allows cities to impose taxes authorized by the Constitution or by general law. Additionally, local laws enacted by the General Assembly may authorize a city to levy and collect taxes and fees within the corporate limits of the municipality.[63] Public funds can be expended to perform any public service or public function authorized by the state constitution or by law.[64] Issues of municipal taxation are more fully covered in Chapter 26.

FEDERAL LIMITATIONS

The Supremacy Clause of the U.S. Constitution makes it, federal law, and treaties the supreme law of the land.[65] Additionally, the ability of local governments to take action in particular areas may be limited by a number of federal constitutional provisions including the First Amendment, the Fifth Amendment, and the Fourteenth Amendment. As previously mentioned, the Fifth Amendment prohibits local governments from taking private property except for public use and upon the payment of just compensation.

The First Amendment states as follows: "Congress shall make no law respecting an establishment of religion, or prohibiting the free exercise thereof; or abridging the freedom of speech, or of the press; or the right of the people peaceably to assemble, and petition the Government for a redress of grievances."[66] Free speech issues may confront local governments and their officials in a variety of contexts including dealing with employees; access to public space for speeches and expressive conduct, including parades, marches, or displays; billboard, sign, and newsstand regulations; and adult entertainment. Additionally, local government officials must negotiate the often confusing path between respecting the free exercise of religion and avoiding the establishment of religion. Issues in this area most often arise concerning public displays and access to public space.

The Fourteenth Amendment to the U.S. Constitution provides the guarantees of due process and equal protection: "No State shall make or enforce any law which shall abridge the privileges or immunities of citizens of the United States; nor shall any State deprive any person of life, liberty, or property, without due process of law; nor deny to any person within its jurisdiction the equal protection of the laws."[67] Although the case law in these areas can be quite detailed, there are some basic guiding principles that can make these concepts easier to understand. Due process generally requires that an individual receive notice and an opportunity to be heard before the government does something detrimental to him or her, while equal protection means treating similarly situated people the same without discrimination based on prohibited grounds.

NOTES

1. John F. Dillon, *Commentaries on the Law of Municipal Corporations*, 5th ed. (Boston: Little, Brown and Company, 1911), 448–50. *See* Jewel Tea Company v. City Council of Augusta, 59 Ga. App. 260, 200 S.E. 503 (1938); Beazley v. DeKalb County, 210 Ga. 41, 77 S.E.2d 740 (1953); Weber v. City of Atlanta, 140 Ga. App. 332, 231 S.E.2d 100 (1976).
2. Ibid.
3. City of Atlanta v. Gower, 216 Ga. 368, 116 S.E.2d 738 (1960); City of Savannah v. Hussey, 21 Ga. 80, 68 Am. Dec. 452 (1857).
4. GA. CONST. art. IX, §II, ¶II.
5. OFFICIAL CODE OF GEORGIA ANNOTATED (O.C.G.A.) §36-35-3.
6. O.C.G.A. §36-34-2.
7. O.C.G.A. §36-35-4
8. O.C.G.A. §36-35-3(a).
9. O.C.G.A. § 36-35-3(b).
10. Ibid.
11. O.C.G.A. §36-35-5.
12. O.C.G.A. §36-35-4.1.
13. O.C.G.A. §36-35-6.
14. GA. CONST. art. IX, §II, ¶III(a).
15. GA. CONST. art. IX, §II, ¶III(b).
16. Kelley v. City of Griffin, 257 Ga. 407, 359 S.E.2d 644 (1987); Coweta County v. City of Newnan, 253 Ga. 457, 320 S.E.2d 747 (1984).
17. GA. CONST. art. IX, §II, ¶III(c).
18. GA. CONST. art. IX, §II, ¶IV; *See* O.C.G.A. §36-66-1 et seq.
19. GA. CONST. art. III, §VI, ¶II.
20. GA. CONST. art. IX, §II, ¶V.
21. U.S. CONST. amend. V; GA. CONST. art. I, §III, ¶I.
22. O.C.G.A. Title 22; §§32-3-1–32-3-20; Brannen v. Bulloch County, 193 Ga. App. 151, 387 S.E.2d 395 (1989).
23. GA. CONST. art. IX, §III, ¶I.
24. *See* AMBAC Indemnity Corporation v. Akridge, 262 Ga. 773, 425 S.E.2d 637 (1993); Nations v. Downtown Development Authority of the City of Atlanta, 256 Ga. 158, 345 S.E.2d 581 (1986).
25. GA. CONST. art. IX, §II, ¶VI.
26. O.C.G.A. §48-8-81.
27. O.C.G.A. §48-13-50.1.
28. O.C.G.A. §36-43-5.
29. O.C.G.A. §36-44-8.
30. *See* O.C.G.A. §33-8-8.3 regarding expenditure of insurance premiums tax revenues to provide services to unincorporated area residents.
31. GA. CONST. art. IV, §V, ¶II.
32. Ibid.
33. GA. CONST. art. III, §VI, ¶VI.
34. Grand Lodge of Ga. I.O.O.F. v. City of Thomasville, 226 Ga. 4, 172 S.E.2d 612 (1970); Swanberg v. City of Tybee Island, 271 Ga. 23, 518 S.E.2d 114 (1999).
35. *See* Mayor of Athens v. Camak, 75 Ga. 429, 435 (1885).
36. Smith v. Board of Commissioners of Hall County, 244 Ga. 133, 259 S.E.2d 74 (1979).

See Swanberg v. City of Tybee Island, 271 Ga. 23, 518 S.E.2d 114 (1999) for example of court ruling that city had received a benefit for the use of its property.
37. Grand Lodge of Ga. I.O.O.F. v. City of Thomasville, 226 Ga. 4, 172 S.E.2d 612 (1970); Atlanta Chamber of Commerce v. McRae, 174 Ga. 590, 163 S.E. 701 (1931).
38. 1990 Op. Att'y Gen. U90-20.
39. Ga. Const. art. IX, §IV, ¶II.
40. O.C.G.A. §36-36-58.
41. O.C.G.A. §§3-4-41, 3-4-91, 3-4-92.
42. Ga. Const. art. IX, §II, ¶VIII.
43. O.C.G.A. §21-5-30.2.
44. Ga. Const. 1945 art. XIII, §I, ¶I; 1976 art. XII, §I, ¶I.
45. Ga. Const. art. XI, §I, ¶IV.
46. Ga. Const. art. XI, §I, ¶IV(b).
47. Columbus-Muscogee County Consolidated Government v. CM Tax Equalization, Inc., 276 Ga. 332, 579 S.E.2d 200 (2003).
48. Ga. Const. art. III, §VI, ¶IV.
49. O.C.G.A. §28-1-15.
50. Ga. Const. art. III, §VI, ¶IV.
51. O.C.G.A. §36-80-19.
52. O.C.G.A. §24-7-22.
53. City of Rome v. Reese, 19 Ga. App. 559, 91 S.E. 880 (1917).
54. Allen v. Wise, 204 Ga. 415, 50 S.E.2d 69 (1948); Atkinson v. City of Roswell, 203 Ga. App. 192, 416 S.E.2d 550 (1992). In Atkinson v. City of Roswell, the court stated that "resolutions are the usual form for the enactment of administrative measures, whereas, ordinances are reserved for legislative acts."
55. *See* ibid.; Western and Atlantic Railroad v. Swigert, 57 Ga. App. 274, 195 S.E.230 (1938).
56. O.C.G.A. §§36-35-3, 36-35-6; Jenkins v. Jones, 209 Ga. 758, 75 S.E.2d 815 (1953); City of Columbus v. Atlanta Cigar Company, Inc., 111 Ga. App. 774, 143 S.E.2d 416 (1965); Pace v. City of Atlanta, 135 Ga. App. 399, 218 S.E.2d 128 (1975); City of Atlanta v. S.W.A.N. Consulting and Security Services, Inc., 274 Ga. 277, 553 S.E.2d 594 (2001).
57. Harper v. The Mayor and Council of Jonesboro, 94 Ga. 801, 22 S.E. 139 (1894).
58. Friedman v. Goodman, 219 Ga. 152, 132 S.E.2d 60 (1963); City Council of Augusta v. Irvin, 109 Ga. App. 598, 137 S.E.2d 82 (1964); Waldrop v. Stratton and McClendon, Inc., 230 Ga. 709, 198 S.E.2d 883 (1973); Foskey v. Kirkland, 221 Ga. 773, 147 S.E.2d 310 (1966); Reynolds v. Board of Commissioners of Paulding County, 180 Ga. App. 516, 349 S.E.2d 536 (1986).
59. Bible v. Marra, 226 Ga. 154, 173 S.E.2d 346 (1970); City Council of Augusta v. Irvin, 109 Ga. App. 598, 137 S.E.2d 82 (1964); City of Flovilla v. McElheney, 246 Ga. 552, 272 S.E.2d 287 (1980).
60. City Council of Augusta v. Irvin, 109 Ga. App. 598, 137 S.E.2d 82 (1964); Foskey v. Kirkland, 221 Ga. 773, 147 S.E.2d 310 (1966).
61. South Georgia Power Company v. Baumann, 169 Ga. 649, 151 S.E. 513 (1929); Ellis v. Stokes, 207 Ga. 423, 61 S.E.2d 806 (1950); Fairfax MK, Inc. v. City of Clarkston, 274 Ga. 520, 555 S.E.2d 722 (2001).
62. Little v. City of Lawrenceville, 272 Ga. 340, 528 S.E.2d 515 (2000).
63. Ga. Const. art. IX, §IV, ¶I.
64. Ga. Const. art. IX, §IV, ¶II.

65. U.S. Const. art. VI.
66. U.S. Const. amend. I.
67. U.S. Const. amend. XIV.

4

Becky Taylor

Mayors and Councilmembers: Powers, Duties, and Relationships

The municipal governing authority consists of the city council or city commission and, depending on the provisions of the city's charter, the mayor. While the powers and duties of members of the governing authority differ depending on the city's form of government, many general characteristics of these offices are similar among all cities in Georgia.

POWERS AND DUTIES OF THE MAYOR AND COUNCILMEMBERS

The governing authority is responsible for two essential types of functions: legislative and administrative. Legislative responsibilities involve setting policy for the government by enacting various ordinances, resolutions, and regulations. Administrative responsibilities deal with the implementation of the policies and procedures established by the governing body. In many cities, the administrative burden is too great to be borne solely by the mayor and council, so these powers are delegated to a professional manager, and policies are carried out by various departments, boards, and commissions in the city.

Before describing the collective powers of the governing authority, it is important to have a clear understanding of the powers and duties afforded the offices of mayor and councilmember—and the limitations on these powers. After clarifying the role of the mayor and city council, this chapter will explore the relationship of the governing body to other municipal boards, authorities, and commissions.

Powers and Duties of the Mayor

The executive powers of the mayor vary depending on the city's form of government. As discussed in Chapter 2, in the council-manager form of government, an appointed manager is held accountable for executive functions in the city. The city manager may report primarily either to the mayor or to the full council. In a true council-manager form of government, the manager is authorized to appoint and remove department heads, is responsible for preparing the proposed budget for submission to the city council, and reports directly to the full council rather than the mayor. While the manager has substantial authority, the mayor and council retain the ultimate executive responsibility and may remove the manager at any time they feel it is appropriate to do so.

In the "weak" mayor and "strong" mayor forms of government, the mayor fulfills the primary executive role. With the weak mayor form, executive authority is diluted by the requirement that the city council must vote to approve certain administrative actions. With the strong mayor form, the mayor may appoint an administrator to assist in carrying out the day-to-day duties associated with oversight of municipal operations and service delivery. Under the commission form of government, the board of commissioners as a whole shares the executive role, although in some cities the mayor may have additional administrative authority, and some cities using the commission form have an appointed administrator.

The responsibilities of the mayor include presiding over all meetings of the council, generally ensuring that city departments run smoothly, helping to build a sense of community, and providing leadership and services to municipal citizens.[1] The mayor serves as the official spokesperson for the city government. The mayor is often empowered with the authority to vote in the event of a tie and may or may not have veto power over legislation approved by council. It is the mayor's duty to sign written and approved contracts, ordinances, and other instruments executed by the governing body, which by law are required to be in writing.[2]

Depending on the city's form of government, the mayor's executive duties range from largely ceremonial (as in the council-manager form of government) to managing day-to-day operations (as with the strong mayor–council form of government). As discussed in detail in Chapter 2, under the council-manager form of government, the mayor provides general oversight for executive functions but assigns day-to-day administrative duties to an appointed, professional manager.

Powers and Duties of the Mayor Pro Tem

Many city charters allow the selection of a mayor pro tem from among the councilmembers. This individual is responsible for fulfilling the duties of the mayor in the event that the mayor is absent. The mayor pro tem also fills any vacancy in the office of mayor until that office can be filled through a special or general election.

Powers and Duties of Councilmembers

Councilmembers are empowered to make policy decisions and to approve ordinances, resolutions, and other local legislation to govern the health, welfare, comfort, and safety of the city's residents. The city council sets policy guidelines for the administrative and fiscal operations of the city.

As with the office of mayor, the specific day-to-day duties of councilmembers differ depending on the city's form of government and the provisions in its charter. Under the strong mayor–council form of government, the city council's administrative powers are very limited. However, under the weak mayor–council form, city councilmembers may be assigned to committees that review how individual departments carry out programs.

Compensation

The municipal charter contains provisions for compensation and expenses for the mayor and councilmembers. State law places limitations and procedural requirements on the adoption of salary adjustments for elected municipal officials.[3]

Vacancies

Vacancies are created when an elected official qualifies for any other office if the term of office being qualified for will begin more than 30 days prior to the expiration of the official's current term of office.[4] No member of the council (including the mayor) can hold any other municipal office during the term for which he or she was elected as councilmember unless he or she first resigns that council position.[5] Vacancies also occur by the death or resignation of the incumbent, by the incumbent ceasing to be a resident, or for other reasons.[6]

Except in the case of death, resignation, or felony conviction, notice must be provided to the person whose office is vacated at least 10 days prior to filling the vacancy or calling for an election. The decision to fill the vacancy is subject to appeal to the superior court. Vacancies may also be created in the event of a recall election. General law provides the grounds for recall and the manner in which a recall election is held.[7] Vacancies created by recall are filled by special election in the manner provided by law.

POWERS AND DUTIES OF THE GOVERNING BODY AS A WHOLE

The powers of the governing body include, but are not limited to, setting millage rates for property taxes, approving the city's budget, approving city expenditures, passing ordinances and resolutions, establishing policies and procedures, hearing rezoning and annexation requests, and making appointments to boards, authorities, and commissions.

Home Rule: Powers under the Constitution

As described in Chapter 3, Georgia's municipal home rule powers are outlined in the state constitution and empower local governments with a significant level of control over how local issues are handled. State law allows the local governing authority legislative power to "adopt clearly reasonable ordinances, resolutions, or regulations relating to its property, affairs, and local government for which no provision has been made by general law and which are not inconsistent with the Constitution or any charter provision applicable thereto."[8]

Administrative Powers in the Georgia Code

According to the Georgia Code, the municipal governing body has the power to[9]

1. establish municipal offices, agencies, and employments;
2. define, regulate, and alter the powers, duties, qualifications, compensation, and tenure of all municipal officers, agents, and employees unless this power is specifically given to another official in the charter;
3. authorize officers, agents, and employees of the city to serve process, summons, notice, or order, as prescribed by state law, in the event that the offense was committed within the city limits;
4. establish merit systems, retirement systems, and insurance plans for municipal employees and employees of independent school systems and to provide a way to pay for such systems and plans;
5. contract with state departments or agencies or any other political subdivision for joint services or the exchange of services and/or for the joint use of facilities or equipment;
6. legislate, regulate, and administer all matters pertaining to absentee voting in municipal elections; and
7. grant franchises for public utilities.

Taxation and Expenditure of Public Funds

The governing authority is empowered by the Georgia Constitution to levy and collect taxes and fees within its corporate limits in order to pay for public services and functions as authorized by the constitution or by general law.[10] The mayor and council are responsible for setting the millage rate for property taxes. On behalf of the city, the governing authority also has the power to accept and expend grant funds and obtain loans, to incur debt,[11] to enter into contracts;[12] and to issue revenue and other types of bonds.[13]

Cities may find it necessary to borrow funds to meet operating expenses and to fund various projects. The constitution and general laws of Georgia contain detailed, explicit provisions with regard to bonded and other indebtedness.[14] One such provision is the requirement of prior voter approval of general obligation bonds, which are to be backed by the full faith and credit of the municipality. Voter approval is not required for temporary loans,[15] lease-purchase contracts,[16] or revenue bonds.[17]

Budgets and Audits

The budget is the primary tool used by the mayor and city council to guide the delivery of services to the community and to communicate priorities to the public. Each fiscal year, municipal officials clarify goals and set priorities for the upcoming year. The governing authority oversees the budget development process and approves the city's budget each year.

The governing authority must also ensure that periodic, independent audits of the city's operating budget are completed. Georgia law requires cities with populations over 1,500 or with expenditures of $300,000 or more to complete an annual audit of all city financial statements. Cities with populations of 1,500 or less or with expenditures less than $300,000 are required to complete an audit every two years, and the audit must cover both fiscal years. The independent audit must be conducted in accordance with generally accepted auditing standards and the standards applicable to the Government Auditing Standards issued by the Comptroller General of the United States. The auditor reviews financial statements to provide an opinion on the city's financial condition and its control over financial reporting and to test for the city's compliance with provisions and requirements of federal, state, and local laws, regulations, contracts, and procedures.[18] See Chapter 27 for a more detailed review of city budgets.

Contracts, Purchasing, Management, and Disposition of Property

The Georgia Code states that "[t]he council or other governing body of a municipal corporation has discretion in the management and disposition of its property."[19] The city's authority to enter into contracts comes primarily from home rule powers and from the municipal charter, which usually grant this power to the mayor and council. There are several different types of contracts, including municipal road contracts, public works contracts, and intergovernmental contracts. There are also specific limitations on the power to contract, which, if not adhered to, will render the contract void or illegal.[20]

The proper procurement and management of property is an important responsibility of city officials.[21] Although sound procurement and property management procedures may not be explicitly spelled out in every city's charter, there are certain basic requirements that all governing bodies should adhere to. First, all contracts made by the city should be in writing and approved by the governing authority. Second, there should be a mandatory requirement that the municipality follow centralized purchasing procedures. Further, the governing body should be authorized to sell and convey or lease real or personal property owned by the city and, in some cases, to sell parcels that have been isolated by improvements to portions of the property. The sale of surplus property is regulated by state law. More detailed information about contracts, purchasing, and the sale of municipal property can be found in Chapter 13 of this handbook.

Planning and Zoning

The governing authority is responsible for setting policies that will determine how the community will grow and develop and for ensuring that the unique characteristics of the city are preserved while providing for controlled growth. The goals and objectives for land-use planning are formally stated in the city's comprehensive land-use plan. The city may also have a zoning ordinance, which serves as the law governing how development will be controlled in the community. The mayor and council may choose to appoint a Planning and Zoning Commission to make recommendations on land-use issues to the city council. Ultimately, the governing authority is responsible for hearing rezoning requests and petitions for annexation.

RELATIONSHIP OF THE MAYOR AND COUNCIL TO OTHER MUNICIPAL BOARDS, COMMISSIONS, AND AUTHORITIES

The city charter may enumerate specific departments, including public works, parks and recreation, police, fire, and public utilities. The charter may also include a description of departments such as finance, personnel, and planning, as well as a minimum list and description of appointed administrative officials. The relationship of mayors and councilmembers to other municipal employees is detailed in Chapter 31, along with a discussion of the relationship of the governing body to other elected municipal officials. The remainder of this chapter will focus on how mayors and councilmembers interact with municipal boards, commissions, and authorities.

Mayors and councilmembers either serve on or make appointments to an array of boards, authorities, and advisory bodies. Many of these offices are empowered with statutory authority to act independently from the municipal governing authority, so it is critical for mayors and councilmembers to understand their relationship to these other offices. It is also important to understand the powers, duties, methods of selection, terms of office, compensation, and expenses related to the offices most commonly found in municipal governments.

MUNICIPAL APPOINTED BOARDS, COMMISSIONS, AND ADVISORY GROUPS

Appointed bodies assist the elected officials of the government by serving in advisory capacities for specific projects, services, and/or facilities of the government. It is important that appointments to these groups are made carefully so that they will function effectively and remain accountable to the city government and sensitive to the public's needs and desires.

PARKS AND RECREATION BOARDS

The municipal governing authority is responsible for adopting resolutions that describe the specific functions, organization, and responsibilities of the parks and recreation department.[22] The department can operate as a line department reporting directly to the city administrator or manager, mayor, or entire council. Alternatively, the department may operate under the direction of a parks and recreation board, the board of education, or another existing board determined by the governing body. In cities that do not have a parks and recreation board, an advisory committee may provide citizen input to the governing authority and the department head.

When the city has an administrator or manager, it is recommended that the parks and recreation department head report directly to him or her under most circumstances. When a county and city operate a parks and recreation department jointly, a policy board with members appointed by each government is recommended.

If a municipality chooses to have a parks and recreation board or advisory committee, the local ordinance or resolution creating it should address the following basic issues.

The Powers and Duties of the Board

The governing authority may authorize the recreation board to maintain and equip parks, playgrounds, recreation centers, and the buildings that are located on these facilities.[23] They may also develop, maintain, and operate all types of recreation facilities and operate and conduct facilities controlled by other authorities. The city may authorize the parks and recreation board to hire playground or community center directors, supervisors, recreation superintendents, and other employees as it deems necessary. The parks and recreation board should be authorized to develop a program of recreational activities and services that is designed to meet the diverse leisure-related interests of all people in the community.

Board Members

The recreation board should consist of a minimum of five persons and a maximum of nine persons.[24] Board members serve without compensation and are appointed by the mayor or presiding officer of the municipality. The terms of office of the board shall be five years or until their successors are appointed and qualified, except that when the appointing authority makes initial appointments or fills vacancies, it may vary the initial terms of members so that thereafter, the term of at least one member will expire annually. Immediately after it is appointed, the recreation board must meet and organize by electing one of its members president and designating other officers as necessary. Vacancies on the board that occur for reasons besides expiration of the term are to be filled by the mayor or presiding officer of the governing body only for the unexpired term.

A park or recreation board may accept grants, real estate donations, or any gift of money or personal property or other donations that are to be used for playgrounds or recreation purposes.[25] The acceptance of any grant or donation that will result in additional expense to the municipality for maintenance and improvements must be approved by the governing authority. A municipality may also levy a tax or issue bonds to support the recreation program.[26] For a more detailed discussion of municipal parks and recreation programs, see Chapter 21.

PLANNING COMMISSION AND ZONING BOARD OF APPEALS

Because of the home rule powers afforded to local governments in Georgia, there is no state statute requiring a planning commission or zoning board of appeals. The Constitution of the State of Georgia provides that "each municipality may adopt plans and may exercise the power of zoning."[27] The Zoning Procedures Law[28] states that cities may, through the adoption on an ordinance or resolution, appoint administrative officers, bodies, or agencies as necessary to exercise their zoning powers. The law also outlines the minimum requirements for advertising, public hearings, and other guidelines to ensure that the public is afforded due process when cities regulate the use of property through zoning.

Planning Commission

The governing authority is responsible for adopting and updating a comprehensive land-use plan that states the overall priorities, goals, and objectives for land use for the present and future. In most cities, however, the governing body is responsible for such a wide range of duties that it often does not have sufficient time to devote to considering land-use planning issues. Therefore, most cities have established a planning commission that serves as an advisory board to the mayor and council for land-use issues. The local planning commission serves as a buffer between the public and the governing authority.[29]

The planning commission is usually charged with reviewing applications for permits and making recommendations to the mayor and council for the approval or denial of permits. In formulating recommendations, the planning commission considers technical information provided by the city's planning staff and the concerns of local special interest groups. The planning commission must look beyond short-term solutions and make recommendations on what is best for the city's future.

The number of members, length of terms, and process for removing planning commissioners is determined by each city. Members of the planning commission are not compensated for their service, unless the city chooses to pay for travel expenses related to their duties. Although training for planning commissioners is not required, it is recommended that cities encourage members of their planning commission to attend training available through the American Planning Association, the Georgia Planning Association, and the Carl Vinson Institute of Government, University of Georgia.

Zoning Board of Appeals and Variances

A city's zoning board of appeals and variances is established by the municipal governing authority to hear individual cases in which the interpretation, administration, or enforcement of the zoning ordinances have caused hardship to property owners. As for the planning commission, the membership, term limits, and process for removing and replacing members of the board of appeals and variances are determined by the governing authority.

Members of the city's governing authority, the planning commission, or the zoning board of appeals must disclose their interests in property being considered for rezoning action and may not vote on items in which they have an interest.[30] More information about planning commissions and zoning appeals can be found in Chapter 14 of this handbook.

MUNICIPAL AUTHORITIES

Local authorities exist as creations of the General Assembly.[31] They are units of government created by the local government to accomplish specific objectives, projects, or missions that are for public purposes and in the public interest. Local government authorities can be created in one of two ways: (1) by general enabling act, which allows cities (under certain conditions) to create an authority by adopting and filing a resolution, or (2) by special local law, which is local legislation passed by the General Assembly that is applicable to a single local government or a number of specific local jurisdictions. Since authorities began being formed in Georgia, constitutional changes and state laws have made it easier for local governments to create authorities. Currently, 11 types of authorities, including industrial development authorities and downtown development authorities, may be activated in local governments by a general enabling act (i.e., the city only has to file a resolution declaring the need for such an authority).

Beginning in 1995, Georgia law began requiring all authorities to register with the Georgia Department of Community Affairs (DCA). Failure to do so results in the authority being prohibited from incurring debt or issuing any credit obligation. Authorities also are required to report to DCA the names of members who serve on their boards of directors. These reporting requirements give the state a better understanding about the operations and finances of authorities. In 2003, a total of 892 authorities were registered with the DCA.[32]

Powers of Authorities

All authorities may

- purchase, lease, sell, or retain property;
- improve or develop property;

- extend credit or make loans;
- borrow money and issue revenue bonds; and
- enter into contracts and intergovernmental agreements with local governments.

Authorities were originally created to enable local governments to bypass strict constitutional debt limitations. The constitution limits local government general obligation debt to 10 percent of the total assessed value of property subject to taxation in the jurisdiction. A referendum is also required prior to the local government incurring general obligation debt. However, an authority is empowered to issue revenue bonds. The bonds are then repaid out of revenues derived from the project funded with the bonds. A city is prohibited from using its tax revenues to repay the bonds. Since tax revenues cannot be used to repay revenue bonds, the bonds are not legally considered to be a debt of the city government. (Note, however, that cities can directly issue revenue bonds without creating an authority, but the law narrowly restricts the types of projects for which the bonds may be used, whereas the laws creating authorities have permitted a wider range of uses for revenue bonds.) Generally, authorities are not required to pay taxes on property they acquire, lease, or otherwise control.[33]

Authorities: Pros and Cons

Advantages of creating an authority include the following:

- The municipal government is able to delegate responsibility.
- The authority can assist in developing and operating a single-purpose facility (such as water and sewer, parking facility, etc.).
- The focus is a public purpose, such as economic development.
- Projects may be financed through revenue bonds.
- There is a means for ongoing oversight of operations after initial development is completed.
- An authority's activities may not be as influenced by politics as would a city's.
- There is some separation between the city and the authority, which may be helpful if controversies arise.

Disadvantages to creating authorities include the following:

- Authorities can become too independent.
- Authority board members are often appointed to terms longer than those of the elected officials who appointed them.

- They can become financially self-sufficient from the city for operations of the facilities they develop.
- They are likely to be less responsive to public opinion and to local governments.

Ensuring Accountability

Despite the level of independence of authorities, municipal governing bodies do have oversight powers and controls. For example, the boards of all municipal authorities are composed of members appointed by the city's governing authority. City officials either may be required to serve or may elect to serve on the boards. The activities of authorities must be consistent with those described in the city's service delivery strategy. The enabling legislation for some authorities specifically states that board members serve at the pleasure of the governing authority. For example, the Housing Authority Law states that housing authority directors can be removed by the mayor for inefficiency, neglect of duty, or misconduct in office.[34] Enabling legislation for other types of authorities provides for even more direct oversight powers. Authorities typically have bylaws that govern their activities and describe their organization. They are subject to open meetings and open records laws.

Funding and Support for Authorities

The Georgia Code provides that a municipality may levy and collect municipal taxes to provide for financial assistance for its development authority or a joint city-county development authority for the purpose of developing trade, commerce, industry, and employment opportunities.

Composition of Boards of Directors of Authorities

The composition of the boards of directors of authorities varies depending on the type of authority and method of creation, but there are some commonalties. First, membership is always appointed by the governing authority. Second, members must be residents of the jurisdiction of the local government appointing them to the board. The number of members usually ranges from five to nine members who usually serve staggered terms of four to six years.

Special requirements are established in the enabling legislation for certain types of authorities. For example, the Hospital Authorities Law requires the city to consider appointing a licensed doctor or registered nurse to the board.[35] Housing authorities, depending on the population of the city, must have at least one director who is a resident of a housing project in the city, and city elected officials and employees are prohibited from serving on the board.[36] At least three of the directors of solid waste management authorities must be elected city officials,[37] and cities have the option of appointing one elected member as director of the downtown development authority.[38]

Commonly Used Types of Authorities

Industrial Development Authority

The municipal governing authority is empowered by general law to create a joint development authority to promote trade, commerce, industry, and employment. A joint development authority may be activated by two or more municipal corporations, two or more counties, or one or more municipal corporations and one or more counties.[39] Joint development authorities are subject to the same statutory requirements as development authorities.[40]

The development authority is created to perform a specific purpose, to accomplish a special mission that is in the public interest (i.e., community economic development). It possesses all the powers necessary to carry out its purpose, including the authority to purchase, retain, improve, and develop property; enter into contracts and intergovernmental agreements; and borrow money and issue revenue bonds.

A development authority consists of a board of a minimum of seven and a maximum of nine directors appointed by the municipal governing body for staggered four-year terms. Each director must be a taxpayer and city resident, and the governing authority of the city may appoint only one of its members as a director.[41] Directors receive no compensation other than reimbursement for actual expenses incurred in performing their duties.[42]

Downtown Development Authority

The objective for activating a downtown development authority (DDA) is to revitalize and redevelop municipal central business districts.[43] The push to create DDAs began in the late 1970s and was motivated by a need to protect downtown areas that were declining because of the development of new commercial areas on the suburban fringes of cities. To activate a DDA, the municipal authority needs only to adopt and file a resolution that declares the need for the authority, specifies the boundaries of the downtown development area that constitutes the central business district, and appoints the initial directors.[44]

DDAs possess all the powers necessary to carry out their purpose. They may accept grants and apply for loans; own, acquire, lease, and improve property; and enter into contracts and intergovernmental agreements.[45]

A DDA consists of a board of seven directors who are appointed by the municipal governing authority to serve staggered four-year terms. Directors are appointed by the governing body and must be taxpayers who live in the city or are owners or operators of businesses located within the downtown development area and taxpayers residing in the county in which the municipal corporation is located. One of the directors may be a member of the governing body of the municipal corporation. No less than four of the directors must be persons who either have or represent a party who has an economic interest in the redevelopment and revitalization of the downtown development area. Directors receive no compensation other than reimbursement for actual expenses incurred in performing their duties. Except for a director who is a member of the city's governing body, each director shall complete within the first 12 months of his or her appointment to the authority at least eight hours of training on downtown development and redevelopment programs.[46]

Hospital Authority

A municipality is empowered to activate a hospital authority to establish and operate hospital facilities within its jurisdiction. Two or more cities or any combination of cities and counties may establish a joint hospital authority. A hospital authority has all the powers necessary to carry out its purposes, including the authority to make contracts; acquire real and personal property; appoint officers, agents, and employees; and operate, construct, improve, and repair hospital projects. The authority fixes the rates and charges for the use of its facilities; however, it cannot operate for a profit. The authority may also borrow money and issue revenue bonds, which are not debts to the county.[47]

A hospital authority has no power to tax. However, the governing authority may contract with the authority to pay for services rendered to indigent sick and others and levy a property tax, not to exceed seven mills, to pay for such services. A hospital authority has the same tax exemptions and exclusions as cities operating similar facilities.[48]

A municipal hospital authority consists of a board of directors of between 5 and 9 members appointed by the governing authority. The governing authority can determine the length of terms, which are to be staggered. A joint authority shall consist of 5 to 15 members, and their terms shall be as provided by resolutions of the participating governments. Board members receive no compensation other than reimbursement for actual expenses incurred in performing their duties.[49]

Housing Authority

A housing authority can be activated by the adoption of a resolution by the municipal government stating the need for the authority. A housing authority may be created if the governing authority determines that unsanitary or unsafe housing conditions exist in the city or if there is a shortage of safe, sanitary, and affordable housing.[50]

A housing authority has all powers necessary and convenient to carry out its purposes, including the power to make contracts; acquire, prepare, lease, and operate housing projects; provide for housing construction, repair, and furnishings; borrow money or accept grants and loans; and issue revenue bonds. Bonds and other obligations incurred by the authority are not debts of the city.[51] Housing authorities may enter into contracts with for-profit entities for the ownership of a housing project and are authorized to incorporate nonprofit corporations as subsidiaries of the authority.[52]

In exchange for tax relief from the city, the authority may agree to pay the city for improvements, services, and facilities furnished by the city for the benefit of any housing project.[53] An authority may not construct or operate a housing project for a profit or as a revenue source for the city. Rents must be no higher than necessary, and authorities must comply with statutory requirements for renting and tenant selection.[54] The city governing authority must provide sufficient money to cover administrative and overhead expenses for the authority's first year of operation, and the city may periodically lend or donate money to the authority.[55]

A housing authority consists of five commissioners appointed by the governing authority to serve staggered five-year terms. Commissioners may not be officers or employees of the city. They receive no compensation other than reimbursement for necessary expenses. The authority may employ its own personnel and may use the services of the city attorney or employ outside counsel.[56]

Airport Authority

Cities are authorized, separately or jointly, to acquire, establish, construct, expand, own, lease, control, equip, improve, maintain, operate, regulate, and police airports and landing fields for the use of aircraft, either within or outside the city limits.[57] The governing authority can construct, maintain, and operate airports or landing fields; adopt regulations and establish fees for their use; set penalties for violations of these regulations; and lease airports to private parties.[58] The governing authority may provide funds for airports or landing fields, acquire easements for lights and markers, and police all airport facilities.[59] A governing authority that has established an airport or landing field or that intends to do so may vest the authority with the power to construct, equip, maintain, and operate it in an officer, board, or other municipal body. However, construction, equipment, and operation expenses remain the responsibility of the city.[60]

In 2003, DCA reported that there were 36 registered single and multijurisdictional airport authorities in Georgia.[61] These authorities are generally permitted to make contracts, obtain and dispose of property, set and collect charges and tolls, issue revenue bonds, and accept loans and grants.[62]

City or Independent School Boards

In Georgia, the responsibility for the administration and financial support of public schools is divided between the state and the local (city or county) board of education.[63] Local governments play virtually no role in the provision of education, but they are responsible for levying the property tax certified by the board of education. The state Board of Education has the authority to formulate educational and administrative policies and standards for the improvement of public education within the state.[64] Management and control of public schools within each county and city are the responsibility of the local board of education.[65]

The state constitution makes no distinction between a county board of education and a city board of education in its grant of authority to manage and control local schools. Cities that do not currently have a school system are constitutionally forbidden to create a new independent school system.[66] However, the Georgia Supreme Court has held that territorial expansion of existing city school systems by annexation is not forbidden by the constitution because it is not the creation or establishment of a new independent school system in violation of the constitution.[67]

Although the powers and duties of independent school boards vary, there are some general consistencies. School boards are responsible for developing the policies to guide the staff and administration of schools in the independent school district. The board can hire teachers and other personnel upon the recommendation of the school superintendent.[68] The state Board of Education is authorized to set a date by which the local school board must prepare and submit an operating budget to the state school superintendent.[69] The local board of education has limited authority to borrow money to operate the school system and may issue bonds for building and equipping schools and purchasing property to build schools. The board of education can purchase, own, and sell property.[70]

In order to qualify for state funds, the local board of education must raise money to operate the schools, which is accomplished primarily through taxation.[71] Each municipality authorized by law to maintain an independent school system may support and maintain the public common schools within the independent school system by levy of ad valorem taxes at the rate fixed by law upon all taxable property within the limits of the municipality. The board of education of the municipality annually recommends to the governing authority of the municipality the rate of the tax levy. Taxes levied and collected for support and maintenance of the independent school system by the municipal governing authority must be appropriated, when collected, by the governing authority to the board of education or other authority charged with the duty of operating the independent school system. Funds appropriated to an independent school system shall be expended by the board of education only for educational purposes, including, but not limited to, school lunch purposes. Such purposes include the payment of costs and expenses incurred to purchase school lunchroom supplies; the purchase, replacement, or maintenance of school lunchroom equipment; the transportation, storage, and preparation of foods; and all current operating expenses incurred in the management and operation of school lunch programs in the public common schools of the independent school system. School lunch purposes shall not include the purchase of foods.[72]

The Georgia Constitution and general law provide that members of the board of education are to be elected by the voters of the school district that the respective board members represent. A member is required to live in the district he or she represents. No person who is a member of the state Board of Education, who is employed by the state board or a local board of education, or who is employed by or serves on the governing body of a private school is eligible to serve as a member of a local board of education.[73]

Members of local school boards are typically elected to four-year terms unless otherwise provided by local act or constitutional amendment.[74] Vacancies for the remainder of an unexpired term are filled by appointment of the remaining members of the board if the vacancy occurs less than 90 days prior to the general election. If the vacancy occurs more than 90 days before the general election, it must be filled by a special election.[75]

Board members of any local system for which no local act exists receive a per diem of $50 per day for attending board meetings, plus reimbursement for actual expenses. General law also authorizes provision of group medical and dental insurance for members of the board of education.[76]

School Superintendent

The local school superintendent serves as the liaison between the state school superintendent and subordinate local school officers. The superintendent serves as the executive officer of the local board of education and is responsible for procuring school equipment and materials it deems necessary. The superintendent must (1) ensure that the prescribed textbooks are used by students, (2) verify all accounts before an application is made to the local board for an order for payment, and (3) keep a record of all official acts, which, together with all the books, papers, and property appertaining to the office, are to be turned over to his or her successor.[77]

The superintendent's duties include enforcing all regulations and rules of the state school superintendent and of the local board according to the laws of the state and the rules and regulations made by the local board that are not in conflict with state laws. He or she must visit every school within the local school system to become familiar with the studies taught in the schools, observe what advancement is being made by the students, counsel with the faculty, and otherwise aid and assist in the advancement of public education.[78]

Regional Development Centers

Regional development centers (RDCs) were created by the state to

1. develop, promote, and assist in establishing coordinated, comprehensive planning across the state;
2. assist local governments in participating in an orderly process for coordinated, comprehensive planning;
3. assist local governments in the preparation, implementation, and update of comprehensive plans that develop and promote the essential public interest of the state and its citizens; and
4. prepare and implement comprehensive regional plans that develop and promote the essential public interest of the state and its citizens.

All local governments in Georgia are automatically members of an RDC.[79] Cities in the Atlanta metropolitan area are members of the Atlanta Regional Commission (ARC), which has enhanced planning and review powers.[80]

Each local government pays annual dues for membership in the RDC. If an arrangement for the payment of such dues is structured so that a county pays dues only on behalf of residents of the unincorporated areas of the county, then the annual dues paid by such county shall come solely from revenues derived from the unincorporated areas of the county. To be eligible for state funds, each RDC must assess and collect annual dues in the amount of 25¢ for each resident of each county within the RDC, based upon the most recent estimate of population approved by the department for this purpose. To be eligible for any supplemental funding, each RDC shall be required to match the amount of the supplemental funds on a dollar-for-dollar basis, subject to statutory limitation.[81]

There are 16 RDCs in Georgia, each of which is governed by a board of directors that must have at least one elected or appointed municipal government official from each member county. The bylaws of the RDC board provide for the selection of its members and may authorize the inclusion of a member who is not a public official. The Board of the Georgia Department of Community Affairs has the authority to appoint one nonvoting member from each district to membership on the RDC board. The board must meet at least 10 times a year and at such times as provided in the bylaws.[82] The RDC board is responsible for appointing and removing a full-time executive director, exercising its statutory powers, establishing committees as it deems appropriate, and adopting an annual work program and budget.[83]

Regional Advisory Councils

For the purpose of delivering state services to local units of government and citizens and for the purpose of establishing state agency regional boundaries, the General Assembly created 12 state service delivery regions.[84] Public- and private-sector representatives of each of the state's 12 regions advise the state in the development and implementation of regionally significant community and economic development initiatives. Each region has a 21-member advisory council (RAC) to provide a forum for communication between the regions and state government. The Board of the Georgia Department of Community Affairs (DCA) appoints 7 members, the Board of the Department of Economic Development (DED) appoints 7 members, and the commissioners of DED and DCA jointly appoint 7 members. Members of the RAC serve staggered two-year terms.[85] In the metropolitan Atlanta region, ARC's community services committee serves as its RAC. The joint services committee is composed of 11 members (i.e., 6 ARC board members and 5 nonboard members).

A regional advisory council's duties are to

- coordinate strategic economic development planning with comprehensive land-use, environmental, housing, and transportation planning;
- maximize the effectiveness of development resources through the collaboration and advice of local private- and public-sector leaders;
- establish a structure to promote public- and private-sector partnerships at the regional level in order to identify and respond to development issues and opportunities facing each of Georgia's diverse economic regions;
- seek local and regional input to develop customized regional economic development strategies;
- advise state agencies on methods to address the development needs and growth concerns of business and local governments to enhance opportunities for established businesses and attract new business development;
- identify opportunities to create regional solutions for natural resource management and other development issues; and
- assist in the development of regional leadership programs, workforce development strategies, downtown revitalization, rural development initiatives, and existing industry support programs.

NOTES

1. Georgia Department of Community Affairs, "Municipal Government Job Descriptions for Elected Officials," August 2004, http://www.dca.state.ga.us/dcawss/jobs-descs/default.asp.
2. Georgia Municipal Association, *Georgia Model Municipal Charter*, 3rd ed. (Atlanta: Georgia Municipal Association, 1994), 37.
3. OFFICIAL CODE OF GEORGIA ANNOTATED (O.C.G.A.) §36-35-4.
4. GA. CONST. art. II, §2, ¶ 5.
5. O.C.G.A. §36-30-4.
6. O.C.G.A. §45-5-1(a).
7. O.C.G.A. §21-4-3(7).
8. O.C.G.A. §36-35-3.
9. O.C.G.A. §36-34-2.
10. GA. CONST. art. IX, §4, ¶ 2.
11. GA. CONST. art IX, §5.
12. Barrett v. City of Atlanta, 145 Ga. 678, 89 S.E. 781 (1916). *See* O.C.G.A. §36-91-20.
13. GA. CONST. art. IX, §6; O.C.G.A. chapters 36-38, 36-82, §36-34-6.
14. GA. CONST. art. IX, §5; O.C.G.A. chapter 36-82, §§36-80-10–36-80-14, 36-91-20. *See* Georgia Municipal Association, *Public Works Construction Projects* (Atlanta: Georgia Municipal Association, Inc., 2003).

15. GA. CONST. art. IX, §5, ¶5.
16. O.C.G.A. §36-60-13.
17. GA. CONST. art. IX, §6; O.C.G.A. §§36-82-60–36-82-85.
18. O.C.G.A. §36-81-7.
19. O.C.G.A. §36-30-2.
20. Georgia Municipal Association, *A Reporter's Guide to Covering City Hall* (Atlanta: Georgia Municipal Association, Inc., 2001), 35.
21. *Georgia Model Municipal Charter*, 62–63.
22. Portions of this section are based on Charles C. Clegg, "Planning for and Providing Municipal Services: Recreation and Parks," in the *Handbook for Georgia Mayors and Councilmembers*, 3rd ed. (Athens: Carl Vinson Institute of Government, the University of Georgia, 1993), 263–70.
23. O.C.G.A. §36-64-3.
24. O.C.G.A. §36-64-5.
25. O.C.G.A. §36-64-6.
26. O.C.G.A. §§36-64-7–36-64-11.
27. GA. CONST. art. IX, §2, ¶4.
28. O.C.G.A. ch. 36-66.
29. Georgia Department of Community Affairs, *Model Code: Alternatives to Conventional Zoning* (Atlanta: Georgia Department of Community Affairs, April 2002), §7-3.
30. O.C.G.A. ch. 36-67A.
31. The section providing overview information about authorities is adapted from information developed by the Department of Community Affairs on local government authorities.
32. O.C.G.A §36-80-16. *See* the Georgia Department of Community Affairs, "2004 List of Registered Local Government Authorities," http://www.dca.state.ga.us/research/authorities.asp#dir.
33. O.C.G.A. §36-62-3.
34. O.C.G.A. §8-3-53.
35. O.C.G.A. §31-7-72.
36. O.C.G.A. §8-3-50.
37. O.C.G.A. §12-8-54.
38. O.C.G.A. §36-42-4.
39. O.C.G.A. §36-62-5.1(a).
40. O.C.G.A. §36-62-5.1(b).
41. O.C.G.A. §§36-62-4, 36-62-5(a).
42. O.C.G.A. §36-62-5(c).
43. O.C.G.A. §36-42-2.
44. O.C.G.A. §36-42-5.
45. O.C.G.A. §36-42-8.
46. O.C.G.A. §§36-42-4, 36-42-7.
47. O.C.G.A. §§31-7-72, 31-7-72, 31-7-75, 31-7-77, 31-7-78, 31-7-79.
48. O.C.G.A. §§31-7-84, 31-7-72(e).
49. O.C.G.A. §§31-7-72, 31-7-74.
50. O.C.G.A. §§8-3-2, 8-3-4, 8-3-5.
51. O.C.G.A. §§8-3-30, 8-3-32, 8-3-70, 8-3-71.
52. O.C.G.A. §§8-3-3, 8-3-8, 8-3-11, 8-3-30.
53. O.C.G.A. §8-3-8.

54. O.C.G.A. §§8-3-11, 8-3-12.
55. O.C.G.A. §8-3-155.
56. O.C.G.A. §8-3-51.
57. O.C.G.A. §6-3-20.
58. O.C.G.A. §6-3-25.
59. O.C.G.A. §§6-3-24, 6-3-26, 6-3-27.
60. O.C.G.A. §6-3-25.
61. "2003 List of Registered Local Government Authorities."
62. Ga. Laws 1984, p. 4935; Ga. Laws 2000, p. 4082.
63. Portions of this section are from the Georgia School Boards Association's online legal reference, http://www.gsba.com/.
64. O.C.G.A. §§20-2-240, 20-2-270–20-2-274.
65. Ga. Const. art. VIII, §5.
66. Ga. Const. art. VIII, §5, ¶1.
67. Upson County School District v. City of Thomaston, 248 Ga. 98 (1981).
68. O.C.G.A. §20-2-211.
69. O.C.G.A. §20-2-167(c).
70. Ga. Const. art. VIII, §5, ¶1; O.C.G.A. §§20-2-520, 20-2-390, 20-2-430.
71. O.C.G.A. §§20-2-160–20-2-168.
72. O.C.G.A. §48-5-405.
73. O.C.G.A. §20-2-51.
74. O.C.G.A. §20-2-52.
75. O.C.G.A. §20-2-54.1.
76. O.C.G.A. §20-2-55.
77. O.C.G.A. §20-2-109.
78. Ibid.
79. O.C.G.A. §§50-8-30–50-8-46.
80. O.C.G.A. §§50-8-80–50-8-103.
81. O.C.G.A. §50-8-33.
82. O.C.G.A. §50-8-34.
83. O.C.G.A. §§50-8-34.1, 50-8-35.
84. Information in this section is from O.C.G.A. §50-4-7 and the Georgia Department of Community Affairs Web site. http://www.dca.state.ga.us/regions/rac/index.html.
85. Ibid.

5

Ted Baggett

Municipal Courts

There are many different types of courts in Georgia, including state and federal courts, trial courts, and appellate courts. Aside from federal courts, the highest state court is the Georgia Supreme Court, which may choose to hear appeals from the Georgia Court of Appeals. It has the final authority on the interpretation of the state constitution and governs the practice of law in Georgia.

There are a variety of trial-level courts in the state's judicial system. Superior courts have original jurisdiction in numerous types of civil cases, and they serve as the exclusive trial court for the adjudication of felony criminal offenses and as courts of appeal for municipal court decisions. State courts are county-level trial courts that only exist in some counties and have jurisdiction over certain civil matters and misdemeanor criminal cases. Probate courts are countywide courts that have jurisdiction over estate matters, gun and marriage licensing, and some election matters. In some counties, they have jurisdiction over traffic offenses that occur in the unincorporated area. Magistrate courts are county-level courts that hold first appearance hearings for state and superior court and have jurisdiction over county ordinance offenses. Magistrate judges also issue warrants authorizing searches and arrest. Municipal courts are city-level courts that have jurisdiction over traffic cases arising within the city limits, cases involving municipal ordinances, and certain specified misdemeanor offenses. Decisions in municipal court may be appealed to the superior court and from there, to the court of appeals or possibly the supreme court.

PROCEDURE

The primary purpose of municipal court, like other trial courts, is to provide an impartial forum for the adjudication of disputes. In municipal court, such disputes usually involve a misdemeanor criminal defendant or someone accused of violating one or more provisions of a municipal ordinance. In criminal matters, either misdemeanors or ordinance violations, the defendant is entitled to the protection of a number of federal and state constitutional rights. All parties appearing in court are entitled to due process, which generally means an opportunity to plead their case to a neutral judge and to present and challenge evidence. These rights also include the right to be represented by counsel and the right to have counsel appointed at government expense if the defendant cannot afford counsel.

Misdemeanor defendants in Georgia are entitled to a jury trial.[1] Although municipal courts have the authority to conduct bench trials, they do not have the authority to hold jury trials. Therefore, in certain cases in which criminal defendants insist on their right to a jury trial, a transfer of the case to a state or superior court may be necessary. Although some defendants may knowingly choose to waive their right to counsel, in order to hear a case, the municipal court must provide lawyers for indigent defendants who request them.[2]

The governmental interest in a criminal prosecution in municipal court is usually represented by a municipal court solicitor or a city attorney acting as a solicitor. Although some municipal courts allow police officers and code enforcement officers to present the prosecution side of a case in municipal court, difficulties may arise out of such practices because the rules of evidence, state law, and constitutional law often are sufficiently complex to require an attorney to represent the government as well as the defense.

The event that triggers a criminal case is either the issuance of a citation or an arrest. Citations are written notices that serve in lieu of arrest and typically give the defendant notice of the crime charged and a summons to appear in court. For some offenses, such as driving under the influence (DUI), a defendant is usually arrested. Once arrested, most defendants are able to post bail or bond in order to leave the jail and return to court to answer the charges. Defendants who fail to appear in court typically forfeit their bond. Courts usually issue warrants for a defendant's arrest if they fail to appear. Although most of the offenses heard in municipal court are relatively minor in comparison with those heard in superior court, some do carry mandatory jail time.

JURISDICTION

Traffic Offenses

State law authorizes municipal court to hear violations of state and local traffic laws that occur within the city limits. State traffic offenses are misdemeanors and, as such, in some cases may carry penalties of up to one year in prison and a $1,000 fine.

Other Misdemeanors

The state has authority to grant jurisdiction over certain misdemeanor offenses to municipal courts. The penalties that may be imposed for these offenses in municipal court typically are identified in the statute that grants jurisdiction.

Ordinance Violations

Cities may proscribe certain conduct that is not already prohibited by state law and provide for appropriate punishment. State law establishes that the maximum punishment for ordinance offenses is six months' incarceration and fines of $1,000 per offense.[3] Some municipal charters limit the city to lesser maximum punishments for ordinance offenses.

Not all ordinance cases that are heard in municipal court are criminal. Some are purely civil in nature. For example, some cities have adopted nuisance abatement ordinances that allow complaints to be brought against property owners for maintaining nuisances or allowing code violations to persist. In these instances, a code enforcement officer is usually the city's main witness. In such cases, the court has the power to order abatement of a nuisance or to attach a lien against property that was previously declared a nuisance and demolished at the city's expense.

COURT PERSONNEL

Judges

The presiding official in municipal court is the municipal court judge. One part-time judge or several full-time judges may staff a municipal court depending on the city's caseload. Although state law does not require that municipal court judges be attorneys, most municipal charters require that the judge be a member of the Georgia Bar, and surveys indicate that almost all municipal court judges are attorneys.[4] Most municipal judges are appointed by the governing authority of the city, although a few are elected. The conduct of municipal court judges, like that of all judges in the state, is prescribed by the Georgia Code of Judicial Conduct, adherence to which is enforced by the Judicial Qualification Commission (JQC) and the state supreme court. The JQC and the supreme court have the authority to remove a judge from the bench. Judges have the duty of sitting in an impartial manner and advising defendants of their rights and are prohibited from participating in *ex parte* communications with municipal officials. Municipal court judges are required to obtain training from the Municipal Courts Training Council.[5]

Clerks

Typically, most municipal courts are staffed by one or more court administrators or clerks employed by the city who must answer to both the city governing authority and the judges. Court staff are governed by the same set of ethical rules that govern judicial behavior. Court employees are also barred from engaging in *ex parte* communication with parties and from giving legal advice to parties appearing before the court.[6] The tasks of municipal court clerks, which include processing warrants and sentences issued by the judge and collecting fines and fees paid to the court, require careful diligence. Failure to properly process paperwork can lead to false arrest, and failure to properly administer court fees is in many instances a crime itself.[7] It is therefore essential that employees assigned to work in municipal court be properly trained.

Public Defenders

As stated previously, some defendants in municipal court who are unable to afford an attorney are entitled to have one appointed to represent them at the city's expense. Defendants attempting to assert their rights to indigent counsel usually complete an application stating their income, assets, and debts and liabilities. Lawyers provided to criminal defendants are often called public defenders. Cities may provide these lawyers through several different mechanisms. Cities may choose to have an appointed list from which the municipal court judge appoints lawyers to represent different defendants at a set rate. Cities may also hire full- or part-time lawyers to appear in court and handle the cases of indigent defendants who request counsel. The Georgia Public Defender Standards Council is charged with promulgating standards for the number of cases a public defender is allowed to handle, the minimum qualifications for such attorneys, and the minimum rates public defenders must be paid, in addition to establishing standards for determining the financial eligibility of persons claiming indigence.[8] Because public defenders represent the criminal defendant, even if their employer is the government, they must abide by the ethical rules that govern lawyers and zealously represent the defendant's position under the rules of the adversary system.[9]

Solicitors

Prosecutors in municipal court are usually called solicitors. They are responsible for bringing the prosecution or case on behalf of the government. Depending on the size of the city's caseload, solicitors can be part time or full time. In some instances, the job of prosecuting in municipal court is one of the responsibilities of the city attorney. In some places, police officers have presented routine cases for prosecution. Because court mandates have resulted in more defense attorneys appearing in municipal court, however, it is no longer prudent to allow the city not to be represented by an attorney in municipal court. It is particularly important that cities have attorneys representing the prosecution in criminal cases that carry mandatory jail time such as DUI, in which failure to create a proper record can result in costly appeals and conviction reversals.

Sentencing

Because most cases in municipal court are criminal, persons found guilty are issued a criminal sentence. The sentence typically includes a fine but may also include jail time for certain offenses. In some instances, defendants are sentenced to probation in order to require them to comply with certain conditions of their sentence. Failure to comply with the terms of probation may trigger a probation revocation hearing. Should the city prove that a defendant has violated his or her probation, the judge may choose to revoke all or a portion of a probated sentence and send a defendant to jail.

Fines

Because most offenses heard in municipal court are minor in nature, fines are the most common punishments imposed. The amounts of fines are limited by the statute creating the offense or by the general boundaries for misdemeanors.[10]

Fees

Fees, or "fine add-ons" as they are sometimes called, are imposed in addition to a defendant's fine. They are usually imposed by state law and require that either additional percentages of the amount of the fine or flat amounts be sent to designated governmental agencies. These fees must be carefully accounted for and distributed to the appropriate agencies in accordance with state law.

Probation

Probation is a mechanism used by courts to encourage defendants to meet certain conditions rather than send them to jail. If the conditions of probation are met, a defendant's case is usually closed. Conditions of probation may include payment of fines, community service, and attendance at driver safety courses. Municipalities may choose to operate their own probation departments with city employees or they may contract with private probation companies to perform the service.[11] If a municipality chooses to have its own employees serve as probation officers, they must receive training required by state law.[12] If a city chooses to contract with a private probation company, the contract must be agreed to by both the municipal court judge and the governing authority of the city.[13]

Incarceration

Although most cases in municipal court do not result in jail time, some offenses do carry mandatory jail time. On occasion, courts may revoke probation, resulting in a defendant having to serve jail time. Incarceration is very costly to a city because adequate facilities are a constitutional requirement and are expensive to maintain. Most cities contract with the county for the provision of jail services for any municipal court defendants who are sentenced to incarceration.

Appeal

Appeals from decisions in municipal court are brought to the superior court.[14]

NOTES

1. Geng v. State, 276 Ga. 428 (2003).
2. Alabama v. Shelton, 122 S.Ct. 1764 (2002).
3. OFFICIAL CODE OF GEORGIA ANNOTATED (O.C.G.A.) §36-35-6(a)(2).
4. Georgia Administrative Office of the Courts, Municipal Court Facts (Atlanta, 2003).
5. O.C.G.A. §36-32-27.
6. Code of Judicial Conduct, 251 Ga. 897.
7. *See for example* O.C.G.A. §15-21-134.
8. O.C.G.A. §17-12-1 et seq.
9. *See* Preamble, Georgia Rules of Professional Conduct, State Bar of Georgia (Atlanta, 2001).
10. O.C.G.A. §17-10-3.
11. O.C.G.A. §42-8-100(g)(1).
12. O.C.G.A. §35-8-13.1.
13. O.C.G.A. §42-8-100(g)(1).
14. O.C.G.A. §15-6-8(4)(B).

6

Susan M. Pruett

Liability of Public Officials and the City

Cities as well as city officials can be subject to liability in a variety of situations under both federal and state law. However, both cities and city officials are immune from certain types of liability under specific circumstances. This chapter addresses some of the types of liability that cities and city officials may face under both federal and state law and discusses the differing levels of immunity and standards for immunity for both cities and their officials.

STATE LAW

Cities are liable for breach of contract in largely the same way as are private entities. However, in some instances, it may be alleged that a municipality's actions promised under the contract were not authorized by law and that the contract is against public policy. When a city acts *ultra vires* (that is, it acts without authority), the contract will be held void.[1]

With respect to torts, however, cities, counties, and their employees and officers may be held liable. A tort is a wrongful act for which the law imposes civil liability to compensate or protect the injured party. Common examples of torts are personal injury actions based on accidents occurring in city facilities or based on actions of city employees. Generally, cities can be held liable for the acts of their officials or employees through *respondeat superior*, which according to *Black's Law Dictionary* is liability by a master for the wrongful acts of his servant or liability by a principal for the acts of his agent, where the servant or agent is acting in the course of his or her agency or employment.

Sovereign Immunity

Municipalities and their officials are immune from suit except to the extent that they have waived sovereign immunity or in specifically limited circumstances. The waiver of sovereign immunity may be accomplished by action of the General Assembly or by a city's purchase of liability insurance.[2] Additionally, immunity is waived for the performance of nongovernmental, often called proprietary, functions.

An example of a waiver of sovereign immunity accomplished by action of the General Assembly is the waiver enacted for use of a local government entity's covered motor vehicle by a local government officer or employee.[3] This law essentially waives the sovereign immunity of cities and counties for injury or damage arising from motor vehicle claims to certain prescribed minimum amounts.[4] Local governments can increase the waiver of immunity by adopting a resolution or ordinance or by obtaining coverage in excess of the statutorily prescribed waiver through the purchase of commercial liability insurance or participation in an interlocal risk management agency.

Local governments may provide for the payment of claims through any method.[5] Thus, local governments may purchase insurance, participate in an interlocal risk management agency, establish a reserve fund for the payment of claims, pay claims as they arise, or any combination of the foregoing. Under the motor vehicle waiver law, the fiscal year aggregate liability of a local government cannot exceed any insurance, contracts of indemnity, self-insurance, or other reserve or fund established to pay claims. Any judgment obtained in excess of the annual aggregate liability is to be paid within six months of the end of the local government's fiscal year in which the final judgment was entered. All tort actions, including those filed against a local government as a joint tortfeasor, must be brought in the state or superior court of the county in which the local government resides.[6]

Official Immunity

As aptly described by the Georgia Supreme Court,

> The doctrine of official immunity, also known as qualified immunity, offers public officers and employees limited protection from suit in their personal capacity. [Official] immunity protects individual public agents from personal liability for discretionary actions taken within the scope of their authority and done without willfulness, malice or corruption. Under Georgia law, a public officer or employee may be personally liable only for ministerial acts negligently performed or acts performed with malice or an intent to injure. The rationale for this immunity is to preserve the public employee's independence of action without fear of lawsuits and to prevent a review of his or her judgment in hindsight.[7]

For the purpose of this immunity, a "discretionary action" is one calling for the exercise of personal deliberation and judgment, entailing examining facts, reaching reasoned conclusions, and acting on them in a way not specifically directed. City officials and employees are liable for the negligent performance of ministerial acts. Ministerial acts are those that are required by law or policy; that are simple, absolute, and definite; and that require little or no exercise of judgment.

An example of this distinction was provided in a case in which the Georgia Court of Appeals held that a county's decision on how to allocate resources to repair roads after widespread flooding was discretionary.[8] The county officials were not liable for the alleged failure to repair a particular road and warn of a dangerous condition. The court found that since the decisions required the officials to use judgment and discretion in determining how to allocate workforces, equipment, and time, the officials were entitled to official immunity.

Nuisance

There is no sovereign immunity for nuisance. A nuisance is defined generally as anything that causes hurt, inconvenience, or damage to another. Generally, to make a claim for nuisance, the plaintiff must show that the defendant has performed continuous or regularly repetitious acts or created a continuous or repetitious condition that has injured the plaintiff. In order for a city to be liable for nuisance, the plaintiff must also establish more than mere negligence: the plaintiff must show that the city knew of a condition that constituted a nuisance and failed to take action within a reasonable time to correct it.[9]

FEDERAL LAW

The largest potential liability under federal law for cities and city officials is based on 42 U.S.C. §1983, a statute that was part of the Civil Rights Act of 1866, which was enacted to implement the Thirteenth, Fourteenth, and Fifteenth Amendments to the U.S. Constitution after the Civil War. In pertinent part, Section 1983 states as follows:

> Every person who, under color of any statute, ordinance, regulation, custom, or usage, of any State or Territory or the District of Columbia, subjects, or causes to be subjected, any citizen of the United States or other person within the jurisdiction thereof to the deprivation of any rights, privileges, or immunities secured by the Constitution and laws, shall be liable to the party injured in an action at law, suit in equity, or other proper proceeding for redress. . . .

Specifically, Section 1983 authorizes relief against a city, city official, or city employee when an individual's federally protected rights have been violated.

Section 1983 has been utilized to establish liability on the part of cities, city officials, and city employees in an ever-expanding variety of situations. Some of the most common types of claims under Section 1983 are for excessive use of force during an arrest, for personal injuries based on use of a city vehicle or equipment, or for alleged mistreatment of employees or citizens. The U.S. Supreme Court has held that conduct by police officers, even when it violated state law, could constitute state action taken under color of state law and could thereby be actionable under Section 1983.[10]

Under Section 1983 there is no respondeat superior liability.[11] Over the years, the Supreme Court has made it very clear that each possible defendant, whether a subordinate or a superior officer or a municipal entity, is responsible only for that defendant's own wrongs. Although a municipality cannot be held liable under a theory of respondeat superior for purposes of Section 1983, a municipality can be held liable for the enforcement of a municipal policy or custom that violates the plaintiff's federally established rights. Thus, when a city official or employee acts based on an ordinance or recognized city policy or custom, the city can be held directly liable for the official's or employee's actions, even though the official or employee may be immune from suit in his or her individual capacity. There is no immunity for municipalities under Section 1983.

Absolute Immunity

City officials have absolute immunity for acts taken as part of their legislative function. Whether an act is considered to be legislative for purposes of discerning absolute immunity is determined based on the nature of the act rather than on the motive or intent of the official performing it. The courts will look at whether the act is part of a governmental function rather than whether the official had an inappropriate motive.[12]

Qualified Immunity

Qualified immunity shields government officials performing discretionary functions from liability for civil damages to the extent that their conduct does not violate clearly established statutory or constitutional rights that a reasonable person would have known. Again, there is a distinction between "discretionary functions," which require some judgment or decision making by the official or employee, and "ministerial functions" which do not require any application of judgment or significant decision making by an official or employee.

In order for an official or employee's conduct to be found to violate a clearly established statutory or constitutional right, the law must be sufficiently well established so that a reasonable official would understand that his or her individual action would violate the plaintiff's federal rights. However, it is not necessary that there be a case decided on the same or materially similar facts as the one presented by the plaintiff in order for the qualified immunity to be waived and the officer or employee to be liable.[13] It is enough if the officials have fair warning that their conduct violates established law,[14] particularly when the existing case law strongly indicates unconstitutionality and the conduct of the officials or employees is particularly egregious.[15]

INDEMNIFICATION, INSURANCE, AND RISK MANAGEMENT

Cities are authorized to purchase liability or indemnity insurance covering mayors and councilmembers as well as city employees. Instead of or in addition to buying insurance, a city may adopt a policy to defend civil, criminal, or quasicriminal actions brought against its officials and employees, except for crimes involving theft of city property or money. Regarding the latter, a city may reimburse the defense costs of those found not guilty or of those against whom charges are dismissed. Municipalities may also spend state, federal, and local funds for this purpose.[16] However, a city is not required to defend such actions.[17] Municipalities are permitted to settle claims out of court, thereby avoiding costly and time-consuming court battles.

Georgia law also allows municipalities to form with other cities to establish interlocal risk management agencies through which they can jointly establish a self-insurance fund or purchase coverage to insure against general liability claims.[18] Many cities provide coverage through GMA's Georgia Interlocal Risk Management Agency program.

Municipal officials may reduce the possibility of lawsuits through the liability prevention process known as risk management.[19] Risk management consists of identification, measurement, control, and financing of losses and loss prevention. In this context, identification involves determining areas of potential liability such as law enforcement, personnel practices and procedures, regulatory functions, and the delivery and denial of services. Review of a city's claims history can be useful in identifying areas for loss prevention activities. Measurement is predicting the frequency and financial severity of potential suits. Control means establishing, implementing, monitoring, and updating policies and procedures related to the exposure areas identified. Financing involves providing funds to reduce or eliminate risks and to cover risks that cannot be eliminated.

Additionally, the application of common sense can help municipalities prevent liability. Several simple steps to bear in mind are the following:

1. Don't use public office for private matters.
2. Correct mistakes; don't ignore them.
3. Have, follow, and update policies.
4. Conduct and attend training.
5. Only adopt those policies and regulations that the city is prepared to actually enforce.
6. Generate only the infrastructure that the city is prepared to maintain.
7. Conduct periodic liability coverage audits.
8. Consult with the city attorney on controversial matters or when in doubt about the legality or potential consequences of an action.

NOTES

1. CSX v. Garden City, 227 Ga. 248, 549 S.E.2d 688 (2003).
2. OFFICIAL CODE OF GEORGIA ANNOTATED (O.C.G.A.) §36-33-1.
3. O.C.G.A. §36-92-1 et seq.
4. Effective January 1, 2005: $100,000 for bodily injury (1 person), $300,000 for bodily injury (2 or more persons), $50,000 for property damage, and $350,000 aggregate. Effective January 1, 2007: $250,00 for bodily injury (1 person), $450,000 for bodily injury (2 or more persons), $50,000 for property damage, and $500,000 aggregate. Effective January 1, 2008: $500,000 for bodily injury (1 person), $700,000 for bodily injury (2 or more persons), $50,000 for property damage, and $750,000 aggregate.
5. O.C.G.A. §36-92-4.
6. Ibid.
7. Cameron v. Lang, 274 Ga. 122, 123, 549 S.E.2d 341 (2001).
8. Norris v. Emanuel County, 254 Ga. App. 114 (2002), 561 S.E.2d 240.
9. *See* City of Columbus v. Barngrover, 250 Ga. App. 589, 552 S.E.2d 536 (2001); Wright v. City of Cochran, 250 Ga. App. 314, 253 S.E.2d 844 (2002).
10. Monroe v. Pape, 365 U.S. 167 (1961).
11. Monell v. Dept. of Social Services, 436 U.S. 658 (1978).
12. *See* Bogan v. Scott-Harris, 523 U.S. 44 (1998); Whipple v. City of Cordele, 231 Ga. App. 274, 499 S.E.2d 113 (1998).
13. Hope v. Pelzer, 122 S.Ct. 2508 (2002).
14. Ibid.

15. Sheldon Nahmod, "Section 1983 Overview and Update," *50th Annual Institute for City and County Attorneys* (Athens: Institute of Continuing Legal Education in Georgia, 2003), 35.
16. O.C.G.A. §§45-9-21, 45-9-22. Section 45-9-21 was held constitutional in Horn v. City of Atlanta, 236 Ga. 247, 223 S.E.2d 647 (1976). The payment of attorney fees in selected cases is authorized by this section. Haywood v. Hughes, 238 Ga. 668, 235 S.E.2d 2 (1977).
17. Wayne County Board of Commissioners v. Warren, 236 Ga. 150, 223 S.E.2d 133 (1976); Horn v. City of Atlanta, 236 Ga. 247, 223 S.E.2d 647 (1976).
18. O.C.G.A. §36-85-1 et seq.
19. Jose J. Anchondo, "Liability Prevention (Risk Management) for Public Employees and Officials," *Intergovernmental Brief* no. 78-3 (Austin: Texas Advisory Commission on Intergovernmental Relations, September 1978).

7

Susan M. Pruett and W. Edwin Sumner*

Ethics, Conflict of Interest, and Abuse of Office

Trust describes the appropriate relationship between a local government's elected officials, other public officials, and their constituency. An elected official serves only as a result of the trust that the majority of the electorate have exhibited by electing the individual to office. The Georgia Constitution stresses the standards applicable to public officers in this way: "All government, of right, originates with the people, is founded upon their will only, and is instituted solely for the good of the whole. Public officers are trustees and servants of the people and are at all times amenable to them."[1]

Two roles for public officers are established by this constitutional language. First, the public officer is a trustee of the people. Trusteeship is perhaps the highest calling that may be granted under the law. As trustees, public officers have a fiduciary responsibility to their constituents. A fiduciary holds something of value, which he or she does not own, and is charged with managing the valuable item for the sole purpose of benefiting the beneficiary of the trust. Elected officers are entrusted with the power to govern and manage public property, with the public as beneficiaries of that trust. A public officer's goal should be to further the public good, not to improve the standing of the public officer, except that the officer may share the benefit as a member of the public at large.

The second idea suggested by the constitutional provision is that the public officer is a servant of the people. A servant cannot exist without a master. The constitution establishes the public as masters and public officers as "servants" who are charged with responding to the needs and wishes of the "master."

---

* Parts of the chapter contain or are based on work by this author from earlier editions of the *Handbook for Georgia Mayors and Councilmembers*.

COMMON LAW– OR COURT-ESTABLISHED STANDARDS

In the context of this chapter, common law means the rules established when judges take factual situations and extract from them basic principles that govern the conduct of human affairs. This common law tradition is handed down from the English legal system and evolved well before there were detailed statutory provisions governing conduct between people. It is important for city officials to understand that an action that may not violate a specific criminal or civil statute on conflicts of interest may run afoul of broader ethical principles that have been established by court decisions. Several principles become evident in a review of court decisions relating to conflicts of interest. Georgia courts have made it plain that persons should not have the opportunity to be tempted to profit from the public business that has been entrusted to them.

Not only can actions violate conflict-of-interest principles, circumstances and situations can create potential violations of the ethical principles applicable to the conduct of governmental affairs. The opportunity to profit from a situation plus an individual's control over that situation are the elements that create an ethical violation. The Georgia courts have sought to negate even the appearance of wrongdoing.

One court decision involving a mayor who owned a car dealership illustrates this concept. The city for which the mayor served engaged in sealed competitive bids for police cars for the city. The mayor's dealership had the lowest bid for the cars and therefore won the contract. The court, careful to avoid suggesting that the mayor took any wrongful action or improperly influenced the council's decision, invalidated the car purchase contract. The court conceded that the contract with the mayor's dealership was the lowest and most advantageous bid from the perspective of the city but found that the situation presented an appearance of wrongdoing that could not be tolerated.[2] The mayor in question had the opportunity to profit because of his position with the city and was tempted to profit from the public business. Even though the mayor did not use any influence in obtaining the contract award, the contract violated public policy and was therefore voided.

There is, then, an equation that every public officer should remember: temptation to profit plus opportunity to profit equals impropriety.

STATUTORY RESTRICTIONS

Georgia law has a number of statutory provisions regarding ethics in the conduct of government business. These provisions consist of both civil restrictions and criminal sanctions.

Civil Statutes

Conflicts of Interest

"It is improper and illegal for a member of a municipal council to vote on any question brought before the council in which he is personally interested."[3] This statutory provision is derived from an 1888 court decision and was carried forward from the Civil Code of 1895 to the present Official Code of Georgia Annotated. "Personal interest" has been construed by the courts to mean a financial interest.[4] It has been cited on a number of occasions by the Georgia courts to void municipal contracts, such as a contract between a mayor and a private corporation in which one of the councilmembers owned stock[5] and a contract between the city and the mayor, even though the mayor did not vote or attempt to influence members of the council.[6] The court has even construed this code section so broadly as to void a contract when the councilmember with the financial interest later resigned from the council and the contract was reconfirmed by the council after such resignation.[7]

This statute and court decisions can present problems for a mayor and council. For example, do the courts mean that a mayor and council are unable to purchase General Motors police cars because the mayor owns 100 shares of General Motors stock or is employed by the local General Motors manufacturing plant? The answer is no; there must be some opportunity for measurable profit to the individual arising from the transaction.

Another example of an exception to this statutory provision is based on a case that challenged an ordinance naming a particular bank as the city depository for all municipal funds. The challenge was based upon the fact that the mayor of the city and one of its councilmembers held the respective positions of officer and director of the depository bank. The Georgia Court of Appeals found that the arrangement did not violate the statute, under the theory that there was no financial profit to the individuals as a result of the bank being named as depository.[8] According to this decision, there was no financial profit because all of the municipal funds were demand deposits. Would the court reach the same conclusion based on these facts today, given the importance of deposits, including demand deposits, to local banks?

In fact, the state attorney general answered this question in the negative in a letter drafted in 1997. In that case, a county commissioner was a minority stockholder, a member of the board of directors, and also the attorney for the bank with which the county did business. Additionally, the commissioner's law partner was a member of the advisory board of and the attorney for another bank with which the county did business. The business the county did with the banks included depositing general operating funds in four different banks on a rotating basis and depositing surplus funds in the bank with the highest rate of return. The attorney general agreed with the county attorney in this case that a conflict of interest existed in each instance based on these facts.[9]

Another statutory provision of interest to public officials is the code of ethics for governmental service.[10] The code presents 10 principles that are excellent guidelines for conduct by public officers and employees. Two examples of these guidelines are (1) public officials should never use confidential information received during the performance of governmental duties as a means for making private profit, and (2) persons in government service should seek to find and employ efficient and economical ways of getting tasks accomplished. There are no sanctions provided for violating any of the general principles outlined in this statute. Therefore, this code of ethics has only an advisory effect on public officers.

Incompatible Offices

Holding incompatible or inconsistent offices is another potential situation that can give rise to an ethical violation. A municipal official is ineligible to hold any other municipal office at the same time he or she serves as a member of the municipal governing body.[11] Thus, a city official cannot also serve on a municipal planning commission[12] or as city clerk[13] or hold office as city building inspector.[14]

A city official also can run afoul of principles of ethical conduct if his or her employment comes into conflict with duties as a public officer. For example, the Georgia Supreme Court has disapproved of an arrangement whereby a mayor of a city was hired to serve as a manager of the city.[15] The mayor, a member of the governing body, was charged with overseeing the performance of the city manager. Thus, the mayor was placed in a position of judging his own performance as the city manager, which is not in the public interest. This prohibition against incompatible offices, or holding incompatible employment, may be a significant problem in very small municipalities.

A more recent example of conflict between a public officer's private employment interest and his "official" interest is found in a case involving a city attorney.[16] The city attorney challenged the mayor's veto of his reappointment. While the court ruled in favor of the city attorney on the main issue, the opinion found that the lawyer for the city attorney was also the city recorder. As such, the city recorder should have been disqualified as the city attorney's legal counsel. The court said that the city recorder, a public officer, was acting as an attorney for his own financial gain in initiating a lawsuit that sought to defeat the official actions of other public officers of the city that the recorder served.

Georgia law does allow members of the governing authority of a municipality or county to serve as volunteer firefighters for that municipality or county as long as the individual serving in both capacities receives no compensation for services as a volunteer firefighter other than actual expenses incurred, a per diem for services, contributions to the Georgia Firefighters' Pension Fund, workers' compensation coverage, or any combination of the foregoing.[17] However, the statute is very clear that nothing in this law requires a city or county to make any of the payments or offer any of the benefits allowed by this statute.

Criminal Statutes

Sale of Property

Suppose a mayor owns the only hardware store in town. As a matter of course, employees in the public works department of the city occasionally go to the hardware store to pick up small tools and other items necessary in carrying out the day-to-day department maintenance. Is this a permissible activity? Georgia criminal law prohibits the sale of real or personal property by a public officer to a local government in which the individual serves.[18] A violation of the provision can result in imprisonments of not less than one to not more than five years. The statute recognizes exceptions, however, for sales of personal property that do not exceed a value of $200 per calendar quarter and for sales of personal property made pursuant to sealed competitive bids. Thus, the mayor in the example would be able to sell tools and other materials to the city if the transaction met either one of these exceptions to criminal law.

Does the second exception to the criminal code mean that a court may approve an arrangement whereby a mayor's car dealership sells cars to the city on competitive bid? Declaring an activity free from criminal sanction does not necessarily mean that the contract could not be invalidated on the grounds that it violates good public policy and the constitutional principles of public trusteeship.

Another exemption from a criminal law provision is made for sales of real property. A sale of real property by a city official to his or her own city is exempt from criminal law if there has been a disclosure to the grand jury or judge or probate court of the county in which the city is located at least 15 days prior to the date the contract or agreement becomes binding. This notice must show the name of the interested person, his or her position in the political subdivision or agency, and the purchase price and location of the property being purchased by the city.[19]

Abuse of Office

Other potential criminal law violations that can arise from public service include violation of oath of office, bribery, improper influencing of legislative action by a municipal officer or employee, and conspiracy to defraud.[20] Bribery is committed by a public official when he or she directly or indirectly solicits, receives, or agrees to receive anything of value while implying that doing so will influence his or her performance on some official action. Bribery is likewise committed when persons offer public officials any benefit to which they are not entitled with the purpose of influencing them in the performance of their duties. The law, however, does acknowledge that a public official may be reimbursed for certain expenses and may accept certain promotional, honorary, and other token gifts without committing bribery. According to the state bribery statute, accepting one or more of the following items does not in and of itself constitute bribery:

- food or beverage consumed at a single meal or event
- legitimate salary, benefits, fees, commissions, or expenses associated with a public official's nonpublic business
- an award, plaque, certificate, memento, or similar item given in recognition of the public official's civic, charitable, political, professional, or public service
- food, beverages, and registration at group events to which all members of the governing authority are invited
- actual and reasonable expenses for food, beverages, travel, lodging, and registration for a meeting that are provided to a public official so that he or she may participate or speak at the meeting
- a commercially reasonable loan made in the ordinary course of business
- any gift with a value less than $100
- promotional items generally distributed to the general public or to public officials
- a gift from a member of the public official's immediate family
- food, beverage, or expenses afforded public officials, members of their immediate families, or others that are associated with normal and customary business or social functions and activities.[21]

Any person convicted of bribery is subject to a fine of not more than $5,000 or imprisonment for not less than 1 or more than 20 years or both.[22] In sum, other than those benefits of public office that are expressly authorized and established by law, no public official is entitled to request or receive—from any source, directly or indirectly—anything of value in exchange for the performance of any of his or her duties of office. A bribe or payoff, for example, given to a public official under the guise of a campaign contribution is still a bribe. The mere fact that a contribution has been reported as a campaign contribution would not change its character as a bribe.[23]

State law also defines two additional and more targeted forms of bribery related to selling influence: when a public official asks for or receives something of value in return for (1) procuring or attempting to procure passage or defeat of an ordinance, resolution, or other municipal legislation[24] or (2) attempting to influence official action of any other public officer or employee of the city. Upon conviction, the officer may be punished by imprisonment of not less than one or more than five years.[25]

Public officials are guilty of extortion when they demand or receive in their official capacity money, fees, or anything of value that they are not entitled to or that represents more value than is due them. A public officer found guilty of extortion must be removed from office.[26] It is also unlawful for a public official to coerce or attempt to coerce, directly or indirectly, any other public official or employee to pay, lend, or contribute any sum of money or anything else of value to any person, organization, or party for political purposes. A person engaging in coercion is guilty of a misdemeanor.[27]

Any public officer who willfully and intentionally violates the terms of his or her oath of office is to be punished by imprisonment for not less than one or more than five years.[28] A public official or other person commits the offense of conspiracy to defraud a political subdivision when he or she conspires or agrees with another to commit theft of property that belongs to a local government or that is under the control of a public official in his or her official capacity. Conviction calls for imprisonment of not less than one to not more than five years.[29] Also, a city official who receives, takes, or contracts to receive or take, either directly or indirectly, any part of the pay or profit arising out of a public works contract is guilty of a misdemeanor.[30]

A public officer or any other person who steals, alters, forges, defaces, or falsifies any records or documents, including minutes or digital records, shall be guilty of a felony if convicted and be subject to imprisonment for 2 to 10 years. Under this statute, willfully removing public records from the premises of the public office is considered stealing the public records.[31]

In addition to the infractions previously described, state law also addresses malpractice, partiality, neglect of duties, conduct unbecoming one's office, and demanding more cost than that to which a public official is entitled. Local elected officials charged with any of the foregoing may be indicted by the grand jury. If a true bill is returned by the grand jury and the public official is found guilty in a criminal proceeding, the official will be subject to fine, imprisonment, or both, at the discretion of the court. In addition, the official will be removed from office.[32]

Campaign Financial Disclosure/Lobbying

Details on the state law applicable to campaign financing and disclosure[33] are beyond the scope of this chapter, but each municipal official should become familiar with the requirements on campaign contribution limitations, disclosure, and reporting of campaign activities required by this statute. Violation of the campaign finance disclosure law can result in punishment for a misdemeanor. Allegations of violations can also become powerful tools when used by an individual against an opponent in an election.

Under certain circumstances, the Georgia Supreme Court has concluded that even monetary gifts designated as campaign contributions may be considered bribery.[34]

Additionally, there are state laws relating to registration and reporting by persons who lobby the General Assembly.[35] Certain provisions of this law apply to city employees and may apply to municipal elected officials as well.

Finally, Georgia law forbids the expenditure of public funds to influence the outcome of an election.[36] Articles in a city newsletter that could be construed as attempts to influence the way citizens vote on an upcoming referendum question may violate this law. Expenditure of private funds to influence voters on a referendum question can only be done by a campaign committee that registers and files financial reports as required in the Ethics in Government Act.

Conflict of Interest in Zoning

Zoning decisions are often troubling issues for government officials. Local government officials with a financial interest in zoning decisions are required to provide disclosure of that interest.[37] If the local government official knew or reasonably should have known that he or she has a property interest in real property affected by rezoning, has a financial interest in any business entity that has a property interest in real property affected by rezoning action, or has a member of the family who has an interest in the property, then the nature and extent of that interest must be disclosed in writing to the governing authority of the city in which the official serves. The local government official is disqualified from taking any action on behalf of him-/herself or any other person to influence action on the application for rezoning. Members of the family to which this requirement applies include a spouse, mother, father, brother, sister, son, or daughter of the official.[38] (This law is described more fully in Chapter 14.) Knowingly failing to comply with these requirements or knowingly violating the other provisions of this law can result in conviction of a misdemeanor.[39]

ETHICS PROVISIONS IN CHARTERS AND ORDINANCES

In addition to the ethics laws and criminal statutes applicable to municipal officials, a city may have additional ethics constraints and methods of airing ethics grievances in the city charter or in municipal ordinances. To the extent that there is already a state law on the same subject, the state law will control. However, local ethics ordinances and ethics boards can serve as an effective way for local residents and electors to hold municipal officials accountable at the local level. In furtherance of this objective, GMA created the Certified City of Ethics program in June 1999.

To earn a Certified City of Ethics designation, a city must adopt a resolution establishing the five ethics principles for the conduct of the city's officials and adopt an ethics ordinance that meets minimum standards approved by the GMA board. The five ethics principles are designed to guide the elected officials as individuals and as a governing body. These principals are to

- serve others, not ourselves,
- use resources with efficiency and economy,
- treat all people fairly,
- use the power of our position for the well-being of our constituents, and
- create an environment of honesty, openness, and integrity.

The adopted resolution must include or at least reference the definitions of these principles. A sample resolution is available from GMA. All elected officials are required to sign the resolution.

To participate in the Certified City of Ethics program, the ethics ordinance must contain definitions, an enumeration of permissible and impermissible activities by elected officials, due process procedures for elected officials charged with a violation of the ordinance, and punishment provisions for elected officials who violate the ordinance. GMA recommends that cities use the model ethics ordinance of the International Municipal Lawyers Association (IMLA) as the basis for their local ordinance. A copy of this ordinance, along with others adopted by the cities of Marietta, Roswell, and Smyrna is included in the GMA publication *Model Code of Ethics for Georgia City Officials*. Additional ethics ordinances are available on the GMA Web site or can be obtained by contacting the GMA legal department. Following their adoption, the resolution and ordinance should be mailed to the GMA legal department. The resolution and ordinance will be forwarded to the executive committee of the GMA City Attorneys Section for their review. If this panel of attorneys determines that both items meet the established requirements, the city will be designated as a Certified City of Ethics. Each city designated as a Certified City of Ethics will receive a plaque and a logo that can be incorporated into city stationery, road signs, and other materials at the city's discretion. In addition, GMA will send press releases to the local media notifying them that the city has earned this designation.

FEDERAL LAWS

There are several means by which federal law enforcement agencies address criminal acts of public officials. They can be grouped into three basic categories: criminal action statutes, corrupt act statutes, and honest services statutes.[40] Criminal action statutes refer to general criminal laws that define and prohibit behavior as criminal. They are not designed specifically to address actions by public officials. Any citizen, including public officials and employees, may be charged with their violation. Examples would include embezzlement, drug dealing, tax evasion, and fraud.[41]

Extortion or bribery involving public officials may also be prosecuted under federal law. Two of the core corrupt act statutes employed to address state and local corruption are the Hobbs Act and the Program Fraud Statute.[42] The Hobbs Act defines extortion as "obtaining of property from another . . . under color of official right."[43] It includes as a violation the misuse and potential misuse of a public official's power for personal profit. The bribe need not be initiated or demanded by the public official, and passive acceptance is sufficient for a Hobbs Act violation as long as the public official knows that he or she is being offered the payment in exchange for a requested exercise of official power.[44] For example, accepting cash in exchange for a promise to vote favorably on a rezoning matter would violate the Hobbs Act.[45] Punishment for violation of the Hobbs Act is a fine not exceeding $10,000, imprisonment for not more than 20 years, or both. Couching a bribe in the form of campaign contributions and reporting the payment as a campaign contribution does not change the nature of the bribe.[46]

The federal Program Fraud Statute addresses the actions of those who are responsible for federal funds. The statute applies when an organization such as a city or an authority receives federal benefits in excess of $10,000 involving some kind of federal assistance during a 12-month period prior to or following the act in question. The statute prohibits the following: (1) embezzling, stealing, defrauding, or misappropriating property valued at $5,000 or more; (2) soliciting or accepting bribes relating to some matter involving $5,000 or more; and (3) giving, offering, or agreeing to give anything of value to influence or reward action in connection with some transaction valued at $5,000 or more.[47] For example, a chief deputy in a jail that housed federal prisoners in exchange for federal funds well in excess of $10,000 in value was indicted and convicted for accepting a bribe from a prisoner in exchange for special treatment from the deputy.[48]

Honest services statutes are available when there are no federal program funds involved, when there is no immediately identifiable *quid pro quo*, or when there is only one actor. Honest services statutes address acts of fraud such as lying, cheating, misrepresenting the truth, self-dealing, nondisclosure of material conflicts of interest, and breach of duty. Using this tool, federal prosecutors must prove the use of either the U.S. mail, an interstate wire communication facility such as a phone or the Internet, or an interstate common carrier such as FedEx or UPS to execute a scheme to defraud someone.[49]

One final federal statute that bears mentioning is the False Claims Act (FCA). There are both civil and criminal penalties under the FCA.[50] The FCA is violated when a false, fictitious, or fraudulent claim is presented to the federal government that the person presenting it knows to be false through actual knowledge, deliberate ignorance, or reckless disregard. In addition to individuals, local governments are considered persons that can be held liable under the FCA.[51] One of the most important aspects of the FCA is that it allows private parties, called relators, to sue in the name of the federal government in lawsuits known as *qui tam* actions. The damages that can be levied and collected in a FCA action include civil penalties of $5,000 to $10,000 per violation, with each false statement serving as a separate claim, and treble damages.[52] The federal government may intervene in the case, but the relator is allowed to collect a bounty of up to 25 percent of the recovery if the government intervenes and 30 percent if the government does not. The potential for treble damages and up to 30 percent of the recovery provides relators with a strong incentive to locate false claims and pursue these actions.

SUSPENSION AND REMOVAL OF ELECTED OFFICIALS

If a local elected official is indicted for the commission of a felony by a grand jury, Georgia law provides a procedure whereby elected officials may be suspended from office by the governor upon recommendation of a special commission. The special commission is appointed by the governor and is composed of the attorney general and two other persons holding the same office as the indicted official. The duty of the special commission is to determine if the indictment relates to and adversely affects the administration of the office of the indicted official. If the official is suspended, a temporary replacement is appointed by the governor unless the applicable charter provides for some other means for filling temporary vacancies. If the indicted official is acquitted, the conviction is overturned on appeal, or a *nolle prosequi* (decision not to prosecute) is entered, the official is to be immediately reinstated to his or her position.[53] Upon the final conviction of a public official for the commission of a felony, whether or not the official was suspended, the office shall be vacated immediately. The vacancy shall be filled in the manner provided by law for filling such vacancies.[54]

Additionally, a public official may be subject to recall by the electors pursuant to the provisions of the Recall Act of 1989.[55] The grounds for recall enumerated in the statute are as follows:

1. that the official has, while holding public office, conducted himself or herself in a manner that relates to and adversely affects the administration of his or her office and adversely affects the rights and interests of the public; and
2. that the official
    a. has committed an act or acts of malfeasance while in office;
    b. has violated his or her oath of office;
    c. has committed an act of misconduct in office;
    d. is guilty of a failure to perform duties prescribed by law; or
    e. has willfully misused, converted, or misappropriated, without authority, public property or public funds entrusted to or associated with the elective office to which the official has been elected or appointed.[56]

CONCLUSION

Some actions, such as trading rezoning votes for cash, are so egregious that any rational person would agree that they are ethical violations. Other situations may or may not be as clear a violation, depending on one's perspective. For example, is it against public policy to include in a contract with an entertainment company using city property a requirement that the company shall provide a certain number of free tickets to entertainment events to members of the municipal governing body? What about the purchase at public auction of a surplus city automobile by the son or daughter of a councilmember, when the councilmember may be in a position to have knowledge of the particularly good condition of the car? What about the sale of insurance to the city by an agency that has a councilmember as one of its employees? Finally, should elected officials allow persons with whom the city does business, or may do business, buy lunch for officials? Does it depend on the cost of the lunch?

These and other situations may not be specifically prohibited by the criminal law. Likewise, a situation may not clearly be covered by civil conflict of interest statutory provisions, but it still may have an appearance of impropriety. The city official should ask him- or herself, "is the opportunity presented really worth the possible allegation of a scandal, which would affect me and my family?" Testing the propriety of a proposed action by asking that question may result in the official deciding to forego activities that would otherwise have been undertaken, even though they might actually have aided the efficient and economical operation of a city government. In a system of government such as ours—which depends on public confidence in its leaders for its continued existence—achieving utmost efficiency and economy may be secondary to earning and keeping that trust.

NOTES

1. GA. CONST. art 1, §2 ¶1.
2. Trainer v. City of Covington, 183 Ga. 759, 189 S.E.2d 842 (1937).
3. OFFICIAL CODE OF GEORGIA ANNOTATED (O.C.G.A.) §36-30-6.
4. Story v. City of Macon, 205 Ga. 590, 54 S.E.2d 396 (1949); Olley Valley Estates Inc. v Fussell, 232 Ga. 779, 208 S.E.2d 801 (1974).
5. Hardy v. Mayor of Gainesville, 121 Ga. 327, 48 S.E. 921 (1904).
6. Ibid., *n*. 1.
7. Montgomery v. City of Atlanta, 162 Ga. 534, 134 S.E. 152 (1926).
8. Smith v. City of Winder, 22 Ga. App. 278, 96 S.E. 14 (1918); for similar ruling, *see* Crawford v. Brewster, 225 Ga. 404, 169 S.E.2d 317 (1969).
9. Letter to the Honorable Robert S. Reeves, Chairman, Emanuel County Board of Commissioners from Attorney General Michael J. Bowers, March 31, 1997.

10. O.C.G.A. §45-10-1.
11. O.C.G.A. §36-30-4.
12. 1971 Op. Att'y Gen. U71-107.
13. 1967 Op. Att'y Gen. 67-36.
14. 1962 Op. Att'y Gen., p.# 333.
15. Welsch v. Wilson, 218 Ga. 843, 131 S.E.2d 194 (1963).
16. Stephenson v. Benton, 250 Ga. 726, 300 S.E.2d 803 (1983).
17. O.C.G.A. §36-60-23.
18. O.C.G.A. §16-10-6.
19. O.C.G.A. §16-10-6(c)(3).
20. O.C.G.A. §§16-10-1, 16-10-2, 16-10-4, 16-10-5, 16-10-21.
21. O.C.G.A. §16-10-2.
22. Ibid.
23. State v. Agan, 259 Ga. 541, 384 S.E.2d 863 (1989), *cert. denied*, 494 U.S. 1057 (1990).
24. O.C.G.A. §16-10-4.
25. O.C.G.A. §16-10-5.
26. O.C.G.A. §45-11-5.
27. O.C.G.A. §45-11-10.
28. O.C.G.A. §16-10-1.
29. O.C.G.A. §16-10-21.
30. O.C.G.A. §36-91-21(f).
31. O.C.G.A. §45-11-1.
32. O.C.G.A. §45-11-4.
33. O.C.G.A. §§21-5-30–21-5-53.
34. State v. Agan, 259 Ga. 541, 384 S.E.2d 863 (1989), *cert. denied*, 494 U.S. 1057 (1990).
35. O.C.G.A. §§21-5-70–21-5-73.
36. O.C.G.A. §21-5-30.2.
37. O.C.G.A. §36-67A-2.
38. O.C.G.A. §36-67A-1(6).
39. O.C.G.A. §36-67A-4.
40. Charles D. Gabriel, "The Role of the FBI in State and Local Government Corruption," *Institute for City and County Attorneys* (Athens: Institute of Continuing Legal Education in Georgia, University of Georgia, 2001), 5.
41. Ibid., 6.
42. Ibid., 9.
43. 18 United States Code Annotated (U.S.C.A.) §1951(b)(2).
44. Evans v. United States, 112 S.Ct. 1881 (1992).
45. Ibid.
46. Gabriel, 12–13.
47. Ibid., 14–15; 18 U.S.C.A. §666.
48. Ibid., 15–16; Salinas v. U.S., 522 U.S. 52 (1997).
49. Ibid., 18–19; 18 U.S.C.A. §§1341, 1343, 1346.
50. 31 U.S.C.A. §§3729–3733; 18 U.S.C.A. §287.
51. Cook County, Ill. v. United States *ex rel.* Chandler, 123 S.Ct. 1239 (2003).
52. 31 U.S.C.A. §3729(a)(7).

53. O.C.G.A. §45-5-6.
54. O.C.G.A. §§45-5-6, 45-5-6.1.
55. O.C.G.A. §21-4-1 et seq.
56. O.C.G.A. §21-4-3(7).

PART 2
Public Access and Media Relations

8

Kelly J. L. Pridgen*

Open Meetings and Open Records

Georgia's open meetings law[1] and open records law[2] are commonly referred to as the "sunshine laws." The open meetings law requires that the public have notice and access to meetings of the city council as well as those of other governmental boards, committees, authorities, etc. The open records law establishes the procedure for providing city and other governmental agency records to anyone requesting to see them. The sunshine laws give citizens and noncitizens alike the opportunity to learn about how government operates, how tax dollars are spent, and how decisions that affect their daily lives are made. This access to city government is key to fostering public trust in the actions of city governments.

OPEN MEETINGS

Who Must Comply with the Open Meetings Act?

Georgia's open meetings law applies to meetings of the governing authority of "agencies," such as the city (i.e., the city council)[3] and committees established by the city on which a member of the council serves.[4] The open meetings law also applies to the governing body of every city department, agency, board, bureau, commission, authority, or similar body. Meetings of the planning and zoning board, the zoning board of appeals, the personnel review board, the merit system board, the board of tax assessors, the board of tax equalization, the water and sewer authority, the development authority, the hospital authority, the housing

---

* Parts of the chapter contain or are based on work by this author from earlier editions of the *Handbook for Georgia Mayors and Councilmembers*.

authority, the recreation authority, etc., must also follow the requirements of the open meetings law.[5]

What Meetings Must Be Open?

In general, whenever a quorum of the city council or other board gathers at a designated time to conduct or discuss public or official business, it is considered to be a meeting that must be open to the public and comply with the other requirements of the open meetings law.[6] This mandate applies to gatherings at which any public matter, official business, or policy is discussed or presented, including work sessions, even if no final action is taken. A quorum of councilmembers may attend social gatherings without violating the open meetings law as long as no city business or other public matter is discussed.

Requirements of the Open Meetings Law

The city must provide the public with advance notice of meetings and their agendas as well as allow access to the meeting and to a written summary and minutes.

Notice of Meetings

- Notice for regular meetings. Notice of the time, place, and dates of regular meetings (e.g., the city council's monthly meeting) must be made available to the general public and be posted in a conspicuous place at the regular meeting place of the city council.[7]
- Notice for special meetings. For any meetings that are not conducted at the regular meeting place or time, the city must post the time, place, and date of the meeting for at least 24 hours at the regular meeting location and give written or oral notice at least 24 hours in advance of the meeting to the legal organ of the county or a newspaper with equal circulation.[8] In counties in which a legal organ is published less than four times per week, the time, place, and date of the meeting must be posted for at least 24 hours at the regular meeting location, and upon written request from broadcast or print media in the county, notice must be provided to the requesting media 24 hours in advance of the meeting. The media outlet, in turn, must make the information available to the public upon inquiry.[9]
- Notice for emergency meetings. When special circumstances occur, the city may hold a meeting with less than 24 hours' notice, if the city provides notice of the time, date, and location of the meeting and an agenda to the legal organ.[10] The legal organ is

responsible for making information available to members of the public upon request.

A Meeting Agenda

An agenda of all matters expected to come before the council must be made available upon request and must be posted at the meeting site.[11] The agenda must be available and posted as far in advance as is practicable during the two weeks prior to the meeting.[12] If a particular issue is not included on the posted agenda, then it may be considered only if it is deemed necessary by the council.[13]

Public Access to the Meeting

Members of the public must be allowed access to the meeting.[14] If attendance at a meeting is larger than the meeting room can accommodate, then the council should move the meeting to a larger meeting room, if available.[15]

Public Recording of the Meeting

Members of the public may make audio or video recordings of the meeting.[16]

A Meeting Summary

A written summary of the subjects and a list of the officials attending the meeting must be prepared and made available within two business days of the meeting.[17]

Minutes of a Meeting

The minutes must, at a minimum, contain the names of the councilmembers present at the meeting, a description of each motion or other proposal made, and a record of all votes.[18] For emergency meetings (i.e., meetings with less than 24 hours' notice), the minutes must describe the notice given and the reason for the emergency.[19] Contracts, maps, and other documents that were approved in the meeting may be included in the minutes or incorporated by reference.[20]

When an Emergency or Disaster Affects Compliance with the Open Meetings Law

If the governor or other authorized state official declares an emergency or disaster that renders it impossible or imprudent to hold a meeting at the regular time and place, meetings may be held for the duration of the emergency or disaster at any place within or outside the city on the call of the mayor or any two councilmembers. To the extent made necessary by the emergency, the councilmembers are not required to comply with time-consuming procedures and formalities prescribed by law, according to the Georgia Emergency Management Act of 1981.[21]

Exemption from Open Meetings Law Requirements

The General Assembly has created special exemptions to the open meetings law. Some gatherings are not considered meetings and are therefore not subject to any requirements; other gatherings may be conducted in a closed meeting but are still subject to certain requirements.

There are two types of gatherings that are not considered meetings subject to the requirements of the open meetings law (i.e., the city is not required to publish notices, post an agenda, or prepare a written summary or minutes). First, when a quorum of the city council inspects city facilities under its jurisdiction (such as fire departments, the water treatment plant, etc.), it is not subject to the open meetings law as long as no other city business or any other public matter is discussed.[22] However, if a quorum of the council is present and members begin to discuss or conduct other city business during such an inspection, they are in violation of the open meetings law. Second, when councilmembers meet with other government officials (e.g., members of the Department of Transportation or Department of Revenue) at a location outside their city,[23] the gathering is not considered a meeting as long as no final action is taken.[24] This exemption to the open meetings law hinges upon meeting with an official or officials from another government agency. However, retreats or meetings outside the city that only members and employees of the city attend are in violation of the open meetings law.

City councilmembers may close an open meeting to discuss certain topics in an executive session. As explained later in this chapter, there are special procedural requirements that councilmembers must follow to legally conduct an executive session. The following meetings, when relevant to the city, may be conducted in closed or executive sessions.

Meetings with the City's Attorney to Discuss Pending or Potential Lawsuits

The attorney-client privilege allows the council to meet with its attorney to discuss pending or potential lawsuits or claims against or by the city in a closed meeting.[25] Two things must be considered before closing a meeting pursuant to the attorney-client privilege. First, the attorney representing the city in the pending or potential lawsuit must be present. Second, a lawsuit by or against the city must already be filed, or there must be a potential lawsuit. A mere threat to take legal action against the city is not enough to close a meeting to discuss a potential lawsuit.[26] In order to determine whether a threat to sue the city is a potential lawsuit that may be discussed in an executive session, councilmembers should ask the following questions:

1. Is there a formal demand letter or something else in writing that presents a claim against the city and indicates a sincere intent to sue?
2. Is there previous or preexisting litigation between the city and the other party or proof of ongoing litigation on similar claims?
3. Is there proof that the other party has hired an attorney and expressed an intent to sue?[27]

Additionally, the meeting may not be closed to receive legal advice on whether a topic may be discussed in a closed meeting.[28]

Meetings to Discuss Tax Matters Made Confidential by State Law

Only tax matters that are required to be confidential by a state statute or appellate court case may be discussed in executive session.[29]

Meetings to Discuss the Future Purchase or Condemnation of Real Estate

Councilmembers may close a meeting to discuss the purchase of real estate by the city.[30] The exception applies only when the city acquires property, not when it sells property. Additionally, it applies only when the city is purchasing real property. The exemption does not apply when the city purchases personal property such as vehicles, equipment, or supplies.

Meetings to Deliberate on the Employment, Appointment, or Dismissal of a City Employee or Officer

Councilmembers may close the portion of the meeting during which they are deliberating on hiring, appointing, compensating, disciplining, or dismissing an employee.[31] However, any portion of a meeting during which the council receives evidence or hears arguments involving disciplinary actions must be open.[32] Additionally, all votes on personnel matters must be taken in public.[33]

Because executive sessions are the exception, not the rule, if there is any doubt whether a topic may be discussed in a closed meeting, the city attorney should be consulted. If doubt remains, the meeting should be open.

Procedures for Properly Conducting an Executive Session

In creating special exemptions to the open meetings law, the General Assembly also established certain requirements for conducting executive sessions.

- Precede with an open meeting. All executive sessions must evolve directly from a properly advertised open meeting.
- Vote to close the meeting. The council, in a properly advertised open meeting, must vote to close the meeting.[34] The reasons for closing the meeting and the results of the vote must be entered into the minutes of the open meeting.[35]
- Allow only relevant attendees. If a session is closed, it must be closed to everyone not affiliated with the city or the business being conducted.[36]
- Discuss only legally exempt topics. Only matters that are legally exempt from the open meetings law may be discussed at the executive session.[37] If someone attempts to bring up a nonexempt topic, the mayor should rule that person out of order. If the nonexempt discussion continues, the mayor should adjourn the meeting immediately.
- Vote on matters discussed in executive session, generally in an open forum. The open meetings law specifically requires any vote on a personnel matter to be taken in public.[38] Although the Georgia Court of Appeals found that voting on whether to accept or reject a settlement offer in a pending lawsuit during an executive session was appropriate under the attorney-client exception to the open meetings law,[39] many cities vote in an open meeting to ratify any action discussed in a closed meeting to avoid any issue with the open meetings law.
- Prepare minutes. Minutes must be prepared for the open meeting that precedes the executive session and must reflect the names of the councilmembers present and the names of councilmembers who voted to close the meeting as well as the specific reason for closing the meeting.[40] Minutes of a closed meeting may be taken but are required only for land acquisitions.[41] In the case of executive sessions held to discuss land acquisition, minutes must be taken as in an open meeting, except that the city may delay releasing the portion of the minutes that would disclose the identity of the real estate until the property has been purchased or the city decides not to purchase it.[42]
- Sign affidavit. At the end of the closed meeting, the mayor or presiding officer must sign a notarized affidavit stating, under oath,

that only legally exempt topics were discussed and providing the legal authority for the exemption.[43] The affidavit must be included with the minutes from the open meeting.[44]

Consequences of Noncompliance with Open Meetings Laws

In addition to the district attorney or solicitor, Georgia's attorney general is authorized to file a criminal action against individuals who violate the open meetings law.[45] Anyone who knowingly violates the open meetings law may be found guilty of a misdemeanor and fined up to $500.[46] If anyone signs an executive session affidavit containing false information, he or she may be convicted of a felony and fined $1,000 and/or imprisoned for up to five years.[47]

The attorney general or any other person, firm, or corporation may bring a civil action in superior court to require the city to obey the open meetings law.[48] Such lawsuits must be filed within 90 days of the date that the alleged violation of the open meetings law occurred.[49] However, for zoning decisions, the action must be brought within 30 days.[50] If challenged successfully, any resolution, ordinance, rule, regulation, or other official action made or adopted at a meeting that does not comply with the law will not be binding.[51]

The city may be required to pay the complaining party's attorney's fees, unless the city can show that it acted with substantial justification in not complying with the open meetings law.[52] Further, participation in a meeting that is held in violation of the open meetings act may be grounds for recall.[53]

Making Open Meetings Work

The open meetings law provides city councilmembers with a tool that encourages public participation in city government. It is a prime opportunity for councilmembers to show citizens how their tax dollars are spent. Following are some steps that councilmembers can take to avoid problems with implementing the open meetings law while furthering the purpose of the law in their city.

For Local Officials

- Update meeting procedures and policies. Make sure that local ordinances and policies regarding meetings are consistent with the new changes in the open meetings law.
- Understand the law. Ask the city attorney to review the open meetings law requirements. Consider holding periodic seminars conducted by the city attorney for the city council and other city boards

and committees. Make sure that all members of the council and key staff understand the requirements of the open meetings law, particularly the exemptions. This step could prevent an unintentional introduction of a nonexempt topic during an executive session.

- Foster compliance by other boards and committees. Make sure that other city boards are aware of their responsibilities under the open meetings law. Send them a copy of any meetings' ordinances that apply. Oftentimes, committees and other boards incorrectly assume that only the city council is subject to the open meetings law.
- Avoid closed meetings. Always begin with the assumption that an issue should be discussed in an open meeting. Executive sessions are only for those narrowly defined circumstances that are spelled out in the law. If the topic seems to be in a gray area, then it should be discussed in an open meeting. Do not risk going into executive session to discuss topics that are not clearly exempt from the law.
- Create an executive session procedure. Although not required, some local governments have adopted policies regarding closed meetings such as using a preestablished motion to go into executive session, requiring all members (rather than just the chairman or mayor) to sign an executive session affidavit, using a preestablished resolution upon coming out of an executive session that certifies that the meeting was devoted solely to exempt topics and authorizing the chairman or mayor to execute the executive session affidavit.

For Citizens and the Media

- Furnish advance notice of meetings. Notify the local media and post meeting notices at the meeting site as soon as a meeting is scheduled. Many cities require the local cable company to reserve a government access channel as part of their franchise agreement. Although it is not required by the open meetings law, cities can further public awareness of meetings by requesting that the cable company post meeting notices and agendas on such a channel.
- Post the agenda early. Post the agenda at the meeting site as soon as it is prepared.
- Provide adequate meeting space. Make sure the meeting room adequately accommodates the audience. In addition to providing enough seating, the room should be arranged so that the audience may see and hear the meeting. Offer members of the press a table or other designated area, if available, where they can hear and see the meeting.

- Distribute meeting material. At the meeting, make available copies of the agenda and other meeting material that may be of interest to those attending.
- Offer a media workbook. Provide press members with their own meeting workbooks, similar to those given to the city councilmembers and manager, which contain copies of contracts, resolutions, ordinances, and other requests to be considered at the meeting. Although not required, this gesture can establish a positive relationship with the local media. Oftentimes, the media's perceived violations of the open meetings and open records law could be lessened by willingly and voluntarily providing information up front.
- Televise meetings. Consider broadcasting meetings on the government access cable channel.

OPEN RECORDS

Who Must Comply with the Open Records Law?

Georgia's open records law applies to anyone who possesses records of the city, including all city departments, agencies, boards, bureaus, commissions, authorities, and other similar bodies.[54] Further, it applies to companies, individuals, and other entities that do business with or have contracts with the city to provide services for the city.[55] Generally, the city employee or official who maintains the records is the records custodian who actually responds to requests for city records. For example, if an individual requested commission meeting minutes, the city clerk would be the likely records custodian to handle the request. If an individual requested personnel records, the personnel director or his or her designee would likely be the records custodian.

Public Records Subject to Disclosure

All documents, papers, letters, maps, books, tapes, photographs, computer-based or computer-generated information, or similar material prepared and maintained or received in the course of the operation of the city are public records subject to disclosure unless they fall within one of the legal exemptions to the open records law.[56] Handwritten notes, e-mails, calendars, etc., are public records subject to disclosure under the open records law.

Records Legally Exempt from Disclosure

Some records are not required ever to be disclosed, while other records may be withheld from disclosure only temporarily. Most of the exemptions to the open records law merely permit the city to withhold records; in other words, although records are exempt, the city may release them. However, certain records must be kept confidential and may not be released. This section discusses some of the exemptions most relevant to councilmembers.

Records That Must Be Kept Confidential

In addition to medical records,[57] the following records must not be released except under specific circumstances:

- Information that could lead to identity theft. Social security numbers; mother's birth name; credit card, debit card, and bank account information; other financial data or information; and insurance or medical information must be redacted from all records before they are released.[58] If technically feasible and not cost prohibitive, month and date of birth must be redacted.[59] However, it should be noted that for certain requests, the information may be released.

- Individual or representative. An individual or his or her legal representative may obtain records containing social security numbers; mother's birth name; credit card, debit card, and bank account information; other financial data or information; and insurance or medical information.[60]

- News media. A news media representative may obtain a social security number and date of birth (except for those of teachers and employees of the public school system).[61]

- Government employees. A government employee may obtain records containing social security numbers; mother's birth name; credit card, debit card, and bank account information; other financial data or information; and insurance or medical information if he or she is doing so for administrative or law enforcement purposes.[62]

- Deceased individuals. Any individual may obtain date of birth and mother's birth name of a deceased individual.[63]

- Credit reporting agencies. Consumer reporting agencies may obtain credit and payment information.[64]

- Confidential tax matters. Tax matters made confidential by state law, such as certain occupation tax records, taxpayer depreciation schedules, taxpayer accounting records, etc., must not be released.[65]

- Trade secrets. Trade secrets and certain proprietary information protected by the Georgia Trade Secrets Act of 1990 may not be released.[66]

- Federal government. Records specifically required by the federal government to be kept confidential may not be released.[67]

If the records custodian believes that a fraudulent request has been made, he or she must apply to the superior court for a protective order to protect the records.[68]

Records That Are Temporarily Exempt from Disclosure

The following records may be (but are not required to be) withheld for a specific period of time.

- Investigation of complaints against city employees. Records containing materials from investigations of complaints against public employees or relating to the suspension or termination of an employee are not subject to disclosure until 10 days after the investigation is complete.[69]
- Appointment of the executive head. Records that would identify all of the applicants for the position of executive head of an agency (such as city manager) may be withheld until three finalists are selected, unless the public has had access to the application and interview process.[70] Fourteen days prior to the final decision, the names and application materials of the three finalists must be released, unless the applicant no longer seeks the position.[71] However, the city may be required to provide information regarding the number of applicants and the race and gender of those applicants.[72]
- Land acquisition. Real estate appraisals, engineering or feasibility estimates, or other records relating to the acquisition of real property may be withheld only until the transaction has been completed or terminated.[73]
- Pending bids and proposals. On construction projects, the engineer's cost estimates and competing bids and proposals may be withheld until such time as the final award of the contract is made or the project is abandoned.[74]
- Attorney-client privilege. Records subject to the attorney-client privilege (i.e., records pertaining to the requesting or giving of legal advice concerning pending or potential litigation, settlement, administrative proceedings, or other judicial actions in which the city is involved) may be withheld on pending litigation.[75]
- Pending violations. Records of law enforcement, prosecution, or regulatory agencies in any pending investigation, other than the initial police arrest and incident reports, may be withheld until the prosecution or any direct litigation is final or terminated.[76]

Records That May Be Withheld

Certain records such as confidential evaluations relating to the appointment or hiring of a public officer or employee[77] and attorney work product[78] may be (but are not required to be) withheld from disclosure. In addition, the following records may be withheld:

- Carpooling. The names, addresses, telephone numbers, hours of employment, or any other information that would reveal the identity of an individual who participates in or has expressed an interest in participating in car pools, van pools, bus pools, or other provision of transit routes.[79]
- Fire alarms and security systems. Records that would reveal the names, addresses, telephone numbers, security codes, and other data collected or developed by the city in connection with the installation, service, maintenance, operation, sale, or lease of a burglar alarm system, fire alarm system, or other electronic security system.[80]
- Invasion of privacy. Medical records or similar files of which disclosure would be an invasion of privacy according to Georgia case law.[81]
- Law enforcement, prosecutors, judges, teachers, and school employees. Records that would reveal the home address, telephone number, social security number, insurance, medical information, or family members of law enforcement officers, judges, correctional employees, prosecutors, Georgia Bureau of Investigation forensic scientists, public school teachers, and employees of public schools.[82]
- Confidential source. Records compiled for law enforcement purposes that would disclose the identity of a confidential source and endanger the life or physical safety of any person or that would disclose the existence of a confidential surveillance or investigation.[83]
- Accident reports. Georgia Uniform Motor Vehicle Accident Reports, unless the person requesting the accident report is named in the report, represents someone named in the report, or files a statement of need.[84] Additionally, other governmental agencies may acquire accident reports without filing a statement of need if they are obtaining the accident report in conjunction with an ongoing administrative, criminal, or tax investigation.[85]
- Computer programs or software. Although the data and information stored on computers are public records, citizens may not copy licensed computer programs and software used in the course of the operation of a city.[86]

Response to an Open Records Request

The open records law requires that all public records, except those legally exempted from disclosure, must be open for personal inspection by any individual at a reasonable time and place[87] usually within three business days from the receipt of the request.[88] The individual in control of the documents, or records custodian, must respond within three business days of receiving the request by doing the following:

- Determine whether the city has the requested documents. The city is not required to prepare any reports, summaries, or compilations that are not in existence at the time of the request.[89] However, requests may be made for documents that do not currently exist but will exist in the future.[90] For example, if an individual requested copies of minutes of future meetings, the city would be obliged to provide copies of the minutes as they come into existence.

- Determine whether the requested documents are subject to an exemption to the open records law. The records custodian should give careful consideration before determining that a record is not subject to disclosure. The rule is that the record is open; the exceptions for not having to release a document are very narrow. As will be explained, failure to provide an open record is a crime.[91] However, a records custodian will not be held liable if he or she is sued for releasing a record in error in good faith reliance that it was subject to the open records law.[92] Once it has been determined that all or part of a document falls under one of the legal exemptions,[93] the city must provide, in writing, the specific legal authority exempting such record from disclosure by code section, subsection, and paragraph.[94] Upon the discovery of an error in designating an exemption, the city has only one opportunity to amend or supplement the designation.[95] Such a correction or amendment must be made within five days of the discovery of the error or within five days of the institution of an action to enforce the act, whichever is sooner.[96] If a requested document contains both open and exempt information, the records custodian must still release the document but may redact or mark out the exempt information.[97]

- Provide an estimate of any copying, search, retrieval, or administrative charges for responding to the request. The records custodian must notify the party making the request of the estimated charge prior to fulfilling the request.[98] Where fees are specifically authorized by law, those fees shall apply.[99] If there are no fees provided by law, then the city may collect a uniform copying fee of up to 25 cents per page.[100] Reasonable charges for search, retrieval, and other direct administrative costs may be collected.[101] However, the hourly charge shall not exceed the salary of the lowest-paid full-time employee with the requisite skill and knowledge to perform the request.[102] There shall be no charge for the first 15 minutes of work.[103] For records made available through electronic means, the agency may charge the actual cost of the computer disk and for other administrative costs directly attributable to providing access,[104] unless it is information from a geographic information system. Cities may establish license fees or other fees for providing information from the geographic information system to recover a reasonable portion of the cost to the taxpayers associated with building and maintaining the system.[105]

- Permit inspection and copying of the requested documents, if available. If the records or documents cannot be made available within three business days, then a written description of the records, along with a timetable for inspection and copying, must be provided within three days.[106] When requested records are maintained by a computer, they shall be made available, when practicable, by electronic means, including Internet access, subject to reasonable security restrictions.[107] The records custodian must supervise the copying and may adopt and enforce reasonable rules governing the work.[108] The copying must be done in the room where the records, documents, or instruments are kept by law.[109] The records custodian must also use the most economical means available in responding to the request.[110] When a person has requested copies and does not pay, the city is authorized to collect the charges in any manner authorized by law for the collection of taxes, fees, or assessments owed to the city[111] as long as an estimate for the charges was provided to the requesting party before the records custodian fulfilled the request.[112] When requests are made by other agencies, the procedures and copying fees do not apply if they are sought in conjunction with an ongoing administrative, criminal, or tax investigation.[113] Even records otherwise exempt from public disclosure may be released to the requesting agency.[114]

Penalties and Fines for Failure to Comply with the Open Records Law

In addition to the district attorney or solicitor, the attorney general is authorized to file a criminal action against individuals who violate the open records law.[115] Anyone who knowingly and willfully violates the open records law, either by refusing access or failing to provide documents within the requisite time, may be found guilty of a misdemeanor and may be subject to a fine not to exceed $100.[116]

As with the open meetings law, the attorney general or any other person, firm, or corporation may bring a civil action in superior court to require the municipal records custodian to release records.[117]

The city may be required to pay the complaining party's attorney's fees if the records custodian acted without substantial justification in denying an open records request.[118]

City Actions to Make Records More Accessible to the Public

- Understand the law. Make sure that all members of the city council and all employees understand the basics of the open records law (particularly the deadlines and the penalties for noncompliance), as well as when it is necessary to contact the city manager or attorney in responding to a request. Often, requests are made to frontline employees, such as receptionists. Make sure that these employees are aware of their duties under the law, in addition to any city policy or procedure on responding to requests.
- Update open records policies. Adopt and disseminate a policy on responding to open records requests.
- Encourage other city officials, boards, and committees to comply. Make sure that other city boards, committees, departments, and elected officers are aware of their responsibilities under the open records law. Send them a copy of any policy or forms for use in responding to requests. Other boards and city officers frequently and incorrectly assume that only the city council is subject to the open records law.
- Designate records custodians. Designate the appropriate individuals as records custodians to handle open records requests for each department. Make sure that a backup plan is in place in case the designated custodian is out of the office or unavailable to respond to requests.
- Respond to incorrect requests. Instruct city staff on how to handle requests that are made to the wrong department or phrased incorrectly. For example, if a citizen requests tax records from the city council, he or she should be politely referred to the tax commissioner or the board of tax assessors, whichever is appropriate. If a requestor asks for a record under the Freedom of Information Act, which is a federal law applicable to federal records, treat it as a request under Georgia's open records law.

- Provide records through the Internet. Providing citizens with the option of accessing records through the city's Web page makes getting information easier for citizens and saves staff time. Examples of records that some cities post on the Internet include meeting schedules, agendas, minutes, and city ordinances. However, thought should be given to the type of electronic access that will be offered (i.e., computer modem, Internet, etc.), the type of records that will be made available electronically, and whether or not systems can be designed to ensure that computer hackers cannot access the computer system and alter records. To avoid any confusion about computer access, designate by ordinance or resolution which records, if any, will be made available electronically. The open records law requires that, when it is practicable, records must be made available electronically when requested.[119] If your city does not yet have e-mail or a Web site, weigh the cost to the taxpayers of providing this access against the time and money that could be saved by not having to photocopy requested records.

- Provide quality citizen service. Emphasize to city employees the importance of good customer service. Almost all of the information contained in city records belongs to the public. Make sure that city employees understand that regardless of the attitude of the party requesting the documents, these are public records, and public employees are required to assist the requestor. The requestor should not be considered an adversary.

- Increase availability of records by placing them in a central location. Show citizens the valuable services that they receive for their tax dollars by looking for ways to make records more accessible. For instance, copies of regularly requested records, such as meeting minutes, the code of ordinances, or the city budget could be placed in the public library.

- Make copying easier. Consider making a coin-operated copy machine available to those citizens who prefer to make their own copies. This option may be more economical for the requestor and at the same time allow city staff to continue with their other duties.

- Limit exemptions. Always begin with the assumption that a record is subject to disclosure. The exemptions to the open records law are very narrow. Do not try to restrict access to records that do not clearly fit within an exemption. The risk for criminal penalties[120] and lawsuits[121] is much greater for the failure to release an open record than for the release of a record that is exempt. Reliance on the open records law is a defense if a person is sued because he or she released a record that he or she believed, in good faith, was required under the open records law.[122]

- Request legal review. Not all requests need legal review. Discuss in advance with the city attorney the situations in which he or she should be consulted to review records requests. Also, identify who will provide legal review of records if the city attorney is out of town or otherwise unavailable. Be sure that all designated records custodians, including the city officers, are familiar with the procedure.

- Make a written record of oral open records requests. Although the records custodian may ask that open records requests be made in writing, he or she may not require them to be in writing.[123] Most requestors will readily provide a written request for two reasons: it protects them from a misunderstanding of the request and helps focus the request to avoid excessive charges when the request is for something other than meeting minutes, agendas, ordinances, etc. A written request also becomes an identifiable record, triggering the three-business-day time period. To simplify the process, a city could provide the requestor with a basic request form if he or she appears at the courthouse in person, or the form could be mailed, faxed, e-mailed, or posted on the city's Web site. City staff receiving the request should use a standard form for recording requests not received in writing.

- Use file inventory for quicker access. Make an inventory or master list of the city's filing system. Within three business days of a request, the requested records should be found and any relevant exemptions identified. Remember, claimed exemptions may only be amended or corrected one time.[124] A file list or inventory will allow quicker access to records as well as complete and accurate responses to requests. State law requires counties to have a records retention plan,[125] and all department heads and records custodians should familiarize themselves with and follow the records retention plan adopted by the city.

- Prepare a timetable when records are not immediately available. If the requested records cannot be processed within three days of receiving the request, politely advise the requestor that the records are not confidential but cannot be provided until a certain date. Be sure to explain why they cannot be obtained quickly. Remember that the law also requires that you provide a written notification to the requestor describing the records, as well as a timetable for their release, within three business days.[126]

- Seek reimbursement of cost uniformly. Apply the open records policy regarding cost reimbursement for copying and supervising records requests equally. Do not charge some citizens but not others for copies and administrative time unless the policy provides that no charge is imposed for minimal amounts of copying. The copying and administrative charges authorized by the open records law are not to be used to discourage frequent or unpleasant requestors. Rather, they are designed to ease the cost of providing access to public records to the taxpayers, who ultimately pay the cost of compliance beyond what is collected in fees from the requestor.

- Avoid bureaucratic traps. If a requested record is available at the time of the request, do not make the requestor wait three business days merely because the law allows it. The law does not require that records custodians wait three business days before responding; it merely allows the records custodian three business days to process those requests that cannot be filled immediately.

- Avoid using legal technicalities. Resist taking advantage of technicalities and loopholes in the law. Trying to work around the law is the surest way to guarantee that new changes will be made that will make it even tougher for city officials to comply efficiently with the open records law. When faced with a gray area or a loophole, remember that the General Assembly and the courts have made it clear that they will always lean toward making access easier or records more open.

NOTES

1. OFFICIAL CODE OF GEORGIA ANNOTATED (O.C.G.A.) §§50-14-1–50-14-6.
2. O.C.G.A. §§50-18-70–50-18-77.
3. O.C.G.A. §50-14-1(a)(1)(B).
4. *See* O.C.G.A. §50-14-1(a)(2).
5. O.C.G.A. §50-14-1(a)(1)(C), (D).
6. O.C.G.A. §50-14-1(a)(2).
7. O.C.G.A. §50-14-1(d).
8. Ibid.
9. Ibid.
10. Ibid.
11. O.C.G.A. §50-14-1(e)(1).
12. Ibid.
13. Ibid.
14. O.C.G.A. §50-14-1(c).
15. Maxwell v. Carney, 273 Ga. 864, 548 S.E.2d 293 (2001).
16. O.C.G.A. §50-14-1(c).
17. O.C.G.A. §50-14-1(e)(2)
18. Ibid.

19. O.C.G.A. §50-14-1(d).
20. O.C.G.A. §36-1-25.
21. O.C.G.A. §§38-3-54, 38-3-55.
22. O.C.G.A. §50-14-1(a)(2).
23. Ibid.
24. Ibid.
25. O.C.G.A. §50-14-2(1).
26. The Claxton Enterprise v. Evans County Board of Commissioners, 249 Ga. App. 870, 549 S.E.2d 830 (2001).
27. Ibid.
28. O.C.G.A. §50-14-2(1).
29. O.C.G.A. §50-14-2(2).
30. O.C.G.A. §50-14-3(4).
31. O.C.G.A. §50-14-3(6).
32. Ibid.
33. Ibid.
34. O.C.G.A. §50-14-4(a).
35. Ibid.
36. *See* Jersawitz v. Fortson, 213 Ga. App. 796, 446 S.E.2d 206 (1994); 1998 Op. Att'y Gen. U98-3.
37. *See* O.C.G.A. §50-14-4(b).
38. O.C.G.A. §50-14-3(6).
39. Schoen v. Cherokee County, 242 Ga. App. 501, 530 S.E.2d 226 (2000); *but see* 1998 Op. Att'y Gen. U98-3.
40. O.C.G.A. §50-14-4(a).
41. O.C.G.A. §50-14-3(4).
42. Ibid.
43. O.C.G.A. §50-14-4(b).
44. Ibid.
45. O.C.G.A. §50-14-5(a).
46. O.C.G.A. §50-14-6.
47. O.C.G.A. §16-10-71.
48. O.C.G.A. §50-14-5(a).
49. O.C.G.A. §50-14-1(b); *see* Guthrie v. Dalton City School District, 213 Ga. App. 849, 446 S.E.2d 526 (1994); Walker v. City of Warner Robbins, 262 Ga. 551, 422 S.E.2d 555 (1992).
50. O.C.G.A. §50-14-1(b).
51. Ibid.
52. O.C.G.A. §50-14-5(b).
53. *See* O.C.G.A. §21-4-3(7); Steele v. Honea, 261 Ga. 644, 409 S.E.2d 652 (1991); Davis v. Shavers, 263 Ga. 785, 439 S.E.2d 650 (1994).
54. O.C.G.A. §50-18-70(a).
55. Ibid.; *see* Hackworth v. Board of Education for the City of Atlanta, 214 Ga. App. 17, 447 S.E.2d 78 (1994).
56. O.C.G.A. §50-18-70(a), (b).
57. O.C.G.A. §50-18-72(a)(2).
58. O.C.G.A. §50-18-72(a)(11.3)(A).

59. Ibid.
60. O.C.G.A. §50-18-72(a)(11.3)(A), (B)(v).
61. O.C.G.A. §50-18-72(a)(11.3)(A).
62. O.C.G.A. §50-18-72(a)(11.3)(B)(ii), (iii), (viii), (ix).
63. O.C.G.A. §50-18-72(a)(11.3)(B)(vi).
64. O.C.G.A. §50-18-72(a)(11.3)(B)(vii).
65. O.C.G.A. §§50-18-(e)(3), 48-13-15, 48-5-314(a).
66. O.C.G.A. §§50-18-72(b)(1), 10-1-760–10-1-767; Theragenics Corp. v. Georgia Department of Natural Resources, 244 Ga. App. 829, 536 S.E.2d 613 (2000).
67. O.C.G.A. §50-18-72(a)(1).
68. O.C.G.A. §50-18-72(a)(11.3)(D).
69. O.C.G.A. §50-18-72(a)(5).
70. O.C.G.A. §50-18-72(a)(7).
71. Ibid.
72. Ibid.
73. O.C.G.A. §50-18-72(a)(6)(A).
74. O.C.G.A. §50-18-72(a)(6)(B).
75. O.C.G.A. §50-18-72(e)(1).
76. O.C.G.A. §50-18-72(a)(4).
77. O.C.G.A. §50-18-72(a)(5).
78. O.C.G.A. §50-18-72(e)(2).
79. O.C.G.A. §50-18-72(a)(14).
80. O.C.G.A. §50-18-72(a)(11.2).
81. O.C.G.A. §50-18-72(a)(2); *see* Fincher v. State, 231 Ga. App. 49, 497 S.E.2d 632 (1998); Dortch v. Atlanta Journal and Atlanta Constitution, 261 Ga. 350, 405 S.E.2d 43 (1991).
82. O.C.G.A. §50-18-72(a)(13), (13.1).
83. O.C.G.A. §50-18-72(a)(3).
84. O.C.G.A. §50-18-72(a)(4.1).
85. O.C.G.A. §50-18-77.
86. O.C.G.A. §50-18-72(f)(2).
87. O.C.G.A. §50-18-70(b).
88. O.C.G.A. §50-18-70(f).
89. O.C.G.A. §50-18-70(d).
90. Howard v. Sumter Free Press, Inc., 272 Ga. 521, 531 S.E.2d 698 (2000).
91. O.C.G.A. §50-18-74(a).
92. O.C.G.A. §50-18-73(c).
93. O.C.G.A. §50-18-72(g).
94. O.C.G.A. §50-18-72(h).
95. Ibid.
96. Ibid.
97. *See* O.C.G.A. §50-18-72(g).
98. O.C.G.A. §50-18-71.2.
99. O.C.G.A. §50-18-71(b).
100. O.C.G.A. §50-18-71(c).
101. O.C.G.A. §50-18-71(d).
102. Ibid.

103. Ibid.
104. O.C.G.A. §50-18-71(f).
105. O.C.G.A. §50-29-2(b).
106. O.C.G.A. §50-18-70(f).
107. O.C.G.A. §50-18-70(g).
108. O.C.G.A. §50-18-71(a).
109. Ibid.
110. O.C.G.A. §50-18-71(e).
111. O.C.G.A. §50-18-71(g)(2).
112. O.C.G.A. §50-18-71.2.
113. O.C.G.A. §50-18-77.
114. Ibid.
115. O.C.G.A. §50-18-73(a).
116. O.C.G.A. §50-18-74.
117. O.C.G.A. §50-18-73(a).
118. O.C.G.A. §50-18-73(b).
119. O.C.G.A. §50-18-70(g).
120. O.C.G.A. §50-18-74.
121. O.C.G.A. §50-18-73(a).
122. O.C.G.A. §50-18-73(c).
123. Howard v. Sumter Free Press, Inc., 272 Ga. 521, 531 S.E.2d 698 (2000).
124. O.C.G.A. §50-18-72(h).
125. O.C.G.A. §§50-18-90–50-18-103.
126. O.C.G.A. §50-18-70(f).

9

Walt McBride and Scot Wrighton

Meetings Procedure, Organization, and Public Participation

During city council meetings, decisions are made that formally set municipal programs in motion, enact ordinances, adopt policy, and authorize the expenditure of city funds.[1] This chapter discusses the conduct of meetings, preparation for meetings, rules of procedure, and encouragement of citizen participation. Citizens draw conclusions about the effectiveness of their governing body from the manner in which public meetings are organized and conducted. Not only are orderly and well-run meetings more enjoyable, they also help establish a more positive city image. Disorderly and poorly conducted public meetings reflect negatively upon the city, its governing body, and staff.

MEETINGS

Before exploring how to have an effective meeting, it's important to understand what a meeting is. (The Open Meetings Act, commonly referred to as the Sunshine Law, and further information on meetings are discussed in Chapter 8.) According to state law, a meeting occurs when

> a quorum of the members of the governing body of an agency or of any committee of its members created by such governing body, whether standing or special, pursuant to schedule, call, or notice of or from such governing body or committee or an authorized member, at a designated time and place at which any public matter, official business, or policy of the agency is to be discussed or presented or at which official action is to be taken or, in the case of a committee, recommendations on any public matter, official business, or policy to the governing body are to be formulated, presented, or discussed.[2]

Thus, nearly every time the council assembles as a group, a meeting occurs. While the law does provide a few exceptions, it is important to be mindful of the spirit of the law. It is intended to make the policy-formulation process more transparent to the citizens whom local officials represent.

There are several kinds of meetings that may be held by city councils: regular meetings, work sessions, executive sessions, special meetings, and public hearings.

Regular Meetings

Regular meetings are official meetings held periodically to consider municipal business, make policy decisions, approve contracts, establish budgets, and enact ordinances or resolutions. Their time and frequency are usually specified in the city charter or ordinance.

Work Sessions

Work sessions provide members the opportunity to meet with staff in order to delve into complex issues, discuss solutions and alternatives, give direction to staff, finalize agendas, or create consent agendas. Work sessions may be held immediately prior to a regular meeting or may be held at other times established by the council. Premeeting work sessions can be used by councilmembers to prepare for upcoming regular meetings. These meetings are typically less formal and are often used for information gathering and no formal votes are taken. However, it should be noted that premeeting work sessions are subject to the open meetings law.

Executive Sessions

Council meetings that are closed to the public are often referred to as executive sessions. Such meetings may only be held for the specific, limited purposes authorized by law, and the council must comply with statutory procedures in closing a meeting. These private sessions are held with the elected officials and any staff or appointed professionals necessary to the discussion.

Special Meetings

These meetings are usually convened to discuss and vote on one or a limited number of specific issues. For example, a special meeting may be held to take action on a controversial rezoning request. Because there may be a number of people wishing to comment regarding the request, holding a special meeting to address the issue is an effective way to avoid an otherwise long and drawn out regular meeting.

Public Hearings

Public hearings allow citizens to express opinions on matters of public concern. Generally, no official action is taken during a public hearing. Some hearings are required by law, but they may also be used by the council for other matters. They may be called to gather facts related to proposed action or to gauge public opinion by allowing citizens the opportunity to comment on a specific topic, such as a land-use plan. They can also be used as town hall meetings to meet members of the public and find out what they are concerned about. Finally, they can be used to allow the citizens to vent their frustrations. Public hearings may be held as a part of a regular or special meeting, or they may be entirely separate meetings.

Although there are many opportunities to meet, official decisions may only be made in regular, open meetings of the elected body. At such meetings, issues are publicly debated and acted upon. Local officials must resist the temptation to make final decisions prior to official meetings and then "rubber-stamp" them at the official meeting.

PREPARING FOR MEETINGS

As an elected official, you bear a heavy burden of responsibility. You will be making decisions that will determine the future of your city. You owe it to your constituents to represent them well. This responsibility includes being prepared to lead.

Do your homework. Study the issues and have the facts in hand before the meeting. Review the data, reports, and background information provided by the staff before arriving at city hall, including pertinent municipal ordinances. Evaluate alternatives and be prepared to debate your position effectively. A councilmember who comes to a meeting unprepared may unwittingly and unnecessarily slow down the meeting. The rules of order that your city uses will help keep debate civil, but you also must keep your temper in check. It is embarrassing and unprofessional when a mayor or councilmember loses control in a public meeting. In such cases, the mayor or whoever is chairing the meeting may have the unruly member removed from the meeting.

You and your fellow elected officials should know who is responsible for setting the meeting agenda. Determine how the agenda is set, how you can add something to it, and what are the agenda deadlines. You also should decide as a group how the agenda will be changed, if necessary.

RULES OF PROCEDURE

Clear, up-to-date, written rules of procedure make it easier to transact municipal business in an orderly manner. To be effective, a councilmember needs to know the rules of procedure for city council meetings. A city's charter may provide for specific rules of procedure, or it may be silent, in which case the city council may adopt a standard guide to parliamentary procedure, such as *Robert's Rules of Order*, or may design its own rules of procedure. Although every local government should adopt a set of procedural rules to govern its meetings, there is no state law requiring adoption of a particular set of rules.

Purpose

Rules of order for public meetings should help manage the conduct of the city council; they should not get in the way of transacting the people's business. Whatever rules are adopted by a governing body, they should conform to the following three principles:

1. Rules should establish and maintain order by providing a clear framework for the conduct of a meeting.
2. Rules should be clear and simple, facilitating wider understanding and participation.
3. Rules should be user friendly, meaning they should be simple enough that citizens feel able to participate in the process.

The following essential elements should be included:

1. A clear statement recognizing the hierarchy of law. The U.S. Constitution and federal law, the Georgia Constitution and state law, and the city's charter override any procedural meeting rules the council may adopt.
2. The manner and requirements for calling and convening special meetings and the quorum necessary for transacting business.
3. Designation of who shall preside over meetings in the absence of the mayor and/or in the absence of the mayor pro tem (or vice or deputy mayor).
4. A standard order of the agenda (e.g., call to order, roll call, minutes, approval of minutes, amendments to the agenda, administrative and fiscal matters, appearances or public comment, reports, old business, new business, adjournment).
5. Designation of a parliamentarian. (Unless the parliamentarian is the chair, his or her findings are advisory because the chair makes decisions of procedure subject to appeal by the body.)

6. Rules limiting debate, if any, including rules governing the public forum or public comment section of the agenda, including rules regarding speakers representing groups, limitations on repetition of the same information, and a method for granting additional time to speakers, if desired.
7. Any instances in which a supermajority (i.e., more than a simple majority) is required for passage. If a city adopts a set of standard rules by reference, any exceptions to the supermajority requirements of the referenced rules should be noted in the council's ordinance.
8. Requirements for second and subsequent readings of ordinances and other official actions of the governing body.
9. A procedure for setting aside the rules, if any.
10. A requirement that all members of the governing body vote on all business before the body unless they publicly declare a conflict of interest and recuse or remove themselves from consideration of the matter in accordance with state laws and local procedures and policies for dealing with conflicts of interest.
11. Rules for enforcing decorum and proper conduct.
12. A procedure for appealing the decisions of the chair.
13. Provision for the use of general consent when the chair establishes that there is unanimity to advance the business of the council more rapidly, including rules governing the use of a consent agenda, if desired.

Published in 1876 by Gen. Henry Martyn Robert, *Robert's Rules of Order* has become recognized as the foremost guide to parliamentary procedure and is used by a variety of organizations including governments at the federal, state, and local levels.[3] However, the rules were not drafted with local governments in mind and do not address certain idiosyncrasies of and issues related to local government, such as the need for public comment and public hearings, the provision of special mayoral powers or limits to such powers in state statutes or local charters, the use of abstentions for political purposes, or the special role of staff during city council meetings. Further, *Robert's Rules of Order* assumes that all meeting participants will conduct themselves with decorum and respect and that they will always follow the rules and abide by the decisions of the chair.

Despite its limitations, *Robert's Rules of Order* does serve to delineate the major rules of parliamentary procedure that a local government needs to conduct productive, efficient meetings, including the making of motions, the management of debate, the process of voting, and is widely recognized as the preferred way of running public meetings. If a council decides to create its own rules of procedure, it may still defer to *Robert's Rules of Order* where the charter and/or the local ordinance are silent.

Although the current edition of *Robert's Rules of Order* is complex and lengthy, its essential principles are actually quite simple. It systemically and logically sets forth meeting rules based on a hierarchy of rights: rights of the majority to decide and to prevail, rights of the minority to be heard, rights of individual members, and rights of absentee members.

When seen as protecting these rights, rules of order and procedure will generally preserve harmony in a group, even when there are distinct disagreements about the substantive public policy matters under consideration. Ultimately, the will of the majority prevails, but that same majority must allow participation by members who do not represent the majority position—to do otherwise or to set aside the rights requires a supermajority vote. The rights of absent members are also partially protected by quorum rules and procedures governing setting and changing the agenda.

Order of Business

City council meetings should follow an order of business formally included in its rules of procedures. The council should not depart from this order except in unusual cases and then only by majority vote. An order of business makes it easier to prepare the agenda and minutes and because it provides predictability, it engenders greater public confidence.

The Agenda

The agenda constitutes the governing body's agreed-upon road map for the meeting. A formal, written agenda following the official order of business should be prepared in advance of each meeting. An agenda provides an outline of items to be considered and usually lists them in order of priority. The agenda must list all items that are expected to be considered at a particular meeting.[4] It may also briefly state what action is requested of the city council and any previous action taken by it. State law requires that the agenda be made available to the public and be posted at the meeting site.[5] Although state law allows councilmembers to add necessary items to the agenda after it is posted,[6] last-minute additions that introduce material members may not have had time to study should be avoided. City councils should establish a deadline for submitting requests or communications for inclusion in the agenda and include them in the rules of procedure ordinance. Any item received after the deadline should be held over for the next meeting unless the majority of councilmembers present at the meeting vote to add it to the agenda. A sample agenda follows:

1. Call to order/roll call/quorum check
2. Innvocation/pledge of allegiance
3. Approval of minutes from previous meeting
4. Approval of the order of the agenda
5. Called public hearings
6. Public forum/citizen comment time[7]
7. Reports (from officers, committees, special presentations, other)
8. Old/unfinished business
9. New business
10. Consent items
11. Tabled items/hold items
12. General comments
13. Adjournment

Discussion

The same basic format should be followed for discussion on each item on the agenda. The chair

- announces the agenda item, sometimes by number, clearly stating the subject;
- invites reports from staff, advisory committees, or other persons charged with providing information to the body;
- asks if any councilmembers have any technical questions that require clarification;
- asks for public comments or, if at a public hearing, opens the hearing to public input and at the end of the public comment section announces that public input has concluded or the public hearing has ended and that the balance of the discussion will be limited to the members of the body, unless the council waives this rule by majority vote;
- invites a motion from the governing body and, when received, announces the name of the member making the motion and the person seconding the motion if a second is required by the body's rules of procedure;
- ensures that the motion is clearly understood, either by repeating it or by asking the clerk or the author of the motion to repeat it; and

- moderates a discussion of the item until a final motion is ready for a vote or other disposition.

Transacting the business of the council in this fashion provides consistency in the decision-making process and assures that the members of the governing body consider all available information before making a decision.

PARTICIPATING IN MEETINGS

In addition to the mayor, who usually presides over city council meetings, and the councilmembers, nearly every city has at least two appointed officials in attendance to perform tasks vital to the conduct of meetings. They include the city clerk, the city manager or administrator (or other administrative officer), and the city attorney.

Presiding Officer

Usually, the mayor is the presiding officer of the city council. In most cities, the voters elect the mayor, but in some instances the city council elects one of its members to the position. Depending on the city charter and ordinances, the mayor may be able to vote only in the case of a tie vote or may be allowed to vote on all issues. The council usually elects one of its members as mayor pro tem to serve in the mayor's absence.

The performance of the presiding officer is the key to effective, businesslike meetings. He or she is responsible for ensuring that meetings are orderly, conducted in conformity with the rules of procedure, and progress at an appropriate pace. At the same time, the presiding officer is responsible for ensuring that councilmembers and citizens have ample opportunity to express their views.

Other Members of Council

The elected councilmembers are the policymakers. City councilmembers share with the presiding officer the responsibility for properly conducted meetings. This responsibility includes having respect for one another's views and being willing to compromise, when possible, for the good of the city.

The city council must use its best judgment on how much time to spend examining a problem before reaching a decision. Actions of a city council should be deliberate and carefully weighed for possible consequences. Members will probably never know as much as they would like to about the consequences of various actions. However, failure to make a decision or to take action can create as many problems as a decision made too quickly. The city council must strike the proper balance between the two extremes. In any case, the city council should not allow a vocal minority that chooses to attend a particular meeting to unduly determine the outcome of a decision. Councilmembers must act for the good of the majority of the citizens.

City Clerk

The city clerk is the official record keeper. Although the role of the clerk varies widely from city to city, all clerks are responsible for keeping the official minutes of council meetings. The clerk's duties may also include preparing and distributing the meeting agenda, bookkeeping and maintaining other records, preparing and processing correspondence and reports, and managing the city council office. The clerk will typically make certain that all meetings are advertised in accordance with the Open Meetings Act.

Manager or Administrator

If the city has a manager or administrator, this officer should attend all meetings of the city council. This officer plays a significant role in preparing business to be considered at city council meetings. He or she is called upon to gather data, develop and evaluate alternatives, make policy recommendations to the city council, and carry out the intentions of the council. The role of the manager or administrator is largely determined by the city council. A good relationship between the city council and the manager or administrator can result in a smooth linkage of policy making to policy execution. Such a relationship can also improve the effectiveness of councilmembers and reduce the amount of time they must spend in meetings.

City Attorney

The city attorney advises the city council on its powers and duties under the law. He or she is usually required to attend meetings of the council to give legal advice on matters before the council, making certain that members abide by all applicable laws and keeping abreast of city programs and problems. The attorney may also be asked to prepare ordinances and resolutions, charter amendments, and other legal documents. He or she also advises other city officers on official legal matters and represents the municipality in court.

Every city needs an attorney who is accessible to city officials at all times. This person does not need to be a full-time officer but should advise the commissioners in the deliberations and decisions of the city council. Many city attorneys serve as the council's parliamentarian, but there is no requirement that the attorney fill this role.

PUBLIC PARTICIPATION

Georgia law requires that virtually all council meetings be open to the public, but the law does not require that members of the public be allowed to speak. Nonetheless, most local governing bodies adhere to the principle that citizens should have the right to petition their elected representatives; allowing time for public comment and debate at meetings maintains elected officials' accessibility and communicates the desirability and value of citizen input. The order of business for council meetings and the preparation of the agenda affect public participation. A council must balance the desire for public participation with its legitimate need to proceed with its regular business in an orderly and expedient fashion.

Meetings that are too lengthy may discourage participation. The use of a consent agenda can be useful when commissioners have a great deal of business to consider. A consent agenda typically includes items that require a decision but are not controversial. A consent agenda includes action items on which little or no discussion is anticipated or items that have been previously discussed (and possibly voted on) but that require final approval. Any item can be removed from the consent agenda for discussion by the full group and have a separate vote taken on that item if requested by one or more members of the group. Some local governments place the consent agenda near the end of the meeting because its contents are generally noncontroversial and rarely involve public comment (e.g., issuance of permits, street closure requests, authorizing payment of bills), while other local governments elect to place the consent agenda near the beginning of the meeting (after approval of the order of the agenda) in the event an item on the consent agenda is judged to be controversial or is the subject of additional public input. A consent agenda can save time, but items should not be placed on the consent agenda to discourage public participation

The public is more likely to participate in meaningful discussion if they are familiar with the governing body's agenda process and with its rules of procedure. In addition to printed agendas, many cities also distribute the written rules for public comment and a simplified version of the council's rules of order and procedure.

The Basic Rules of Parliamentary Procedure

The following are the basic rules of parliamentary procedure.[8]

- The rights of the organization supersede the rights of individual members.
- All members are equal and have equal rights to attend meetings, make motions and debate, and vote.

- A quorum must be present to conduct business. A quorum is the number of members required to be present to legally conduct business.
- The majority rules. The minority has the right to be heard but must abide by the majority's decision.
- Silence is consent. Nonvoting members agree to accept the majority decision.
- A two-thirds vote is necessary when limiting or eliminating members' rights or when changing a previous decision.
- A motion must directly relate to the question under consideration, and once a speaker has been granted the floor another member may not interrupt.
- The presiding officer may not put a debatable motion to a vote as long as members wish to debate it.
- Once a question is decided, it is generally out of order to bring up the same motion or one essentially like it at the same meeting.
- Personal remarks are always out of order in debate. Debate must be directed to motions and principles, not motives or personalities.

Two of the most misunderstood rules of parliamentary procedure are motions to "table" and to "call the question."

Tabling or Postponing

After considerable debate, the council still may not be ready to vote on a motion. In that case, members may propose that the motion

- be postponed until the next meeting so that more information can be gathered.
- be postponed temporarily (that is, table the motion), setting it aside until later in the meeting to allow more urgent business to be dealt with, permit amendments to be drafted, or allow time for implications of the motion to be checked. A motion to "take from the table" brings it back before the meeting. A motion to table is not debatable; a motion to postpone may be the subject of debate unless the city's rules of procedure provide otherwise.
- be withdrawn at the request of its mover, but only if no member who is present objects.

Calling the Question

Someone who yells "question!" from the floor indicates that he or she wants the motion put to a vote. Generally, the chair should not allow normal and reasonable debate to be cut short. A motion to call the question or in any way limit debate must be seconded and requires a two-thirds majority vote in order to then proceed with a vote on the main motion on the floor.

When special circumstances, the unique wishes of the governing body, tradition, or other reasons dictate that meetings proceed in a manner not envisioned by *Robert's Rules of Order* or any other adopted model of meeting procedure, the procedure for setting aside the rules should be clearly delineated in the body's own rules. A city's rules of procedure could also address a councilmember making general comments at the conclusion of a meeting; these remarks will not necessarily lead to a motion.

Encouraging Citizen Attendance

City council meetings offer an excellent opportunity for citizens to learn from and speak to their elected representatives. To encourage greater citizen participation, consider the following steps:

- Provide adequate notice of meetings. Printing the time and location in the legal notice section of the local newspaper is not enough. Publish the agenda in the newspaper. Take advantage of free time that radio and television stations must provide for public service announcements. Post an eye-catching copy of the agenda in public buildings and stores.
- Schedule and situate meetings for maximum attendance. Weekday evenings are usually more convenient. Arrange for adequate parking.
- Furnish a congenial setting for meetings. The meeting room should be well maintained, adequately lighted, at a comfortable temperature, and large enough to accommodate the public. There should be good acoustics or a public address system and adequate seating for citizens. City councilmembers should face the audience and one another; a semicircular arrangement is effective. The clerk, attorney, and other municipal officials should be seated where they can best assist in the conduct of the meeting.
- Schedule business for maximum participation. Scheduling subjects of greatest public interest early in the meeting is usually a good idea.
- Distribute the agenda and other information liberally. As citizens enter the meeting room, they should be given a copy of the agenda. A seating chart of councilmembers reflecting the respective areas they represent, a simple organization chart of city government, and a list of the names of the chief administrative officers are also helpful.

- Use visual aids for presentation. Topics often can be presented visually for greater clarity. Zoning change requests, budget presentations, and reports, for example, can be made more informative and interesting through the use of visual aids. Most local libraries and schools have modern visual aid equipment that can be rented or borrowed for public use.
- Assist the news media. Media reporters should be seated at a table where they can easily see and hear the proceedings. Upon entering the room, they should be given a copy of the agenda. Data, reports, and memoranda sent with the agenda to city councilmembers prior to the meeting should also be available for reporters.

Public meetings can be satisfying and even fun when they are well run, focus on the objectives, and end on time.

NOTES

1. Portions of this chapter are drawn from the *Handbook for Councilmen in Council-Manager Cities*, 3rd ed. (New York: National Municipal League, 1976), ch. 2; J. Devereux Weeks, *Handbook for Virginia Mayors and Councilmen* (Richmond and Charlottesville: Virginia Municipal League and Bureau of Public Administration, University of Virginia, 1963), ch. 5; Elizabeth M. Lee, "Planning and Conducting City Council Meetings," *Management Information Service* 2, nos. 5–9 (Washington, DC: International City Management Association, September 1970): 8–11.
2. OFFICIAL CODE OF GEORGIA ANNOTATED (O.C.G.A.) §50-14-1.
3. http://www.robertsrules.com.
4. O.C.G.A. §50-14-1(e)(1).
5. Ibid.
6. Ibid.
7. If they do not appear on the agenda, the rules for public forum should be explained each time by the chair.
8. D. Zimmerman, *Robert's Rules in Plain English*, Harper Collins: New York. (1997)

10

Audrey T. Griffies and Amy Henderson

Public Relations

> "Our liberty depends on the freedom of the press, and that cannot be limited without being lost."
>
> —Thomas Jefferson

The role of public relations (PR) in local government is often misunderstood. Some see public relations as mere frosting on the cake—an extra that only large city governments can afford; others equate it to the production of "slick" propaganda, designed to cover up serious problems. These perceptions are neither accurate nor helpful to the person who has been elected to serve the public.

Public relations is more than just another program that a city government budgets into its fiscal year. Every government is constantly engaged in public relations. City employees are engaged in public relations each time a citizen visits city hall to pay a utility bill, phones with a complaint about garbage pickup, or signs up for a city recreation program. Elected city officials are engaged in public relations whenever they respond to a voter's request, answer a reporter's question, or explain municipal concerns to a civic organization.

In city government, public relations represents the sum of all contacts between the citizens and the people who work in the government. Public relations involves all the actions that influence the way voters form their opinions about their government—from a handshake to a newsletter, from a telephone call to a story in the newspaper.

This chapter first considers public relations as an integral part of daily city government activity. It then suggests ways in which city government officials can interact effectively with the media. The latter part of the chapter gives specific suggestions for getting the government's story out to the public and describes the role of the public information officer.[1]

DAY-BY-DAY PUBLIC RELATIONS

The stereotype of public relations is that of talking with reporters and writing press releases. But in most cities—especially smaller cities—the most powerful impression that citizens have of city government comes from personal contact with city employees and officials. Paving crews, sanitation workers, police officers, and clerks are in the front line of contact with citizens. It's here that a city's officials and staff have the greatest chance of establishing good relations with the public by following basic procedures of good communications.

Public Relations Begins at the Top

The attitudes of elected officials toward the public set the tone for the entire administration. Maintaining good public relations offers direct advantages to the officeholder. It will help the mayor and councilmembers accomplish those tasks they consider important. Ultimately, all elected officials depend on good public relations in order to get reelected.

In public office, an official must learn to deal successfully with many "publics"—the individual citizen, special interest groups, civic and professional organizations, minority groups, and representatives of the media. The following rules of thumb will make contacts with members of the public more pleasant and more valuable:

1. Remember that you are the people's representative and spokesperson, not one of their rulers.
2. Have a pleasant, down-to-earth attitude with all citizens. Do not treat them in a high-hat or callous manner.
3. Listen to complaints and suggestions made by citizens. Citizens often have good ideas concerning government programs and services. Complaints about specific services should be referred to the appropriate department.
4. Keep the public informed about city government.
5. Be consistent in your dealings with the public.
6. Do not be afraid to say no to people who ask favors that are against the public interest or simply cannot be done. Take time, however, to explain why their requests cannot be granted.
7. Follow through on citizens' requests. In a busy, overworked city government, it's sometimes easy for citizen requests to "slip through the cracks" and remain unanswered for long periods of time. Don't let this happen. Often, all it takes for a citizen to feel good about your efforts is a phone call to let him or her

know that you are working on the problem or will address it soon—even if you can't handle the request immediately.
8. Refrain from publicly criticizing fellow government officials.
9. Consider personal honesty your most carefully guarded possession and public office your most cherished trust.

Citizens expect their elected city officials to be accessible. Voters expect to contribute to decisions as they are being discussed rather than merely reacting to policies already decided upon. To satisfy these demands for accessibility, many cities have established citizen advisory committees that meet regularly to discuss municipal government matters. Public hearings about pending legislation, especially if it is of a controversial nature, are also a way to promote citizen involvement. In general, sincere efforts by elected officials to encourage public participation in government will almost certainly result in improved public relations.

Good In-House PR Shows Down the Line

Each individual associated with a city government is an ambassador from that government to the public. Officials should remember that a few poorly handled complaints can undo all the favorable publicity gained by a whole series of expensive ads. Therefore, encouraging public relations skills for all city employees is very important.

A wise official will also remember that good PR begins in house. Encouraging good employee relations is the first step in building good relations with the public: satisfied employees produce good public relations. Establishing and maintaining good morale among city employees, then, is extremely important for a supportive and effective administration. Slick publicity can never replace the genuine willingness of a satisfied staff to serve the public. A great deal of damage can be done by a dissatisfied employee.

Department heads and supervisors are most directly responsible for the attitudes, morale, and training of employees. Their awareness of the importance of good public relations to a city government is critical. If a department head speaks contemptuously about the public, that attitude surely will be reflected down the line.

Contacts with the Public Create an Impression

All city government employees need to know how to handle face-to-face contact with citizens. An employee should assume that his or her contact with a citizen may be that citizen's only personal encounter with city government in a month, a year, or perhaps a lifetime. In face-to-face contact, a perceptive employee should be able to judge whether a citizen is satisfied and, if he or she is not, take steps to remedy the situation. In all direct contacts, the employee's personal appearance and manner of speech will play a part in the citizen's impression of the government.

Citizens will also draw conclusions from the appearance of the city government's offices and facilities. Thus, it is important to post signs or have a receptionist or other employee available to clearly direct visitors to the proper agency or official. Making it easy for a citizen to find his or her way suggests that the government cares about responding to citizen needs.

Many contacts with citizens will be by telephone. Each employee should be encouraged to respond promptly to phone calls as well as to in-person requests. Good telephone habits also include

- identifying the employee and department immediately when answering or placing a call,
- listening carefully to the caller's question or complaint,
- speaking clearly and distinctly and avoiding unnecessary jargon,
- keeping a message pad and pencil near the phone,
- remaining calm and using tact with callers who are upset, and
- avoiding unnecessary transfer of calls.

When a call must be transferred, the caller should be informed quickly to avoid needless repetition of lengthy explanations. The employee should ensure that the transfer is made correctly and the caller is in contact with the proper person.

Answering requests so that a citizen is satisfied may involve willingness to give the telephone caller a little extra time and consideration. An employee should seek to clarify the caller's inquiry and, if possible, determine the specific information or office that the caller needs.

Since some contacts with the public will be written, letter-writing skills are also an important part of good public relations. The appearance of a letter, like the appearance of a desk, creates an impression; there should be no smudges or typos. Letter writers should be careful to use language that will be easily understood. Technical jargon typical of government should be avoided in written correspondence as well as in face-to-face dialogues.

More cities are now using Web sites and electronic mail to reach citizens. The rule of first impressions applies here as well: your Web site should be attractive, useful, and easy to navigate. E-mails should be proofed for grammar and spelling, as would regular correspondence. Also, keep in mind that tone of voice and inflections are not easily "read."

Sometimes, something meant to be humorous may be read by the reader as sarcastic or mean. Even though e-mails are more informal than regular letters, the tone should remain businesslike.

WORKING WITH THE MEDIA

Newspapers, radio, and television broadcasts that come to mind at the mention of "the media" are just part of a much wider spectrum of media. A medium is any means by which communication moves from one person to another. Word-of-mouth is a medium (and, some say, the most effective one). Web sites, the telephone, cable television, memoranda, and city utility bills are all means of communication and are therefore media.

People consider radio, television, and newspapers as the media because they are the ones most often used to inform the public about issues of public concern. But it's important not to overlook the potential of other media in helping local government officials communicate with the public.

Most citizens form images of their city government and its officials through newspapers, radio, and television. These media tell people what city officials say and what the government does.

These media are not, however, just vehicles for one-way communication from government to citizen. They also report public responses to city government officials and programs, and their own editorial responses may influence others. City officials need to read and listen to these media sources.

Good relationships between the media and a local government are built on mutual self-interest. A government wants certain news reported in the local newspaper. It wants the public to know what it is accomplishing. On the other hand, the media want newsworthy stories and information important to their readers or viewers.

Although the government and media depend upon each other, their relationship is characterized by ongoing tension. Even the efforts of the best-intentioned public official cannot circumvent this tension between the media and government. On the one hand, the media see their role as that of providing continuing surveillance of government activities in order to keep the public informed. They feel they have an obligation to investigate, question, and criticize government operations and services. They also know that controversy makes news. On the other hand, governments may prefer to underplay controversy. They may expect the media to support their efforts and to give little attention to any mistakes, faults, and failures. These competing goals inevitably create conflict.

Although both sides have legitimate complaints, the tension between the government and the media is healthy—and essential to a functioning democracy.

Developing Good Media Relationships

City governments, especially their officials, need to learn how to use the media successfully. Elected officials can perish politically unless they learn to deal with local newspapers, radio, and television. They must also be aware that as public officials, their private lives may be observed closely by the media.

The following suggestions should help to make relations with the media beneficial rather than frustrating for local officials.

Understand How the Different Media Function

Television, radio, and newspaper reporters approach the news from different angles. Newspaper reporters are likely to follow city government most closely, keeping track of day-to-day happenings and seeking to provide in-depth coverage of significant actions. As a general rule, they have more time and more space in which to tell a story. For most weekly papers, local government is a staple of their coverage. Daily papers also give a lot of coverage to local government news but include more national and international news as well.

Television reporters are usually looking for major events, particularly those with some visual impact. For example, a newspaper reporter may regularly cover planning commission meetings. A television reporter may be interested in a meeting only if a large group of citizens are planning a protest. Radio stations either use newspapers as their source of news or have assigned reporters. In general, radio reporters are looking more for short, quick news items than for in-depth stories.

Media representatives appreciate an official who recognizes them and knows what they do. These guidelines will help:

1. Keep up to date on the names of the reporters assigned to cover government. City officials often complain about the rapid turnover of reporters. Although such frequent turnover is common, it is to your benefit to acquaint new reporters when they come to city hall. The Georgia Municipal Association produces a "Reporters' Guide to Covering City Hall," which offers basic information about city government. Provide specific information about your city—names of key officials, size of budget, budget year, key projects, etc.—and offer to take the reporter on a tour of the city. These steps may result in more accurate, fair stories.

2. Know who does what on a news staff. Don't, for example, hold a reporter responsible for a headline or the placement of a story in the paper: an editor makes these decisions.
3. Be aware of media deadlines. Ask the reporter what deadline he or she is working on and respond appropriately. Get announcements to a station manager in time for the seven o'clock news. Return telephone calls promptly so that your viewpoint on a new city program will be in the paper's evening edition. If you can't provide the information a reporter is seeking by deadline, let him or her know as soon as possible that you can't. These deadlines also mean that reporters work under demanding time pressures. Under such conditions, errors can be made even by the most conscientious reporters and editors.
4. Give advance notice. Frequently, media are understaffed, particularly on weekends. If you want coverage of an event, let the media know in advance so that a reporter, photographer, or camera crew can be scheduled.
5. Suggest story ideas. Reporters often hear, "Why didn't you cover that event?" or "Why don't you ever publish the good news?" Often, the answer is because they weren't aware of the event or no one told them the "good news." Reporters get paid for reporting. Help them and help yourself by offering story ideas.

Be Both Helpful and Accessible

Return phone calls promptly. Alert the media to important news. See that reporters are provided with agendas for meetings and background information on issues and programs.

Treat all reporters fairly, and don't play favorites. When there is important news, see that all reporters are alerted. Don't ignore media that cater to a particular segment of the city's residents, such as newspapers that serve the black community.

Even if you have established a good relationship with the media, recognize that you will not always be happy about the news they report. It is a rare public official who has not been annoyed by a statement taken out of context or even misquoted or by an action or stand on an issue that has been misinterpreted. What should you do in such a circumstance? Avoid overreacting to occasional annoyances. Try to forgive and forget, and don't hold grudges.

Former President Reagan's top press aide, Larry Speakes, once said, "I've been in this business long enough to know that you never win a fight with a reporter or an editor, for as Huey Long said when he was governor of Louisiana, 'They have reams and reams of paper and barrels and barrels of ink.'"

When you are interviewed by a reporter, keep these two cardinal points in mind: be honest and be discreet.

Even if a situation is unpleasant, being straightforward and honest will pay off. Rumors often are worse than the truth. If members of the press suspect something is being covered up, they will try to investigate. The resulting story of a cover-up may be larger and more significant than the initial story would have been, and it is certain to have a negative impact on the public.

If you have bad news, you tell it first. Don't let it be "discovered" by the media.

Be as open as possible, be honest, but also be discreet. When talking to a reporter, remember that what you say will be aired or appear in print. If you are not prepared to make a statement, say so. If you shouldn't say something, don't. Most reporters will honor a request to keep a remark "off the record," but some will not. This confidentiality is a courtesy, not an obligation.

In uncomfortable situations, public officials sometimes take refuge in being "unavailable" or in responding "no comment" to questions. These refuges are rarely, if ever, prudent. Public officials can look foolish if, for example, they reply "no comment" when asked why they voted for an unpopular bill. However, "no comment at this time" can be appropriate in some situations. For example, if a city is being audited, any remarks might be premature or damaging. When using that reply, explain why comments are inappropriate at the time. It is permissible to say, "I don't know" when asked a question that you don't know the answer to, but it's wise to add, "but I will find out and get back to you." Then do so. Although being open with the media is sometimes uncomfortable, it is the best way to serve the public, our democracy, and your city government.

REPORTING TO THE PUBLIC

Public relations means more than establishing harmonious contacts with the public or even with the media. Part of public relations is getting important information to the public. A way of remembering this aspect of public relations is to think of the letters in the abbreviation PR as standing for "performance" and "reporting." If a city government is performing its tasks well, it should also be reporting its success to the citizens.

Using Broadcast Media

The obvious methods by which to report news to the public is by using newspapers, radio, and TV. Without some effort on its part, however, a city cannot depend on the media to get specific information to the public. If a city official is on good terms with a reporter, editor, or station manager, a phone call may be the simplest way to initiate the news process.

Remember when talking to television reporters to "think visually." They are going to want to know what kind of footage they can get to go with the story. When pitching a budget story, for example, suggest the reporter conduct the interview in the city park, where children will be playing in the background, to illustrate the need for more funds for the city recreation program.

Newspaper calendars and public service announcements on radio or TV may be used to let the public know about city meetings, hearings, or special events. Information items should be typed and delivered to the appropriate place before deadline.

Announcements or stories about city programs can be given to the press in the form of a news release. A news release is a written account of an event or issue. (Figure 10-1 presents the standard format for a news release.)

A news release should be proofread carefully before it is reproduced or distributed. Typographical errors cast doubt about the accuracy and authority of the source. Further, such errors could result in a serious misstatement.

The news conference is a method of informing all the media simultaneously about an important news item. This method of communication should be used sparingly, however, as many people must take time out of their working day for such an event. Generally, invitations to a news conference are given orally, and news conferences are held in the early part of the day in a central location. They are typically used for major announcements (e.g., a new industry coming to town, launching a new city-service) or in crisis situations when you want to get the information out to all outlets at one time.

News releases and conferences are usually handled by the city's public information officer, if such a position exists. Local media may provide other opportunities for letting the public know about their city government.

Newspapers may welcome guest editorials or even regular columns contributed by local officials. In some cities, radio and television public

Figure 10-1. *Standard Format for a News Release*

Your Name   for immediate release
City Department
Full Department Address
Your Phone Number

News Release

A news release should be typed on one side of 8½" x 11" paper, double spaced for newspaper use, triple spaced for radio and television. Leave wide margins for the editor's use.

Most news releases have a headline, as shown above, and a label like that in the upper right-hand corner that tells the media when to use the release. If the information should not be used at once but on a future date, then the label should read "for release (month-day-year)." It is a good idea to release most information at a time when all the local media have an equal chance of using it as news.

If appropriate, a photograph may be sent along with a news release. People and places in the photograph should be identified.

Should the news release run longer than a single page, print "more" at the bottom of each page except the last. Number the pages: in general, three pages should be the maximum. At the end of the news release, print three asterisks or the symbol —30—.

—30—

---

affairs forums or talk shows can be excellent ways of communicating with citizens. A phone call to the station manager may be all that is necessary to schedule an appearance on such a program.

Using Other Media

Even without broadcast media (and some Georgia cities have very little access to broadcast media), cities have access to a number of media that, properly used, can be very effective means of communicating with citizens.

Cable Television

New communications technology has greatly broadened the range of media. The proliferation of cable TV channels in particular offers new choices in communication. A number of Georgia cities have been able to secure the use of cable channels and videotaping and editing facilities when negotiating cable franchises. A city may be able to offer 24-hour city programming to its citizens through the use of a cable channel and a videotaping and editing studio. Or cities may be able to negotiate to have their city council sessions taped (which very effectively ends citizen complaints about accessibility) or negotiate agreements whereby the cable franchisee provides aid and assistance in producing informational videos for the city.

The ideal time to reach agreements with cable providers about such services is during franchise negotiations, but cable providers may be asked to provide such services at any time. It's an excellent idea to examine what services other cities have sought and obtained and what current law requires of cable systems before entering franchise negotiations.

Newsletters

Cities of all sizes throughout Georgia are already providing their cities with regular newsletters. They range from two-page, type-written, photocopied newsletters with hand-drawn art to slick, printed, two-color newsletters that feature photographs of city employees. More and more cities are also producing e-newsletters, which are e-mailed to subscribers. Newsletters generally include news of city departments' activities, news of city personnel, upcoming community events, and explanations of city policies.

Such newsletters need not be a one-way medium. They can encourage citizens to write letters to the editor. Or they may solicit information. A city's newsletter may ask its readers to write or call if there is anything they want to know about the city. The city can then respond to requests, either directly or through the newsletter.

Desktop publishing technology, which has become relatively inexpensive in the last several years, is widely used to produce newsletters, since it allows users to produce very attractive, professional-looking newspapers for a small investment of money. But desktop publishing should not be regarded as a panacea. It still requires time and attention to detail to produce a newsletter that is attractive and free of errors. Typographical errors and errors of fact can still be misleading, no matter how they are produced.

Utility Bills

Utility bills are a direct mail advertiser's dream—mail that is opened and read by almost everyone who receives it. Some Georgia cities have elected to take advantage of this medium by including short printed pieces with their utility bills. A brief article enclosed in the city's utility bills can give citizens information about the way the city functions.

Occasional Pieces

Anything a city prints can be used as a tool to get the city's message across, including annual reports, posters announcing various meetings, advertisements, and press handouts at city meetings.

Facing Live Audiences

Information about the city government can also be communicated in person—an effective way of reaching specific audiences. Most civic groups welcome city spokespersons as speakers for their meetings. Service departments, such as police and fire, often present programs that explain city services to schools and other groups.

Some cities have devised a speakers' bureau, selecting city officials who can make themselves available to tell citizens about various aspects of their government. By publicizing the existence of a speakers' bureau, a city can create increased opportunities to get its message out.

Public hearings and open meetings give voters and governments effective methods for exchanging viewpoints (see Chapters 8 and 9). Ample notification of such meetings is important. Scheduling public hearings or committee meetings in the evening, when working people can attend, is a good idea, as is rotating meeting locations around the different neighborhoods in the city.

ROLE OF PR IN DISASTER PREPAREDNESS

During disasters are often when good public information is most desperately needed and least available—unless a city has included public information in its disaster preparedness plan.

Such disasters can take many forms. Very often, they are natural disasters such as a severe flood or a devastating fire. They may also be manmade disasters such as a train loaded with hazardous materials derailing, requiring massive evacuations of city residents.

At such times, there will be intense efforts on the part of the media to obtain comments from local officials. But very often, the department heads and other officials who would ordinarily respond quickly to such requests will be too busy. Under such circumstances, reporters will often interview anyone they can reach, which can result in conflicting and inaccurate information.

The best way to avoid this situation is to include communications in the city's disaster preparedness plan. Some member of the city government should be assigned the responsibility for talking with the media—as "media contact." Make sure the other members of the disaster response team understand their roles so that they can refer media requests properly to the media contact, along with the information needed by the media. Reporters don't ordinarily like being referred to a spokesperson, but an official spokesperson is better than no interview.

The media contact can not only field questions from the media but can also relay vital emergency information to the local radio, television, and newspaper outlets.

Thus, the media contact can serve a vital function—relaying important information to the media, squelching rumors and inaccuracies, leaving other city officials free to cope with the emergency, and projecting an image of a city government that is well prepared to handle the crisis.

ROLE OF THE PUBLIC INFORMATION OFFICER

Many governments hire persons skilled in communications to assist them in letting the public know the positive things they are doing. This person may do the following:

- Prepare news releases, public service announcements, etc.
- Maintain good media relations.
- Produce brochures, posters, leaflets, reports, notices, and other publications.
- Produce photos, videos, and other visual aids.
- Maintain files of photos of city personnel.
- Prepare paid advertisements.
- Respond to citizen requests, complaints, etc.
- Meet with citizen groups.
- Prepare speeches and other presentations.
- Give tours.
- Coordinate special events.
- Develop forms of recognition for citizens and city employees.

- Improve communications among city employees and between city employees, mayors, and councilmembers.
- Keep abreast of new technology for communications, such as telecommunications and computer databases.
- Maintain scrapbook of news clippings—invaluable for later research.[2]

Obviously, the size and income of a city government will determine whether such a position is advisable. A city that cannot afford to hire a full-time employee in this area may wish to consider taking on a skilled individual on a part-time or temporary basis.

However, public relations should never be delegated away. Specific public relations tasks can be assigned, but good public relations is a product of the performances of all members of city government—employees, supervisors, and elected officials.

NOTES

1. Portions of this chapter are drawn from Charles C. Craig and Audrey T. Griffies, "Public Relations," in *Handbook for Georgia Mayors and Councilmembers*, 3rd ed., ed. J. Devereux Weeks and Paul T. Hardy (Athens: Carl Vinson Institute of Government, University of Georgia, 1993), 76–90.
2. This information is drawn primarily from correspondence with Claire Benson, director of public information for the city of Athens, Georgia, February 1983.

11

Margaret S. Herrman

Conflict Resolution

Any official administering the affairs of a municipality, whether elected or appointed, experiences conflict—sometimes frequently and usually in many forms.[1] Conflicts may involve municipal employees, the public, or elected municipal officials. For example, on any given day situations can arise in which particular employees are not doing their jobs. One employee may be impeding another employee's work. Members of an entire department may be fighting, either internally or with other departments. A neighborhood might be up in arms over changes in garbage fees and collection sites. Members of the governing authority may snipe at each other during meetings or, worse, undercut each other's work when speaking with members of the press. Or, the service-delivery plan, comprehensive plan, or local option sales tax (LOST) negotiations are due, and the affected governments may not see eye to eye.

As an elected official, you may not be directly involved in day-to-day conflicts, but you may become aware of them through conversations with the city administrator or manager or department heads or from complaints from angry city residents. No municipal official wants to learn about problems as a result of notification of pending litigation. Nevertheless, litigation naturally follows conflict that has not been handled well, and it is always a possibility.

Direct involvement in conflict will most likely occur in the context of the mayor and council's deliberations; in oversight of the city administrator or manager's work; in dealings with elected or appointed leaders of other cities, counties, or authorities; and even in dealings with the local legislative delegation. This chapter describes strategies that can help you reap the natural benefits of conflict while also providing ways in which to assess how effectively the city's administrators, department heads, and employees handle conflict. Knowledge of these same strategies can also assist in the selection of the best people to help in the event that the services of a consultant in conflict resolution are ever needed.

THE FUNCTION OF CONFLICT

Conflict is an important component of general interactions between people and political life in particular.[2] Contrary to common belief, the absence of conflict in relationships and organizations causes them to deteriorate over time. Consultants regularly see superficially calm conditions; such calm often masks and precedes a brewing conflict.

Conflicts should be treated as a signal, a warning of incompatible work habits, confusion over a proposed policy, or fear among the members of the governing authority that their political futures are being undermined. Viewed as a signal, conflict is an ally, not necessarily the enemy. Consider the following:

> Why not treat conflict as a form of life, particularly since we all know that it is precisely during the periods in our lives when we are exposed to a conflict that really challenges us and that we finally are able to master, that we feel the most alive.[3]

Conflict in Government

Municipal governments are like all complex organizations. In any organization, how well supervisors and employees work together and the decisions made by leaders affect its functioning throughout. Budget decisions of the mayor and council affect every program and every employee in a city. The ripple effect reaches beyond the organization as well. Certainly, employee morale affects constituent perceptions of how well a government is functioning.

At the same time, municipal governments differ greatly from private-sector organizations. These differences represent underlying political and structural realities that may subtly affect reactions to a conflict. For example, in those cities in which they exist, merit systems protect employees, but they also make it very difficult to fire someone who is incompetent or lazy.

Governments must be accountable to their constituents. Open meetings and open records laws, also known as sunshine laws, support accountability and encourage public awareness. However, the inflexibility of open meetings laws may make it difficult for mayors and councilmembers to talk candidly about legitimate irritation, anger, and distrust. Without airing and resolving such underlying conflict, even the most professional and dedicated official may find it difficult to think creatively about complex issues during public deliberations.

In some communities, watching even normal political discussion has become a blood sport for the media and some citizen advocacy groups. Ordinary disagreements about the pros and cons of a policy decision are too often portrayed as intractable conflict and a sign of dysfunction or incompetence.

Coping with these realities challenges an official to stop and consider how to confront and resolve conflict. The first step involves deciding (1) whether to take an active role in the conflict and (2) if yes, what role to take. Are you a stakeholder? Should you try to mediate the situation, or should an outside mediator be engaged?

There are a number of ways to address conflict. Different approaches may be effective in different situations. Familiarity with several problem-solving models and likely applications and limitations will help municipal officials select appropriate ways to solve problems and assist in screening consultants when needed.

RESPONDING TO CONFLICT: CHOOSING THE CORRECT RESPONSE

Conflicts exist in many shapes and sizes. Some involve a small number of people. Some involve whole neighborhoods or even hundreds of people. In some situations, those in conflict have about the same amount of power; in others, power disparities are striking. Some conflicts are only confronted after the fight has continued for some time. In other instances, people begin to tackle issues and take sides before a conflict surfaces. Familiarity with a variety of ways to deal with conflict may increase the ability to match a resolution strategy with an actual or emerging conflict. Following are some choices and applications.

When to Hold 'Em, When to Fold 'Em

Once a conflict of any form fully materializes, alternatives for resolving the situation are highly predictable and limited in scope. Even in the best of circumstances, there is less than a 50/50 chance that local governing officials will get what they initially want for their city. Individuals may win outright, but the win may sour future dealings with opposing parties. (When was the last time a political opponent thanked the opposition for beating him or her?) You may lose outright. You may also reach a compromise, but by definition compromising means that each side gives up something that it wants.

Given these choices, most people react to an emerging conflict by trying to avoid it. Think of the times you appointed a committee to "look into the situation." You might have dismissed the situation by saying, "If it ain't broke, don't fix it" or "It's not a big problem."[4] Or, you might have made a quick decision to capitulate. Capitulation without discussion of the problem will likely cause the conflict to return. Avoidance can be a good short-term strategy, but—in government settings—conflicts cannot be put off forever, nor do they just vanish from lack of attention.

Avoidance, suppression, or even "management" are not recommended for use in government settings as long-term strategies.[5] In the long run, all of these strategies tend to aggravate conflicts rather than solve them. So, the first choice is whether to confront a conflict. If avoidance is used in a more limited way—as a time out to think or to strategize and gather advice—this strategy can be helpful.

Once the decision is made to deal with a conflict, ask yourself if you, your employees, or your constituents would be well served if you personally tried to resolve the situation. Several factors should be considered:

1. Do you have enough clout to make meetings happen, especially a series of relatively long, intense meetings?
2. If you offer to help, can you deal with the possibility that people might turn to someone else instead?
3. Would you be comfortable getting beaten up emotionally?
4. Are your skills commensurate with the dispute?
5. Do you have the temperament (that is, a "thick skin") to distance yourself enough to see the situation as an interesting puzzle and not a personal attack?
6. Will your position or title allow you to be impartial? Impartiality means that you do not have an interest in any particular outcome and that you can treat everyone with equal respect. Supervisors and department heads could have a hard time with this question if the conflict involves subordinate employees.
7. Can you delegate the task of creating solutions to those directly involved in the conflict? Again, delegation can be especially hard for managers when the organization they work for expects them to make decisions.
8. Do you really have the time to focus on the people and the dispute?

Questions 1 through 8 apply to any level of conflict but are particularly relevant to matters of personnel management. Several "no" answers to these questions suggest that it may be preferable to bring in an outside person to help resolve the conflict. Questions 9 through 11 pertain primarily to technically complex disputes (land use, noise abatement, and regional environmental disputes, or service delivery or LOST negotiations).

9. Do you or your staff have anything (data, experience, information from previous negotiations, etc.) that would be valuable to contribute either to deliberations or solutions? If so, you should seriously consider getting outside help to lead the conflict resolution so you can actively add your expertise to the negotiations.

10. Will others see you as impartial? This question relates to question 6 but with a slightly different emphasis. You may think you can be evenhanded, but your formal title or your source of funding may make it difficult for either side to believe in your impartiality.

11. Is this dispute "bigger" than your capacity to manage a problem-solving process? This question is less one of skill and more one of resources to convene, facilitate, and administer a complex process that might last for some time. Can you do these tasks along with all your other responsibilities?

A "wrong" answer to any one question is all right, but more than that will make the job of resolving the conflict more difficult if you decide to take it on anyway.

Reactive and Proactive Responses

There are reactive and proactive ways in which to work with conflict. Many times people wait until well after a conflict fully emerges and then decide what to do. Avoidance, litigation, and even mediation are reactive responses. Waiting is a form of avoidance and not always bad. Indeed, some situations call for waiting until a conflict fully ripens and the adversaries are really ready to work on the problem.

But, there is an alternative choice—taking a proactive approach. Some of the most progressive political leaders in the United States are adding conflict prevention to their normal way of operating.[6] Conflict prevention is based on the premise that stakeholders recognize potential controversies and know when future decisions will generate heat long before a conflict actually surfaces. In using this approach, when a difficult situation appears to be developing, the stakeholders (i.e., representatives of those who will be affected by the decision) can be invited into a dialogue, problem assessment, and problem-solving process before the conflict polarizes and before any decisions are made. It is important to give all stakeholders time to research, discuss, decide, and influence the ultimate decision. Early dialogues support creative thinking and will promote final decisions that provoke much less controversy.

Using Conflict Resolution Strategies

This section describes mediation, policy dialogues, and collaboratives (see Table 11-1). Each of the conflict resolution strategies stems from the same core set of skills and philosophies. Each is also slightly different and best suited to specific circumstances. Effective leaders attempt to match the conflict resolution strategy to the type of conflict whenever possible.[7] Each strategy is discussed in the context of the following types of disputes.

Personnel Disputes

Training all supervisors and staff in conflict resolution skills is an effective, proactive approach to conflict in the workplace. Such training typically includes good communication skills, methods of resolving conflicts without the need to go to higher levels of management, and management methods to reinforce good conflict resolution skills. Training should coincide with the adoption of policies that encourage and support employees who successfully solve interpersonal problems themselves. When employees solve their own interpersonal problems, solutions occur quickly and early in the natural cycle of a conflict. Other employees and the public will experience an extended positive effect when they sense good employee morale and work habits.

Even workplaces that support proactive conflict resolution among employees experience situations in which employees have problems that would benefit from a supervisor's help. Supervisors who are skilled and comfortable with their own capacity to resolve conflict (1) react more quickly and thus reduce further polarization and negative interactions in the workplace, (2) use confidentiality to promote clear thinking and a willingness to work through a tense situation, (3) use communication skills that support exploration of obvious and hidden issues, (4) create a problem-solving environment that encourages reflective and creative thought, (5) assist with problem solving, and (6) know when they need to seek outside help.

Generally, however, local governments rely on reactive rather than proactive strategies. Of the several options for dealing with full-blown conflicts, mediation is one of the most effective for personnel disputes. Mediation creates a relatively safe, cost-effective problem-solving environment that encourages the expression of anger, a substantial ex-

Table 11-1. *Conflict Resolution Definitions*

Arbitration: Arbitration is also a form of negotiation. It is similar to mediation in that it introduces a disinterested person into the mix. It is very different from mediation in that the range of issues discussed are typically not as expansive, and the arbitrator decides the settlement. Before an arbitration begins, the participants, a court, or a preexisting contract determines whether the arbitrator's decision will or will not be legally binding. In the context of public-sector negotiations, arbitration typically is not binding.

Collaboration and Competition: Collaboration and competition represent different assumptions about why and how you are negotiating. Competition assumes an adversarial stance, a narrow focus on the issues (otherwise known as positions), and limited outcomes (win-lose). Collaboration assumes a nonadversarial stance, broader exploration of not just positions but also what is behind the positions (the "why" of a position), and much more elaborate outcomes that address those underlying needs (win-win).

Collaboratives: Collaboratives represent a relatively new but well-tested approach to complex community or countywide policymaking. They typically involve teams of people, each with a point of view or a stake in the decisions to be made, coming together over a period of time. The purpose of a collaborative process is to find solutions to discrete problems like housing shortages, creation of service delivery plans, sitings of power lines, divisions of sales taxes, and comprehensive land-use plans.

Facilitation: Facilitation is a form of assistance for groups of all sizes. Facilitators understand group dynamics and the stages of decision making. They lead by helping participants stay on task, meet deadlines, and accomplish goals. They lead without getting involved in the content of decisions. Facilitators use some of the same skills as a mediator, but the situations they lead are often of shorter duration and less volatile than would be true of most mediations.

Mediation: Mediation is a form of negotiation. Mediation adds a disinterested person to a negotiation. The mediator manages the process of negotiation so that good problem solving occurs. The different models of mediation allow for flexible applications relevant to many different settings and circumstances (consider the difference between two employees fighting versus a regional dispute over water). Mediators encourage communication, the free flow of ideas and concerns, analysis of the conflict and the issues, the creation of options, and the selection of outcomes that satisfy everyone's needs (win-win). A mediator does *not* decide a settlement.

Negotiation: Negotiation occurs in all decision-making or conflict resolution processes. At a minimum, negotiation includes two people discussing a problem with the intent of reaching some solution. Regardless of the number of people negotiating, the only people present are those who would be directly affected by the solution.

Policy Dialogues: Policy dialogues occur between several governments. A dialogue may occur early, as a prevention or planning intervention or as a way of encouraging public officials to negotiate after a protracted conflict. In Georgia, policy dialogues occur during public meetings. They focus on important policies that affect multiple jurisdictions. Ideally, governments enter a dialogue with the intent of eventually ratifying and implementing decisions that are made jointly during the dialogue.

ploration of the conflict, and mutual solutions. Mediations and their participants are protected in several ways:

1. Good mediators know how to encourage honest communication while reducing personal attacks.
2. Employment mediation is private and generally takes place away from the work site.
3. Before a mediation begins, participants sign waivers and consents stipulating confidentiality.
4. Local personnel policies can stipulate that all employment mediations are confidential and that supervisors will be punished if they retaliate or evaluate an employee negatively as a result of participation in a mediation.
5. Written results of the mediation are treated as confidential material.

Figure 11-1. *Small Group Mediation Compared with Litigation, Arbitration, and Simple Negotiation*

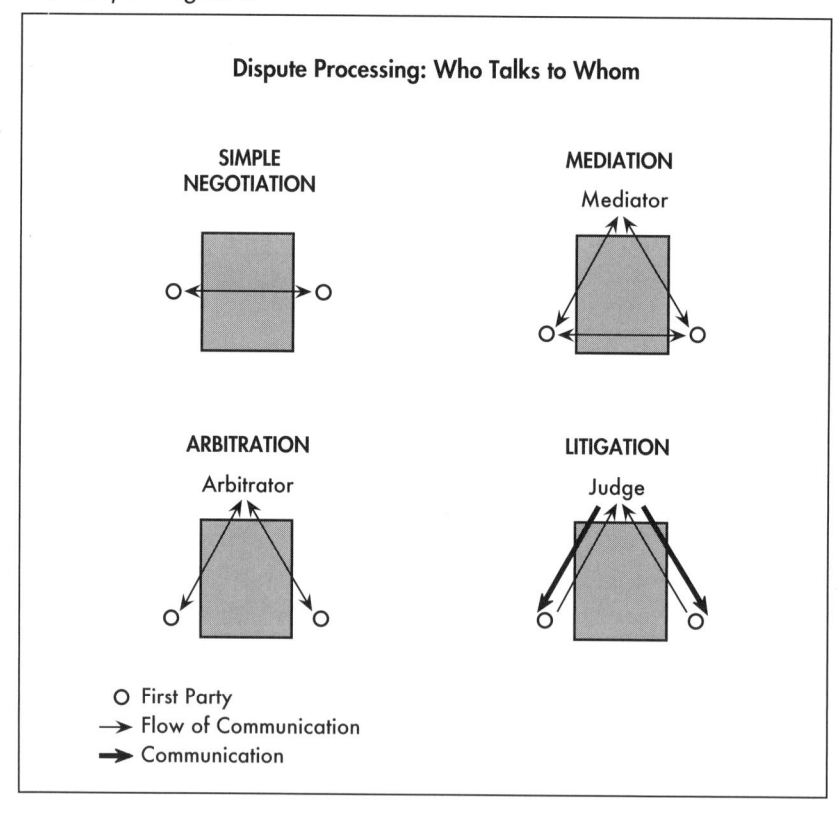

Dispute Processing: Who Talks to Whom

SIMPLE NEGOTIATION

MEDIATION — Mediator

ARBITRATION — Arbitrator

LITIGATION — Judge

○ First Party
→ Flow of Communication
➔ Communication

Figure 11-1 illustrates how a small group mediation typically looks, including where the participants sit and who talks to whom. As noted in the figure, participants talk directly to each other (something that does not happen in litigation and rarely in arbitration) and through the mediator. The mediator also talks directly to the participants. Mediation is ideal for resolving personnel disputes since the issues driving the conflict are often personal and have little or no legal standing. Mediation, in comparison with both litigation and arbitration, allows people to discuss what is really on their minds. Because topics are not limited to legally relevant issues, mediation encourages people to get to the heart of the matter, thereby increasing the likelihood of finding a solution that works long term.

If a personnel dispute involves only a few employees (typically two to four), a single-mediator model is extremely effective (resolutions occur 70 to 80 percent of the time). If the problem involves a larger group, such as an entire department, mediation still works extremely well, but it can be helpful to use two mediators (i.e., co-mediation model). Figure 11-2 illustrates the seating arrangement for a slightly more complex mediation. Note that some people negotiate while others act as a resource for the negotiators on each team. Chances of a successful outcome are increased by hiring mediators with experience in this type of setting.

Disputes Involving Constituents

Zoning controversies are a classic example of disputes involving constituents, although they are only one of many types of potential disputes between constituents and elected or appointed officials. Experienced mediators and facilitators can help anticipate community/municipal problems. They can also help solve entrenched problems by organizing constituents and officials into collaboratives.[8] Collaboratives and policy dialogues are two dispute resolution processes that have proved effective when issues are complex and involve several constituent groups. Both rely on structured negotiation that is managed by a professional mediator or facilitator who has specific training and experience in working with large groups and multiple teams. In most instances, there is little distinction between a policy dialogue and a collaborative process. Policy dialogues have been used with great success when groups of constituents and their elected and appointed officials work on emerging crises such as regional water shortages or long-term economic development plans. Figure 11-3 illustrates a large team mediation.

Collaborative models of dispute resolution have been used during some of the more complex service delivery negotiations (see Figure 11-3). In each case, teams of elected officials and their staff examined each

Figure 11-2. Complex Mediation Model

[Diagram showing a complex mediation model with Mediator/Facilitator at top, Developer and Legal Counsel on left, Community Leaders and Community Residents on right, Legal Counsel on right, and Agency Staff/Resource People/Technical Assistance at bottom. Numbered positions 1, 2, and 3 (three positions) arranged within the central square with arrows indicating interaction flows.]

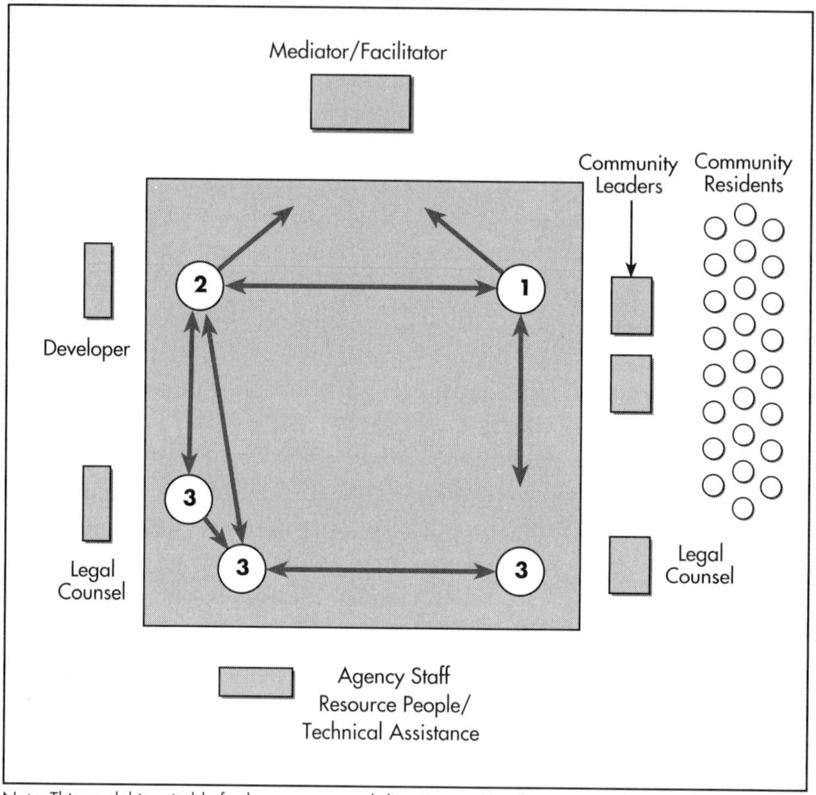

Note: This model is suitable for larger personnel disputes, zoning disputes, or planning disputes.

service, identified the government to deliver the service, established the jurisdictional boundaries for each service, and addressed the tax implications for their constituents. Although the media and city residents did not serve as negotiators, they filled an important role as observers.

Less complex models of mediation, such as those used for departmentwide employment disputes, can also be effective in addressing and solving disputes between smaller groups of constituents and officials. Used reactively, these models work well for zoning disputes, disputed tax assessments, and unpopular sitings of municipal services such as a jail or a water treatment plant. However, the number of groups in dispute will determine the complexity of the mediation model used.

The two-mediator, or co-mediator, model used in one-on-one personnel disputes is also extremely effective when an Americans with Disabilities Act (ADA) dispute arises over access to government services. However, it is important to match the dispute with a mediator who has

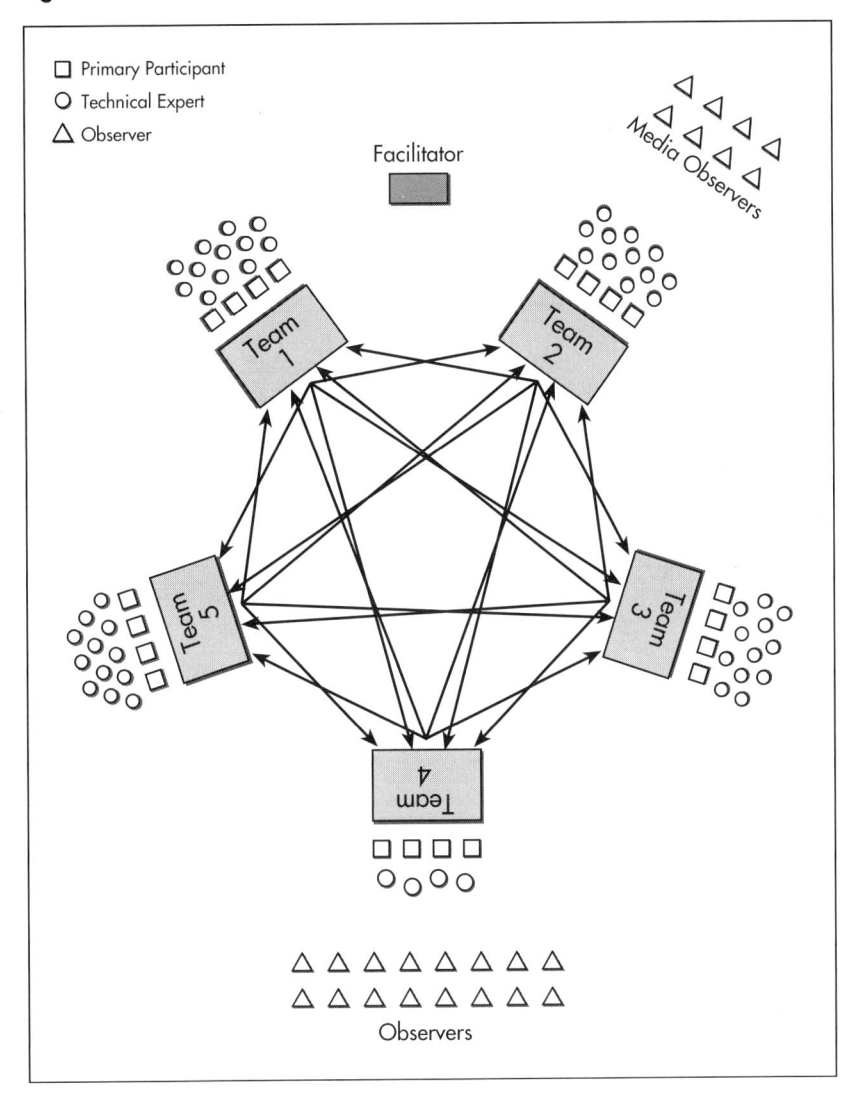

Figure 11-3. *Team Mediation, with Several Teams*

been trained in and is sensitive to the nuances of ADA mediation (e.g., language sensitivity, awareness of the legal issues, and familiarity with solutions from earlier mediations).

The least complex model of conflict resolution occurs when employees interact with the public. This model often only involves conversations of short duration. Employees represent the day-to-day face of government. Public confidence in the responsiveness of city government increases when employees are trained and skilled in conflict resolution. An example is a situation in which a resident has water and sewer lines crossing his or her property. The city owns the right-of-way, but the resident has planted prize azaleas outside the right-of-way, which will be disturbed when the city services its lines. This potential confrontation could land on the city manager's desk or show up at the next meeting of the mayor and council. Public works employees who are adept at conflict resolution can avert such a public controversy simply by negotiating when, where, and how the work will be done and then overseeing it to ensure that follow-through is consistent with the negotiated outcome.[9]

Intragovernmental and Intergovernmental Disputes

Disputes between the mayor and councilmembers or between individual councilmembers, appointed authorities in the city, or elected or appoint-

Table 11-2. *Differences between Debate and Dialogue*

Debate	Dialogue
Premeeting communication between participants is minimal.	Premeeting contacts and preparation of participants are essential elements of the full process.
Participants tend to be familiar leaders who are known by the public for their political and personal positions.	Participants speak as individuals whose own unique experiences differ in some respect from others on their "side."
Once a meeting begins, the atmosphere tends to be threatening.	The atmosphere is as comfortable as possible. Facilitators are used to support feelings of safety and promote respectful exchange.
Participants speak as representatives of groups.	Participants speak as individuals, from their own unique experience.
Differences within "sides" are minimized.	Differences among participants on the same "side" are revealed.
Participants express commitment to a point of view, approach, or idea.	Participants express their uncertainties, as well as deeply held beliefs.
Participants try to refute the other side's data or expose faulty logic in others' arguments.	Participants listen to the beliefs and concerns of the others.
Statements are predictable and offer little new information.	New information surfaces.
Debates are constrained by previous public statements that define problems and options for resolution.	Participants feel that they can explore various options for problem definition and resolution.

Note: This table is adapted from a table produced by the Public Conversations Project. Contact info@publicconversations.org for more information.

ed governmental bodies occur in the public eye. How, then, do you get your work done while also dealing with difficult situations and people? The place to start is in considering how you conduct business. The more negotiations are conducted like a dialogue and less like a debate, the greater the probability that the negotiations will succeed for everyone. Table 11-2 compares debate and dialogue. When you read through the table, think about your city, your comprehensive plan negotiations, your service delivery negotiations, or your tax allocation negotiations.

SUMMING UP

All of the models discussed in this chapter apply to disputes within and between governmental bodies. If a mayor and council are experiencing difficulties, effective conflict resolution may take the form of a one-on-one mediation or a series of smaller mediations (see Figure 11-1). Difficulties between elected bodies might rely on a mini-team model that looks like that depicted in Figure 11-2. A regional dispute, such as one over water, might benefit from a full team model similar to the one depicted in Figure 11-3.

The bottom line is that the choice is yours. Effective dispute resolution builds on years of experience with public-sector disputes, especially regarding large, complex issues. City officials now have significant resources from which to choose. There are no limits to how the mayor and council, the city manager or administrator, or city employees can address conflict.

NOTES

1. This chapter is adapted from Margaret S. Herrman, "Introduction" and "Finding Help" in *Resolving Conflict: Strategies for Local Government*, ed. Margaret S. Herrman (Washington, DC: International City/County Management Association, 1994), viii–xxii, 51–64.
2. A conflict exists when a person or a group frustrates the actions of another person or group in some way. However, a conflict may exist for some time before key people openly acknowledge the problem. For a description of the numerous steps people take before openly indicating that a conflict exists, *see* William L. F. Felstiner, Richard L. Abel, and Austin Sarat, "The Emergence and Transformation of Disputes: Naming, Blaming, Claiming," *Law and Society Review* 15, no. 3–4 (1980–81): 631–54.
3. Johan Galtung, *Essays in Peace Research*, Vol. 3 (Copenhagen: Christian Ejlers, 1975–80), 501.
4. *See* Leon Mann and Irving L. Janis, "Decisional Conflicts in Organizations," *Productive Conflict Management*, ed. Dean Tjosvold and David W. Johnson (New York: Irvington, 1983).
5. Many books and articles on conflict resolution espouse conflict management. Traditional materials on conflict management use the term as an equivalent to evasion or suppression, but these terms do not necessarily clarify the meaning.

6. Two resources for this type of approach are William R. Potapchuk and Caroline G. Polk, *Building the Collaborative Community* (Washington, DC: The National Institute for Dispute Resolution and the Program on Community Problem Solving, 1994); and Lawrence Susskind, Sarah McKearnan, and Jennifer Thomas-Larmer, *The Consensus Building Handbook* (Thousand Oaks, CA: Sage, 1999). Both offer advice and case examples.

7. This idea is not original. Frank E. Sander and Stephen B. Goldberg, in "Fitting the Forum to the Fuss: A User-Friendly Guide to Selecting an ADR Procedure," *Negotiation Journal* 10 (January 1994): 49–67, advocated matching forums and fusses. Their thoughts applied to litigation and courts not being the best strategy for all disputes. The idea was so timely that the American Bar Association sponsored a major program for the District of Columbia, and a number of other pilot programs around the United States have become standard procedure. Even though the first application of this idea occurred in a different setting, the same principle applies to treatment of employee disputes within county governments.

8. *See* Arthur T. Himmelman, "Communities Working Collaboratively for a Change" (Humphrey Institute for Public Affairs, April 1990) and Potapchuk and Polk, *Building the Collaborative Community*.

9. Value disputes, originating in diverse cultures, were previously noted in the context of employee disputes. They are also perhaps the most common type of dispute between employees and the public. Problems attributable to cultural divides may not be obvious. For example, in some regions of the United States, even in some rural communities in Georgia, informal norms dictate how and when someone greets another person (e.g., in traditional communities, the younger generation is expected to initiate the ritual, and the use of a title of Mr., Mrs., or Ms. is often expected). Consider the potential for friction when a young, brusque, preoccupied employee from another region sees the owner of the prize azaleas noted in the text. When cultural expectations are violated, suspicions of anger or aloofness build up. While expectations about greetings do not constitute formal procedures, they reflect subconscious and strongly held beliefs about how the world "should" operate.

PART 3

Management of Municipal Government

12

Stephen E. Condrey and Paul T. Hardy

Personnel Management

One of the costliest elements in the operation of municipal government today is personnel. This cost factor, as well as federal and state requirements, makes it essential that municipal officials practice good human resource management. The first part of this chapter defines federal and state laws that regulate the employer-employee relationship. The second presents ways in which to establish and administer an effective human resource management system.

EMPLOYER AND EMPLOYEE DUTIES AND RIGHTS

Federal and state legislation and court decisions have given municipal employees a number of rights that their employers must recognize. Municipal officials must consider these rights when making personnel decisions that may adversely affect employees in some way. If they fail to do so, an employee may have a claim against the city and its elected officials for money damages that must be paid by the city and, in some cases, from the personal assets of its elected officials. In recent years, governmental entities have become a popular target for this kind of litigation. Municipalities that act incautiously in making decisions affecting employees increasingly run a risk of becoming involved in federal or state court litigation with disgruntled or terminated employees.

Constitutional Duties and Rights

Courts have said that under certain circumstances a public employee may have a property or a liberty interest in his or her job. These interests cannot be adversely affected by a personnel action (a disciplinary action or discharge) without due process of law. This section discusses what property and liberty rights exist in the public employment situation and what is needed to comply with the requirement of due process of law. Also discussed are substantive and procedural due process and First Amendment rights of public employees.

Property Rights

Under certain circumstances, the courts consider a public employee's job to be property belonging to him or her that cannot be taken away (through discharge) or lessened in value (through disciplinary demotion, suspension of pay, reduction in pay, etc.) unless the employee receives due process of law. Whether a public employee has such a property interest is determined on the basis of principles of state law.[1] As a general rule, in Georgia, "one in public employment has no vested right to such employment."[2] However, as with all general rules, a number of exceptions have been created. When dealing with personnel matters, municipal officials should be aware of the following:

1. If the city adopts by ordinance, resolution, or other official act a provision that municipal employees may only be removed "for cause," an employee may have a property interest in his or her job.[3] It should be noted that some courts have held that a "termination for cause" provision appearing only in an employee handbook or manual is insufficient to create an enforceable property interest,[4] but cities should be cautious in relying on such authority, particularly if the manual or handbook is adopted by official action of the municipal governing authority.

2. If the city hires an employee for a definite period of time and the employee is discharged before the end of that time, he or she may have a property interest.[5]

3. An employee hired for an indefinite period of time—including through a contract for permanent employment—does not have a property interest.[6] This is called employment at will.

4. If an employee serves at the pleasure of the employer[7] or if he or she is terminated because it is determined by a superior to be in the best interest of the city,[8] he or she does not have a property interest.

5. When a municipality provides for an initial trial period to give the city an opportunity to determine if an individual will be an acceptable employee (often described as a probationary period), such an employee does not have a property interest in his or her job during the trial period.[9] If employees are subject to being discharged at any time, it is the better practice not to designate any initial period in a job as probationary so as not to give the impression that job rights change after that period.

6. When a municipality abolishes positions for budgetary or other reasons, an employee whose position is abolished generally does not have a property interest in his or her job.[10]
7. Always check a city's charter to see if employees are "at will" or may have a property interest in employment. The charter overrides ordinances or policies that directly conflict with it.

Liberty Rights

If an employee is demoted or discharged without due process of law (including not being renewed at the end of a contract period), and this action imposes a "stigma" or "disability" on the employee that denies him or her the freedom to take advantage of other job opportunities, the employee's constitutional liberty interest may be implicated.[11] This type of claim usually arises when derogatory information about the employee is released in the course of the discipline or discharge process.

For there to be a violation of the employee's liberty interest, the employee must show the following:

1. The action must have taken place in the context of demotion or discharge from employment.[12]
2. The information about the employee must be false.[13] If the information is true, the employee's liberty interest has not been violated, even though his or her ability to obtain future employment is damaged.
3. The information must have been made public in an official or intentional manner.[14] The mere presence of derogatory information in a city employee's personnel files does not infringe on an employee's liberty interests if it is not released.[15]
4. The information about the employee must be "stigmatizing." One federal appellate court described this requirement in the following way:

   The "liberty interest" is the interest an individual has in being free to move about, live, and practice his profession without the burden of an unjustified label of infamy. . . . [A] charge which infringes one's liberty can be characterized as an accusation or label given the individual by his employer which belittles his worth and dignity as an individual and, as a consequence, is likely to have severe repercussions outside of professional life. Liberty is not infringed by a label of incompetence, the repercussions of which primarily affect professional life, and which may well force the individual down one or more notches in the professional hierarchy.[16]

5. The employee must have been denied a meaningful opportunity to clear his or her name.[17]

Procedural Due Process

If a municipal employee's liberty or property interest is involved, the employee is then entitled to procedural due process.

With respect to a property interest, both pretermination and posttermination hearings are required.[18] It is not necessary that a pretermination hearing be elaborate: its purpose is to serve as an initial check against mistaken decisions. A more thorough review of the discharge can take place at a posttermination hearing. All that is required in the pretermination hearing is that the employee be told why he or she is being terminated and that he or she be given an opportunity to respond to the charges before the adverse action takes effect.[19]

If a municipal employee has a property interest in his or her job (see earlier discussion on property rights under "Constitutional Duties and Rights"), the employee must receive a pretermination hearing, even in extraordinary situations in which retaining an employee for the time necessary to comply with the pretermination procedures would (1) result in damage to public property, (2) be detrimental to the interest of the municipal government, or (3) result in injury to the employee, a fellow worker, or to the general public. However, the employer can suspend the employee with pay until the hearing is held.[20]

The following procedures have been ruled necessary for an adequate posttermination hearing:

1. Prior to the hearing, the employee must be furnished with
   a. written notice of the charges against him or her that contains sufficient detail so as to enable him or her to show any error that may exist[21] and
   b. the names of all witnesses who will be called, as well as an explanation of their expected testimony.[22]
2. The hearing must then be held within a "reasonable time."[23]
3. At the hearing, the employee must be given an opportunity
   a. to be heard,[24]
   b. to present evidence in his or her own behalf,[25] and
   c. to confront (cross-examine) his or her accusers.[26]
4. The hearing must be held before a tribunal having apparent impartiality to the charges.[27]

The evidentiary portion of the hearing and the final vote of the governing authority are required by the Georgia open meetings law (discussed in Chapter 8) to be open to the public. Only the deliberations may be conducted in a closed session. Experience has shown that it is best to have posttermination hearings or "appeals" preserved for future evidentiary use and that a court reporter or a good tape-recording system should be used.

Although it has been held that a deficiency in the pretermination proceedings may be cured by the availability of a full and fair hearing after the employee's termination,[28] cities should observe the requirement of a pretermination hearing whenever possible. In the case of liberty interests, the required hearing is not intended to evaluate the correctness of the adverse personnel decision. Rather, a liberty interest hearing is a limited procedure through which the employee is given an opportunity to clear his or her name or otherwise explain his or her conduct.[29] The liberty interest hearing need not be provided prior to the effective time of the adverse action.[30] However, the employee is entitled to notice of the charges raised against him or her and an opportunity to refute them, either by cross-examination of his or her accusers or through the presentation of independent testimony and evidence.[31]

Georgia law has extended to governmental entities, including cities, employer immunity for disclosure of certain information to a prospective employer. This information includes a current or former employee's job performance, commission of an act that constitutes a violation of state law, or the ability or lack of ability to carry out the duties of a job. An employer who discloses factual information concerning any of these matters is presumed to be acting in good faith unless there is evidence to the contrary or the information was disclosed in violation of a nondisclosure agreement or was otherwise considered confidential according to an applicable federal, state, or local statute, rule, or regulation.[32]

Georgia law gives public employees the right to petition the state superior courts for review of employment decisions under certain circumstances. A municipality's failure to follow proper procedures therefore may subject it to suit in state court.[33]

First Amendment Rights

Public employment has been held to be a valuable governmental benefit that cannot be denied an individual for an unconstitutional reason.[34] A public employee may not be disciplined for reasons such as race, religion, or assertion of other constitutionally guaranteed rights.[35] Nonrenewal of an employee's contract for such reasons is also constitutionally impermissible.[36]

This section discusses adverse employment action, particularly discharge, because of the assertion of protected rights, particularly the First Amendment right of freedom of speech and association.[37]

Freedom of Speech. Although public employees cannot be required to surrender their right to free speech, a governmental employer does have an interest in regulating the speech of government employees to some extent. The interests of the public employee as a citizen in commenting on matters of public concern must be weighed against the interests of the governmental employer in promoting the efficiency of the public services performed by its employees.[38] A public employee cannot be disciplined for making a public statement that is true, even though it is critical of his or her ultimate employer. Even if the statement is false, it is not grounds for discipline unless made either with knowledge of its falsity or with reckless disregard for whether it is true.[39]

For a municipal employee to assert a claim based on the right of free speech, he or she must show (1) that he or she was engaged in protected speech, (2) that the speech was a matter of public concern, and (3) that the speech was a substantial or motivating factor leading to discipline.[40]

Freedom of Association. The First Amendment right of freedom of association gives public employees the right to organize and become members of a labor organization.[41] Advocating membership in a labor union[42] and even expressing the belief that public employees should have the right to strike[43] are both constitutionally protected. However, an employee can be discharged or otherwise punished for going on strike.[44] Moreover, a disciplinary action for picketing in support of a strike probably does not violate an employee's constitutional rights.[45] Furthermore, the First Amendment does not impose any affirmative obligation on a city government to listen or respond to, recognize, or bargain with a labor union.[46]

Political Belief and Association. Public employees cannot be disciplined for failure to obtain the support of or affiliate with a political party unless they are in confidential or policy-making positions.[47] Furthermore, unless they are excepted for these reasons, public employees cannot be disciplined solely because of their political beliefs.[48] However, even some employees included in the exception may be protected from a disciplinary action.[49]

These prohibitions apply not only to actual or threatened dismissals but also to actual or threatened reassignments of duties or transfers if this action imposes on the employee a choice between continued employment and forsaking the exercise of protected beliefs and association.[50] It is also impermissible to require public employees to make contributions for political purposes.[51]

Federal Statutory Duties and Rights

Numerous federal statutes affect the employer-employee relationship in the public sector. Most of these statutes prohibit one or more types of discrimination against employees. The following are examples of some of the federal laws that may apply to municipal employees.

Title VII

Title VII of the 1964 Civil Rights Act, amended by the Civil Rights Act of 1991,[52] provides that it is an unlawful employment practice for an employer (defined as an employer of 15 or more employees)[53] "(1) to fail or refuse to hire or to discharge any individual, or otherwise to discriminate against any individual with respect to his compensation, terms, conditions, or privileges of employment, or because of such individual's race, color, religion, sex, or national origin; or (2) to limit, segregate, or classify employees or applicants for employment in any way which would deprive or tend to deprive any individual of employment opportunities or otherwise adversely affect his or her status as an employee" on any of the same grounds.[54]

Fair Labor Standards Act

The Fair Labor Standards Act (FLSA) was originally enacted during the Depression to encourage employers to hire more workers rather than simply requiring their existing employees to work longer hours. Important protections established by the FLSA are a minimum wage and the requirement of overtime compensation. In 1974, Congress expanded coverage of the FLSA to public employers not previously covered.[55] The U.S. Supreme Court initially held extension of the FLSA to be unconstitutional as it applied to public employers administering traditional governmental functions such as police protection and fire prevention.[56] In 1985, however, the Supreme Court reversed its previous decision and allowed extension of the FLSA to almost all governmental employers and employees.[57]

The normal workweek under the FLSA is a period of seven consecutive days, and overtime work is work performed in excess of 40 hours in a workweek. The FLSA sets up a minimum hourly wage and provides for payment of a premium for overtime work equivalent to one and a half times the employee's regular rate of pay. Municipal employees may be offered in lieu of overtime pay compensatory time off work at the rate of one and a half hours off for each overtime hour worked, but compensatory time off work may be granted only if it is based on an agreement between the city and its employees.[58]

The FLSA contains a number of exemptions and exceptions. Exceptions and exemptions to coverage provisions are generally construed narrowly against those who seek to advance them in an attempt to avoid overtime pay liability.[59] Courts have noted that the FLSA is remedial in nature and should be read liberally in favor of workers.[60] However, the courts have ruled that public employers are free to reduce the number of hours that employees work.[61]

The act provides a complete overtime pay exemption for individuals employed by a public agency that has fewer than five employees in fire protection or law enforcement activities.[62] In determining whether a public agency qualifies for the exemption, fire protection and law enforcement activities are considered separately. Thus, if a city employs fewer than five employees in fire protection activities but five or more employees in law enforcement activities, it may claim the exemption for fire protection but not for law enforcement.[63]

A provision of the FLSA provides an exception to the general requirement that overtime be computed on a weekly basis and that a premium be paid for hours in excess of a 40-hour workweek for firefighters and law enforcement personnel.[64] The exemption allows cities to establish work schedules for firefighters and law enforcement personnel that differ from those of other municipal employees. The regulations base regular and overtime pay on the number of hours worked in a 28-day work period. Because these regulations are so complex and specific, a city should not attempt to establish a work schedule and pay plan for firefighters and law enforcement employees without professional guidance.[65] Not included in the exemption are the "civilian" employees of fire and police departments who serve as dispatchers, radio operators, repair workers, janitors, clerks, or stenographers.[66] Rescue and ambulance service personnel will qualify for the exemption as employees engaged in "fire protection activities" if they "form an integral part of the public agency's fire protection activities"[67] or serve as employees engaged in "law enforcement activities" if they "form an integral part of the public agency's law enforcement activities."[68] Ambulance and rescue service employees may also qualify if they are employees of a public agency other than a fire department or law enforcement agency and if their services are substantially related to firefighting or law enforcement activities.[69]

Although these firefighters and law enforcement employees may accumulate up to 480 hours of compensatory time, other nonexempt employees may accrue only 240 hours. After that maximum is reached, a covered employee must be paid overtime if he or she works more than 40 hours in a workweek. However, the city may require employees to use compensatory time. Employees must be permitted to use their compensatory time within a "reasonable period" of a request unless it would be "unduly disruptive." Employees protected by the FLSA must be paid any unused compensatory time upon separation from employment with the municipality.[70] Compensatory time cannot be used as a means of avoiding statutory overtime pay. An employee has the right to use earned compensatory time and must not be coerced into taking more compensatory time than a municipality can realistically expect to be able to grant within a reasonable time of the request.[71]

In addition to firefighters and law enforcement employees, the FLSA exempts bona fide executive, administrative, and professional employees from its overtime pay requirements.[72] Such exemptions are construed narrowly, and the burden is on the employer to prove that it is entitled to the exemption. Neither the employee's job title nor job description is determinative of whether or not an employee is exempt from the overtime pay requirements; the exemption is based solely on actual duties and salary.[73] As with firefighters and law enforcement personnel, the regulations governing the exemptions for executive, administrative, and professional employees are both specific and complex, and no city should seek to address such exemptions without professional guidance.

Equal Pay Act and Age Discrimination in Employment Act

Two other laws, the Equal Pay Act and the Age Discrimination in Employment Act, were made applicable to state and local governments by 1974 amendments to the Fair Labor Standards Act.[74] The Equal Pay Act prohibits, with certain exceptions, differentials in pay based on sex (includes pregnancy, childbirth, and related medical conditions) in jobs, the performance of which require equal skill, effort, and responsibility and that are performed under similar working conditions.[75] The Age Discrimination in Employment Act provides that employers may not discharge, fail or refuse to hire, or otherwise discriminate against any individual with respect to compensation, terms, or conditions or privileges of employment because such person is 40 years of age or older unless there is a bona fide occupational qualification based on age.[76]

Americans with Disabilities Act

The Americans with Disabilities Act[77] (ADA) prohibits discrimination by employers against qualified individuals with disabilities in virtually all aspects of employment, including the application process, hiring, advancement, termination, compensation, and training. The ADA contains extensive and sweeping provisions preventing discrimination against persons with disabilities. Examples of conduct specifically prohibited by the ADA include

1. segregating, limiting, or classifying on the basis of disability a qualified individual with a disability in a way that would adversely affect employment opportunities or status (for instance paying a disabled employee an amount less than is paid to a similarly situated nondisabled employee);
2. excluding or denying equal job benefits to a qualified individual because that person has an association or relationship with a disabled person; or
3. using tests or other selection criteria that tend to screen out individuals with disabilities, unless the test is job related and consistent with business necessity.[78]

The ADA prohibits preemployment inquiries into a person's disability status. The only acceptable preemployment inquiries an employer may make are inquiries into the ability of an applicant to perform job-related functions.[79]

An employer may require a medical examination after tendering an offer of employment and before the applicant begins work. The employer may condition the offer on the results of the examination only if all entering employees in the same job category are subjected to such an examination.[80]

The ADA requires an employer, including a city, to provide "reasonable accommodation" of an otherwise qualified person with a disability, unless the employer can show that it would constitute an undue hardship. This requirement applies not only to persons applying for new employment but also to existing employees who may be or become disabled. It necessitates that an employer determine the essential functions of a job and examine possible modifications and adjustments to the job and/or the work environment that would allow a person with a disability to perform those functions. An employer may challenge an accommodation as being unreasonable on the basis that it constitutes an undue hardship to the employer because it is too costly or would be disruptive to the employer's operations.[81] Municipalities may be held liable for compensatory but not punitive damages for violations of the ADA.[82]

Family and Medical Leave Act

The Family and Medical Leave Act of 1993 (FMLA) requires all public employers to have an FMLA policy for their employees and post a federally mandated notice providing employees and applicants for employment with information about the FMLA. If the public employer has 50 or more employees within a 75-mile radius, the employer must provide up to 12 weeks of unpaid leave during any 12-month period for eligible employees. Eligible employees are those employees who have worked for the city for at least one year and have provided at least 1,250 hours of service in the past 12 months. Leave may be taken for the birth or adoption of a child or placement of a foster child; to care for a spouse, child, or parent with a serious health condition; or due to the employee's own serious health condition. An employee who takes leave under the FMLA must be returned to the same position that he or she held prior to taking such leave or to an equivalent position, and the employer must maintain group health insurance coverage for the employee during the period of leave, as if the employee had worked. The leave guaranteed by the FMLA is unpaid, although an employer may require that an employee use any available vacation, personal, family, or sick leave before the unpaid portion of the 12-week leave period begins. In addition, leave under the FMLA may be taken intermittently or on a reduced schedule when medically necessary.[83] A city can also be liable under the FMLA if it is found to have retaliated against an employee because he or she engaged in an activity or raised a claim protected by the act.[84]

Drug Testing

Drug testing of city employees is considered a search under the Fourth Amendment to the U.S. Constitution.[85] Although a search must usually be supported by a warrant issued upon probable cause, the courts have found that exceptions to the warrant and probable cause requirements may be permitted when "special needs, beyond the normal need for law enforcement" are involved. For instance, the courts have allowed random drug testing of employees who are in "safety-sensitive" positions."[86]

However, the courts have carefully defined what is and is not a safety-sensitive position. Before establishing a drug-testing policy, a city needs to consider and establish who will be tested, when they will be tested (preemployment, postaccident, randomly, periodically, or based on reasonable suspicion); how and when they will be notified of the testing; how the testing will be conducted; how the test records will be handled; and what will happen in the event of a disputed test result. Note that based on current case law, only employees in safety-sensitive positions may be subjected to random testing. Additionally, certain employees such as pipeline workers or employees who drive commercial vehicles may be subject to testing required by federal law. The establishment of any employee drug-testing policy requires careful review by the city attorney before its adoption.

State Statutory Duties and Rights

Discrimination

A state law similar to the federal Equal Pay Act[87] expressly covers municipal employers with 10 or more employees. It prohibits differentials in pay based on sex for equal work "in jobs which require equal skill, effort, and responsibility and which are performed under similar working conditions." The statute provides for arbitration as well as recourse to the courts, where both back pay and attorneys' fees may be awarded. A copy of the law, provided by the state upon request, must be posted in a conspicuous place.[88]

Age discrimination in employment is also prohibited by a Georgia law preventing an employer from refusing "to hire, employ, or license . . . [or] . . . bar or discharge from employment any individual between the ages of 40 and 70 years solely upon the ground of age, when the reasonable demands of the position do not require such an age distinction. . . ." Retirement policies or systems are not affected as long as they are not designed merely to evade this law.[89]

When a city employee is terminated and, as a condition of a settlement agreement, the employee's personnel file is partially or totally purged, the former employee's personnel records, including the personnel file and any associated work history records, must be clearly designated with a specific notation. This notation must state that the records were purged as a condition of a settlement agreement and must be disclosed to any other governmental entity making an inquiry as to that former employee's work history for the sole purpose of making a hiring decision.[90]

Other Duties and Rights

Each employee must be given time off to vote in any municipal, county, state, or federal election in which he or she is qualified to vote unless the employee's time of work begins at least two hours after the polls open or ends at least two hours before the polls close.[91]

Salaries of municipal officials and employees are subject to garnishment. However, an employee may not be discharged because his or her earnings have been subjected to garnishment for any one indebtedness, even though more than one summons of garnishment is served.[92]

Employee Benefits

Georgia's workers' compensation statute applies to municipal employees.[93] The law specifically encompasses "[a]ll firefighters, law enforcement personnel, and personnel of emergency management . . . agencies, emergency medical services, and rescue organizations whose compensation is paid by . . . any municipality . . . regardless of the method of appointment." In addition, certain volunteer personnel may be covered if the governing authority adopts the appropriate resolution.[94]

Municipalities are authorized by state law to set up deferred compensation plans for their employees,[95] but such plans may not reduce any retirement, pension, or other benefit provided by law.[96] Social security benefits are also available if the municipality has a plan of coverage for its employees that is approved by the Employees Retirement System of Georgia.[97]

HUMAN RESOURCE ADMINISTRATION

One of the most important yet least often attended to functions of municipal government is human resource administration. Human resource costs can exceed 70 percent of a municipality's noncapital expenditures but often take a back seat to issues such as taxation, finance, and capital improvements. Human resource administration covers a broad range of issues such as recruiting and selecting employees, establishing competitive salary rates for employees, properly training new and veteran employees, motivating employees to achieve desired objectives, and fairly and adequately evaluating employee performance.

This part of the chapter will familiarize the elected official with the basic issues involved in human resource administration at the municipal government level. It also suggests appropriate sources of information for the official who seeks further information or direct technical assistance. Subjects covered are employee selection, position classification, salary administration, employee benefits, employee training and development, performance appraisal, and personnel policies and procedures.

Employee Recruitment and Selection

In the past, many municipal governments recruited their employees by word of mouth. Today, the increasing complexity of the work in which municipalities are involved, coupled with legal requirements and federal guidelines resulting from legislation such as Title VII of the Civil Rights Act of 1964, the Civil Rights Act of 1991, and the ADA warrant increased attention to employee recruitment and selection practices.[98]

Recruitment

A broad-based recruitment program that seeks to incorporate all segments of the community is in the best interest of all concerned. Job announcements should clearly state the duties of the position, minimum and desired qualifications, salary ranges, and special licenses or certificates necessary to adequately perform the major duties of the position. Recruitment activities should be both passive (advertisements in local newspapers) and active (recruitment visits to schools and colleges), depending on the nature of the position to be filled. Position vacancies should usually be announced for at least 10 working days to allow those interested to learn of the vacancy and to have the opportunity to apply. When recruiting for positions such as department heads or city managers, a longer recruitment period may be necessary if a municipality chooses to advertise nationally in publications such as the International City/County Management Association's Newsletter or the *Public Administration Times*.[99]

Selection

Since the U.S. Supreme Court case of *Griggs v. Duke Power Company*, the selection of employees has come under increasing scrutiny and legal requirements.[100] Municipalities should strive to create "selection devices" that help them choose the best-qualified applicants without adversely affecting minorities and other protected groups. Selection devices include tools such as interviews, training and experience evaluations, written examinations, performance examinations, and assessment centers.

The mayor and councilmembers' role in employee selection is usually limited to the positions of appointed city administrators and department heads. Executive search firms are sometimes employed by cities to help them find well-qualified applicants for these high-level positions. Technical assistance is also available through the Carl Vinson Institute of Government.

Position Classification

Position classification involves placing like positions together into groups or "classes." For example, comparable secretarial positions could be grouped under the classification of administrative secretary or similar equipment operation positions could be grouped under the classification of heavy equipment operator. Positions with the same position classification are assigned the same pay grade and pay range. This practice helps to ensure that a city is providing equitable pay.

Position classification provides the framework for an effective system of human resource administration and affects recruitment, selection, and performance appraisal. Job descriptions, which form the basis of the classification plan, should be up to date and specific in their listing of the major duties and responsibilities of positions. If job descriptions are timely and specific, they can be used to create announcements advertising position vacancies and to develop performance standards for use in appraising employee performance. In order to comply with the requirements of the ADA, in developing job descriptions, all tasks for each position should be rated as to whether or not they are essential job functions. Employers should attempt to distinguish between essential job functions, which are why the job exists, and marginal job functions, which could be assigned to another employee without changing the nature of the job. A more complete description of the requirements imposed upon an employer by the ADA is given earlier in this chapter.

One of the more popular methods of position classification is the Factor Evaluation System (FES). FES is a point-factor evaluation system that measures the different factors (e.g., knowledge, complexity, and physical demands) that constitute jobs. This methodology has been used by the Vinson Institute in building classification plans for more than 250 units of local and state government.

The mayor and councilmembers' role in position classification generally involves approving new classification plans or approving modifications to existing ones. For example, a mayor and council might approve or disapprove a department's request to reclassify a position from "secretary" to "administrative secretary." In making reclassification decisions, mayors and councilmembers should consider whether the reclassification request is based on a significant change in duties and not solely on a desire to increase the compensation of the employee.

Salary Administration

One of the mayor and council's most visible role in human resource administration is salary administration. The mayor and council are called upon to approve new classification plans and to annually update the city's pay plan. An effective pay plan is both internally and externally equitable. Being internally equitable means that positions with similar levels of duties and responsibilities are grouped together in the same pay grade. A pay plan is externally equitable when its pay rates are competitive with its main competitors.

Mayors and councilmembers will find various publications useful as they administer salaries. The Georgia Department of Community Affairs publishes an annual salary survey of the most common municipal government positions and makes the data available on the Internet.[101]

The Georgia Department of Economic Development publishes an annual salary survey of the most common manufacturing jobs. The Bureau of Labor Statistics of the U.S. Department of Labor periodically publishes salary data for the more populous regions of the state. Additionally, the International City/County Management Association publishes regional salary data concerning city managers, administrators, and department heads. Mayors and councilmembers should exercise care in interpreting the data contained in published salary surveys. For example, job titles may have been misinterpreted, resulting in incorrect information being reported. Mayors and councilmembers should also be sure that they are comparing "apples to apples" and "oranges to oranges." In other words, are the duties and responsibilities of the municipal positions they are researching sufficiently similar to those reported in the survey? If not, a salary comparison may be invalid or inaccurate.

An effective pay plan generally has 21 to 29 salary grades. Each of these grades should have a salary range of approximately 40 percent to 50 percent from the minimum to the maximum rate. To make salary administration more manageable, steps can be inserted between the minimum and maximum rates. Progression through the steps can be linked to length of service and/or performance. For example, an employee who performs at a competent level might be awarded a one-step increase, whereas an employee whose performance is considered to be outstanding might receive a two-step increase. In the past, many pay plans had steps with values of 4 percent to 5 percent. However, plans with increments of that size should be avoided because they usually require the city to spend a large percentage amount on step raises, resulting in less funds being available for general increases that are applied to the entire salary structure. Over a period of time, the practice of granting large step increases and making small overall adjustments will result in a pay plan that may pay tenured employees well but be unable to attract new employees because of low entry rates.

After an equitable classification and pay plan has been implemented in a city, the mayor and council's role in salary administration primarily concerns granting annual and merit increases. Annual (or cost-of-living) increases should be applied to the entire salary scale and to every employee's salary. The Consumer Price Index or the Employment Cost Index, published by the U.S. Bureau of Labor Statistics, are generally used as guides in determining the amount of across-the-board increases. Two to 3 percent of the personnel budget should also be set aside for step or merit raises, and merit increases should be separate from cost-of-living raises.

Employee Benefits

One of the fastest-growing areas of personnel-related costs is employee benefits such as health-related and retirement benefits as well as sick and annual leave. Unless a municipality has a risk manager or human resources director with an extensive background in employee benefits, setting up municipal insurance and retirement plans may require the services of a benefits consulting firm. The Department of Community Affairs periodically compiles information on leave benefits. Typical municipal leave benefits are one day of sick leave per month and one to one and a half days of annual leave per month, depending on the length of an employee's service to the city, with a limit on the number of days that can be carried over from year to year.

Employee Training and Development

The systematic training and development of municipal employees can greatly benefit a city. Training support can take the form of providing tuition reimbursement for attending college courses, encouraging personnel to seek additional certifications, sponsoring in-house training courses specifically designed to increase the management and supervisory skills of city employees, or professional development programs offered by outside groups that keep employees informed and up to date on developments in their field.

Performance Appraisal

There is no foolproof way to appraise employee performance. However, some methods are more legally acceptable and job related than others. For many years, employee performance appraisal consisted of a manager's annual assessment of subordinate employees based on characteristics such as dependability, personality, and appearance. However, trait-based performance appraisal devices are no longer acceptable: the courts have ruled that performance appraisals, such as employment tests, must be job related. In many cases, adhering to these standards may necessitate writing different performance standards for every job classification. The appraisal format itself can be kept simple, but it should require that the supervisor and employee define in writing what the acceptable level of performance is for each major duty that the employee performs. This exercise underscores the necessity for communication and accurate, job-specific position descriptions.[102]

Successful employee performance appraisal is a continual process, not just an activity that takes place once a year. Employees who receive constant feedback concerning their work are much more likely to make desired behavior changes than are those who receive periodic or infrequent information about their performance.

Performance appraisal is most successful when it is used primarily as a communication tool between supervisor and employee. However, it is being used increasingly to link employee performance and pay.

While, on the surface, a pay-for-performance system seems desirable because of the nature of city jobs, such a system may be extremely difficult if not impossible in many instances for a municipal government to implement. For example, while it is a fairly common practice in the private sector to base an insurance agent's pay on the number or value of policies he or she sells, basing a police officer's pay on the number of arrests he or she makes would be inappropriate.[103]

Personnel Policies and Procedures

An up-to-date set of personnel policies and procedures provides the ground rules for city employment. Personnel policies generally contain procedures for employee grievances and appeals, annual and military leave, and a statement of the municipality's philosophy regarding human resource administration. Due to the changing nature of personnel-related law, a municipality should have its personnel policies and procedures reviewed periodically by an employment attorney.

NOTES

1. Board of Regents v. Roth, 408 U.S. 564 (1972); Perry v. Sindermann, 408 U.S. 593 (1972); Crowell v. City of Eastman, 859 F.2d 875 (11th Cir. 1988); Barnett v. Housing Authority, 707 F.2d 1571 (11th Cir. 1983); Ross v. Clayton County, 173 F.3d 1305 (11th Cir. 1999); OFFICIAL CODE OF GEORGIA ANNOTATED (O.C.G.A.) §34-7-1.

2. Barnes v. Mendonsa, 110 Ga. App. 464 (1964); Dixon v. Metropolitan Atlanta Rapid Transit Authority, 242 Ga. App. 262, 529 S.E.2d 398 (2000). See DeClue v. City of Clayton, 246 Ga. App. 487, 540 S.E.2d 675 (2000), which held that a municipal employee has a property interest in his job if he can be dismissed only for cause.

3. Kirton v. Biggers, 232 Ga. 223, 206 S.E.2d 33 (1974); Brownlee v. Williams, 233 Ga. 548, 212 S.E.2d 359 (1975); Maxwell v. Mayor and Alderman of City of Savannah, 226 Ga. App. 705, 487 S.E.2d 478 (1999); Declue v. City of Clayton, 246 Ga. App. 487, 540 S.E.2d 675 (2000).

4. Ellison v. DeKalb County 236 Ga. App. 185, 511 S.E.2d 284 (1999); McMillan v. City of Hazelhurst, 620 F.2d 484 (5th Cir. 1980).

5. Bhargave v. Cloer, 355 F.Supp. 1143 (N.D. Ga. 1972); Walton v. Davis, 188 Ga. 56, 2 S.E.2d 603 (1939); Jackson v. Inman, 232 Ga. 566, 207 S.E.2d 475 (1974); Coleman v. Glenn, 103 Ga. 458, 30 S.E. 297 (1897). See also City Council of Augusta v. King, 54 Ga. App. 111, 187 S.E. 268 (1936); O.C.G.A. §34-7-1.

6. O.C.G.A. §34-7-1; Parks v. City of Atlanta, 76 Ga. 828 (1886); Murphine v. Hospital Authority of Floyd County, 151 Ga. App. 722, 261 S.E.2d 457 (1979); Bell v. Stone Mountain Memorial Association, 185 Ga. App. 890 (1988); Blanton v. Griel Memorial Psychiatric Hospital, 758 F.2d 1540 (11th Cir. 1985); Arford v. Blalock,

199 Ga. App. 434, 405 S.E.2d 698 (1991). Assignment to a particular position on a temporary basis does not give the employee a property interest in the position. *See* Sibley v. City of Atlanta, 152 Ga. App. 723, 263 S.E.2d 698 (1979).
7. Bailey v. Dobbs, 227 Ga. 838, 183 S.E.2d 461 (1971); Ventetuolo v. Burke, 596 F.2d 476 (1st Cir. 1979); *see also* Hagopian v. Trefrey, 639 F.2d 52 (1st Cir. 1981). *See* Brewer v. MARTA, 204 Ga. App. 241, 419 S.E.2d 60 (1992), in which if a plaintiff's employment is at will, the employer with or without cause and regardless of its motives may discharge the employee without liability.
8. Warren v. Crawford, 927 F.2d 559 (11th Cir. 1991); City of Buchanan v. Pope, 222 Ga. App. 716, 476 S.E.2d 53 (1996).
9. Burnley v. Thompson, 524 F.2d 1233 (5th Cir. 1975); Thaw v. Board of Public Instruction, 432 F.2d 98 (5th Cir. 1970); Drummond v. Fulton County Department of Family and Children Services, 547 F.2d 835 (5th Cir. 1977); Ross v. Clayton County, 173 F.3d 1305 (11th Cir. 1999). *See* Rankin v. McPherson, 483 U.S. 378 (1987), in which the court held that even a probationary employee who can be discharged for no reason may be entitled to be reinstated if discharged for exercising a constitutional right.
10. Smith v. Board of Commissioners of Hall County, 244 Ga. 133, 259 S.E.2d 74 (1979); Newsome v. Richmond County, 246 Ga. 300, 271 S.E.2d 203 (1980); City of Atlanta v. Mahony, 162 Ga. App. 5, 289 S.E.2d 250 (1982); International Brotherhood of Police Officers Local No. 471 v. Chatham County, 232 Ga. App. 507, 502 S.E.2d 341 (1998); Abedi v. City of Atlanta, 244 Ga. App. 562, 536 S.E.2d 255 (2000).
11. Board of Regents v. Roth, 408 U.S. 564 (1972).
12. Paul v. Davis, 424 U.S. 693 (1976); Cotton v. Jackson, 216 F.3d 1328 (11th Cir. 2000). *See* Meyer v. Ledford, 170 Ga. App. 245, 316 S.E.2d 804 (1984), in which it was ruled that defamation suffered by a fireman during a department investigation was, without more, not a violation of the plaintiff's liberty interest.
13. Codd v. Velger, 429 U.S. 624 (1977); Owen v. City of Independence, Missouri, 445 U.S. 622 (1980); Cotton v. Jackson, 216 F.3d 1328 (11th Cir. 2000).
14. Bishop v. Wood, 426 U.S. 341 (1976); Thomason v. McDaniel, 793 F.2d 1247 (11th Cir. 1986); Peterson v. Atlanta Housing Authority, 998 F.2d 904 (11th Cir. 1993); Sykes v. City of Atlanta, 235 Ga. App. 345, 509 S.E.2d 395 (1998); Cotton v. Jackson, 216 F.3d 1328 (11th Cir. 2000). In Buxton v. City of Plant City, Florida, 871 F.2d 1037 (11th Cir. 1989), the court held that the placing of stigmatizing information in a public employee's personnel file results in the loss of a liberty interest.
15. Ortwein v. Mackey, 511 F.2d 696 (5th Cir. 1975); Sims v. Fox, 505 F.2d 857 (5th Cir. 1974); Swilley v. Alexander, 629 F.2d 1018 (5th Cir. 1980); Vaughn v. State, 758 F.2d 1535 (11th Cir. 1985); Brewer v. Schacht, 235 Ga. App. 509 S.E.2d 378 (1998); Cartwright v. Wilbanks, 247 Ga. App. 187, 541 S.E.2d 393 (2000).
16. Stretten v. Wadsworth Veterans Hospital, 537 F.2d 361 (9th Cir. 1976) at 366. The court noted that a label that would prevent an individual from practicing his or her chosen profession at all may have consequences so severe that liberty would be infringed. Whether information about an employee is stigmatizing must be decided almost on a case-by-case basis. However, generally speaking, charges of fraud, dishonesty, mental illness, or racism are considered stigmatizing, while allegations such as incompetence, inability to deal with coworkers, neglect of duty, or sleeping on the job are not stigmatizing. As to charges of dishonesty, *see* Huffstutler v. Bergland, 607 F.2d 1090 (5th Cir. 1979), which held that the employee was not stigmatized by a form that rated his honesty as "unsatisfactory" because it did not accuse him of property theft but rather correlated with the narrative description on the form indicating that the evaluator considered the employee to be a person who could not be trusted to produce in the workshop or be faithful or prompt in his attendance. The mere act of disciplining and discharging an at-will employee is not actionable. Clemons v. Dougherty County, 689 F.2d 1365 (11th Cir. 1982), in which it was ruled that information about an employee might be stigmatizing even

if the charges did not allege dishonesty or immorality; Brewer v. MARTA, 204 Ga. App. 241, 419 S.E.2d 60 (1992); Garmon v. Health Group of Atlanta, Inc., 183 Ga. App. 587 (1987); Hall v. Answering Service, Inc., 161 Ga. App. 874 (1982).
17. Buxton v. City of Plant City, Florida, 871 F.2d 1037 (11th Cir. 1989); Cartwright v. Wilbanks, 247 Ga. App. 187, 541 S.E.2d 393 (2000); Cotton v. Jackson, 216 F.3d 1328 (11th Cir. 2000).
18. Cleveland Board of Education v. Loudermill, 470 U.S. 532 (1985).
19. Kelly v. Smith, 764 F.2d 1412 (11th Cir. 1985); Everett v. Napper, 832 F.2d (11th Cir. 1987); Adams v. Sewell, 946 F.2d 757 (11th Cir. 1991); Gilbert v. Homar, 520 U.S. 924 (1997).
20. Cleveland Board of Education v. Loudermill, 470 U.S. 532 (1985). A suspension without pay pending investigation of the charges by the employer was held to violate Loudermill's requirements. Everett v. Napper, 833 F.2d 1507 (11th Cir. 1987); Bass v. City of Albany, 968 F.2d 1067 (1992); Camden County v. Haddock, 271 Ga. 664, 523 S.E.2d 291 (1999); Norris v. Henry County, 2002 WL 1275655 (2002). *See also* Declue v. City of Clayton, 246 Ga. App. 487, 540 S.E.2d 675 (2000), in which the court held that an employee who was hired for an indefinite period of time with no written contract had no property interest in his job.
21. Hatcher v. Board of Public Education and Orphanage for Bibb County, 809 F.2d 1546 (11th Cir. 1987); Levitt v. University of Texas at El Paso, 759 F.2d 1224 (5th Cir. 1985) (citing Ferguson v. Thomas, 430 F.2d 852, 856 [5th Cir. 1970]).
22. Hatcher v. Board of Public Education and Orphanage for Bibb County, 809 F.2d 1546 (11th Cir. 1987).
23. Levitt v. University of Texas at El Paso, 759 F.2d 1224 (5th Cir. 1985).
24. Ibid.
25. Ibid.
26. Hatcher v. Board of Public Education and Orphanage for Bibb County, 809 F.2d 1546 (11th Cir. 1987).
27. Levitt v. University of Texas at El Paso, 759 F.2d 1224 (5th Cir. 1985), but the employee bears the burden of proving actual bias; Ferguson v. Thomas, 430 F.2d 852 (5th Cir. 1970); Parker v. Letson, 380 F.Supp. 280 (N.D. Ga. 1974); Arnett v. Kennedy, 416 U.S. 134, 155 (1974), plurality opinion; Davis v. Vandiver, 494 F.2d 830 (5th Cir. 1974); Hortonville Joint School District v. Hortonville Education Association, 426 U.S. 482 (1976). It is likely that due process would be denied if the hearing body's familiarity with the facts or position on the issues developed into a preconceived idea as to what decision it would render prior to the holding of the hearing. Long County Board of Education v. Owen, 150 Ga. App. 245, 257 S.E.2d 212 (1979).
28. Adams v. Sewell, 946 F.2d 757 (11th Cir. 1991).
29. Campbell v. Pierce County, Georgia, 741 F.2d 1342 (11th Cir. 1984).
30. Ibid.
31. Ibid.
32. O.C.G.A. §34-1-4.
33. *See* O.C.G.A. §5-4-1 et seq.; Lee v. Hutson, 810 F.2d 1030 (11th Cir. 1987); Jones v. City of East Point, 795 F.Supp. 408 (N.D. Ga. 1992).
34. Perry v. Sindermann, 408 U.S. 593 (1972); City of Buchanan v. Pope, 222 Ga. App. 716, 476 S.E.2d 53 (1996); Sykes v. City of Atlanta, 235 Ga. App. 345, 509 S.E.2d 395 (1998).
35. Ferguson v. Thomas, 430 F.2d 852 (5th Cir. 1970); Johnson v. City of Albany, 413 F.Supp. 782 (M.D. Ga. 1976).
36. Pred v. Board of Public Instruction, 415 F.2d 851 (5th Cir. 1969); Johnson v. City of Albany, 413 F.Supp. 782 (M.D. Ga. 1976); Bishop v. Aronov, 926 F.2d 1066 (11th Cir. 1991).

Personnel Management 181

37. Goolsby v. University of Georgia, 144 Ga. App. 605, 234 S.E.2d 165 (1977).
38. Mt. Healthy City School District Board of Education v. Doyle, 429 U.S. 274 (1977); Connick v. Myers, 461 U.S. 138 (1983); Board of County Commissioners Waubansee County, Kansas v. Umbehr, 518 U.S. 668 (1996); Brochu v. City of Riviera Beach, 304 F.3d 1144 (11th Cir. 2002).
39. *See* Pickering v. Board of Education, 391 U.S. 563 (1968). However, when the statement is so without foundation as to call into question an employee's fitness to perform the duties of the job, the statement would be evidence of the employee's lack of competence but does not provide an independent basis for dismissal. Rankin v. McPherson, 483 U.S. 378 (1987).
40. Pickering v. Board of Education, 391 U.S. 563 (1968); Ferrara v. Mills, 781 F.2d 1508 (11th Cir. 1986); Board of County Commissioners Waubansee County, Kansas v. Umbehr, 518 U.S. 668 (1996); Cooper v. Smith, 89 F.3d 761 (11th Cir. 1996).
41. AFSCME v. Woodward, 406 F.2d 137 (8th Cir. 1969); Melton v. City of Atlanta, 324 F.Supp. 315 (N.D. Ga. 1971).
42. Joiner v. Thompson, Civil Action No. 2882, M.D. Ga. Macon Division, September 5, 1973.
43. Aurora Education Association v. Board of Education, 490 F.2d 431 (7th Cir. 1974); Johnson v. City of Albany, 413 F.Supp. 782 (M.D. Ga. 1976).
44. Johnson v. City of Albany, 413 F.Supp. 782 (M.D. Ga. 1976). Strikes by public employees are prohibited by Georgia law. O.C.G.A. tit. 45, ch. 19, art. 1.
45. International Longshoreman's Association v. Georgia Ports Authority, 217 Ga. 712, 124 S.E.2d 733 (1962); O.C.G.A. §§34-6-2, 34-6-7.
46. Smith v. Arkansas State Highway Employees, Local 1315, 441 U.S. 463 (1979); Minnesota State Board of Community Colleges v. Knight, 465 U.S. 271 (1984); Georgia Association of Educators v. Gwinnett County School District, 856 F.2d 142 (11th Cir. 1988).
47. Elrod v. Burns, 427 U.S. 347 (1976); Branti v. Finkel, 445 U.S. 507 (1980); Board of County Commissioners Waubansee County, Kansas v. Umbehr, 518 U.S. 668 (1996); Cooper v. Smith, 89 F.3d 761 (11th Cir. 1996); O'Hare Truck Services, Inc. v. City of Northlake, 518 U.S. 712 (1996).
48. Branti v. Finkel, 445 U.S. 507 (1980); Rutan v. Republican Party of Illinois, 497 U.S. 62 (1990); Waters v. Churchill, 511 U.S. 661 (1994); Board of County Commissioners Waubansee County, Kansas v. Umbehr, 518 U.S. 668 (1996).
49. Branti v. Finkel, 445 U.S. 507 (1980). *See* Kinsey v. Salado Independent School District, 916 F.2d 273 (5th Cir. 1990), in which a school superintendent alleging that his suspension was in retaliation for supporting losing school board candidates had the right to participate in the election of school board members even though he and the school board had a "close and confidential relationship."
50. Abood v. Detroit Board of Education, 431 U.S. 209 (1977).
51. Ibid.
52. Civil Rights Act of 1991, Pub. L. 102-166, 105 Stat. 1074 (1991); 42 United States Code Annotated (U.S.C.A.) §2000e.
53. 42 U.S.C.A. §2000e.
54. 42 U.S.C.A. §2000e-2.
55. 29 U.S.C.A. §203(d).
56. National League of Cities v. Usery, 426 U.S. 833, 851 (1976).
57. Garcia v. San Antonio Metropolitan Transit Authority, 469 U.S. 528 (1985).
58. 29 U.S.C.A. §207(o); 29 CFR §§553.22, 552.23, 553.25, 553.26, 553.227, 553.28.
59. Bennan v. Sugar Cane Growers Cooperative of Florida, 486 F.2d 1006 (5th Cir. 1973); Atlanta Professional Firefighters Union Local 134 v. City of Atlanta, 920

F.2d 800 (11th Cir. 1991); Avery v. City of Talladega, Alabama, 24 F.3d 1337 (11th Cir. 1994); 29 U.S.C.A. §213 (exemptions).
60. Firefighters Local 349 v. City of Rome, 682 F.Supp. 522 (N.D. Ga. 1988), citing H. B. Zachary Co. v. Mitchell, 262 F.2d 546, 549 (5th Cir. 1959), aff'd 362 U.S. 310 (1960).
61. Christensen v. Harris County, 529 U.S. 576 (2000).
62. 29 U.S.C.A. §213(b)(20).
63. 29 C.F.R. §553.200.
64. 29 U.S.C.A. §207(k).
65. 29 U.S.C.A. §207(k); 29 CFR §553.201.
66. 29 C.F.R. §§553.210(c), 553.211(g).
67. 29 C.F.R. §§553.210(a), 553.215(a).
68. 29 C.F.R. §553.211(b). Rescue and ambulance service personnel may spend no more than 20 percent of their work time in unrelated, nonexempt activities or they will not qualify for the 7(k) exemption. Jones v. City of Columbus, 120 F.3d 248 (11th Cir. 1997); Falken v. Glynn County, Georgia, 197 F.3d 1341 (11th Cir. 1999).
69. *See* O'Neal v. Barrow County Board of Commissioners, 980 F.2d 674 (11th Cir. 1993), which held that a separate county EMS agency was held to qualify for a 7(k) exemption solely under 29 C.F.R. §553.215 and §553.13 limitations because of the amount of nonexempt work not applicable to exemptions under 29 C.F.R. §553.215.
70. 29 U.S.C.A. §207(o)(4)(5). Christensen v. Harris County, 529 U.S. 576 (2000).
71. Christensen v. Harris County, 529 U.S. 576 (2000).
72. 29 C.F.R. §§541.1, 541.2, 541.3.
73. Evans v. McClain, 131 F.3d 957 (11th Cir. 1997).
74. 29 U.S.C.A. §201 et seq.; 42 U.S.C.A. §2000e(k).
75. 29 U.S.C.A. §206(d).
76. 29 U.S.C.A. §621 et seq.
77. 42 U.S.C.A. §12101 et seq.
78. 42 U.S.C.A. §12112(b).
79. 42 U.S.C.A. §12112(d)(2)(B).
80. 42 U.S.C.A. §12112(d)(3)(A).
81. 42 U.S.C.A. §12111(9)(10).
82. Barnes v. Gorman, 536 U.S. 181 (2002).
83. 29 U.S.C.A. §2601 et seq.; 29 C.F.R. Part 825.
84. 29 U.S.C.A. §2615; 29 C.F.R. §825.220. Strickland v. Water Works and Sewer Board of City of Birmingham, 239 F.3d 1199 (11th Cir. 2001); Smith v. BellSouth Telecommunications, 273 F.3d 1303 (11th Cir. 2001). *See* Wascura v. City of South Miami, 257 F.3d 1238 (11th Cir. 2001), in which the court ruled that the employee failed to present any evidence of a causal connection between her request for FMLA leave and her subsequent termination.
85. Fourth Amendment to the U.S. Constitution; GA. CONST. art. I, §1, ¶13. Chandler v. Miller, 520 U.S. 305 (1997); City of East Point v. Smith, 258 Ga. 111, 365 S.E.2d 432 (1988); Beasley v. State, 204 Ga. App. 214, 419 S.E.2d 92 (1992).
86. National Treasury Employees Union v. Von Raab, 489 U.S. 656 (1989); Skinner v. Railroad Labor Executives' Association, 489 U.S. 602 (1989); 49 U.S.C.A. §31301 et seq.; 49 C.F.R. §40.1 et seq.; 49 C.F.R. §382.1 et seq. *See also* Georgia Association of Educators v. Harris, 749 F.Supp. 1110 (N.D. Ga. 1990); Mayo v. Fulton County, 220 Ga. App. 825 (1996); Department of Corrections v. Colbert, 260 Ga. 255 (1990); City of East Point v. Smith, 258 Ga. 111 (1988).
87. 29 U.S.C.A. §206(d).

88. O.C.G.A. ch. 34-5.
89. O.C.G.A. §34-1-2.
90. O.C.G.A. §45-1-5.
91. O.C.G.A. §21-2-404.
92. O.C.G.A. §§18-4-7, 18-4-21.
93. O.C.G.A. §34-9-1.
94. Ibid.
95. O.C.G.A. §45-18-31.
96. O.C.G.A. §45-18-34.
97. O.C.G.A. tit. 47, ch. 18.
98. Pub. L. 102-166, Nov. 21, 1991, 105 Stat. 1074; 42 U.S.C.A. §12101 et seq.
99. For further information on executive recruitment and selection, *see* David N. Ammons, *Recruiting Local Government Executives* (San Francisco: Jossey-Bass, 1989).
100. Griggs v. Duke Power Company, 401 U.S. 424 (1971), 3 EPD 8137.
101. *See* http://www.dca.state.ga.us/dcawss/default.asp.
102. For a thorough discussion concerning performance appraisal practices, *see* K. McKirchy, *Powerful Performance Appraisals: How to Set Expectations and Work Together to Improve Performance* (Franklin, NJ: Career Press, 1998).
103. For an excellent discussion on the prospects of pay-for-performance compensation systems, *see* P. T. Chingos and P. Marwick, eds., *Paying for Performance: A Guide to Compensation Management* (New York: J. Wiley, 1997).

13

Perry Hiott and Paul T. Hardy*

Contracting, Purchasing, and Sale of Municipal Property

A city's authority to contract comes primarily from its charter.[1] The municipal charter generally grants to the mayor and council, acting as the governing body, the power to enter into contracts for the transaction of municipal business.[2] Neither the mayor nor the council acting alone has the authority to bind a municipality to a contract.[3]

A city may enter a contract or incur a liability only if its charter or some other law of the state authorizes it to do so. A contract beyond the scope of a city's corporate powers is void.[4] However, if municipalities are granted jurisdiction over a subject matter, they shall have an implied power to contract in regard to the subject matter.[5]

Not only is a municipality restricted from contracting except where it has authority, its power to contract is also limited. If the city ignores one of these limitations, the contract may be deemed *ultra vires* (i.e., unlawful, illegal, or unauthorized). Examples of illegal contracts are

- contracts tending to lesson competition or to encourage a monopoly;[6]
- contracts that, if carried out, would increase the municipality's debt beyond constitutional debt limitations;[7]
- contracts binding the governing authority or its successors so as to prevent free legislation regarding governmental functions;[8]
- contracts in violation of public policy, although there may be no statute prohibiting them;[9]
- contracts compensating members of the municipal government authority for services;[10]

---

* Parts of the chapter contain or are based on work by this author from earlier editions of the *Handbook for Georgia Mayors and Councilmembers*.

- contracts promoting self-interest;[11] and
- contracts that give away control or embarrass a city's legislative or governmental powers[12]

An illegal contract with a municipality is considered void forever; it does not bind the municipality even if there has been complete performance on the part of the other party.[13] A contract that is void because it is illegal cannot be ratified. Acceptance or use by the municipality of any benefits furnished under the void contract will not make it valid.[14] This rule is based on the principle that it is the duty of any person contracting with a municipality to ensure that the contract strictly complies with the mandatory provisions of the law limiting and prescribing the municipality's powers.[15]

One exception to this rule relates to a void contract that could have been but was not properly authorized. If the representative officials who have the right to contract make such a contract and if they have knowledge of the work being done and thereafter accept the benefits on behalf of the municipality, an implied ratification will result that will render the municipality liable for the reasonable value of the goods or services received.[16]

Contracts for professional services involving particular knowledge, such as those engaging the services of attorneys, auditors, or architects, are not subject to bidding requirements.[17] If no local legislation or population statutes prevent it, a municipality is generally free to negotiate such contracts as it sees fit.

CONFLICT OF INTEREST

Municipal officials may not use their office for private gain. Georgia law provides that "it is improper for a member of a city council to vote upon any question brought before the council, in which he is personally interested."[18] The Georgia courts have applied this statute to municipal contracts, and they have relied on it to void contracts

- between a mayor and council and a private corporation in which one of the councilmen owned stock,[19]
- between a municipality and a company that was represented by the law firm of which one of the councilmen was a member,[20] and
- between the city and the mayor even though the mayor neither voted nor attempted to influence members of the council.[21]

In addition to being a violation of public policy and thus voidable, such contracts tainted by "personal interest" may also be criminal violations.[22] The Criminal Code of Georgia also contains the following provision:

Any employee, appointive officer, or elective officer of a political subdivision or agency thereof who for himself or in behalf of any business entity sells any real or personal property to

1. the employing political subdivision,
2. the agency of the employing political subdivision,
3. a political subdivision for which local taxes for education are levied by the employing subdivision, or
4. a political subdivision which levies local taxes for education for the employing political subdivision

shall, upon conviction, be punished by imprisonment for not less than one or more than five years.[23]

This provision does not apply to sales of personal property totaling less than $200 per calendar quarter or sales of personal property made pursuant to sealed competitive bids. Neither does it apply to sales of real property in which a disclosure of the personal interest has been made to the grand jury or probate judge at least 15 days prior to the date of the agreement. However, even though criminal charges might be avoided, there is a possibility that such sales could be voided. The selling of services to the county is not included in the crime defined in this section of the code.[24] These statutory provisions make it clear that any municipal official who sells to his or her municipality could have the contract invalidated and even face criminal charges.

City officials must avoid all situations in which their public actions may be affected by or come into conflict with their personal interests. In instances in which avoidance is impossible, they should disqualify themselves from acting on such matters. It is of no consequence that there is only a potential conflict of interest, that there is no dishonesty or loss of public funds, or that the official is not influenced by the situation.[25]

TYPES OF CONTRACTS

Among the various types of contracts that cities enter into are (1) municipal road contracts, (2) public works contracts, and (3) intergovernmental contracts. The following is a discussion of these three types of contracts and some information on what the law requires regarding a successful bidder.

Municipal Road Contracts

Contractual Authority

The municipality is authorized to contract with any person, the federal government, the state, or any state agency, municipality, or county for the construction, maintenance, administration, and operation of municipal roads and related activities.[26] The municipality may, on the other hand, perform roadwork with its own forces or with prison labor.[27] Any contract for work on the municipal road system must be in writing and approved by resolution of the municipal governing authority and entered on its minutes.[28]

Limitations on Authority to Negotiate Contracts

Municipalities are prohibited from negotiating county road contracts except those

- involving the expenditure of less than $20,000;
- with a state agency or county or political subdivision with which it is authorized to contract;
- with a railroad or railway company or publicly or privately owned utility as authorized by applicable law;
- for engineering or other kinds of professional or specialized services;
- for emergency maintenance requiring immediate repairs to a public road, including but not limited to bridge repairs, snow and ice removal, and repairs due to flood conditions; or
- otherwise expressly authorized by law.[29]

Bidding Requirements

Generally, municipal road contracts are let by public bid.[30] The city is required to advertise for competitive sealed bids in a local publication (usually the newspaper in which sheriff's sales are advertised) once a week for two weeks. The first advertisement appears two weeks prior to the opening of the sealed bids and the second follows one week later.[31] The advertisement must include

- a description sufficient to enable the public to know the approximate extent and character of the work to be done;
- the time allowed for performance;
- the terms and time of payment;
- where and under what conditions and costs the detailed plans and specifications and proposal forms may be obtained;
- the amount of proposal guaranty, if one is required;
- the time and place for submission and opening of bids;
- the right of the municipality to reject any one or all bids; and

- such further notice as the municipality may deem advisable to be in the public interest.[32]

The city may require each bidder to pay a reasonable sum to cover the cost of the bid proposal form, the contract, and it specifications.[33] No bid can be considered unless accompanied by a proposal guaranty payable to the municipality to ensure that the successful bidder will execute the contract on which he or she bids.[34]

Public Works Construction Projects

The Georgia Local Government Public Works Construction Law[35] establishes uniform requirements for local government public works construction projects. The law requires contracts for such projects to be awarded in an open and competitive manner while authorizing the use of current construction industry practices to provide increased flexibility to local governments that are constructing public facilities.

The public works construction law defines public works construction as

> the building, altering, repairing, improving, or demolishing of any public structure or building or other public improvements of any kind to any public real property other than those projects covered by Chapter 4 of Title 32. Such term does not include the routine operation, routine repair, or maintenance of existing structures, buildings, or real property.[36]

Exemptions

Not all construction contracts are subject to the public works construction law.[37] With certain exceptions, the requirements of the law do not apply to contracts for the following:

1. public works construction contracts costing less than $100,000
2. projects involving use of inmate labor
3. projects involving federal or state labor
4. projects involving the expenditure of federal grants
5. projects necessitated by emergencies and natural disasters
6. road construction projects
7. self-performance projects
8. sole source contracts
9. projects with hospital authorities
10. projects for professional services

Advertising Requirements

The public works construction law establishes minimum requirements for advertising public works construction opportunities. A city must publicly advertise a contract opportunity for public works construction projects. The contract opportunity notice must be posted conspicuously in the governing authority's office, and it must be advertised in either the legal organ of the county or by electronic means on an Internet Web site of the governmental entity or on a Web site identified by the governmental entity. The contract opportunity must be advertised at least two times. The first advertisement must be published at least four weeks prior to the opening of the bid or proposal. The second advertisement must follow at least two weeks after the first ad. The advertisement must include such details to enable the public to know the extent and character of the work to be done. All notices must advise potential bidders or offerors of any mandatory prequalification requirements, any pre-bid conferences, and/or any federal requirements.[38]

Prequalification of Bidders and Offerors

The public works construction law allows cities to adopt, at their discretion, a process for mandatory prequalification of prospective bidders or offerors.[39] A prequalification process allows a city to establish minimum criteria that potential bidders or offerors must meet in order to become eligible to submit a bid or proposal on a public works construction project. While local governments are not required to use a prequalification process, those who choose to do so must adhere to the following requirements contained in the public works construction law:

1. Criteria for prequalification must be reasonably related to the project or the quality of work. Examples include past relevant experience with similar projects or required licenses. The criteria should not be designed to eliminate all prospective bidders or offerors but one.
2. The minimum criteria for prequalification must be available to any prospective bidder or offeror requesting such information.
3. The process must include a method of notifying prospective bidders or offerors of the minimum criteria for prequalification. All required notices of advertisement must advise potential bidders or offerors of the mandatory prequalification process.[40]
4. The prequalification process must include a procedure for a disqualified bidder to respond to his or her disqualification to a representative of the city, although this provision does not require the city to provide a formal appeal procedure.[41]

Competitive Sealed Bids and Proposals

Cities must utilize one of two methods when soliciting public works construction contracts: competitive sealed bids and competitive sealed proposals.[42]

Competitive Sealed Bids. Under this method, the city issues an invitation to bid, and prospective bidders must submit bids in accordance with the bid invitation. All submitted bids must contain a final price or fee for project completion. The city must select the bid from the responsible and responsive bidder who submits the lowest price and meets all of the requirements included in the bid invitation. Under this method, bids are valid for only 60 days, unless otherwise agreed upon by the city and the bidder.[43]

Competitive Sealed Proposals. Under this method, the city issues a request for proposal (RFP), which contains a description of the project and the factors that will be used to evaluate submitted proposals. The RFP may or may not require a final price or fee to be included with the proposal. Price may be one of the factors considered by the city when making its final decision, but it will not be the only factor. All submitted proposals are evaluated in accordance with the criteria provided in the RFP, and the city must make its final selection based on such criteria. Under this method, proposals are valid for as long as specified in the RFP, but offerors that have not been short-listed by the city must be released after 60 days.[44]

Project Delivery Methods and Construction Management

The public works construction law allows any construction delivery method to be utilized. However, any public works construction project that places the bidder or offeror at risk for construction and requires labor or building materials in the execution of the contract must be awarded on the basis of competitive sealed bids or competitive sealed proposals.[45]

The city should consider its own internal capabilities when selecting the appropriate construction delivery method and management approach. Before selecting a construction project delivery method and management approach, city officials should determine whether or not the city has the in-house resources available to manage the design and construction phases of the project or supervise and inspect construction.

Construction Project Delivery Methods

Several construction delivery methods are available. These methods are conceptual, and variations of each method may exist.

Traditional Method (Design-Bid-Build). In this method, the city hires a professional architect or engineer to design the project. After completion of the design phase, the city solicits bids for the construction portion of the project. The city typically awards the contract to the bidder who submits the lowest responsive, responsible bid. The selected contractor then retains necessary trade contractors.

Design-Build. In this method, the city hires a single firm that provides all design and construction services. Several different firms (design professionals and trade contractors) may provide the actual services, but the city has only one contract with the entity responsible for both types of services.

Construction Management (CM) At-Risk. In this method, the construction manager assumes financial risks and liabilities, placing the manager "at risk." This method eliminates the duplication of services caused by employing both a construction manager and general contractor. The model also allows the city to avoid entering into contracts with numerous trade contractors.

Construction Management Methods

Unlike the project delivery methods previously mentioned, which are based on the assignment of "delivery" risk for design and construction, the following methods are referred to as "management" methods. These methods can be used in conjunction with any of the project delivery methods.

Program/Project Management. In this method, the city employs a project manager to act on the city's behalf during all phases of the project. The primary distinction between the project manager and the construction manager depends upon the scope of the project being performed. Typically, the project manager will fill the role of the city's staff should the city not have adequate or experienced personnel.

Agency Construction Management. In this method, the city hires a construction manager who serves as a professional adviser and who manages and coordinates the activities of the design and construction teams. However, the general contractor and the design team still have contracts directly with the city. The selected construction manager has little liability or responsibility and serves only in an advisory role. Therefore, the construction manager is at no financial risk.

Bond Requirements

Bid, payment, and performance bonds are required on all projects costing more than $100,000 that are subject to the public works construction law. These bonds protect the city in the event that a contractor fails to meet his or her responsibilities regarding the project. A city may, at its discretion, require such bonds for any project, regardless of its cost.[46]

Bid Bonds. Bid bonds protect the city in the event that the selected bidder or offeror fails to enter into a contract with the city.[47]

Performance Bonds. Performance bonds provide reimbursement to the city in the event that the contractor fails to complete the project in accordance with the contract.[48]

Payment Bonds. Payment bonds protect the subcontractors and suppliers who work for the city's contractor by ensuring that they are compensated by the contractor.[49] If a city fails to obtain a payment bond on a contract costing more than $100,000, the city may be held liable to pay the subcontractors and all suppliers.[50]

Contractor's Oath

Prior to beginning work on a public works construction project, the contractor must provide a written oath stating that he or she has not attempted to prevent competition with regard to the procurement of a contract for the project. If the contractor's oath is false, the contract is void, and the city can attempt to recover any monies paid to the contractor.[51]

Penalties

No public works construction contract that is subject to the Georgia Local Government Public Works Construction Law shall be valid unless it complies with the requirements of the law.[52] A municipal elected official who receives or agrees to receive any pay or profit from a local government public works construction contract shall be guilty of a misdemeanor.[53] Also, any contractor who knows that the city failed to properly advertise the contract opportunity and/or use either the competitive sealed bid method or the competitive sealed proposal method is not entitled to payment for any of the work performed under the contract.[54]

Intergovernmental Contracts

A constitutional provision authorizes municipalities to contract for a period not exceeding 50 years with the state or other local units of government in Georgia with respect to facilities or services.[55] Under this provision, municipalities are specifically authorized to convey existing facilities to the state and to any public agency, corporation, or authority. Cities may contract with any public agency, corporation, or authority for the care, maintenance, and hospitalization of its indigent sick.[56] Under this power, the municipality may not enter into any contract it might deem unadvisable. The state and its agencies and subdivisions may contract with each other only with reference to facilities and services authorized by the constitution.[57]

Another constitutional provision authorizes counties and municipalities to contract with one another for certain services, such as police and fire protection, garbage and sewage disposal, street and road maintenance, parks and recreation areas, and treatment and distribution of water.[58]

Intergovernmental contracts are also authorized by statute. A survey of the general laws indicates the municipality is authorized to contract with

- the state, a state agency, another municipality or county or with any combination thereof for public road work;[59]
- other municipalities, counties, private persons, firms, associations, or corporations for any period of time not to exceed 50 years, to provide industrial wastewater treatment services to such private entities in order to comply with applicable state and federal water pollution control standards and to be eligible for grants-in-aid or other allotments;[60] and
- the Georgia Ports Authority for the leasing, operation, or management of real or personal property in or adjacent to any seaport.[61]

This list provides only a sample of the range of contracts that a city is authorized to enter into with other political bodies.

The Successful Bidder

A contract let for public bid is to be awarded to the "lowest reliable bidder." However, the municipality has the right to reject all bids whether such right is reserved in the notice or not and may readvertise, perform the work itself, or abandon the project.[62]

Before beginning work, the successful contractor must sign a written oath that he or she has not prevented, or attempted to prevent, competition in the bidding.[63] In addition, when the contract price is $5,000 or more, the contractor must file

- payment and performance bonds for the protection of subcontractors and others furnishing materials or labor; and
- any other bonds required by the municipality in its advertisements for bids, such as public liability and property damage insurance bonds or policies and bonds to maintain in good condition such completed construction for a period of not less than five years.[64]

Failure to take a payment bond renders the city liable for losses to subcontractors, laborers, material men, and other persons furnishing materials and labor.[65]

PURCHASING

A number of statutory provisions authorize municipalities to enter into purchasing agreements. For example, various general laws permit municipalities to

- contract with the federal government or the state for the purchase, lease, or acquisition of equipment, supplies, and property and appoint an officer or employee to bid and make necessary down payments for these things;[66]
- purchase various supplies and surplus property through the state Department of Administrative Services such as washing powders, insecticides, picnic tables, park benches, parking bumpers, and street signs and markers directly from the Georgia Correctional Industries Administration;[67] and
- enter into joint agreements with counties, municipalities, school districts, and other governmental jurisdictions for the purchase of various items.[68]

Individual cities may also possess the power to purchase by virtue of a local statute. Local acts may require, for example, that bids be obtained for purchases over a certain specified amount, that a minimum number of bids be obtained, that the bids be sealed and in writing, and that the lowest and best bid be accepted.[69] Most municipalities, however, merely have provisions in their charters providing that the council may by ordinance prescribe the rules and procedures for municipal purchasing.[70]

Miscellaneous Statutes Concerning Purchasing

When making purchases, municipalities should be aware of two additional statutes that deal with purchasing. The first provides that, in the purchasing of and contracting for supplies, materials, equipment, and agricultural products, state and local authorities must give preference "as far as may be reasonable and practicable" to items manufactured or produced in Georgia, unless giving such a preference will sacrifice price or quality.[71] The second act makes it a misdemeanor for any municipal officer to purchase or authorize the purchase of any beef other than beef raised and produced in the United States when the purchase is to be made with governmental funds. Canned meats not available from a source within the United States and not processed in this country may be purchased without penalty.[72]

Office Supplies

No general law requires competitive bidding in the purchase of office supplies and similar items. Local statutes may provide that purchases of items be preceded by legal advertisement and competitive bidding.

Evaluating Municipal Purchasing Practices

Following is a list of questions to use in evaluating your city's purchasing practices.

Organization and Policies

- Has the city centralized the purchasing function in a single person or office?
- Has the city adopted formal regulations stating
    1. the duties of the purchasing agent,
    2. the amount over which quotes are needed,
    3. the amount over which bids are required,
    4. the petty cash fund limits and procedures,
    5. how and when emergency purchases may be made, and
    6. how to dispose of obsolete equipment?
- Whenever possible, are goods standardized?
- Has the city issued a procedures manual specifying details such as the following?
    1. soliciting bids
    2. informal bidding
    3. preparing purchase orders
    4. inspecting and testing received goods
    5. making payment for goods
    6. exceptions to the normal purchasing process
- Has the city stimulated competition by eliminating geographical limits on bidders?

Purchasing

- Has the city established and does it use a bidders' list?
- Has the city set forth the policy of prequalification for bidders?
- Does the city avoid splitting purchase orders?
- Does the city maintain a record of suppliers who have not met performance or quality standards?

- When possible, does the city acquire professional services (auditing, engineering, etc.) competitively?
- Were the purchases from the state practical and feasible?
- Has the city explored the possibility of leasing, rather than purchasing, some of its equipment such as heavy road equipment, automobiles, photo copiers, etc.?

Receiving

- Are receiving reports prepared for all purchased goods?
- Does the city accurately count and examine received goods to see that they meet quality standards?

Invoice Processing

- Does the city's accounts payable system properly account for unmatched receiving reports?
- Are purchase orders, receiving reports, and invoices compared for accuracy before payment?
- Does the city follow up on partial deliveries?
- Does the city regularly compare vendor statements to recorded amounts payable?

SALE OF MUNICIPAL PROPERTY

All sales by a municipal corporation of real property or personal property that has an estimated value of more than $500 must be made either by sealed bids or by auction to the highest bidder. A municipal corporation may reject any and all bids or cancel any proposed sale. Notice of a sale must be published once in the official newspaper of the county in which the municipality is located or in a newspaper of general circulation in the municipality. The legal notice must appear not less than 15 days nor more than 60 days prior to the date of the sale. If the sale is by sealed bid, the bids shall be opened in public at the time and place stated in the legal notice. The bids shall be kept available for public inspection for not less than 60 days.[73]

Personal property with an estimated value of $500 or less may be sold without regard to any of the above provisions. Such sales may be made in the open market without advertisement and without the acceptance of bids. The municipality has the power to estimate the value of the property to be sold.[74]

Sale of City-Owned Utilities

A municipality may sell, lease, or otherwise dispose of the property of any electric, water, gas, or other municipally owned public utility plants or properties. The city may decide the terms and conditions of such transactions.[75] Prior to the sale, a notice setting out the price and other general terms of the sale must be placed for three consecutive weeks in a newspaper published in or having general circulation in the municipality. The sale or lease may take place 10 days after publication of the final notice unless 20 percent of the qualified voters sign a petition objecting to it. If such a petition is filed, the sale or lease cannot take place unless it is approved at a special election by two-thirds of those voting. Such election shall be held at least 50 days after the objecting petition is filed with the city.[76]

NOTES

1. Barrett v. City of Atlanta, 145 Ga. 678, 89 S.E. 781 (1916); Miller v. City of Cornelia, 188 Ga. 674, 4 S.E.2d 568 (1939); Patterson v. City Council of Sparta, 175 Ga. App. 819, 334 S.E. 2d 725, *appeal dismissed*, 178 Ga. App. 733, 344 S.E.2d 711 (1986).
2. City of Jonesboro v. Shaw-Lightcap, Inc., 112 Ga. App. 890, 147 S.E.2d 65 (1966); Coke v. City of Atlanta, 195 Ga. App. 67, 392 S.E.2d 283 (1990).
3. City of Atlanta v. Bull, 161 Ga. App. 648, 288 S.E.2d 335 (1982); Ingalls Iron Works v. City of Forest Park, 99 Ga. App. 706, 109 S.E. 3d 835 (1959); Horkan v. City of Moultrie, 136 Ga. 561, 71 S.E. 785 (1911); OFFICIAL CODE OF GEORGIA ANNOTATED (O.C.G.A.) §36-30-3.
4. Barrett v. City of Atlanta, 145 Ga. 678, 89 S.E. 781 (1916); Cole v. City of Atlanta, 195 Ga. App. 67, 392 S.E.2d 283, *cert. denied* (1990); Precise v. City of Rossville, 261 Ga. 210, 403 S.E.2d 47 (1991); CSX v. Garden City, 277 Ga. 248, 588 S.E.2d 688 (2003).
5. Wright v. Floyd County, 1 Ga. App. 582, 58 S.E. 72 (1907); Schanck v. Town of Hepzibah, 236 Ga. 530, 224 S.E.2d 354 (1976).
6. GA. CONST. art. III, §6, ¶5(c).
7. GA. CONST. art. IX, §5, ¶1.
8. O.C.G.A. §36-30-3; Barr v. City Council of Augusta, 206 Ga. 750, 58 S.E.2d 820 (1950); Ledbetter Bros., Inc. v. Floyd Co., 237 Ga. 22, 226 S.E.2d 730 (1976)—the determining factor is whether the contract will be completed within the term of the governing authority which makes it; City of Fayetteville v. Fayette County, 171 Ga. App. 13, 318 S.E.2d 757 (1984); City of Power Springs v. WMM Properties, 253 Ga. 753, 325 S.E.2d 155 (1985). *See also* City of Atlanta v. Brinderson Corporation, 799 F.2d 1541 (11th Cir. 1986) in regard to construction contracts.
9. O.C.G.A. §13-8-1; Trainer v. City of Covington, 183 Ga. 759, 189 S.E. 842 (1937); Frazier v. City of Albany, 245 Ga. 399, 265 S.E.2d 581 (1980); Department of Transportation v. Brooks, 254 Ga. 303, 328 S.E.2d 705 (1985).
10. Mayor and Council of Macon v. Huff, 60 Ga. 221 (1878)—the supreme court held invalid a contract in which a municipality had agreed to pay its mayor an annual sum to fence, drain, and repair the municipal park for a period of five years; Twiggs v. Wingfield, 147 Ga. 790, 95 S.E. 711 (1918)—the supreme court invalidated a contract in which the municipal flood commission employed an individual who was the public works commissioner and ex-officio city engineer to prepare plans and specifications and advertise bids in providing for flood protection to the municipal-

ity; Welsch v. Wilson, 218 Ga. 843, 131 S.E.2d 194 (1963)—the supreme court held invalid a contract in which the municipality hired the mayor to fill the office of city manager; Fowler v. Mitcham, 249 Ga. 400, 291 S.E.2d 515 (1982).

11. Hardy v. Mayor and Council of Gainesville, 121 Ga. 327, 48 S.E. 921 (1904)—a contract for a municipality's printing work was ruled void because it had been awarded by the mayor and council to a corporation in which one of the councilmen owned stock; Cochran v. City of Thomasville, 167 Ga. 579, 146 S.E. 462 (1928)—the court held that it was illegal for a councilman to participate in the execution of a contract between the municipality and a paving company that was represented by the law firm of which he was a member. *See* R. Perry Sentell, *Studies in Local Government Law*, 3rd ed. (Charlottesville, VA: Michie Co., 1977), 623–27.

12. Patterson v. City Council of Sparta, 175 Ga. App. 819, 334 S.E.2d 725, *appeal dismissed*, 178 Ga. App. 733, 344 S.E.2d 711(1986).

13. City Council of Dawson v. Dawson Waterworks Co., 106 Ga. 696, 32 S.E. 907 (1899); City of Hogansville v. Farrell Heating Co., 161 Ga. 780, 132 S.E. 436 (1925); City of Warm Springs v. Bulloch, 212 Ga. 149, 91 S.E.2d 13 (1956).

14. Town of Wadley v. Lancaster, 124 Ga. 354, 52 S.E. 335 (1905); Mayor and Council of Hogansville v. Planters Bank, 27 Ga. App. 384, 108 S.E. 480 (1921); Hardy v. Mayor and Council of Gainesville, 121 Ga. 327, 48 S.E. 921 (1904).

15. Wiley v. City of Columbus, 109 Ga. 295, 34 S.E. 575 (1899); Ingalls Iron Works Co. v. City of Forest Park, 99 Ga. App. 706, 109 S.E.2d 835 (1959); City of Jonesboro v. Shaw-Lightcap, Inc. 112 Ga. App. 890, 147 S.E.2d 65 (1966); City of Atlanta v. Black, 265 Ga. 425, 457 S.E.2d 551 (1995).

16. City of Gainesville v. Edwards, 112 Ga. App. 672, 145 S.E.2d 715 (1965), ruling in City of Gainesville upheld in Circle H Development, Inc. v. City of Woodstock, 206 Ga. App. 473, 425 S.E.2d 891 (1992); City of Dallas v. White, 182 Ga. App. 782, 357 S.E.2d 125, *cert. denied* (1987).

17. *Program Materials, Twenty-third Institute of City and County Attorneys* (Athens: Institute of Continuing Legal Education, University of Georgia, 1976), TFC 9–10.

18. O.C.G.A §36-30-6.

19. Hardy v. Mayor and Council of Gainesville, 121 Ga. 327, 48 S.E. 921 (1904); Mayor and Council of Hogansville v. Planters Bank, 27 Ga. App. 384, 108 S.E. 480 (1921); Department of Transportation v. Brooks, 254 Ga. 303, 328 S.E.2d 705 (1985).

20. Cochran v. City of Thomasville, 167 Ga. 579, 146 S.E. 462 (1928).

21. Trainer v. City of Covington, 183 Ga. 759, 189 S.E. 842 (1937); Montgomery v. City of Atlanta, 162 Ga. 534, 134 S.E. 152 (1962).

22. Municipal officials commit the offense of bribery by directly or indirectly soliciting, receiving, or accepting anything of value by inducing the reasonable belief that the giving of the thing will influence his or her official action. O.C.G.A §16-10-22.

23. O.C.G.A. §16-10-6.

24. O.C.G.A. §16-10-6; Defoor v. State, 233 Ga. 190, 210 S.E.2d 707 (1974).

25. Montgomery v. City of Atlanta, 162 Ga. 514, 134 S.E. 152 (1926).

26. O.C.G.A. §§32-4-91, 32-4-92.

27. O.C.G.A. §32-4-91.

28. O.C.G.A. §32-4-111.

29. O.C.G.A. §32-4-113.

30. O.C.G.A. §32-4-114.

31. O.C.G.A. §32-4-115.

32. Ibid.

33. O.C.G.A. §32-4-116.

34. O.C.G.A. §32-4-117.

35. O.C.G.A. §36-91-1 et seq.
36. O.C.G.A. §36-91-2(10).
37. O.C.G.A. §36-91-22.
38. O.C.G.A. §36-91-20(b).
39. O.C.G.A. §36-91-20(f).
40. O.C.G.A. §36-91-20(b), (f).
41. O.C.G.A. §36-91-20(f)(4).
42. O.C.G.A. §36-91-21.
43. O.C.G.A. §36-91-50(b).
44. O.C.G.A. §36-91-50(c).
45. O.C.G.A. §36-91-20(c).
46. O.C.G.A. §§36-91-41(a), 36-91-50, 36-91-70, 36-91-90.
47. O.C.G.A. §§36-91-2(1), 36-91-90.
48. O.C.G.A. §§36-91-2(9), 36-91-70.
49. O.C.G.A. §§36-91-2(8), 36-91-90.
50. O.C.G.A. §36-91-91.
51. O.C.G.A. §36-91-21(e).
52. O.C.G.A. §§36-91-21(a), 36-91-21(g).
53. O.C.G.A. §36-91-21(f).
54. O.C.G.A. §36-91-21(a).
55. GA. CONST. art. IX, §3, ¶1; *See* City of Cartersville v. Municipal Electric Authority of Georgia, 592 S.E.2d 677 (2004) in which the court held that a 25-year extension to the existing 50-year contract between the city and the authority did not violate the constitution as long as the duration of the contract did not exceed 50 years.
56. Ibid.
57. Mulkey v. Quillian, 213 Ga. 507, 100 S.E.2d 268 (1957); Precise v. City of Rossville, 261 Ga. 210, 403 S.E.2d 47 (1991).
58. GA. CONST. art. IX, §2, ¶3.
59. O.C.G.A. §32-4-110.
60. O.C.G.A. §36-60-2.
61. O.C.G.A. §52-2-9(15).
62. O.C.G.A. §32-4-118.
63. O.C.G.A. §32-4-122.
64. O.C.G.A. §32-4-119.
65. O.C.G.A. §32-4-120.
66. O.C.G.A. §50-16-81.
67. O.C.G.A. §§50-5-100–50-5-103, 50-5-143.
68. GA. CONST. art. IX, §3, ¶1; *see also* Jerry Singer, *Cooperative Purchasing*, 2nd ed. (Athens: Carl Vinson Institute of Government, University of Georgia, 1985), 5, 6.
69. Ga. Laws 1978, pp. 3081, 3108; Ga. Laws 1977, pp. 3776, 3807; Ga. Laws 1973, pp. 2188, 2247.
70. Ga. Laws 1979, pp. 3881, 3908; Ga. Laws 1979, pp. 3499, 3524.
71. O.C.G.A. §50-5-61.
72. O.C.G.A. §50-5-81.
73. O.C.G.A. §36-37-6.
74. Ibid.
75. O.C.G.A. §36-37-7.
76. O.C.G.A. §§36-37-8, 36-37-10.

14

Stuart H. Dorfman

Planning

Just as people in business must plan for the future of their company, their store, or their office, mayors and city councilmembers must plan for the future of their city. In government, as in business, present needs must be addressed and future trends and problems anticipated, with appropriate measures taken so that operations continue to run smoothly and efficiently. Planning is essential to enable persons in business or governmental officials to anticipate future needs and to provide the products or services that customers or citizens will expect.

In Georgia, the power to plan and regulate the uses of property within cities is vested in the local governing authority. As stated in the home rule provision of the Georgia Constitution, "each municipality may adopt plans and may exercise the power of zoning."[1] This provision also states that "[t]his authorization shall not prohibit the General Assembly from enacting general laws establishing procedures for the exercise of such power."[2]

Almost every mayor and city councilmember in the state has had to respond to tough decisions affecting the growth and character of his or her city.[3] For example, where and when should roads be built? How will the city determine the best location and right timing for future water and sewer lines, public buildings, and parks? How will it acquire the land or right-of-way for public uses before the private sector acquires it for development?

In municipalities that have zoning ordinances or resolutions, councilmembers may face controversial rezoning issues: Should the council approve a developer's request to rezone a large tract of land for the construction of a shopping center when residents of an adjacent residential neighborhood are openly hostile to such a development? Should a request be approved to rezone a piece of land from single-family homes to a 125-unit apartment complex? How does the council weigh the benefits and consequences of rezoning for the developer, the neighborhood, and the entire city?

COMPREHENSIVE PLANNING

Comprehensive planning anticipates such complex problems and defines alternative ways of dealing with them.[4] Planning provides information to public officials and private citizens to guide their policies and decisions. Moreover, it coordinates public and private investment decisions for the betterment of the community. Ultimately, comprehensive planning can enhance the "public good" as well as provide economic benefits to individuals and the community.

Planning encourages public officials, working together with everyone else doing business and living in the community, to systematically find the answer to a basic question: What do we want to become? Answering this question necessitates first taking a realistic look at what the city is today. Planning requires making an inventory and assessment of the city's assets and liabilities, determining its needs, setting goals so that the city has a clear idea of exactly what it wants to achieve, and establishing a method and program to reach those goals. The comprehensive plan provides an overall picture of the city and serves as a guide for the city's future growth.

A comprehensive plan contains several elements that address the major components of what makes up the municipality: its population, economy, natural and historic resources, community facilities, housing, land use, and any other factors that are important. A comprehensive plan also usually contains an implementation strategy, including a work program that describes how the city intends to carry out the recommendations and achieve the goals in the plan.

Public Benefits of Planning

A fundamental reason to undertake a local comprehensive planning program is to further the public good.[5] Comprehensive planning can promote orderly and rational development to ensure that the physical quality of the city remains attractive. It can be used to assist local governments in planning major investments in roads, schools, and water and sewer systems and in recreation, health, and other public facilities. Comprehensive planning can also protect the community from haphazard and uncontrolled growth that detracts from the quality of life for its citizens. Overall, the comprehensive planning process can help ensure that checks and balances are in place to accommodate and manage growth in a rational, equitable, and economic manner.

Following are some benefits that planning can provide to further the public good in the community:

- **Assurance that tax dollars are spent wisely on major improvements where they are most needed and will do the most good.** The deliberate and thoughtful process of determining where development will likely occur can save tax dollars. Some matters to consider are where residential development will likely be located, the density of that development, where schools will be needed, where water and sewer lines should be placed, and whether water service capacity should be designed for residential or industrial use.
- **Assistance in preserving the environment.** Local planning can help preserve environmentally sensitive land and prime agricultural land, and it can help prevent development from occurring in areas that might flood.
- **Protection of unique or historic buildings or districts and scenic areas.** Planning for the preservation of these assets can make the city more attractive for visitors (including tourists) and a desirable place for locating new businesses, and it can enhance the quality of life for its residents.
- **Protection of existing uses to prevent the erosion of a city's tax base.** Public policy that recognizes the need to protect the existing tax base encourages new development of the kind that will enhance the tax base.
- **Anticipation and avoidance of potential problems or (at the very least) prevention of minor problems from becoming major ones.** Planning can provide a good indication of what is likely to occur in a community in the future. Careful consideration of existing conditions and probable future trends can greatly improve a city's problem-solving capabilities.

At the local level, planning is a long-range process—a process that makes a community come together to identify what it has, what it wants, and how it is going to become what it desires. It is a process that demands that local governments address existing and potential opportunities and problems.

Economic Benefits of Planning

Comprehensive planning can also help enhance economic development within a city and protect both residential and business investments that are currently in place.[6] The most important investment most people make is the purchase of a home. Business and industrial property owners are also interested in protecting their investments. Comprehensive planning can remove some uncertainty about the future by ensuring that development will not undermine the value of investments of current property owners. For instance, home buyers want some assurance that their investment will not be jeopardized by the appearance of chicken houses on adjacent property. Similarly, a developer of a shopping center wants some assurance that his or her investment will not be threatened by the construction of a sewage treatment plant on property adjacent to the center. Comprehensive planning helps deter such negative possibilities by allowing for the separation of incompatible land uses, thereby giving guarantees to property owners that their investments will be protected.

Following are some benefits that planning can provide to enhance economic development and protect existing investments:

- Comprehensive planning can help ensure that adequate land, suitably served by water and sewer lines, streets and roads, and other necessary facilities and services, is set aside for commercial and industrial purposes.
- Comprehensive planning can help ensure that sufficient land, with soil, topographical, and geological qualities appropriate for development, is set aside for development purposes. For example, some land is not appropriate because of its location in a flood plain or because an area's water supply will not provide enough water for industrial development. Other areas may be too steep or underlain by bedrock, making their development financially unfeasible. Planning can help prevent investments in sites that are poorly suited for their intended uses.
- An active comprehensive planning program will result in a well-run community that is attractive to prospective investors.

THE GEORGIA PLANNING ACT

The Georgia Planning Act of 1989[7] takes into consideration the history, culture, and traditions of Georgia and affirms the importance of planning to Georgia's economic future and quality of life. The act respects home rule and local autonomy over local matters while recognizing the need for regional cooperation and planning.

Cities and counties prepare their comprehensive plans and submit them to their regional development centers (RDCs). The RDCs then forward the comprehensive plans to the Georgia Department of Community Affairs (DCA) for review and comment. If DCA determines that the plan meets the requirements of the Minimum Standards and Procedures for Local Comprehensive Planning,[8] which govern the preparation, adoption, and implementation of local plans, it certifies the local government as a qualified local government (QLG). Only QLGs are eligible to receive certain grant and loan funds from the state, including those administered by DCA, the Department of Natural Resources (DNR), the Georgia Environmental Facilities Authority (GEFA), the OneGeorgia Authority, and the Georgia Forestry Commission (GFC).[9] Although planning is a voluntary process under the Georgia Planning Act, cities that choose not to plan will lose their QLG status.

Almost all local governments in the state have completed their comprehensive plans and received their QLG certification. To maintain its QLG status, a local government must update its comprehensive plan at a minimum of every 10 years. However, a plan may be amended at any time to reflect changing conditions or policies. Also, a local government must update the short-term work program portion of its plan at a minimum of every five years. The short-term work program lists the specific actions that the local government intends to undertake over a five-year period to implement its comprehensive plan.

The Comprehensive Plan

A plan for physical development—often referred to as a comprehensive plan, a master plan, or a general plan—represents a statement of public policy expressed in the form of a document that includes maps, charts, and graphs.

Because Georgia is composed of many diverse communities, the complexity of comprehensive plans will vary. The minimum standards require a basic level of planning for cities located in counties with the smallest populations. An intermediate level of planning requirements must be addressed by cities in midsized counties with stable growth rates. An advanced level of planning is required of cities in larger and faster growing counties, where more complex planning issues must be addressed. Also, each plan should be tailored to a city's individual needs. The minimum standards and procedures are based on a relatively simple set of questions to be considered by each municipality:[10]

1. What do we have now? (inventory of existing conditions in the community)
2. What do we need? (assessment of existing community programs, facilities, and services and their ability to meet current and future needs)

3. What do we want for the future and how are we going to get there? (establish goals and an implementation program for achieving them)

In accordance with the minimum standards and procedures, these three basic questions must be addressed for each of the following elements that must be included in a city's comprehensive plan.

Population

An analysis of the residential makeup of the city is required. This element looks at the characteristics of the current population and projects the population into the future. Household age, racial, education, and income characteristics of the city's population must also be examined.

Economic Development

An inventory and assessment of the municipality's economic base, its labor force, and its economic development resources must be undertaken, including wage and skill levels, types of employers, and available training. Based on these analyses, realistic economic development strategies can then be formulated.

Housing

An inventory and assessment of housing in the community must be undertaken, including the number, location, type, condition, cost, and age of housing. The adequacy of the existing housing supply can then be determined and strategies formulated to address housing needs for the present and the future.

Natural and Cultural Resources

An inventory and assessment must be undertaken of the community's natural, environmentally sensitive, and historic and cultural resources (e.g., public water supply sources, water supply watersheds, groundwater recharge areas, wetlands, mountain areas, rivers, flood plains, soils, agricultural and forest lands, plant and animal habitats, parks and recreation areas, historic homes and buildings, and archaeological and cultural sites). This information will be used to create strategies for resource use, preservation, and protection. Under the Georgia Planning Act, water supply watersheds, groundwater recharge areas, wetlands, certain defined high elevations and steep slopes in the mountains, and river corridors are identified as "vital areas" of the state. These vital areas require special consideration in the planning process and are discussed in more detail in Chapter 16. For more information on how land-use activities and environmental quality interrelate, see the book Land-Use and the Protection of Georgia's Environment.[11]

Community Facilities and Services

An inventory and assessment of the various services and facilities provided by the city must be conducted, including the transportation system (streets, roads, and highways), water supply and treatment, the sewerage system, garbage disposal, and police and fire protection. Also included are parks, schools, and libraries. The impact of future population growth on these municipal services and facilities and the level at which these services and facilities will continue to be provided must be addressed in this element.

Land Use

An inventory and analysis of all land in the city is basic to comprehensive planning. Different types of uses (e.g., residential, commercial, industrial, park and recreation, etc.) are indicated on a map to show land-use patterns. An analysis can then be made of compatibility among the various uses of land. A future land-use map is then developed by projecting the city's probable future growth and needs. This map indicates the best areas for future growth for each of the different types of land uses.

Intergovernmental Coordination

An inventory must be conducted of existing coordination mechanisms and agreements between the city and adjacent local governments, school boards, water and sewer districts, industrial development authorities, and downtown development authorities. In addition, the city must identify its existing coordinating mechanisms or agreements related to applicable state programs (e.g., the city and county's service delivery strategy or any regional water supply and/or water quality protection plans). The adequacy and suitability of the city's existing coordination mechanisms can then be assessed to determine if they are serving the current and future needs of the community and, if not, what improvements should be made.

Transportation

An inventory must be conducted of the components of the city's transportation network, including streets, roads, highways, bridges, sidewalks, bikeways, parking facilities, public transportation, railroads, and airports.

An assessment is then made to determine if these facilities and services are adequate to meet the existing and future needs of the community or whether improvements will be needed to accommodate anticipated population and economic growth. (Note: The transportation element of the plan is required only of governments designated at the intermediate and advanced planning levels. Governments at the basic planning level include an inventory and assessment of their transportation network as part of their community facilities and services element.)

These seven elements (eight for intermediate and advanced level communities) are the minimum that must be addressed in a comprehensive plan. A local government may add elements if it so chooses. Goals, objectives, and policies will be formulated during the development of the planning elements. Through this process, existing needs and problems will be directly addressed, and realistic plans can be made for probable future growth and needs.

In addition to addressing the required elements, cities that are designated at the intermediate and advanced planning levels must also consider certain quality community objectives in the process of preparing their comprehensive plans. These objectives have been established to promote the quality of life in all of Georgia's communities. Cities at the intermediate and advanced planning levels must also develop a vision for the future of their communities. This community vision should portray a picture of what the city desires to become, and it must be based on public input and an assessment of the city's current and probable future needs and be supported by the city's goals and implementation program.

To address the third basic question—What do we want for the future, and how are we going to get there?—each city establishes goals that address the community's social, economic, and physical needs and develops an implementation program that presents the city's strategy for implementing its comprehensive plan. The most important part of the implementation program is the five-year, short-term work program, which schedules specific actions that a local government will take each year over the next five years to carry out its goals and policies and includes the estimated costs of those actions or projects, funding sources, and the parties responsible for undertaking them. The short-term work program includes community and economic development programs and/or projects, public facilities, and any land development regulations (such as subdivision regulations, building codes, or zoning ordinances) expected to be adopted. The local government has complete control in determining which steps it will take to implement the plan and achieve its goals through the short-term work program.

Although the local plan must include the planning elements and the implementation program, the contents of the plan should emphasize the most important issues for that particular municipality. The plan should serve as a continuously used management tool to aid the city's elected and appointed officials in planning for the future. The comprehensive plan should be updated, as needed, in order to ensure its continued accuracy and maximum usefulness.

Other Components

The Georgia Planning Act requires local governments to consider a number of other matters as they conduct their planning activities. Additional legislation has been enacted that is closely related to and, in certain ways, is part of the comprehensive planning process.

Developments of Regional Impact

A Development of Regional Impact (DRI) is a proposed project of such a size that it is likely to have an impact beyond the local jurisdiction in which it will be located.[12] Because such a project will probably have a regional impact and affect other local governments, it must go through a special regional review process.

Nineteen categories of developments have been established. These categories include offices; commercial, wholesale, and distribution facilities; hospitals; and housing developments. "Thresholds" (i.e., measures of scale or size, such as square feet or number of lots or units) are used to determine whether a proposed development is large enough to constitute a DRI. The thresholds have been established at such levels to ensure that only developments that are likely to have an impact beyond the host government's jurisdiction will be subject to review.

When a developer or other type of applicant requests local government action (such as a building permit, a rezoning, or a business license) to proceed with a project, the city, using the appropriate threshold levels, determines if the development is a DRI. If the project appears to meet or exceed any of the thresholds, the city must then submit the proposed project to its RDC for review and comment. The RDC then analyzes the potential regional or interjurisdictional impacts of the proposed development. In its analysis, the RDC considers the project's probable impact on the region's environment and natural resources, economy, housing, water, sewerage, solid waste services, public transportation, and other public facilities.

The other local governments likely to be affected by the proposed project are also given an opportunity to review the DRI. Based on its own review and comments from these governments, the RDC determines if any conflicts exist with regard to the proposed project and whether the project is in the best interest of the state. When appropriate, informal conflict resolution and formal mediation can be used to resolve the differences that have been identified. Although the local government in whose jurisdiction a DRI is proposed is required to participate in the DRI process, the local government has the ultimate authority to decide whether or not to approve the proposed development.

The Georgia Regional Transportation Authority (GRTA) has jurisdiction for DRI review (in addition to the RDC review) over a 13-county Atlanta region, which has been classified by the U.S. Environmental Protection Agency as an air quality nonattainment area. At such time that any other metropolitan area in the state reaches nonattainment designation, GRTA will have DRI review responsibility over that area as well.[13]

The DRI review process helps local governments stay informed about major developments in their region, thereby promoting cooperation and coordination among neighboring cities and counties. Participation by all affected parties also helps them identify and reduce potential conflicts before local project approval is granted and construction is begun.

Regionally Important Resources

A Regionally Important Resource (RIR) is "a natural or historic resource that has natural boundaries extending beyond a single local government's jurisdiction or has value to a broader public constituency and which is vulnerable to the actions and activities of man."[14] Examples of natural resources are floodplains, marshlands, steep slopes, and rivers and streams. Examples of historic resources include unique or significant historic properties and certain archaeological and cultural resources. Based on input from local governments, RDCs, and other parties, DCA may designate specific RIRs in the state and direct the preparation of a resource management strategy for each, with input from the affected local government(s) and RDC(s). Designated RIRs will be incorporated into the natural and historic resources element of local comprehensive plans, and the strategies developed for RIR management will become part of the plans' implementation strategies.

If a local government initiates or an applicant (e.g., industry, business, or developer) requests some type of local government action that may affect an RIR, the local government will submit a description of the proposed action and a summary of the proposed project to its RDC for review. Based on its review and the comments it receives from other affected local governments, which are also given the opportunity to review the project, the RDC determines (1) whether any conflicts exist with regard to the proposed project and (2) whether the project is likely to have an adverse impact on the RIR or is inconsistent with the resource management strategy.

To help resolve any conflicts, the RDC initiates an informal conflict resolution process. The RDC may also suggest measures that would mitigate the impacts of the proposed action on the RIR. At the end of the review period, the RDC will determine whether the proposed action is in the best interest of the state (i.e., if the proposed action is consistent with the resource management strategy and will not have a negative effect on the RIR). If any conflicts remain unresolved, formal mediation can then be initiated. The local government that proposed the action retains the final authority to (1) proceed with the action as proposed, (2) modify the proposed action, or (3) not proceed with the action.

Mediation

Another important component of the Georgia Planning Act and the Georgia Comprehensive Solid Waste Management Act calls on local governments to mediate or otherwise resolve certain interjurisdictional conflicts.[15] The purpose of mediation is to provide a means by which local governments can communicate with one another regarding plans or actions that potentially have interjurisdictional effects. Mediation is generally less expensive and more constructive than litigation, which too often is the only option otherwise available to local governments when serious conflicts arise.

Mediation is ordinarily voluntary. However, as part of the planning process, any government that fails to participate in mediation, when appropriate, could lose its QLG certification. Loss of this certification will result in a local government's ineligibility to receive certain state grant and loan funds.

Matters that are subject to mediation under the Georgia Planning Act and the Georgia Comprehensive Solid Waste Management Act include

- conflicts related to the preparation or implementation of local, multijurisdictional, and/or regional comprehensive plans;
- conflicts related to the preparation or implementation of local, multijurisdictional, and/or regional solid waste management plans;
- actions or conflicts related to RIRs; and
- actions or conflicts related to DRIs.

In the early stages, the process involves the use of informal conflict resolution, which can be requested by a local government or initiated by the RDC. During its review of a local plan or of a proposed action regarding a DRI or an RIR, the RDC is responsible for bringing local governments together when a potential conflict exists. If informal conflict resolution is unsuccessful, a formal, 90-day mediation process may be initiated. Even if all or part of the conflict remains unresolved after the formal mediation process has concluded, a local government retains its QLG certification if it participated in good faith.

Solid Waste Management

Under the Comprehensive Solid Waste Management Act of 1990,[16] a local government shall develop or be included in an approved comprehensive solid waste management plan that is prepared (either singly or jointly with other jurisdictions) to meet the requirements of the act. Failure to do so can result in the denial of grants, loans, and permits for solid waste management facilities and programs.

The Solid Waste Management Act states that each solid waste plan should

- identify the size and type of solid waste handling facilities within the plan's area;
- identify land areas unsuitable for solid waste handling facilities;
- ensure adequate solid waste handling capability and capacity within the planning area for at least 10 years from the date of plan completion;
- indicate how the community plans to meet the statewide per capita 25 percent municipal solid waste reduction goal (based on fiscal year 1992 levels); and
- be in conformance with the state's Solid Waste Management Plan.

As part of the statewide solid waste management planning process, each local government reports annually to DCA on its progress in meeting the solid waste reduction goal. To help communities identify the full and actual costs of solid waste disposal and to help the public understand these costs, each local government is required to report annually on the costs of managing its solid waste.

Because of the escalating costs associated with sound solid waste management, local governments are encouraged to work cooperatively to manage their solid waste on a multijurisdictional basis. The Solid Waste Management Act provides that preference in state funding be given to facilities included in regional or multijurisdictional plans.

When a local government's solid waste plan has been completed, it may be submitted as part of the community facilities element of the local government's comprehensive plan. Because the Solid Waste Management Act goes into far more detail on this subject than does the Georgia Planning Act in terms of requirements, a solid waste plan is expected to be more detailed than the solid waste portion of the community facilities element.

The short-term work program, a mandatory part of the solid waste management plan, showing a year-by-year breakdown of specific actions, budgets, and assignments, must be updated at least once every five years. A plan is subject to amendment when conditions or policies change. If any significant changes in a city's solid waste facility or program take place, an update to the solid waste plan should be initiated to encompass the resultant actions that a major change in facilities or programs will necessitate.

Impact Fees

Impact fees are payments by a developer to provide a proportionate share of the costs of capital improvements and public services that are needed to serve new growth and development. The Georgia Development Impact Fee Act regulates the conditions under which impact fees may be levied by local governments in Georgia.[17]

The primary purpose of the Impact Fee Act is to provide a rational framework on which to base a fee that is directly related to the amount of impact a development has on specific public services and facilities. The statute provides guidelines for how fees are to be calculated, collected, spent, and, in some cases, refunded, thereby giving both local government officials and developers a fair and predictable basis for projecting government revenues and development costs.

Public facilities for which impact fees can be imposed include

- water supply, treatment, and distribution facilities;
- wastewater collection, treatment, and disposal facilities;
- roads, streets, and bridges;
- stormwater control facilities;
- parks and recreation areas;
- police and firefighting facilities; and
- libraries.

Cities that choose to adopt an impact fee ordinance must

- adopt a local comprehensive plan that meets the minimum standards and procedures for local comprehensive planning and includes a capital improvements element;

- establish a development impact fee advisory committee to advise the city on its adoption of an impact fee ordinance; and
- hold two public hearings regarding the proposed impact fee ordinance before it is adopted.

LAND-USE CONTROLS

Regulations and ordinances related to land use and development are mechanisms to implement the comprehensive plan. Major ordinances related to land use normally include zoning and subdivision regulations.

Zoning

Zoning is a primary regulatory method used by local governments to influence, guide, and control development as they carry out their plans for physical and economic growth. It is a means by which a local government attempts to ensure compatibility and reduce conflict among different types of land use. Zoning can provide adequate space for each kind of land use. Additionally, it can be used to direct growth into particular areas of a city where infrastructure may exist to support that development or where environmentally sensitive areas are not widespread.

A zoning ordinance consists of (1) a map that divides the jurisdiction into various districts for particular classes of residential, commercial, industrial, and other uses and (2) a written ordinance that establishes the conditions under which land may be developed and used for particular purposes. A zoning ordinance specifies what types of development may take place in each zoning district of the jurisdiction. It stipulates the allowable size and height of structures and sets forth the requirements for lot size, setbacks, street parking, and other related considerations. A zoning ordinance is not a comprehensive plan or a land-use plan, but it can be used to implement such plans by controlling how land is used.

A zoning ordinance specifies what types of development may or may not take place in each zoned district of the city. Specifically, zoning can

- ensure that incompatible land uses are buffered and separated, thereby protecting residential, commercial, and industrial uses;
- group commercial uses together to increase shopping convenience and to provide for adequate parking space;
- assist prospective business investors in finding suitable locations by clearly designating sites for potential development; and
- preserve environmentally sensitive areas and prime agricultural lands.

A zoning ordinance should be based on a land-use or comprehensive plan so that zoning decisions can be readily justified. Outcomes of recent court cases indicate that local governments have not fared well when defending zoning actions in situations in which their zoning ordinances were not based on such plans.

The Georgia Supreme Court in *Guhl v. Holcomb Bridge Road Corporation* identified six factors that should be considered by local governments when making a zoning decision:

1. the existing uses and zoning of nearby property;
2. the extent to which the value of the property is diminished by its present zoning;
3. the extent to which this reduced value promotes the health, safety, morals, or general welfare of the public;
4. the relative gain to the public as compared with the hardship imposed on the individual property owner;
5. the suitability of the property for the presently zoned purposes; and
6. the length of time the property has been vacant as zoned, considered in the context of land development in the area in the vicinity of the property.[18]

Zoning Procedures Law

The Zoning Procedures Law applies to all counties and cities, except that counties of 625,000 or more population and cities of 100,000 or more population within such counties are subject to additional requirements.[19] The purpose of this law is to ensure that due process is provided when local governments regulate the uses of property through zoning. It requires a local government to follow specified minimum procedures in exercising its zoning powers. However, the law does not invalidate prior zoning decisions or require a city to exercise zoning powers.

On an action resulting in a zoning decision, including the adoption of a zoning ordinance, an amendment to the ordinance, or the granting of a special-use permit, the law requires a city to provide for a hearing, with at least 15 but no more than 45 days' prior notice. The notice must spell out the time, place, and purpose of the hearing and must be published in a newspaper of general circulation within the corporate limits of the municipality. Subject to the same hearing requirements, the city must adopt written policies and procedures governing the calling and conduct of hearings and make copies available for distribution to the public.[20] These policies and procedures must specify a minimum and equal time period of not less than 10 minutes per side for presentations by proponents and opponents of a proposed zoning ordinance.[21]

The city is required to adopt standards governing the exercise of its zoning power that may include factors it finds relevant in balancing the interests between promoting public health, safety, morality, or general welfare and the right to unrestricted use of property. Copies of these standards, which are also subject to the hearing requirements, must be available for distribution to the public.[22]

When a request for rezoning property has been initiated by a party other than the city, the notice also must include the location of the property and the current and proposed zoning classifications. Moreover, a sign containing information required by municipal resolution or ordinance must be placed in a conspicuous location on the property not less than 15 days prior to the hearing.[23]

If a rezoning request is denied, the same property may not be considered again for rezoning until after six months following the denial.[24] If a city and a county adopt a common zoning ordinance with respect to zoning classifications, then a qualifying municipality may adopt a zoning ordinance providing that all annexed property will automatically be zoned by the city, without further action, for the same use as prior to the annexation. A change in zoning classification of such property would still require following the procedures for a zoning decision.[25]

If a proposed zoning decision relates to or will allow location of a halfway house, drug rehabilitation center, or other facility for the treatment of drug dependency, a public hearing must be held at least six months and not more than nine months before the date of final action on this decision.[26]

If a proposed zoning change is for a property within 3,000 feet of any military base or installation and if a city has a planning department or similar agency that reviews zoning proposals, then that department or agency must make a recommendation regarding the impact of the proposed use on the military facility and the compatibility of the proposed use with the facility. Also, the commander of the base shall be given the opportunity to make a recommendation regarding the proposed zoning change.[27]

Conflict of Interest in Zoning Actions

The conflict of interest disclosure law requires a member of the local governing authority or planning commission who has (1) a property interest in, (2) a financial interest in a business having a property interest in, or (3) a family member having such interest in any property affected by a rezoning action to disclose immediately, in writing, the nature and extent of that interest to the governing authority. A member who has an interest as defined in (1) or (2) must disqualify him- or herself from voting on the rezoning action and shall not take any measures on behalf of him- or herself or any other person to influence action on the application for rezoning.[28]

This law also requires a rezoning applicant to file a disclosure report with the governing authority when the applicant has, within two years immediately preceding the application, made campaign contributions totaling $250 or more to any member of the governing authority or planning commission who will consider the application. The report must reveal the member's name and official position and the dollar amount and description of each campaign contribution made during the two-year period, and the report must be filed within 10 days after the application is first submitted.[29] An opponent of a rezoning action who has made similar contributions also must file a disclosure report as previously described, except that it must be submitted at least five calendar days prior to the first hearing on the application.[30] Any person who knowingly fails to comply with the requirements of this law will be guilty of a misdemeanor.[31]

The law stipulates that if the disqualification of one or more members of the local governing authority results in the inability to attain a quorum for a final decision, the governing authority must request the superior court to appoint a disinterested special master to hear evidence regarding the proposed rezoning action and make a recommendation to the governing authority. Disqualification from voting is removed when a special master has been appointed and has made a recommendation.[32]

A member of the local governing authority or planning commission is not prohibited by this law from voting on a zoning decision when the city is adopting a zoning ordinance for the first time or voting on revising its zoning ordinance, initiated by the local government, pursuant to the city's comprehensive plan.[33]

Subdivision Regulations

Subdivision regulations specify the process for converting undeveloped land into building lots. They establish site improvement standards for streets, lots, and site layouts; for the construction of curbs, gutters, and sidewalks; and for the provision of water and sewer systems. These regulations also specify who (e.g., developer or local government) is responsible for installing certain public improvements (e.g., paved roads, water and sewer systems, etc.) in new residential subdivisions.

In the past, subdivision regulations could require the dedication of land for open space and the reservation of areas for public uses such as schools, parks, fire stations, and other public facilities. However, under the Georgia Development Impact Fee Act (described earlier), a local government may require land dedications only for "project improvements" such as landscaping, recreation areas, or other amenities that primarily benefit the project occupants rather than the community as a whole.

Subdivision regulations should also require proposed developments to conform to the city's comprehensive plan. Street layout should be consistent with the transportation and thoroughfare portion of the plan so that new streets will be compatible with the city street system. Street layout is an important part of the subdivision design because the streets not only furnish access to individual lots but also provide the location for water, sewer, gas, and other public utility lines.

Any proposed subdivision that includes, abuts, or requires access to any part of the state highway system is subject to additional regulations of the Georgia Department of Transportation (DOT). These regulations relate to the location and design of a proposed street or driveway intersection with a state highway.

Subdivision regulations are commonly administered by a planning commission. The regulations establish a process of plat review and approval. A proposal for a new subdivision is normally reviewed in several steps involving preapplication, when the developer has a chance to discuss the proposal with commission members or staff; the submission of a preliminary plat, which includes a boundary survey, proposed streets, rights-of-way, easements, lot sizes, and other development characteristics; and then, after streets and utilities have been put in, the submission of a final plat, which incorporates detailed specifications for the property as required in the subdivision regulations. After the final plat is approved by the planning commission (or, if none exists, by the governing authority), it is officially filed with the superior court of the county in which the city is located.

Subdivision regulations, properly formulated and administered, will

- encourage economically sound development;
- ensure that required streets, utilities, and public facilities are properly provided; and
- ensure that safe and convenient traffic and transportation access is provided.

Subdivision regulations determine the development patterns of specific areas of the city. Through appropriate regulations, municipal officials can make sure that when development occurs, it will be in accordance with the city's comprehensive plan and be of maximum benefit while having the least possible adverse effects on the city's residents, businesses, and institutions.

Transfer of Development Rights

Cities may adopt ordinances permitting the transfer of "development rights" from one lot or parcel of property to another and establishing procedures, methods, and standards for such transfer within the municipality.[34] A city must hold a public hearing on the proposed ordinance prior to its enactment.

Development rights are the maximum development that would be allowed on a particular piece of property according to the city's plan and zoning ordinance. These rights can be transferred from a property for which proposed development may be considered undesirable or environmentally harmful to a property that can accommodate development in addition to what ordinarily would be allowed.

The property from which development rights are to be transferred must have special characteristics, such as farmland, woodland, desert, mountain land, a flood plain, natural habitat, recreation area or parkland, or land with unique aesthetic, architectural, or historic value that the city wants to protect from future development. The property to which the development rights are proposed to be transferred must be appropriate and suitable for development and sufficient to accommodate the transferred development rights without substantial adverse environmental, economic, or social impact to that property or neighboring property.

The proposed transfer must be approved by the property owners of both the property from which the development rights are transferred and the property to which the rights are transferred. Prior to any transfer of development rights, the municipality must adopt an ordinance providing for the issuance and recording of the legal instrument necessary to transfer the rights; establishing a system for monitoring the severance, ownership, assignment, and transfer of these rights; and providing a map or other description of those areas of the city designated as eligible to transfer and receive development rights between properties.

A city may purchase development rights and hold them for conservation purposes or resale. Also, cities may enter into intergovernmental agreements with counties to enact interdependent ordinances to transfer development rights between jurisdictions.

PARTICIPANTS IN THE PLANNING PROCESS

Everyone who lives or works in a community participates to varying degrees in shaping its future. In most cities, however, the elected and appointed officials are the ones who carry out the comprehensive planning program on a day-to-day basis.

In addition to the mayor and councilmembers, the groups and individuals who play key public roles in the planning process include the chief administrative officer (CAO) of the city, the planning commission, the professional planning staff, the zoning administrator, and the board of zoning appeals, as well as various municipal departments that are involved in different aspects of the comprehensive planning process.

Mayor and Council

The mayor and council have the final say on how effective the community planning process will be. With or without comprehensive planning, the elected officials will shape the city's future with their policy decisions that are implemented by the ordinances and resolutions that are adopted, the taxes that are raised, and the resources that are allocated for public improvements and services.

For the planning process to work, the mayor and council must take charge and be the driving force behind the development of the city's comprehensive plan. This function of the mayor and council is especially important in setting community goals and, at the other end of the process, in developing and implementing programs and projects so that the city's plan is successfully carried out. In the same vein, the mayor and council should protect the integrity of the plan by making its decisions in accordance with the plan's intent.

Chief Administrative Officer

In many respects, the CAO is also the chief planner for the community. The CAO (mayor, city manager, city administrator, etc.) is in the best position to motivate department heads to think and act as a planning team.

Once organized under the direction of the CAO, the management team proposes an annual, coordinated set of goals and work priorities (e.g., paving certain streets and roads, extending water or sewer lines, or buying land for a new fire station or playground) consistent with the objectives of the city's comprehensive plan. These goals and priorities become the basis for the annual budget and the annual update of the capital improvements program and budget.

Planning Commission

The planning commission is an advisory board, usually composed of five to nine persons, appointed by the mayor and council. If it is a joint city-county planning commission, some of its members are appointed by the mayor and council and others by the county governing authority. The planning commission's mission is to plan for the city's future, looking beyond short-term solutions, the technical views of municipal staff and department heads, and the particular concerns of local special interest groups. Persons appointed to the planning commission should have no actual or even potential conflicts of interest. They should be encouraged to attend training programs sponsored by universities, professional associations, and state or regional agencies.

The planning commission ordinarily prepares and recommends for adoption, by the elected governing body, the city's comprehensive plan, updates to the plan, the zoning ordinance and amendments, and subdivision regulations and amendments. Once the governing authority adopts subdivision regulations, the planning commission may also become a "platting commission," which means that it reviews and approves subdivision plats. The commission may receive technical assistance from a professional staff and from department heads and consultants in performing these functions. If the city does not have a planning commission, the governing body normally assumes planning commission functions.

Professional Planner

A number of municipalities in Georgia have professionally staffed planning departments or departments that may combine planning, building inspection, traffic engineering, and economic and community development. Cities may also combine their resources with counties to support a joint planning staff. Smaller communities often rely upon RDCs for professional planning assistance.

Professional planners are often generalists with skills in land use, transportation planning, economic development, and the administration of zoning ordinances and subdivision regulations. They provide technical studies and ongoing advice as needed by the planning commission and other public officials.

Even though a city may employ its own planning staff, it may occasionally find it beneficial to employ planning consultants for specialized assignments. The choice of a consultant should be made carefully, considering not only cost but also qualifications.

Zoning Administrator

The zoning administrator oversees the day-to-day administration of the zoning ordinance. Some cities give this responsibility to the building inspector, and others assign this function to the planning director. Subdivision regulations are also commonly administered by the person carrying out the responsibilities of a zoning administrator. Whoever administers the zoning ordinance and subdivision regulations should work closely with the planning commission and staff to ensure that these two regulatory devices are administered appropriately and fairly in implementing a city's comprehensive plan.

Board of Zoning Appeals

In most cities in which a zoning ordinance has been enacted by the governing authority, a board of zoning appeals is created as a part of that ordinance. This quasijudicial board hears appeals when it is alleged that an error has occurred in enforcing the zoning ordinance. It may also hear requests for variances from the ordinance when a building cannot be located without violating setback and other site requirements of the zoning ordinance because a particular hardship exists on the parcel of land, such as a stream or rock formation. In most zoning ordinances, the functions of the board are very narrowly defined.

Under no circumstances does the board have the authority to issue a variance for use of property not already allowed by the zoning ordinance.

CITIZEN PARTICIPATION

The success of a planning program largely depends on citizen participation, acceptance, and enthusiasm. A high level of citizen participation in the planning process is the best assurance that the comprehensive plan reflects the feelings and aspirations of a city's residents. A diverse cross-section of a city's residents should be encouraged to participate in the planning process. An organized and ongoing system of collecting information about how residents feel about their city and how they would like it to be in the future should be developed and sustained.

One way to involve citizens in the planning process is to develop local advisory committees or councils in each area of the city to work with the planning staff. This approach ensures broad representation but requires a heavy commitment of staff time.

Public hearings also encourage citizens to get involved.[35] The minimum standards and procedures for local comprehensive planning require that at least two public hearings be held in regard to the plan's preparation. One public hearing must be held before any planning begins. This hearing is intended to inform citizens about the purpose of the plan, the process to be used in its preparation, the schedule for preparing it, and how the public will be involved. Another public hearing must take place after the draft plan is prepared. At this hearing, the public should be informed about the content of the plan and its recommendations and be given an opportunity to make suggestions regarding additions or revisions.

Task forces are yet another option for obtaining citizen participation. Task forces are special committees, usually appointed by the mayor, to deal with a specific issue or problem. A task force can sometimes be quite large, having as many as 50 or more members of the community. The task force is often divided into smaller groups, with each one looking into a particular part of the larger issue or problem at hand. The task force is normally provided assistance by the elected officials and city staff so that its work will proceed in a timely and meaningful fashion. The task force usually comes up with a final report, including recommendations.

Workshops can also facilitate citizen involvement in the planning process. At a workshop, a professional planner and others knowledgeable about the issue(s) under consideration can discuss the benefits of planning and guide participants through the steps of the planning process. These workshops, which may range in number from one to several depending on the community's size, provide an open forum in which to address the community's future and an opportunity for citizens to learn about what to expect from the planning process. Workshops can fulfill a dual purpose of public education and public participation in plan preparation.

Whatever methods of citizen participation are used, a plan prepared with active and informed citizen participation will undoubtedly better reflect the city's overall needs, goals, and desires and stand a much better chance of being used than would a plan prepared with little or no public involvement. This importance of ownership of the plan by both elected officials and citizens cannot be overemphasized; it is one of the most critical factors in successful plan preparation and implementation.

PLANNING ACTIVITIES

The principal functions of the planning commission and planning staff are to help the community anticipate the future and, at the same time, to conduct current business in a manner consciously designed to achieve community goals. At all times, planning officials should closely cooperate with the CAO, department heads, elected officials, and citizen groups in order to both plan for the future and to implement those plans.

Planning Responsibilities

Although planning officials spend considerable time hearing requests to amend the zoning map and reviewing subdivision plats, their full range of responsibilities is much broader and includes

- maintaining and updating the comprehensive plan;
- developing such specific plans as may be necessary and desirable for industrial parks, neighborhoods, park sites, and other community facilities;
- helping city officials, as well as neighborhood and special interest groups, define their needs and goals as a part of the planning process;
- encouraging public participation in planning and in governmental affairs;
- assisting the municipal government in formulating a short-term work program and a list of projects that will satisfy city objectives;
- assisting in the development of the capital improvements program; and
- coordinating federal and state participation in local capital improvement projects.

Specific matters of concern to the planning commission and staff include

- zoning ordinance text and map updates;
- revisions of subdivision regulations;
- community appearance (including sign and billboard controls);
- streets and roads, highways, and public transportation;
- soil and water conservation, including sedimentation controls; and
- flood or other pertinent environmental controls.

Information Collection

Even without the help of a planner, a small city can assemble and keep current the minimum information and working documents essential for good planning and management (see Chapter 17). Such a collection would include

- population, economic, and housing data: past trends, the present situation, and projections into the future, which are available from DCA's PlanBuilder Web site (http://www.georgiaplanning.com);
- maps of the city's street system (from the Georgia Department of Transportation [DOT]);
- land-use maps, coded by color, showing how each parcel of land is used;
- maps showing the location of all public facilities;
- maps showing the precise location of all storm drainage outfalls, water mains, and other utility lines (public and private);

- soils maps (from the U.S. Soil Conservation Service);
- wetlands maps (from the U.S. Fish and Wildlife Service and the Georgia Department of Natural Resources [DNR]);
- historic sites maps (from DNR); and
- floodplain maps (from the Federal Emergency Management Agency [FEMA]).

In addition to population, economic, and housing statistical data, many maps and tools for planning are also available at DCA's PlanBuilder Web site (http://www.georgiaplanning.com). Other useful maps are available at the Georgia GIS Data Clearinghouse Web site (http://gis1.state.ga.us).

Planning Documents: Adoption and Change

The basic documents of a city's plans and related rules and regulations consist of the comprehensive plan, the zoning ordinance and map, and the subdivision regulations. Public meetings by the planning commission and public hearings by the governing authority on proposed comprehensive plans, zoning ordinances, subdivision regulations, and changes to any of those already in existence are essential before these items are adopted by the governing authority. Amendments to the comprehensive plan, text, or map of the zoning ordinance or to the text of the subdivision regulations are normally referred to the planning commission before action is taken by the governing body.

An amendment to the zoning ordinance or subdivision regulations is a legislative act and requires the same legal form required to amend other ordinances. A proposed rezoning requires public notice, a public hearing, and formal recommendations to the governing body by the planning commission. The Zoning Procedures Law sets forth minimum public notice and hearing requirements.

The role of the planning commission in zoning matters is to gather as much factual information as possible about a proposal, give the public an opportunity to be heard, and make recommendations regarding the proposal to the governing authority. The governing authority may accept, modify, or reject the recommendations of the planning commission.

Plan Implementation

Comprehensive plans are implemented through the use and enforcement of public codes and regulations, such as zoning ordinances and subdivision regulations.

Another way to carry out the plan is through investing public funds. In many instances, the investment of public funds in road improvements or in water and sewer systems triggers opportunities for private funds to follow. Coordinating the timing and location of these investments is critical to carrying out the objectives of a comprehensive plan.

Community and economic development programs also can put comprehensive plans into action. DCA has a variety of programs to help local governments improve the economic vitality of their communities and make them more attractive places in which to live. The Community Development Block Grant (CDBG) program provides funds for housing, public facilities, and economic development projects that will improve the living conditions and economic opportunity for low- and moderate-income persons.[36]

DCA's Quality Growth Assistance Program helps cities address community development and quality-of-life issues by undertaking "smart growth" practices such as controlling sprawl development, adapting historic structures for reuse, adopting innovative land-use regulations, and preserving open space or parklands. Besides providing technical assistance, DCA also offers Quality Growth Grants for local governments to implement smart-growth activities.[37] DCA's Main Street and Better Hometown Programs are self-help community development programs designed to improve the quality of life in a city's downtown. Each city selected for one of the programs is assisted in building a stronger local economy through the revitalization of its downtown area. The Downtown Development Revolving Loan Fund assists cities in implementing quality downtown development projects.[38] A similar program, the Georgia Cities Foundation Revolving Loan Fund, also helps cities revitalize their downtown areas.[39]

Encouraging a municipal business and industry group to promote marketing and recruitment efforts and using other economic development programs or tools such as various types of revolving loan funds and special tax districts can improve a city's economic well-being. By participating in the Georgia Business Retention and Expansion Process (BREP), managed by the Georgia Department of Economic Development, the wants and needs of a city's businesses can be determined and appropriately addressed, thereby strengthening the local economy.

Plan implementation is ultimately achieved through the daily work of the city government's operating departments. For example, every action taken to develop park facilities and streets or roads, regulate new subdivisions, construct new utility lines and other facilities, or change law enforcement patterns affects the community and its future. Thus, coordination between planners and other department personnel is essential, not only in plan preparation but also in conducting the daily business of government.

INTERGOVERNMENTAL COORDINATION

A number of cities and counties appoint joint planning commissions and jointly support a planning department, or they contract with each other for planning services. Cities and counties are also served by one of the 16 regional development centers (RDCs) in the state. Services provided by the RDCs include help in preparing and implementing comprehensive plans, zoning ordinances, subdivision regulations, and economic development programs. RDCs also provide areawide planning and coordination for selected programs.

Intergovernmental cooperation is encouraged and, in some cases, required, as local governments carry out their various responsibilities under the Georgia Planning Act. Joint planning can be accomplished when two or more governments decide that it is in their best interest to prepare a comprehensive plan together and then pool their resources to do so. Because all the municipalities in a particular county are scheduled to update their comprehensive plans at the same time as the county in which they are located, the benefits of preparing a joint comprehensive plan that also can be updated jointly should be investigated.

Joint planning can be very cost effective. It can also result in coordination between a county and the city (or cities) within it, which can preclude conflicts between local plans and help ensure that the plan's implementation, including any economic development programs, will benefit all the local governments involved. Just as local governments have found that shared or the consolidated provision of services (e.g., police and fire protection and solid waste management) can benefit all parties, they can experience similar results from joint planning.

As part of the review process that a local plan goes through to receive certification, each RDC conducts a public hearing for each plan submitted to it for review. The primary purpose of this public hearing is to provide other local governments and other parties that may be affected by the plan an opportunity for comment to ensure consistency and compatibility between a municipality's plan and the proposed plan of a neighboring jurisdiction.

The Service Delivery Strategy law requires counties and the municipalities located within each county to reach and maintain agreements regarding the delivery and funding of all provided services, such as police and fire protection, solid waste collection and disposal, and parks and recreation services and facilities.[40] The law also requires that land-use plans be compatible and nonconflicting among the governments. For a detailed discussion of the provisions and requirements of the Service Delivery Strategy law, see Chapter 30.

As previously discussed, three of the major components of the Georgia Planning Act are Developments of Regional Impact (DRI), Regionally Important Resources (RIR), and the mediation process. Each involves intergovernmental cooperation. The DRI process is intended to improve communication and cooperation between governments by identifying, at the outset, before conflicts arise, any potential impact of proposed large-scale developments on neighboring governments. A summary of the proposed development is distributed by the RDC to potentially affected local governments, which then have the opportunity to comment on the development. Similarly, a local government that may be affected by a proposed action in a neighboring or nearby jurisdiction will have an opportunity to comment on that action or on any action that will have an impact on an RIR. The mediation component of the Georgia Planning Act provides a means whereby local governments can resolve conflicts by effectively communicating with one another. Mediation offers the potential for solving intergovernmental problems in a timely and relatively low-cost manner.

The Georgia Planning Act calls for each RDC to prepare a plan for its region and to annually update the regional work program or the implementation part of its plan. This plan must take into consideration all local plans within the region. As the regional planning process is carried out, local concerns are addressed through the local plans that have been adopted and are being implemented, through local representation on the RDC boards of directors, by each local government's review of the regional plan, and through public hearings that are held regarding the regional plan.

SOURCES OF HELP

Planning is a technical and complex endeavor. Local officials frequently will need help with their planning programs and activities. A variety of assistance is available. Local staff should not be overlooked when delving into planning matters. Even if a municipality does not have a professional planner on its staff, other staff members may be able to provide some information or insight regarding the planning matter or problem at hand. In any situation involving legal matters, the city attorney should be consulted.

RDCs have experience working with local governments in preparing and implementing comprehensive plans and are often the first place to call for planning help. The Georgia Municipal Association (GMA) provides many services to its member cities and is available for help on planning matters. The Carl Vinson Institute of Government at the University of Georgia can also provide assistance.

Not only can DCA help local governments regarding plan preparation and implementation, but also—as the state agency responsible for implementing the Georgia Planning Act—it can provide assistance regarding any aspect of the act. DNR and DOT provide assistance that is specific to their areas of expertise. Professional organizations such as the Georgia Planning Association and the Georgia Association of Zoning Administrators are other sources of help. Consultants can also provide assistance, ranging from overall plan preparation to helping with very specific types of planning activities.

NOTES

1. GA. CONST. art. IX, §2, ¶4.
2. Ibid.
3. Portions of this chapter are drawn from Burton Sparer, "Planning" in *Handbook for Georgia Mayors and Councilmembers*, 2nd ed., ed. J. Devereux Weeks and Emily Honigberg (Athens: Carl Vinson Institute of Government, University of Georgia, 1994), 175–88.
4. Ibid.
5. This section is drawn from Georgia Department of Community Affairs, *Why Plan?* (Atlanta: DCA, 1990), 5–7.
6. Ibid., 7–8.
7. OFFICIAL CODE OF GEORGIA ANNOTATED (O.C.G.A.) ch. 45-12; tit. §§50-8-1–50-8-46, 36-70-1–36-70-5, 12-2-1–12-2-9.
8. Ga. Comp. R. & Regs. ch. 110-12-1 (2004).
9. O.C.G.A. §§36-70-1–36-70-5, 50-8-1–50-8-17, 12-2-1–12-2-9; chs. 50-23, 50-34; §§12-6-1–12-6-23.
10. Ga. Comp. R. & Regs. r. 110-12-1-.04(2)(a).
11. James E. Kundell, Richard W. Campbell, Joseph M. Heikoff, Lawrence R. Hepburn, Robert Klant, and S. Wesley Woolf, *Land Use and the Protection of Georgia's Environment* (Athens: Carl Vinson Institute of Government, University of Georgia, 1989).
12. Ga. Comp. R. & Regs. ch. 110-12-3 (2004).
13. O.C.G.A. ch. 50-32.
14. Department of Community Affairs, *Procedures for the Designation and Review of Regionally Important Resources* (Atlanta: Board of Community Affairs, DCA, 1991), 4–5.
15. Ga. Comp. R. & Regs. ch. 110-12-5 (1996).
16. O.C.G.A. §§12-8-20–12-8-41.
17. O.C.G.A. ch. 36-71.
18. Guhl v. Holcomb Bridge Road Corporation, 238 Ga. 322, 232 S.E. 2d 830 (1977).
19. O.C.GA. chs. 36-66, 36-67.
20. O.C.G.A. §§36-66-4, 36-66-5; Tilley Properties v. Bartow County, 261 Ga. 153, 401 S.E. 2d 527 (1991).
21. O.C.G.A. §36-66-5.

22. Ibid.; Tilley Properties v. Bartow County, 261 Ga. 153, 401 S.E. 2d 527 (1991).
23. O.C.G.A. §36-66-4.
24. Ibid.
25. O.C.G.A. §36-66-4(e).
26. O.C.G.A. §36-66-4(f).
27. O.C.G.A. §36-66-6
28. O.C.G.A. §36-67A-2.
29. O.C.G.A. §36-67A-3.
30. Ibid.
31. O.C.G.A. §36-67A-4.
32. O.C.G.A. §36-67A-5.
33. O.C.G.A. §36-67A-6.
34. O.C.G.A. ch. 36-66A.
35. Portions of this section are drawn from the Georgia Department of Community Affairs (DCA), *Preparing a Local Plan* (Atlanta: DCA, 1990), 6–8.
36. 42 UNITED STATES CODE ANNOTATED (U.S.C.A.) §5301 et seq.
37. Ga. Comp. R. & Regs. ch. 110-23-1 (2001).
38. Ga. Comp. R. & Regs. ch. 110-19-1 (2000).
39. The Georgia Cities Foundation is a nonprofit subsidiary of the Georgia Municipal Association (GMA).
40. O.C.G.A. §§36-70-20–36-70-28.

15

Ted Baggett

Annexation

Annexation is the process by which a city expands its boundaries in order to extend its municipal services, regulations, and taxing authority. Annexation is also a means of ensuring that all residents and businesses who benefit from access to the city's facilities and services share the tax burden associated with constructing and maintaining those facilities and services. Cities may also encourage annexation in order to provide areas for future growth.

PURPOSE

Georgia annexation policy states that "the orderly growth of municipal corporations, based on the need for municipal services and the ability of the municipal corporation to serve, is essential to the economic progress of the state and to the well being of its urban citizens."[1] Because cities exist primarily in order to provide urban-type services, it follows that cities may choose to annex to accommodate those property owners and citizens who wish to enjoy city services. Although cities may provide some services outside their territorial limits, areas added to a city through annexation receive the benefit of all applicable municipal services.

Property owners and residents of the unincorporated county may be interested in annexation into a city to obtain municipal-type services not provided in the unincorporated area or to obtain a heightened level of service. For example, city residents may enjoy lower fire insurance rates because of better Insurance Services Office ratings resulting from enhanced response times offered by a municipal fire department. Other residents may wish to take advantage of being under the jurisdiction of a municipal police department that may have a better officer-to-resident ratio and a smaller patrolling area. Finally, rural municipalities are often able to provide municipal water service at rates that are more cost efficient for homeowners.

In addition to enhanced services, many residents wish to take advantage of the efforts that cities have made to create a special identity or sense of place within the community. Smart growth initiatives in many cities that promote active downtowns, service coordination, and urban infrastructure improvements like sidewalks and parks allow city residents to enjoy a quality of life typically associated with municipalities. As a result of these initiatives and heightened service levels, annexation often results in raising the annexed property's value. Additionally, property owners and residents may seek annexation because of differences in development regulations, such as zoning, that may exist between the city and the county.

Finally, many residents enjoy having access to a smaller and more responsive local government. Many believe that being able to rely on a mayor and council that represent only a few thousand people allows for decision making that respects the needs of individual neighborhoods.

Because of the complex issues surrounding annexation, some cities have taken the step of conducting an analysis of the fiscal impacts of a proposed annexation to examine the expenditures and revenues that may be anticipated as a result of the annexation. Additionally, cities may wish to adopt policies to govern future annexations. Such policies should be viewed as guidelines for analysis of potential annexations while maintaining the flexibility needed to consider the affected interests on a case by case basis. The adoption of annexation policies also allows citizens of a city and the surrounding areas to understand the issues associated with boundary judgments.

METHODS

In addition to annexations by the General Assembly and the annexation of unincorporated islands totally surrounded by cities, there are three primary methods of annexation: the 100 percent method, the 60 percent method, and the resolution and referendum method. All three of these methods require the consent of a majority of the persons living in the area to be annexed into a city.

100 Percent Method

The 100 percent method allows property owners of all the land in an area to have their property annexed into an adjacent city by signing a petition.[2]

60 Percent Method

This method allows for petitioners representing at least 60 percent of the property owners and at least 60 percent of the voters in an area to sign a petition to have their property annexed into an adjacent city. This method is available to cities with populations over 200. The municipality is required to prepare a plan for extending city services to an area to be annexed and hold a public hearing before the annexation is complete.[3]

Resolution and Referendum Method

The resolution and referendum method provides for an election to be held in an area to determine if the area should be annexed. This method requires both agreement between all the local governments providing services and approval of the proposed annexation by a majority of the votes cast in a referendum on the annexation.[4] Municipalities may annex adjacent or contiguous areas intended to be developed for urban purposes or areas in between the existing city limits and areas to be developed for urban purposes. The municipality must prepare a plan for extending city services to an area to be annexed and hold a public hearing prior to the referendum. An area intended to be developed for urban purposes is defined as an area with a total resident population equal to at least two persons for each acre of land subdivided into lots and tracts such that at least 60 percent of the total acreage consists of lots and tracts five acres or less in size and such that at least 60 percent of the total number of lots and tracts are one acre or less in size.[5]

Unincorporated Islands Annexation

Municipalities with a population of 200 or more may unilaterally annex contiguous unincorporated islands.[6] Unincorporated islands are areas not under the jurisdiction of a city but totally surrounded by property that is subject to municipal jurisdiction. All or any portion of an unincorporated island of any size that was in existence before 1991 may be annexed simply by the passage of an ordinance. The intent behind this power is to allow cities to alleviate service delivery complications caused by such areas.[7]

Local Act of General Assembly

In addition to annexation by home rule, the Georgia General Assembly may annex territory to municipal limits by enacting local legislation amending a city's charter.[8]

RELATIONSHIP WITH COUNTIES AND SERVICE DELIVERY

Although annexation primarily concerns the city and the property owners or residents in the area to be annexed, counties may also be impacted. A county's responsibility for service delivery and land-use planning in the unincorporated areas can be influenced by municipal annexation. There is no impact on the county when services are countywide and funded from the county's general fund. The county continues to collect property taxes as it did prior to annexation. However, if a county provides services solely to the unincorporated area and those services are funded from the unincorporated area, annexation can impact the county even though the county will no longer be responsible for providing those services to the annexed area.[9]

Counties are empowered to raise objections to a proposed change in land use when property is proposed to be rezoned to a more intense land use either in conjunction with or subsequent to annexation. State annexation law provides the process that counties must follow if they object to the zoning or rezoning of property annexed by a municipality. However, a county may not stop a city from completing an annexation or the zoning or rezoning of annexed property.[10] Cities in Georgia are permitted to cross county boundaries and to exist in more than one county. However, if a city seeks to annex across a county boundary for the first time, the city must seek the approval of the county into which the city is annexing.[11]

Every county and city must enter into a service delivery strategy agreement in order to address any problems with duplication of services.[12] These agreements may accommodate changes necessitated in service delivery by annexation. Furthermore, cities and counties may enter into intergovernmental agreements and mutual aid agreements that establish respective roles for service delivery.[13] See Chapter 30 for further discussion of service delivery strategy agreements.

NOTES

1. O.C.G.A. §36-36-51(2).
2. O.C.G.A. §§36-36-20–36-36-23.
3. O.C.G.A. §§36-36-31–36-36-40.
4. O.C.G.A. §§36-36-50–36-36-61.
5. O.C.G.A. §36-36-54.
6. O.C.G.A. §§36-36-90–36-36-92.
7. Jennifer G. S. Diefenbacher and W. Edwin Sumner, *Annexation: Putting the Pieces Together*, 3rd ed., revised by Collin W. Brown (Atlanta: Georgia Municipal Association, August 2001).

8. O.C.G.A. §36-36-16.
9. Paula E. Steinbauer, Betty J. Hudson, Harry W. Hayes, et al., *An Assessment of Municipal Annexation in Georgia and the United States* (Athens: Carl Vinson Institute of Government, University of Georgia, 2002).
10. O.C.G.A. §36-36-11.
11. O.C.G.A. §36-36-23(b).
12. O.C.G.A. §§36-70-20–36-70-28.
13. GA. CONST. 1983, art. IX, sec. III, para. I(a).

16

James E. Kundell, Tom Gehl, and Terry A. DeMeo

Environmental Management

Over the past few decades, knowledge of environmental abuses and their implications for human health and natural systems has increased, resulting in the enactment of numerous federal and state environmental laws. One result of this increased awareness of environmental challenges is that the role of city officials in addressing environmental concerns is also changing.

The state agency with primary authority to administer environmental laws in Georgia, particularly in issuing permits, is the Environmental Protection Division of the Department of Natural Resources. However, other state agencies also provide technical, financial, and permitting assistance on environmental matters. The Department of Community Affairs coordinates and has an approval function in comprehensive planning, service delivery strategies, and solid waste management plans; the Georgia Environmental Facilities Authority administers low-interest loans to local governments for infrastructure improvements; the Coastal Resources Division of the Department of Natural Resources protects sensitive coastal areas by administering coastal programs; the Georgia Soil and Water Conservation Commission provides information and training on the erosion and sediment control program; and the Department of Human Resources administers the on-site sewage (septic tank) management program.

LOCAL GOVERNMENTS AND THE ENVIRONMENT

Federal and state environmental laws, coupled with citizen concerns for a healthy environment and quality of life, have resulted in additional responsibilities for cities. These responsibilities include adopting and implementing erosion and sediment control ordinances; improving water quality by protecting greenspace along rivers, streams, and lakes; and adopting environmentally sustainable solid waste practices such as increasing recycling options.

In addition to these responsibilities, there are a number of trends that affect how Georgia local governments address environmental matters.

Full-Service Local Government Status

A 1972 change to the Georgia Constitution allowed counties to become full-service local governments. As a result, some counties began providing services such as securing, treating, and distributing drinking water and collecting, treating, and discharging wastewater. In 1997 the Gen-

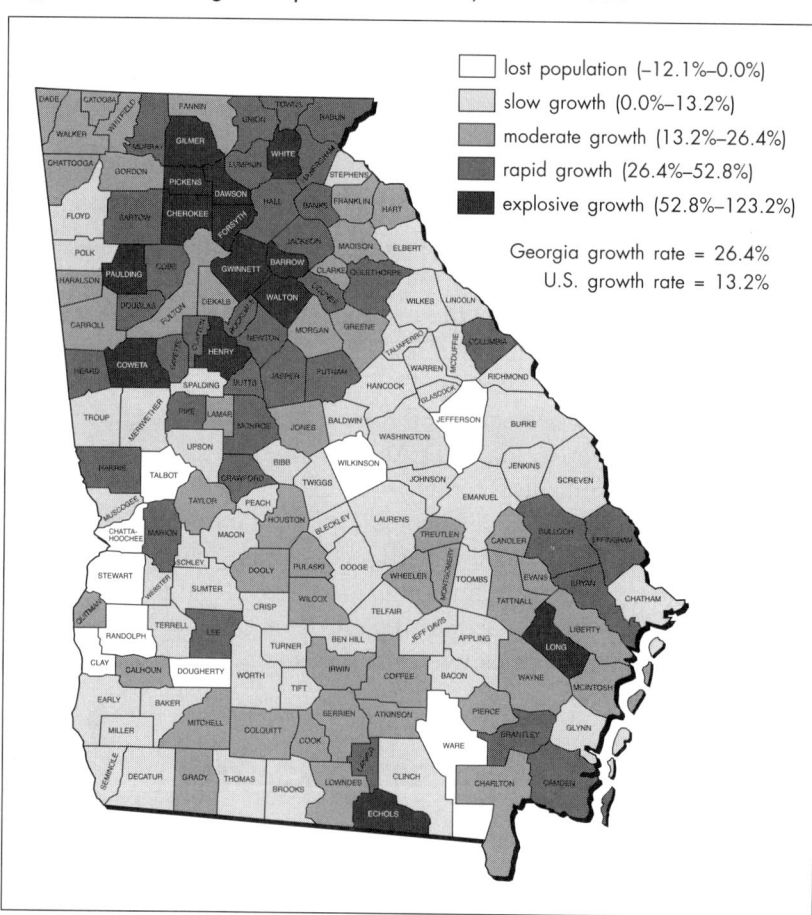

Figure 16-1. *Georgia's Population Growth, 1990—2000*

Source: U.S. Department of Commerce, Economics and Statistics Administration, Bureau of the Census.

eral Assembly passed the Service Delivery Strategy Act requiring counties, and the municipalities within their boundaries, to evaluate how best to provide public services including water, wastewater, storm water, and solid waste. The nature of growth and development at the local level affects the need for different types of county-provided public services and relationships between cities and counties for providing these services.

Growth

The 2000 U.S. census ranked Georgia as the sixth fastest-growing state in the nation, increasing in population by 26.4 percent during the 1990s.[1] The population of the state is predicted to be almost 10 million by 2010, which represents an increase of nearly 200,000 new residents per year.[2] However, growth patterns are not uniform across the state (see Figure 16-1). Some areas of the state have experienced rapid growth that contributes to economic vitality but also increases pressure on limited environmental resources and demands for local government services. Other areas of the state have lost population and are faced with a different set of challenges such as maintaining environmental infrastructure and services on a declining tax base. Absorbing rapid growth and stimulating new growth present major environmental, social, and economic problems for local governments and require careful consideration and planning at the state and local levels.

Relationship of Land Use to Environmental Quality

A direct relationship exists between land use and environmental quality. Because authority for land-use decisions rests principally with local governments, city officials are increasingly faced with evaluating the environmental impacts of land-use decisions.

Environmental Quality/Quality of Life

With increased public concern about quality-of-life issues, elected officials are putting greater emphasis on environmental protection. The link between environmental quality/quality of life and economic development is becoming a major component of industry, trade, and tourism in Georgia.

Multijurisdictional and Regional Efforts

Because environmental problems rarely coincide with jurisdictional boundaries, local governments are increasingly faced with the need to work cooperatively with neighboring jurisdictions to address environmental concerns on a regional basis. This needed cooperation is evidenced in water resources, where watersheds, river basins, and aquifers are more appropriate for water management; in air quality, where nonattainment areas frequently consist of several cities and counties; and in solid waste, where regional facilities are replacing county landfills.

These trends have not only altered what cities do in the environmental management arena but also how they do it. Cities have thus assumed a greater environmental management role, individually and collectively, with their neighboring jurisdictions. This chapter discusses the environmental issues and activities with which cities might be (or may become) involved, including land use, water supply and water quality, air quality, energy use and conservation, and solid and hazardous waste management. Land use is discussed first because there is a direct link between what we do on land and the quality of water, air, and communities.

LAND USE

Local governments have the largest impact on the environment in the area of land use for two reasons. First, authority for land-use decisions exists primarily at the local level.[3] Second, land-use decisions have the most direct, immediate, and permanent effect on a community and its environment, economy, and quality of life. Land-use decisions determine the number and location of houses, industries, business establishments, and farm operations. For each new person that moves into an area, one-half to three-fourths of an acre of land changes from forest, pasture, or agriculture to roads, parking lots, homes, stores, and other developed uses.[4] Often this development occurs on prime farmland, those areas that are flat, well drained, and nearly devoid of trees. Land-use planning and location decisions help local officials identify areas of value such as farmland that should be left for food and fiber production. Moreover, such planning identifies areas of value to the community such as wetlands and floodplains that help protect against the effects of droughts and floods, historical areas that preserve community character and local heritage, and recreation and park sites that provide needed outdoor opportunities.[5]

Local land-use policies also can separate incompatible land uses, which is important in maintaining quality of life as well as environmental quality. Although zoning and other land-use controls can be controversial, some communities have discovered only too late that without these measures, there is no landowner or local government control that can be exercised to prevent the location of undesirable land-use activities. Preventing nuisance issues related to noise, odors, and aesthetics is accomplished through land-use planning, zoning and other ordinances, and location decisions that keep conflicting land uses separated.

Land-use decisions affect the need for public services provided by local governments and determine the base revenue capacity to provide those services.[6] Thus, because land used for commercial purposes does not require a high level of local government or school system services, commercial land actually generates more tax revenue than the local government expends in services to it. Surprisingly, this is also true of land used for agriculture or forests. The opposite is true of land developed for residential purposes, as it generally requires levels of services exceeding the tax revenues it generates.[7] For every $1.00 that a new home brings in tax revenue, some counties spend as much as $1.55 in roads, sewers, and other public services.[8] Yet, if the tax base does not permit local infrastructure to keep pace with the rate of growth, communities will remain in a position of playing fiscal catch-up in providing the expected public services.

Land-use decisions also influence the amount and types of pollutants generated within a county. For example, poor land-use planning and sprawl will likely result in more air pollution from automobile exhaust than will a compact, well-planned community. In addition, land-use activities can have a significant impact on water quality. Runoff from streets and parking lots may carry many contaminants to waterways. The proper location, design, and maintenance of parking lots and streets can greatly reduce this runoff. Moreover, land-use planning and ordinances that recognize the value of maintaining vegetated buffers along waterways will help reduce the amount of chemicals, bacteria, and sediments that reach streams, rivers, and lakes.

Comprehensive Planning

To better address planning and growth-related concerns, the Georgia Planning Act was passed in 1989.[9] It requires each local government to prepare a long-range comprehensive plan that addresses demographics, economic development, natural and historic resources, housing, community facilities, and land use. Part 5 of the act is of particular importance in that it addresses vital areas of the state—those natural resources deemed to be of fundamental public interest to protect and preserve.[10] Vital areas were originally defined as wetlands, water supply watersheds, and significant groundwater recharge areas. In 1991 this law was amended to add the higher elevations of Georgia's mountains and river corridors to the list of vital areas. As directed by the law, the Department of Natural Resources has developed minimum standards and procedures for protecting vital areas, known as environmental planning criteria, that may include requirements for resource assessments, management plans, and protection ordinances.

In order to meet the requirements to protect vital areas, local officials must identify the location of vital areas within their jurisdiction in the local comprehensive plan. If vital areas are present, local officials must determine whether all or a portion of the Part 5 environmental planning criteria will be implemented through local protection measures. The Department of Community Affairs reviews local comprehensive plans and protection measures to determine consistency with the requirements of the Georgia Planning Act and Part 5 environmental planning criteria. Satisfying these requirements allows cities to maintain Qualified Local Government status, which establishes eligibility for a host of state funding such as community development block grants, water and sewer loans, state revolving loans for construction of wastewater facilities, economic development grants, and greenspace grants.[11] The Georgia Planning Act of 1989 and comprehensive planning are discussed in more detail in Chapter 14.

Coastal Georgia

Coastal communities must comply with three additional laws regulating development along the coast: the Coastal Marshlands Protection Act,[12] the Shore Protection Act,[13] and the Georgia Coastal Management Act.[14] These state laws recognize the vital nature of Georgia's coastal resources and seek to protect the natural systems of the marshes and shoreline by addressing public and private uses of land and waters within the coastal area. The Coastal Resources Division (CRD) of the Department of Natural Resources has the legal authority to implement all three acts.

The Coastal Marshlands Protection Act of 1970, as amended in 1992, provides the CRD with authority to protect the state's nearly 700,000 acres of coastal marshlands (which include fresh, brackish, and saltwater marshes) through a permit program. The state's coastal marshlands provide a nursery habitat for many commercially and recreationally important fish and shellfish. The marshlands protect against flooding and erosion and act as a significant filter of water pollutants. Permits are required for erecting structures such as docks and for dredging or filling in estuarine areas including marshlands, intertidal areas, mudflats, and tidal water bottoms.

The Shore Protection Act, enacted in 1977 and amended in 1992, provides authority to protect and manage the state's shoreline including sand dunes, beaches, sandbars, and shoals that make up a sand-sharing system among the barrier islands and along the coast. This system helps protect property, natural resources, and recreation areas from the damaging effects of floods, winds, tides, and erosion. The Shore Protection Act authorizes the CRD to provide permits for limited construction activity in the sand dune areas and prohibits all motor vehicles on the dunes and beaches.

In 1997 the Georgia Coastal Management Act was adopted, enabling Georgia to reenter the federal Coastal Zone Management Program (in the late 1970s, Georgia dropped out of the federal program). This state law directs the CRD to prepare a coastal zone management plan that includes locally developed policies to guide the public and private uses of land and waters within the coastal area. It brings the concerns of the previous two laws together with research and outreach programs to fill the gaps in managing the coastal area.[15]

Greenspace

Open space protection is a common land-use approach for directing growth. Georgia lags behind many other states in the amount of public open space set aside for wildlife, recreation, historic preservation, and other greenspace purposes. Currently, only about 8 percent of the land in Georgia is protected as publicly owned greenspace (see Figure 16-2).

The Georgia Greenspace Act was passed by the General Assembly in 2000, creating the Georgia Greenspace Commission and the Georgia Greenspace Trust Fund.[16] The voluntary Georgia Greenspace Program, directed by the Greenspace Commission and administered by the Department of Natural Resources, was established to provide financial incentives for urban and rapidly developing counties, and the municipalities contained within them, to set aside 20 percent of their land as permanently protected greenspace.

The Georgia Greenspace program requires the development of a community greenspace plan but provides flexibility in the land selected for preservation. However, it is expected that the majority of community greenspace will be floodplains and wetlands along stream corridors (to help meet water quality goals); scenic, archaeological, and historic areas (to provide for passive outdoor recreation); and neighborhood paths for walking and cycling (to support access to other protected lands). The program awards grants from the trust fund to eligible counties (i.e., those that, based on the 2000 census, have populations of at least 60,000 or have grown by at least 800 residents per year). Forty counties met eligibility criteria for the $30 million in grants appropriated in fiscal year 2001. Forty-nine additional counties became

Figure 16-2. *Georgia's Protected Greenspace*

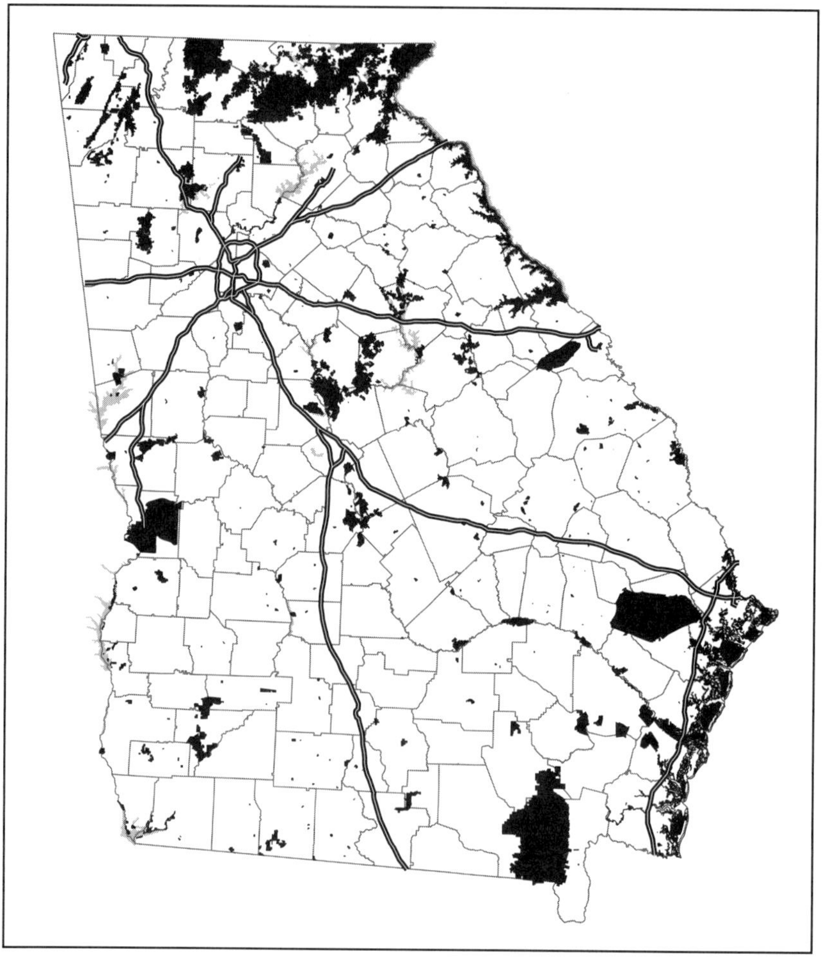

eligible when the 2000 census was released; a total of 89 counties qualified for another $30 million in trust fund grants appropriated in fiscal year 2002.[17]

Budget constraints in 2003, however, resulted in money being withheld from the greenspace program. As of this writing, the governor's plan favors continuation of the program, if funding is available, while expanding the Georgia Conservation Partnership to include public-private partnerships in land preservation, state natural areas protection efforts, and the community greenspace program. He also envisions the greenspace program to be usable by communities across the state, not just the most densely populated and fastest-growing ones.

Erosion and Sediment Control

To protect Georgia's land and water resources from land-disturbing activities, the General Assembly passed the Erosion and Sedimentation Act in 1975 and subsequently amended it several times.[18] The act requires local governments to be covered under state regulations or to adopt erosion and sediment control ordinances and request delegation of local issuing authority from the Environmental Protection Division (EPD).

The local government issuing authority retains control of the pace of local development by responding to requests for permits for land-disturbing activities and enforcing the local erosion and sediment control ordinance.[19] EPD administers the erosion and sediment control program in areas where there is no local issuing authority. In these areas, EPD is responsible for responding to permit requests for land-disturbing activities and undertaking inspection and enforcement actions. EPD also provides oversight of local programs to ensure that local issuing authorities are complying with their ordinances.

The Georgia Soil and Water Conservation Commission produces and distributes the *Manual for Erosion and Sedimentation Control in Georgia*. The manual contains the criteria, standards, and specifications required in all local programs; a model local ordinance; technical guidance for the development of land-disturbing plans; and best management practices for controlling erosion and sedimentation from construction activities.

Although there is no corresponding federal law for the control of erosion and sedimentation, the National Pollutant Discharge Elimination System (NPDES) was established pursuant to the Clean Water Act of 1990 to monitor storm water runoff from construction sites, among other activities. In 2000 EPD issued a general statewide NPDES permit for construction sites of five acres or more (individual NPDES permits are required for construction sites over 250 acres), which limits the maximum amount of sediment that is allowed to leave the site in storm water runoff. The requirement for coverage under the general NPDES storm water permit has been extended to construction sites that disturb areas of one acre or more. Legislation was enacted in 2003 to bring together the requirements of the state Erosion and Sedimentation Act and the federal storm water control requirements. Changes in the requirements include a focus on use of best management practices, training for those involved in land-disturbing activities, and use of stop-work orders for violators.

Land provides many services such as areas to build communities, food production, and habitat for wildlife. Land-use decisions on where roads, water and sewer lines, schools, hospitals, and government buildings are placed determine the character of our communities. Land also provides environmental services related to water and air quality. Vegetated land such as floodplains, wetlands, and greenways help trap pollutants and sediment, preventing contaminants from entering streams, rivers, and lakes. In addition, much of the state's air quality problems are associated with sprawling development that requires more and longer automobile trips. A thoughtful local government approach to planning for development patterns can protect the many services land provides.

WATER QUALITY AND QUANTITY

Under federal and state laws, local governments have responsibilities relating to both water quality and water quantity. Although water quality and quantity are directly related, laws have tended to focus on one or the other, in part because of the different roles of federal, state, and local governments in addressing water-related matters.

Water Quality

The national focus on improving water quality took shape with the passage of the Clean Water Act in 1972,[20] followed in 1974 by the Safe Drinking Water Act to ensure that public water supplies do not pose health hazards. Georgia enacted and then amended the Georgia Water Quality Control Act and the Georgia Safe Drinking Water Act to bring the state into compliance with federal laws and to obtain primacy for implementing federal programs. Consequently, EPD is the agency that administers the clean water and safe drinking water programs in Georgia.

Public Wastewater Systems

Under the federal Clean Water Act, technology was used with remarkable success to clean up industrial and local government point sources of pollution (i.e., discharges of wastewater or fluid chemicals from a pipe into a river, stream, or lake). A federal grant program helped construct many public wastewater systems that are composed of sewage collection infrastructure, sewage treatment infrastructure, and wastewater and sludge disposal infrastructure/measures. However, maintaining and upgrading wastewater infrastructure and adding new technology and infrastructure in growth areas are expensive local government activities. Although the federal grant program is no longer available, a revolving fund administered by the Georgia Environmental Facilities Authority provides low-interest loans to local governments for construction of wastewater infrastructure. EPD is the agency with regulatory authority relating to wastewater collection, treatment, and discharge. Sources of information and assistance for local governments faced with questions relating to their wastewater systems include the Georgia Water and Pollution Control Association, Georgia Rural Water Association, and EPD.

Storm Water System

Much has been accomplished to clean up streams, rivers, and lakes by reducing industrial and local government wastewater discharges. Currently, however, over half of the pollutants entering waterways come from nonpoint sources such as runoff from construction sites, lawns, roads, parking lots, and agricultural fields. Because over 6,000 miles of streams and rivers that have been assessed in Georgia do not meet water quality standards, there is a great need to focus on pollution that comes from nonpoint sources.

The Clean Water Act addresses this problem by requiring additional steps to improve water quality when technology does not bring the water bodies into compliance with water quality standards. In these cases, an assessment is required to identify the source(s) of the pollutant(s), and then a strategy must be developed and implemented to ensure compliance. This process is known as the development of a total maximum daily load (TMDL), a calculation of the total amount of a pollutant that a water body is able to dilute. The total amount of a pollutant is then allocated among the various sources of the pollutant. As required by the federal Clean Water Act, the U.S. Environmental Protection Agency (EPA)—and, by extension, the State of Georgia—must develop TMDLs for the impaired streams in the state. As a result of this effort, local governments will see greater emphasis placed on controlling nonpoint as well as point sources of pollution.

Controlling nonpoint sources of water pollution is more difficult and controversial than controlling point sources because nonpoint sources are related to how land is used. Efforts to date to address nonpoint sources, principally through the Georgia Erosion and Sedimentation Act, have not been as effective as they need to be.[21] As previously discussed, in addition to state efforts to improve the implementation of this law, requirements were built into the federal Clean Water Act to phase in storm water control measures. Controlling storm water is important because the first flush of water from a storm carries with it most of the pollutants that have built up on the land since the last rainfall. Consequently, if storm water is collected and treated/filtered, much can be accomplished toward protecting water quality.

Table 16-1 presents the components of a storm water management system. Increasingly, the focus is shifting to the river basin or watershed as the geographic area when attempting to manage storm water. Components of the system include assessing the watershed and developing and implementing a storm water management plan, adopting and implementing an erosion and sediment control ordinance, and obtaining and meeting any required storm water management permits. In designing a storm water management system, local governments must depend not only on built infrastructure, but also on natural service systems or "green" infrastructure such as floodplains, wetlands, and greenways to help reduce and filter the storm water flow.

Funds maybe available through state and federal programs to assist counties in purchasing greenspace for storm water control purposes. In addition, local planning and zoning ordinances, subdivision regulations, and building codes can be designed to better control storm water. Cities may also impose storm water utility fees to cover the cost of controlling storm water, as the cities of Griffin and Decatur have done.

The focus of the Clean Water Act has evolved from an initial emphasis on using technology to clean up local government and industrial point discharges to the more recent emphasis on cleaning up nonpoint sources. If we want the streams, rivers, and lakes of Georgia to provide good quality water to meet multiple demands, we must effectively control both point and nonpoint sources of pollution.

Table 16-1. *Storm Water Management Components*

Watershed Management
Assessment
Plan
Monitoring/enforcement activities
	Current Storm Water Collection
	Built service system
	  1. Collection system
	  2. Detention structures
	  3. Pump facility
	  4. Treatment capacity
	
	Natural service system
	  1. Floodplain protection
	  2. Wetland protection
	  3. Greenways
	
	Land-use practices

Erosion and Sedimentation Control Plan/ordinance adopted Permitting process Monitoring/enforcement activities	
Storm Water Permit Currently Required Permitting process Monitoring/enforcement activities Required in future	**Potential Expansion of Storm Water Collection** Built service system Natural service system Land-use practices

Safe Drinking Water

A reliable supply of safe drinking water is necessary for communities to survive and prosper. In fact, from a public health, economic development, environmental quality, public finance, and quality-of-life perspective, there are few things more important to a community.

As with the Clean Water Act, the federal Safe Drinking Water Act focused first on using technology to treat raw water to meet drinking water standards. Over the past few decades, however, the emphasis has shifted to protecting water sources. Research has shown that a high percentage of water-borne disease outbreaks over the past 50 years have been preceded by storm events and that both surface and groundwater systems are susceptible to contamination.[22]

Historically, local governments have provided public drinking water services. Securing, treating, and distributing water have been local responsibilities, if the local government chose to undertake them. Financing these services was also left to the local government. This arrangement is still true today, but there is some involvement of federal and state governments in funding the drinking water systems. For instance, the 1996 amendments to the Safe Drinking Water Act established for the first time a revolving fund to help local governments finance water supply systems. The Georgia Environmental Facilities Authority administers this program in Georgia.

Federal and state efforts to protect water sources from contamination first appeared with wellhead protection measures. Subsequently, requirements for source water assessments were included in the 1996 amendments to the Safe Drinking Water Act. Those states that have implemented the federal safe drinking water program, including Georgia, are required to develop and submit a source water assessment plan for approval by the EPA. States are then required to complete assessments of all public water systems, including delineation of the source water protection area, an inventory of potential contamination sources, and determination of susceptibility of the drinking water supply to contamination.

The source water assessments provide specific information on threats to local water supplies and the likelihood that the water supplies will become contaminated. Consequently, source water protection measures can be targeted toward those threats that pose the greatest risk to the water system. Although the amendments do not require that source water protection measures be taken, if an assessment of the local water supply is conducted and problems are identified, it can be argued that the local government has a responsibility to address the problems.[23] The 1996 amendments also require water suppliers to provide their customers with an annual Consumer Confidence Report that presents information on the quality of drinking water and on any violations of drinking water standards.

Water Quantity

Georgia is a water-rich state, receiving on average about 50 inches of precipitation each year. Nevertheless, increased demand for water, uneven distribution of water resources, and recurring droughts have important consequences for meeting the state's need for water. Figure 16-3 depicts areas in the state where there is significant groundwater, in addition to Georgia's 14 major river basins and the metropolitan statistical areas (MSAs), or population centers, in the state.

Table 16-1. *Georgia's River Basins, MSAs, and Groundwater Regions*

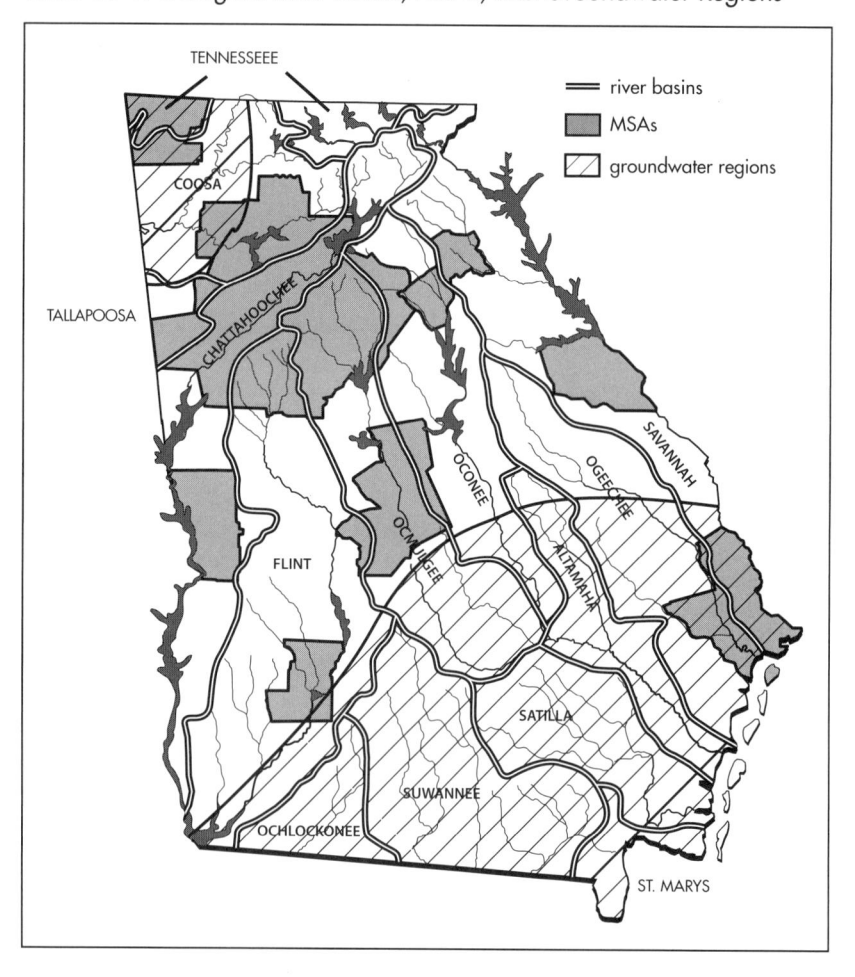

One of the state's water challenges concerns the location of the Atlanta metropolitan region in the Piedmont Province in North Georgia:

1. There is limited groundwater in the Piedmont Province. The area is underlain by hard, compact crystalline rock that does not form extensive aquifers like those found in South Georgia. Consequently, groundwater is limited in the Atlanta metropolitan region.
2. Streams and rivers form in North Georgia and flow southward. These streams are relatively small and may be inadequate to meet the needs for water of the most highly populated region of the state.
3. There are no natural lakes in North Georgia. The region is geologically old, and over the centuries natural barriers that would have formed lakes have since eroded away. The lakes in the region are human-made reservoirs.
4. As the population and economic center of the state, the Atlanta metropolitan region has significant demands for water. These increasing demands, as well as population growth, extend across North Georgia, where over three-fourths of the state's population lives.

To address the water concerns of the Atlanta metropolitan area, the General Assembly created the Metropolitan North Georgia Water Planning District in 2001. Composed of 16 counties, the district was directed to plan for how the region could meet requirements for water supply and conservation, wastewater management, and storm water control.[24]

Not only the Atlanta metropolitan region but also the coastal region of Georgia faces water problems. A 24 coastal county region, including the Savannah and Brunswick areas, is affected by saltwater intrusion in the Upper Floridan Aquifer and is included in an Interim Water Management Strategy administered by EPD. Groundwater withdrawal restrictions and caps have been placed on certain parts of the region. Studies of how best to address the water challenges facing coastal Georgia have been undertaken with the goal of initiating long-term management programs based on the findings.

Southwest Georgia is also facing water challenges due to its unique geology, where the Upper Floridan Aquifer outcrops in the major irrigation area of the state. High water demands for irrigation in this region, in which the groundwater and streams have a dynamic interrelationship, has raised concerns that the lower Flint River and its tributaries could go dry during drought periods. Increasingly, regional approaches are a focus of water management efforts.

Water supply systems vary across the state. North Georgia primarily depends on surface water systems,[25] and South Georgia uses groundwater resources. Table 16-2 presents the components of a local water supply system. In planning for water supply, it is important to consider conservation, improved efficiency, and water reuse. New sources of water are difficult to find and will be expensive to bring online. As a result, local governments must make better use of the water they already have. Conserved water is an inexpensive source of water, and the practice of efficient water use sends the proper signals to residents and neighboring states regarding Georgia's water management practices. The principle of "efficiency first" should guide Georgians for several reasons. It is cost effective in that it costs less to be more efficient with existing resources. It can delay or eliminate the need for capital projects. It may make water available for ecosystem protection. It also minimizes the effects of drought.[26] Moreover, water conservation planning is required of all water-use applicants who withdraw greater than 100,000 gallons per day of groundwater or surface water.[27]

To provide water services (water supply, wastewater, and/or storm water) in the future, local governments must have the managerial, technical, and financial capabilities to carry out their service delivery responsibilities. It is vitally important to bring stakeholders and the public into the process of evaluating services and planning for future needs. This inclusive approach provides a forum for communication and coordination of efforts.

Table 16-2. *Water Supply Components*

Water Supply—Current	Water Withdrawal Treatment
Groundwater	Intake/collection infrastructure
1. Wellhead protection	1. Wells
2. Aquifer limits	2. Surface water intake structure
Surface water	Current treatment capacity
1. Watershed protection	Potential treatment capacity
2. Reservoir capacity	
3. River withdrawal	**Water Delivery/Distribution System**
Conservation measures	Current service provision
Communitywide Water Supply Plan	Potential expansion of service provision
Water Supply/Withdrawal Permits	Fire suppression distribution
Withdrawal permit	1. ISO rating (insurance service office)
Operational permit (safe drinking water)	

Whether at work, home, or play, citizens tend to become more committed to solving problems and addressing needs when they are aware and involved.

AIR QUALITY

Georgia is faced with a complex meteorological situation. It has natural conditions that make the state prone to significant air pollution problems such as stagnating air masses and inversions.[28] The Bermuda High that frequently dominates summer weather conditions tends to keep air pollutants from dispersing. Unless measures are taken to control emissions, increased population and industrial expansion will cause a greater quantity of pollutants to be released into the atmosphere, aggravating the problem.

The federal government took the lead in dealing with air quality by passing the Clean Air Act in 1970 and amending it in 1977 and 1990.[29] To bring Georgia into compliance with this federal law, the General Assembly passed the Georgia Air Quality Act in 1978 and assigned implementation and enforcement responsibilities to EPD.[30] In 1990 Congress enacted sweeping changes to the Clean Air Act.[31] Among other requirements, the federal law directs the states to develop state implementation plans to determine how they will meet federal standards.

Air pollution sources are divided into two categories: stationary and mobile. Stationary sources generally release pollutants through a smokestack. For these sources, a permit from EPD is required, which stipulates the levels of pollutants that may be released. The 1990 Clean Air Act amendments require states to establish a permit fee for stationary sources that will cover the cost of administering the program and serve as an incentive to reduce emissions.

The federal government has addressed the problem of mobile sources, such as automobiles, in part through legislation requiring manufacturers to develop cars that pollute less. However, cars that are not properly maintained do not run efficiently and emit exhaust that contains pollutants. Georgia, like many other states, has implemented an inspection and maintenance program for the Atlanta metropolitan region to ensure that motorists keep their cars in good operating condition. If a vehicle does not meet the exhaust standards, the owner is required to have the car tuned up or take other steps to improve emissions. Proof of inspection is required before a motorist is able to purchase automobile tags.

The Atlanta metropolitan region is designated as a nonattainment area for ozone because it violates federal air quality standards. Ozone is a secondary pollutant produced from nitrogen oxides and volatile organic compounds released principally from automobiles but also from stationary and natural sources.[32] To control releases from mobile sources, inspection and maintenance programs have been introduced in Cherokee, Clayton, Cobb, Coweta, DeKalb, Douglas, Fulton, Gwinnett, Fayette, Forsyth, Henry, Paulding, and Rockdale Counties. Six additional counties have been identified as having a significant impact on the region's air quality (Bartow, Carroll, Hall, Newton, Spalding, and Walton Counties). With urban sprawl causing more people to drive more miles, the number of local governments included in the nonattainment area is likely to increase, potentially including much of North Georgia.

To further address the air quality problems associated with urban sprawl, Congress requires that the state implementation plans be consistent with the transportation plans that receive federal highway funds. Efforts in the Atlanta metropolitan region to meet this requirement have been difficult and have resulted in litigation. Alternative transportation options, such as mass transit, bicycle paths, and connected greenspace for walking, are therefore being emphasized.

Under the Clean Air Act, all local governments, including those outside the designated nonattainment area, are required to take certain actions to reduce emissions of hazardous air pollutants from publicly owned treatment facilities and sources of asbestos. Other statewide requirements include meeting new source performance standards for municipal waste incinerators, sewage sludge incinerators, and boilers/industrial furnaces and meeting vehicular fleet requirements.

ENERGY USE AND CONSERVATION

Air pollution problems and solutions are inextricable to energy policy because the burning of fossil fuels (e.g., coal, oil, gasoline, and natural gas) by both mobile sources (e.g., cars, trucks, and airplanes) and stationary sources (e.g., industries and power plants) is the major cause of air pollution. In Georgia, over 75 percent of the primary energy used by both stationary and mobile sources comes from fossil fuels. In addition, deregulation of the electric power industry and the natural gas industry has resulted in many changes relating to energy costs and availability. Although there are alternative sources of energy (e.g., solar, wind, and geothermal), the primary alternatives currently available to communities are conservation and increased efficiency.

Cities can cut their energy usage and the energy used by businesses and residents by conducting energy audits of city buildings and operations (including vehicle fleets) and by carefully considering the energy implications of transportation and land-use decisions. Conservation measures can be implemented in every building in a city. The installation of insulation, the use of more efficient machines and appliances, and the development of new processes that reduce the use of energy can decrease energy consumption. Most power companies and a variety of public and private institutions can assist local governments in this area.

In addition, cities can educate the public about energy issues. People often waste a great deal of energy simply because they are unaware of their wastefulness. Moreover, energy consumption should be considered in city decisions on building codes, purchasing procedures, and land-use planning and zoning. Decisions to construct a new street or road, locate a new county facility, design a water treatment plant, or buy a new vehicle for the city all have long-range energy and air quality implications.

SOLID AND HAZARDOUS WASTE MANAGEMENT

A key responsibility of local government officials is the disposal of the community's waste products. At one time, an "out-of-sight, out-of-mind" approach was used, and wastes were dumped in low-lying areas, gullies, or wetlands. As the amount of waste increased and its composition changed to include more hazardous waste, as more was learned about the problems resulting from improper waste disposal (primarily groundwater and surface water contamination), and as the population expanded to produce more waste generators and fewer sites acceptable for waste disposal, managing waste became increasingly complex.

To deal with solid waste concerns, Congress enacted the Solid Waste Disposal Act of 1965[33] and amended it as the Resource Conservation and Recovery Act in 1976 and 1984.[34] In 1984 Congress directed the EPA to develop environmentally protective standards for sanitary landfills. These standards, referred to as Subtitle D regulations, were finalized in 1991. The standards impose requirements for the use of liners, leachate collection systems, groundwater and methane monitoring, and closure and post-closure care that dramatically increase the cost of solid waste disposal. Historically, hazardous wastes were disposed of with solid waste, but the Resource Conservation and Recovery Act also requires the separation and proper treatment, storage, and disposal of hazardous waste.

Solid Waste

Solid waste management is difficult for local government officials; there are few options available, and each is costly. Nearly 8.7 pounds of solid waste is generated per person per day in Georgia. In 2000, 12.7 million tons of waste was sent to landfills.[35] According to the EPA, there are four basic options for reducing the amount of solid waste. Perhaps the best option is to reduce the amount of waste generated at the source (i.e., source reduction or reuse). This option requires a change in the buying habits of consumers (including local governments) and commercial production packaging. Consumers must demand (and accept) less packaging of the products they purchase. The success of this option is at least partially dependent upon a local government's success in educating the public.

The next preferable option is to recycle materials (including composting of organic matter) that would otherwise be destined for disposal facilities. Although this option often receives favorable attention, recycling is not generally a moneymaking effort because markets for recycled materials tend to fluctuate. Nevertheless, the number of local governments in Georgia that provide recycling services continues to increase (501 in 2000), along with the diversity of the types of recyclable materials accepted.[36]

Incineration (referred to in Georgia law as thermal treatment technology) is the third most preferred option. The burning of waste to reduce volume and/or to generate energy requires a reliable source of solid waste for fuel and can be expensive, depending on the economies of scale achieved. As of 2002, the Savannah Resource Recovery Authority was the only facility of this kind in Georgia. It operates a 500-ton per day waste-to-energy facility for the Savannah metropolitan area.

The least-preferred option is land disposal. In 1972 Georgia had approximately 416 open dumps, all of which have been closed. Municipal solid waste (MSW) landfills (county and municipal facilities) now receive common types of garbage such as household trash, food scraps, and packaging material, but they also accept sludge from wastewater treatment facilities and commercial solid waste. Construction and demolition facilities accept construction materials and woody debris.

In response to the increased costs of landfilling and difficulty in siting new disposal facilities, the Georgia General Assembly passed the Georgia Comprehensive Solid Waste Management Act in 1990, which amended the state's 1972 law.[37] The law established a goal of reducing the amount of solid waste entering disposal facilities by 25 percent on a statewide per capita basis by 1996. The first step toward reaching this goal was the development of the Georgia Solid Waste Management Plan in 1990, revised in 1997, which details the state's activities that are designed to meet the requirements.[38]

Local government solid waste management plans are also required under the Comprehensive Solid Waste Management Act. The standards and procedures to be met by local government plans have been incorporated in the rules of the Georgia Department of Community Affairs. Plans are required to be updated every 10 years. Updated plans must continue to focus on meeting the 25 percent reduction goal and on assuring solid waste disposal capacity over a 10-year period.

Several amendments to the Comprehensive Solid Waste Management Act affect local governments. In 1996 cities and counties were required to impose restrictions on the disposal of yard trimmings.[39] A 1997 amendment provides that multijurisdictional solid waste management authorities can be deactivated if the local governments that activated the authorities declare by ordinance or resolution that there is no need for them.[40] Further restrictions were imposed on the siting of solid waste disposal facilities in 1998.[41]

As local governments closed small landfills, the private sector assumed a greater role in managing solid waste in Georgia. Almost 80 percent of the total number of MSW landfills in the state are publicly owned, yet over 65 percent of the waste is disposed of in privately owned facilities. In addition, most of the state's remaining capacity (more than 95 percent) is now in less than half of the total number of landfills. Georgia now has an adequate amount of disposal space in landfills, with an estimated 22 years of remaining capacity due in part to the trend toward larger MSW facilities.[42]

The establishment of the 25 percent statewide waste reduction goal in 1990 has resulted in significant progress toward making waste reduction and recycling viable waste management options. Because of waste reduction, Georgia's per capita MSW disposal rate leveled off in the late 1990s after years of steep annual increases. In addition, more counties operate pay-as-you-throw programs that charge residents volume-based disposal rates, creating economic incentives to recycle.

Nevertheless the overall disposal rate continues to grow. In 1993, 6.63 pounds of waste per Georgian per day was generated; the figure rose to 8.69 pounds in 2000. Increased volumes of out-of-state waste imported for disposal (5 percent of the total) and construction and demolition waste associated with economic development are impediments to the state's waste reduction goal.[43]

Although the 1996 target date for reaching the 25 percent waste reduction goal has passed, the attorney general has issued an opinion that the goal remains in effect. Consequently, local governments that met the goal should continue their efforts. Those jurisdictions that failed to meet the goal should continue efforts to reach this goal.[44] All of the components in the Comprehensive Solid Waste Management Act, including local plans, are designed to accomplish one major objective: to ensure that solid waste is managed in an integrated, environmentally protective manner. Ultimately, the people of Georgia should produce less waste, and the waste that is produced should be managed to minimize adverse land and water quality impacts.

Hazardous Waste

The problems of waste disposal are complicated by hazardous wastes (characterized as toxic, ignitable, reactive, or corrosive materials), which generally comprise industrial chemical wastes but may include common household items such as paints, drain cleaners, and pesticides. In the past, hazardous wastes frequently were not handled or disposed of properly. As a result, approximately two-thirds of the counties in Georgia have at least one site on the state's Hazardous Site Inventory, many of which are located in cities.[45]

To bring the state into compliance with the federal Resource Conservation and Recovery Act of 1976, the General Assembly enacted the Georgia Hazardous Waste Management Act of 1979.[46] This law assigned responsibilities to EPD to regulate hazardous waste in the state. In 1993 a new division was created in the Department of Natural Resources: the Pollution Prevention Assistance Division. The division's major focus is assisting local governments, industries, farmers, and others to voluntarily reduce the amount of hazardous waste they generate. The total amount of hazardous waste generated in Georgia has been reduced by 73 percent through voluntary pollution prevention efforts since 1985.[47] The Pollution Prevention Assistance Division is also the lead agency in the area of household hazardous waste and has worked with the Georgia Municipal Association on radon gas abatement and other waste reduction matters.[48]

Two aspects of hazardous waste should concern local government officials: the exemption of small generators from legal requirements and the possibility of accidents at generating or storage sites or during transportation of hazardous materials. Originally, the Resource Conservation and Recovery Act did not regulate small generators of hazardous waste. An industry could generate up to 2,200 pounds of hazardous waste each month without having it treated or disposed of in a hazardous waste facility. The hazardous waste could simply be put in a landfill. However, Congress amended the act in 1984 to bring small generators (i.e., those generating 220 to 2,200 pounds per month) under the law. Industries generating less than 220 pounds per month continue to be exempt from the requirements of the law, as are households that generate hazardous waste. As a result, local officials should assume that some hazardous substances are entering their landfills and take precautions to ensure proper management.

Although many hazardous substances used by industries and transported on the highways are not defined as hazardous waste, the possibility of accidents at industrial sites or during the transport of hazardous substances are causes for concern for communities and, therefore, local government officials. To prepare for such occurrences, emergency response personnel (i.e., police and fire departments) should be trained to handle a hazardous substance situation. The EPD has an emergency response unit that can provide information on how to deal with hazardous substances.

In 1995 the EPA launched the Brownfields Economic Redevelopment Initiative to encourage states, local governments, and others to clean up and reuse abandoned, idle, or underused industrial and commercial facilities in areas where expansion or redevelopment is complicated by real or perceived environmental contamination.[49] The program provides seed money to local governments to conduct brownfield assessments, removes liability barriers, and encourages development partnerships and local workforce development and training in brownfields.[50]

The Georgia Hazardous Site Reuse and Redevelopment Act was enacted in 1996 and amended in 1998. The law provides procedures and criteria for limiting the liability of purchasers of qualifying brownfields.[51] This law and the EPA's initiative can potentially benefit many communities by facilitating redevelopment of sites into viable business or industrial endeavors.

Table 16-3. *Federal and State Laws and City Responsibilities*

Law	Local Area of Responsibility
Toxic Substance Control Act (TSCA)	Lead-based pain abatement Asbestos abatement
Federal Insecticide, Fungicide and Rodenticide Act (FIFRA)	Pesticide use Public works projects
Endangered Species Act (ESA)	Public works projects
National Environmental Policy Act (NEPA); Georgia Environmental Policy Act	Public works projects (environmental impact assessments/statements)

In addition to the areas that have been discussed in this chapter, city officials may have responsibilities relating to other federal or state environmental laws (see Table 16-3).

CONCLUSION

The link between what happens on land and its effect on the environment is undeniable. Elected and appointed city officials must understand the interconnectedness of land use, infrastructure, financing decisions, and quality of life and recognize that the role of local governments has changed: Cities and counties must assume greater responsibility for environmental management.

Many agree that the current environmental laws and regulations are sufficient. Indeed, the most frequently cited need is for more effective implementation of existing environmental laws and regulations through more stable sources of financing, improved enforcement, and involvement of citizens. Local governments that have undertaken the difficult task of developing and attaining public support for funding sources find themselves with increased capacity to provide the services needed today and for tomorrow's constituents.

The establishment of environmental courts is an emerging tool that builds local capacity for the enforcement of existing laws and regulations. An environmental court is a part of the existing city judicial system. This specialty court shifts environmental violations (e.g., inappropriate land use, littering, and other environmental abuses) to the civil court system, thereby helping to alleviate the overcrowded criminal court docket. When environmental courts prosecute violators by imposing fines or other penalties, public awareness increases and more widespread compliance is achieved.

A citizen environmental advisory committee is another emerging tool used to help local officials deal effectively with complex environmental issues. Environmental advisory committees are appointed groups of citizens who provide local officials with accurate, reliable information that is sensitive to local needs. Cities in Georgia have benefited from this type of single-focus environmental advisory committee.

Now more than ever there is a need to address environmental issues through partnerships with citizens and cooperative, working relationships among local governments. City-county and regional solutions to the management of environmental issues have been evolving but must be increased and maintained to be effective.

Effecting change in environmental management is complicated and expensive. Environmental laws and regulations, coupled with public concern for a healthy environment and quality of life, have caused cities to assume more responsibility for environmental stewardship. In order to meet these demands and maintain reasonable tax levels, local officials must seek comprehensive, cost-effective tools to carry out their environmental responsibilities.

NOTES

1. U.S. Census Bureau (http://quickfacts.census.gov/qfd/states/13000.htm).
2. State Data and Research Center (http://www.gadata.org/Information_Services/county popproj2010.htm).
3. For further discussion of this topic, *see* James E. Kundell, Richard W. Campbell, Joseph M. Heikoff, Lawrence R. Hepburn, Robert Klant, and S. Wesley Woolf, *Land-Use Policy and the Protection of Georgia's Environment* (Athens: Carl Vinson Institute of Government, University of Georgia, 1989).
4. Robert G. Healy, *Competition for Land in the American South: Agriculture, Human Settlement and the Environment* (Washington, DC: The Conservation Foundation, 1985).
5. James E. Kundell, Fred C. White, and Johnnie Graharn, *Prime Agricultural Land in Georgia* (Athens: Institute of Government, University of Georgia, 1981).
6. For a discussion on service delivery strategy requirements, *see* Chapter 30.
7. Jeff Dorfinan, Dawn Black, David Newman, et al., *The Economic Costs of Development for Local Governments* (Athens: Department of Agricultural and Applied Economics, University of Georgia, 2002).
8. Christopher Swope, "Sprawl: Rendezvous with Density," *Governing Magazine* (March 2001).
9. Ga. Laws 1989, 1317, codified in OFFICIAL CODE OF GEORGIA ANNOTATED (O.C.G.A) tit. 2, 8, 12, 31, 32, 36, 44, 45, 49, 50.
10. O.C.G.A. §12-2-8.
11. Terry A. DeMeo and James E. Kundell, *Linking State Water Programs to Watershed Management* (Athens: Carl Vinson Institute of Government, University of Georgia, 2001).
12. O.C.G.A. §12-5-280 et seq.
13. O.C.G.A. §12-5-230 et seq.
14. O.C.G.A. §12-5-320 et seq.
15. O.C.G.A. tit. 12, ch. 5, art. 4, part 6.
16. O.C.G.A. §36-22-1 et seq.
17. For further discussion of this program, *see* the Georgia Greenspace Program at http://www.DNR.state.ga.us/dnr/greenspace/index.html.
18. O.C.G.A. §12-7-1 et seq.
19. *Nonpoint Source Management in Georgia: An Update of the Georgia Nonpoint Source Management Program* (Athens, GA: Institute of Community and Area Development, 1998).
20. The Georgia Water Quality Control Act, enacted by the Georgia General Assembly in 1964, actually preceded the federal law.
21. O.C.G.A. tit. 12, ch 7.
22. F. C. Curriero, J. A. Patz, J. B. Rose, and S. Lele, "The Association between Extreme Precipitation and Waterborne Disease Outbreaks in the United States, 1948–1994," *American Journal of Public Health* 91, no. 8 (August 2001): 1194–99.

23. James E. Kundell and Terry A. DeMeo, *Source Water Protection: A Guidebook for Local Governments* (Athens: Conference of Southern County Associations, National Association of Counties, Georgia Water Management Campaign in cooperation with the Carl Vinson Institute of Government, 2000).
24. O.C.G.A. tit. 12, ch. 5, art. 10.
25. Small systems in North Georgia may obtain their water from wells. In Northwest Georgia, springs can serve as a significant source of water. Larger systems in North Georgia are generally dependent on surface water systems.
26. Mary A. Elfner, personal communication, Georgia DNR Water Conservation Program, January 5, 2004.
27. O.C.G.A. §12-5-96 (groundwater), §12-5-31 (surface water).
28. Donald H. Pack, "Meteorology of Air Pollution," in *Man's Impact on Environment*, ed. Thomas R. Detwyler (New York: McGraw-Hill, 1971).
29. 42 United States Code Annotated (U.S.C.A.) §7401 et seq.
30. O.C.G.A. §12-9-1 et seq.
31. 42 U.S.C.A. §7407 et seq.
32. W. L. Chameides, R. W. Lindsay, J. Richardson, and C. S. Kiang, "The Role of Biogenic Hydrocarbons in Urban Photochemical Smog: Atlanta as a Case Study," *Science* 241 (September 16, 1988): 1473–75.
33. 42 U.S.C.A. §6901 et seq. (originally codified in 42 U.S.C.A. §3251).
34. Ibid.
35. *Georgia Solid Waste Management Report* (Atlanta: Georgia Department of Community Affairs, 2001).
36. Ibid.
37. O.C.G.A. §12-8-20 et seq.
38. *Georgia Solid Waste Management Plan*.
39. O.C.G.A. §§12-8-21(g), 12-8-40.2.
40. O.C.G.A. §12-8-59.2.
41. O.C.G.A. §§12-8-25, 12-8-25.3.
42. *Georgia Solid Waste Management Report*.
43. Ibid.
44. 1997 Op. Att'y Gen. No. 97-23.
45. *Georgia's Environment* (Atlanta: Environmental Protection Division, Georgia Department of Natural Resources, 2001).
46. O.C.G.A. §12-8-60 et seq.
47. *Georgia's Environment*.
48. O.C.G.A. §12-8-180 et seq.
49. U.S. Environmental Protection Agency, *Brownfields: Glossary of Terms* (http://www.epa.gov/swerosps/bf/glossary.htm).
50. U.S. Environmental Protection Agency, *Brownfields Economic Redevelopment Initiative* (http://www.epa.govlbrownfields).
51. O.C.G.A. tit. 12, ch. 8, art. 9.

SOURCES OF ADDITIONAL INFORMATION

General Resources

Association County Commissioners of Georgia, http://www.accg.org

Georgia Environmental Protection Division, http://www.ganet.org/dnr/environ

Georgia Department of Community Affairs, http://www.dca.stqte.ga.us
Georgia Environmental Facilities Association, http://www.gefa.org
Region IV, U.S. Environmental Protection Agency, http://www.gov/region4
U.S. Environmental Protection Agency, http://www.epa.gov

Land Use

American Farmland Trust, http://www.farmland.org (provides resources on preserving farmland and promoting environmentally responsible farming practices)

Planning Commissioners Journal, http://www.plannersweb.com (provides resources on land use, planning, and sprawl)

Smart Growth Network, http://www.smartgrowth.org (provides resources on growth management, case studies, and funding)

Sprawl Watch Clearinghouse, http://www.sprawlwatch.org (provides resources on sprawl, smart growth, federal policies, state-by-state information, and land conservation)

The Trust for Public Land, http://www.tpl.org (provides resources on protection of land for parks, gardens, greenways, and riverways)

Urban Land Institute, http://www.uli.org (provides resources on urban revitalization, smart growth, and transportation)

Water Quality and Quantity

American Water Works Association, http:www.awwa.org

Georgia Department of Natural Resources Water Conservation Program, http://www.conservewatergeorgia.net

Georgia Water & Pollution Control Association, http://www.gwpca.org (provides information on municipal wastewater and Consumer Confidence Report technical assistance)

National Watershed Clearinghouse, http://ctic.purdue.edu/KYW/KYW.html (provides information on how to develop local watershed programs)

Water Environment Federation, http://www.wef.org (provides links to water sites)

James E. Kundell and Diana Tetens, *Whose Water Is It? Major Water Allocation Issues Facing Georgia* (Athens: Carl Vinson Institute of Government, University of Georgia, May 1998).

Air Quality

U.S. Environmental Protection Agency, http://www.epa.gov/oar/aqtrnd97 (provides a link to the National Air Quality and Emissions Trends Report, 1999)

Air and Waste Management Association, http://www.awma.org (provides outreach and technical assistance)

Clean Air Force, http://www.cleanairforce.com (provides education, inspection, and emission testing information)

Energy Use and Conservation

U.S. Department of Energy, http://www.eia.doe.gov.html, State Electricity Profiles, Georgia, and http://www.eia.doe.gov/emeu/aer/eh/eh.html, Energy in the United States: A Brief History and Current Trends (July 1998)

Energy Efficiency and Renewable Energy Clearinghouse, P.O. Box 3048, Merrifield, VA 22116, (800) 363-3732 (800-DOE-EREC), fax (703) 893-0400, e-mail: doe.erec@_nciinc.com, TDD (800) 273-2957 (provides fact sheets)

Energy Efficiency and Renewable Energy Network, http://www.eren.doe.gov (a gateway to information and resources from national laboratories and other organizations) and http://www.eren.doe.gov/cities_counties/articles.html (provides fact sheets)

Center of Excellence for Sustainable Development, http://www.sustainable.doe.gov

Atlanta DOE Support Office, 730 Peachtree Street, NE, Suite 876, Atlanta, GA 30308, (404) 347-2837

Solid and Hazardous Waste Management

U.S. Environmental Protection Agency, http://www.epa.gov/epaoswer/non-hw/muncpl/factbook/internet/, Municipal Solid Waste Factbook.

U.S. Environmental Protection Agency, http://www.epa.gov/swerosps/bf/html-doc/aa-preamb.htm, The Preamble to the Brownfields National Partnership Action Agenda (May 1997)

Solid Waste Association of North America, http://www.swana.org

Georgia Department of Community Affairs, http://www.dca.state.ga.us, Solid Waste Annual Report

Pollution Prevention Assistance Division of the Georgia Department of Natural Resources, http://www.ganet.org/dnr/p2ad (provides technical assistance and education materials)

Georgia Department of Natural Resources, http://www.DNR.State.GA.US/dnr/environ/branches, Sites on the Hazardous Site Inventory by County in Georgia

Solid Waste Association of North America, http://www.swana.org

National Recycling Coalition, http://www.recycle.net

17

Jan Coyne, William C. Bell,* and Mary Maureen Brown*

Geographic Information Systems

A geographic information system (GIS) combines database management and analysis functions with computer-aided mapping. It adds a visual and locational dimension to municipal management and decision making. Since much of the data municipalities manage is land based, a GIS can help managers and decision makers manage municipal affairs more effectively.

A GIS allows users to ask questions such as

- What is at this location?
- Where are the schools located?
- What is the address of this parcel?
- What is the average income in the municipality?
- What areas of the municipality are suitable/unsuitable to build on?
- What is the pattern of land-use change?
- What are possible patterns of land use in the future?

This chapter provides an overview of GIS technology, issues, and potential for helping municipal governments make better decisions. GIS is widely used in local government, either as an in-house service or as a service provided by other public-sector organizations or private firms. GIS is also used by businesses, nonprofit organizations, and community groups. Whether or not a municipality uses GIS, chances are that municipal decision makers will encounter the products of GIS technology. Implementing and managing a GIS requires a level of funding that

---

* Parts of the chapter contain or are based on work by these authors from earlier editions of the *Handbook for Georgia Mayors and Councilmembers*.

may seem unwarranted without some knowledge of why the funding is necessary and what the benefit is to the municipality. Knowing the limitations and capabilities of GIS allows municipal decision makers to use it economically and effectively. "GIS has moved beyond the techies and into county board rooms and city council chambers," says Randy Johnson, Hennepin County, Minn., commissioner and former president of the National Association of Counties (NACo). Butte–Silver Bow, Mont., Chief Executive Jack Lynch affirms, "Every elected official needs to be familiar with GIS and what it can do—GIS is the most valuable management tool you can find."[1]

WHAT IS GIS?

A GIS is a system of hardware, software, and procedures designed to support the capture, management, manipulation, analysis, modeling, and display of spatially referenced data for solving complex planning and management problems.[2] In other words, it is a computer system that is used for collecting and analyzing data that can be mapped, and it displays the resulting information as a map or series of maps.

"Spatially referenced" means that the data can be assigned a location on the earth. The location is assigned using a coordinate system. The simplest coordinate system is a rectangular grid with horizontal and vertical lines labeled with numbers or letters like the one shown in Figure 17-1. The numbers are the coordinates of the grid. The dots are referenced, or located, using the coordinates 2,1 and 3,3. The first number of the coordinate comes from the labels across the bottom of the grid, and

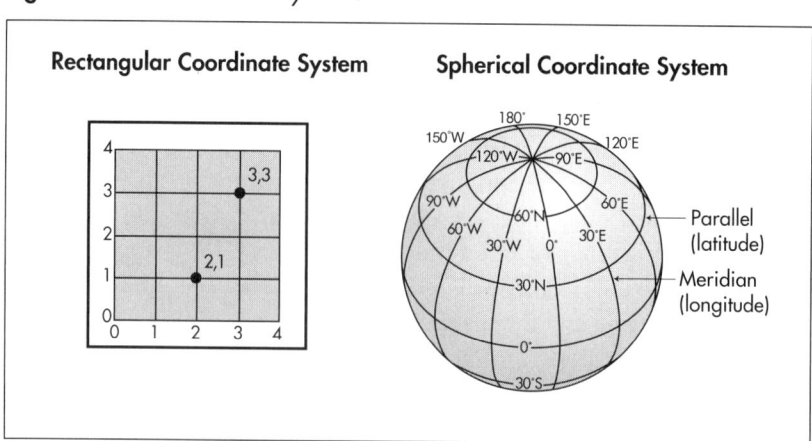

Figure 17-1. *Coordinate Systems*

the second number comes from the labels on the left side of the grid. Any dot placed in the grid can be similarly referenced. Because a rectangular grid system does not fit the round earth, a spherical coordinate system (Figure 17-1) is used, with coordinates measured in degrees. The lines that run from pole to pole are called meridians; the others, parallels. The reference coordinates are longitude and latitude: longitude is measured east and west of 0° (the meridian that runs through Greenwich, England) to 180° (the meridian that runs through Fiji); latitude is measured north and south of 0° (the Equator) to 90° (the North and South Poles). The coordinate system enables relationships of objects on earth to be more or less preserved when they are depicted on a map.

Types of spatially referenced data that a municipality would use include the following:

Jurisdictional boundaries

- county and city limits
- census divisions
- electoral districts
- special services districts
- property boundaries
- parks

Physical features

- roads
- streams and bodies of water
- buildings
- land use (fields vs. forests, for example)

The spatial data are linked to attribute data in a database. Attribute data refer to additional information about a feature such as the name and length of a road, the population and the average income of residents of a municipality, the owner and value of a parcel, etc.

One way municipal information is organized in a GIS is by layers of spatial features with their attributes (Figure 17-2). These layers can then be presented singly or overlaid with other features, depending on what information is being sought. For example, the roads, land-use, and facilities layers can be overlaid to see where the best location for a new fire station might be. It is this ability to integrate disparate types of data and display the relationships between and among them that makes GIS powerful.

In order to overlay the spatial data, each layer has to match the others. The coordinate systems have to be the same, and the data have to be at the same scale. Scale is the relationship of distance on the earth to distance on the map. Data collected from different sources will likely have different coordinate systems and scales. Improper conversion of these characteristics of spatial data causes errors that affect analysis and interpretation of the data.

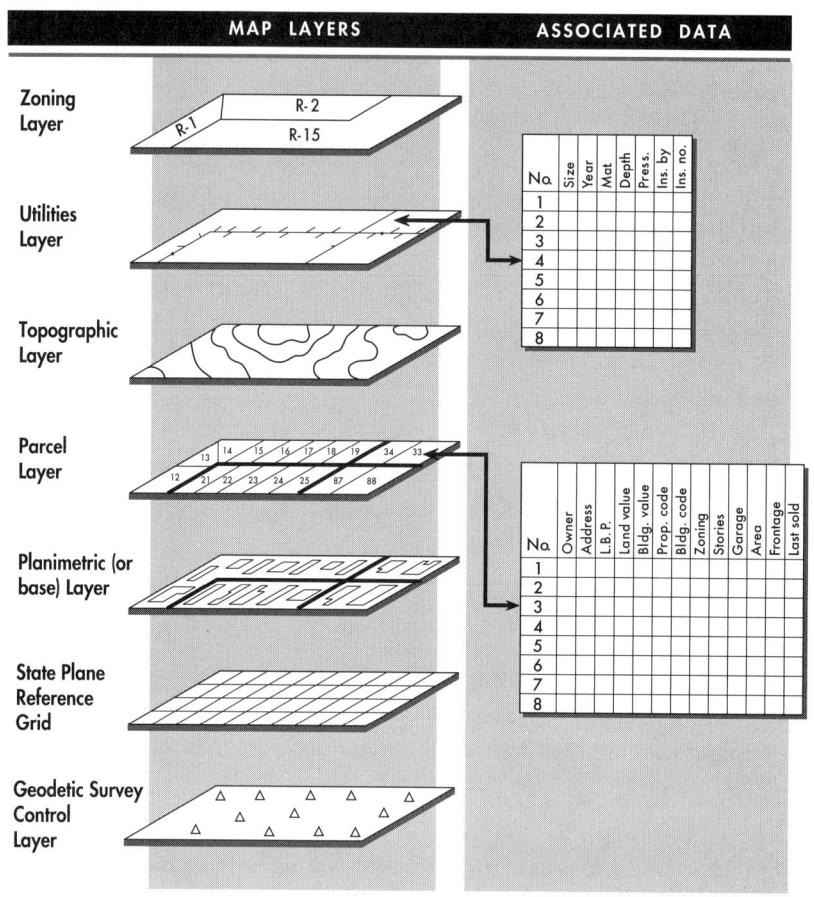

Figure 17-2. *Map Overlay Potential of a GIS*

Scale is of interest to municipal decision makers because data that are useful to the municipality for most applications of GIS are at a scale that currently requires significant amounts of time and money to acquire. There are free digital data available from both the state and federal governments, but most of it is too generalized for use by local governments. Generalization removes detail so that objects can be depicted clearly on maps of large areas. The same generalized data shown at the scale of the municipality would leave out important details.

Related Technologies

GIS can be developed as a general-purpose tool or for a narrowly defined set of functions. For example, land information systems (LIS) focus on the mapping and analysis of land and property records. Transportation management uses a specialized set of analysis tools supplied by developers of GIS for transportation. There are also other automated mapping systems that were developed for specific fields that are now incorporating GIS functions. These include

- computer-aided drafting (CAD), widely used in industrial design and architecture;
- automated mapping/facilities mapping (AM/FM), used to manage utilities; and
- global positioning system (GPS).

The latter system, GPS, includes receivers and satellites that can pinpoint locations on the earth. It is used in the computerized navigational systems found on boats and in some automobiles. Surveyors use GPS to help them make more accurate surveys. It is one way to collect sufficiently detailed data for a municipality or to check the accuracy of data acquired in other ways.

Remote sensing is the acquisition of data from satellites or airplanes using infrared sensors, radar, cameras, or other sensors. Remotely sensed images and air photography must be processed in order to be used with other data in a GIS. Images have a certain amount of distortion that must be removed, and they must be made to match the coordinate system used in a particular GIS. Once adjusted, images can be used for interpreting land-use patterns over wide areas or for updating and checking the accuracy of other map layers, such as roads or streams.

GPS, remote sensing, and air photography are technologies that enable municipalities to create sufficiently detailed and accurate data for the scale of a municipal-level GIS. The expense of acquiring the imagery or hiring a surveyor is part of the reason data acquisition can be the costliest aspect of GIS implementation.

LOCAL GOVERNMENT APPLICATIONS

The strength of a GIS lies in its ability to combine both visualization and analytical functions. The combination of maps and graphics with a relational database is a powerful tool for managing information. A GIS can integrate diverse sources of information that create patterns and relationships that might otherwise be missed. Patterns of population growth, road networks, waterways, or vegetation distribution can be compared with one another. Hypothetical scenarios, such as how the landscape would look with different levels of population growth or different land-use policies, also can be seen. An individual attribute can be viewed in multiple ways: with more or with less detail; alone or with other attributes; or in its current, past, or possible future state. For example, data can be classified or abstracted before being displayed to show an average or number of entities above or below a certain threshold.

Initially, GIS was predominantly used to automate manual tasks already being performed in local governments, such as mapping and information management. Current systems allow more complex analyses of data, including three-dimensional visualization of landscapes and forecasting. Researchers and practitioners are also investigating ways to incorporate GIS into the public participation process so that citizens and decision makers can benefit from the technology throughout all phases of planning and policy creation.

GIS can be applied to the following functions of a municipal government:

- public works
- elections
- tax assessment
- planning and zoning
- emergency services
- parks and recreation
- water works
- police
- solid waste management
- natural resources
- management
- public health

In addition, the availability of a GIS can directly affect citizen participation, particularly with regard to taxation issues:

> A GIS can be used to analyze the relationship between tax revenues drawn from different neighborhoods or areas and the expenditures being made in those areas. Citizens can use the GIS to learn how taxes drawn from their neighborhood are budgeted for different functions. As recent surveys suggest, citizens are more likely to approve of needed taxations when they know that their dollars are being spent on specific services—especially services that might benefit their neighborhood or themselves individually.[3]

Data can be analyzed to reveal patterns or trends that need to be addressed or to assess the impact of a municipal policy. For example, where and when certain types of crime occurs may be associated with land use (does it occur in residential or business areas? does it occur at the same general time? is it concentrated in one area or widely dispersed?), proximity to transportation, population characteristics, and other information that law enforcement agencies can use in deciding how to focus their efforts. Such data may also suggest other solutions, such as streetlights in dark areas or crime prevention education for citizens.

A GIS can be used to help decide which of a number of possible changes might be the best one(s) to implement. For example, population growth trends can be modeled in terms of land-use or zoning regulations to see how each might affect the municipality in terms of infrastructure requirements. Regulations can be changed, land-use or zoning types can be shifted, and the effects can be assessed on the computer to help evaluate whether current regulations will be viable in the future.

BENEFITS AND COSTS OF IMPLEMENTING GIS

The use of GIS in small jurisdictions has become commonplace only in the last decade. Larger local governments, such as those in major urban areas, were early adopters of the technology and have been the focus of studies of the effectiveness and costs and benefits of using GIS. The results of these initial studies were based on the early use of GIS to automate tasks, a function for which GIS was considered beneficial. The studies indicate that there is not necessarily an immediate return on investment; jurisdictions generally began seeing cost decreases and efficiencies in three to five years.

Other benefits of GIS adoption include eliminating duplication (i.e., one database can serve multiple users) and improving data management, information processing, access to information, analysis and problem-solving capabilities, and the quality of decisions, because they are backed by sufficient data. According to Hugh Calkins of the National Center for Geographic Information and Analysis, "The largest savings from using a GIS in local government come from greater efficiency in answering citizen inquiries. The querying ability of a well-designed GIS can save from two person-years in a small town to ten or more person-years in a large county."[4]

Aside from the fact that improvements may not be apparent for years, part of the difficulty in measuring the benefit of GIS is that much of it is not quantifiable. It is hard to separate the effects of the system from the effects of its environment. Local governments benefit from GIS and other technology when the implementation of it is well researched and planned. The purpose of the system needs to be clear, and those responsible for managing it need to be trained in its use. The jurisdictions that have been disappointed in their return on GIS investment have generally not done enough groundwork to understand all of the costs involved, or they have overestimated the system needed for their particular set of requirements and needs.

In 2001, the General Assembly enacted legislation to help local governments reduce the cost of creating or maintaining a GIS. Local governments and regional development centers are now permitted to charge fees for providing information from or access to the GIS. Fees must be based on the development costs of creating or maintaining the GIS and "may include cost to the municipality . . . of time, equipment, and personnel in the creation, purchase, development, production, or update of the geographic information system." The code also authorizes local governments to contract with private firms to provide GIS information to the public.[5]

The costs of adopting a GIS vary with how much is required of the system, whether new people need to be hired, and, if so, how many. Expenditures for GIS software range from applications having little or no cost to applications costing tens of thousands of dollars that run on computers ranging from inexpensive desktop PCs to massive networked servers. Initial database development is usually the most costly aspect of GIS implementation both in terms of funding and time, and it varies with the amount and detail of data needed. Regular hardware, software, and database upgrades need to be considered in the long-term budget for a system. Municipalities change, as do the data about them, and the uses of the GIS will change as well.

Personnel training is often neglected in considering costs. Initial training and periodic updates are necessary to fully utilize the system. There is no point in paying for functions the staff is not aware of or able to use properly.

Implementation

The first step in considering adoption of a GIS is to decide what kinds of analysis a municipality wants to perform and what information it wants to obtain from the analysis. The next step is to conduct a cost-benefit analysis and feasibility study. These studies should address more than just technical issues, since organizational and policy issues play a role in implementation. Employee receptivity to technology and ability to adapt to new technology, how effectively potential users of the system communicate, and users' conception about what is wanted and needed in the system all affect how much a GIS costs and how long it takes to implement. All potential users of the system should be consulted at this stage to make sure that all data needs or requirements are taken into account.

Once the decision to adopt a GIS is made, the municipality needs to decide how to organize it. There are a number of organizational models of GIS implementation: single department, multidepartment, or multiagency.

Single Department Model

In the single department approach, the GIS is developed in a single department of the government and used only for the applications of that department. This approach is common. For example, the municipal planning department may develop a GIS to manage land records information. As other departments learn about the system, they may request GIS services from that department.

Multidepartment Model

In this model, various departments share costs and responsibilities. Cost sharing among the departments funds database development and updating. Sometimes this model evolves from the single department model as requests for service impede the use of the system for its original purpose.

There are a couple of approaches to the multidepartment model. One department may be chosen as the lead department and be responsible for housing the GIS and providing the services to other departments. The other approach is to create a GIS department to manage the system. Both approaches have advantages and disadvantages. Having a lead department with its own priorities may affect how service is provided to other departments, and a centralized GIS department may not be able to respond to the specialized needs of individual municipal departments.

Multiagency Model

The multiagency model shares costs and responsibilities between several levels of local government or between a number of partners—governmental or nongovernmental. Typical agreements involve utilities such as gas, power, cable, and telephone companies that share the cost of map development with municipalities and exchange information such as underground structures data with them. If there is sufficient interest on behalf of the partners, this approach is the most economical option. However, this model generally takes much longer to get projects under way because of the need for joint discussions on cost sharing and the need to consider different kinds of data, different levels of accuracy, and the different viewpoints and politics of the various agencies. Nevertheless, the greater variety of data provided by multiple partners yields better benefits at lower costs (Figure 17-3).

Data

Once the approach to implementation has been decided, data issues need to be addressed. Data maintenance and sharing agreements among partners need to be created unless a single department is implementing the

Figure 17-3. *Multiagency GIS*

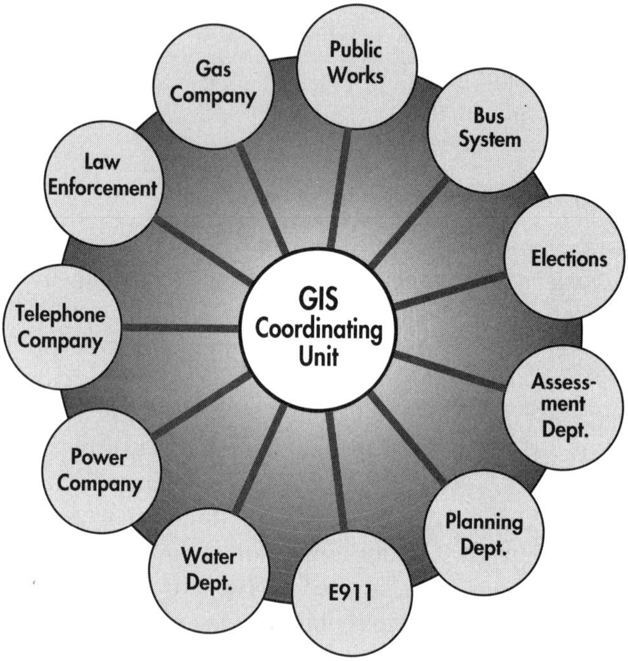

system. Database standards need to be agreed upon. Standards should include the following:

- naming and definition conventions (so that each named type of road, for instance, means only that type of road and all road names are entered in the same format)
- mapping standards (coordinate system, scale, symbols used to represent objects, line colors and widths, etc.)
- data documentation (information about the data, such as source, coordinate system, scale, extent, and date of compilation)
- access privileges (who gets to do what with the data, software, and hardware)
- access charges (if any, how much and who pays)
- liability for inaccurate data
- quality assurance (who is responsible for data updates and accuracy checks and how often does it occur)
- data backup and recovery procedures

Policies created by the municipality based on database standards that have been agreed to and developed with all users of the system will streamline later steps in the implementation process.

Before data are collected, a data model and database design should be decided upon. Users' needs and expectations should be clearly defined at this stage. Database design affects how data should be collected and what kinds of analysis can be performed. It can also affect the software and hardware used.

What kind of data are collected and how they are collected will depend on the preceding steps. As mentioned earlier, a basic set of data layers is available at no cost from state and federal sources. The Georgia GIS Data Clearinghouse makes Georgia data available over the Internet. County and municipal boundaries, roads, hydrology, elevation, and other data are provided by the U.S. Geological Survey, the U.S. Bureau of the Census, the Georgia Department of Transportation, and the Georgia Department of Natural Resources, among others. Other data will have to be acquired through manually digitizing or scanning paper maps, converting GPS data provided by surveyors, or using aerial photography. The method used will depend on the types of data available, the equipment and personnel available, the accuracy required, and the cost. Different applications of GIS require different levels of accuracy. Engineering applications, such as utility or infrastructure management, generally require more accurate data than do planning applications.

Regardless of the approach pursued in GIS implementation, an experienced consultant is generally required because of the highly technical nature of a GIS project. In addition, a GIS manager position should be established to ensure that the system continues to meet the evolving needs of the municipality.

Available Resources

The Regional Development Centers (RDCs) provide GIS services to member local governments, especially for comprehensive planning.

Georgia colleges and universities provide GIS education. Some provide GIS services, including implementation planning and database development. Information Technology Outreach Services (ITOS) is a University of Georgia unit that assists local governments with GIS.

The Urban and Regional Information Systems Association (URISA) is an organization of professionals using information technology and spatial information in planning, public works, and other governmental areas. URISA provides educational and other resources.

NOTES

1. LLGIS Consortium, "About LLGIS." http://www.llgis.org/pages/about_llgis/index.htm. Accessed January 29, 2002.
2. Steve Palladino, *GIS in the Schools: Workshop Resource Packet*, Technical Report 93-2 (Santa Barbara: National Center for Geographic Information and Analysis, University of California, 1993), 71. (http://www.ncgia.ucsb.edu/pubs/pubslist.html#93-2). Accessed January 12, 2002.
3. John O'Looney, *Beyond Maps* (Redlands, CA: ESRI Press, 2000), 120–21.
4. Ibid., 15. "Calkins' estimates of potential time savings were derived by measuring the time it takes to respond manually to a query and the time it takes to respond using a GIS and multiplying the difference by the average number of queries in a year."
5. OFFICIAL CODE OF GEORGIA ANNOTATED (O.C.G.A.) §50-29-2.

SUGGESTED LITERATURE

Aronoff, Stan. *Geographic Information Systems: A Management Perspective*. Ottawa, Canada: WDL Publications, 1989.

Bell, William C., and Mary Maureen Brown. "Geographic Information Systems." In *Handbook for Georgia County Commissioners*, 3rd ed. (with 1998 update), ed. J. Devereux Weeks and Paul T. Hardy. Athens: Carl Vinson Institute of Government, University of Georgia, 1998.

Greenhood, David. *Mapping*. Chicago: University of Chicago Press, 1964.

Huff, Darrell. *How to Lie with Statistics*. New York: W. W. Norton, 1982.

Monmonier, Mark. *How to Lie with Maps*. Chicago: University of Chicago Press, 1991.

Public Technology, Inc. (PTI). *GIS://The Next Management Tool*. Washington, DC: PTI, 1997.

_____. with the Urban Consortium and International City Management Association. *The Local Government Guide to Geographic Information Systems: Planning and Implementation*. Washington, DC: PTI, 1991.

Ventura, Stephen J. "The Use of Geographic Information Systems in Local Government," *Public Administration Review* 55, no. 5 (September–October 1995): 461–67.

PART 4
Municipal Services

18

John A. O'Looney

Electronic Government, Infrastructure, and Governance

Local governments in Georgia and across the country are using electronic systems to provide more and better services, to communicate more frequently and effectively with citizens and constituents, and to support improved planning and decision making. To accomplish these goals, however, Georgia municipalities will need to meet the interwoven challenges of electronic government, electronic infrastructure, and electronic governance.

ELECTRONIC GOVERNMENT

Electronic government involves the development of information services and transaction capacity across the range of municipal government responsibility. Areas of information technology (IT) capacity building include business development and regulation, law enforcement and the courts, education, social services, taxation, citizenship development, and support for services such as utilities or recreational programs. Electronic government has the capacity to improve communications (i.e., citizen to government, government to citizen, citizen to citizen, government official to government official, and government to government); enhance the speed and quality of work, particularly work that involves transactions (e.g., paying bills, fees, taxes); manipulate data; and deliver information-based services (e.g., instruction, licenses, counseling, etc.).

Organizational support is a key element in developing electronic government. While facilitating the process of moving from physical to digital government will involve new funding, the funding challenge is relatively minor compared with the challenges of developing new hiring, training, and management processes. The "humanware" aspects of IT development, in particular, have been shown to represent an increasingly large proportion of the total cost of developing these new technologies.[1] As the cost of hardware and software declines, public managers will need to focus on issues such as increasing computer literacy among staff members, retaining skilled staff, developing a technology friendly organization, increasing the tolerance for experimentation and failure, identifying opportunities for interagency and intergovernmental collaboration, and balancing the support for technology among the various functions of government.[2]

Traditionally, electronic government at the municipal level only involved maintenance of back-office data centers for operations such as accounting, taxes, and utility billing. In the 1980s and early 1990s, electronic government included local area networks for interoffice communications and file sharing and developing geographic information systems (GIS) for use by planning and zoning departments. Leading-edge municipal governments are implementing plans for Internet- and intranet-based service delivery that incorporate strategies for improved workflow, computer seat management, and citizen-to-government and business-to-government transactions, as well as the delivery of all manner of content (e.g., text, video, and chat), including Web-based GIS.[3] The key advantage of an intra-Internet approach is that it increases flexibility (e.g., the municipality can have any computer seat act as a station for any type of work and can quickly include or exclude from the intranet any telecommuting workers or consultants). In addition, because many people are learning to use a Web browser through home use of the Internet, the costs of training individuals in the use of such technology in the workplace is reduced.

Developing a successful method of electronic government requires an effective plan of action that will address the needs of the community and of the government itself. The first step in such a plan should be assessing how citizens interact with their government and government officials.[4] It should then be possible to determine how to use technology to provide new channels for such interactions as well as enhance existing channels. Additional planning and implementation steps will involve gaining support, gathering ideas, setting objectives, finding needed resources, identifying costs, designing the technology, creating and maintaining content, managing the technology, and evaluating the technology's effectiveness.[5]

Typically, local government intra-Internet strategies involve three developmental steps: (1) providing static Web pages on a Web server provided by a commercial Web host; (2) providing dynamic Web content through a government-operated Web server interacting with one or more databases; and (3) providing enhanced content (e.g., geographically organized information and maps) and transaction processing capability (e.g., bill paying).[6] Although the cost of achieving step 1 is relatively minor, substantial cost increases are involved in steps 2 and 3. The importance of moving from static Web pages to dynamic, searchable Web databases is that the latter will allow local governments to provide citizens with current and detailed information that they can use in their daily lives. Examples include the following:

- current neighborhood-level crime incident reports
- current water or utility bill accounts
- citizen and intragovernmental discussion forums
- searchable property records
- searchable library resources
- searchable records of animals available for adoption
- searchable local governmental ordinances
- online program availability and registration
- facilities reservations

Offering these advanced services requires improving underlying technologies, but many services and communication channels can be provided with only the basic (step 1) technologies. In a recent examination of Georgia local government Web sites, for example, researchers looked at whether a site offered program information and service offerings, budget information, performance data, and communications information (phone numbers, address, and e-mail) that would allow a citizen to participate in public decision-making processes more effectively and intelligently. Many local governments have yet to create Web sites that provide these essential links and pieces of information.[7]

Implementing the more sophisticated Internet technologies is often beyond the capabilities of in-house technical staff. In these instances, local governments have to choose between enhancing in-house staff or contracting for these services. Although each choice has its advantages and disadvantages, existing research suggests the following:

1. Outsourcing technical services can place a local government in a particularly vulnerable position, the degree of which is influenced by the complexity of the task, the amount of competition for delivering the service, and the extent to which the assets being developed will have alternative or additional uses.
2. Local governments that maintain a substantial level of in-house capability tend to be more satisfied with consultant services.

3. Effective contracts for technical assistance often demand more of an alliance with the contractor than do service contracts generally.[8]

ELECTRONIC INFRASTRUCTURE

Electronic network infrastructure and citizen access represent a second front in the effort to build a modern electronic local government system. Infrastructure and access are related but distinct areas of concern. Networks must exist before citizens can access the Internet, but this fact says little about the type of network, its capacity, or its ability to serve desired purposes. In developed nations such as the United States, regulated competition among private telephone companies has provided the model for policy making with regard to establishing access to common networks. However, this model is not fully applicable to digital networks because unlike an analog telephone network (essentially a "you-have-it-or-you-don't" technology), a digital network offers many different levels of access. As such, the market will tend to provide some areas and groups with high-quality services while providing others with minimal or no service. The amount of access (or bandwidth) determines the quality of service and, to a certain extent, the type of service(s) available (e.g., video demands higher bandwidth). Governments that decide to go digital will have to establish some level of universal service. A major policy question in the coming years will be how to determine that level within an ever-changing technological environment.

Decisions about bandwidth also have an economic development component. Providing the poorer, more rural areas of the state with second-class access to digital networks may doom them to second-class development opportunities. For both access and economic development purposes, the model of road networks, which are built and maintained directly by governments, provides an alternative to market-based provisioning. Public provision of roads results in greater equality of access and a more extensive network than might occur were the building of roads financed primarily through private funds or tolls. The same holds true for electronic infrastructures.

In some communities, bandwith infrastructure is provided by both public and private entities. For instance, in Georgia most communities receive the access that a telecommunications or cable company has chosen to provide to the area, but some like LaGrange and Newnan have used public resources to develop a higher level of local network capacity and citizen access. These municipalities see the public provision of network capacity as both an economic development magnet and as a catalyst for more online government, education, and intracommunity business transactions. In addition to local government choices about public or private provisioning, citizen use of networks will depend on a variety of policies for pricing, access to kiosks in public facilities and spaces, technology education, and employee access at work.[9]

ELECTRONIC GOVERNANCE

Electronic governance involves establishing legal, programmatic, and regulatory frameworks to support the range of economic, social, and political transactions that citizens want to use. Electronic governance is a distinctly public-sector function. Whereas private firms can often move a large portion of their transactions onto electronic networks by simply overcoming technical hurdles, local governments must consider the implications of their actions for a broad range of issues. Local governments must struggle with issues of privacy, intellectual property, fairness and openness of access, the legal standing of electronic documents, and the impact of policies on economic development, community viability, and the allocation of rights and resources among governmental jurisdictions and economic sectors.

A significant challenge for electronic governance is the development of electronic transaction law and infrastructure. Many government services can be provided merely by installing software and networks. However, various transactions such as construction permits, purchase orders, travel reimbursements, contracts, and voting cannot take place online without additional assurance that a person's statement is authentic and uncorrupted.[10] Electronic transaction law and infrastructure lay the foundation for these assurances. Because different government and business functions need different types of assurance and security, governments will need to specify when and where different types of electronic messages will have the force of law or will bind parties to agreements, exchanges, or other transactions. Georgia currently has a fairly permissive Electronic Signature Act.[11] This act identifies what types of electronic messages or records are considered to have the same force and level of risk as do comparable written documents. The act is considered permissive because it tends to include a wide variety of document types that can be signed electronically and because it allows contracting parties to agree ahead of time on what level of electronic communication (from a simple e-mail to an encrypted communication signed with a digital signature) will function as a legally valid electronic document.

The federal Electronic Signatures in Global and National Commerce Act preempts conflicting state laws; few differences exist between it and Georgia's Electronic Signature Act.[12] In both acts, acceptance of an electronic signature is voluntary, and interested parties can define the procedures that will create an authentic signature or contract. As such, these acts are technology neutral. Specifically, Georgia law states, "Where a person or other entity accepts or agrees to be bound by an electronic record executed or adopted with an electronic signature, then (1) any rule of law which requires a record of that type to be in writing shall be deemed satisfied, and (2) any rule of law which requires a signature shall be deemed satisfied."[13]

Under Georgia's open-ended electronic signature legislation, local governments have considerable leeway in conducting electronic transactions. The very open-endedness of the legislation, however, means that local governments will need to develop their own policies with regard to what level of signature or security they want to require for which electronic transactions. To make prudent choices in this regard, both public managers and elected officials will need to become educated regarding the key features of electronic documents and signatures.[14]

In addition to setting up the legal groundwork for electronic transactions, local governments will need to stay abreast of developments regarding certification authorities or the organizations that certify the authenticity and integrity of documents that have been sent or stored electronically. In some places, digital certificates are supplied by the state itself, while, in others, state or local governments contract with private certificate authorities for this service. Georgia's strategy in this regard is likely to develop over the next few years through the activity of the Georgia Technology Authority.[15]

Citizen and Employee Access

Network access alone does not ensure that the quality of electronic interactions with government and the larger community by citizens or public employees will equal or exceed that of nonelectronic interactions: citizen access can be achieved under any number of varying network management regimes and structures. Management regimes answer questions such as when, where, how, to whom, with what software, with whose permission, and for how long. Network information architectures embed these and other rules and policies into the nature of the network itself. Municipalities that are interested in developing a "21st century workforce" may need to reexamine policies that restrict access to advanced network services such as broadband access and Web publishing.

Some policy issues with regard to Web publication, for example, include whether and under what conditions the government will provide a link to other Web sites or resources; what kind of permissions employees need in order to publish on the Web; when e-mail can or should be removed; and whether permissions to publish will vary by different Web domains (Web pages, newsgroup postings, listserv messages, etc.) or content types.

Network Architecture

Every network structure can have a different impact on the type, style, frequency, duration, and content of citizen-to-citizen, citizen-to-government, government-to-citizen, employee-to-government, and business-to-government interactions. A poorly designed network infrastructure can limit or create an imbalance in each or all of these interactions, thereby limiting online transactions, communications, and decision making. Even more important than network infrastructure are the choice of software and the implementation and enforcement of participation rules that will guide the development of online governance. Key decisions in the future could include, what data will be shared in what form? How many people will be allowed in a government-sponsored chat room? Will the government facilitate communication between citizens who have similar interests? similar prejudices? Will governments personalize their Web sites or allow citizens to filter information? If so, in which areas? To what extent? Will public officials monitor and moderate online communications? Will citizens be allowed to participate anonymously? create and answer polls online? The shape of a room or the use of a loudspeaker can affect democratic processes in physical space. The architecture of the public part of cyberspace will have an even greater effect on democratic decision making and citizen participation in the future.[16]

Intellectual Property, Privacy, Connectivity, and Knowledge Management

As with the enabling electronic signature law, establishing policies in the interrelated areas of intellectual property, privacy, connectivity, and knowledge management will affect the ability of both the public and the private sector to work electronically. On the one hand, intellectual property and privacy are needed to give people the assurance that their work product and their communications will be appropriately respected. With this assurance, people will be more receptive to participating in online work and communications. Connectivity, or the ease with which people are able to contact and communicate with others, is also necessary for successful online communications on a broad scale. Both of these sets of values are necessary for a knowledge-based society and economy.[17] Unfortunately, potential conflict exists between these two values: one can ensure greater privacy by putting limits on connectivity (e.g., making it harder to find someone's e-mail address) or ensure greater connectivity by limiting privacy. The ideal is to discover and implement public policies that would limit these two public values the least.

With respect to Internet privacy issues, most governments have yet to take even minimal steps in developing and implementing a policy to ensure user privacy.[18] With respect to intellectual property, there are two concerns: that the Internet has undermined intellectual property rights because the reproduction and mass distribution of exact copies of digital media has become easy and that digital encryption technology may in the near future so completely protect intellectual property as to undermine fair use of that property. While local governments have little say concerning intellectual property law, local governments do establish policies on access and pricing of government data and records, and such policies potentially affect who can develop alternative policy analyses.[19]

Connectivity can be enhanced by effective organization of information (e.g., online e-mail links and e-mail lists for people with particular interests or characteristics), but it can be undermined by practices such as "spamming" or by establishing filters at various points in the network. Spamming, the mass sending of unwanted e-mail, weakens the benefits of connectivity because too much time must be devoted to deleting unwanted communications. Some state governments have developed anti-spam legislation, but the use of technologies that hide the identity of the senders of e-mail makes enforcing these laws difficult. Information filters can potentially undermine connectivity by blocking access to a resource. However, because filters can also be used to help people find needed information,[20] under some conditions, they might enhance connectivity.

Impact on Municipal Tax Revenues

Another area of electronic governance relates to the potential impact of e-commerce on local government revenues. Local governments have primarily been concerned with the possible consequences on sales tax revenues, but they may also need to be concerned about the effect of e-commerce on property taxes (e.g., when a retailer moves from a high-value, high-tax retail center to a low-value e-commerce warehouse).[21] Although early estimates of lost revenue appear to have been exaggerated, the long-term effect on local governments is likely to be substantial and may particularly affect the ability of local governments to customize their sales tax policies.[22] The detrimental consequences of Internet commerce–related sales tax losses will be greater for some local governments, specifically, those that rely heavily on revenues from retail centers that draw primarily from a population of highly affluent, well-educated consumers.

In each of these areas—electronic government, electronic infrastructure, and electronic governance—municipal governments will have to make difficult decisions. Not only will policymakers need to agree on the general purpose and direction of the policy in question, but also they will have to choose the type of mechanisms for implementing the policy. Choosing whether to use market incentives, public provision of network capacity, or mandates or subsidies for particular types of network architectures or to establish norms and implement new laws and regulations may be as important as choosing the particular policy direction itself. Because cyberspace is still in its infancy, the decisions made in the coming years are likely to be some of the most important for municipalities in the twenty-first century.

LOOKING TOWARD THE FUTURE

As the Internet is used more and more to provide and collect information electronically, the potential for combining and using informational resources in creative ways increases substantially. In particular, governmental services and efficiency can be improved by automating the exchange of information among multiple governments, citizens, businesses, and organizations. Currently, there are technologies being developed (e.g., Web services and XML Web document marking) that will make it more likely for governments to serve citizens and conduct business in a personalized and efficient manner. With these technologies, for example, local governments could automate their reporting functions to state and federal agencies, provide citizens with customized notices, and allow elected officials to track the ways in which their government functions compared with other similar governments. Efficiency would be increased because data that was entered once could be used multiple times by different departments. For larger governments, these technologies will enable a group of computers to share workloads. Also, the most efficient government providers of information services will be able to syndicate these services (for a fee) to other governments. For smaller jurisdictions, Web services will enable the government to purchase or subscribe to applications or services (e.g., job posting, recruitment, and screening) from low-cost vendors. Additionally, they could subscribe to different services from different vendors and then piece them together into what appears to the citizen or business user as a seamless system. These technologies will also make it possible for private companies to convey their information to various governments in order to provide a bundled service (e.g., the same information provided on forms for a telephone hookup may be used to purchase water service with the city).[23]

NOTES

1. W. W. Gibbs, "Taking Computers to Task," *Scientific American* 277, no. 1 (July 1997): 82–90.
2. See John A. O'Looney, *Local Government On-Line: Putting the Internet to Work* (Washington DC: International City/County Management Association, 2000).
3. An intranet is a network that uses the same protocols and technologies as the Internet but restricts access to a specific group of users, such as government employees.
4. The Center for Technology in Government describes a number of ways in which local governments can discover what citizens want from electronic government. *See* the Center's 2000 report at http://www.ctg.albany.edu/resources/abstract/abwhat_citizens_want.html.
5. For an example of how these steps can relate to the planning for a local government Web site, see O'Looney, *Local Government On-Line*, and Center for Technology in Government, "Untangle the Web: Delivering Municipal Services through the Internet," http://www.ctg.albany.edu/resources/pdfrpwp/utw.pdf. For an example of how to evaluate a local government Web site, *see* John O'Looney, "Georgia Municipal Websites: Drawing a Baseline," http://www.cviog.uga.edu/govtech/Gaweb.htm; Christopher Weare, Juliet A. Musso, and Matthew L. Hale, "Electronic Democracy and the Diffusion of Municipal Web Pages in California," *Administration and Society* 31, no. 1 (March 1999): 3–27. For survey data on how other local governments are addressing current and future Internet service delivery issues, *see* John A. O'Looney, "Use of the Public Sector Internet for Citizen Participation and Service Delivery," in *ICMA Municipal Yearbook 2001* (Washington DC: ICMA, 2001).
6. Technical demands for developing Web sites will likely also involve formatting Web pages (whether static or dynamic) in extensible markup language (XML). XML formatting will enable Web site users to selectively capture data based on document codes and reformat them for other purposes and audiences. For example, a state government could automatically gather and organize required reporting data from local government Web sites, regardless of the form in which they were originally published. Also, local governments could publish multiple personalized Web pages, technical documents, and annual reports—all based on a single XML document.
7. O'Looney, http://www.cviog.uga.edu/govtech/Gaweb.htm.
8. *See* John A. O'Looney, *Outsourcing State and Local Government Services* (Westport, CT.: Quorum Press, 1998); "Selecting Services for Outsourcing," in *Local Government Innovation*, ed. Robin A. Johnson and Norman Walzer (Westport, CT: Quorum Books, 2000).
9. *See* John A. O'Looney, "Access: Making Your Community Internet-Ready," *IQ Service Report* (May 2000).
10. Messages sent across electronic networks are not necessarily self-authentication (i.e., you cannot always be sure who the party on the other end of the line is or what they have said or written). *See* Lawrence Lessig, "Reading the Constitution in Cyberspace," *Emory Law Journal* 45, no. 3: 810–911.
11. OFFICIAL CODE OF GEORGIA ANNOTATED (O.C.G.A.) ch. 10-12.

12. Jonathan E. Stern, "The Electronic Signatures in Global and National Commerce Act," *Berkeley Technology Law Journal* 16 (2001): 391.
13. O.C.G.A. §10-12-4.
14. A good primer on this topic is the American Bar Association's Digital Signature Guidelines, produced by the Information Security Committee Electronic Commerce and Information Technology Division, Section of Science and Technology in 1995 and 1996, http://www.abanet.org/scitech/ec/isc/dsgfree.html.
15. More information can be found at the Georgia Technology Authority Web site at http://www.gagta.com/.
16. *See* John A. O'Looney, "The Search for Digital Sunshine," *Government Technology's E-Government* 1, no. 2 (June 2000): 42–46; Lawrence Lessig, *Code and Other Laws of Cyberspace* (New York: Basic Books, 1999); John O'Looney, "Preliminary Findings of a National Study of the Future of Public Sector Internet Services for Citizen Participation and Service Delivery," http://www.cviog.uga.edu/govtech/cybsur.htm.
17. *See* Electronic Commerce Study Committee, *Electronic Commerce Primer for the Georgia General Assembly* (Atlanta: Electronic Commerce Study Committee, March 14, 2000).
18. A March 2001 study by Brown University researchers suggests that only 7 percent of the 1,800 state and federal Web site surveys included a rudimentary privacy statement. Steve Towns, "Privacy Matters," *Government Technology* (June 2001): 64–66.
19. For a discussion of data access issues with respect to GIS data, *see* John A. O'Looney. *Beyond Maps: Geographic Information Systems and Local Government Decision Making* (Washington, DC: ICMA, 1997).
20. *See* Harry Hammitt, "Filtering: Keeping the Internet Clean, or Shutting It Down?" *Government Technology* (April 2000), http://www.govtech.net/magazine/local.us/apr00/internet/internet.html.
21. "E-Commerce: Potential Impacts on Property Tax Revenues?" http://icp.cviog.uga.edu.
22. Most experts agree that any reform that will allow for taxation of Internet sales is likely to demand both simplification and greater uniformity among the 7,500 taxing jurisdictions. As of July 2001, more than 36 states had already formed the Streamlined Sales Tax Project, and at least 15 states had adopted model legislation to simplify their tax systems. *See Government Technology News*, "House Wades into Net Tax Debate" (June 27, 2001).
23. *See* William D. Eggers, "The Invisible State," *Government Technology* (February 2002). *See* John O'Looney, "Local Government and the Semantic Web: A Working Paper" (Athens: Carl Vinson Institute of Government, University of Georgia), http://www.cviog.uga.edu/papers/Local Government and the Semantic Web.doc.

19

*Tom Berry, Ron Kuisis, Bill Thornton, and Charles B. Tyson**

Public Works and Public Utilities

The American Public Works Association (APWA) has defined public works as "the physical structures and facilities that are developed or acquired by public agencies to house governmental functions and provide water, power, waste disposal, transportation, and similar services to facilitate the achievement of common social and economic objectives."[1] Public works are without question the source of a large portion of municipal expenditures and therefore deserve the careful attention of mayors and city councils.[2]

Citizens rely on public works agencies for a multitude of services. In rural areas, public works facilities and services may be limited to highways, and flood control projects. In more urbanized areas, however, citizens often rely on public works agencies for construction and operation of streets and highways, water supply, water treatment and distribution, wastewater collection and treatment, solid waste collection and disposal, storm sewers and other drainage facilities, electricity and natural gas, and many other services vital to the well-being of the community.

For the purposes of this chapter, the discussion of public works and facilities is confined to the following:

- engineering
- streets and traffic control
- flood control
- water
- sewerage

---

* Parts of the chapter contain work by this author from earlier editions of the *Handbook for Georgia Mayors and Councilmembers* and are based on a similar chapter in the *Handbook for County Commissioners*, 4th ed.

- solid waste
- electricity/natural gas
- cable television and telecommunications

ENGINEERING

In order for a public works project to be successful, it must be properly planned. In most cases, planning requires employing the services of a qualified, professional engineer. Many cities in Georgia cannot afford the luxury of a full-time engineering staff but must rely on professional engineers hired on a consulting basis. The selection of a consulting engineer for a city is extremely important, the proper choice can yield the maximum benefit for its citizens. In contracting for professional services, such as engineering or architectural services, selecting an experienced and capable consultant should be the primary consideration. Selecting professional engineers and architects based on political considerations should be avoided.

Georgia law defines a professional engineer as one who is qualified and properly certified and defines professional engineering practice as it applies to public works construction and maintenance.[3] Also, except for construction (including alterations) that costs less than $100,000, Georgia law prohibits cities from engaging in public works design, construction, or supervision unless such activity is under the direct authority of a registered professional engineer or architect.[4]

Although a small consulting firm can adequately serve the needs of the community for some projects, a much larger staff with more varied capabilities is necessary for other undertakings. Therefore, when selecting an engineer or architect, the governing authority should very carefully consider the type of project and its requirements.

Although competitive bidding for engineering services generally should be avoided, many city governments do request quotations from engineering and architectural firms that include services to be provided, expertise of those providing the service, and cost of the service. Selecting a professional firm on the basis of price alone, however, can result in higher cost of the overall project. When selecting such professionals, many cities receive a quote for the service to be rendered on a project-by-project basis. Engineering or architectural fees typically are 5 to 10 percent of the project cost. It is not necessary, however, to award the project using a percentage, and engineering/architectural services awarded on a percentage basis may even have a tendency to escalate the final cost of the project.

The APWA believes that the public interest is best served when governmental agencies select architects, engineers, and related professional technical consultants for projects and studies through Qualifications-Based Selection procedures. Basing selections on qualifications and competence (rather than price) fosters greater creativity and flexibility and minimizes the potential for disputes and litigation.[5]

The process involves the following steps:[6]

1. An owner (city) identifies the general scope of work and develops a selection schedule.
2. A request for qualifications is issued.
3. Statements of qualifications are evaluated.
4. A list of finalists of qualified firms to be interviewed is determined.
5. Interviews are conducted, and the firms are ranked.
6. The owner invites the highest-ranked firm to assist in defining a detailed scope of work.
7. The design firm develops and submits to the owner a detailed fee proposal based on the agreed-upon scope of work.
8. If the proposed fee is not acceptable to the owner, the owner and designer work together to modify the scope of work, schedule, and budget to determine if an agreement on fee can be achieved.
9. If an agreement cannot be reached with the top-ranked firm, those negotiations are ended and negotiations begin with the next most qualified firm.
10. An agreement covering the scope and fee is executed.
11. Firms involved in the selection process are given postselection feedback, when requested.

Once a firm has been selected, the city should work very closely with the engineer and/or architect to ensure that the final product will be what the city wants and expects. The selected engineer and/or architect will represent the city and become a vital conduit between the city and the contractor on a particular project, but the city must accept ultimate responsibility for whether or not a particular facility adequately provides the function that was intended and is developed in accordance with the wishes of the council and citizens.

STREETS AND TRAFFIC CONTROL

Few, if any, services provided by a municipality are as visible to the public as its streets: virtually every citizen of the municipality, not to mention many visitors, use them every day. To pedestrians and drivers, traffic flow and the cleanliness and condition of a street are reflections of the city's total image. A city might, for the most part, be a well-run, efficient organization, but if the streets are dirty or rough and signals and directions are confusing, an impression of sloppy management is conveyed.

It is extremely important, then, that street maintenance has a high priority in the city's budget. A municipality can incur costly liability if its streets are not maintained in safe condition and repairs are not made in a timely fashion, especially after the municipality has received notice of the existence of a particular hazard or has reasonable knowledge that such a hazard exists.[7] Many cities provide routine maintenance and resurfacing through the services of a private contractor. Funding assistance is available through the Georgia Department of Transportation (DOT) Local Assistance Road Program (LARP).

Streets should be designed by a professional engineer if they are to be used cost effectively for a long period of time. A qualified paving contractor, in accordance with city plans and specifications, usually constructs major streets. However, cities would be well advised to explore the possibility of in-house construction with funding assistance from DOT. If in-house personnel are expected to perform new street construction, they should be adequately trained, and the necessary and proper equipment purchased or rented. Regardless of how well a crew is trained, it cannot be expected to perform quality road construction without the proper equipment.

Most cities have subdivision regulations requiring developers to provide the infrastructure for subdivisions. A municipality should be diligent in its efforts to ensure that the streets and other aspects of subdivision infrastructure are properly constructed in accordance with the city's specifications so that the subdivision tax base can support the maintenance of the infrastructure and costly repairs are not incurred.

Streets

Municipal streets are governed by the Georgia Code of Public Transportation.[8] This code prohibits private road construction or maintenance by a municipality,[9] specifies property acquisition procedures for public road purposes,[10] and requires notification to DOT within three months after a municipal street is added or abandoned.[11] This code empowers municipalities to contract with other governments; use authorized federal and state funds; acquire, manage, and dispose of real property; and purchase, borrow, rent, lease, control, manage, receive, and make payment for all personal property (e.g., equipment, machinery, and vehicles) used in operating the municipal street system.[12] In public road construction and maintenance, municipalities may employ personnel and contract with persons whose services may be required.[13]

A municipality may regulate the use of public roads on its municipal street system and on portions of the county road system that extend within the municipal corporate limits.[14] In regulating these roads, municipalities may set vehicle parking requirements and may place parking meters on all public roads in the corporate limits, including state highway system roads, when authorized by DOT.[15] Traffic control devices and signs may not be placed on state highway system roads without permission from DOT.[16]

Furthermore, municipalities may purchase supplies from the state; regulate utilities on, over, and below any parts of its streets in the municipal street system; and require potential damage security from contractors who work on municipal streets.[17] Municipalities may provide for surveys, maps, and specifications in supervising and maintaining streets.[18]

To aid physically handicapped persons, municipalities are required to construct curb ramps on newly constructed or replaced curbs.[19] Municipalities are empowered to contract for public road maintenance or construction.[20] For contracts involving $20,000 or more, public bids are required, according to prescribed rules.[21] This code further regulates municipalities with regard to

- control of advertising, erection of informational and directional signals, regulation of limited access roads, and regulation of roads under a municipality's exclusive jurisdiction;[22]
- public utilities relocation (and payment for these costs) and railroad grade crossings;[23]
- junkyards that are within 1,000 feet of the rights-of-way of interstate or federal aid primary highways;[24] and
- acquisition of property, scenic easements, air space, and rights of access for present or future public road or transportation purposes.[25]

Traffic Control

Vehicular and pedestrian flow on streets is regulated under the Georgia Uniform Rules of the Road.[26] These regulations are also enforceable on privately owned shopping center parking lots or similar areas used by the public as through streets or connector streets.[27]

In their broad scope, the Georgia Uniform Rules of the Road regulate the use of traffic signs, signals, and markings; driving on the right side of the roadway, overtaking, and passing; the right-of-way of approaching vehicles; the rights and duties of pedestrians; turning, starting, and signaling; stopping at railroad crossings and entering highways from private drives, alleys, and buildings; school buses; speed restrictions; stopping, standing, and parking; backing, driving on sidewalks, crossing fire hoses, littering, and "laying drags"; duties in an accident; and the use of bicycles, play vehicles, motorcycles, motorized carts, and mopeds. They also define and specify penalties for serious traffic offenses.[28]

These rules apply throughout Georgia. Municipalities are given powers to adopt regulations that are supplemental to the Uniform Rules of the Road. They also may adopt by ordinance any or all of these rules by reference; publishing or posting the provisions in full is not required. The adopting ordinance must use the same or similar wording that appears in Figure 19-1.[29]

FLOOD CONTROL

Many drainage problems do not exist until humans intervene in the hydrologic cycle by building unwisely in relation to natural drainage patterns. Often, highways, streets, parking lots, and other impervious surfaces are constructed within a city without proper attention being given to where the runoff will go and how it will affect citizens and properties downstream or elsewhere in the city.

A municipality should have a comprehensive drainage and flood control plan and use it when approving new developments. This plan should be uniformly applied to avoid developments and other construction that create flood problems. A city can be held liable for damage caused by its action or inaction with respect to drainage and flood control.[30]

Storm Water Utilities

Several local governments in Georgia have established a storm water utility to fund drainage improvements projects. User fees are charged within a special assessment district and are dedicated to support the maintenance and upgrade of storm drain systems. Most fees are based at least in part of the percentage of impervious cover of the parcels of developed land within the utility. For simplicity, some utilities limit such methods to commercial property and charge a flat rate on residential property.[31] Storm water bills are often included with a city's water or sewer bill.

In establishing a storm water utility, municipal officials are urged to take great care to ensure that the utility charge is a service fee rather than a tax. The City of Atlanta storm water utility, established in 1999, was

Figure 19-1. *Model Ordinance: Georgia Rules of the Road*

(Municipality) of _____

Ordinance number _____

An ordinance adopting the Georgia Uniform Rules of the Road, Code Sections (_____ to _____ [except for Code Sections _____]) of Chapter 6 of Title 40 of the Official Code of Georgia Annotated, to regulate traffic upon the public streets of the (Municipality) of _____ and repealing ordinance number _____ and all other ordinances and sections of ordinances in conflict herewith.

It is ordained by _____ as follows:

Section 1. Adoption by reference. Pursuant to Chapter 6 of Title 40 of the Official Code of Georgia Annotated, Code Sections 40-6-372 through 40-6-376, Code Sections (_____ to _____ [except for Code Sections _____]) of that chapter known as the Uniform Rules of the Road and the definitions contained in Code Section 40-1-1 are hereby adopted as and for the traffic regulations of this (Municipality) with like effect as if recited herein.

Section 2. Penalties. Unless another penalty is expressly provided by law, every person convicted of a violation of any provision of this ordinance shall be punished by a fine of not more than _____ dollars or by imprisonment for not more than _____ days or by both such fine and imprisonment.

Section 3. Repeal. The (existing ordinances covering the same matters as embraced in this ordinance) are hereby repealed and all ordinances or parts of ordinances inconsistent with the provisions of this ordinance are hereby repealed.

Section 4. Effective date. This ordinance shall take effect from and after the _____ day of _____, 20 _____.

(O.C.G.A. §40-6-374)

found to be unconstitutional by a superior court judge. The court found that the city was generating revenues for unspecified purposes rather than earmarking money for storm water management purposes. The Georgia Supreme Court, however, upheld the constitutionality of storm water utilities, if appropriately constructed, in a 2004 decision involving Columbia County.

WATER

The objective of a municipal water system is to deliver potable water to citizens and customers. People generally give little thought to the water system except on those rare occasions when they turn on the faucet and no water comes out or the water has an odor or peculiar taste. But very little thought is generally given to where the water comes from, how it is treated, and the vulnerability of the supply.

The operation of a city water supply system has become increasingly complex and expensive in recent years largely because of unfunded mandates by the state and federal governments. Both surface water and groundwater sources, no matter where they are located, should be protected against pollution and misuse. The Federal Safe Drinking Water Act establishes very strict water quality standards.

It is imperative that a municipality's staff include competent and diligent water personnel to ensure that the water system does not deteriorate. Persons supervising the operation of public water supply systems and wastewater treatment plants must be certified by the State Board of Examiners for Certification of Water and Wastewater Treatment Plant Operators and Laboratory Analysts.[32] The Environmental Protection Division (EPD) of the Georgia Department of Natural Resources (DNR) has established several classifications of water supply systems.[33]

A master water development plan should be produced to avoid expensive mistakes in expanding the system. Computer programs should be used when possible to calculate line sizes and pressure requirements for community extensions. The community water system usually is a proprietary service supported by customer or citizen charges based upon the quantity of water used. Water ordinarily is metered, and billing is determined by monthly meter readings.

Ordinarily, local governments must borrow money in order to make major expansions and modifications to water systems. Selling revenue bonds is the common method used to provide these funds. In some cases, general obligation bonds pledging the full faith and credit of the city are used to finance water systems.

Planning for an adequate, dependable long-term water supply is critical to any community's long-term viability. In 2004, the Georgia General Assembly enacted legislation requiring the development of a statewide comprehensive water management plan. As a result, integration of local water supply plans with the state water management plan will be necessary in the future.

A municipal water system must be adequate to supply amounts of water needed for peak hourly flows both for domestic purposes and required fire flows. It is therefore very important that all water used by the system be properly accounted for. It is not uncommon for cities to have 20 to 25 percent of water that is unaccounted for, although a water loss of more than 10 percent may indicate that a major problem exists in the system. Slow meters, broken lines, unmetered water, or a combination of all of these factors could account for such water loss.

Each city should have an emergency plan for when the water system is out of service because of natural disasters, power failure, contamination, major main break, loss of water source, or a terrorist event. At minimum, such an emergency plan should include

- a list of city equipment and available private equipment that can be used for repairs,
- a list of local contractors who can be called upon to make repairs in times of emergency,
- reciprocal agreements that will enable calling upon neighboring water systems for assistance,
- a list of employees who can be called upon to help during such emergencies (complete with addresses and telephone numbers), and
- a plan of action based on hypothetical scenarios that is regularly reviewed by system personnel.

Terrorists and ordinary vandals pose a threat to the safety of drinking water. The U.S. Environmental Protection Agency (EPA) requires public water systems serving at least 3,300 people to conduct security assessments.

Persons supervising and operating a municipal water supply system must regularly perform water supply quality tests. These tests are to be taken at specified intervals and the results sent to DNR for analysis. DNR will immediately report to the city any deviation from approved water quality standards and demand corrective action.[34] For more discussion on water issues, see Chapter 16.

SEWERAGE

In a modern municipal sewerage system, liquid wastes are collected through two types of sewer systems: sanitary and storm systems. Sanitary sewers collect contaminated, putrescible liquid from the plumbing systems of buildings and carry it to a sewage treatment plant or other suitable place of disposal. Storm sewers collect rainwater and carry it to natural water courses or bodies of water in such a way as to prevent flooding.[35]

Overall, people give little thought to the public sewerage system; it is virtually invisible to the user, and the old adage "out of sight, out of mind" applies. Therefore, many problems in a sewerage system may go unnoticed by the general public until they become significant, and even then the public may be apathetic toward these problems until they cause personal inconvenience. As population density increases, though, the disposal of liquid waste becomes more complex and expensive.

The sanitary sewer collection and treatment system should evolve out of a long-term master planning process so that it can be developed in an orderly fashion and as many costly mistakes as possible avoided. This system must be laid to grade so that the waste-carrying liquids will be moved along by gravity throughout the community to lift station points that raise the waste-carrying liquids to a higher elevation and release them to be carried along by gravity again until ultimately they reach the wastewater treatment plant. The materials are then treated and disposed of in a manner that is acceptable to the Environmental Protection Division and to the U.S. Environmental Protection Agency. There are a number of acceptable processes for the treatment of wastewater, and the selected method must be carefully executed with the help of a qualified engineer so that maximum water quality is maintained at the lowest possible cost.

Local governments generally charge a fee for sanitary sewerage systems, as they do for water systems. Sewerage systems are usually built with bond proceeds and, since they are ordinarily proprietary services, they tend to be financed through the issuance of revenue bonds. With the numerous mandates from both state and federal governments, sanitary treatment and disposal of sewage has become much more expensive. Because these mandates are unfunded, the users paying for the service must bear its cost.

SOLID WASTE

The handling of solid waste was radically changed with the passage of the Georgia Comprehensive Solid Waste Management Act of 1990.[36]

This law requires that each government develop or be included in an approved solid waste management plan.

Many methods of solid waste collection are used in Georgia, ranging from backyard pickup to a fully automated curbside system. Some systems are more economically feasible than others, but one major factor determining which should be used is the level of service that a particular community desires, demands, and is willing to pay for.

Most solid waste in Georgia is delivered to a sanitary landfill, where refuse is compacted and covered with a layer of dirt. The chief factor in developing a satisfactory landfill operation is the acquisition of a large tract of relatively inexpensive, conveniently located land. When land cost is at a premium, special landfill tractors can be used to tightly compress refuse for more economical disposal. In recent decades, it has become increasingly difficult to site new landfill facilities.

Recycling and Transfer Station

Community recycling initiatives can extend landfill life by reducing the amount of the waste stream. Examples of programs directed at landfill waste stream reduction include residential participation in separation of recycling products from household waste collection; recycling of recoverable materials such as motor oil, batteries, and tires; roadside litter prevention and patrols; composting; and Christmas tree chipping. Information on these and other programs can be obtained from the Georgia Department of Community Affairs, Office of Environmental Management.

Transfer stations are facilities that allow the disposal of contained household waste via dumpsters at such facilities. Normally, fees are associated with the disposal of such wastes. Also, transfer stations often include recycling centers that accept all forms of recyclables such as cardboard, plastics, scrap metal, glass, and paper. Often, these facilities are small in scale and are unable to accommodate a large influx of waste disposal.

In a recycling program, recyclables are collected and then separated from nonrecyclable materials, processed, and marketed. In a source-separation process, segregated recyclables usually are stored by the local government until there is a sufficient amount to send to a processor or market. Normally in small communities, no further processing of the recyclables occurs (i.e., can flattening, glass pulverizing). Rather, this activity may be conducted by private recyclers or dealers. During commingled collection, the local government transports the recyclables to a materials recycling facility, where the recyclables are segregated. Segregation usually occurs by hand, but occasionally automated systems are used. In mixed collection, all waste is collected together and taken to a central processing facility.

The processing of recyclables generally includes those activities that prepare the material for final shipment to the recycler or dealer. Once segregated, recyclables may need further processing to make them more dense or to package them in a way that is appropriate for final shipment.

One should bear in mind that recycling does not occur until someone uses the recycled product to make new products. Therefore, if no market exists for the recycled materials, no recycling takes place. It is generally the responsibility of the local government to locate markets for these recycled materials.

Composting

Another method of reducing the solid waste stream is composting, a process of aerobic biological decomposition of organic materials to produce a stable and usable organic topsoil that does not require disposal. Resources used to create the final compost product originate from roughly 70 percent of the municipal solid waste stream that is organic material (e.g., food waste/scraps, yard and lawn clippings). The primary activities associated with composting are (1) collections/receiving wastes for composting, (2) processing the waste, and (3) marketing. A local government can collect or receive waste for composting from a variety of sources such as active yard waste collection programs, vacuuming of leaves, etc.

Some cities provide solid waste collection through a tax levy. Most local governments, however, charge a service fee, which is determined by the local governing authority and based on the level of service provided. One rationale is that the fee method makes citizens more aware of the cost of providing this service. Some cities have implemented "pay-as-you-throw" fee structures, with fees based on the amount of solid waste collected, as a way of encouraging waste reduction and recycling.

ELECTRICITY AND NATURAL GAS

In most Georgia cities, electricity and natural gas are provided through a franchise agreement with a private company. These contracts should be carefully examined by someone knowledgeable in the field to determine if they are consistent with the industry and bring an equitable benefit to the city for the use of its rights-of-way. The Georgia Municipal Association (GMA) has drafted model franchise agreements that can be very helpful to cities that are exploring and comparing such franchises.

Several municipalities in Georgia own their electric or gas system and, in some cases, both utilities. Thus, those cities are distributors of these services. Municipally owned gas and electric systems can be profitable to the city if rates are cost based and the amount transferred to the general fund is kept at a reasonable level (i.e., sufficient funds are maintained in the utility enterprise fund for operations, maintenance, and capital expenses). Developing a master electric and/or gas plan is critical: the systems must be able to expand as needed, and the investment required for expansion must be timed to avoid a long delay in the return on the investment. The Municipal Electric Authority of Georgia (MEAG)[37] and the Municipal Gas Authority of Georgia (MGAG)[38] were created to assist Georgia cities in keeping up with their respective industries. Cities should carefully consider whether it is to their advantage to participate in the programs of these authorities.

Municipal electric systems are not regulated by the Georgia Public Service Commission except in the protection of underground utilities during excavation and according to the Georgia Territorial Electric Service Act.[39] Municipal natural gas systems are regulated by the Georgia Public Service Commission for pipeline safety and the protection of underground utilities.

Cities that own their own utility (or utilities) should hire professional staff to operate their electric or natural gas utility.

TELECOMMUNICATIONS AND CABLE TELEVISION

Georgia cities are finding it necessary to ensure that there is effective communication between businesses and their customers and government and its citizens and among citizens themselves. The convergence of cable television, telephone, and other transport mediums of video, voice, and data over a common cable is increasingly likely.

It is incumbent on municipal governments to facilitate the provision of these services to their constituents. Access to telecommunications services may take the form of negotiating a franchise agreement with a private provider or the city providing the service itself. Organizations such as GMA, other cities, and private consultants may assist in these evaluations. Care should be taken when choosing consultants to ensure that they are objective in their proposals.

If a municipal government is to evaluate honestly the possibility of providing telecommunications or cable services to its community, certain actions should be taken. First, and most important, the municipal and community leadership should evaluate why the city should provide these services. The greater the support for proposals among a city's elected officials, the greater the likelihood that informed decisions will be made in the evaluation process. A municipality must comply with the Georgia Fair Cable Competition Act in determining whether or not to provide cable television service. If a city is considering operating its own telecommunications system in conjunction with or independent of cable television service, PSC rules and procedures may apply. It should also be noted that specialized personnel required to effectively operate a CATV or telecommunications system may be needed.

Telecommunications

Though somewhat restricted by Section 253 of the Telecommunications Act of 1996, cities retain regulatory authority over the occupation and use of public rights-of-way for the provision of telecommunications services. Exercise of such authority can be in the form of a franchise agreement or revocable encroachment license that sets the terms and conditions of street occupancy and provides compensation to the city in the form of a franchise or license fee. This is usually based on a percentage of revenue (typically 3 to 5 percent) and/or a specified amount per unit occupancy. Such fees are typically in addition to any permitting fees normally assessed by the community.

Because of the rapidly changing nature of advanced telecommunications technologies and services, it is generally recommended that franchises be granted for a term of between three and seven years. In addition, court decisions throughout the country periodically alter the regulatory environment. GMA can provide expert assistance to cities on these matters.

Cable Television

In order to ensure the best possible cable service from a private provider, a city government would be wise to retain a cable television (CATV) franchise expert for assistance, both in the franchise negotiation process and to ascertain that the CATV operator satisfies its obligations under the franchise agreement. GMA can also help cities keep pace with the constantly changing federal and state regulations regarding a city's authority and control over its CATV franchise(s).

Federal law requires that all franchises be nonexclusive. A provider enjoys a presumption of franchise renewal upon satisfying statutorily defined conditions, including substantial compliance with the existing franchise; the provision of service that meets the needs of the community; and possessing the legal, technical, and financial capabilities to operate the system. The typical period covered by a franchise agreement is between 10 and 15 years.

The fee paid to the city by the CATV company should be based on a percentage of its gross revenues, typically 3 to 5 percent. The franchise agreement should provide that the municipality has a right to conduct its own independent audit of these fees and compliance with other obligations. The franchise should provide channels and equipment to be used by the city or public access and education free of charge.

RATES, RESERVES, AND TRANSFER POLICIES

Because most of the facilities discussed in this chapter are operated as enterprise funds, and their costs of operation are recovered through fees for service, municipalities should therefore operate in a businesslike manner. Rates should be based on the cost to provide the service and should be competitive with other service providers in Georgia. Rates should include sufficient reserve components to cover for the infrastructure necessary to provide the service. These reserves should be separate from normal operations dollars and used to maintain and repair major components of the infrastructure.

The citizens of the municipality that has invested the necessary capital to construct public utility systems should expect dividends from that investment. These dividends may take many forms such as the economic development of the community, reduced property taxes, and an improved quality of life. These dividends usually take the form of transfers from the enterprise to the city's general fund. The transfers can be based on an expected rate of return from the enterprise, a percentage of gross revenues, or some other method, but it must be reasonable and not beyond the ability of the enterprise to transfer under existing rates.

The ability of each enterprise to operate entirely from its own rates without permanent subsidies from other enterprise areas or general fund taxes is extremely important and should be established in the planning and budget process every year. If the enterprise areas of water, sewer, natural gas, and other publicly owned utilities are operated in a prudent and businesslike manner, they will continue to provide valuable dividends for current and future citizens of the municipal community.

NOTES

1. Donald C. Stone, *Professional Education in Public Works/Environmental Engineering and Administration* (Chicago: American Public Works Association, 1974), 2.
2. Portions of this chapter are drawn from Jerry A. Singer, "Public Works and Public Utilities," in *Handbook for Georgia Mayors and Councilmembers*, 2nd ed., ed. J. De-

vereux Weeks and Emily Honigberg (Athens: Carl Vinson Institute of Government, University of Georgia, 1984).
3. OFFICIAL CODE OF GEORGIA ANNOTATED (O.C.G.A.) §43-15-2.
4. O.C.G.A. §43-15-24
5. *Selection and Use of Engineers, Architects and Professional Consultants* (Kansas City, MO: American Public Works Association, 1977), 1.
6. *Qualifications-Based Selection* (Washington, DC: American Council of Engineering Companies, n.d.).
7. *See* O.C.G.A. §32-4-93. R. Perry Sentell Jr., *The Law of Municipal Tort Liability in Georgia*, 4th ed. (Athens: Carl Vinson Institute of Government, University of Georgia, 1988).
8. O.C.G.A. tit. 32.
9. O.C.G.A. §32-1-8.
10. O.C.G.A. tit. 32, ch. 3.
11. O.C.G.A. §32-4-91.
12. O.C.G.A. §32-4-92.
13. Ibid.
14. O.C.G.A. §§32-4-92, 32-6-2.
15. Ibid.
16. O.C.G.A. §32-6-50.
17. O.C.G.A. §§32-4-92, 32-4-119.
18. Ibid.
19. O.C.G.A. §32-4-94.
20. O.C.G.A. §32-4-92.
21. O.C.G.A. §§32-4-113, 32-4-114
22. O.C.G.A. tit. 32, ch. 6, arts. 1, 3, 4, 5.
23. O.C.G.A. tit. 32, ch. 6, art. 6.
24. O.C.G.A. tit. 32, ch. 6, art. 8.
25. O.C.G.A. tit. 32, ch. 3, art. 1.
26. O.C.G.A. tit. 40, ch. 6.
27. O.C.G.A. §40-6-3.
28. O.C.G.A. tit. 40, ch. 6, arts. 2–13; tit. 40, ch. 6, art. 15.
29. O.C.G.A. §§40-6-370–40-6-372, 40-6-374.
30. *See* Sentell, *n*5.
31. Janice Kaspersen, "The Stormwater Utility: Will It Work in Your Community?" *Stormwater: The Journal for Surface Water Quality Professionals* 1, no. 1 (2000): 22–28.
32. O.C.G.A. §§43-51-1–43-51-9; Ga. Comp. R. & Regs. ch. 750-1-750-10.
33. O.C.G.A. §43-51-10.
34. Ga. Comp. R. & Regs. ch. 391-3-5.
35. International City Managers' Association, *Municipal Public Works Administration*, 5th ed. (Chicago: International City Managers' Association, 1957), 289.
36. O.C.G.A. §12-8-20 et seq,
37. O.C.G.A. tit. 46, ch. 3, art. 3.
38. O.C.G.A. tit. 46, ch. 4, art. 4.
39. O.C.G.A. tit. 46, ch. 3, art. 1, pt. 1.

20

Mike Gleaton and Jerry A. Singer*

Building Codes and Code Enforcement

Construction code enforcement is an important issue facing Georgia's cities and counties. Georgia continues to attract thousands of new residents and new businesses each year. This growth requires construction of new housing, offices, retail establishments, industries, etc. Ensuring that these new buildings are structurally sound and safe and assets to both their owner and the community where they are located makes local construction code enforcement a high priority for Georgia's cities and counties. Georgia's Constitution and state law gives local governments broad discretionary powers in the enforcement of the Georgia State Minimum Standard Codes. It is essential that local governments take the necessary steps to update their local ordinances to reflect current state law, particularly with respect to administrative and enforcement procedures.

CONSTRUCTION CODES AND THE PROGRESSIVE COMMUNITY

Georgia's uniform construction codes are designed to help protect the life, health, and property of all Georgians from the hazards of faulty design and construction; unsafe, unsound, and unhealthy structures and conditions; and the financial hardship resulting from unnecessarily high construction and operating costs of houses, buildings, and similar structures.

Municipalities are not mandated by state law to enforce the state building codes or to issue building permits and perform construction inspections. Rather, cities may choose which, if any, of the state minimum

---

* Parts of the chapter contain or are based on work by this author from earlier editions of the *Handbook for Georgia Mayors and Councilmembers*.

standard codes they intend to enforce within their jurisdictions. However, the Uniform Codes Act provides that "any municipality or county either enforcing or adopting and enforcing a construction code shall utilize one or more of the state minimum standard codes...."[1] Therefore, in order for a city to have a construction codes enforcement program, at least one of the state minimum standard codes must be enforced locally.

Purposes of Building Codes

Enforcing building codes is an important city function. The purposes of construction codes are to[2]

- save lives by preventing structural fires resulting from defective installation of materials or the installation of improper materials in existing and new buildings;
- protect individual health by assuring construction of facilities that are structurally safe, weather-tight, properly ventilated, adequately lighted, and designed to encourage maximum safe usage;
- save construction costs by preventing the use of more materials than are required for new buildings or existing structures;
- protect property by assuring that structures will serve the purposes for which they are designed;
- encourage sound, steady growth by assisting builders, owners, and developers in the use of acceptable technological improvements in the building trades;
- reduce the chances of costly litigation involving property disputes, interference in the use of light and air, or other matters that can arise during the course of construction; and
- permit qualification for federal grant assistance requiring code enforcement as a prerequisite to funding eligibility.

Advantages to City Enforcement of State Codes

There are a number of advantages to municipal enforcement of state building codes, including

- protecting the life, health, and property of citizens and thus helping to provide a better living environment;
- helping to prevent the creation of slums and thereby contribute to the maintenance of a stable tax base;
- establishing the foundation for a permit system;
- providing a means of systematically updating property assessments;

- obtaining lower insurance rates for residents;
- fulfilling prerequisites for federal rehabilitation grants;
- meeting the requirements of other state and federal laws, such as the water conservation act;
- ensuring that local construction is built in compliance with state codes; and
- demonstrating that the city is a progressive local government.

UNIFORM CODES ACT

The Uniform Codes Act became effective on October 1, 1991.[3] The act was adopted to establish standard building codes that are applicable statewide. Prior to that date, municipalities and counties could adopt any code or standard that they desired to enforce locally. This local control resulted in a great deal of variation in the construction codes and standards that were enforced throughout the state. This law authorizes the governing authority of any municipality or county to enforce the 10 state minimum standard codes. There are 8 mandatory codes and 2 permissive construction codes that cities may enforce.[4] Each of the 10 state minimum standard codes typically consists of a base code (e.g., the International Building Code as published by the International Codes Council and a set of statewide amendments to the base code. Georgia law provides that 8 of these codes are "mandatory" (i.e., applicable to all construction, whether or not the codes are locally enforced) and 2 are "permissive" (i.e., only applicable if a local government chooses to adopt and enforce one or more of these codes).

Since Georgia law gives the mandated codes statewide applicability, cities and counties are not required to and, in fact, should not adopt the actual codes themselves in order to enforce them.[5] Local governments should only adopt administrative procedures that authorize local enforcement of the state-adopted mandatory codes. However, the local governments are empowered to choose which of the mandatory codes they wish to enforce locally.

STATE MINIMUM STANDARD CODES

The eight construction codes are mandatory (see Table 20-1), and any structure built in Georgia must comply with these codes, whether or not the local government chooses to enforce these codes locally.[6] It is not necessary for local governments to adopt any of the mandatory state

310   MUNICIPAL SERVICES

Table 20-1. *Mandatory Codes*

International Building Code
International Fuel Gas Code
International Mechanical Code
International Plumbing Code
National Electrical Code
International Fire Code
International Energy Conservation Code
International Residential Code[a]

Note: All of the mandatory codes have Georgia amendments that are applicable statewide.

[a] The General Assembly specifically omitted the plumbing requirements of the International Residential Code for One- and Two-Family Dwellings. Therefore, the plumbing requirements of the International Plumbing Code and the electrical requirements of the National Electric Code must be used in one- and two-family construction.

minimum standard codes because these codes have already been adopted as the official codes of Georgia by state law. However, in order to enforce any of the mandatory minimum standard codes, a city must adopt an ordinance or ordinances stating that it intends to enforce that code or codes.

The two optional codes are available for city or county adoption and enforcement (see Table 20-2). Unlike the mandatory codes, in order for a city to enforce one or more of these permissive codes within its jurisdiction, the city must first adopt the code or codes that it wants to enforce, either by ordinance or resolution. The city must file a copy of the ordinance or resolution adopting a permissive code and authorizing its enforcement with DCA.[7]

The State Codes Advisory Committee

DCA's state codes advisory committee plays a major role in the review and periodic update of the state construction codes. This committee is made up of 21 members who are experts in the various codes and who are chosen to represent the diverse interests of citizens, builders, financiers, designers, city and county code enforcement officials, and other groups. The Georgia Safety Fire Commissioner and the Commissioner of the Department of Human Resources or their designees are ex-officio members of the advisory committee. The commissioner of DCA appoints the remaining members. The state codes advisory committee uses task forces to assist in the review of new codes or proposed amendments to existing codes. A task force is made up of experts in a particular field, such as building, mechanical, plumbing, electrical, gas,

Table 20-2. Permissive Codes

International Property Maintenance Code
International Existing Building Code

housing, fire prevention, or energy. Codes experts in the Planning and Environmental Management Division of DCA provide staff support for these task forces.

State construction codes are reviewed, amended, and revised as necessary by DCA with the approval of the Board of Community Affairs. Code amendments to Georgia's codes may be initiated by the department or upon recommendation from any citizen, profession, state agency, political subdivision of the state, or the state codes advisory committee. New provisions and amendments or modifications of the state construction code requirements go into effect after approval by the Board of Community Affairs and upon filing with the Secretary of State in accordance with the state Administrative Procedure Act. The approval of the state codes advisory committee must be obtained before the proposed changes are submitted to the Board of Community Affairs. The board cannot alter the recommendations of the state codes advisory committee. It has two options: approve the recommendations as submitted by the state codes advisory committee or deny them and return them to the advisory committee.

Administration and Enforcement of the State Minimum Standard Codes

In order to properly administer and enforce the state minimum standard codes, cities and counties must adopt reasonable administrative provisions. These provisions should include procedural requirements for the enforcement of the codes, provisions for hearings, provisions for appeals from decisions of local inspectors, fees, and any other procedures necessary for the proper local administration and enforcement of the state minimum standard codes. Local governments are empowered to inspect buildings and other structures to ensure compliance with the codes, to employ inspectors and other personnel necessary for enforcement, to require permits and establish charges for such permits, and to contract with other governments for code enforcement.[8]

Some cities and counties have mistakenly assumed that DCA has adopted the "administrative" chapter (chapter 1 of each code), thereby providing local governments with the administrative procedures required by the law. This assumption is incorrect. DCA has excluded the administrative chapters, and state law specifically allows local governments to adopt by ordinance or resolution any reasonable provisions or procedures necessary for the proper local administration and enforcement of the codes.

DCA periodically reviews, amends, and/or updates the state minimum standard codes. If a local government chooses to enforce any of these codes locally, it may only enforce the latest editions adopted by DCA (along with the statewide amendments also adopted by DCA). DCA has developed both a sample resolution and ordinance that can be used as a guide for local governments in the development of their administrative code procedures. Cities should contact the Construction Codes Section at DCA for a copy of this sample resolution or ordinance and for any technical assistance needed in the development of a local code enforcement program.

Appendices

It should be noted that the Uniform Codes Act states that the appendices of the codes are not enforceable by a local government unless they are (1) specifically referenced in the code text adopted by DCA or (2) specifically included in an administrative ordinance adopted by a municipality or county. If any appendices to a particular code have been adopted by DCA, they will be noted in the Georgia amendments to that base code.

Local Code Amendments

The Uniform Codes Act allows cities to adopt local amendments to the state minimum standard codes under certain conditions. DCA does not approve or disapprove any local code amendment. The department only provides recommendations to the local government. However, in order for a city to enforce any local code amendment, the local government must submit the proposed local amendment to DCA for review and recommendation.[9]

There are several requirements that local governments must meet in order to enact a local code amendment. These requirements are as follows:

- The requirements in the proposed local amendment cannot be less stringent than the requirements in the state minimum standard code;
- The local requirements must be based on local climatic, geologic, topographic, or public safety factors;
- The legislative findings of the city council must identify the need for the more stringent requirements; and

- The local government must submit the proposed amendment to DCA 60 days prior to the proposed local adoption and enforcement of any such amendment.

After a local government submits a proposed local amendment, DCA has 60 days in which to review the proposed amendment and forward its recommendation to the local government. DCA may respond in three ways: recommend adoption of the amendment, recommend against adoption of the amendment, or have no comment on the proposed amendment. If DCA recommends against the adoption of the proposed amendment, the local governing body must specifically vote to reject DCA's recommendation before the local amendment may be adopted. If DCA fails to respond within the 60-day timeframe, the local government may adopt the proposed local amendment without any recommendation from the department.

After adoption by the local governing authority, copies of all local amendments must be filed with DCA. Once the adopted local code amendment has been filed with DCA, the local government may begin enforcement. No local amendment becomes effective until the local government has filed a copy of the adopted amendment with DCA.

Code Enforcement Agency

Code enforcement should be organized so that only an official directly concerned with enforcing city codes reviews the inspector's performance.[10] The following criteria have been identified for successful local code enforcement programs:[11]

- All code enforcement activity should be located in one code enforcement department/agency.
- Code enforcement should be the sole function of that department/agency.
- The code enforcement agency should have departmental status.
- The code enforcement administrator or building official should be responsible directly and exclusively to the person serving as chief administrative officer of the city.
- All code enforcement staff should be properly trained and/or certified.

Permits and Inspections

Upon adoption, the building codes are enforced through a system of permits and inspection. Anyone planning construction or alterations covered by city codes must first submit a set of plans and specifications to the city building inspector. If these plans meet city code standards and other development regulations (i.e., zoning), a building permit is issued. The permit allows construction to proceed on the condition that the approved plans must be followed. The local building inspector makes periodic inspections to monitor compliance. Personnel requirements for code enforcement vary with the size of the city, the volume of building activity, and the type of mandatory and optional codes being enforced. In larger cities, code enforcement may require a department with several full-time staff members, while small cities may choose to contract with a county or another municipality that has a code enforcement program or enter into an intergovernmental agreement establishing a joint code enforcement system. There are several good examples of joint code enforcement programs around the state.

Regulatory Fees

Local governments are authorized to charge regulatory fees (i.e., permit and inspection fees) to help defray the costs associated with code enforcement activities. However, no local government is authorized to use permit or inspection fees as a means of raising revenue for general purposes. Therefore, the amount of regulatory or inspection fees charged by a city must approximate the reasonable cost of the actual regulatory activity performed by the city. A sample schedule of permit fees based on the estimated cost of construction is recommended to local governments (see Table 20-3).[12]

Codes Enforcement Training

To assist local government inspection officials in their code enforcement responsibilities, DCA sponsors construction code training programs conducted by Clayton College and State University. In addition, the department provides on-site construction code technical assistance, information, and referral services to cities and counties requesting these types of services. For more information on the current courses available and class schedules, contact the college's Continuing Education at 770-961-3556 or conted.clayton.edu.

Information and Assistance

The DCA Web site (www.dca.state.ga.us/planning) has free up-to-date information about Georgia's Construction Codes Program, including copies of the current state minimum standard codes with Georgia amendments, the Georgia Building Officials Directory, "Codes Update" (a newsletter published twice a year), along with helpful links and other related codes information, including guidelines to assist local governments

Table 20-3. Recommended Schedule of Permit Fees

A. Permit Fees

Total Valuation	Fee
$1,000 and less	No fee, unless inspection required, in which case a $15 fee for each inspection shall be charged
$1,001 to $50,000	$15 for the first $1,000 plus $5 for each additional thousand or fraction thereof, to and including $50,000
$50,001 to $100,000	$260 for the first $50,000 plus $4 for each additional thousand or fraction thereof, to and including $100,000
$100,001 to $500,000	$460 for the first $100,000 plus $3 for each additional thousand or fraction thereof, to and including $500,000
$500,001 and up	$1,660 for the first $500,000 plus $2 for each additional thousand or fraction thereof

B. Moving Fee
For the moving of any building or structure, the fee shall be $100.

C. Demolition Fee
For the demolition of any building or structure, the fee shall be
0 to 100,000 cu. ft., $50;
100,000 cu. ft. and over, $0.50 per 1,000 cu. ft.

D. Penalties
Where work for which a permit is required by this code is started or proceeded prior to obtaining said permit, the fees herein specified shall be doubled, but the payment of such double fee shall not relieve any persons from fully complying with the requirements of this code in the execution of the work or from any other penalties prescribed herein.

E. Plan-Checking Fees
When the valuation of the proposed construction exceeds $1,000 and a plan for the construction is required to be submitted, a plan-checking fee is required to be paid to the building official at the time of submitting plans and specifications for plan review. Said plan-checking fee shall be equal to one-half of the building permit fee. Such plan-checking fee is in addition to the building permit fee.[a]

In eliminating the need for an applicant to state the value of the estimated construction cost, the Building Valuation Data Table, which is available from the International Code Council, may be used.[b]

---

[a] Applies to permit fees for all construction, including alterations.

[b] The Building Valuation Data Table represents average square foot costs for most buildings. Costs are based on national averages and include total design, inspection, and construction of the particular building and appurtenances. The table presents 18 occupancy categories, e.g., dwelling, church, office, restaurant, and retail store. Each occupancy is sorted into nine types of construction, for which there is a square-foot construction cost.

with proper local amendment notification and inspections and notices of intention to adopt new code editions or proposed code amendments. To request additional information on Georgia's construction codes, training programs for local code enforcement officials, or technical assistance, contact the Georgia Department of Community Affairs, Codes and Industrialized Buildings Section, 60 Executive Park South, NE, Atlanta, GA 30329-2231, (404) 679-3118, fax (404) 679-0572, e-mail: codes@dca.state.ga.us.

NOTES

1. OFFICIAL CODE OF GEORGIA ANNOTED (O.C.G.A.) §8-2-28.
2. Adapted from Howard Schretter and Jerry A. Singer, Institute of Government and Institute of Community and Area Development, University of Georgia, Athens, Memorandum to the Mayor and Council, Planning Commission, and Chamber of Commerce of the City of Dahlonega, Georgia, 1972.
3. O.C.G.A. tit. 8, ch. 2, art. 1, pt 2.
4. O.C.G.A. §8-2-20(9)(B).
5. O.C.G.A. §8-2-25(a).
6. Code editions in effect as of January 1, 2004. The standard and Council of American Building Officials (CABO) codes are the same as the international codes.
7. O.C.G.A. §8-2-25(b)
8. O.C.G.A. §8-2-26(a).
9. O.C.G.A. §8-2-25(c).
10. Richard L. Sanderson, *Code and Code Administration* (Chicago: Building Officials Conference of America Inc., 1969), 102.
11. Ibid, 10.
12. International Code Council, http://www.iccsafe.org.

21

Daniel Hope III

Recreation and Parks

The role of government in providing public green spaces for Georgia's citizens is as old as the state itself. The precedent was set by General James Edward Oglethorpe when he designed and developed the city of Savannah in 1733. The local government role became more formal in 1911, when Atlanta started the first city parks department to provide essential park and recreation services. Today, a majority of Georgia's municipalities have recreation and park departments or provide recreation and park services through other means. These services have become an important and integral local government responsibility. In addition to the services provided by individual cities, recreation and park services are provided in a growing number of instances through cooperative efforts with other local governments.[1]

More than 90 percent of the population of Georgia is served by some type of local government recreation and park department.[2] In 2001, statewide, about 8.1 percent of local governments' general fund expenditures was spent for recreation and park services.[3]

At the onset of this chapter, it is important to note a distinction in terminology. The Department of Community Affairs (DCA) groups recreation and parks with libraries when it reports expenditures for "leisure services." As used in this chapter, the term "recreation and parks" refers to youth and adult sports, festivals and special events, senior centers, recreational classes, visual and performing arts, community centers, gymnasiums, public parks and open space, golf courses, swimming pools, greenways, trails, and other such programs and facilities.

WHY SHOULD MUNICIPAL GOVERNMENTS PROVIDE RECREATION AND PARK SERVICES?

Parks, open spaces, tree-lined streets, museums, festivals, recreation programs, and special events all contribute significantly to a community's overall sense of place. These factors, combined with a wide range of elements such as health, safety, education, housing, and transportation, define "quality of life" and determine whether a community is a desirable place to live and work.[4]

According to Partners for Livable Communities,[5] capital investments intended to provide recreation, entertainment, and cultural enrichment to community residents often have a low priority. When parks, museums, libraries, performing arts facilities, and other amenities that require land and structures are allowed to deteriorate or do not keep pace with population or changing demands, a community loses much that makes it attractive. As amenities grow more important for urban development, their loss may be counted in dollars lost to the local economy as well as a declining quality of life.[6]

There is a common myth that recreation and park services are just frills and not very necessary. Another is that the benefits of such leisure activities affect only individuals and not the community at large. Myths of this sort often lead elected officials to underfund recreation and park services. In reality, however, the level of importance that the public assigns to the benefits garnered from the use of local government recreation and park services is very high.[7]

According to the studies conducted in North America, only 7.5 percent of adults in the United States report that they are not interested in recreation and park services. More important, about 75 percent of citizens claim that recreation and park services are very valuable to them: 9 out of 10 people recognize significant benefits to themselves, their household, and their community from these services. About 4 out of 5 North Americans, a higher percentage than uses almost any other local government service, use their local government recreation and park systems. Even among nonusers, 80 percent acknowledge the many benefits of recreation and park services.

This popularity is why municipal governments have become increasingly involved in recreation. But why should a city put time and money into leisure services when many civic organizations, nonprofit agencies, or the private sector already provide recreational activities? For several reasons, recreation has become an accepted governmental responsibility:[8]

- Only when recreation and park services are provided by governmental agencies and therefore offered at little or no cost can the largest proportion of people take advantage of them. Many simply cannot afford to "buy" recreation services.
- With the growing value of land, the city is often the only organization with resources for acquiring, developing, and maintaining the land for public recreation, park, and open space purposes.
- Only local governments can ensure the provision of recreation and park services on a permanent basis. Private or volunteer agencies may be abolished, remove facilities from public use, or divert their use from recreational purposes. Public agencies, however, have greater permanency and are subject to public control and accountability.
- The potential rewards to the city for providing adequate recreational opportunities make them profitable investments.
- Citizens have demanded it.

Recreation and park departments provide numerous benefits to the municipality. These include increased self-esteem, better physical and mental health, and decreased stress and tension for individuals; strengthened familial and friendship bonds for groups, leading to community solidarity; increased economic activity due to the community's attractiveness to business and industry; and an increased quality of life for the community as a whole. Further, the development of a stronger environmental ethic and better understanding of the need for stewardship also result from recreation and leisure activities. Such benefits are gained on-site as part of the recreation experience, and they carry over into off-site effects such as a more positive self-image, improved work performance, better marital and family relationships, and an increased tax base as more people are attracted to the city because of its recreation and park services.[9]

WHAT DOES STATE LAW ALLOW A MUNICIPALITY TO DO?

Chapter 36-64 of the Official Code of Georgia Annotated allows local governments to establish and expend funds on recreation and park services. Often referred to as the Recreation Enabling Law, it empowers

> the governing body of any municipality or county, or combination thereof, to provide, establish, maintain, and conduct a recreation system and to acquire the property necessary to establish and maintain playgrounds, recreation centers, parks, and other recreational

facilities and activities. It also allows municipalities and counties to create recreation boards or commissions and outlines their powers and duties.

In order to carry out the provisions of the enabling law, local governments, or any board they designate, may employ play leaders, playground or community center directors, supervisors, recreation superintendents, or other officers or employees needed to carry out the services. The basic provisions of the law are as follows:

1. The governing body of any municipality may establish a system of supervised recreation. It may, by resolution or ordinance, vest the power to provide, maintain, and conduct parks, playgrounds, recreation centers, and other recreational activities and facilities in the board of education, park board, other existing body, or in a recreation board, whatever the governing body determines.

2. The governing authority may appropriate general municipal funds to conduct, equip, and maintain recreational lands and buildings. Staff may also be employed to manage the recreation and parks system. In addition, grants, gifts, money, or property for recreational purposes may be accepted by the agency responsible for recreation programs, with governing authority approval required when acceptance of real estate will subject the municipality to additional expense.[10]

3. Ten percent of the voters of a municipality may sign a petition requesting the governing authority to provide a supervised recreation system and to levy a recreation tax for that purpose, subject to approval by referendum.

4. The governing authority may propose that bonds be issued for the purpose of acquiring lands, buildings, or equipment for recreation purposes. Though not specifically mentioned in the law, special local option sales tax (SPLOST) funds may also be used for recreation and parks capital projects.

5. Cities and counties, as well as school boards, may jointly establish and maintain a recreation system.

WHAT MAKES UP A RECREATION AND PARK SYSTEM?

A recreation and park system is a major contributor to the overall quality of life in the city. To help local governments ensure the professional competence and effectiveness of park and recreation agencies, the National Commission on Accreditation developed standards of desirable practice organized into 10 major categories: agency authority, role, and responsibility; planning; organization and administration; human resources; finance (fiscal policy and management); program and services management; facility and land-use management; safety and security; risk management; and evaluation and research.[11]

Structure and Organization

The most commonly found structure for public recreation, park, and leisure service departments includes the following elements:

- *Organization and Administration.* Organization is the structure that clarifies the lines of authority and areas of responsibility for the agency to accomplish its mission. Administration is the process that ensures that an agency's resources are used to attain its predetermined goals. It must also provide maintenance for the care and upkeep of the areas, facilities, and structures; ensure that they are accessible; and protect the health and safety of the users.
- *Parks and Facilities.* Parks are areas of land and water not intensively developed for residential or economic purposes. They are set aside for their aesthetic, environmental, recreational, educational, or cultural value and may also serve transportation and historic preservation purposes. Facilities are the buildings and structures in parks needed to deliver leisure services (e.g., swimming pools, ball fields, community centers, and performing arts centers).
- *Programs and Services.* The activities or experiences offered are designed to enable the individual to maximize the use of his/her leisure time. These programs and services may be active or passive in nature and range from sports to the performing arts to environmental education.

Open Space

Closely related to recreation is the provision by the municipality of open space, especially in urban areas. In its broadest definition, open space is considered space that is not used for buildings or structures. Without open spaces our cities would be unrecognizable and unmemorable.[12] The need for open space in urban areas can be illustrated by the following statement:

> The people in an urban area need open space for many different purposes: to conserve water and other natural resources; as a reserve for future needs, often unpredictable; to maintain special types of agriculture which must be near cities; to prevent building in undesirable locations in order to avoid the hazard of floods or a

wasteful extension of services; to provide a rural environment for people who want to live that way; for pleasant views from urban areas; for a sense of urban identity; for buffers against noise and other nuisances; but above all, for recreation which can be combined with many other uses.[13]

The Community Greenspace law establishes a framework and the funding to help developed and rapidly developing counties and their municipalities preserve community open space.[14] The law also promotes the adoption of policies and rules that enable local governments to preserve at least 20 percent of their land areas as connected and open greenspace that can be used for informal recreation and natural resource protection. These green, open spaces must be permanently protected and preserved in an undeveloped, natural state or development must be consistent with natural resource protection or informal recreation. The Georgia Greenspace Commission is administratively attached to the Department of Natural Resources (DNR), which reviews and approves community greenspace programs. The funding comes from the Greenspace Trust Fund, which DNR also administers.

WHO IS RESPONSIBLE FOR OPERATING THE RECREATION AND PARK SYSTEM?

Once the decision to establish a recreation and park department has been made, the municipal governing authority must decide how it will be structured and who will be responsible for its operation. As previously pointed out, the municipal governing authority may, by resolution or ordinance, vest the power to provide, maintain, and conduct parks, playgrounds, recreation centers, and other recreational activities and facilities in the board of education, park board, or other existing body or in a recreation board. Although not mentioned in the enabling legislation, the municipal governing authority may establish an advisory board in lieu of a policy board. In either case, the ordinance or resolution must clearly define the specific functions, organization, and responsibilities of the recreation and parks department. The department can operate as a line department reporting directly to the city manager or administrator, to the mayor, to the entire municipal governing authority, or to a recreation and parks policy board. If a policy board or an advisory board is created, bylaws should be developed for operation of the board.

Several organizational structures are used throughout Georgia:

- Many recreation and park department heads report directly to the city manager or administrator.

- Some report directly to the mayor.
- The most significant number of departments are operated through a recreation and park policy board (often referred to as a recreation and park commission). In this case, the recreation and park board is appointed by the mayor and is responsible to the mayor and council.
- Some utilize an advisory board, and approximately 10 percent operate through an authority.[15]
- Regardless of how the chain of command is set up, many cities utilize an advisory committee as a way of involving citizens with the department. When a city and county operate a recreation and park department jointly, a policy board, with members appointed by each government, is recommended.

Functions of a Recreation and Park Policy Board

State law provides for the establishment of a policy board (also known as a legal board) and defines the powers and duties of the board, the number of board members and how they are appointed, the selection and replacement of individual members, and the length of a member's term.[16] A municipality that decides to have an advisory board or committee rather than a policy board should also address these four points in the local ordinance or resolution creating it.

As it carries out its responsibilities, a recreation and park policy board functions in five major areas:

1. *Policymaking.* The board sets policies to govern all phases of the department's operations. These policies should specify how the board wishes its human and fiscal resources to be used. Equally important, the policies should be designed to assure the health, safety, and well-being of participants.
2. *Program planning, review, and evaluation.* The board establishes long-range goals, approves yearly operating objectives, and annually reviews and evaluates the progress made toward achieving its goals and objectives.
3. *Financial management.* The board is responsible for assuring that sufficient income is generated from various sources to carry out the programs and operate the facilities that are approved by the board. Normally, the department's director develops the budget, and the board, after reviewing and modifying it as needed, recommends it to the mayor and council, which has final approval.

324   MUNICIPAL SERVICES

4. *Evaluation of the performance of the director.* The policy board provides an objective evaluation of the department's director. The municipal governing authority, the policy board, and the director must have a clear understanding of the director's responsibilities, authority, and duties.

5. *Community relations.* The board is obligated to make recreation programs and facilities available to all citizens within its jurisdiction who want to participate. It should maintain high standards for the programs conducted and facilities operated and ensure the accessibility, safety, and welfare of participants. The board should make itself known to the community through reports, earn respect through the integrity of its management, and achieve acceptance by striving to serve everyone in the community and by involving the community constructively in planning and evaluating its programs and facilities.

Recreation and Park Authorities

The Georgia Constitution provides for the creation of community improvement districts.[17] Community improvement districts, which are managed by a governing authority, are created to provide any one or more of several types of governmental services and facilities, including parks and recreation. The General Assembly may authorize the administrative body that oversees a community improvement district to incur debt and to levy taxes, fees, and assessments within the community improvement district only on real property used nonresidentially.[18]

WHAT RECREATION AND PARK SERVICES SHOULD BE OFFERED?

There are a variety of methods for gathering information about recreation and park services. Depending on the resources of the municipal staff, these methods can be used in-house or they can be contracted out.

The most common way to determine people's attitudes about the provision of recreation and park services is to collect information through a survey. The survey can vary in length and be administered in various ways: through face-to-face or telephone communication or through a computer, publication in the local newspaper, or the mail. Each method has pros and cons and costs associated with it.

In addition to obtaining specific information about recreation and park issues, it is important to understand the demographic makeup of the city. Demographic information is usually available in the city's planning office, the regional development center (RDC), local libraries, nearby colleges and universities, or on the Internet (through the Web sites of DCA, GMA, ACCG, and the U.S. Bureau of the Census, for example).

A community's residents are the best source of information about what kinds of recreation and park services are needed. Therefore, a community-based decision-making process is often the most effective means for determining the kind of services citizens desire.[19] It places the people who live in the county on the planning committee and invites them to open forums to discuss the issues. It is a strategic process for determining where the county is now, its preferred future, and how to get there.

The strategic plan develops the vision and mission for recreation, parks, and leisure services along with goals, objectives, and an action plan. It is broader in scope than the site plan, which is the design for an individual park or facility. From the strategic plan, a comprehensive plan that looks at the specific long-term and short-term dimensions of the recreation programs and the physical resources of the delivery system is developed.[20] The strategic plan and the action plan should be included in the city's comprehensive plan.

Municipal Recreation and Park Department

A municipality that has a recreation and park department already in place or is planning to establish one will need to address specific questions as it explores the community's needs or evaluates current performance.

Resources

Programs

What recreation programs are available in the city? Are they offered by public or private agencies? What gaps do the citizens of the city find in recreation services? Are the programs and services based on constituent needs, community opportunities, departmental philosophy and goals, and the provision of desirable experiences for clientele? What special programs are provided for distinct age or population groups (youth, the elderly, disabled, minorities, etc.)? Are the programs easily accessible to all citizens? Do they meet the community's broad range of leisure needs?

Facilities

What are the existing types of public and private facilities for swimming, individual and team sports, social activities, cultural arts, open space, greenways, etc.? What are the major strengths of the facilities? What are their major weaknesses or deficiencies? Are the facilities easily accessible to all citizens? Are some geographical areas of the community particularly deficient? Are buildings, areas, and historical and archaeological sites managed as part of the parks system? What is the importance of nonpublic agencies in providing recreation opportunities? Are unique natural areas protected? Is it possible to share facilities with the county, the public school system, nearby colleges and universities, or other public or private institutions in order to conserve limited resources?

Expansion and Development

What are the community's major needs for acquiring land or developing new facilities? Are certain facilities underused, inefficient, or out of date, and if so, do they need to be rehabilitated, expanded, or closed? What will the effects of such action be? What are the costs and/or savings of rehabilitation as opposed to new facility development? Can a true system of parks and facilities be created by linking them with existing trails, bikeways, and greenways? How?

Management

Personnel

Is there a professionally qualified administrator (who has a four-year degree in recreation and park administration and is nationally recognized as a certified professional) who is responsible to the managing authority for the management, direction, and control of the department? How should the human resources of the recreation and parks system be used? How many full- and part-time staff are needed? Are citizen volunteers used, and if so, in what ways? Has contracting some services to the private sector been considered?

Policy Development

What is the department's approach to developing overall recreation and park management policies? Is there currently a systematic process for scheduling regular maintenance and for replacing major fixtures and equipment that have a predictable useful life? Is there, or will there be, a systematic process of evaluation to assess outcomes and the operational efficiency and effectiveness of the department?

Budgeting

Are the fiscal policies that set guidelines for management and control of revenues, expenditures, and investment of funds set forth clearly in writing? How should the recreation and park system be financed? Does the annual budget include both revenues and expenditures for operations and capital improvements? What percentage of the total municipal budget was expended for recreation and parks in the last three years? How should revenues be allocated for administration, park maintenance, building maintenance, and recreation programs? Is there an established policy on the type of services for which fees and charges may be instituted and a basis for determining the amounts? Are fees and charges put in the municipality's general fund, or are they earmarked for recreation and park activities?

SUMMARY

The role of city government is to ensure the quality of its citizens' lives through the organization and delivery of services. One of the most important of these services is the recreation, parks, and leisure delivery system, which contributes to the overall quality of life and provides a significant contribution to the county's economy. A community's open spaces, parks, streetscapes, cultural facilities, and recreation programs are all part of its leisure services delivery system, and these amenities help create a sense of place, making a community one in which people want to live and raise their families.

NOTES

1. Steven L. Dempsey, Daniel Hope, and Kelly Howington, *Georgia City and County Recreation Services Study: Fiscal Year 2001* (Athens: Carl Vinson Institute of Government, University of Georgia, 2002).
2. *See* "Georgia Local Government Finance Highlights" published by the Georgia Department of Community Affairs (Atlanta, October 2002).
3. Dempsey, Hope, and Howington, *Georgia City and County Recreation Services Study: Fiscal Year 2001*.
4. R. H. McNulty, D. R. Jaconson, and R. L. Penne, *The Economics of Amenity: Community Features and Quality of Life* (Washington, DC: Partners for Livable Places, 1985).
5. The name was changed from Partners for Livable Places to Partners for Livable Communities in the 1990s. *See* http://liveable.com/.
6. McNulty, Jaconson, and Penne, *Economics of Amenity*.
7. J. Harper, G. Godbey, and S. Foreman, "Just the Facts: Answering the Critics of Local Government Park and Recreation Services," *Parks & Recreation* (August 1998): 78–81.
8. G. Lutzin Sidney, ed., *Managing Municipal Leisure Services* (Washington, DC: International City Management Association, 1980), 1–12.
9. L. Allen, B. Stevens, K. Hurtes, and R. Harwell, *Benefits-Based Programming of Recreation Services: Training Manual* (Ashburn, VA: National Recreation and Park Association, 1998).
10. *See* OFFICIAL CODE OF GEORGIA ANNOTATED (O.C.G.A.) ch. 36-71 on development impact fees.

11. *National Commission on Accreditation, Self-Assessment Manual for Quality Operation of Park and Recreation Agencies: A Guide to Standards for National Accreditation*, 2nd ed. (Ashburn, VA: National Recreation and Park Association, 1996).
12. P. Harnik, *Inside City Parks*. Report from the Trust for Public Land and the Urban Land Institute (Washington DC: Urban Land Institute, 2000).
13. *President's Commission on National Goals, Goals for Americans* (Englewood Cliffs, NJ: Prentice-Hall, 1960), 239.
14. O.C.G.A. ch. 36-22.
15. Dempsey, Hope, and Howington, *Georgia City and County Recreation Services Study*.
16. O.C.G.A. §36-64-5.
17. Ga. Const. art. IX, §7.
18. Ga. Const. art. IX, §7, ¶3(2)(c).
19. Daniel Hope and Steven L. Dempsey, "Achieving Consensus in Planning Recreation and Park Services," *World Leisure Journal* 42, no. 4 (2000): 56–64.
20. B. Van der Smissen, M. Moiseichik, V. Hartenburg, and L. Twardzik, eds., *Management of Park and Recreation Agencies* (Ashburn, VA: National Recreation and Park Association, 1999); 100.

22

William F. Bruton, Bobby D. Moody, Jackie T. Gibbs, Charles R. Swanson Jr.,* Mike Sherberger,* and J. Devereux Weeks*

Public Safety

POLICE SERVICES

The delivery of police services in the United States is overwhelmingly a function of local government. In fact, local units of government make 70 percent of all expenditures for this purpose and employ 77 percent of all police officers.[1] More than two-thirds of Georgia's municipalities provide police services.[2] Georgia's municipalities have police departments ranging in size from 1 to more than 1,000 officers.

A police department that is well operated can be a great advantage to a city. Because the police are so visible at all times of the day and night throughout a community, to some extent they become a gauge by which citizens measure the quality of the entire spectrum of municipal services. Further, a well-managed department can help avoid costly litigation. Police departments can be a source of time- and resource-consuming litigation. Suits may be lodged based on many grounds, such as claims that officers were improperly or insufficiently trained or were negligently employed or assigned, that they were not supervised, or that officers used excessive force in making arrests. Moreover, officers today seem more inclined to sue their employers, claiming that they have been sexually harassed or discriminated against on the basis of race or gender or that other important rights have been violated. A department that is improperly administered and operated can be a significant liability that can literally cost a city millions of dollars for just one incident of wrongful behavior, but a police department that is solid can be a considerable asset to a city.

---

* Parts of the chapter contain or are based on work by these authors from earlier editions of the *Handbook for Georgia Mayors and Councilmembers*.

A well-operated police department is a source of pride for a city and can enhance economic development because it is one of the aspects that industries or businesses evaluate very carefully when considering moving to a community.

The Functions of a Police Department

According to the American Bar Association (ABA), all municipal police departments must

1. identify criminal offenders and criminal activity and, where appropriate, apprehend offenders and participate in subsequent court proceedings;
2. reduce the opportunities for the commission of some crimes through preventive patrol and other measures;
3. aid individuals who are in danger of physical harm;
4. protect constitutional guarantees;
5. facilitate the movement of people and vehicles;
6. assist those who cannot care for themselves;
7. resolve conflict;
8. identify problems that are potentially serious law enforcement or governmental problems;
9. create and maintain a feeling of security in the community;
10. promote and preserve civil order; and
11. provide other services on an emergency basis.[3]

The ABA not only lists what the public perceives to be the police role—investigations, apprehension, and assistance in prosecution—but also includes functions associated with preserving the peace and order of a community. Despite popular perceptions of the police as crime fighters, in actuality, police officers spend no more than 15 percent of their time actually enforcing the law. The rest of the time they are engaged in delivering social services, such as mediating a dispute between two families regarding what one child said or did to another, helping the victims of natural disasters, and providing a link between those in need of help and the social service agency best able to assist them.

In response to these demands for police to spend so much time on community problems other than those that are purely crime related, a method referred to as community oriented policing (COP) has emerged. In contrast to traditional policing, which is largely reactive to crime, COP is proactive, attempting through the use of timely information to resolve community problems before they become crime problems. In this context, the individual officer no longer simply responds to calls for services and reported crimes. Instead, patrol officers also become coordinators of municipal services and neighborhood welfare. COP is primarily characterized by ongoing attempts to promote greater community involvement in the police function and customized police service.[4]

Organizing Police Services

General principles such as avoiding excessively wide spans of control should be followed, but there is no single best way to organize a police department. Many factors will influence the actual organizational structure, including the types of services provided, the extent of specialization, the total number of personnel, and the preferences of the chief.

Although there are a number of possibilities for structuring a police department, it is generally recognized that all of its elements fall into three broad categories: line, auxiliary, and staff (see Table 22-1).

Line units seek to achieve directly the broad goals prescribed for the police. The primary element of line services is uniformed patrol. In a large city, about 45 percent of the force will be assigned to uniformed patrol. Other line units include traffic and investigation. Auxiliary services are immediately supportive of the line units, including operation of the jail/detention facility, communications, the crime laboratory, records and criminal identification files, and evidence storage. Staff services also support the line function but less directly than do auxiliary services. Staff services include training, fiscal management, recruitment and selection, planning and research, and public information efforts. Only the largest cities have police departments with the full range of line, auxiliary, and staff elements. Medium-sized municipalities with a

Table 22-1. *Elements of Police Service*

Line	Auxiliary	Staff
Uniformed patrol	Jail/detention facility	Fiscal management
Traffic	Communications	Personnel recruitment, selection, training
Investigation	Crime laboratory	Planning and research
	Records and identification	Public information
	Evidence storage	

quarter to a half million residents may lack one or more elements, such as a crime laboratory, while the smallest police departments will have only the patrol elements.

Employment and Training Standards

Municipal law enforcement officers must meet the minimum standards of the Georgia Peace Officer Standards and Training Act,[5] which created the Peace Officer Standards and Training (POST) Council to certify persons subject to the act. Certification is based upon statutorily specified preemployment standards and successful completion of a mandatory 400-hour basic law enforcement training course, which must be completed within six months of a person's appointment as a peace officer.[6]

To fulfill preemployment requirements, a person must

1. be at least 18 years of age;
2. be a citizen of the United States;
3. have a high school diploma or its recognized equivalent;
4. not have been convicted by any state or by the federal government of any crime, the punishment for which could have been imprisonment in a federal or state prison or institution, nor have been convicted of sufficient misdemeanors to establish a pattern of disregard for the law;
5. be fingerprinted and a search made of local, state, and national fingerprint files to disclose any criminal record;
6. possess good moral character as determined by investigation under procedure(s) established by the council;
7. have an oral interview with the hiring authority or its representative to determine the applicant's appearance, background, and ability to communicate;
8. be found, after examination by a licensed physician or surgeon, to be free from any physical, emotional, or mental conditions that might adversely affect the exercise of the powers or duties of a peace officer; and
9. successfully complete a job-related academy entrance examination provided for and administered by the council.

As do all Georgia peace officers, chiefs of police and heads of law enforcement units must annually attend a minimum of 20 hours of training. Officers who fail to complete this training may lose their power of arrest unless they secure a waiver of this requirement from POST.[7] Any chief of police or department head of a law enforcement unit whose term of employment began after June 30, 1999, is required to complete 60 hours of executive law enforcement training in addition to the basic required training. This additional requirement may be waived if the chief or department head has served as a police chief or department head of a law enforcement unit since December 31, 1992, without more than a 60-day break in service and has previously completed the required executive training or other equivalent training.[8]

ACCREDITATION OF LAW ENFORCEMENT AGENCIES

The Commission on Accreditation for Law Enforcement Agencies (CALEA)[9] is a private, nonprofit organization formed in 1979 by four national associations: International Association of Chiefs of Police (IAP), National Organization of Black Law Enforcement Executives (NOBLE), National Sheriffs' Association (NSA), and Police Executive Research Forum (PERF). The commission has developed a national set of 445 law enforcement standards for all types and sizes of state and local agencies, including municipal departments. CALEA fosters police professionalism, which is reflected in the stated purpose of the commission:

> The Commission was formed for two reasons: to develop a set of law enforcement standards; and to establish and administer an accreditation process through which law enforcement agencies could demonstrate voluntarily that they meet professionally-recognized criteria for excellence in management and service delivery.[10]

The accreditation process is a voluntary undertaking. Recently, significant movement toward accreditation has been spurred by two factors. First, since most of the standards identify topics and issues that must be covered by written policies and procedures, successful accreditation offers a defense, or "liability shield," against civil litigation.[11] Second, CALEA provides a nationally recognized system for improvement. Fundamental to the accreditation process is assessment, beginning with self-assessment.[12] During this stage, an agency undergoes a critical self-evaluation that addresses the complete range of law enforcement services provided. Later, the agency is assessed by an outside team of law enforcement professionals who are brought on site to determine whether the agency has complied with applicable standards for a department of its type and size.

CALEA enjoys wide support among police executives and community leaders. Its accreditation process can be a substantial plus to a municipal police department that has performance problems. This process is not without its critics, however. Some view it as "window dressing—long on show and short on substance," a reference to the fact that some departments allegedly meet the standards by developing the necessary policies and then fail to actually follow them. Other critics have maintained that the process is control oriented and at odds with the important value of individual initiative.

Some law enforcement agencies that wish to undergo self-evaluation and improvement may not be financially able or willing to make the commitment to the CALEA process. The State of Georgia Law Enforcement Certification Program offers a professionally recognized methodology to make systematic improvements to such agencies.

The State of Georgia Law Enforcement Certification Program was developed in late 1996 through the collaborative efforts of the Georgia Association of Chiefs of Police, the Georgia Sheriffs' Association, the Georgia Peace Officer Standards and Training Council, the Georgia Municipal Association, the Association County Commissioners of Georgia, and the Georgia Police Accreditation Coalition. Although voluntary, the certification provides a comprehensive blueprint for effective, professional law enforcement. The process of certification begins with an agency's self-assessment, including review of the certification program's standards manual, determination and demonstration of the agency's compliance with the standards, and establishment and implementation of new procedures to address those standards not currently met by the agency. GACP then conducts an on-site assessment of the agency, observing the entire agency and interviewing its personnel. Finally, after reviewing the report of the on-site team, the Joint Review Committee either approves or denies certification, and, if approved, the award of certification is made to the agency.[13]

MUNICIPAL JAILS

Ordinarily, municipal jails or detention facilities are operated by police departments. The typical municipal jail is a holding facility for accused persons who have not been able to secure release on their own recognizance or bond or who are awaiting a preliminary hearing or trial. Because a jail's population typically consists of pretrial inmates, turnover may be as much as 75 percent every three days. Most jails also hold other types of prisoners, such as "overflow" inmates from other jurisdictions, inmates awaiting transfer to another facility, federal violators being housed pursuant to a contract, and offenders serving short-term sentences.

Jail inmates retain all of their rights as citizens, except as may necessarily be limited to properly operate the facility. When a city operates a jail, it assumes responsibility for the safe, legal, and humane custody of the inmates. Inmates have considerable rights. Jailers have been successfully litigated against for reasons such as unsanitary jail conditions; inadequate feeding, recreational facilities, and visitation policies; and protection from assaults by other inmates.

Jail Standards and Training

Georgia state statutes provide some guidance as to the requirements for operating a jail,[14] and a body of specialized case law has evolved regarding this area. Serious problems can arise when personnel are assigned to jail duty without proper training. The basic entry-level training course prescribed by POST does not constitute such training. It is an excellent foundation for general police work, but all personnel assigned to the jail should complete the 80-hour jail training course offered by the Public Safety Training Center in Forsyth.[15] Because of the extreme liability risk involved in operating a jail, municipalities should carefully evaluate the need to do so. When a jail is established, it should be in full compliance with applicable standards.

FIRE PROTECTION

Fire departments have changed from being the primary providers of fire prevention and suppression services to an integral component of a community's homeland security system. The transition has been a natural extension of fire departments developing an all-hazards response system. Fire departments now provide hazardous materials response, technical rescue, emergency medical treatment, and other specialized functions along with traditional fire prevention and suppression functions. Fire departments need the support of citizens and local elected officials to meet their obligations to mitigate all types of emergencies.

In general, any fire department of a municipality shall have the authority to

1. protect life and property against fire, explosions, hazardous materials, or electrical hazards;
2. detect and prevent arson;
3. administer and enforce the laws of the state as they relate to fire departments;

4. conduct programs of public education in fire prevention and safety;
5. conduct emergency medical services and rescue assistance;
6. control and regulate the flow of traffic in areas of existing emergencies, including rail, highway, water, and air traffic; and
7. perform all such services of a fire department as may be provided by law or which necessarily appertain thereto.[16]

In order to carry out its mission and authority, a municipal fire department must be legally organized. The chief administrative officer shall notify the executive director of the Georgia Firefighters Standards and Training Council if the organization meets the minimum requirements and rules to function as a fire department. In order to be legally organized, a fire department must

1. be established to provide fire and other emergency and nonemergency services in accordance with standards specified solely by the Georgia Firefighter Standards and Training Council and the applicable local government;
2. be capable of providing fire protection 24 hours a day, 365 days per year;
3. be responsible for a defined area of operations depicted on a map located at the fire station, the area of operations of which shall have been approved and designated by the governing authority;
4. be staffed with a sufficient number of full- or part-time or volunteer firefighters who have successfully completed basic firefighter training as specified by the Georgia Firefighters Standards and Training Council; and
5. possess certain minimum equipment, protective clothing, and insurance.[17]

The municipality responsible for the establishment and operation of a fire department should adopt a formal statement of purpose and define the responsibilities of the fire department. A functioning fire department needs

1. master planning,
2. adequate equipment and facilities,
3. employment and training standards,
4. ongoing training,
5. a fire prevention program,
6. knowledge of the fire-rating process, and
7. a sufficient water supply.

Master Planning

A fire plan can be used to improve fire department efficiency. The plan normally contains a survey of exiting services and a schedule for improving them. The plan should be revised regularly to reflect changes in the department's scope of mission.

Adequate Equipment and Facilities

Fire departments need various types of equipment, including

1. vehicles to transport firefighters to fires;
2. vehicles to transport and pump water to fires;
3. equipment on the vehicles to fight fires, such as pumps, ladders, hose, self-contained breathing apparatus, and fire extinguishers; and
4. protective clothing, such as coats, helmets, and boots.

Also required are heated fire stations located at sites that best serve the greatest number of residences and businesses. If possible, the stations should be large enough to conduct training sessions.

Effective Fire Communications

Citizens should be able to call a well-publicized emergency telephone number to report fires. Volunteer firefighters need to be equipped with communication devices such as pagers. The central dispatcher sends a signal activating a "beeper," or pager, that is carried by volunteer firefighters who respond to the alarm. Vehicles traveling to the fires should have the capacity for constant two-way communication with the dispatcher, other fire departments, and law enforcement agencies in the area.

Employment and Training Standards

Georgia law requires that all firefighters, fire and life safety educators, fire inspectors, and fire investigators meet certain standards. The Georgia Firefighters Standards and Training Council is charged with establishment of uniform minimum standards of employment and training and certification of those individuals who meet the standards.[18]

Any person employed or certified as a firefighter shall

1. be at least 18 years of age;
2. not have been convicted of a felony in any jurisdiction within 10 years prior to employment (with certain exceptions);
3. have good moral character as determined by investigation under procedure(s) approved by the council;

4. be fingerprinted and a search made of local, state, and national fingerprint files to disclose any criminal record;
5. be in good physical condition as determined by a medical examination and successfully pass the minimum physical agility requirements as established by the council; and
6. possess or achieve within 12 months after employment a high school diploma or a general education development equivalency.[19]

As a condition of continued certification, all firefighters shall train, drill, or study at schools, classes, or courses at the local, area, or state level as specified by the council.[20]

Fire Prevention Program

Without commitment, any effective fire prevention program is difficult to implement. Every fire department should encourage fire prevention because it saves lives and prevents property damage, which is a personal and community loss. The National Fire Protection Association reports a steady decrease in structure fires for the 1977–2002 period. This decrease can be attributed to successful fire prevention efforts. Fire prevention programs are a good investment because they coordinate resources from throughout the community to address the fire loss problem.

Fire prevention programs should have three main areas of focus: enforcement, education, and engineering. Building codes and fire code enforcement address two of the main fire prevention elements. Properly planned and constructed buildings and facilities reduce risks to the public and firefighters who live and work in Georgia cities. Fire sprinkler systems in buildings not only are preventive mechanisms but also reduce insurance costs and the need to maintain surplus water supply for fire fighting. Installing fire sprinklers in residential occupancy buildings, including single family homes, will represent the next step in reducing the number of lives lost in fires. Fire safety education can yield positive results by ensuring community awareness. A study of fire loss and fire causes can direct resources to educational activities such as home heating, installation and maintenance of smoke detectors, and escape planning.

The Fire-Rating Process

Every fire chief should understand how fire departments are evaluated for insurance purposes by the Insurance Services Office (ISO). Fire personnel should understand the basis for the department's existing rating and what is required to improve it.

For the purpose of establishing homeowners' and fire insurance rates, each fire department is rated or classified by ISO. In making an evaluation, ISO uses the *Fire Suppression Rating Schedule* as a guide for evaluating fire suppression capabilities. It places departments in one of 10 classes, with a Class 1 rating being the best and Class 10 the worst. To meet the minimum level of protection recognized by ISO, a fire department must have at least a Class 9 rating.

In evaluating fire departments, ISO representatives measure three principal features of the fire suppression system: fire alarms, fire departments, and water supply. In each of these three areas, ISO inspectors assign credits based on the quality of performance. The final rating depends on the percentage of total possible credits received.

Water Supply

Fire suppression efforts depend on an adequate supply of water to fight fires. Flow and pressure required for industrial and commercial fires are typically greater than those required for residential fires. An ongoing program of fire hydrant inspection and maintenance helps to ensure adequate water pressure.

EMERGENCY MANAGEMENT

Emergency management is a government function that centers on coordinating available resources in planning for, responding to, and recovering from a wide variety of events than can injure significant numbers of people, do extensive damage to property, and generally disrupt community life. Local elected officials are responsible for providing emergency management services for their communities as part of the duty to maintain law and order and protect lives and property. In our state, emergency management is a collaborative effort among local governments, the Georgia Emergency Management Agency, and the Federal Emergency Management Agency.[21]

Emergency Management Organizations

Many counties and cities have established emergency management agencies, with a paid full- or part-time or volunteer director. The number of staff and the complexity of operations vary widely, depending on community needs and resources. Although some federal monies are available to support local programs, most activities are funded from local resources. The general authority for program rules and regulations is found in federal and state law.

Regarding disaster relief assistance, Georgia law provides that any county or city that does not establish a local emergency management organization will not be entitled to any state funding for such assistance.[22] In Georgia, there are 161 local emergency management agencies, including 159 county organizations and 2 city agencies. Local directors are appointed by the director of the Georgia Emergency Management Agency (GEMA) but are nominated by the local governing body and serve at the pleasure of local officials.

Program Functions

Generally speaking, the goal of local emergency management organizations is to save lives, protect property, and coordinate the rapid restoration of essential services and facilities in time of disaster, whatever the cause (natural or technological) and whenever the occurrence. Many routine work activities associated with these organizations are common to risk-management programs in the private sector.

A functioning, operational program must have an emergency operations plan that clearly defines available resources and the responsibilities, authority, and channels of communication for all involved personnel, including law enforcement officers, firefighters, and social service representatives. In order to properly prepare a plan, local officials should first conduct a hazard and risk analysis of the community, assess current capabilities, and take affirmative action to ensure that additional resources are available when needed. In addition, the plan should be routinely exercised to ensure its effectiveness and currency. Finally, key emergency management staff from all affected agencies and social service groups, such as the Red Cross, should receive appropriate training in response and recovery activities.[23]

A Changing Focus

Over the last 50 years, the emphasis in emergency management has shifted away from a concern with civil defense preparedness toward a fuller awareness of the wide variety of potential disasters and emergencies faced by communities. While tornadoes, flooding, hurricanes, and other natural calamities are the most visible types of disasters, they are not the only ones. For example, recent improvements in technology have produced a growing potential for chemical spills and leaks, nuclear accidents, and other technological hazards. Such emergencies, characterized by rapid onset, low predictability, and a high potential for destruction, may soon become the major emergency management problem facing many communities because they present the greatest risk and are the most difficult to control. Some communities have even defined events such as prison escapes as emergencies and have developed plans and response actions accordingly. Of course, what constitutes a disaster or emergency for a particular community depends largely on its size and complexity, its array of resources, and its capability to effectively manage problems.

Standards for Emergency Management Directors

Georgia law establishes certain qualifications and performance standards that local emergency management organization directors must meet.[24] Local directors who are employed full time are required to

1. be at least 21 years of age;
2. not have been convicted of a felony;
3. have a high school education or its equivalent and have completed certain emergency management training courses;
4. be capable of writing response and recovery plans; and
5. be routinely available to respond to emergency scenes and to coordinate emergency response of public and private agencies and organizations.

Similar requirements apply to paid part-time directors.

ANIMAL CONTROL

Municipal officials often receive complaints about animals. State law requires cities to regulate or license animals in the control of rabies. This responsibility is shared with the county board of health, which has primary responsibility for prevention and control of rabies and must appoint a county rabies control officer.[25]

Although taxpayers (particularly those who are not animal owners) may complain about the cost of an animal control program, they usually look to the local government not only to control rabies but also to solve nuisance animal problems. In response, some communities have initiated programs to combat the problems of pet overpopulation and animals roaming free. The goal of these programs is responsible pet ownership. Four main components of the programs are

1. an animal control ordinance that makes the owner legally responsible for the pet,
2. an enforcement program that employs properly trained field officers to patrol the community,
3. a facility that provides humane and sanitary housing for animals, and

4. a public education program to inform pet owners that responsible pet ownership is the law.[26]

Two potential sources of revenue are available to help fund such an animal control program. For example, a municipality can establish an animal licensing process that requires owners to register every cat and dog and to pay a registration fee. Registration of animals not only raises revenue for the animal control program, but also aids in owner identification (so that a lost animal can be returned to its owner) and in regulating animals in the city. Permits for commercial animal establishments, such as kennels and pet shops, are another revenue source.

Although a municipality can administer its own animal control program, it may choose to contract with a local humane society to do so. The city then pays the society to provide services such as pet sterilization, public education in the responsibilities of pet ownership, and animal shelter facilities and staff.

For further discussion and a model ordinance for the control and regulation of animals, see *Responsible Animal Regulation*, available from the Humane Society of the United States.

NOTES

1. Kathleen Maguire and Ann L. Pastore, eds., *Sourcebook of Criminal Justice Statistics—2002, Online*, http://www.albany.edu/sourcebook.
2. Ibid.
3. American Bar Association (ABA), *The Urban Police Function* (New York: ABA, 1972), 8.
4. *See* http://www.cops.usdoj.gov/default.asp?Item=36.
5. OFFICIAL CODE OF GEORGIA ANNOTATED (O.C.G.A.) tit. 35, ch. 8.
6. O.C.G.A. §34-8-9(a).
7. O.C.G.A. §35-8-20.
8. O.C.G.A. §35-8-20.1.
9. Part of this section is drawn from Charles R. Swanson Jr., Leonard Territo, and Robert Taylor, *Police Administration: Structures, Processes, and Behavior*, 5th ed. (New York: MacMillan, 2001).
10. CALEA Online, *Law Enforcement Accreditation Process*, http://www.calea.org.
11. Gary W. Cordner, "Written Rules and Regulations: Are They Necessary?" *FBI Law Enforcement Bulletin* 58, no. 7 (July 1989): 18.
12. Russell Mass, "Written Rules and Regulations: Is the Fear Real?" *Law and Order* 38, no. 5 (May 1990): 36.
13. Georgia Association of Chiefs of Police.
14. O.C.G.A. tit. 42, ch. 4, art. 2.
15. *See* O.C.G.A. §35-8-24.
16. O.C.G.A. §25-3-1.
17. O.C.G.A. §§25-3-22, 25-3-23.

18. O.C.G.A. tit. 25, ch. 4.
19. O.C.G.A. §25-4-8.
20. O.C.G.A. §§25-4-9, 25-4-10.
21. 42 UNITED STATES CODE ANNOTATED (U.S.C.A.) §5121 et seq.; O.C.G.A. tit. 38, ch. 3., art 1.
22. O.C.G.A. §38-3-35.
23. The Georgia Emergency Management Agency (GEMA) provides emergency management planning and other types of assistance to local governments. For information, contact the Director of GEMA, 935 E. Confederate Avenue, S.E., P.O. Box 18055, Atlanta, GA 30316-0055, http://www.gema.state.ga.us.
24. O.C.G.A. §38-3-27.
25. O.C.G.A. §§31-19-1, 31-19-7.
26. Phyllis Wright and Susan B. Stauffer, "Practical Management of Animal Problems," *Management Information Service Report* 13 (Washington, DC: International City Management Association, April 1981).

23

Jim Finch, Billy Parrish, and Paul D. Radford

The Role of Elected Officials in Economic and Downtown Development

There are approximately 531 cities in Georgia, 250 of which have fewer than 1,000 residents. Another 219 cities have populations of between 1,000 and 10,000 residents, and in most cases, city officials do not have the tax base to devote significant financial resources to economic development initiatives. That is why it is more important than ever to have an economic development strategy that is reasonable and represents the interests of the mayor and council, citizens, local business interests, and other interested organizations. More important, the strategy should be coordinated with the economic development strategies of other governmental entities including boards of education, chambers of commerce, development authorities, and convention and visitors bureaus in the county. For the most effective and cost-efficient use of government funds, financial resources should be allocated for economic development activities that support these combined strategies.

THE STRATEGY

The first step in developing an economic development strategy is gathering input from members of the governing authority, citizens, and other interested individuals and organizations. Ideas and information should then become part of the economic aspect of the city's comprehensive plan. After adoption of the comprehensive plan, the economic aspect of that plan should become the strategy that the community follows and supports. With limited resources to finance economic development efforts, it is important that municipal officials partner with other governments and organizations to ensure successful implementation of the strategy.

SPECIAL KNOWLEDGE

Every elected official should have knowledge of (1) the essentials of development, (2) the "players" who can assist and support a community's strategy, and (3) the tools that are available to assist with economic development projects.

The three essentials of development are leadership development, community development, and economic development. The players may include bankers; educators; attorneys; existing business representatives; local, regional, and statewide economic development professionals; regional development centers; state agencies; and others. The tools include, but are not limited to, downtown development authorities, development authorities, financing programs, quality growth principles, monetary and nonmonetary incentives, hotel-motel taxes, freeport exemptions (O.C.G.A. §48-5-48.2), city business improvement districts, tax increment financing, infrastructure, affordable workforce housing, education and workforce training programs, business retention initiatives, entrepreneurial development programs, and publicly owned and available land or buildings.

Development Essentials

Leadership

Leadership is generally considered the key component for successful economic development. The implementation of formal leadership development programs, both for youths and adults, must be encouraged. Every city does not need a program, but there should be an annual program in every county. Elected officials should be involved in these programs as class participants and as alumni presenters. Elected officials should develop programs to recognize citizens who participate in local leadership programs and appoint class graduates to boards and leadership positions in the community. In building a strong leadership base in a community, it is essential that inclusiveness, not exclusiveness, be encouraged. The recruitment and participation of all sectors of the community increase the probability that the community will be successful in implementing its economic development strategy.

Community Development

Community development is the second essential element of economic development. Community development includes social infrastructure, physical infrastructure, and workforce development. Social infrastructure includes the provision of basic human services; effective and efficient governance; and an educated, capable, and visionary leadership. It is not necessary that an elected official have a Ph.D., but elected officials should participate in training opportunities provided by associations such as the Georgia Municipal Association (GMA) and colleges and universities that provide the training and knowledge needed for an individual to be an effective municipal official. Water, sewer, storm water removal, gas, electricity, transportation networks, telecommunications, and fiber optics are all essential parts of a city's physical infrastructure. Municipal officials must ensure that all of these amenities are provided in the most efficient manner possible, at the lowest available cost. A dependable, efficient, and cost-effective infrastructure may be the key ingredient in reaching economic development goals. Finally, having a strong K–12 educational system, opportunities for postsecondary training and degrees, and workforce training to meet the specific needs of employers are additional components that must be considered when developing a community's strategy.

Economic Development

The third essential element for a successful strategy is economic development. Business retention and expansion, entrepreneur development, small business support, and new business recruitment are all parts of a complete strategy. As an elected body, the mayor and council must have an understanding of the issues that affect the city's existing business base. Recognizing the importance of existing businesses is vital. There are tools that can help a community determine the impacts of local government policies on local businesses. The economic element of the comprehensive plan should identify niches in the community that an entrepreneur can successfully fill. Identification of a community's assets can help determine appropriate targets for business recruitment. New business development includes television and movie production, heritage- and nature-based tourism, recreation and natural resource development, retirement housing, alternative agriculture opportunities, and downtown development. However, without a strong, vibrant downtown, many of these alternatives may not even be possible. The importance of investing and maintaining a strong downtown business core is discussed later.

ECONOMIC DEVELOPMENT IS A PROCESS, NOT AN EVENT

There are many resources that local, regional, state, and federal organizations can provide to support a community's economic development efforts. It is incumbent on elected officials to educate themselves about these resources and to note that economic development is a process, not an event. There has to be a long-term commitment of time and resources from a broad cross section of the community. It is critical that the three essentials of development be present to ensure sustainable economic development success.

Without a plan that has the approval of its citizens, players, and partners, a community cannot sustain development. The goal is to create and enhance economic benefits for all citizens and to guide growth and development while encouraging reinvestment in the community.

Two resources about special economic development training opportunities and leadership skill development are located at the Georgia Academy for Economic Development (GAED) and the Georgia Department of Community Affairs (DCA).

Downtown Development in Georgia

Downtown development has proved to be an essential part of a community's overall economic development strategy. It can be argued that a healthy and vibrant city or town center is one of the most important elements of an effective economic development program. Even if people do not live in the city proper, polls (conducted in the spring of 2003 by Insider Advantage Inc. for GMA) have shown that they identify with the nearest city or town and view it as their hometown. These same polls have shown overwhelmingly that people value a safe, vibrant, and healthy downtown. The downtown area of a city is often the largest employer in a city, or it is almost always among the top three. The collection of retail, office, governmental, and service workers located in downtown can number from the low hundreds in a small town to over a thousand in a larger city. In addition, because these jobs are by their very nature diversified, most downtowns remain strong and flexible employment centers.

Downtown is also critical in the development of local tourism. Studies have shown that small towns and historic places are second only to beaches in terms of the most desirable places to visit, and a city's downtown and surrounding neighborhoods are the embodiment of the history and culture of a community.

Downtown is also a ready-made business incubator, particularly for small, service-based businesses that need limited space at an affordable rate. Eighty percent of all workers across America are employed in small businesses, and downtowns continue to provide reasonable space for the emerging small businesses that form the backbone of the nation's economy.

All across Georgia, downtowns are experiencing a housing boom, from small-scale upper-floor rehabilitations for apartments above shops to the construction of major new developments in and around downtown. From the smallest to the largest cities, investors are discovering the benefits of investing in downtowns, and people are discovering the joys and benefits of living downtown.

Finally, investing in downtown development has returned some significant dividends statewide. Since 1980, in the 105 Georgia Better Hometown and Main Street Cities, 6,200 net new businesses and over 28,000 net new jobs have been created in cities with less than 50,000 population. This growth has translated into a total public- and private-sector investment of over $1 billion and is reason enough for city leaders to continue to nurture the heart and soul of their city—its downtown.

History of the Georgia Main Street and Better Hometown Programs

Georgia's Main Street and Better Hometown Cities Programs are managed by DCA, and they encourage comprehensive downtown management based on the National Main Street Center's Four Point Approach™ to downtown revitalization. In 1980, Georgia was one of six pilot states to begin a statewide program of downtown economic development called Main Street. The Georgia Main Street Program is based on the simple but effective Main Street Four Point Approach™ developed by the National Trust for Historic Preservation. Main Street is a comprehensive revitalization process that improves all aspects of a commercial district. It successfully integrates a practical management strategy with the physical improvement of buildings and public spaces, aggressive promotion and image building, and the economic development of the area. Essential to the success of a Main Street Program is a professional downtown program manager to coordinate the downtown revitalization effort.

DCA, the host agency, designated the five original Georgia Main Street Cities in 1980. Each year, new cities with populations between 5,000 and 50,000 were added to the growing Main Street roster. However, in 1991, budget cuts forced DCA to drop coordination of the Main Street Program at the state level. Local programs continued to grow with guidance from the Georgia Main Street Association (GMSA) that had been formed in 1988. In 1993, leadership from GMSA requested that the Georgia Department of Economic Development take control of the coordination of the Main Street Program. There were 32 cities in the Georgia Main Street Program when the department began full-time coordination of the program on July 1, 1994.

Under the coordination of the Georgia Department of Economic Development, the Georgia Main Street Program continued to successfully implement the four-point approach in Georgia cities with populations of between 5,000 and 50,000. However, little was being done to address downtown revitalization in Georgia's smallest communities (those with populations of less than 5,000). Because of the need for a statewide, small-town downtown revitalization program, DCA, along with the Georgia Power Company, launched the Georgia Better Hometown Program in January 1997. Based on the success of the Georgia Main Street Program, the Better Hometown Program was also modeled on the National Trust for Historic Preservations' Main Street Four Point Approach™ to downtown revitalization.

The Georgia Main Street and Better Hometown Programs had common missions: to revitalize Georgia's downtowns based on a tried and true approach to downtown revitalization. However, because the two programs were coordinated by two different state agencies, the programs operated independently of one another. On July 1, 2001, the Georgia Main Street Program returned to the DCA, and both the Georgia Main Street and Better Hometown Programs are now housed and staffed in DCA's Office of Downtown Development under the management of the Georgia Main Street Program.

The Main Street Program is one of the most successful self-help programs ever. During its 25-year history, programs have been started and sustained in 47 states and over 1,600 communities nationwide.

What is The Four Point Approach™?

The Main Street Program's success is based on a comprehensive strategy using what is called the Main Street Four Point Approach™.

1. **Organization**. The program builds consensus and cooperation among the many groups and individuals who have a stake in the revitalization process. It provides a forum for many different groups and individuals to work together for the shared goal of a vital city center.
2. **Promotion**. The program promotes downtown as the center of activity through quality events and marketing to attract people into the downtown area to shop, work, and invest.
3. **Design**. The program promotes the rehabilitation of existing buildings in order to create an attractive, pedestrian friendly downtown center while recognizing the physical attributes in and around downtown. It promotes the rehabilitation of existing buildings by educating property owners and local building

and fire officials. Financial incentives may be used to initiate this activity.
4. **Economic Restructuring**. The program examines the existing business mix of downtown. First it enhances existing businesses through retention and expansion; then it expands that base through the recruitment of new businesses to strengthen the city's existing economic base.

The Four Points are supported by a set of principles that were developed from over 25 years of hands-on revitalization experience. The eight principles of the Main Street Program are outlined below.

1. **Comprehensive**. A single project cannot revitalize a downtown or commercial neighborhood. An ongoing series of initiatives is vital to build community support and create lasting progress.
2. **Incremental**. Small projects make a big difference. They demonstrate that "things are happening" on Main Street and hone the skills and confidence that the program will need to tackle more complex problems.
3. **Self-Help**. Although the National Main Street Center can provide valuable direction and hands-on technical assistance, only local leadership can initiate long-term success by fostering and demonstrating community involvement and commitment to the revitalization effort.
4. **Public-Private Partnership**. Every local Main Street Program needs the support and expertise of both the public and private sectors. For an effective partnership, each must recognize the strengths and weaknesses of the other.
5. **Identifying and Capitalizing on Existing Assets**. Unique offerings must be identified. Local assets provide the solid foundation for a successful initiative.
6. **Quality**. Quality must be a major goal, from storefront design to promotional campaigns to special events.
7. **Change**. Changing community attitudes and habits is essential to bringing about a downtown renaissance. A carefully planned program will help shift public perceptions and practices to support and sustain the revitalization process.
8. **Action Oriented**. Frequent, visible changes in the look and activities of the downtown will reinforce the perception of positive change. Small but dramatic improvements early in the process will remind the community that the revitalization effort is under way.

In addition, DCA has developed a set of performance criteria based on its own experiences with successful downtown development efforts around the state and the experiences of the National Main Street Center. These performance criteria can help guide a community toward successful downtown revitalization. A community with a successful program

1. has broad-based community support for the downtown revitalization process, with strong support from both the public and private sectors.
2. has developed vision and mission statements relevant to community conditions and to the local Main Street and Better Hometown Programs' organizational stage.
3. has a comprehensive Main Street or Better Hometown work plan.
4. possesses a historic preservation ethic.
5. has an active board of directors and committees.
6. has an adequate operating budget.
7. has a paid professional program manager (part time for Better Hometown Programs, full time for Main Street Programs).
8. conducts a program of ongoing training for staff and volunteers.
9. reports key economic activity statistics.
10. is a current member of the National Trust's Main Street Network membership program and a member of the Georgia Downtown Association (Georgia's professional association of downtown managers). This optional criterion is required by the National Main Street Center for cities wishing to be nominated for National Designation.

Local officials can and must play an active role in encouraging downtown development. The following is a checklist to guide local officials in the steps they can take to help foster and sustain meaningful downtown development activity.

Encourage Public Discussion on the Need for Downtown Revitalization

If no downtown revitalization effort exists, a series of public meetings should be initiated to discuss the need for revitalization. Speakers should be invited from nearby successful Georgia Main Street and Better Hometown Cities to share their stories and from GMA, DCA, the University of Georgia (UGA), or other sponsor agencies to discuss resources available to assist a community in starting up a revitalization effort.

Build a Public-Private Partnership to Support Downtown Development

Key members of the community, representing both the public and the private sectors, should be brought together to discuss downtown revitalization and to build an initial public-private leadership group to explore the various ways a revitalization effort can be started and sustained over time. This collaboration always needs to be done with the active involvement of property owners and merchants in the downtown.

Authorize a Downtown Development Authority

By state statute (O.C.G.A. chapter 36-42), every city in Georgia has the authorization to create a downtown development authority by action of its governing authority. All that is required to activate the authority is a resolution declaring the need for the authority, the appointment of authority members, and the establishment of reasonable downtown development boundaries. The process can be started by having representatives of the public and private sectors attend GMA-sponsored downtown development authority training programs.

Create a Staffed Downtown Development Office

The creation of the necessary public and private support to hire a downtown development manager with an adequate operating budget to facilitate and manage a city's downtown revitalization efforts is critical. For cities with populations of less than 5,000, a part-time (20 hours/week) manager is adequate for the initial phases of the effort. For cities that have populations of 5,000 or more, a full-time manager is essential and recommended. In some of the larger and long-standing successful Main Street cities, a staff for the downtown development effort of between one and a half to three full-time equivalent employees is an emerging trend. It is critical that there be a public-private board or a downtown development authority to oversee the downtown revitalization program and that such efforts be grounded in a comprehensive work plan and a managed approach.

Provide Consistent Support for Downtown Revitalization

It must be understood that downtown revitalization, like economic development, is a process, not a project, product, or event. By working incrementally, success will be achieved over time, and most important, it will be sustained.

OTHER SERVICES AVAILABLE FROM THE OFFICE OF DOWNTOWN DEVELOPMENT

Urban Georgia Network

The Urban Georgia Network was created by DCA to assist large urban areas that are not eligible for Main Street or Better Hometown designations but have similar problems and opportunities. It provides a forum for networking and information sharing on common urban issues. The network encompasses downtown programs, authorities, business improvement districts, community improvement districts, and other organizations that develop and manage the larger urban downtowns in Georgia. The network meets quarterly in various member cities.

Georgia Downtown Development Conference

In partnership with the Georgia Downtown Association (Georgia's association of professional downtown managers) and its other partners/sponsors, the DCA's Office of Downtown Development helps coordinate the annual Georgia Downtown Conference. The conference provides up-to-date information on downtown development techniques and strategies and includes nationally known keynote speakers, hands-on work sessions, topical roundtables, and panels as well as plenty of networking opportunities. The conference is open to the general public.

Topical Research

From time to time, every city needs assistance in gathering and researching topics related to downtown development. The DCA Office of Downtown Development, along with its public and private partners, can provide assistance to cities in finding answers to many downtown development issues. DCA has a host of resources available to assist with questions regarding design standards, retail and downtown housing development, market research, small business development, tax base studies, and others.

Assistance to Other Cities

Although the Office of Downtown Development focuses primarily on designated Main Street and Better Hometown Cities or members of the Urban Georgia Network, assistance is available to all Georgia cities. Assistance is available for board development training and communitywide meetings to help cities focus on economic development through downtown revitalization. Facilitated sessions and statewide training on various topics including historic preservation, tax credit incentive programs, and financial assistance programs are also offered.

Downtown Development Revolving Loan Fund

The Downtown Development Revolving Loan Fund is designed to assist nonentitlement cities and counties in implementing quality downtown development projects. Applicants and eligible subrecipients must have a viable downtown development project and clearly identify the proposed uses of the loan proceeds. This program has a unique relationship with the Georgia Cities Foundation, a nonprofit subsidiary of the GMA that also provides low-interest loans to developers interested in investing in downtowns across the state.

Regional Offices

DCA has staff assigned to assist communities in all regions of the state, including metro Atlanta. The regional staff serves as DCA's first point of local government/community contact for brokering, supporting, and implementing departmental programs and services. Throughout the state, DCA staff are available to help cities with their downtown development interests.

PARTNERS IN DOWNTOWN DEVELOPMENT ACROSS GEORGIA

In addition to the resources available through DCA, there are many other public and private organizations that support downtown development across the state. A few of these organizations and the services they provide follow.

Georgia Municipal Association and the Georgia Cities Foundation

The Georgia Cities Foundation is a nonprofit subsidiary of GMA. The foundation makes low-interest loans to qualified downtown development projects that will significantly affect the economic vitality of the downtown area. DCA provides underwriting and loan-servicing assistance to the foundation.

University of Georgia, Business Outreach Services

UGA's Business Outreach Services offers assistance to Georgia communities that wish to undertake or maintain downtown revitalization efforts. Areas of assistance include retail recruitment, market analysis, project development, board training, and facilitation. In addition, the university develops and provides GMA-sponsored downtown development authority board training programs.

356 MUNICIPAL SERVICES

University of Georgia, College of Environment and Design

The College of Environment and Design provides design assistance to communities through DCA's Design Assistance Office. By providing interns and holding design charrettes (i.e., focused design teams that address specific design issues in a community), UGA supports the efforts of Georgia Main Street and Better Hometown Programs across the state. In addition, the College of Environment and Design assists with the Certified Local Government Program of the Georgia Department of Natural Resources Historic Preservation Division, as well as providing direct assistance to communities.

Georgia Trust for Historic Preservation

As the largest statewide private, nonprofit historic preservation organization in the country, the Georgia Trust provides a portion of the design assistance channeled through DCA's Design Assistance Office. The trust has provided preservation-based design assistance to Georgia's Main Street cities since 1980 and continues to be a valued partner throughout the state.

Georgia Downtown Association

The Georgia Downtown Association (GDA) is Georgia's professional downtown managers association. GDA is a nonprofit membership organization that cosponsors the annual Georgia Downtown Conference.

Department of Natural Resources, Historic Preservation Division

As a division of the Georgia Department of Natural Resources, the Historic Preservation Division assists Georgia communities and its citizens in historic preservation education and programs such as the granting of Historic Preservation Tax Credits, a 20 percent federal tax credit for the rehabilitation of historic buildings. In addition, the division works with other partners to develop and sponsor training programs on architectural preservation issues, provide technical assistance, and administer a preservation grant program for the state.

Georgia Power, Georgia Electric Membership Cooperatives (EMCs), Municipal Electric Authority of Georgia (MEAG) Power

Although many Georgia utility companies provide assistance at the state and local level to downtown development efforts, three companies—Georgia Power, Georgia EMCs, and MEAG Power—have provided significant sponsorships and direct assistance to downtown development throughout the state.

Georgia Department of Economic Development

The Georgia Department of Economic Development (formerly the Georgia Department of Industry Trade and Tourism) provides assistance to Georgia cities through the promotion and marketing of Georgia's tourism industry and the recognition that downtowns and town centers are an important part of Georgia's heritage tourism business.

Georgia Department of Transportation

The Georgia Department of Transportation assists Georgia cities with traffic management concerns in and around downtown. The department also administers the Transportation Enhancement Act (commonly referred to as the T-21 program) for the state. These grant funds have been instrumental in upgrading downtown streetscapes throughout Georgia.

U.S. Department of Agriculture

The Department of Rural Development within the U.S. Department of Agriculture provides funding to eligible cities around the state for important local and regional economic development projects and programs, including activities related to downtown development.

To learn more about downtown development or to obtain further information on Georgia Main Street or Better Hometown designation and the Georgia Main Street Program, contact DCA's Office of Downtown Development, 60 Executive Park South, Atlanta, Georgia 31709, (404) 679-3115, fax (404) 679-0572.

PART 5

Financing and Revenues

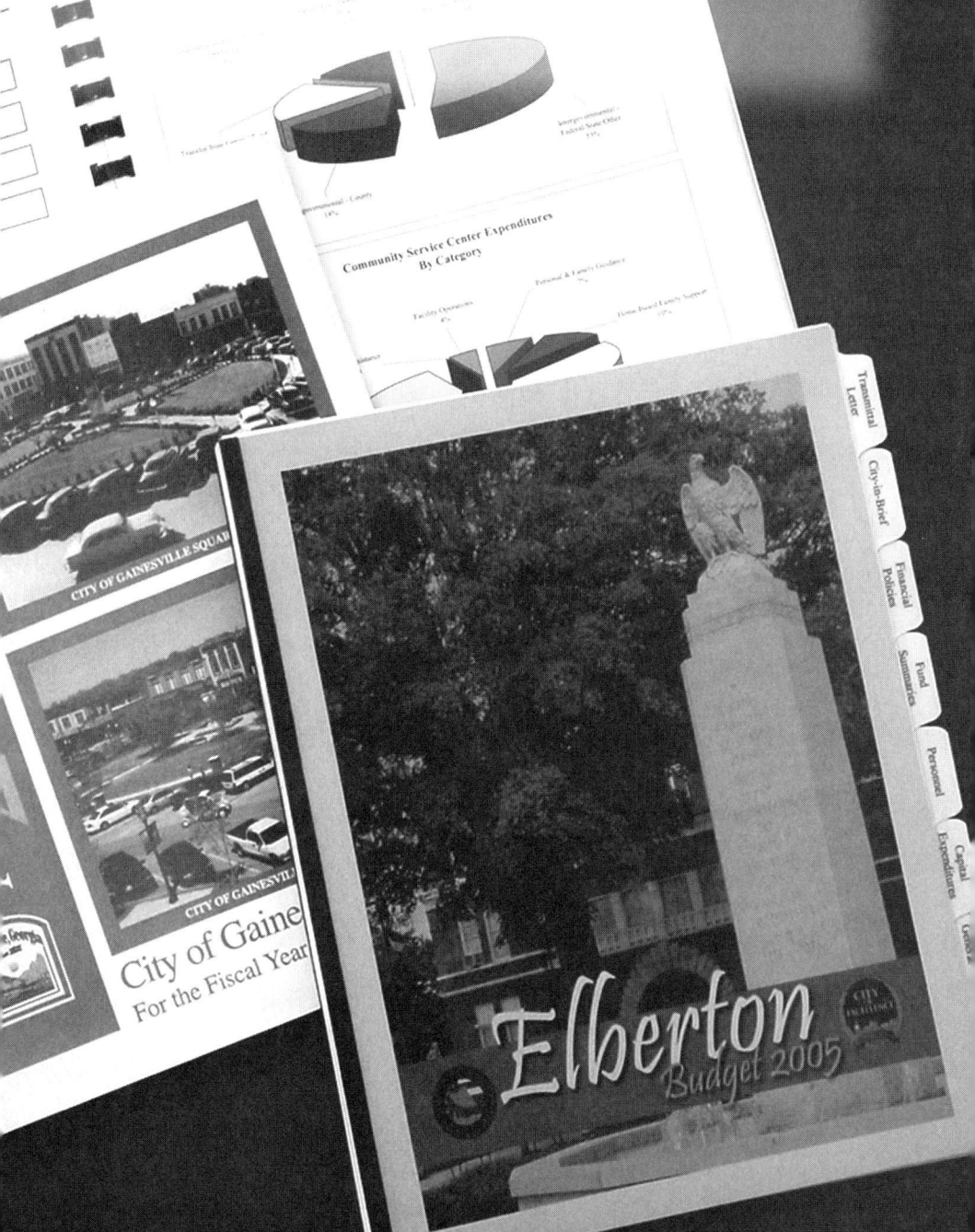

24

Paul E. Glick and Sabrina Wiley Cape*

Understanding City Finance

During each year, usually monthly, city finance staff prepare financial statements for the city council. At the end of the fiscal year, the auditors spend one to three months preparing their report and audited financial statements, which they ultimately present to the city council. What do the numbers in these financial statements mean? Are they important? How can city councilmembers better understand them? This chapter answers these questions and addresses other city financial reporting issues.

Recently, Georgia cities have seen major changes in accounting and financial reporting. The Department of Community Affairs has developed a local government uniform chart of accounts that municipal governments began using in 2000. In addition, the Governmental Accounting Standards Board (GASB), which sets the accounting and financial reporting rules, has issued a new financial reporting standard that municipal governments will be implementing, according to the total annual revenues of the municipality. This chapter also discusses these new requirements and standards.

FINANCIAL REPORTING

Financial reports are classified according to their content and the purposes for which they are issued. Different types of financial reports may be issued for different user groups according to how the reports will be used (internal or external) and when they are completed (interim or annual).

---

* Parts of the chapter contain or are based on work by this author from earlier editions of the *Handbook for Georgia Mayors and Councilmembers*.

Interim financial reports are prepared on a monthly basis by management, normally for internal use, including that of the city council. Most cities issue some type of interim report to assist with their day-to-day management. Annual financial reports, which include data regarding operations in the previous year, are designed for external readers, such as citizens or bond rating services. Annual reports are less useful to city councilmembers because of the timing of their preparation. Because these reports usually are independently audited by a certified public accounting firm, it may take up to six months after the close of the fiscal year to entirely complete this annual report. In addition to the regular annual report, some cities prepare a comprehensive annual financial report, which includes introductory, financial, and statistical information.

TYPES OF STATEMENTS

Generally, governments prepare two types of financial statements: balance sheets (sometimes called statements of net assets) and operating statements (sometimes called statements of activities). Balance sheets are financial statements that present what the city owns, what it owes, and its worth (i.e., fund balance or net assets).

Operating statements are directed toward control over revenues and expenditures in the primary operating funds. The budgetary operating statement, which includes revenues and expenditures that are compared with the final revised budget and changes in fund balance, is most commonly used. A budgetary operating statement should be most useful to city councilmembers, particularly during the year, because it compares budgeted revenues with actual revenues and budgeted expenditures with actual expenditures. This kind of statement allows councilmembers to monitor overspending and to determine if revenues are being received as projected.

MUNICIPAL VERSUS BUSINESS FINANCES

Before one can understand city financial statements, it is important to note the differences between the financial operations of a municipality and those of the business world. Cities have objectives that are different from those of commercial enterprises; they operate in a different economic, legal, political, and social environment. Cities use capital assets to provide services, whereas businesses use capital assets to generate revenues. These differences often require accounting and financial reporting techniques unique to local governments.

Business enterprises exist to maximize economic profits. The "bottom line," or profits and losses presented on an operating statement, is a reasonable indicator of the success of a business. For a city, however, the bottom line usually is not an accurate indicator of its success. If a city reports more revenues than expenditures in a fiscal year, is that good? If a city spends more than it receives in a fiscal year, is that bad? Whether a city reports more revenues than expenditures or spends more than it receives in a fiscal year is not all-important. The primary objective of a city is to provide services to its constituents within budgetary constraints. There is little regard for the bottom-line concept. The GASB's new financial reporting standard (discussed later in this chapter) tends to move some city financial reporting toward business-type accounting.

Legal Requirements

In business, substantial discretion is allowed in obtaining and using resources. By contrast, Georgia municipal government financing and spending activities are subject to very specific legal and contractual provisions. To adequately review city financial reports, councilmembers should be familiar with municipal legal requirements.

Annual Operating Budget

Each year, Georgia cities adopt a budget showing where the money to operate the city comes from and how it will be spent (see Chapter 27). The annual operating budget plays a more expanded role in municipal government than it does in business. Budgets are an important internal planning tool for both business and government, but in municipal government they also play an important external role. Because a city is a public entity, parties inside (e.g., department directors) and outside (e.g., citizens) the city government may participate in the development of the annual operating budget. The law requires Georgia cities to conduct public budget hearings in which interested parties have an opportunity to ask questions and offer suggestions about the proposed budget. Very few people participate in budget hearings in most cities, but occasionally interested constituents attend budget hearings to express their opinions. For example, because the size of the budget usually affects property taxes, it is not uncommon for property owners to attend budget hearings.

Once the city council adopts the budget, it establishes spending limits that cities normally cannot exceed unless the council legally changes (i.e., amends) the budget. These limits create spending constraints for city administrators that usually do not exist in the commercial sector.

Accounting and Financial Reporting Rules

Generally accepted accounting principles (GAAP) are the accounting rules followed by most accountants in business and government alike. GAAP provide a set of uniform minimum standards and guidelines for financial accounting and reporting. Therefore, all financial statements prepared on a GAAP basis are comparable, regardless of the legal jurisdiction or geographic location of the government. Georgia law requires cities to prepare their audited financial statements in conformity with GAAP.

GAAP is used differently in business and government. GASB establishes GAAP for governments, and the Financial Accounting Standards Board sets standards for business. GASB, a nonprofit entity located in Norwalk, Connecticut, is made up of a full-time chairperson and six part-time board members and has a research director and a permanent staff of accountants working under the direction of the chairperson. When applied to business financial statements, GAAP provide information (i.e., the profit or loss) that investors and creditors need to decide whether (and how much) to invest in stock or to loan money to a particular business. By contrast, individuals do not invest capital in government; therefore, governmental GAAP financial statements emphasize legal compliance (e.g., budget information).

Because city councilmembers have oversight responsibility for municipal financial operations, the rules that GAAP provide for preparing financial information to demonstrate accountability are very useful. Councilmembers are responsible for setting financial policies, which includes determining how much money the city may spend through the adoption of the annual operating budget and monitoring progress toward meeting those budgetary goals.

INDEPENDENT AUDITS

Most cities have independent audits conducted in conformity with GAAP and generally accepted governmental auditing standards (GAGAS). GAGAS consist of the auditing rules that independent certified public accountants (CPAs) must follow when auditing municipal financial statements. In an independent audit, the CPA expresses an opinion as to the fairness of a city's basic financial statements in conformity with GAAP. In other words, the auditor verifies that the financial statements present the actual financial position and results of operations for the year ended.

Why Are Cities Audited?

The GASB and the Government Finance Officers Association (GFOA) have long recommended that the financial statements of all local governments be audited independently in accordance with GAGAS. In addition, Georgia law requires cities that spend at least $300,000 annually or have a population in excess of 1,500 to be audited annually; most other cities are required to be audited at least every two years (see Chapter 27). Because cities operate largely on involuntary resources in the form of taxes, which are entrusted to elected and appointed officials for the provision of public services, an audit by an independent certified public accounting firm is essential to ensure that public funds have been expended as legally required. There is another significant reason for an independent audit: because some of the country's larger cities have experienced financial difficulties, buyers of local government debt securities often rely on financial statements as a basis for investment.

City officials can realize many benefits from obtaining independent audits:

1. The results of financial and compliance audits can help elected and appointed officials in their decision-making roles.
2. The additional assurances provided by audited financial statements and the audit testing of legal compliance allow officials to make more confident decisions concerning the future of municipal operations.
3. Audit results also may point the way to constructive changes that benefit the city and its officials.
4. Audits include a review of a city's internal accounting controls, which helps curtail circumstances permitting inefficiencies or fraud.

TYPES OF AUDITS

Most independent audits conducted on behalf of cities are classified as both financial and compliance audits, whereas audits in the private sector are almost always financial audits. A financial and compliance audit expands the scope of the audit beyond validating financial records to include the city's compliance with the various finance-related legal and contractual provisions. This aspect of auditing is very important because, as mentioned earlier, municipalities must operate within a legally regulated environment.

Most cities in Georgia have an annual audit conducted by a CPA, in accordance with GAGAS. One type of financial audit is the single audit mandated by the provisions of the 1996 amendments to the U.S. Single Audit Act of 1984.[1] The purpose of the single audit is to have one city-wide audit that will encompass not only local resources, but also all state and federal grants.[2]

THE UNIFORM CHART OF ACCOUNTS

In 1997 the Georgia General Assembly passed legislation with significant implications for municipal financial reporting. It required that the Georgia Department of Community Affairs (DCA) develop a local government uniform chart of accounts and a set of community indicators that will allow state and local policymakers to monitor the social and economic conditions of Georgia communities.[3]

The uniform chart of accounts was approved by the state auditor and adopted by the DCA in 1998. In developing the uniform chart, the DCA solicited input and advice from local government officials around the state. Adapted from the GFOA's "Illustrative Chart of Accounts" contained in Appendix C of the "Blue Book," the Georgia chart's primary purpose is to provide a uniform format for local government financial reporting and accounting, allowing state agencies to collect more reliable and meaningful financial data and information from local governments.

Cities adopted this uniform chart of accounts in reports to state agencies prepared for fiscal years ended in 2001. Cities must also classify their transactions in conformity with the fund, balance sheet, revenue, and expenditure classification descriptions in the chart, and their accounting records should reflect these account classifications. Although local governments are not required to use the chart's numbering system in their own accounting systems, they may find that using the uniform chart of accounts for accounting purposes facilitates their financial reporting to DCA and other state agencies.[4]

The DCA requires local governments to submit reports on their services and operations as a condition of receiving state-appropriated funds from the department. These reports are produced using data from the local government finance and operations surveys administered by the department. The community indicators report will be developed using data from these surveys and other sources for all local governments in the state with annual expenditures of $250,000 or more. A community's report focuses on demographic patterns, economy, finance, education, health, social environment, civic participation, and selected municipal government services.[5] Any city that receives state funds from the governor's emergency fund or from a special project appropriation must submit a grant certification form to the state auditor in conjunction with its annual audit. This form requires the city council and the auditor of the city to certify that the grant funds were used solely for the purpose or purposes for which the grant was made. Failure to submit this certification results in forfeiture of the grant and the return of any grant funds already received by the local government.[6]

FUND ACCOUNTING

Fund accounting requires cities to keep separate records for each individual fund. GAAP define a fund as an entity with separate accounting records for a specific activity. For example, a city might account for a state grant in one fund and record the proceeds from a building bond sale in another fund. Fund accounting can complicate manual bookkeeping. The use of a computer and computerized government accounting systems for fund accounting greatly simplify the process. Also, GAAP encourage cities to maintain a minimum number of funds.

Generic Fund Types

For city councilmembers to be able to read and understand city financial statements, they need to know the nature and purpose of eight fund types (defined by GAAP as generic fund types), which are grouped into three categories. These categories are important because the accounting rules that cities must follow may be applied differently to each of the fund categories.

Figure 24-1 presents a fund organizational chart illustrating the four categories and the relationship of categories A, B, and C to the eight generic fund types. The categories are briefly described here:

- A. **Governmental fund types**. Used to account for general municipal operations (e.g., police department, public works, parks and recreation).
- B. **Proprietary fund types**. Used to account for city activities that are similar to the commercial sector (e.g., a water and sewer utility).
- C. **Fiduciary fund types**. Used to account for assets held by a city in a trustee or agent capacity (e.g., the city is the administrator of a trust for nongovernment purposes).

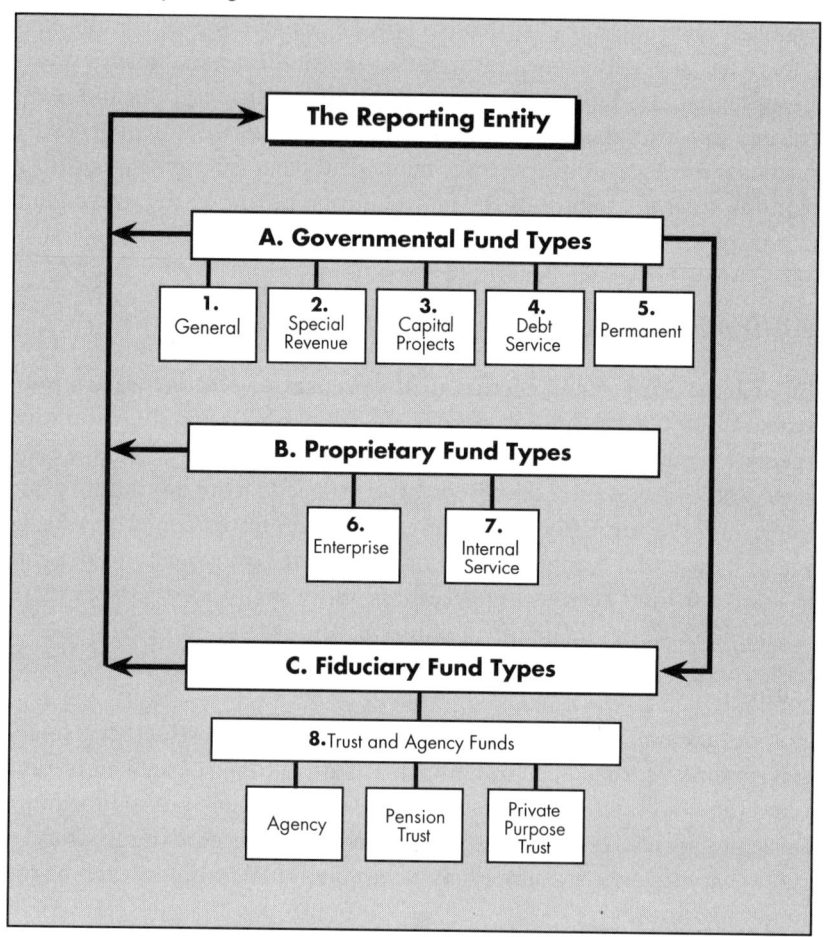

Figure 24-1. *Government Accounting and Governmentwide Financial Reporting*

```
                    ┌─► The Reporting Entity ◄─┐
                    │                          │
                    ├─► A. Governmental Fund Types ─┐
                    │                               │
                    │   1.    2.      3.      4.      5.
                    │ General Special Capital  Debt  Permanent
                    │         Revenue Projects Service
                    │
                    ├─► B. Proprietary Fund Types
                    │
                    │        6.           7.
                    │     Enterprise    Internal
                    │                   Service
                    │
                    └─► C. Fiduciary Fund Types ◄─
                    
                         8. Trust and Agency Funds
                         
                      Agency   Pension   Private
                               Trust     Purpose
                                         Trust
```

Five generic fund types are categorized within governmental funds:

1. **General fund.** Used to account for all resources that GAAP do not require to be accounted for in another fund. Municipalities report most of their financial transactions in this fund, including some of the activities of the constitutional officers. Expenditures in this fund might include road maintenance, the court system, police and fire, the city clerk's office, and parks and recreation.

2. **Special revenue funds.** Used to account for resources that are legally or administratively restricted for specific purposes. A federal grant fund might be classified here.

3. **Capital projects funds.** Used to account for resources restricted for major capital outlays. The proceeds from building bond issues to build new libraries that will be repaid from property taxes would be accounted for here.
4. **Debt service funds.** Used to repay the principal and interest on general long-term debt, such as a building bond issue.
5. **Permanent funds.** Used to report resources that are legally restricted to the extent that only earnings, and not principal, may be used for purposes that support the city's programs (that is, for the benefit of the city or its citizenry). For example, the perpetual care of a cemetery that the city operates would be classified as a permanent fund.

The two following generic fund types are classified as proprietary fund types:

6. **Enterprise funds.** Used to account for operations that are financed and operated in a manner similar to business enterprises. Public utilities are the most common city activity reported in this way.
7. **Internal service funds.** Used to account for operations similar to those under enterprise funds that provide goods or services primarily to other departments within the same city on a cost-reimbursement basis. Cities often report as internal service funds activities such as data processing, motor pools, and print shops. Normally the larger cities use internal service funds.

Included in fiduciary fund types is the eighth generic fund type, which is subdivided into three funds:

8a. **Agency funds.** Used as holding accounts for assets belonging to some entity other than the city. For example, a trust for nongovernment purposes is classified as an agency fund.
8b. **Pension trust funds.** Used by cities to account for their own (single employer) pension plans. In other words, the retirement assets held for the city's employees who have retired or will retire are reported here. Only a few Georgia municipalities maintain their own single employer pension plans.
8c. **Private purpose trust funds.** Used to report trust arrangements under which principal and income benefit individuals, private organizations, or other governments. These funds do not benefit the reporting city.

FINANCIAL REPORTING FOLLOWING GASB STATEMENT 34

The GASB issued Statement No. 34 (GASB Statement 34)[7] in June 1999. This statement established new financial reporting requirements for state and local governments throughout the United States. Although the statement restructures much of the information that municipalities presented in the past—thereby creating new information—day-to-day accounting operations have not changed. Cities with revenues totaling over $100 million must have implemented the standard by year-end in 2002; cities with revenues of between $10 and $100 million, in 2003; and cities with revenues of less than $10 million, in 2004. City councilmembers can expect to see the results of GASB Statement 34 in their annual audited financial statements. GASB Statement 34 includes two levels of reporting in the annual financial report: fund-level reporting and governmentwide reporting.

Fund-Level Financial Reporting

GASB Statement 34 requires municipalities to continue to do what annual reports already do: provide information about funds. The focus of financial statements has been sharpened, however. Pre–GASB Statement 34, fund information was reported in the aggregate by fund type, which often made it difficult for users to assess accountability. Now, cities are required to report information about their most important (or "major") funds, including the city's general fund.

Fund statements also will continue to assess the "operating results" of many funds by reporting the amount of cash on hand and other assets that can easily be converted to cash. These statements show the performance—in the short term—of individual funds using the same indicators that many cities use when financing their current operations.

Fund-level reporting basically requires municipalities to present balance sheets and operating statements for each fund category (i.e., governmental, proprietary, and fiduciary). In addition, cities are required to continue to provide budgetary comparison information in their annual reports. An important change, however, is the requirement to add the government's original budget to that comparison. Many cities revise their original budgets over the course of the year for a variety of reasons. Requiring cities to report their original budget in addition to their revised budget increases the usefulness of the budgetary comparison.

Governmentwide Financial Reporting

This level of financial reporting is brand new to municipal governments. For the first time, municipal financial managers are being asked to share their insights in a required management's discussion and analysis (MD&A) by giving readers an objective and easily readable analysis of the government's financial performance for the year. For the first time, municipalities are including governmentwide financial statements in their annual financial report, prepared using accrual accounting for all of the government's activities. Currently, most governmental utilities and private-sector companies use accrual accounting, which measures not only current assets and liabilities, but also long-term assets and liabilities, such as capital assets (including infrastructure) and general obligation debt. It also reports all revenues and all costs of providing services each year—not just those received or paid in the current year or soon after year end (like the modified accrual basis). Cities are to prepare both a governmentwide balance sheet (known as the statement of net assets) and a governmentwide operating statement (known as the statement of activities), with aggregate governmental activities and aggregate business-type activities.

These governmentwide financial statements should help users

- assess the finances of the city in total, including the current year's operating results;
- determine whether the city's overall financial position improved or deteriorated;
- evaluate whether the city's current-year revenues were sufficient to pay for current-year services;
- understand the cost of providing services to its citizenry;
- see how the city finances its programs—through user fees and other program revenues versus general tax revenues; and
- understand the extent to which the city has invested in capital assets, including roads, bridges, and other infrastructure assets.

BASIS OF ACCOUNTING

When does a city record the sale of water? When the customer uses the water, when the city reads the meter, or when the customer pays the bill? The basis of accounting answers this type of question. Basis of accounting refers to when revenues, expenses (on the accrual basis of accounting) or expenditures (on the modified accrual basis of accounting), and related assets and liabilities are formally recognized in the accounting process and reported in the financial statements.

Like basis of accounting, the "measurement focus"—an interrelated concept—is reflected in a municipality's financial statements. Measurement focus indicates what the financial statements are trying to communicate; that is, what is being measured by the statements. Most cities use two types of measurement focus:

- **Current financial resources measurement focus.** Financial statements using this focus, commonly known as "flow of funds," report only current assets (i.e., those that the city can convert to cash quickly) and current liabilities (i.e., those due in the short term) on their balance sheets. The difference between these assets and liabilities, or the fund balance, is considered to be the amount available for spending. On these statements, the emphasis is on accountability. The financial data and information assist city councilmembers in their oversight function.
- **Economic resources measurement focus.** Financial statements using this focus report all assets and liabilities on their balance sheets. The difference between all assets and all liabilities is the capital, or equity, of the fund. On these statements, the emphasis is on "profit" or "loss." City councilmembers can thereby monitor financial projections.

Measurement focus determines what is measured in the financial statements; the basis of accounting determines when transactions are formally recognized in the financial statements. When measurement focus is determined, the basis of accounting to be used is determined. Basis of accounting is a difficult concept. However, in order to understand municipal financial statements, city councilmembers need to understand the different bases of accounting and which funds in their city use which basis at which financial reporting level.

As alluded to previously, there is more than one basis of accounting. GAAP find two bases of accounting acceptable for cities: accrual and modified accrual. Others exist that are unacceptable. The most common unacceptable basis of accounting is the cash basis. On the cash basis, when the money comes in, the city records the revenue; when the city writes the check, it reports the cost. While using this type of basis may be simple, ultimately it is not truly informative. The cash basis of accounting fails to recognize receivables and payables (i.e., amounts still due to or owed by the city). Therefore, under the cash basis of accounting, the financial statements do not accurately represent the financial position or results of city operations.

The Accrual Basis of Accounting

Cities use the accrual basis, which is used by most major corporations, on all governmentwide statements and for their proprietary and fiduciary fund types. When cities use the accrual basis, they report revenues in the financial statements when they earn revenue: a city earns the revenue when it provides the service. For example, when a resident waters his or her yard, the city has provided for the use of water and earned that revenue, even though the city does not record the revenue until the water meter is read and the number of gallons the customer used is calculated. A city reports expenses when they are incurred; that is, when the city owes a supplier for an item purchased or owes an employee for a service performed. For example, once an employee works one day, an expense is incurred because the city owes the employee a day's pay. GAAP has special rules regarding when cities must formally recognize taxes and grants.

Using the accrual basis of accounting, a city can purchase fixed assets (equipment, vehicles) and report them on the balance sheet as assets and not as costs in the operating statement. However, each year the city must include in the operating statement a charge for the use of each fixed asset, based on its estimated useful life. This charge is called depreciation.

On the accrual basis of accounting, all liabilities (both short term and long term) are included on the balance sheet. For example, when a city issues long-term bonds for an enterprise fund (e.g., the water fund), the bonds payable are reported as a liability on the balance sheet of the enterprise fund, but this transaction is not reported on the operating statement. When a portion of the principal is paid, the liability is reduced but the operating statement is not affected. However, any interest costs are reported as an expense.

The Modified Accrual Basis of Accounting

The other acceptable basis of accounting, the modified accrual, is used by cities to report their governmental fund types at the fund reporting level. Under modified accrual accounting, revenues are reported when they are considered to be available—not when they are earned, as in the accrual basis of accounting. Availability of revenue (i.e., when it is formally recognized as revenue) is primarily what differentiates these two bases of accounting.

"Available" means the city will collect the revenue in the current year or shortly after the end of the year to pay liabilities from the current year. For example, if the fiscal year ends on June 30 and the city will receive revenue for that fiscal year in July, it will probably be reported as revenue as of June 30, as long as it relates to the year just ended. However, if the available revenue is not received until December, it will probably not be reported as revenue for the year ending June 30 because it cannot be used to pay outstanding liabilities at June 30.

On both the accrual and modified accrual bases of accounting, an expense or expenditure, respectively, is recognized when the liability is incurred, but the due date for payment of a liability affects how it is reported. If payment for the liability is not due at year-end, on the modified accrual basis, the liability is not reported as an expenditure at the time incurred. On the accrual basis, the due date of the payment, or when the city pays the liability, does not affect when the city reports the expense.

On the modified accrual basis, cities report capital assets, such as equipment and vehicles, as expenditures on the operating statement; they are reported as assets on the balance sheet on the accrual basis. However, because the city has acquired assets, these purchases also are reported separately in the city's capital asset system but not on its governmental fund type balance sheet. When the modified accrual basis of accounting is used, depreciation is not reported in the operating statement because the city already has reported the total cost of the capital asset as an expenditure when purchased.

Long-term debt generally cannot be reported on the balance sheet of a fund that uses the modified accrual basis of accounting. When a city sells bonds and cash is received, the proceeds from the sale of bonds are reported on the operating statement in a special section called "other financing sources/uses." Although the city must pay back the principal on the bonds, the liability is not reported in the governmental fund type. Therefore, a balance sheet reporting governmental funds usually will not include any long-term liabilities. However, cities do report both their capital assets and their long-term debt at the governmentwide reporting level.

The repayment of governmental fund debt usually is paid from a debt service fund and is reported as an expenditure on the modified accrual basis of accounting. On the accrual basis, the repayment of debt principal is reported as a reduction of a liability and not as an expense.

NOTES

1. 31 UNITED STATES CODE ANNOTATED (U.S.C.A.) §§7501–7507.
2. For a more in-depth discussion on compliance auditing, see Paul T. Hardy, Betty J. Hudson, Richard W. Campbell, and Paul E. Glick, *Compliance Auditing in Georgia Counties and Municipalities: A Practical Guide to State Laws for Auditors and Local Government Officials*, 2nd ed. (Athens: Carl Vinson Institute of Government, University of Georgia, 2000).
3. OFFICIAL CODE OF GEORGIA ANNOTATED (O.C.G.A.) §36-81-3(e).
4. O.C.G.A. §36-81-3(e); *Uniform Chart of Accounts for Local Governments in Georgia*, 2nd ed. (Atlanta: Georgia Department of Community Affairs, 1998).

5. O.C.G.A. §36-81-8.
6. O.C.G.A. §36-81-8.1.
7. GASB Statement No. 34, *Basic Financial Statements—and Management's Discussion and Analysis—for State and Local Governments* (Washington, DC: Governmental Accounting Standards Board, 1999).

25

Sabrina Wiley Cape and Paul E. Glick*

Financial Policies

City councilmembers make decisions relating to financial matters on a regular basis. However, only a limited number of cities have adopted financial policies to help make these decisions. What are financial policies? Why should city councilmembers adopt them? What obstacles will need to be overcome? How are financial policies developed? This chapter reviews each of these questions.

WHAT ARE FINANCIAL POLICIES?

Financial policies are the rules that govern financial decisions in a city. City councilmembers adopt these policies and follow them when making financial decisions about the future of their cities. Once city officials adopt financial policies, most subsequent financial decisions are simplified because the issues have been deliberated during the policy adoption stage.

Cities might adopt financial policies covering the following topics:

- operating budget and equity (fund balance) reserves
- capital improvements plan or program (CIP)
- debt
- revenue
- accounting, auditing, and financial reporting
- purchasing
- cash and investments

---

* Parts of the chapter contain or are based on work by this author from earlier editions of the *Handbook for Georgia Mayors and Councilmembers*.

Table 25-1. Questions to Ask and Issues to Resolve When Establishing Financial Policies

Operating budget and equity (fund balance) reserves	Which funds should be budgeted?
	Is the budget balanced?
	Is a contingency budgeted?
	How much fund balance is maintained?
	Is the fund balance used in balancing the budget?
	What is the legal level of budgetary control?
	Should a more detailed level of budgetary control be established?
	Is the budget process centralized or decentralized?
	What happens to appropriations at the end of the year?
	What budgetary basis of accounting is used?
	Is a budgetary reporting system maintained?
	Who will perform budget adjustments/amendments during the year?
Capital improvements program (CIP)	How are capital projects defined?
	What period of time does the CIP cover?
	What evaluation criteria are used to prioritize capital projects?
	How much of the CIP is funded each year from the annual operating budget?
Debt	When is debt issued?
	What type of debt is issued?
	How much debt is issued?
	What are the maturity dates of debt issuances?
	What are the actions undertaken to maintain positive relations with bond rating agencies?
Revenue	What is the goal for establishing and maintaining a diversified revenue source?
	What are the collection policies?
	What collection methods (such as tax sales, liens, collection agencies, etc.) are used?
	How are revenue projections developed, how often, and what period of time do they cover?
	How are property rates calculated?
	How are user fees and charges set, and how often are they updated?
	Should a revenue manual be developed by the city?

Table 25-1. *Questions to Ask and Issues to Resolve When Establishing Financial Policies (continued)*

Accounting, auditing, and financial reporting	How is the independent auditor selected?
	What is the level of audit coverage?
	Who prepares financial reports for internal use, and what type of reports will be prepared?
	Does the city participate in the GFOA certificate of achievement program with the production of a comprehensive annual financial report (CAFR)?
	Does the city use audit or finance committees?
	Does the city have an internal audit staff?
	Are generally accepted accounting principles (GAAP) being followed?
Purchasing	Is the purchasing system centralized or decentralized?
	Should written purchasing rules and regulations be developed?
	Who should award bid contracts?
	Which thresholds should be established for purchasing activity such as requiring formal bids, written quotes, telephone quotes, petty cash, etc.?
	Should local bidder preference be authorized?
	Should the city utilize the Georgia state contracts?
Cash and investments	Should the city spread cash among local banks, rotate banks, or pool cash and investments?
	Should the city perform a banking services bid?
	Is competitive bidding used for investment instruments?
	What are the investment objectives of the city?
	What are the authorized investment instruments?
	How are qualified institutions defined?
	What collateralization procedures are needed by the city?
	Should the local government investment pool (LGIP) be used?

Questions that city councilmembers need to ask with regard to each of these policy issues are presented in Table 25-1.

Many cities have some financial policies even though the elected officials have not formally adopted them. Often these policies result from precedent, and they become standing practices within a city. For example, a city's property tax rate might not have been changed for a number of years. The city has no written policy that limits increasing the tax rate, yet everyone "just knows" that the position of the city councilmembers is not to raise property taxes. Obviously, an informal policy is at work in that city.

ADOPTING FINANCIAL POLICIES: CONSIDERATIONS

There are a variety of reasons why city councilmembers should adopt financial policies:

Financial policies can provide city elected officials with the opportunity to review their present approach to financial management with an overall, long-range perspective.

> Generally, during budget preparation, city councilmembers spend most of their meeting time reviewing the annual operating budget. And, because of the annual budget process, city officials are generally "annually oriented" in their financial planning. Fortunately, financial policies require city councilmembers to conduct financial planning on a long-range basis, which can only improve a city's financial management.

Financial policies can improve city councilmembers' credibility and the public's confidence in them.

> When citizens are aware that the city council has adopted meaningful financial policies, they feel confident that the councilmembers are providing sound financial management for the city.

Financial policies can save time and energy for both the city council and the city's administrative staff.

> It has been said that 80 percent of the decisions that city councilmembers make relate in some way to finance (e.g., hiring additional personnel, purchasing new vehicles, evaluating where to locate a new fire station). Therefore, if financial policies are in place, the amount of time at council meetings spent on financial issues can be minimized. Such policies also allow the city's administration to move ahead with financial matters as it follows the adopted financial policies, rather than wait for decisions from the city council.

Formulating financial policies can be educational for city councilmembers.

> Because most city councilmembers have a heavy workload, discussions of financial issues are sporadic. The process of developing financial policies provides city elected officials the opportunity to become educated on all facets of city financial management.

Financial policies can provide continuity for the city and its city council.

> If financial policies already exist, newly elected officials who are assuming office should not have to make major changes in the fi-

nancial management of the city. Of course, the fact that financial policies are in place does not mean that the newly elected officials cannot or should not change the policies. It simply means that existing financial policies promote necessary continuity for city operations.

Financial policies can provide a basis for coping with fiscal emergencies.

Revenue shortfalls and emergencies requiring unanticipated expenditures can have a severe fiscal impact on a city unless financial plans and policies have been established to handle them. Financial policies are critical for a city to maintain financial solvency.

Obstacles to Overcome

Unfortunately, certain perceptions and some very real situations can become obstacles to city councilmembers when considering developing financial policies. Councilmembers themselves may resist developing long-range financial plans. As stated earlier, because of the annual budget cycle, councilmembers tend to think of financial planning on an annual basis. Also, they may believe that developing a long-range financial plan is not worthwhile because so many things can change over time.

There is also a political dimension. In the process of developing financial policies, many important issues will be discussed at public meetings, and each elected official's position on specific financial issues will therefore become public knowledge. Some city officials may be reluctant to reveal too much about how they feel about a particular topic (e.g., increasing property taxes).

Finally, the task of developing financial policies is very time consuming and is therefore perceived as a drawback. It usually takes a number of special meetings or work sessions for the city council to deliberate the policies. Weighing these very real concerns against the benefits of adopting financial policies should make overcoming hesitations more acceptable and certainly possible. The time and effort necessary will be well rewarded.

HOW TO DEVELOP FINANCIAL POLICIES

City councils must complete various steps before they can adopt financial policies. One of the first steps is to have the city administration begin developing and drafting financial policies. The city administration might present the city council with a work plan for developing financial policies, which would include most of the topics covered in this chapter. For example, the work plan might include

- the definition of financial policies;
- the purpose and benefits of financial policies;
- a review of the obstacles to developing financial policies;
- the types of financial policies to be considered, with samples for each topical area;
- the methods of developing financial policies; and
- strategies for using financial policies.

Once the city council concurs and chooses the areas for policies, the city administration should begin drafting policies consistent with other adopted policies, as necessary. A good way to begin is to review policies adopted by other cities in the state and nation. In addition, sample policies and hands-on training in the financial policy area are available from the Carl Vinson Institute Governmental Training and Education Division.

After the city administration drafts the policies, the city council should devote as many work sessions as necessary to reviewing these policies. This process will be educational for the city council but time consuming.

The city council might decide to hold a public hearing on the financial policies to allow for citizen input. Finally, the policies should be adopted formally through a resolution or ordinance. All policies should be maintained in a policy book and be reviewed periodically (possibly annually and/or after newly elected county commissioners take office). Often, policies are incorporated into the city's finance ordinance or resolution. See Table 25-2 for a selection of financial policy areas, issues, and sample policies.

SUMMARY

The importance of financial policies cannot be overemphasized. Laws provide specific guidance regarding some of the issues that financial policies address. However, city councils are given much latitude regarding the context of the financial policies. The city and its elected officials should make every effort to adopt meaningful financial policies. Subsequently, both the city administration and city council must follow these policies.

Table 25-2. *Sample Financial Policies*

Area	Issue	Sample Policy
Operating budget and equity reserves	Fund balance amounts to maintain	The city will attempt to establish a fund balance reserve for the general fund to pay expenditures caused by unforeseen emergencies, to cover shortfalls caused by revenue declines, and to eliminate any short-term borrowing for cash flow purposes. This reserve will be maintained at an amount that represents approximately $300,000 or three months of general fund operating expenditures, whichever is greater.
Capital improvements program	Capital assets thresholds	For the capital improvements program, all land and land improvements and building projects costing $20,000 or more are classified as capital assets within the capital projects fund. Equipment costing $5,000 or more with an estimated useful life of two or more years is considered a capital asset and purchased as a capital outlay line item within the operating budgets of the departments.
Debt	When to use capital leases rather than outright purchases	Capital leases are used to finance equipment purchases at any time that the cost of the equipment purchases exceeds 12 percent of the general fund budget.
Revenue	Review of fees and charges	The city will review all fees and charges annually in order to keep pace with the cost of providing that service.
Accounting, auditing, and financial reporting	Auditor selection	Every four years the city will issue a request for proposal to independent auditors to provide an audit for the city's operations. The current auditing firm is eligible to propose on this audit.
Purchasing	Centralized purchasing	The city will maintain a centralized purchasing system through which all city purchases for both goods and services will be coordinated by the purchasing department.
Cash and investments	Selection of banks for normal banking operations	Every three years the city will issue a request for proposal to independent banks to provide normal banking services for the city's operations.

26

Betty J. Hudson, Gwin Copeland,
Richard W. Campbell,* and J. Devereux Weeks*

Municipal Revenues

As creations of the state, cities must adhere to state laws, rules, and regulations, and their capacity to generate revenue is determined by the explicit revenue-raising authority granted to them under state law. As noted in Chapter 27, Georgia, like most states, requires that municipal budgets be balanced. Local budgeting processes are therefore to a large extent revenue driven because "available revenues determine the level of spending for any given year."[1]

This chapter describes the revenue sources currently available to Georgia cities, discusses several criteria used in evaluating alternative revenue sources,[2] and examines revenue patterns based on the yield from specific revenue sources. (For a discussion of municipal financial policies to guide revenue decisions, see Chapter 25.)

REVENUE PATTERNS

Local governments in the United States operate in an intergovernmental system. They generate revenues from their own sources as authorized by their state governments and receive intergovernmental revenues in the form of federal and state aid. In 2001, Georgia municipalities derived most of their $4.5 billion in revenue from their own sources, with intergovernmental revenue ($213 million) accounting for only 4.7 percent of total municipal revenue (Table 26-1).

The dominant municipal revenue source is the enterprise fund, which accounts for more than half of all municipal revenues, generating $2.4 billion in 2001. However, if one excludes enterprise fund revenues

---

* Parts of the chapter contain or are based on work by these authors from earlier editions of the *Handbook for Georgia Mayors and Councilmembers*.

Table 26-1. *Revenue Yield, by Source, 1996 and 2001*

	1996			2001			
Revenue Sources	Millions of dollars	Dollars per capita	Percent of total	Millions of dollars	Dollars per capita	Percent of total	Percent change (in amount)
Own-Source Revenue (OSR)							
Property taxes	414	166.61	12.5	468	175.23	10.3	13.0
Sales taxes	317	127.23	9.6	458	171.72	10.1	44.5
Excise and special use taxes	301	120.85	9.1	400	149.92	8.8	32.9
Licenses, permits, and fees	102	40.89	3.1	136	51.06	3.0	33.3
Service charges and other revenues	354	142.32	10.7	462	173.41	10.2	30.5
Enterprise fund	1,680	675.38	50.7	2,392	896.07	52.8	42.4
Total OSR	3,168	1273.28	95.7	4,316	1617.41	95.2	36.2
Intergovernmental revenue (IGR)							
Federal	58	23.20	1.7	85	31.71	1.9	46.6
State	55	22.11	1.7	86	32.36	1.9	56.4
Local	32	12.83	1.0	42	15.89	0.9	31.3
Total IGR	145	58.14	4.4	213	79.96	4.7	46.9
Total revenues	3,313	1,331.42	100.0	4,529	1,697.37	100.0	36.7

Source: Georgia Department of Community Affairs, *Georgia Local Government Finance Highlights, 1996 and 2001* (Atlanta: DCA).

and examines total *general* revenues, the four highest municipal revenue sources are (1) property taxes, (2) service charges (e.g., garbage and trash collection, parks and recreation) and other revenues (e.g., interest earnings and fines and forfeitures), (3) sales taxes, and (4) excise and special use taxes (e.g., alcoholic beverage, insurance premiums, hotel-motel, and franchise payments). Property taxes generated $468 million for cities in 2001 (21.9 percent), with most property tax revenue coming from taxes on real and personal property. Sales taxes produced $458 million (21.4 percent), with service charges and other revenues providing $462 million (21.6 percent) for municipalities in 2001 (Table 26-2).[3]

TAX REVENUE

Tangible Property Tax

With the so-called taxpayer revolt of the 1980s and recommendations from organizations such as the U.S. Advisory Commission on Intergovernmental Relations (ACIR) and the National Conference of State Leg-

Table 26-2. *General Revenues, 2001*

Revenue Sources	Amount ($)	Percent of total
Property taxes	467,820,050	21.9
Real and personal property taxes	407,745,732	19.1
All other property taxes	60,074,318	2.8
Sales taxes	458,446,784	21.4
Local option sales tax	370,529,000	17.3
Special purpose sales tax	87,917,784	4.1
Excise and special use taxes	400,234,948	18.8
Alcoholic beverage taxes	64,041,141	2.8
Insurance premium taxes	98,909,875	4.6
Hotel/motel taxes	78,650,135	3.7
Franchise payments	158,140,031	7.4
Other excise and special use taxes	5,493,766	.3
Service charges and other revenues	462,948,625	21.6
Service charge revenues	166,445,736	7.8
Other revenues	396,502,889	13.8
Licenses, permits, and fees	136,328,400	6.5
Intergovernmental revenues	213,463,269	9.8
Total general revenues	2,139,242,076	100.0

islatures (NCSL) that local governments diversify their revenue bases, the property tax has declined in importance as a revenue source for local governments in the United States.[4] In 1976, for example, the property tax accounted for 42.8 percent of municipal general revenues, while in 1986 the percentage had dropped to 29.5 percent.[5] Despite the decline, nationally the property tax remains the major source of revenue for both cities and counties. In Georgia, property taxes accounted for slightly more than 10 percent of total municipal revenues in 2001, down from 13 percent in 1996.

While the property tax has been the object of criticism (e.g., inequitable appraisals and anxiety about reappraisal, cumbersome and expensive to administer), it is likely to remain a permanent fixture of municipal revenue systems. Its attributes include the following:[6]

1. It provides a stable source of revenue.
2. It taxes nonresident property owners who benefit from local services.

3. It is used by municipalities and counties to finance property-related services such as law enforcement and fire protection and the construction of publicly owned infrastructures such as streets, curbs and sidewalks, and storm drainage systems.
4. The tax on real property is difficult to evade, thus making collection and enforcement easier for local governments.
5. The tax has enabled local governments in the United States to achieve their unique form of autonomy from state and federal control, thereby forestalling centralization of power at higher levels of government.

In Georgia, the ad valorem (according to value) property tax remains a major revenue source for municipalities, generating $468 million in FY 2001.[7] Ad valorem taxes are levied on the following types of property:

1. real property—land, buildings, permanent fixtures, and improvements
2. personal property—property that can be moved with relative ease, such as motor vehicles, boats, machinery, and inventoried goods
3. intangible property—long-term notes secured by real estate and the transfer of real property

General law dictates that tangible real and personal property for municipalities be assessed at 40 percent of its fair market value, except that cities that had an assessed value greater than 40 percent in 1971 may continue to assess at more than 40 percent.[8] The state tests the correctness of municipal assessments periodically and will impose sanctions, including fines, if property is not properly assessed at 40 percent of fair market value.[9] The state constitution authorizes special favorable assessment values for certain kinds of property. Examples are rehabilitated historic property, landmark historic property, bona fide residential transitional property, and bona fide conservation-use property not exceeding 2,000 acres.[10] Also, real property of no more than 2,000 acres owned by a single property owner and devoted to bona fide agricultural purposes must, if certain conditions are met, be assessed at 30 percent of market values (i.e., at 75 percent of 40 percent of fair market value).[11] Standing timber is to be assessed one time, rather than annually, at 100 percent of fair market value at the time it is cut.[12] Timber land is assessed annually as other property and may qualify as bona fide conservation-use property or agricultural-use property and qualify for those favorable assessment classifications.[13]

The tax rate is stated in terms of mills, with 10 mills equal to 1 percent of a property's assessed valuation. Municipal ad valorem tax (millage) rates are set by the city governing authority before the city tax digest is approved by the Georgia Department of Revenue.[14] The tax rate is set by dividing the amount of money the city needs from property taxation by the amount of the tax digest:

tax (millage) rate = amount needed from property taxation ÷ tax digest

The amount of taxes due from an individual property owner is the tax rate times the assessed value of the individual's property:

tax (millage) rate x assessed value = taxes due

Taxpayer Bill of Rights

There is an additional issue that a municipal governing authority must consider when setting the millage rate. Local governments must acknowledge to the public that property taxes may be increased even when the millage rate does not increase through increases in assessed value. In order to determine if there is an increase in property taxes, the city must determine the rollback rate. The rollback rate is the millage rate that would yield the same amount of revenue when applied to reassessments that the local government collected the previous year. Technically, the rollback rate equals the previous year's millage rate minus the millage equivalent of the assessed value added by reassessment. If the city proposes a millage rate greater than the rollback rate (i.e., one that would result in a tax increase from the previous year), the city must advertise its intent and conduct at least three public hearings prior to adoption of the millage rate.[15]

Intangible Tax

The intangible personal property tax was repealed in 1996; however, the intangible tax on long-term real estate notes and the real estate transfer tax were preserved. Long-term real estate notes, which are notes that fall due more than three years from the date of execution and are secured by real estate, are subject to an intangible recording tax of $1.50 for each $500 of the face amount to be paid before such notes can be recorded in the superior court clerk's office. The maximum intangible recording tax on a note is $25,000. Examples are mortgages, deeds to secure debt, bonds for title, or any other real estate security instrument that gives the lender a resource to be used if the principal obligation is not paid. In counties with a population of 50,000 or more, this tax is collected by the superior court clerk, and in counties with a population of less than

50,000, this tax is collected by the county tax commissioner. Revenue from the intangible tax on long-term real estate notes is distributed to the state, the county, municipalities, the school district(s), and to other local taxing districts in proportion to relative millage rates levied by the state and each local taxing district.[16]

Real Estate Transfer Tax

With certain exceptions, a real estate transfer tax is imposed at the rate of $1 on the first $1,000 and 10 cents on each additional $10 on any conveyance of real property when the value of the interest transferred exceeds $100. The clerk of superior court collects the tax and at least once every 30 days distributes it among the state and the county and cities where the property is located in proportion to the millage rate levied by each taxing jurisdiction or district.[17]

Local Sales Tax Limits

Another important source of revenue for cities is the local option sales tax (LOST). As a general rule, the aggregate of all local sales and use taxes imposed in any period cannot exceed 2 percent.[18] The law provides four exceptions to this cap. First, a sales tax for capital projects for education purposes (ESPLOST) does not count toward this limit. Second, any county that levies a sales tax for MARTA and that does not levy a homestead option sales tax (i.e., Fulton County) is permitted to exceed the 2 percent cap by levying a special purpose local option sales tax (SPLOST) for water and/or sewer capital projects for up to five years. Third, a 1 percent increase is allowed to the LOST for a consolidated government with a tax freeze in place that was created through a local constitutional amendment (i.e., Columbus–Muscogee County). Fourth, the law makes an exception for a municipal sales tax for water and sewer purposes, which may be levied in a city with an average wastewater flow of no less than 85 million gallons per day (i.e., City of Atlanta).

Local Option Sales and Use Tax

The joint county and municipal LOST is the most common form of this tax.[19] Subject to voter approval, a sales and use tax of 1 percent may be imposed on the purchase, sale, rental, storage, use, or consumption of tangible personal property and related services. The LOST is a special district tax; the boundaries of the special districts are coterminous with the boundaries of the counties.

Proceeds from this tax are collected by the Georgia Department of Revenue and disbursed to the county and the qualified municipalities within the special district based on the percentages negotiated by the county governments and the cities within each county. One percent of the amount collected is paid into the general fund of the state treasury to defray the costs of administration, and a percentage is paid to the dealer for collecting and reporting the tax.[20] This tax is subject to the same exemptions that are in the state sales tax, except for sales of motor fuels. The state sales tax exemption for eligible food and beverages does not apply to the majority of the LOST currently in effect. However, the LOST enacted in Taliaferro and Webster counties after October 1, 1996, exempt food and beverages.[21]

The tax bill of each property taxpayer must show the reduced city and county millage rate resulting from the receipt of sales tax revenue from the previous year, as well as the reduced dollar amount of the person's property tax resulting from the receipt of such revenue. When a local sales or use tax is paid on an item in another local jurisdiction, a tax credit against this tax is available to the purchaser unless used as a credit against another local sales and use tax levied in the county. Also, the tax may not be imposed upon the sale of tangible personal property that is ordered by and delivered to the purchaser at a point outside the county under certain conditions or if a local option income tax is in effect. To date, no local government has imposed a local option income tax.[22]

All counties and municipalities that impose a joint sales and use tax are required to renegotiate the distribution certificate for the proceeds of the LOST following each decennial census. The criteria to be used in the distribution of such proceeds and the process to resolve conflicts between the county and qualified municipalities are set by state law. If the county and cities fail to renegotiate such certificates as required by law, the tax is terminated.[23]

Special Purpose Local Option Sales and Use Tax

SPLOST is another significant source of city revenue.[24] The revenues from this tax must be used for capital outlay projects, and the tax and the projects to be funded by the tax are subject to voter approval. This additional 1 percent sales and use tax may be imposed on the purchase, sale, rental, storage, use, or consumption of tangible personal property and related services. The tax is collected by the Georgia Department of Revenue and disbursed to the county. Like LOST, SPLOST is a special district tax, and it may be used to fund city projects. Funding of municipal projects may be determined through one of two processes. If the city or cities that have more than half of the aggregate population of all cities in the county and the county commission enter into an intergovernmental agreement to fund a city project or projects through the SPLOST, those projects will be funded in accordance with the agreement.[25] In the event that no intergovernmental agreement is reached, the SPLOST may also be used to fund city projects through a population-based distribution schedule.[26] As a condition to levying a SPLOST, the county must meet and confer with city officials at least 30 days before the call for the referendum in order to consider any capital projects for which a city may seek SPLOST funds. One percent of the amount collected is paid into the general fund of the state treasury to defray the costs of administration. This tax is subject to the same exemptions that are in the state sales tax, except for sales of motor fuels. The state sales tax exemption for eligible food and beverages does not apply to SPLOST, regardless of when the tax was imposed.[27]

The proceeds are to be used for capital projects that have been approved by the voters and may include the following:

1. roads, streets, and bridges, which may include sidewalks and bicycle paths.
2. a capital outlay project in the special district consisting of a courthouse; administrative buildings; a civic center; a hospital; a local or regional jail, correctional institution, or other detention facility; a library; a coliseum; local or regional solid waste handling facilities; local or regional recovered materials processing facilities; or any combination of such projects.
3. a capital outlay project to be operated by a joint authority or authorities of the county and one or more municipalities within the special district.
4. a capital outlay project to be owned or operated or both by the county, one or more municipalities in the special district, one or more local authorities in the special district, or any combination thereof.
5. a capital outlay project consisting of a cultural, recreational, or historic facility or a facility for some combination of these purposes.
6. a water or sewer capital outlay project or combination thereof to be owned or operated by a county water and sewer district and one or more municipalities in the special district.
7. the retirement of existing general obligation debt of the county, one or more cities, or any combination thereof.
8. a capital outlay project consisting of public safety or airport facilities or both or related capital equipment used to operate such facilities or any combination of such purposes.

9. a capital outlay project consisting of capital equipment for use in voting in official elections or referenda within the county or municipality.
10. a capital outlay project within the special district consisting of any transportation facility designed for the transportation of people or goods, including but not limited to railroads, port and harbor facilities, mass transportation facilities, or any combination thereof.
11. a capital outlay project within the special district consisting of a hospital or hospital facility owned by the county, a municipality, or the hospital authority and operated by the county, by the municipality, or by the hospital authority or by a nonprofit, tax-exempt organization through a lease or contract with the county, municipality, or hospital authority.
12. any combination of two or more of these projects.

This special tax cannot be levied for more than six years, stated in either calendar years or quarters.[28] The length of the levy depends on several factors, including the terms of the intergovernmental agreement, if any, and the types of projects to be funded. With voter approval, a SPLOST may be reimposed following the expiration of the existing tax. If the call for the referendum is properly timed, the levy can continue without interruption. A referendum to impose a SPLOST, however, can only take place on one of four special or general election dates per year, roughly on a quarterly basis.[29]

General obligation debt may be incurred for SPLOST projects. To issue general obligation debt in conjunction with a SPLOST, the SPLOST referendum must be accompanied by a referendum for general obligation debt. The general obligation debt must specify each local government issuing debt as well as the amount of debt to be issued with respect to each local government. Only one SPLOST may be levied at any time in a special district.

Sales Tax for Education Purposes

Local boards of education may levy a 1 percent sales tax to fund capital projects for education purposes. This tax is commonly called an ESPLOST. The revenue from it is not distributed to city government; it is distributed to county and independent school districts. Subject to voter approval, the board of education of a county school district (if there is no independent school district in the county) may impose a 1 percent ESPLOST. If there is an independent school district in the county, and at least 25 percent of that district's student enrollment is in the county, then the board of education of the county school district together with the boards of education of each independent school district located in the county may, by concurrent resolutions, impose a 1 percent sales and use tax for capital projects for education purposes. If less than 25 percent of the independent school system district's population is in the county, concurrent resolutions are not required for the county school district to call for the tax. The tax is imposed on the purchase, sale, rental, storage, use, or consumption of tangible personal property and related services. The tax is collected by the Georgia Department of Revenue and disbursed to the board or boards. One percent of the amount collected is paid into the general fund of the state treasury to defray the costs of administration. This tax is subject to the same exemptions as the state sales tax, except for sales of motor fuels and sale of food and beverages.

Net proceeds of the sales tax for educational purposes are distributed proportionally between the county and independent school districts according to student enrollment unless otherwise specified in accordance with concurrent resolutions. The proceeds of the tax may be expended for

- capital outlay projects for educational purposes or
- the retirement of existing school system general obligation debt incurred for capital outlay projects, with the requirement that ad valorem property taxes must be reduced by an amount equal to the proceeds applied to debt retirement.

Excess proceeds must be used to retire existing debt of the school system or, if there is no debt, to reduce the millage rate of the school system. If approved by the voters, the tax may be reimposed after expiration. General obligation debt may be issued in conjunction with the imposition of this special sales tax if approved by the voters of the school district or districts.

Imposition of this tax does not affect the authority of a city or county to impose other local option sales and use taxes. This tax is not subject to the 2 percent cap on local sales taxes.[30] The school board or boards calling for the referendum, not the city council or county commission, are responsible for the cost of holding the referendum.[31]

Municipal Sales Tax

A 2004 law authorized a municipal sales tax to fund water and sewer capital projects. To be eligible to levy the tax, a city must have an average wastewater flow of no less than 85 million gallons per day and must be located in a county in which a SPLOST is not currently in effect. Like the SPLOST, the municipal sales tax for water and sewer purposes is subject to voter approval through a public referendum. Prior to calling for a sales tax referendum, however, the city must pass a resolution requesting the county to call for a SPLOST referendum. If the county refuses to do so or fails to act on the request within 10 days of receiving the resolution from the city, the city may then seek to impose the city sales tax.

The city sales tax may be levied for a maximum of four years and may be renewed through referenda twice. A city may only impose one municipal sales tax at a time. Sales of motor vehicles are exempt from the municipal sales tax; however, sales of motor fuels, food and beverages, and natural and artificial gas are subject to the tax. As with the other LOST, 1 percent of the revenue collected from the tax must be paid into the state general fund to defray the cost to the state of administering the tax.[32]

Alcoholic Beverage Excise Taxes

Cities may levy an excise tax of no more than 22 cents per liter of wine and no more than 22 cents per liter of distilled spirits.[33] General law requires cities to impose an excise tax of 5 cents per 12 ounces on all bottles, cans, and like containers of beer sold in the city. Containers of draft beer are taxable at the rate of $6 for every 15½ gallons.[34]

Local Excise Tax on Distilled Spirits

An excise tax not exceeding 3 percent may be imposed by the city on the sale of distilled spirits by the drink. This tax may not be imposed on sales of fermented beverages made wholly or in part from malt (i.e., beer) or any similar fermented beverage.[35]

Insurance Premium Taxes

A tax of 1 percent may be levied by cities on life insurance companies based on gross direct premiums on policies of persons residing within their boundaries. The tax is collected by the Georgia Commissioner of Insurance and distributed on a population ratio basis. No administrative fee is authorized for the collection of this tax. On all other types of insurance companies, municipalities may levy a gross premium tax of no more than 2.5 percent. This tax is collected by the Georgia Commissioner of Insurance and distributed to cities levying the tax based on premiums allocated on a population ratio formula.[36] No administrative fee is authorized for the collection of this tax.

Business and Occupation Tax

The Georgia Constitution and laws provide that municipalities may levy and collect business and occupational license taxes in the corporate limits of the municipalities.[37]

With certain limited exceptions, applicable primarily to out-of-state businesses, a city may tax a business or the practitioner of an occupation or profession only if the business or practitioner maintains a location or office within the corporate limits of the city.[38] Cities may use one or a combination of the four acceptable methods of taxation: the flat tax, profitability ratios, gross receipts, and number of employees.[39]

The law distinguishes between the imposition of a tax, a regulatory fee, and an administrative fee. A city may impose a tax on a business or practitioner solely for the purpose of raising revenues. However, it may only impose a regulatory fee if the city actually regulates the particular type of business or practitioner, and any regulatory fee must approximate the reasonable cost of the actual regulatory activity performed by the city.[40] Cities may impose an administrative fee as a part of an occupation tax to cover the reasonable cost of handling and processing the occupation tax.[41]

A number of professions are permitted by law to choose between payment of an occupation tax imposed under the city's normal business taxation ordinance or a flat fee, not to exceed $400, set by the city. Examples include lawyers, doctors, dentists, veterinarians, and accountants.[42] An occupation tax may not act as a precondition on the practice of law or of other profession regulated by the state.[43]

Cities are not required to impose an occupation tax, but if they choose to do so they must adopt an ordinance or resolution imposing the business and occupation taxes and regulatory fees according to the requirements of general law.[44] The authority granted to cities to levy occupation taxes on other types of business (e.g., banks, utility companies regulated by the Public Service Commission, and insurance companies) by other general laws remains unchanged.[45] In addition, cities may levy a local occupational license tax on banks.[46]

Financial Institutions Business License Tax

Cities may levy a business license tax on depository financial institutions (i.e., banks and savings and loans) that have an office located within their jurisdictions. The rate of such tax is 0.25 percent of the financial institution's Georgia gross receipts, with the minimum tax being $1,000. Each city is assigned the gross receipts of a financial institution as allocated by the home office to its branches.[47]

Hotel-Motel Tax

Municipalities may impose an excise tax on charges made for rooms, lodging, or accommodations furnished by hotels, motels, inns, lodges, and tourist camps, campgrounds, or any other place in which rooms, lodgings, or accommodations are regularly furnished for value. The law provides several different provisions for levying a hotel-motel tax. The amount of the levy and the expenditure requirements vary based on which alternative is chosen. The hotel-motel tax cannot be levied on rooms, lodgings, or accommodations after the first 10 consecutive days of continuous occupancy; charges for the use of meeting rooms and other facilities or to any rooms, lodgings, or accommodations provided without charge; or rooms, lodgings, or accommodations furnished for one or more days to Georgia state or local government officials and employees traveling on official business.

If a city's levy is at a rate of up to 3 percent, the city must spend for the promotion of tourism, conventions, and trade shows a percentage of the tax revenue that is not less than the percentage spent in the previous year for these purposes. If, during the previous year, any portion of the receipts from the tax was spent for these purposes through a grant to or contract with the state, a state department or authority, or a private-sector, nonprofit organization, at least the same percentage must be spent each year thereafter for those purposes through a contract with one or more of those entities.[48] Any balance may be placed in the general fund for any governmental purpose.[49] The law allows cities to levy this tax at 5, 6, 7, or 8 percent for certain purposes, subject to specific conditions.[50] Typically, the higher tax rate is authorized as a means of financing a specific convention facility in a given county or city.

Any city levying a hotel-motel tax must include in its annual report of local government finances to the Department of Community Affairs a schedule of all revenue from the hotel-motel tax that is spent for the promotion of tourism, conventions and tradeshows, and for any other purpose required by the hotel-motel tax law. The schedule must identify the project or projects funded and the party or organization with whom the city contracted with respect to each expenditure.

Excise Taxes on Rental Motor Vehicles

Cities may impose an excise tax of 3 percent on the rental charge for the rent or lease of a motor vehicle for 31 or fewer consecutive days. A city may not levy this tax if the vehicle is either picked up or returned outside the state of Georgia. A city must expend the proceeds of this excise tax on the promotion of industry, trade, commerce, and tourism; capital outlay projects for the construction and equipping of convention, trade, sports, and recreation facilities or public safety facilities; and maintenance and operation expenses or security and public safety expenses associated with those capital outlay projects. Proceeds may also be expended pursuant to intergovernmental contracts for those types of capital outlay projects. This excise tax is scheduled to terminate no later than December 31, 2038.[51]

Local Option Income Tax

Subject to referendum, a county (or any city, if the county refuses to do so at the request of the largest city) may levy a 1 percent local option income tax if no LOST is in effect. The tax is collected and disbursed by the Georgia Department of Revenue. One percent of the amount collected is paid into the general fund of the state treasury to defray the costs of administration. Except for individuals having a gross income of less than $7,500, the tax is levied on the same income taxable by the state. The tax can be levied only if more than 50 percent of the persons qualified to vote at the election cast a vote and more than one-half of these voters vote in favor of the tax. Because the referendum requirement makes levying the tax extremely difficult if not impossible, this tax is not in effect anywhere in Georgia.[52]

NONTAX REVENUE

Nontax revenues are an important source of general fund revenues for cities. Primary among nontax revenues are fines, forfeitures, court fees and costs, and interest earned on invested funds. Service charges, franchise fees, and intergovernmental and miscellaneous revenues make up the remainder of other general funds received.

Fines, Forfeitures, and Court Fees and Costs

Revenue from these sources includes traffic and parking fines, fines from violations of the wildlife laws, forfeitures of money posted to guarantee appearance in court, and court fees and costs. Municipalities may adopt any or all provisions of the Georgia Uniform Rules of the Road law and prescribe fines for violations, except where otherwise expressly provided by law.[53]

Investments

Cities may earn interest from investment of idle funds. Monies can be invested in bank savings accounts, certificates of deposit, a variety of U.S.

government securities, and the state-managed local government investment pool, which permits municipalities to pool their idle funds with those of the state and other local governments to earn higher interest rates.[54]

User Charges

Municipalities may charge citizens or other governments for services. The amount of such charge may partially or totally offset the cost of providing the service. Services for which user fees may be charged include water, sewage disposal, garbage collection, and recreation. General law provides that fees charged for water or sewer services outside the geographical boundary of the provider must not be unreasonable or arbitrarily higher for customers located outside its boundaries than for those located within its boundaries.[55]

Franchise Fees

Cities can enter into franchise agreements with electric, gas, telephone, and cable television companies, as well as with other public utilities doing business within the municipality.[56] Typically, these agreements provide that a utility will pay the municipality a franchise fee, which is often a specified percentage of the utility's gross receipts within the city, as compensation for the city's permission to use the public right of way.

Alcoholic Beverage Licenses

The state constitution provides that, in the absence of a general law, cities may be authorized by local law to levy and collect license fees within their corporate limits.[57] Cities are authorized to license and regulate the manufacture, distribution, and sale of distilled spirits, malt beverages, and wine within their corporate limits. In addition to the excise tax on alcoholic beverages, discussed earlier in this chapter, municipal governing authorities are authorized to establish the amount of such an annual license fee, with the limitation that they may not charge dealers in distilled spirits more than $5,000 annually for each license.[58]

Development Impact Fees

Development impact fees may be imposed by counties to finance the following public facilities needed to serve new growth and development:[59]

1. water supply production, treatment, and distribution.
2. wastewater collection, treatment, and disposal.
3. roads, streets, and bridges, including rights of way, traffic signals, landscaping, and local components of state or federal highways.

4. storm water collection, retention, detention, treatment, and disposal, flood control, and bank and shore protection and enhancement.
5. parks, open space, and recreation areas and related facilities.
6. public safety, including police, fire, emergency medical, and rescue facilities.
7. libraries and related facilities.

Sale of Contraband Property

In certain instances, municipalities may be entitled to the proceeds from the sale of confiscated contraband property.

Controlled Substances

All property used or intended for use in violation of the Georgia controlled substances act or the controlled substances laws of the United States or other states can be forfeited by court action and sold. Property means real property and personal property, including weapons, currency, securities, or any kind of privilege, interest, claim, or right. Proceeds from forfeited property, plus confiscated money, are distributed pro rata to the state and to local governments according to the role their law enforcement agencies play in seizing the property and money, with the limitation that the state cannot receive more than 25 percent of the distribution.[60]

Unauthorized Dumping of Sewage

Vehicles, trailers, and equipment used in the unauthorized dumping of sanitary sewage or commercial or industrial waste into public sanitary or storm sewers are to be condemned through court action and may be sold, with the proceeds to be paid to the local government or district that owns the sewer system.[61]

Weapons

Weapons used in the commission of a crime and owned by the person convicted may be sold at public auction by the sheriff, with the proceeds to be paid to the county or, if the crime was committed within a city, to be paid to that city.[62]

Intergovernmental Revenues

Municipalities receive funds from the federal and state governments and often from other local jurisdictions as described under "User Charges."

Historically, federal funds have generally come to cities through general revenue-sharing and block and categorical grant programs. General revenue-sharing funds are no longer available to local governments. Unlike revenue-sharing funds, which could be spent with wide discretion and did not require recipients to provide a matching contribution, block and categorical grants must be spent for specific purposes and usually require a matching contribution. For example, block grants are available to smaller counties under federal community development block grant programs. Their primary objective is to expand economic opportunities, principally for persons of low or moderate income. Also, federal funds are available on a competitive basis for public facilities, economic development, and housing. Metropolitan cities are eligible to participate in the metropolitan cities program sponsored by the U.S. Department of Housing and Urban Development (HUD).[63]

State aid generally refers to grants of money to municipalities either for general purposes or for special programs. State law authorizes such grants.

Grants to Municipalities

The General Assembly is authorized to make funds available to certain municipalities for any public purpose except for salaries of elected officials based on a statutory population formula. In order to be eligible for such funds, the governing authority of a city must have held regular meetings within the previous year and must have either collected ad valorem taxes in the city or provided at least two municipal services. The city must submit a certificate to the Office of Treasury and Fiscal Services stating that it has met these requirements. Also, based on a certificate of eligibility, certain cities may receive funds for purchasing, constructing, improving, maintaining, and repairing capital outlay items. Allocation of these funds is based on a statutory population formula. In addition, assistance is available to cities through the county contract program administered by the state Department of Transportation.[64]

The state is authorized to make grants to cities for water pollution control projects, whether or not they qualify for federal aid. In addition, the state is empowered to grant funds to assist in the construction of solid waste handling systems. Further, the state is authorized to establish an assistance fund for matching federal and municipal funds to acquire land for recreational purposes and to improve, expand, develop, or construct outdoor recreational facilities, if approved by the federal government. Such funds cannot finance more than 25 percent of the cost, and to be eligible, the city must fund at least 25 percent of the cost.[65]

The state is empowered to make grants to municipalities to assist in the construction and modernization of publicly owned and operated medical and auxiliary medical facilities, mental retardation centers, and mental health centers when such projects have been approved for federal grants. Generally, state aid may not exceed one-third of the cost.[66]

Municipalities and Counties

The state is empowered to grant funds and other assistance to two or more municipalities or counties or any combination thereof for a program in which the state participates when the local governments are able and willing to provide for the consolidation, combination, merger, or joint administration of the program to reduce its cost or simplify its administration.[67] However, funds have not been appropriated for such grants in recent years.

Municipalities are authorized by the state constitution and general law to enter into contracts with other municipalities and counties for the purpose of sharing ad valorem tax proceeds and other revenues for the development and operation of regional facilities, including business and industrial parks, conference centers, convention centers, airports, athletic facilities, recreation facilities, and jails or correctional facilities.[68]

Borrowed Revenue

Cities may borrow funds to meet operating expenses and to finance capital expenditures. Commonly used instruments include tax anticipation notes for annual temporary loans payable by December 31 from general city funds. These instruments are typically considered sources of short-term revenue to pay for maintenance and operation expenditures early in the year and until property tax receipts are collected later in the year. Other borrowing mechanisms include general obligation bonds, certificates of participation, multiyear installment purchase agreements, and revenue bonds. Bonds, certificates, and installment contracts are repaid from either general city funds or a particular source of revenue.

General obligation bonds are paid by the city issuing them, and the funds to repay them are derived from specific taxes levied by the city. They are backed by the full faith and credit of the city. Revenue bonds are repaid solely from specific revenue generated by public works facilities purchased or constructed with the bonds and, by law, are not debts of the municipality. The borrowing of funds is subject to numerous legal restrictions, procedures, and requirements, including prior voter approval of general obligation bonds to be paid from general city funds.

Voter approval is not required for temporary loans, revenue bonds, certificates of participation, or multiyear installment purchase agreements.[69] Borrowing is discussed more fully in Chapter 29.

Other Revenues

Other possible revenue sources include (1) leases, (2) parking lots and garages, and (3) public concessions.

EVALUATIVE CRITERIA

Revenue and taxation decisions are complex political decisions, and those involved in making these decisions are well aware that individual members of the taxpaying public do not want to bear more than their fair share of the revenue burden.[70] Decisions determining "fair share," or how to distribute the revenue burden in a community, represent the most important choices made by a city council. Two general approaches come into play in decisions about revenue sources:

- benefits-received approach
- ability-to-pay approach

The benefits-received approach implies that the revenue burden be allocated according to the benefits received from public services. User fees and charges are nontax revenue sources that directly reflect this approach. Although this approach has wide appeal in a society with a market economy—one in which consumers pay for the benefits received from private goods and services—there are problems associated with its application in the public sector. In the delivery of many municipal services (e.g., police, fire, and parks and recreation), it is impossible to measure the benefits received by specific city residents. Governmental services usually produce general benefits for the entire community, making the benefits-received approach difficult to apply in financing the delivery of public services.

The ability-to-pay approach underlies most local government revenue systems and their heavy reliance on taxes. Under this approach, the tax burden is distributed according to some indication of taxpayer ability to bear the burden, usually income, property, or some other indicator of wealth. The ability-to-pay approach allows for some redistribution of affluence in society, a value associated with tax system design, but is inconsistent with the benefits-received approach.

In making decisions to increase existing tax rates or to adopt new revenue sources, the following criteria warrant careful consideration:

- equity
- balance
- ease of administration

Equity

Equity implies a fundamental concern for the fairness of the distribution of the revenue burden in a community. The equity issue has two components: horizontal equity and vertical equity.

Horizontal equity involves equal treatment of taxpayers who have equal ability to pay taxes. If two taxpaying units are essentially equivalent in all respects, but one unit pays significantly more tax, the tax system lacks horizontal equity. With regard to the property tax, for example, when owners of homes of equivalent market value pay different property tax amounts (because of different assessed valuations), the principle of horizontal equity is violated. Vertical equity, on the other hand, involves unequal treatment of taxpayers who have unequal or different capabilities to pay taxes. Although there are no clear guidelines, "most would argue that those with more capacity ought to pay more taxes."[71] With regard to the income tax, for example, when lower-income individuals pay a higher income tax amount and/or percentage than do individuals with higher income, the principle of vertical equity is challenged.

Vertical equity involves the relationship between income and taxes actually paid (i.e., the effective rate). The nominal or statutory tax rate is the rate legally defined as applicable to the tax base. The effective tax rate is different, reflecting the actual fiscal impact on the taxpayer. The effective rate is usually calculated by dividing the tax paid by a relevant measure of affluence, usually income. Thus, vertical equity reflects an understanding that statutory tax rates affect individual taxpayers according to their unique financial conditions. With this in mind, a tax can be classified in one of three equity categories reflecting three different revenue burden distributions:[72]

- Regressive—a tax with effective rates that are lower for individuals or families with high affluence than for those with low affluence.
- Progressive—a tax with effective rates that are higher for individuals or families with high affluence than for those with low affluence.
- Proportional—a tax with effective rates that do not change across individuals or families whose affluence varies.

Balance

Revenue must be maintained at a steady flow from year to year to support the continuous and uninterrupted provision of needed public services. Some revenues such as the sales tax and income tax are elastic, meaning that their yields respond to changes in economic activity. In periods of economic growth or high inflation, for example, revenue yields would increase at roughly the same rate as inflation. Likewise, revenue yields would decrease during recessions, reflecting the slowdown in economic activity.

Although it is desirable for tax systems to include elastic revenues, stable revenue sources are also important. The yields from stable revenue sources such as property taxes and user fees and charges will not fluctuate automatically with changes in the economy. Yields from these sources change only when the tax rate is altered. It is important, then, for municipal revenue systems to maintain a balance of both stable and elastic revenue sources so that cities can adequately support their operations no matter what the state of the economy.[73]

Ease of Administration

Not only equity and balance, but also the collectibility of revenue and the ease of administration are important considerations. The goal of administration is to extract desired revenues while minimizing the costs of revenue collection. Revenue collection involves both administrative costs (i.e., the costs to the government of collecting the tax) and compliance costs (i.e., the costs to the taxpayer of complying with the tax law). These two types of costs vary significantly from one revenue source to another, showing that revenue collection requires effort by both the taxpayer and the collecting government.

While the property tax involves relatively high administrative costs, nonproperty tax revenue involves high compliance costs. In administering the property tax, the government maintains parcel records, assesses the value of property, calculates individual tax liability, and distributes tax bills to property owners. The taxpayer is simply responsible for paying the bill. And in many cases, this task is handled by the bank through an escrow account. Because the taxpayer is minimally involved in the process, the compliance costs are low, while the administrative costs to the collecting agency are extremely high.

On the other hand, nonproperty taxes are essentially taxpayer administered, relying to a large extent on voluntary compliance. The individual or firm maintains records of taxable transactions, tabulates the tax base, calculates liability, and makes the payment. The city conducts private audits to ensure an acceptable level of compliance. In such voluntary systems, administrative costs are minimized, and the taxpayer bears the bulk of total collection costs.

NOTES

1. Robert L. Bland, *A Revenue Guide for Local Government* (Washington, DC: International City Management Association, 1989), 17. *See also* James J. Gosling, *Budgetary Politics in American Governments* (New York: Longman, 1992), 159.
2. Portions of this chapter are drawn from Betty J. Hudson and J. Devereux Weeks, *County and Municipal Revenue Sources in Georgia*, 3rd ed. (Athens: Carl Vinson Institute of Government, University of Georgia, 1997).
3. Georgia Department of Community Affairs, *Georgia Local Government Finance Highlights* (Atlanta: Georgia Department of Community Affairs, 2001).
4. *See* U.S. Advisory Commission on Intergovernmental Relations (ACIR), *Local Revenue Diversification: Income, Sales Taxes and User Charges*, Report A-47 (Washington, DC: ACIR, 1974); *Principles of a High Quality State Revenue System* (Cambridge, MA: Lincoln Institute of Land Policy and the National Conference of State Legislatures, no date).
5. Bland, *Revenue Guide for Local Government*, 28.
6. Ibid., 42.
7. Georgia Department of Community Affairs, *Survey of Georgia Local Government Finance* (Atlanta: Georgia Department of Community Affairs, 2001).
8. OFFICIAL CODE OF GEORGIA ANNOTATED (O.C.G.A.) §48-5-7(a).
9. O.C.G.A. tit. 48, ch. 5, art. 5A.
10. GA. CONST. art. VII, §1, ¶3(d), (e)(1); O.C.G.A. §§48-5-7, 48-5-7.2, 48-5-7.3, 48-5-7.4.
11. GA. CONST. art. VII, §1, ¶3(c); O.C.G.A. §§48-5-7, 48-5-7.1.
12. GA. CONST. art. VII, §1, ¶3(e)(2); O.C.G.A. §48-5-7.5.
13. GA. CONST. art. VII, §1, ¶3(c)(2), (e)(1); O.C.G.A. §§48-5-7, 48-5-7.1, 48-5-7.4.
14. O.C.G.A. §48-5-273.
15. O.C.G.A. §48-5-32.1.
16. O.C.G.A. tit. 48, ch. 6, art. 3.
17. O.C.G.A. tit. 48, ch.6, art. 1.
18. O.C.G.A. §§48-8-6, 48-8-112, 48-8-121.
19. O.C.G.A. tit. 48, ch. 8, art. 2.
20. O.C.G.A. §§48-8-87, 48-8-50.
21. O.C.G.A. §§48-8-3, 48-8-82.
22. O.C.G.A. §§48-8-90, 48-8-93, 48-7-149.
23. O.C.C.A. §48-8-89.
24. O.C.G.A. tit. 48, ch. 8, art 3.
25. O.C.G.A. §48-8-115.
26. O.C.G.A. §48-8-115(b)(2)(B).
27. O.C.G.A. §48-8-3.
28. O.C.G.A. §48-8-111. *See also* O.C.G.A. §48-8-111.1. A consolidated government that levies this special local option sales and use tax is not subject to any time limitation on imposition of this tax. Consolidated governments are also exempt from the

requirements to contract with cities on capital outlay projects or to operate projects jointly with a city.
29. O.C.G.A. §§48-8-111, 21-2-540.
30. GA. CONST. art. VIII, §6, ¶ 4; O.C.G.A. tit. 48, ch. 8, art. 3, pt 2.
31. Op. Att'y Gen. 85-18.
32. O.C.G.A. tit. 48, ch. 8, art. 4.
33. O.C.G.A. §§3-6-60, 3-4-80.
34. O.C.G.A. §3-5-80.
35. O.C.G.A. §3-4-131.
36. GA. CONST. art. IX, §4, ¶1(c); O.C.G.A. §§33-8-8.1, 33-8-8.2.
37. GA.CONST. art. IX, §4, ¶1(b); O.C.G.A. §48-13-6.
38. O.C.G.A. §48-13-7.
39. O.C.G.A. §48-13-10.
40. O.C.G.A. §§48-13-8, 48-13-9.
41. O.C.G.A. §48-13-10.
42. O.C.G.A. §48-13-9.
43. Sexton v. City of Jonesboro, 267 Ga. 571, 481 S.E.2d 818 (1997).
44. O.C.G.A. §48-13-6.
45. O.C.G.A. tit. 48, ch. 13, art. 1.
46. O.C.G.A. §§7-1-758, 7-1-1958, 48-6-93, 48-13-16.
47. O.C.G.A. §48-6-90 et seq.
48. O.C.G.A. §§48-13-51(a)(1)(D), (2).
49. O.C.G.A. §48-13-51(2).
50. O.C.G.A. tit. 48, ch. 13, art. 3.
51. O.C.G.A. tit. 48, ch. 13, art. 5.
52. O.C.G.A. tit. 48, ch. 7, art. 6.
53. O.C.G.A. tit. 36, ch. 32; tit. 40, ch. 6, art. 14; city charters.
54. O.C.G.A. §36-80-3; tit. 36, ch. 83.
55. GA. CONST. art. IX, §§2, 3; O.C.G.A. §36-70-24.
56. O.C.G.A. §36-34-2(7).
57. GA. CONST. art. IX, §4, ¶1(b).
58. O.C.G.A. §§3-4-50, 3-5-40–3-5-43, 3-6-40.
59. O.C.G.A. tit. 36, ch. 71.
60. O.C.G.A. §16-13-49.
61. O.C.G.A. §12-8-2.
62. O.C.G.A. §17-5-52.
63. 42 UNITED STATES CODE ANNOTATED (U.S.C.A.) §5301 et seq.; O.C.G.A. §50-8-8.
64. O.C.G.A. tit. 36, ch 40, arts. 2, 3; tit. 32, ch. 5, art. 2.
65. O.C.G.A. §§12-5-32–12-5-34, 12-5-37, 12-8-38.1, 12-3-8.
66. O.C.G.A. tit. 31, ch. 7, art. 3.
67. O.C.G.A. §36-80-6.
68. GA. CONST. art. IX, §4, ¶4; O.C.G.A. tit. 36, ch. 73.
69. GA. CONST. art. IX, §§5, 6; tit. 36, ch. 82, arts. 1, 2, 3; §§36-80-2, 36-80-10–36-80-14, 36-60-13, 36-60-15.
70. This section relies heavily on chapters 6 and 9 in John L. Mikesell, *Fiscal Administration: Analysis and Applications for the Public Sector*, 3rd ed. (Belmont, CA: Brooks/Cole, 1991).

71. Ibid., 154.
72. Ibid., glossary.
73. *See* Sanford M. Groves, *Financial Trend Monitoring System: A Practitioner's Workbook* (Washington, DC: International City Management Association, 1980), 21–25; Bland, *Revenue Guide for Local Government*, ch. 2.

27

Paul E. Glick, Sabrina Wiley Cape,* and Richard W. Campbell*

Operations Budgeting

The operating budget is the most important document that a municipality will produce.[1] The operating budget is a statement of the city's goals and policy preferences, an inventory of its resources, and a plan for allocating scarce resources to meet the needs of its citizens.[2] Cities in Georgia are required to prepare an operating budget each year. (A capital budget that covers proposed expenditures for items with a life of more than one year is not an annual requirement and is described in Chapter 28.)

The annual operating budget (in this chapter, referred to as the budget) is not only a plan that guides the operations of municipal government and its divisions; it is also a political document. In a democratic society, government officials have an obligation to efficiently execute the will of the people. Citizens likewise have a right to oversee and check the policy and administrative decisions of their representatives and appointed public servants. The budget serves both of these democratic aims. It is an important management tool, providing information essential to improving the efficiency of program operations. And, as an accountability document, the budget provides information that citizens can use in assessing municipal activities and operations.

Described as a "wish book with price tags attached," the budget reflects the commitment of resources to the implementation of proposed policies and programs. The budget, then, is the product of a complex process of resolving conflicting needs and wants. It also is an essential component of responsive and responsible local government.

---

* Parts of the chapter contain or are based on work by these authors from earlier editions of the *Handbook for Georgia Mayors and Councilmembers*.

The claim that "each local government's budgeting process is unique ... the product of geographical, historical, economic, political, and social factors peculiar to that jurisdiction" certainly applies to cities in Georgia.[3] No one would argue, for example, that Atlanta, Snellville, Dillard, Brunswick, Plains, and Metter confront the same issues or that their budgets or budget processes are or should be the same. However, municipal budget processes in Georgia, do reflect important features and values associated with budget decision making generally. This chapter reviews state legal requirements relating to municipal budgeting and financial disclosure, describes the process of municipal budgeting, explores the multiple purposes served as the budget is formed and administered, and discusses selected policies intended to guide the operating budget process.[4]

STATE LEGAL REQUIREMENTS

Municipalities are creations of the state, and the state of Georgia has a vested interest in their financial well-being.[5] Prior to 1980, there were no general state statutory or constitutional requirements related to budget development or the disclosure of financial information. In that year, the General Assembly enacted the local government Financial Management Standards Act (FMSA) requiring cities to adopt an annual balanced budget and to provide for regular audits.[6] Subsequently, the General Assembly enacted two important local government budgeting laws. In 1997 it directed the state Department of Community Affairs to create a uniform chart of accounts for the state's local governments (see Chapter 24 for a more detailed discussion of the uniform chart of accounts),[7] and in 1998 it amended the 1980 budget law expanding and clarifying state requirements related to local government budgeting.[8]

The budget law, as amended, imposes the following requirements on cities:

- **Establish an official fiscal year for the city's operations**. There is no prescribed fiscal year, but most begin on either January 1 or July 1.
- **Adopt a balanced budget and provide for a regular audit**.
- **Prepare a proposed budget for submission to the city council**. The budget proposal must include anticipated revenues by source and expected expenditures by function.
- **Adopt project budgets, rather than annual budgets, for major capital projects**. An annual budget corresponds with a city's fiscal year, but a project budget is adopted for the project period,

without regard to the fiscal year. Normally, the issuance of general obligation bonds has funded major capital projects. Prior to this change in the law, cities were required by state law to adopt annual budgets for each project. For example, if a city were to build a new city hall over a three-year period, it would need to estimate the costs that would occur in each of the three years. If the project were not completed on time, many of the same costs would be budgeted in more than one different fiscal year. Under the law, however, cities can budget the total cost of the project in the year in which the project began, with no additional budget action required in the later years of the project, unless the total budget is increased.

- **Limit the requirements for adopting budgets**. Cities now only need to adopt budgets for their governmental fund types (i.e., the general fund, special revenue funds, debt service funds, capital project funds, and permanent funds). A city does not need to adopt budgets for its other funds such as water and sewer. However, a city may adopt annual budgets for all of its other funds.
- **Notify the public that the budget proposal is available for public review**.
- **Conduct a public hearing at least one week prior to the adoption of the budget resolution or ordinance, notice of which must be published at least seven days before the hearing**.
- **Adopt a budget resolution or ordinance, which can contain dollar amounts different from the amounts contained in the proposed budget**.
- **Adopt budget amendments by ordinance or resolution**. Formerly, it was not always clear at a city council meeting when a councilmember was actually amending the budget. For example, when a city councilmember moved to buy a new fire truck and the council voted "yes," had the budget been amended? Under the new law, city councilmembers are required to amend the budget through a more formal process (that is, by approving an ordinance or resolution).
- **Provide for an audit of the financial affairs and transactions of all funds and activities in accordance with generally accepted governmental auditing standards**.[9] The audit report must contain financial statements prepared in conformity with generally accepted accounting principles and the opinion of the auditor regarding the statements.[10] Also, the opinion is to disclose any apparent material violation of state or local law. Cities with a population in excess of 1,500 persons or expenditures of $300,000

or more must have an audit prepared each fiscal year. Other cities must be audited at least once every two fiscal years.
- **Submit a copy of the audit report to the Georgia state auditor within 180 days after the close of the fiscal year, or the close of each second fiscal year in the case of cities not required to be audited annually.**

The budget law also clarifies the legal level of budgetary control. The level of control is the level of budget detail that the city council must adopt in its budgets; overspending at this level would result in a violation of the law. The law establishes the legal level of control at the departmental level within each fund, unless a more detailed level of control is established by resolution or ordinance of the council.[11] When the legal level of control is the department, transfers of appropriations within any fund below the departmental level require only the approval of the budget officer.[12] However, the law does not define departments. Therefore, the city council must make departmental allocations clear within the budget (see Table 27-1).

If the city councilmembers keep the department as the legal level of control, only the city council can transfer budget amounts between departments within each fund. For example, in Table 27-1, if the city council had a need to spend more than the $2 million in the public works department, the council would have to amend the budget. If the city spends more on any department than the budget allows without first amending the budget, it is breaking the law.

STAGES OF THE MUNICIPAL BUDGETARY PROCESS

The municipal budgetary process is divided into four stages: preparation, adoption, execution, and auditing. Although the way in which the budget document develops through these four stages is simple, the to-

Table 27-1. *Sample General Fund Allocations, by Department*

Department	Amount
General government	$1 million
Police	$3 million
Finance	$1 million
Public works	$2 million
Parks and recreation	$1 million
Total budget	$8 million

tal process is complex.[13] It involves many different actors such as the chief administrative officer, the city councilmembers, the clerk to the city council, the department heads, and others, who change roles from one stage to the next.

"The budget" is really two budgets. The first budget, or legislative budget, is a request for funds. The legislative budget is the focus of concern during the first two stages of the process (i.e., preparation and adoption). A budget request is prepared by department heads and other staff for action by the council. Once the response to the funding request is completed by the adoption of an appropriation resolution or ordinance, the budget becomes a plan each municipal department is authorized to undertake. This second budget, or management budget, is critical to the final two stages in the process (i.e., execution and auditing). This is the budget that the administrative officers must execute, making sure that spending does not exceed limits. It also serves the audit function, providing a foundation for the city's financial accounting structure.[14]

Preparation

Budget preparation begins with the creation of a budget request. In many cities, the clerk is designated as the budget officer and prepares the budget under the supervision of the mayor or a designated budget committee. In such cases, the council and/or budget committee retains ultimate responsibility, and the city clerk assumes the day-to-day responsibilities associated with budget preparation. In those cities in which there is a city administrator or manager, that person is usually designated as ultimately responsible for budget preparation and submission. These municipalities often also have either a director of finance or budget director who assumes the day-to-day responsibility for budget preparation. The budget officer (whether the clerk, administrator, or manager) is also responsible for coordinating the work of a centralized budget and finance staff as well as the budget activities of department heads and their staffs.

To ensure that the budget is ready and in place when the fiscal year begins, it is necessary to establish a plan for developing the budget early in the process. First, the budget officer distributes a budget calendar to all participants. The budget calendar is a schedule of the various actions or steps that are necessary to prepare, review, and finally adopt a budget. It gives a specific timetable and assigns responsibility for each action. Table 27-2 presents a suggested budget calendar based on a January 1 fiscal year. Preparation of the budget request is time consuming and should begin about four to six months before the start of the city's fiscal year.

Table 27-2. Suggested Budget Calendar (January 1 Fiscal Year)

Due Date	Budget Steps	Day-to-Day Responsibility
September 1	Budget calendar is prepared.	Budget officer*
September 1	Budget preparation forms are printed and ready for distribution.	Budget officer
September 15	Budget information for current year and for prior years is entered on forms for each department. Budget request forms and instructions are then distributed to departments.	Budget officer
October 1	Revenue estimates for the next budget year are completed.	Budget officer
October 15	Expenditure estimates are made and are returned to the budget officer.	Department heads
November 15	Budget requests are summarized.	Budget officer
	Requests are analyzed and adjusted.	Budget officer
	Proposed expenditure plan is assembled.	Budget officer
	Proposed revenue program is prepared.	Budget officer
November 22	Proposed budget for next budget year is submitted to the board of commissioners.	Budget officer
November 30	Proposed budget is reviewed.	City council
December 1	Public hearing is advertised.	Budget officer
December 8	Public hearing on budget is held.	City council
December 15	Board's review of proposed budget is completed. Revisions are made to the budget.	City council
December 24	Budget adoption meeting is advertised.	Budget officer
December 31	The budget is adopted. The appropriation ordinance and the revenue ordinance are adopted.	City council
January 1	Monthly or quarterly allotment schedules for departments are prepared. Budget accounts are created. The adopted budget is entered into these accounts.	Budget officer

* The budget officer can be any one of the following: city administrator, manager, clerk, finance officer, budget officer, or the mayor or a councilmember.

Once the budget participants know who is responsible for what and by when, the next step is to estimate the amount of revenue that will be available. Since cities cannot spend more dollars than they collect, the designated budget officer carefully estimates the amount of revenue the city can expect from each revenue source. Revenue collections in previous years serve as a basis for the forecast. For the purpose of estimating the property tax, the previous year's millage rate is applied, but once the budget is adopted a new millage rate will be set in order to generate revenues to cover expenditures.

Department heads play an important role in budget preparation. Working with members of their staff, they prepare and submit budget requests to the person responsible for day-to-day budget activities. Department heads should prepare realistic requests that reflect constraints confronting the city in a particular fiscal year. They must provide accurate numbers to support their request and articulate and "sell" their respective programs.[15] To assist department heads, the budget officer issues guidelines indicating the limits within which budget requests should be prepared. The guidelines contain information such as the following:[16]

- revenue estimates
- planned changes in the level of service delivery
- a review of current year operations
- an analysis of general economic conditions expected for the coming year
- assumptions to be made about wage rates and other prices
- conditions under which additional personnel can be requested and the number of personnel who may be promoted
- planned productivity gains
- instructions for completing the forms

Furthermore, the budget officer prepares and distributes budget request forms to all city departments. These forms ensure consistency and uniformity in the information submitted in departmental requests, thereby facilitating the review process by the person or committee responsible for budget preparation. Two commonly used forms are the budget expenditure request form and the personal services cost explanation form:[17]

1. **Budget expenditure request form**. This form shows the details of a department's budget request. It usually lists expenditures by line item and activity within a department. It includes actual expenditures from the preceding two or three years, the current year's budgeted expenditures, the budget request for the next fiscal year, and information regarding the extent to which the request is an increase or decrease in the current budget.

2. **Personal services cost explanation form**. This form shows the basis for a department's request for funds to pay personnel costs in the next fiscal year. It usually includes cost data related to current salaries, salary increases, overtime, social security, and new employees.

The budget officer reviews departmental requests and prepares an integrated budget for submission to the city council. Although this review can include formal hearings in which department heads defend and justify their requests publicly, the process is usually informal, with considerable day-to-day interaction as the budget officer and the department heads resolve specific details. Once the review is completed, the budget is presented to the city council, usually six weeks before the beginning of the fiscal year.

The budget document submitted to the city council should include (1) a budget message, (2) a budget summary, and (3) detailed budget requests.

Budget Message

The budget message describes the significant features of the proposed budget; identifies the differences between the proposed budget and the current budget and explains the reasons for these differences; discusses new programs contained in the budget; identifies and explains the need for additional revenue sources; and identifies public needs that were recognized as important but could not be addressed in the proposed budget.

Budget Summary

The budget summary shows estimated revenues by major source and requested expenditures by departments and activity. It also presents a detailed schedule, by department, of funds requested for capital expenditures.

Detailed Budget Requests

This portion of the proposed budget provides detailed expenditure data by major expenditure item (object code) for each department. It also includes expenses, which are not charged to specific departments (i.e., bond redemption, judgments, and losses, etc.). Finally, it contains revenue estimates by major and minor revenue sources.

Adoption

The second stage of the budgetary process, adoption, is the responsibility of the city council. The adoption stage provides an opportunity to review the performance of municipal operations and to assess the quality and level of services delivered. Review of the proposed budget normally takes four to six weeks. Although a budget or finance committee often conducts a major part of the review, budget adoption requires formal action by the council.

The city council is required by state statute to conduct a public hearing to consider the budget. This hearing provides citizens and various community interest groups an opportunity to present their views on various aspects of the proposed budget. The city council can also request that the budget officer and/or department heads come before it to explain and discuss specific elements in the budget request.

After the required hearing is held and any changes are made, the budget is ready for adoption. The council must take two actions in order to adopt the budget:

1. It must enact a revenue resolution or ordinance establishing the tax levy.
2. It must enact a budget resolution or ordinance appropriating funds to departments.

With adoption, the budget is no longer a proposal or a request for funds. The so-called legislative budget has become the management budget. This budget guides the implementation of the council's policies and programs and serves as a benchmark for making judgments about performance.

Execution

The third stage in the budgetary process, the execution stage, has been referred to as the "action phase of budgeting," when plans contained in the budget are actually put into operation.[18] While there is inevitably "a push and pull between flexibility and control,"[19] historically budget execution has been viewed as a way of maintaining control over the use of resources, as municipal governments put into practice the various policies and programs authorized in their budgets. In a democracy, in which the power of the purse rests with legislative bodies, managerial controls must be established to ensure that actual spending does not exceed appropriations and that resources are expended only for those purposes intended by the legislative body.

Fund Accounting

The most important component of a management control system is the accounting structure employed to record and report a municipality's financial transactions. Accounting systems vary significantly from one city to another. Some cities, for example, rely on a cash basis of accounting (revenues are recorded when received in cash and expenditures are recorded when paid); others use a modified accrual basis (revenues are recorded when received in cash and expenditures are recorded when purchased). Many cities, especially the most populated, employ integrated computer-based financial management systems, but many others continue to rely on bookkeepers. No matter how basic or sophisticated the system of budget execution, accounting for the resources appropriated by the city council remains a fundamental need.

Unlike accounting in profit organizations (where the corporate organization itself is a single, accountable entity), governmental accounting involves the use of multiple funds, reflecting the existence of multiple accounting entities.[20] Fund accounting has evolved in the public sector to keep track of revenue from many different sources that is designated for a variety of specific purposes and activities. Most municipal services and administrative activities (i.e., police, fire, public works, and financial administration) are supported by tax revenue and are accounted for in the general fund. However, appropriations designated for debt service and revenue generated by specific revenue sources for a specified purpose must be accounted for separately in other governmental funds.

Cities also engage in activities that are self-supporting, which are funded by fees and charges rather than general tax revenue (e.g., water and sewer, utilities, mass transit, golf courses, etc.). Financial transactions and financial reports related to these activities must be kept separate so that the "profitability" of the enterprise can be determined. They are accounted for in proprietary funds.

The Governmental Accounting Standard Board (GASB) suggests that cities employ eight fund types. These are described in some detail in Chapter 24.[21]

Budgetary Accounting and Preauditing

Budgetary accounts and preaudits are as important to a management control system as the use of fund accounting. Budgetary accounts are established for each activity and line item contained in the adopted budget. The budgetary expenditure accounts, referred to as appropriations, contain resources that the city is authorized to expend during the fiscal year.

The appropriations balance is reduced routinely as expenditures are made. In fact, prior to expending funds, it must be determined that the appropriations balance is sufficient to cover the expenditure. This control technique is referred to as the preaudit function. Generally accepted accounting principles, reflecting this concern for control, require that yearly financial reports compare budgeted revenues and budgeted expenditures with actual revenues and actual expenditures.

Auditing

The final stage of the budgetary process involves a retrospective examination of the process of budget execution. Auditing represents an attempt to check and evaluate municipal operations within a given fiscal year. Audits provide feedback to the council and other city officials on the integrity of financial transactions and formal reporting, the efficiency of program operations, and the effectiveness of city policies and programs.

Three types of audits are financial audits, performance audits, and program audits. As noted in the section on state legal requirements, cities are required to have a financial audit prepared. An independent accounting firm usually performs the financial audit in the months immediately following the fiscal year end. This audit must be prepared according to generally accepted governmental auditing standards and must contain the required basic financial statements. The audited financial statements are collectively referred to as the "annual financial report."

The annual financial report also includes a letter from the auditor containing its judgment about whether or not the financial statements are a fair representation of the city's financial position, the results of its operations, and cash flows of its proprietary funds (funds that are self-sustaining, usually through charges and fees).

Because performance audits and program audits are not required by state statute, most cities do not conduct these audits. Those cities that do usually have an in-house staff of management analysts. Performance audits are also referred to as efficiency audits and represent attempts to measure the level of activity performed in specific divisions and departments. Performance audits focus on workload measures; information such as numbers of assaults investigated per shift (police), books loaned per week (library), and clients interviewed per month (welfare) is recorded. These workload measures allow management to monitor changes in the level of effort and the effect of these changes on performance.

Program audits focus on results rather than level of activity or workload measures. These audits require the skills associated with evaluation research and represent an attempt to assess the effectiveness of program operations. Effectiveness is defined as the extent to which the results of program operations are consistent with the program's goals and objectives. In order to make a judgment about effectiveness, it is necessary to measure the effect that the program actually has on the community. Assessing program impact produces information that allows the city to decide whether the results from specific programs are worth the investment or whether community resources might be better used to pursue other policies and programs.

Overlap of Budgeting Stages

The four stages of budgeting—preparation, adoption, execution, and auditing—overlap significantly. For example, while the budget request for FY 2005 is being prepared, the budget for FY 2004 is being executed (and perhaps amended), and the audit for FY 2003 is being conducted. During the subsequent phase, the city council reviews the budget request for FY 2005, considers the audit report for FY 2003, and makes decisions concerning any necessary budget amendments for FY 2004—all in the same time period. The situation is further complicated because the city's fiscal year may be different from those of the state (July 1–June 30) and federal (October 1–September 30) governments. In situations in which local funds must be budgeted to match federal or state funds, discrepancies in fiscal years may confound the municipal budget process.

BUDGET VALUES AND BUDGET FORMATS

Three values pervade the municipal budgetary process—control, management, and planning[22]—regardless of the budget practice or procedure a local government uses. Each value is reflected in a specific budget format that provides a framework within which budgetary decisions are made and budgetary data presented. The three budget formats are line-item budgets, performance budgets, and program budgets. All budget decisions require information, which will vary with the format. The format chosen by a particular jurisdiction will largely depend on the extent to which budget decision makers are concerned with controlling the use of public resources (line item) and/or making judgments about how efficiently (performance) and effectively (program) those resources are used.

Line-Item Budgets

Control-oriented budgets frequently take the form of very detailed line-item descriptions of authorized expenditures. The focus in the budgetary process is on line items, or objects of expenditure (e.g., personnel, pencils, gasoline). Originally, budgets were designed primarily to give elected officials more control over how public money was spent. They were intended to reduce the potential for corruption and waste in municipal government. Although this format achieves its objective of control, it also creates a relatively inflexible financial management system that may not allow administrators enough leeway to make minor adjustments when unanticipated problems or opportunities arise. For this reason, a strict line-item budget usually is not preferred. Rather, less restrictive line-item formats are found in city budgets today. Table 27-3 shows a simplified example of a line-item budget reflecting a strong control orientation.

Performance Budgets

Management is another focus of public budgets, often reflected in the use of performance budgets. Like performance audits, performance budgets are more concerned with efficiency than with control over expenditure decisions. In such budgets, workload data and performance indicators are provided to illustrate the efficiency of the services described. Table 27-4 presents a simplified example of a performance budget format.

Program Budgets

Focusing on broad overall functions rather than on agencies or specific tasks, the program budget emphasizes planning. As the example in Table 27-5 shows, a program budget is concerned with programs rather than with departments or objects of expenditure. Sometimes, however, additional detail in program budgets is desirable to specify how program funds are to be allocated to departments and objects of expenditure. Many program budgets do contain line-item detail (see Table 27-6).

Table 27-3. *Example of Line-Item Budget Format*

Item	Budget
Salaries—governing authority	$11,000
Wages and salaries—other personnel	38,400
Per diem	2,250
Payroll taxes	8,500
Health insurance	6,700
Life insurance	5,800
Postage	900
Utilities	2,900
Gasoline and motor oil	1,300
Telephone service—local	2,175
Telephone service—long distance	300
Debt service	13,850
Total	$214,100

Table 27-4. *Example of Performance Budget Format (Sanitation Services Program Only)*

Service	Budget
Refuse Collection	
Personal services	$3,500
Contractual services	500
Supplies and materials	500
Capital outlay	1,000
Total	$5,500
Performance Statistics	
Residential Collections	
Pickups per week from residences	1,000
Tons of refuse collected per year	375
Cost of collection per ton	$8
Cost per dwelling = pickup per year	$3
Total annual cost	$3,000
Commercial Collections	
Commercial stops—two pickups per week	100
Tons of refuse collected per year	250
Cost of collections per ton	$8
Cost per stop per year	$20
Total annual cost	$2,000

Source: Adapted from Arthur A. Mendonsa, *Simplified Financial Management in Local Government* (Athens: Institute of Government, Institute of Community and Area Development, and Center for Continuing Education, University of Georgia, 1969), 164, 167.

Table 27-5. *Example of a Simple Program Budget Format*

Program	Budget
General administration	$ 28,000
Public safety	21,000
Water services	110,500
Sanitation services	17,000
Roads, streets, and bridges	14,300
Recreation services	2,000
Total	$192,800

Table 27-6. Example of a Detailed Program Budget Format (Public Safety Only)

Program	Item	Budget
Public Safety	Salaries—Police	$18,000
	Uniforms—Police	700
	Gasoline and oil—Police	2,400
	Vehicle maintenance—Police	500
	Telephone—Police	700
	Operating supplies—Police	400
	Salaries—Fire	15,000
	Uniforms—Fire	600
	Total	$51,900

Budgetary Trends

State law does not require that Georgia municipalities follow any prescribed budget format. Rather, a city usually selects a format that reflects the primary focus of its budget and the level of financial detail that city officials want to include. The National Association of Counties has expressed the concern that because line-item budgets "merely state what each department and other administrative units plan to buy, [they] fail to inform the taxpayer what he is really receiving for his money [and tend to] 'hamper' as much as aid the deliberative processes of county government."[23] While it is true that city councils are central to the budget process and that they must exercise control through the use of the line-item format, the view that municipal budget decisions can benefit from other kinds of information has gained some acceptance over the years.

Local governments, especially larger jurisdictions, increasingly are using more sophisticated results-oriented budget formats. In fact, a mid-1980s survey of 460 municipalities with populations greater than 25,000 revealed that over three-fourths were using performance and program budgeting.[24] A recent and more representative study that included smaller cities and counties found that line-item remains the most commonly used format but that more and more local governments expect to change formats in the future.[25]

BUDGET-RELATED POLICIES

As suggested in Chapter 25, city councilmembers must address many important questions as they assume their budget-making responsibilities. A few of these questions are presented below. A prudent city council is one that develops agreed-upon responses to such recurrent questions and, further, formalizes its responses in policy statements intended to guide future actions.

Must the Budget Balance?

Georgia law requires municipalities to adopt balanced budgets. When the budget is balanced, revenues must equal expenditures. However, there are two scenarios in which revenues and expenditures need not be equal: (1) when the city is trying to accumulate resources, usually for cash flow purposes, for capital items, or for unforeseen emergencies; or (2) when the city has incurred a deficit fund balance (i.e., actual expenditures have exceeded revenues) in prior years and wishes to eliminate this problem. In Georgia, this second option is not allowable unless the city has an adequate unreserved fund balance (i.e., the accumulated difference between revenues and expenditures over the life of the fund) from the previous year to cover the difference between revenues and expenditures in the proposed budget.

How Much Should a Fund Balance Be?

Fund balance can refer to "reserves" or "rainy day" funds, but accountants define fund balance as the difference between the assets and the liabilities on the balance sheet or the difference between revenues and expenditures since the fund (e.g., the general fund) was created. Accounting rules allow cities to reserve portions of fund balance. When a portion of fund balance is reserved, it is not available to spend. Reserves usually result from legal restrictions. The portion of fund balance that is not reserved, or the unreserved fund balance, is what is available to spend in the subsequent year.

There is no easy answer to the question regarding size of fund balance. There are situations in which a very high balance could present a problem. Like businesses, cities must have adequate resources to meet their payrolls and pay their bills. Cities use fund balances to meet these cash-flow needs; businesses refer to such resources as "equity" or "retained earnings." But there is also a significant difference between cities and businesses. Because businesses operate to make a profit; they can never have too much equity. By contrast, cities operate to provide social and essential services. Therefore, if a fund balance becomes too large, a city can be criticized for taxing its residents and businesses beyond what it needs for current operations. Adopting a financial policy that explains why a certain fund balance is being maintained will help a city's position if a taxpayer were to sue the city for levying excess property taxes.

Although some taxpayers might question the need for any fund balance at all, there are some convincing arguments that support maintaining adequate fund balances. The primary argument is that fund balances need to be maintained to ensure adequate cash flow. If a city relies heavily on property taxes (as opposed to sales taxes) to finance its operations, cash-flow problems can result. For example, some cities operate within a calendar fiscal year (January–December) but do not receive their property taxes until November or December. Therefore, the year is almost over before the property taxes are available to spend. Municipalities can either maintain an adequate fund balance to cover cash-flow requirements during the year or borrow money for this purpose (usually through the issuance of tax anticipation notes). The more conservative approach would be to accumulate adequate fund balance to cover cash flow problems and thereby avoid interest costs associated with borrowing money.

Some cities accumulate fund balances to cover contingencies not provided for in the budget that require expenditures. Contingency funds are used for emergencies such as flooding caused by excess rainfall, the explosion of a gas main on a city road, or the collapse of a city bridge. Some municipalities include separate contingency accounts in their budget; others use fund balance for this purpose.

Many cities across the United States maintain fund balances equal to the equivalent of one to three months of operations. For example, if a city's expenditure budget is $12 million, the policy might be to maintain a fund balance of $1 million (i.e., one-twelfth of $12 million). Only in extreme cases (i.e., in which cash flow problems require larger fund balances) do municipal fund balances exceed three months of operations. Again, there is no "right answer" as to how much a city's fund balance should be.

Do Appropriations Lapse at the End of the Fiscal Year?

When a portion of a city's adopted budget remains unspent at the end of the year, what happens to that amount? Georgia law does not appear to address this issue specifically. Generally, city councils use one of three financial policies to address this question. Under the most common policy, any unspent appropriations lapse at the end of the fiscal year and are not carried forward to the subsequent year. Any outstanding encumbrances (e.g., purchase orders outstanding) at year's end must therefore be reappropriated in the subsequent year, usually through a budget amendment, thereby increasing the budget. The city council must reappropriate the amount of encumbrances; however, it has detailed information about the encumbrances that must be carried forward because they have been outlined in the previous year's budget.

Another policy stipulates that if any part of an appropriation is encumbered, that portion is added (i.e., carried forward) to the subsequent year's budget automatically. When a council adopts this policy, the council need not take any legal action regarding encumbered appropriations that are carried forward. Some city councils adopt this financial policy because they see no need to formally approve a carryover of items budgeted in the previous year.

A third policy approach allows all unencumbered appropriations (i.e., any portion of an appropriation that has not been charged with expenditures) to be carried forward. This policy makes it possible for department directors to accumulate appropriations from year to year, but keeping track of the budget can be complicated. Few municipalities use this policy. Generally, it is recommended only for capital projects.

NOTES

1. Portions of this chapter are drawn from Ronald B. Hoskins, "Budgeting," in *Handbook for Georgia Mayors and Councilmembers*, 2nd ed., ed. J. Devereux Weeks (Athens: Carl Vinson Institute of Government, University of Georgia, 1984); Arthur A. Mendonsa, *Simplified Financial Management in Local Government* (Athens: Institute of Government, Institute of Community and Area Development, and Georgia Center for Continuing Education, University of Georgia, 1969).
2. Ronald B. Hoskins, "Budgeting," in *Handbook for Georgia Mayors and Councilmembers*, 2nd ed., J. Devereux Weeks and Emily Honigberg (Athens: Carl Vinson Institute of Government, University of Georgia, 1984).
3. Lon Sprecher, "Operating Budgets," in *Local Government Finance: Concepts and Practices*, ed. John E. Peterson and Dennis R. Strachota (Chicago: Government Finance Officers Association, 1991), 45.
4. For a recent and more detailed discussion of local government budgeting, see Robert L. Bland and Irene S. Rubin, *Budgeting: A Guide for Local Governments* (Washington, DC: International City County Management Association, 1997) and Roy T. Meyers, ed., *Handbook of Government Budgeting* (San Francisco: Jossey-Bass, 1998). With regard to recent improvements in local government budgeting and financial management, see Roland Calia, Salomon Guajardo, and Judd Metzgar, "Best Practices in Budgeting: Putting NACSLB Practices into Action," *Government Finance Review* 16 (April 2000): 9–17.
5. For a thorough and useful summary of state legal requirements related to local government budgeting, which is updated annually after each session of the Georgia General Assembly, see Paul Hardy, Betty J. Hudson, Richard W. Campbell, and Paul E. Glick, *Compliance Auditing in Georgia Counties and Municipalities: A Practical Guide to State Laws for Auditors and Local Government Officials*, 2nd ed. (Athens: Carl Vinson Institute of Government, University of Georgia, 2000), 18.
6. OFFICIAL CODE OF GEORGIA ANNOTATED (O.C.G.A.) tit. 36, ch. 81.
7. O.C.G.A. §36-81-3(e). *Also see Uniform Chart of Accounts for Local Governments in Georgia* (Atlanta: Georgia Department of Community Affairs, 1998).
8. O.C.G.A. §§36-81-2(14), 36-81-3, 36-81-5.
9. Guidelines for audit preparation are contained in State and Local Government Committee, *Audit and Accounting Guide: Audits of State and Local Governmental Units* (New York: American Institute of Certified Public Accountants, 2002).

10. Although subject to change, generally accepted accounting principles (GAAP) represent the consensus at any given time as to how the financial accounting process should operate and how financial statements should be prepared. The authoritative GAAP statement is found in National Council on Governmental Accounting, *Governmental Accounting and Financial Reporting Principles* (Chicago: Municipal Finance Officers Association, 1979). More recently, the Governmental Accounting Standards Board (GASB) has been created, and the Government Finance Officers Association (GFOA) publishes a monthly newsletter on accounting, auditing, and financial reporting titled the *GAAFR Review*.
11. O.C.G.A. §36-81-3(d)(3).
12. Ibid.
13. For an insightful discussion of the intricacies and complexities of the budgetary process generally, *see* Aaron Wildavsky, *The Politics of the Budgetary Process*, 3rd ed. (Boston: Little, Brown and Co., 1979). For a discussion of the municipal government process and the role of various actors (ie., mayor, city manager), *see* Terry Nichols Clark, G. Edward DeSeve, and J. Chester Johnson, *Financial Handbook for Mayors and City Managers* (New York: Van Nostrand Reinhold Co., 1985).
14. This distinction between legislative and management budgets comes from Robert N. Anthony and David W. Young, *Management Control in Nonprofit Organizations* (Homewood, IL: Richard D. Irwin, 1984), 357–59.
15. Witherspoon, "Budgeting," in *Guide to County Organization and Management*, 56.
16. Anthony and Young, *Management Control in Nonprofit Organizations*, 366.
17. Jack Rabin, W. Bartley Hildreth, and Gerald Miller, "Budgeting: Formulation and Execution," in *Public Budgeting Laboratory* (Athens: Carl Vinson Institute of Government, University of Georgia, 1996).
18. Robert D. Lee Jr. and Ronald W. Johnson, *Public Budgeting Systems*, 2nd ed. (Baltimore: University Park Press, 1977), 209.
19. Witherspoon, "Budgeting," in *Guide to County Organization and Management*, 61.
20. For two basic introductions to governmental accounting, see Leo Herbert, Larry N. Kellough, and Alan Walter Steiss, *Governmental Accounting and Control* (Monterey, CA: Brooks/Cole, 1984) and Paul E. Glick, *A Public Manager's Guide to Government Accounting and Financial Reporting* (Chicago: Government Finance Officers Association, 1990).
21. National Council on Governmental Accounting, *Governmental Accounting and Financial Reporting Principles*, 9.
22. These values are discussed in some detail in Allen Schick, "The Road to PPB: The Stages of Budgetary Reform," *Public Administration Review* 26 (December 1966): 243–58.
23. Witherspoon, "Budgeting," in *Guide to County Organization and Management*, 172.
24. Theodore H. Poister and Robert P. McGowan, "The Use of Management Tools in Municipal Government: A National Survey," *Public Administration Review* 44 (May–June 1984): 217. *Also see* Donald Axelrod, Budgeting for Modern Government (New York: St. Martin's Press, 1988), 266–74.
25. Daniel E. O'Toole and Brian Stipak, "Budgeting and Productivity Revisited: The Local Government Picture," in *Public Productivity Review* 12 (1988): 1–12.

28

Sabrina Wiley Cape, Paul E. Glick,* and Richard W. Campbell*

Capital Improvements Planning

A capital budget involves different criteria and a longer time frame than does an operating budget. As discussed in Chapter 27, the annual operating budget describes costs incurred in the normal operations of city departments responsible for delivering services that benefit the citizenry in the current fiscal year, and these operating costs are financed out of current-year revenues. Capital costs, on the other hand, usually are incurred in the acquisition of equipment and in the construction of facilities and infrastructure that may benefit residents of the city well into the future. Because capital purchases involve long-term benefits, they are classified as capital improvements and may be funded through the issuance of bonds, proceeds of special purpose local option sales tax (SPLOST), or other forms of borrowing (see Chapter 23). Capital budget decisions usually are handled in a multiyear capital improvements plan (CIP) in a separate administrative process, although funding from the general fund (local resources) is often considered.

The CIP outlines a recommended schedule of public improvements to be accomplished over a multiyear period, usually four to six years. In the same manner as the annual operating budgetary process, the CIP is developed with a calendar, instructions and guidelines, and standardized forms. Each department submits a capital projects request, with justification and cost estimates. The governing authority assesses the requests based upon a ranking of projects submitted by the departments and, when the assessment is complete, acts on the proposed CIP.[1]

Although capital budgets and CIPs are important elements of sound financial management, they have not been used widely in Georgia cities

---

* This chapter includes material developed by Jim Calvin, former city manager and executive director of the Georgia Municipal Association, and these authors.

until recently. A recent survey of municipal officials conducted by the Georgia Department of Community Affairs (DCA) revealed that 222 of the 269 cities surveyed prepared a capital budget in 2003.[2] This figure indicates that Georgia city officials, like local government officials nationally, have come to recognize the capital budget and CIP as essential policy tools and vehicles for communicating the city's long-term infrastructure needs to the public.[3]

The purpose of this chapter is to emphasize the importance of long-range capital planning to the financial future of Georgia cities, to outline the steps involved in the process of developing a capital budget and CIP, and to review financial policy issues that city councils need to address as they plan for the future of their city's investment in capital assets.

CAPITAL IMPROVEMENTS PLAN

A discussion of capital budgeting should begin by first distinguishing between the CIP and the capital budget. Typically, the CIP is a plan identifying needed capital expenditures projected for some period of time into the future. The capital budget is the first year (i.e., the most current year) of the CIP and normally is incorporated into the annual operating budget. It provides resources for specific facilities, improvements, and equipment. The relationship of the CIP and the capital budget is important. The CIP identifies the capital needs, and the capital budget indicates which capital needs will be completed in the current year's operating budget.

A CIP indicates which capital assets to purchase, construct, renovate, or repair, presented in order of priorities; the estimated cost of the capital assets; the year in which the required capital expenditures should occur; and the method that will be used to finance the cost of the capital assets. Usually a CIP will improve a city's capital asset purchase and replacement program. Benefits from developing a CIP include the following:

- **Providing for orderly comprehensive replacement of capital facilities and equipment**. Many cities do not have a coordinated process for considering and approving capital projects. As a result, capital projects are approved in an undisciplined, uncoordinated manner. Such ad hoc procedures inevitably waste public resources, fail to consider available information, and sometimes result in poor project timing. Optimal results require an orderly process that considers all projects at the same time and produces a planning document that considers available financing sources and reasonable schedules for project completion.

- **Ensuring continuity.** Changes in city councilmembers can affect continuity. A CIP, however, will allow city personnel to continue to purchase, replace, and/or construct capital assets in an orderly manner.
- **Assisting with long-range fiscal planning.** Few cities engage in long-term financial planning for general government purposes and, as a result, are unaware of how municipal capital needs requiring capital financing will accumulate over future years. Consequently, some cities have deferred needed maintenance on buildings and equipment and delayed capital replacement projects in order to balance the current year's operating budget. The CIP process can help identify financial imbalances and begin the steps necessary to assure sound, long-term operations and capital financing strategies.
- **Planning and timing projects adequately**. Using a CIP can help governing authorities avoid having to cope with the results of poorly timed projects. Far too often, cities install capital facilities only to find later that these need to be changed or replaced by other installations. Good planning can ensure that these efforts are coordinated and costly duplications avoided.
- **Enhancing the city's bond rating**. Investors and bond-rating agencies stress the value of a CIP for a city seeking to borrow funds. The absence of rational, long-term planning can prevent a city from receiving a favorable credit rating from the rating agency. A poor credit rating can result in a higher interest rate on bond issues sold by cities that do not document and disclose their long-term capital financing needs and plans.
- **Providing the city with a public relations tool**. Most capital programming processes offer the public a chance to raise questions and offer opinions. Typically, this opportunity is received favorably by civic groups who view the process as an important link between city government and its constituents and as representing good business practices and management. The press particularly appreciates receiving background information on capital projects presented clearly in an organized document. Many city councilmembers find that by providing opportunities for public input early in the capital planning process they can effectively defuse volatile opposition to specific projects later on.

It is useful to examine the reasons why cities in Georgia have not used the mechanism of capital budgets and CIPs in the past. First, capital items are expensive. It is not uncommon for city councilmembers to defer certain capital costs to subsequent years in order to balance the operating budget. Because they are central players in the annual operating budget process, city councilmembers sometimes find it hard to see beyond the end of the current operating budget year. This tendency to focus on the present can result in needed capital assets not being purchased or replaced systematically.

Also, politics can play a role. The deferment of major capital costs to subsequent years (i.e., the decision not to invest in capital), while possibly a good political decision, may be a bad financial decision (i.e., the maintenance costs incurred on an asset not replaced can become excessive). It is important, then, that city elected officials recognize the significance of a CIP. The adoption of a CIP provides the opportunity for the orderly replacement of capital assets within the financial capacity of the city.

THE CIP PROCESS

The CIP process is as important as the plan itself. In other words, many observers of local government operations believe that the CIP is as much process as it is product. As with any process, there are clearly definable steps necessary for its completion. Some of the more important steps in a typical CIP process are listed and discussed here.

Step 1—Prepare a CIP Calendar

The CIP calendar is a very useful document for developing and monitoring the CIP process. Like the operating budget calendar discussed in Chapter 27, a CIP calendar is simply a chronological list of the tasks that need to be completed in the CIP process. The calendar may include the city personnel responsible for completing those tasks. By regularly consulting it, whoever is responsible for coordinating the CIP can determine at any point in the process whether or not it is on schedule.

Step 2—Assign Staff or Mayor to Coordinate the CIP

Practice and experience have shown that a centralized organization for staffing the CIP process works best. A city department or, in the case of smaller cities, a single individual (such as the city clerk or city administrator/manager) should be responsible for coordinating the entire CIP preparation process. In a "strong" mayor form of government, the mayor may be the single individual assigned to the task of coordinating responsibilities. This assignment need not include any decision-making or resource-allocating responsibilities; rather, it entails completing technical and procedural tasks. The staff of the regional development center (RDC) can also be a resource in this process.

Step 3—Establish CIP Policies

The primary role of city councilmembers in the CIP process is to articulate the policies that will guide the process. Following are some of the CIP policy issues that city elected officials will address: What are capital projects? What is the length of the CIP? What criteria are used to prioritize capital projects? How much of the CIP is funded each year in the operating budget? For accounting purposes, how many capital project funds will be maintained?

Defining Capital Projects

Capital expenditures are different from operating expenditures primarily because of the costs and estimated useful lives associated with capital assets. Capital assets generally are more costly than current assets, and city councilmembers often consider them "big ticket" items. In order for cities to classify an item as capital, its cost should be large enough to justify special attention. Generally, this cost amount is classified as a capital asset threshold. The level of the threshold depends primarily on the size of the city. In larger cities, a CIP may not include a purchase unless it costs $10,000 or more. In a large city, items costing up to $9,000 may be purchased from the operating budget without causing the operating budget much stress. However, in some smaller cities, an item costing $1,000 warrants special attention and may be capital in nature. Purchasing a computer at a cost of $2,500 could stress the operating budget of a small city because this size of purchase is considered material to the total operating budget. Finally, for an asset to be considered capital, it should have an extended useful life, usually at least two years. With the issuance of the Governmental Accounting Standards Board Statement 34, cities should consult independent auditors regarding whether it is in their best interest to raise the dollar thresholds of what constitutes a capital asset and a capital project. Implementation of GASB Statement 34 is phased in based on a city's total revenues.

Length of the CIP

Although a CIP legitimately may encompass any number of years, the most commonly used time period is 5 years, the current year (i.e., that portion incorporated into the operating budget) plus 4 years projected into the future. Time and experience indicate that these are the most realistic and manageable periods to use. Five years is an adequate time period in which to plan and prepare for most capital needs as they arise. A period of time much longer than that has proven to be less useful as a planning tool. Cost estimates for projects to be funded 20 years in the future tend to be less accurate and therefore less useful than 5-year estimates. However, for environmental improvements, such as water and sewer systems, a CIP of 20 years may be appropriate. On the other hand, a period of time shorter than the suggested 4 or 6 years tends to negate many of the advantages that developing and maintaining a CIP offers. For example, a period of 2 or 3 years generally is considered too little time in which to recognize the need for, much less plan and build, a major capital facility. Often, the planning and design phase of such projects can require 2 or 3 years.

Although set up on a multiyear basis, a CIP should be reviewed annually. An annual review of the CIP guarantees a regular reassessment of municipal capital needs. Additions to and deletions from the CIP may be made during this formal review process to ensure that the CIP best reflects the city's current capital needs. Even if no changes in the CIP are made, an annual review confirms that those projects in the CIP are still legitimate capital needs of the city. Each department director should participate actively in the annual review process.

Establishing Criteria for Prioritizing Capital Projects

Ranking requested capital projects in order of priority is perhaps the most important and one of the more difficult tasks involved in the completion of the CIP. After the department directors indicate their proposed capital items by cost and fiscal year, the total cost of all capital needs requested is determined and compared with the resources available. Unfortunately, most of the time, adequate funding is not available for all requested projects. Therefore, these capital items must be weighed and ranked to determine which will receive funding in the current year and which will be deferred to subsequent years.

Decision makers will be faced with many "apples versus oranges" kinds of decisions. For example, should the city purchase a computer for the human resource office, or should the city resurface two miles of paved roads? Is it better to build a garage used to repair public works vehicles or replace a heating system in city hall? At issue, then, will be which project has the highest priority. The choice is subjective; there is no absolute objective formula available. However, in order to address these kinds of choices and incorporate some objectivity, a city council needs to adopt a policy that will incorporate evaluation criteria in the priority-setting process.

Evaluation criteria can focus the city council's judgment in a consistent, rational way. They are not intended to replace basic decision making but to provide a rational basis for deciding which projects in the

CIP to fund. Ideally, the evaluation criteria policy should be established by the city council and then be refined by the city administration before adoption. The criteria used by each city will vary, based upon each city's needs and priorities.

Examples of evaluation criteria in the CIP prioritization process could include any or all of the following:

- Mandatory project—The project will fulfill a judge's order that a city build a new facility.
- Maintenance project—The project is necessary to preserve an asset such as the roof on city hall.
- Project improves efficiency—A new computer system could substantially reduce the amount of time spent on the purchasing procedure.
- Project provides a new service—A newly established senior citizens program requires building renovations to house it.
- Policy area project—Purchasing two passenger vans will enable the city to fulfill its policy of transporting senior citizens to obtain medical treatment.
- Extent of usage—A new walking trail that will be used by a great percentage of the city's residents could warrant higher priority than projects affecting fewer people.
- Project's expected useful life—Certain long-lasting equipment could receive a higher priority rating than shorter-lived equipment.
- Effect of project on operation and maintenance costs—A new lighting system could provide better lighting in city hall at reduced electrical costs.
- Availability of state/federal grants—Some equipment could be grant funded.
- Elimination of hazards—Adding a stoplight to a city road will allow elementary school students to cross the road safely.
- Prior commitments—Only one-third of a construction contract that the city signed has been completed.

Often, numerical values are added to criteria to provide an objective evaluation. However, this priority-setting process should be considered a "first cut," with additional analysis required.

Allocating Operating Budget Resources for Capital Items

Some cities have adopted policies that indicate what percentage of the operating budget they try to allocate for capital items. The allocation does not include those resources necessary to build additional buildings or major additions or renovations to buildings, all of which normally are financed from either locally approved general obligation bonds, revenue bonds (i.e., for enterprise fund projects), or the special purpose local option sales tax.

To determine an applicable amount of the operating budget to allocate to capital, city councilmembers should review the percentage of general fund expenditures incurred in previous years (e.g., for the last five years). As past experience is reviewed, care must be taken to ensure that unusual capital expenditures (such as large equipment purchases resulting from opening a new building) have not occurred, thereby distorting the percentages. This analysis, along with projected capital needs, should provide a basis for establishing a CIP funding policy. There is no "right answer" to how much of the operating budget should be allocated to capital because circumstances can differ in each city.

In addition to general fund resources, other types of funding are available for capital projects. Alternative funding sources include bonds, grants, special assessments, and leases.

Step 4—Develop Data-Gathering Forms

The perfect form to be used to gather CIP data does not exist. The purpose of CIP forms is to collect the information necessary to encourage and facilitate systematic thought and rational decision making in the CIP process. Most cities find that, in developing their capital planning efforts, it helps to keep the initial forms used during the first two or three years simple. If additional information is required, supplemental forms may be needed and revisions made to subsequent years' capital documents. The following elements consistently appear in most CIP forms: project name, description, and location; submitting department or office; estimated project costs, with sufficient data to support the estimate (e.g., square feet); estimated cost and financing presented by year; financing sources; and a site location map, as applicable.

Step 5—Solicit Project Requests and Proposals

Instructions from the mayor (if the city has a strong mayor form of government) or the city administrator/manager that encourage realistic capital spending and prudent investment of the city's resources generally will result in responsible requests for funding. Soliciting requests for project proposals to include in the CIP might begin with a staff meeting. Usually the personnel responsible for the operating budget are also responsible for the CIP. These persons could include the mayor, department directors and supervisors. During this meeting, personnel responsible for the

CIP distribute the CIP forms and explain the process and timetable. Everyone receives instructions at the same time, and questions and concerns can be covered with everyone involved in the CIP process. Topics normally addressed at these meetings include general financial and long-term outlook, policies that affect operations and capital planning, current work in progress, current year's timetable, problems encountered in the previous year and how they will be addressed, explanation of forms and instructions, description of a properly completed request packet, and where to go for help.

Step 6—Evaluate Requested Projects

Who should evaluate the requested projects is an important question. In smaller cities, city councilmembers might participate in this process. In other cities, a committee could be formed to review the requested projects as they relate to the established criteria. Another option is for each committee member to evaluate capital requests against one specific criterion. As mentioned earlier, the criteria usually are assigned numeric values that allow for an objective rating, and this rating process would be a first cut, with necessary additional reviews.

Step 7—Develop Funding Plan

After the higher priority projects have been determined, the CIP coordinating unit described in Step 2 should evaluate the city's ability to finance requested projects. As already discussed, the amount of the operating budget allocated to capital outlay will affect the amount of capital projects that can be completed. Obviously, larger construction and renovation projects need to be funded from sources other than the operating budget.

The CIP will only be as effective as the plan for financing the proposed projects. The city's ability to finance the CIP generally depends on the level of recurring future operating expenditures, the current level of bonded indebtedness, and the city's legal debt limit. Many projects proposed in the CIP will have an ongoing impact on the city's operating budget.

Analysis of the debt structure of a city is one of the most important parts of the financial analysis of the CIP process. When determining the most appropriate method for funding a capital project, factors to consider include

- Is the financing option legally available?
- Is the financing option politically acceptable?
- Is the financing option administratively feasible?

Two major funding sources for capital projects are general fund resources and general obligation bond proceeds. Other funding alternatives, which are quite limited, include the use of a capital lease and federal grants for capital outlay. See Figure 28-1 for a sample page from a CIP, with its emphasis on cost estimation and the identification of funding alternatives.

Step 8—Provide for Public Input

Opportunities for public input can be provided at various stages of the capital programming process. At any point, the entire CIP, including its timing, may be subject to public review. In preparing the CIP, then, city staff members and the city council should be conscious of the need to present the CIP to the public. The following opportunities for public review and input might be considered:

- Accept public input at the outset of the process. Ask department directors and supervisors to attend a public hearing before completing their forms so that ideas from the public are incorporated into their submissions.
- Provide for public review of the proposals as submitted to the city council by the city administrator/manager or other responsible CIP official. Many cities use methods such as public hearings, government television channels, citizens' academies, and civic group presentations to solicit public input.
- Schedule public review after consideration by the city council and before final adoption.

Step 9—Provide for Adoption by City Council

After the capital document is presented to the city council and reviewed in public, the procedures should provide for a method of adoption. Characteristically, the CIP is adopted as a planning instrument, and the capital budget is adopted separately as a specific authorization in the operating budget. Since 1998, local governments are required to adopt and operate under a project-length balanced budget for each capital projects fund in use by the government.[4]

Depending on how the CIP is integrated into the operating budget, the capital budget usually constitutes approval to proceed with procurement and other administrative actions necessary to implement the first year of the capital program, which is termed the capital budget year of the capital improvement program.[5]

Table 28-1. Sample General Fund Allocations, by Department

<table>
<tr><td colspan="2" align="center">City of Valdosta
Capital Improvement Program</td></tr>
<tr><td>PROJECT:</td><td>Streets Master Plan</td></tr>
<tr><td>DEPARTMENT:</td><td>Engineering</td></tr>
<tr><td>DESCRIPTION:</td><td>To widen existing roads and construct new roads as identified in the comprehensive traffic study performed by the Department of Transportation.</td></tr>
<tr><td>JUSTIFICATION:</td><td>Improve traffic and pedestrian safety.</td></tr>
<tr><td>O&M IMPACT:</td><td>$30,000 annually to the general fund from mowing of right-of-way, utility cost for traffic signals, and sign replacement.</td></tr>
</table>

FINANCING METHOD	2002	2003	2004	2005	2006	2007	TOTAL
SPLOST IV	400,000	725,000	780,051	0	0	0	1,905,051
GRANT	150,000	275,000	299,561	0	0	0	724,561
TOTALS	550,000	1,000,000	1,079,612	0	0	0	2,629,612
PROJECT COST	550,000	1,000,000	1,079.612	0	0	0	2,629.612

NOTES

1. For a detailed discussion of the selection and evaluation of capital projects, *see* J. Richard Aronson and Eli Schwartz, "Capital Budgeting," in *Management Policies in Local Government Finance*, ed. J. Richard Aronson and Eli Schwartz (Washington, DC: International City Management Association, 1987), 400–21.
2. Georgia Department of Community Affairs (DCA), Government Manager's Indicators Survey (Atlanta: DCA, 2003).
3. *See* Susan G. Robinson, "Capital Planning and Budgeting," in *Local Government Finance: Concepts and Practices*, ed. John E. Peterson and Dennis R. Strachota (Chicago: Government Finance Officers Association, 1991), 65–68.
4. OFFICIAL CODE OF GEORGIA ANNOTATED (O.C.G.A.) §38-81-3(b)(2). For a brief summary of this provision, *see* Paul T. Hardy, Betty J. Hudson, Richard W. Campbell, and Paul E. Glick, *Compliance Auditing in Georgia Counties and Municipalities: A Practical Guide to State Laws for Auditors and Local Government Officials* (Athens: Carl Vinson Institute of Government, University of Georgia, 2000), 132.
5. For a more detailed description of capital budgeting, *see* "Planning and Budgeting for Capital Improvements," chapter 7 in Robert L. Bland and Irene S. Rubin, *Budgeting: A Guide for Local Governments* (Washington DC: International City/County Management Association, 1997), 167–95.

29

Paul T. Hardy

Municipal Indebtedness

The ability to borrow is a major area of municipal finance. In addition to taxation and intergovernmental aid, local governments borrow funds to finance capital expenditures and to meet operating expenses.

ECONOMIC CONSIDERATIONS

Before deciding to borrow any appreciable amount, however, municipal officials should consider the economic constraints on borrowing. Preparation of a comprehensive forecast of future revenues and expenditures is essential. The forecast should provide sufficient detail so that steps can be taken to ensure a flow of funds for debt liquidation, as well as for existing and planned expenditures in other areas.[1]

This chapter considers how and when municipalities in Georgia may incur indebtedness. The topics discussed include types of debt instruments available to municipalities, fundamental legal restraints and exceptions, and marketing municipal bonds.

TYPES OF DEBT INSTRUMENTS

If a city decides to borrow, it must determine the form or type of indebtedness to incur. Several types of debt instruments are available. The most commonly used forms are bonds (both general obligation bonds and revenue bonds) and promissory notes.

Bonds are classified into different categories according to source of payment, time of maturity, and type of issuer. With respect to source of payment, bonds are either repaid from general revenues of the municipality issuing them or from a particular source of revenue. Bonds that are repaid from the city's revenues are referred to as general obligation

442   FINANCING AND REVENUES

or full faith and credit bonds, meaning that the city promises to pay the interest and retire the principal. The money to pay these bonds will normally come from taxes levied by the municipality. Bonds that are repaid solely from a specific source of revenue are called revenue bonds. Revenue bonds do not create any liability on the part of the municipality that issues them, and they cannot be paid out of general municipal funds. Money to repay revenue bonds is generated by the project purchased or constructed from the proceeds of the bond sale.

On the basis of date of maturity, bonds may be generally classified as those that mature in 1 to 5 years (short-term bonds), 5 to 10 years (intermediate bonds), or more than 10 years (long-term bonds). Concerning the type of issuer, bonds issued by a municipality are considered municipal bonds. Bonds issued by an authority (housing authority, hospital authority, etc.) are classified as authority bonds.

FUNDAMENTAL LEGAL RESTRAINTS AND EXCEPTIONS

Georgia cities possess the authority to contract or incur indebtedness only as authorized by the Georgia Constitution and other applicable law. Before attempting to borrow money, a municipality should know the limits on its power to go into debt as well as the types of borrowing not subject to debt limitations.

Debt Limitations

Generally, the Georgia Constitution limits indebtedness to 10 percent of the assessed value of all taxable property located within a municipality.[2] This provision also states that no new debt may be incurred without the assent of a majority of the qualified voters voting on the bond issue.[3] Exceptions to the 10 percent limitation and the required election include

- funds granted by and loans obtained from the federal government or any agency pursuant to conditions imposed by federal law;[4]
- funds borrowed from any person, corporation, association, or the state to pay in whole or in part the cost of property valuation and equalization programs for ad valorem tax purposes;[5]
- temporary loans; and[6]
- funds to pay for damages caused by the city's breach of a contract.[7]

Counties and school districts have their own 10 percent limitation.[8] A city may enter into a contract with an authority and levy taxes to meet its contractual obligations to the public authority as long as the contract between the city and the public authority is authorized by the intergovernmental contacts clause of the state constitution.[9] Contracts that are authorized by the intergovernmental contracts clause and require a municipality to pay an amount sufficient to pay the debt services on an authority's debt do not create new municipal debt.[10]

Special District Debt

Municipalities may incur debt on behalf of special districts created to provide local government services in such districts. Before doing so, the city must provide for the assessment and collection of an annual tax within the district sufficient to pay the principal and interest of the debt within 30 years. The state constitution requires that such debt must be approved by a majority of the voters of the special district voting in a special election held for that purpose. A municipality cannot incur any debt on behalf of a special district that, when added to the rest of the municipality's outstanding debt, exceeds 10 percent of the assessed value of all taxable property within the municipality. The proceeds of the tax collected from the special district must be used exclusively to pay off the principal and interest of the debt incurred on behalf of the special district.[11]

Temporary Loans

The constitution provides that, subject to certain conditions, cities may incur debt by obtaining temporary loans in each year to pay current expenses. The conditions for such temporary loans include the following requirements:

1. The aggregate amount of all such loans shall not exceed 75 percent of the municipality's total gross income from taxes collected in the preceding year.
2. Such loans are payable on or before December 31 of the calendar year in which they are made.
3. No such loan may be made when a prior temporary loan is still unpaid.
4. The municipality shall not incur an aggregate of temporary loans or other contracts, notes, or obligations for current expenses in excess of the total anticipated revenue for the calendar year.[12]

Exceptions to Long-Term Debt Limitations

A municipality may incur debt of a relatively long-term nature in several ways without being subject to constitutional debt limitations or election requirements.

Revenue Bonds

One method of incurring debt is through the issuance of revenue bonds for the purchase or construction of public works designated as revenue-producing facilities by the Georgia Revenue Bond Law.[13] The Georgia Constitution provides that both the principal and interest must be paid only by revenue pledged to the payment of such bonds. Revenue bonds are not deemed to be debts of the municipality, and a municipality may not levy or use taxes to pay any part of the principal or interest of such bonds.[14] Because revenue bonds are not debt of the municipality, the municipality is not required to obtain the assent of the qualified voters before issuing them. The maturity date of revenue bonds cannot exceed 40 years.[15]

Development Authorities Debt

Creating a development authority that can incur debt itself through the issuance of revenue bonds for the development of trade, commerce, industry, and employment is another method of incurring debt. Revenue bonds issued by a development authority do not constitute debt of the municipality, but municipalities can contract with development authorities and pledge their full faith and credit and levy taxes to meet their obligations under the contract as mentioned previously.[16] Examples of development authority projects include the acquisition, construction, improvement, or modification of any property to be used as or in conjunction with the production, processing, storing, or handling of agricultural, mining, manufactured, or industrial products; a sewage or waste disposal facility; sports facilities or convention or trade show facilities; airports, docks, or other mass commuting and parking facilities; other listed projects; and any other such project that would further the public purpose of this law.[17]

Multiyear Installment Purchases and Leases

Other methods of incurring debt involve the use of multiyear installment purchases or leases.

To provide for the terms and conditions under which cities may enter into multiyear lease, purchase, or lease purchase contracts, a law was enacted providing that such a contract

1. must terminate absolutely and without further obligation on the part of the municipality at the close of the calendar year in which it was executed and at the close of each succeeding calendar year for which it may be renewed;

2. may provide for automatic renewal unless positive action is taken by the municipality to terminate it, and the nature of such action shall be determined by the municipality and be specified in the contract;
3. shall state the total obligation of the municipality for the calendar year of execution and further state the total obligation that will be incurred in each calendar year of the renewal term, if renewed; and
4. must provide that title to any supplies, materials, equipment, or other personal property is to remain in the vendor until fully paid for by the city. However, a municipality may accept title to property, subject to the contract, and transfer title back to the vendor if the contract is not fully consummated.[18]

In addition to the above, such contracts may contain

1. a provision for automatic termination in the event that appropriated and otherwise unobligated funds are no longer available to satisfy the obligations of the municipality under the contract;
2. any other provision reasonably necessary to protect the interest of the municipality; or
3. a provision for the payment by the municipality of interest or the allocation of a portion of the contract payment to interest.[19]

Such contracts are deemed not to create a debt of the city for the payment of any sum beyond the calendar year of execution or, in the event of a renewal, beyond the calendar year of the renewal. Nothing in this law restricts cities from executing contracts arising out of their proprietary functions.[20]

In 1996, the following additional restrictions were imposed on the ability of cities to enter into multiyear lease, purchase, or lease-purchase contracts:

1. The principal portion of the contract, when added to the amount of general obligation debt incurred by the city pursuant to article IX, section 5, paragraph 1 of the state constitution, must not exceed 10 percent of the assessed value of all taxable property in that city.
2. Any real or personal property being financed by such contract must not have been the subject of a failed referendum within the preceding four calendar years unless such property is required to be financed by a court order or imminent threat of a court order, as certified by the municipal governing authority.

3. A public hearing must be held after publication of notice in a newspaper of general circulation on any contract for the acquisition of real property.
4. The average annual payments on any contract with respect to real property must not exceed 7.5 percent of the governmental fund revenues of the municipality for the preceding calendar year plus any available special county 1 percent sales and use tax proceeds.[21]

Utilizing this law, the Georgia Municipal Association (GMA) has created several financial programs that allow municipalities to purchase on a multiyear basis without referenda essential items such as fire and jail equipment, public facilities, and computers.

MARKETING MUNICIPAL BONDS

Besides fulfilling legal requirements, other factors are involved in the successful marketing of a municipality's debt.

- The municipality should obtain expert financial and legal advice. Since experts keep up with the bond market and confer with others in the field, their counsel may save considerable interest expense.
- The timing of the bond issue must be carefully considered. Because interest rates on new bond issues fluctuate, officials should attempt to time the sale of bond issues to take advantage of favorable market conditions.
- A bond attorney should be selected before the first bond resolution is passed. An accompanying favorable legal opinion from a bond attorney whose opinion is recognized as marketable will have a positive effect on the bids of bond underwriters. Printing a copy of the legal opinion on the back of municipal bonds is a common practice.
- A proposed bond sale should be publicized in local newspapers, in the foremost state financial paper, and in financial publications with national circulation. Notices should usually appear at least two weeks in advance of the sale and provide enough information so that underwriters can prepare their bids.
- A municipality that is selling bonds must be prepared to present comprehensive data about the community, particularly its economic base and its financial situation. This requirement will necessitate engaging recognized engineers and accountants not only to aid in planning and supervising capital improvements but

also to compile pertinent information. Engineers can help predict construction costs and future capital requirements. Accountants can provide data on anticipated earnings and expenses, the city's credit history, and other facts about the economic and social life of the community.

NOTES

1. Portions of this chapter are drawn from "Municipal Indebtedness," in *Handbook for Georgia Mayors and Councilmembers*, 3rd ed., ed. J. Devereux Weeks and Paul T. Hardy (Athens: Carl Vinson Institute of Government, University of Georgia, 1993), 144–50.
2. GA. CONST. art. IX, §5, ¶1. It should be noted that under past constitutions (the 1983 constitution prohibits local amendments), a number of local amendments were passed authorizing certain municipalities to issue bonds in specified amounts for specified purposes in excess of the 10 percent limit. All local amendments were continued in force until July 1, 1987. Only those local amendments specifically continued by the governing authority or the General Assembly as provided in art. XI, §1, ¶4 of the Georgia Constitution are still in effect.
3. GA. CONST. art. IX, §5, ¶1. Regarding such elections, *see* OFFICIAL CODE OF GEORGIA ANNOTATED (O.C.G.A.) §§36-80-10–36-80-15 (election for authorization of unbonded debt) and ch. 36-82 (bonds).
4. GA. CONST. art. IX, §5, ¶4.
5. Ibid.
6. GA. CONST. art. IX, §5, ¶5.
7. Dekalb County v. Georgia Paperstock Company, 226 Ga. 369, 174 S.E.2d 884 (1970).
8. GA. CONST. art. IX, §5, ¶; Steagall v. Southwest Georgia Regional Housing Authority, 197 Ga. 571, 30 S.E.2d 136 (1944); Nelms v. Stephens County School District, 201 Ga. 274, 39 S.E.2d 651 (1946); Pinion v. Walker County School District, 203 Ga. 99, 45 S.E.2d 405 (1947).
9. GA. CONST. art. IX, §3, ¶1(a); Building Authority of Fulton County v. State of Georgia, 253 Ga. 242, 321 S.E.2d 97 (1984); Nations v. Downtown Development Authority of the City of Atlanta, 256 Ga. 158, 345 S.E.2d 581 (1986); Clayton County Airport Authority v. State of Georgia, 265 Ga. 24, 453 S.E.2d 8 (1995); Reed v. State of Georgia, 265 Ga. 458, 458 S.E.2d 113 (1995). Compare Nations et al. v. Downtown Development Authority of the City of Atlanta, 255 Ga. 324, 338 S.E.2d 240 (1985) in which the city was held to have improperly taken on debt when the city guaranteed, via its taxing power, to make up 90 percent of the shortfall in the revenue (from rents) to pay bondholders.
10. Clayton County Airport Authority v. State of Georgia, 265 Ga. 24, 453 S.E.2d 8 (1995).
11. GA. CONST. art. IX, §5, ¶2. *See also* GA. CONST. art. IX, §2, ¶6, which provides for the creation of special districts.
12. GA. CONST. art. IX, §5, ¶5.
13. GA. CONST. art. IX, §6, ¶1. *See also* "Georgia Revenue Bond Law," O.C.G.A. §§36-82-60–36-82-85.
14. GA. CONST. art. IX, §6, ¶1; O.C.G.A. §36-82-66.
15. O.C.G.A. §36-82-64.

16. GA. CONST. art. IX, §6, ¶3. *See* O.C.G.A. ch. 36-62 for law governing development authorities; Stephenson v. State of Georgia, 219 Ga. 652, 135 S.E.2d 380 (1964).
17. O.C.G.A. §36-62-2.
18. O.C.G.A. §§36-60-13, 36-60-15.
19. O.C.G.A. §36-60-13.
20. Ibid.
21. O.C.G.A. §§36-60-13(e), 36-60-13(f), 36-60-13(g), 36-60-13(h).

PART 6
Intergovernmental Relations

30

*Harry W. Hayes, Betty J. Hudson, and Paul T. Hardy**

Service Delivery Strategies, Merger of Governmental Functions, and Consolidation of Governments

Cities do not exist in a vacuum, and it is necessary for them to maintain effective relations with all kinds of governments. Perhaps the most crucial relationship, however, is that between a city and the county or counties within which it is located. Both formal and informal agreements are available to local governments in dealing with the questions of who will provide services to city and county residents and how such services will be funded.

This chapter addresses the following issues in city-county relations:

- extraterritorial powers
- service delivery strategy agreements
- merger of governmental functions (functional consolidation)
- consolidation of governments (governmental consolidation)

EXTRATERRITORIAL POWERS

Cities and counties are authorized by the Georgia Constitution, several general statutes, and local acts to carry out certain functions beyond their geographical boundaries. For example, most city charters authorize cities to extend water and sewer services "within and without the boundaries of the municipality," and the Georgia Supreme Court has determined that such provisions are sufficient for cities to provide extraterritorial services without first entering into a contract with the county.[1] The Georgia Constitution authorizes cities to exercise specified powers

---

* Parts of the chapter contain or are based on work by this author from earlier editions of the *Handbook for Georgia Mayors and Councilmembers*.

and provide certain specified services outside its own boundaries only through a contract with the other municipality or the county, unless otherwise provided by law. Cities are also permitted to exercise the power of eminent domain extraterritorially for purposes of acquiring property for an airport, but only with the consent of the county, city, or other political subdivision where the property is located.[2]

SERVICE DELIVERY STRATEGIES

Intergovernmental relations was a major focus of the Georgia Future Communities Commission, created in 1995 by the Georgia General Assembly. In its examination of issues confronting local governments, the commission noted that the lack of a clear legal distinction between cities and counties in service delivery authority as a result of the 1972 amendment to the Georgia Constitution authorizing counties to provide urban-type services had, in many Georgia communities, fostered inefficient service delivery systems and unhealthy conflict.

The commission recommended that each county and the cities within the county be required to develop a service delivery strategy to identify the responsibilities of each of the governments for funding and delivery of services. This proposal became the Service Delivery Strategy law, enacted by of the General Assembly in 1997.[3] In recognition of the unique characteristics of each county and city throughout the state, the legislation did not mandate a specific outcome for the delivery of services in every county but left much discretion to cities and counties.[4]

The intent of this legislation was "to provide a flexible framework within which local governments in each county can develop a service delivery system that is both efficient and responsive to citizens in their county." Local governments are required to develop service delivery systems that reduce unnecessary duplication, promote cooperation, eliminate funding inequities, and promote compatible land-use plans.[5]

Counties were responsible for initiating the process between July 1, 1997, and January 1, 1998, and were to execute a service delivery strategy by July 1, 1999.[6] Service delivery strategies are on file with the Department of Community Affairs (DCA) for all of the state's 159 counties.

What Is a Service Delivery Strategy?

Pursuant to the Service Delivery Strategy law, local governments must carefully scrutinize the services they currently provide in order to identify overlap or gaps in service provision, examine the existing method of funding those services, and develop a reasoned approach to allocating the delivery and funding of the services among the various local governments and authorities in each county. A service delivery strategy is intended to be a concise action plan, backed up by the appropriate ordinances and intergovernmental agreements, for providing local government services now and in the future. It is important that the service delivery strategy be more than a mere snapshot of where and how services are provided right now. Rather, the service delivery strategy should identify areas in which each city, county, and authority plans to provide services in the future. While the law does not dictate specific service delivery and land-use planning arrangements within any given county, it does require every strategy to include four basic components and to meet six criteria.

Components of a Service Delivery Strategy

Each strategy must identify all services currently provided in the county by cities, counties, and authorities; assign which local government will be responsible for providing a specific service in which area of the county; describe how all services will be funded; and identify all intergovernmental contracts, ordinances, resolutions, etc., to be used in implementing the strategy, including existing contracts.[7]

Existing Service Delivery Arrangements

In preparing its service delivery strategy, a county and the cities within the county must first identify all local government services provided by or primarily funded by each general purpose local government and each authority within the county and describe the geographic area in which the identified services are provided by each jurisdiction. State law does not specify the services that should be included in a county's strategy; however, all services provided by a county or by its cities must be included. Cities and counties are encouraged to review their comprehensive plans, their most recent annual budgets, and their enabling laws and charters, respectively, to identify services to be included in the strategy.

Future Service Delivery Arrangements

Each strategy must indicate which local government or authority will provide each service after adoption and implementation of the strategy, identify the geographic areas of the county in which each service will be provided, and describe any services that will be provided by a local government to any area outside its geographical boundaries. Again, it is important that the service delivery strategy indicate future as well as current service areas. Communicating expectations about municipal growth and service delivery expansion is important to fully preserve a city's ability to provide that service in the future without seeking the consent of the county or other cities or authorities. The law does not preclude cities and counties from offering the same services, but it does encourage local governments to take advantage of this planning process to provide services in the most efficient manner possible. If a county's service delivery strategy assigns two or more local governments within the same county the responsibility to provide identical services within the same geographic area, the strategy must explain this duplication of services, including any overriding benefits or insurmountable problems that affect continuing the arrangement. If a city or a county decides either to add a new service or to drop an existing service after the strategy is adopted, an update to the service delivery strategy must be negotiated with each county and affected municipalities.

Funding Sources

The strategy must describe the source of revenue each local government will use to fund each service it will provide within the county (e.g., countywide revenues, unincorporated area revenues, municipal revenues, enterprise funds, or some combination). Describing sources of revenue with specificity is important because it is crucial to identify which individuals and businesses are paying for which services and to address issues of double taxation.

Legal Mechanisms for Implementation

Finally, the strategy must identify the mechanisms, if any, to be used to implement the service delivery strategy, including but not limited to intergovernmental agreements, ordinances, resolutions, and local acts of the General Assembly.

Criteria

In assigning and implementing service delivery responsibilities, the following requirements must be met:

- The strategy should provide for the elimination of duplication of services or give an explanation for its continued existence.
- Jurisdictions charging water and sewer rate differentials to customers outside their boundaries must be able to justify such differentials.
- Services provided primarily for unincorporated areas must be funded by revenues derived exclusively from the unincorporated areas.
- Conflicts in land-use plans within a county and between the county and its cities must be eliminated.

- Provision of extraterritorial water and sewer services by any jurisdiction must be consistent with land-use plans.[8]

Elimination of Duplication

When two local governments provide or offer the same service in overlapping areas, the service delivery strategy must identify the steps to eliminate unnecessary competition and duplication of services and the time frame in which such steps will be taken. For example, if a city water department and a county water authority both have excess water capacity and have extended water lines to serve the same area of the county immediately adjacent to the city's jurisdictional boundaries, the services are considered a duplication. However, if a city provides a service at a higher level than that provided by the county throughout the geographic area of the county, it is not considered a duplication of service. Thus, city maintenance of its own police department to patrol within the city, in addition to sheriff department patrols of the entire county, is not viewed as a duplication of services.[9]

While it is possible that a county and the cities within it might adopt a strategy that makes no changes to the existing service delivery arrangement within the county, the water and sewer rate equity and the tax equity criteria could require changes in how those services are funded.

Elimination of Double Taxation

Under the law, the strategy must ensure that the cost of any service provided by a county primarily for the benefit of the county's unincorporated area is borne by the residents, individuals, and property owners who benefit from the service. Funding for such service must come either from special service districts created by the county in which property taxes, insurance premium taxes, assessments, or user fees are levied or imposed or through any other mechanism agreed upon by the affected parties that will eliminate double taxation of municipal property owners. If the county and one or more cities jointly fund a countywide service, the strategy must ensure that the county share of such funding is borne by the residents, individuals, and property owners in the unincorporated area who benefit from the service.

One important method of addressing double taxation is the insurance premiums tax. When the Service Delivery Strategy law was enacted, several other pieces of legislation were enacted at the same time as part of an overall legislative package. House Bill 492 from the 1997 legislative session amended the law on county insurance premiums tax collections to make it clear that such funds are to be used first to pay for services provided for the primary benefit of inhabitants of the unincorporated area and, only after such services have been paid for, to reduce the ad valorem tax millage rate in the unincorporated areas of the county.[10]

Determining which county services should be paid for out of the general fund and which services should be paid from revenue sources derived from the unincorporated area has been one of the more difficult issues facing counties and cities in reaching service delivery agreements. Some county services are made available countywide to all residents and, in many instances, nonresidents. Such services include public health and welfare, county roads, the county jail, and the operation of county courts. Other county services may be provided by the county to unincorporated area residents but not to municipal residents, such as a county fire department, a county refuse collection service primarily serving unincorporated area residents, and certain law enforcement activities.

Elimination of Arbitrary Water and Sewer Differentials

The strategy must ensure that water or sewer fees charged to customers located outside the geographic boundaries of a service provider are not arbitrarily higher than the fees charged to customers inside its boundaries. If a local government believes a rate differential is arbitrary and disputes the reasonableness of such water and sewer rate differentials, the law provides a detailed process for that local government to challenge the arbitrary rate differentials on behalf of its residents. If it is determined that the water and sewer rates charged to a local government's outside customers are arbitrary, the strategy may provide for a phased-in adjustment of rates.

Compatible Land-Use Plans

Local governments within the same county must, if necessary, either amend their land-use plans so that the plans are compatible and non-conflicting or adopt a single land-use plan for the entire county. This provision is intended to protect citizens who reside near the boundaries of one local government's jurisdiction from undesirable and incompatible land uses being allowed to locate nearby in areas under the control of another local government.

Extraterritorial Water and Sewer Service Consistent with Land-Use Plans

The provision of extraterritorial water and sewer services by any jurisdiction must be consistent with all applicable land-use plans and ordinances.[11] Under the state comprehensive planning act, all cities and counties must prepare a comprehensive plan, including a land-use element that, in many cases, is implemented through zoning ordinances, subdivision regulations, or other land development controls. This requirement for consistency is designed to ensure that a government proposing to extend its water or sewer lines into the jurisdiction of another government does not violate the other government's comprehensive plan.

Resolution of Land-Use Classification Disputes in Annexations

The previous law providing that an annexation could not become effective until the county's bona fide land-use classification objection was resolved has been repealed. Counties are now permitted to raise objections to certain changes in land use occurring in connection with or following an annexation. However, raising such an objection does not stop the annexation from occurring. State annexation law establishes the process counties must use to object to the zoning or rezoning of property following an annexation.[12]

Adoption of the Strategy

The Service Delivery Strategy Law required the development of 159 service delivery strategies, one for each county. Approval of the strategy in each county required adoption of resolutions by the county, the county seat city, all cities with a population over 9,000, and 50 percent or more of all other cities with a population over 500 within the county.[13]

Dispute Resolution

If a county and the cities within it are unable to reach agreement on a service delivery strategy, the law requires them to attempt to resolve their differences through some method of alternative dispute resolution. If alternative dispute resolution is unsuccessful, the neutral party is required to prepare a report and provide it to each local government within the county. The report is considered a public record. The cost of alternative dispute resolution is shared by the disputing parties on a pro rata basis according to population. The county's share is based upon the unincorporated population of the county.[14]

Verification by the Department of Community Affairs

Each county was required to file its service delivery strategy with the Department of Community Affairs (DCA) by July 1999, unless an extension was granted until September 1999. The department was required to verify that the county had adopted a strategy and that the strategy met the requirements of the act. The law specifically states that DCA shall neither approve nor disapprove the specific elements or outcomes of the strategy. As long as the strategy meets the required criteria, local governments have complete discretion to develop their own arrangements.[15]

Sanctions for Noncompliance

The law provides that, effective July 1, 1999, no state-administered financial assistance, grants, loans or permits can be issued to any local government or authority that is not included in a DCA-verified service delivery strategy. In addition, projects that are inconsistent with a strategy are ineligible for state funding and permits. Examples of state funding, grants, and permits that counties could lose by failing to reach or update a service delivery strategy include LARP grants, GEFA water and sewer loans, recreation grants, and CDBG grants and water withdrawal, wastewater treatment, and solid waste disposal facility permits. Each state agency is required to make certain that any projects under consideration for funding or permit approval are consistent with the service delivery strategies of the applicable counties.[16]

Strategy Updates

There are three instances in which cities and counties must review and, if necessary, revise their approved service delivery strategies: when they update their comprehensive plans, at least every 10 years; when service delivery or revenue distribution arrangements change; and when local governments are created, abolished, or consolidated.[17]

There are three ways in which a county and its cities may fail to be in compliance with the requirements of the Services Delivery Strategy law. These failures occur when (1) the service delivery strategy is not formally adopted by all required governments; (2) the strategy does not address all required components and criteria, leaving DCA unable to verify the strategy; or (3) the strategy is not updated as required.

State Service Delivery Regions

There are 12 service delivery regions in the state (see Figure 30-1).[18] Each region outside the metropolitan Atlanta area has dedicated field staff from DCA and the Department of Economic Development (DED). The Atlanta offices of the two agencies provide service in the Atlanta metro area.

In each region, DCA staff work with local governments, development authorities, and community and economic development organizations on regional initiatives, rural development, and other community

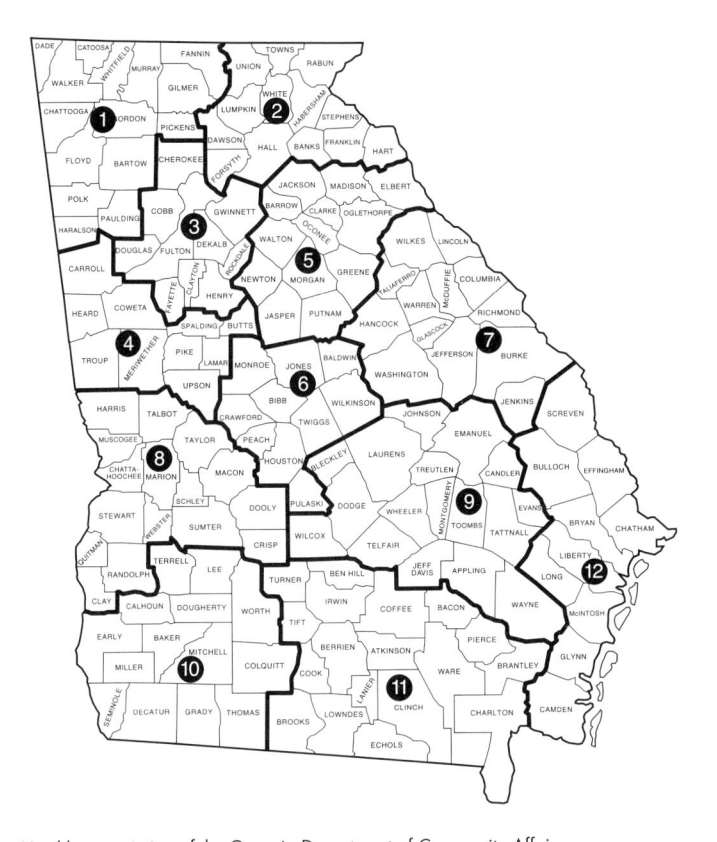

Figure 30-1. *State Service Delivery Regions*

Source: Used by permission of the Georgia Department of Community Affairs.

and economic development issues. DED staff work with established businesses and deal with issues regarding the development of a workforce for businesses. Also, both agencies will cooperate in the delivery of the Business Retention and Expansion Process and in helping to bring the multiday program of the Georgia Academy of Economic Development to the region.

Each region has a 21-member Regional Advisory Council (RAC) to provide a forum for communication between the regions and state government. The staffs of DCA and DED, with advice and input from the RACs, provide technical assistance services in community and economic development and foster regional collaboration among local governments, business and industry, and other community and economic development partners.[19]

MERGER OF GOVERNMENTAL FUNCTIONS

Under a merger arrangement, a single governmental unit is by law made responsible for furnishing one or more services for a certain region. The merged activity ordinarily is under the primary control of the governmental unit charged with providing the service. There may be an exchange of merged services. For example, the city might provide water for the entire county while the county furnishes fire protection.

Some cities and counties have merged tax-collecting and building inspection functions. Performing such functions separately, in both city and county, creates duplication of staff, records, equipment, and office space. Merging these functions promotes more efficient performance of the service and is more convenient for the public. When there is such a merger, the costs are prorated between the governments involved. In contrast to full consolidation of the governments of a city and county, the merger of governmental functions is often referred to as functional consolidation.

CONSOLIDATION OF GOVERNMENTS

The most comprehensive approach to solving city-county problems is total consolidation of city and county governments. Under this arrangement, the governments are legally consolidated into one government, which is assigned both municipal and county functions. Reorganization of this type requires

- the merger of existing city and county departments and offices into one departmental system;
- the establishment of a single legislative body, representing and responsible to all segments of the county population; and
- the establishment of one administrative office to direct government business.

Decisions involved in the reorganization, especially the question of jobs and responsibilities of present personnel under the new government, require careful evaluation. The status of the county elective offices of judge of the probate court, clerk of the superior court, sheriff, and tax commissioner, commonly referred to as county constitutional officers, under a reorganized government involves constitutional questions, but it is clear that governmental consolidation can have only minimal, if any, effect on the status of these offices.

To accommodate the urbanized areas of the county and at the same time avoid placing an excessive tax burden on low-density areas, a consolidated government often includes the creation of at least two types of service districts:

1. a general service district encompassing the entire county, with taxes levied for functions of countywide benefit, and
2. an urban service district in which taxes are levied for municipal-type services of primary benefit only to persons within that district. (As the need arises, the urban services district may be extended to take in new areas.)

Functions for which taxes could be levied by the general service district might include general administration, courts, public health, libraries, welfare, law enforcement, detention, recreation, inspections, and certain public works functions of countywide application. Examples of urban services would be local street maintenance, refuse collection, and animal control.

The state constitution authorizes the General Assembly to provide by local law for the consolidation of a city and a county.[20] However, a consolidation cannot become effective unless approved separately by a majority of the voters voting on the issue in the county and by a majority of the voters voting on the issue in the city, if the city contains at least 10 percent of the county population. Votes are generally not counted separately in cities with less than 10 percent of the county's population; however, if a majority of the voters of a city containing less than 10 percent of the population of the county do not approve consolidation, that city cannot be included in the consolidation.[21]

The local law creating a charter commission to prepare a consolidation charter may provide that the charter is to become effective without further action by the General Assembly or require that the charter be implemented by a subsequent local act.[22] In addition, the General Assembly is authorized to provide by general law for city-county consolidation.[23]

Total governmental consolidation has the following advantages and disadvantages:

Advantages

- Taxpayers pay only for benefits received.
- Issues of responsibility between two governments are eliminated, as well as intergovernmental disputes involving issues such as annexation, tax equity, service delivery, and tax revenue distribution.
- There is unified responsibility for community problems.
- It is easier for citizens to deal with one government than with two.

Table 30-1. Structure Comparisons in Athens–Clarke County, Augusta, Columbus, and Cusseta–Chattahoochee County

Legislative Body

	Title	N	Term	Vote	Veto
Athens–Clarke County	Commission	10	4 years Staggered	Yes	Override 7 votes
Augusta	Commission	10	4 years Staggered	Yes	N/A
Columbus	Council	10	4 years Staggered	Yes	Reconsider upon motion of mayor
Cusseta–Chattahoochee County	Commission	5	4 years Staggered	Yes	N/A

Presiding Officer

	Title	N	Term	Vote	Veto
Athens–Clarke County	Mayor	1	4 years Limited to 2 consecutive terms	Only in a tie	Yes—all actions
Augusta	Mayor	1	4 years Limited to 2 consecutive terms	Only to make or break a tie	No
Columbus	Mayor	1	4 years Limited to 2 consecutive terms	Only in case of a tie	No, but may require reconsideration of ordinances
Cusseta–Chattahoochee County	Chairperson	1	1 year	Yes	No

Administration

	Title	N	Term	Vote	Veto
Athens–Clarke County	Manager	1	2 years Appointed by commission upon mayor's recommendation	No	No
Augusta[a]	Administrator	1	By approval of commission	No	No
Columbus	Manager	1	By approval of council	No	No
Cusseta–Chattahoochee County	Manager	1	3 years Appointed by commission	No	No

Note: The table reflects the way in which each government functions as of 2001, as provided for in each government's charter.

[a] The Augusta charter is silent on the administrative form within the government

Table 30-1. *(continued)*

Budget Authority	Appointment Authority	Committees
Adopts budget	Majority of commission on manager, attorney, and auditor	Serve on committees as appointed by mayor
Prepares and adopts	All positions	Approve and serve on committees as recommended by mayor and mayor pro-tempore
Adopts budget	City manager and attorney	No reference in charter to committee form
Adopts budget	Manager, attorney, and auditor	No reference in charter to committees
Presents	Recommends to commission manager, attorney, and auditor	Makes appointments
No	As authorized by ordinance of the commission	Recommends with concurrence of mayor pro-tempore
Presents	Nominates manager and attorney Appoints police and fire with approval of council advisory boards	No reference in charter to committee form
No	No	No reference in charter to committees
Prepares and presents to mayor	Appoints department heads except attorney and auditor	Staffs committees
Coordinates with departments	No	Staffs committees
Prepares and presents to mayor	Appoints department directors, except police and fire, with advice/consent of council	No reference in charter
Prepares and presents to commission	Appoints department heads with advice and consent of commission	No reference in charter

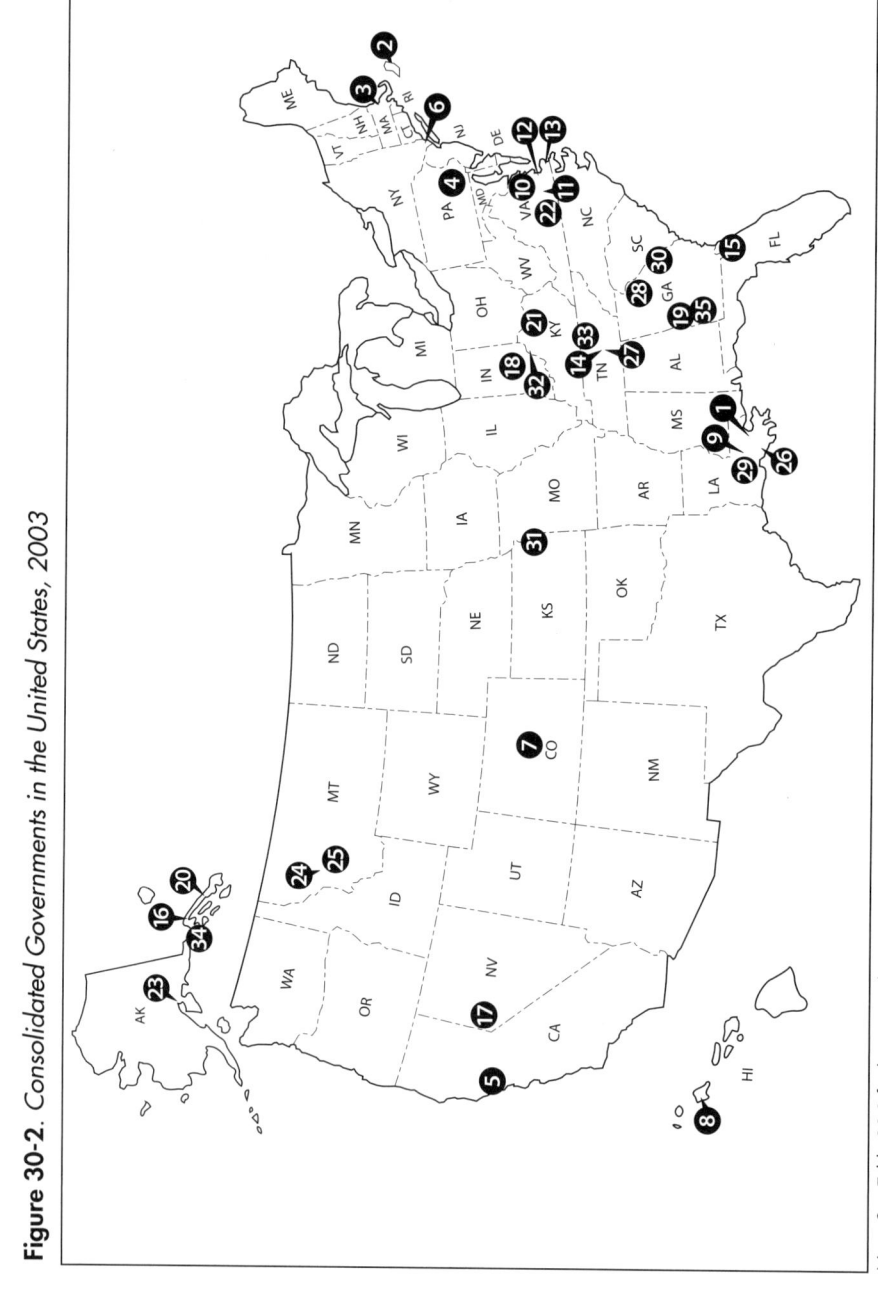

Figure 30-2. Consolidated Governments in the United States, 2003

Note: See Table 30-2 for key to numbers

Table 30-2. *Consolidated Governments in the United States, by Date of Consolidation*

Government	Consolidation Date	2000 Population
1. New Orleans–Orleans Parish, Louisiana	1805	484,674
2. Nantucket Town–Nantucket County, Massachusetts	1821	9,520
3. Boston–Suffolk County, Massachusetts	1821	689,807
4. Philadelphia–Philadelphia County, Pennsylvania	1854	1,517,550
5. San Francisco–San Francisco County, California	1856	776,733
6. New York (5 boroughs), New York	1890s	8,008,278
7. Denver–Denver County, Colorado	1902	554,636
8. Honolulu–Honolulu County, Hawaii	1907	876,156
9. Baton Rouge–East Baton Rouge Parish, Louisiana	1947	412,852
10. Hampton–Elizabeth City County, Virginia*	1952	146,437
11. Newport News–Warwick County, Virginia*	1957	180,150
12. Chesapeake–South Norfolk–Norfolk County, Virginia*	1962	199,184
13. Virginia Beach–Princess Anne County, Virginia*	1962	425,257
14. Nashville–Davidson County, Tennessee	1962	569,891
15. Jacksonville–Duval County, Florida	1967	778,879
16. Juneau–Greater Juneau Borough, Alaska	1969	30,711
17. Carson City–Ormsby County, Nevada*	1969	52,457
18. Indianapolis–Marion County, Indiana	1969	860,454
19. Columbus–Muscogee County, Georgia	1970	186,291
20. Sitka–Greater Sitka Borough, Alaska	1971	8,835
21. Lexington–Fayette County, Kentucky	1972	260,512
22. Suffolk–Nansemond County, Virginia*	1972	63,677
23. Anchorage–Greater Anchorage Borough, Alaska	1975	260,283
24. Anaconda–Deer Lodge County, Montana	1976	9,417
25. Butte–Silver Bow County, Montana	1976	34,606
26. Houma–Terrebone Parish, Louisiana	1984	104,503
27. Lynchburg City–Moore County, Tennessee	1988	5,740
28. Athens–Clarke County, Georgia	1990	101,489
29. Lafayette–Lafayette Parish, Louisiana	1992	190,503
30. Augusta–Richmond County, Georgia	1995	199,775
31. Kansas City–Wyandotte County, Kansas	1997	157,882
32. Louisville–Jefferson County, Kentucky	2000	693,604
33. Hartsville–Trousdale County, Tennessee	2000	7,259
34. Haines–Haines Borough, Alaska	2002	2,392
35. Cusseta–Chattahoochee County, Georgia	2003	14,882

*Independent cities that historically are city-county consolidations.

Source: Adapted from U.S. Census Bureau 2000 population data and National Association of Counties. Prepared by the Carl Vinson Institute of Government, University of Georgia, Athens, 2003.

- Having one government means greater efficiency in performing governmental functions.
- Business and industry may be more willing to locate in an area in which there is only one layer of government regulation.
- A consolidated government may be perceived as more progressive.

Disadvantages

- Costs of producing services may increase.
- Costs of services to some taxpayers will increase.
- Jobs must be abolished for improvement in efficiency and economy to be realized.
- A single government may be less responsive to public demands.
- Transition costs may be high in the initial years following consolidation. For example, benefits and pay scales for the employees of the higher-paying government are typically extended to all employees of the consolidated government, thereby increasing personnel costs.

Although consolidation has been attempted a number of times in Georgia, there have been only four successful consolidations to date: the City of Columbus and Muscogee County in 1971,[24] the City of Athens and Clarke County in 1991,[25] the City of Augusta and Richmond County in 1995,[26] and the City of Cusseta and Chattahoochee County in 2003.[27] See Table 30-1 for a comparison of how these consolidations are structured. Nationally, there are currently 35 consolidated governments (Figure 30-2, Table 30-2).

NOTES

1. Coweta County v. City of Newnan, 253 Ga. 457, 320 S.E.2d 747 (1984).
2. GA. CONST. art. IX, §2, ¶5; OFFICIAL CODE OF GEORGIA ANNOTATED (O.C.G.A.) §6-3-22; City Council of Augusta v. Garrison, 68 Ga. App. 150, 22 S.E.2d 421 (1942); Collier v. City of Atlanta, 178 Ga. 575, 173 S.E. 853 (1933); Ball v. Peavy, 210 Ga. 575, 825 S.E.2d 143 (1954); R. Perry Sentell Jr., *Additional Studies in Georgia Local Government Law* (Charlottesville, VA: Michie Company, 1983), ch. 9.
3. O.C.G.A. tit. 36, ch. 70, art. 2.
4. The portion of this chapter on service delivery strategies is based on Association County Commissioners of Georgia, Georgia Municipal Association, Georgia Department of Community Affairs, and Carl Vinson Institute of Government, *Charting a Course for Cooperation and Collaboration* (Atlanta: Georgia Department of Community Affairs, 1997).
5. O.C.G.A. §36-70-20.
6. O.C.G.A. §§36-70-21, 36-70-22.
7. O.C.G.A. §36-70-23.

8. O.C.G.A. §36-70-24. The previous requirement that a county and its cities establish a process for resolving land-use disputes regarding annexed property was repealed in 2004. *See* O.C.G.A. §36-36-11 for a new provision regarding land-use disputes in annexations.
9. *See* O.C.G.A. §36-70-2(5.2). Effective May 13, 2004, the sheriff, the clerk of superior court, the judge of the superior court, and the tax commissioners are exempted from the Service Delivery Strategy Act.
10. O.C.G.A. §33-8-8.3.
11. O.C.G.A. §36-70-24(4)(B).
12. O.C.G.A. §36-36-11.
13. O.C.G.A. §36-70-25(a).
14. O.C.G.A. §36-70-25(b).
15. O.C.G.A. §36-70-26.
16. O.C.G.A. §36-70-27.
17. O.C.G.A. §36-70-28.
18. O.C.G.A. §50-4-7.
19. For additional information on the state service delivery regions, see http://www.dca.state.ga.us/regions/index.html.
20. GA. CONST. art. IX, §3, ¶2(a).
21. O.C.G.A. §36-60-16.
22. GA. CONST. art. IX, §3, ¶2(a).
23. GA. CONST. art. IX, §3, ¶2(b). *See* O.C.G.A. tit. 36, ch. 68.
24. Ga. Laws 1968, p. 1508; 1971 (Extra Session), 2007 as amended.
25. Ga. Laws 1990, p. 3560; 1991, p. 3537.
26. Ga. Laws 1995, p. 3648, as amended.
27. Ga. Laws 2001, p. 4305. Charter of the Unified Government of Cusseta–Chattahoochee County, Georgia, effective November 4, 2003 (unpublished).

31

Gwin Copeland and Paul D. Radford

City Officials and Their Role in Georgia's Intergovernmental Relations Network

"Intergovernmental relations" refers to the complex interactions between city officials and officials representing a municipality's home county or counties, other cities and counties, school districts, special districts, authorities, and the state and federal governments. Although maintaining a cooperative relationship with your home county or counties is particularly important, each city needs to maintain and nurture effective relations with all types and levels of governments and the officials who represent them.

As an elected official, you are challenged with helping determine the direction of your city. In so doing, you will be required to make some important decisions regarding a broad range of issues, including service provision (water, sewer, recreation, and public safety, to name just a few), land use, annexation, taxation, housing, economic development, revitalization of depressed areas, and capital improvements. These issues can be difficult enough to address when only one body of government is involved in the decision-making process. The issues that cities face are interwoven with those of other governing bodies such as county governments, school boards, other city governments, and authorities as well as the state and federal government. Therefore, city officials must be able to work with representatives of these different, and sometimes competing, levels of government.

RELATIONS WITH CITY AND COUNTY GOVERNMENTS

Many aspects of local governance involve negotiation and coordination with other forms of government. For example, cities and counties must negotiate distribution of local option sales tax revenue, assuming such a tax is in place, as well as develop and keep current a complex service delivery strategy. Having a good working relationship with other governmental entities in your county and a clear understanding of their responsibilities helps make these negotiations much easier. Similarly, cities and counties often have a common interest in attracting new employers and investments to their area. Being able to work cooperatively with all the parties involved in this endeavor will dramatically improve the prospects for a successful economic development strategy.

Role of Advocacy

In a perfect world, local government relationships would be cooperative and without controversy. Because cities, counties, and school boards effectively serve much of the same constituency, they likely would have similar goals. In many instances, these local government entities get along well, each interested in making a meaningful contribution for the betterment of the community and the people they serve. But state laws and service provision requirements inevitably cause tension and create rifts at the local level, particularly between city and county officials. These issues normally fall into three primary subject areas: service provision, competition for revenue, and personal politics.

Service Delivery Agreements

Counties were created by the Georgia Constitution to serve as administrative arms of the state. As a result, counties are constitutionally responsible for state functions such as courts, the sheriff's office, and health care. Over the years, however, counties have become increasingly involved in providing traditional municipal services, such as water and sewer services, parks and recreation services, transportation services, and garbage collection. While the Georgia Constitution states that a county may not provide these services inside an incorporated area without a contract with the municipality and that a municipality may not provide these services outside its jurisdiction without a contract with the county or other cities affected[1], cities and counties do compete to provide services.

Georgia law requires cities and counties to enter into service delivery agreements. Each county and the cities within that county must determine which local government will provide which services in which location. The agreement reached through these negotiations must be in writing and will govern service provision within the county. This issue is covered extensively in Chapter 30. Most service delivery disputes relate to who gets to provide water and/or sewer service in a particular area and whether the sheriff's department will provide law enforcement for all areas of the county or if a city intends to provide its own law enforcement. Because revenue is essential to providing services, both cities and counties have a lot at stake when negotiating service agreements.

Service delivery negotiation requires cities not only to work with counties but also to negotiate with the other cities in their county. Therefore, cities may benefit from a unified approach in their negotiations with their county.

Revenue Agreements

Another tax revenue source related to service delivery is the local option sales tax (LOST). Every 10 years, the counties and cities that have a LOST in place must renegotiate their distribution arrangement. Because of the length of these agreements and because LOST revenues are used both to offset property taxes and as general fund revenues of the city and county, the negotiations can be contentious. Multiple cities within a county may benefit from negotiating together with the county to achieve a larger municipal share of LOST and thereby a greater portion for each municipality.

It is also beneficial for multiple cities within a county to work together in negotiating with the county for a fair share of the special purpose local option sales tax (SPLOST) that can be used to fund major capital needs. Pursuant to 2004 amendments, SPLOST proceeds may be distributed to counties and cities by two processes. The county and a city or cities comprising more than half of the aggregate county population may enter into an agreement to fund one or more city projects, or if there is no intergovernmental agreement, the SPLOST may be distributed to fund city projects through a population-based schedule.

Because cities and counties have competing interests, LOST and SPLOST negotiations may become contentious. The ideal in negotiating service delivery agreements, LOST, and SPLOST is to ensure the fiscal health and vitality of every local government in the county.

Personal Politics

Personal politics can certainly complicate negotiation and cooperation. Regardless of partisanship, however, elected officials should act in the best interests of their city and the people they serve. Although this advocacy role may be exhausting and uncomfortable at times, elected officials should serve their constituents by forging positive interactions whenever possible with fellow local officials.

Alternative Methods of Interaction

Several methods of addressing intergovernmental challenges are available to Georgia cities. Each municipality should thoroughly review its particular situation and determine which method provides the most logical and appropriate conditions for providing the type of government desired by its citizens.

Informal Cooperation

Informal cooperation refers to simple cooperative actions or agreements that are voluntary and require no structural change in the participating governmental unit. An example of informal cooperation at the local level is the exchange of information over the telephone between city and county managers and clerks. Another example is the exchange of information and mutual-aid assistance between city police departments and sheriffs' offices.

Mutual Aid Agreements

Mutual aid agreements are usually based on a "you scratch my back and I'll scratch yours" relationship in which two or more units of government agree to provide supplemental services. These agreements typically are made to address police, fire emergency management, and riot control situations. The Georgia Mutual Aid Act authorizes local law enforcement agencies, fire departments, and emergency medical services to cooperate with and provide assistance to other local governments or agencies when they request help in a local emergency.[2]

Formal Agreements

As a general rule, government functions and services that lend themselves to a formal agreement meet the following criteria: they have cost-benefits that are easily defined because they are of mutual benefit to the participating governments. These agreements are typically but not always noncontroversial. Examples of formal agreements include joint service agreements and service contracts. Any agreement relating to service provision or revenue distribution should be in writing to ensure legal enforceability of the agreement. Such agreements, often referred to as intergovernmental agreements, are authorized by article IX, section III, paragraph I of the Georgia Constitution. Two common types of intergovernmental agreements are joint service agreements and contracts for services.

In a joint service agreement, two or more local governments mutually perform a particular function or service. Often, these agreements involve joint acquisition, construction, ownership, and maintenance of property; joint employment of personnel; or other similar cooperative activity. In a joint service agreement, participating local governments share ownership and control. Examples of joint services include a joint water authority or a jointly owned industrial park.

Contracts for services, while similar to joint service agreements, are distinguishable in that one party is the seller and the other is the buyer. One local government may purchase a service (for example, renting office space or acquiring police protection) from another local government. The terms of the contract must be acceptable to each party, but the supplier or seller is usually in control of administering the service.

Typical contracts for services include animal control, road maintenance, police protection, and fire protection. Other functions and services may be wholly or partially adaptable to contractual agreements. For instance, several police and court activities such as jails, communications, and record keeping are well suited for service contracts.[3] Conversely, ordinary police patrol responsibilities may not be suited for cooperative service agreements because of the different requirements and expectations of municipal and unincorporated residents. Provision of and arrangement for these services are detailed in Chapter 30. It is difficult to develop contracts for government functions and services that have a high degree of uncertainty or controversy with respect to cost, benefits, and disadvantages to participating governments.

Dependent and Independent Authorities

Dependent and independent local government authorities are separate, quasilocal governments that are authorized by or created by the legislature for a specific purpose. Examples of local government authorities include housing, hospital, water and sewer, downtown development, recreation, solid waste, parking and buildings, industrial development, and airport authorities. These authorities have their own governing boards, members of which are initially appointed by the local government entity or entities that created or activated the authority. These authorities may be dependent or independent. The degree of fiscal, contractual, and administrative independence an authority has will define its relationship with the city. Independent authorities ordinarily possess considerable fiscal and administrative independence. Dependent authorities generally rely on city staff for management, must report periodically to the city council, and cannot enter into any contractual arrangements without the consent of the boards of both the city and the authority.

Local government authorities are popular for three reasons:

- They often provide a service or initiate a project that might be difficult for a city to directly provide or manage.

- They allow for separate boards to oversee the day-to-day operations and to concentrate on a focused mission.
- Any bonds or other debt issued to carry out the project or services are obligations of the authority or special district, not the city.

Although having a separate local government authority that is concerned with providing only one service can be advantageous, it can also present difficulties. Citizens are often confused with respect to the governing body providing the service. A separate authority may result in coordination and responsiveness problems for elected officials. It is therefore important for local elected officials to remain aware of decisions made by authorities and to contribute and participate as much as possible in the decision-making process. Generally speaking, the more fiscal independence a local government authority achieves, the greater the chance for conflict between the city and the authority.

Merger and Consolidation

In a merger of governmental functions, one governmental unit is made responsible for furnishing one or more services for a certain service area. The merged service is usually under the primary control of the government charged with providing the service.

The most comprehensive approach to addressing city-county service provision challenges is consolidation of city and county governments. Under this arrangement, the governments are legally consolidated into a single, newly empowered and defined governmental entity. That government assumes all the powers, functions, assets, liabilities, and responsibilities of the former municipal and county governments. Merger and consolidation are discussed in much greater detail in Chapter 30.

STATE AND FEDERAL ADVOCACY

It is also important for municipal officials to develop and maintain good relationships with state and federal officials. To help facilitate these relationships, cities are represented at the state level by the Georgia Municipal Association (GMA) and at the federal level by the National League of Cities (NLC). Nonetheless, municipal elected officials' personal and professional relationships with their state and federal representatives are extremely influential.

Georgia Municipal Association

Created in 1934, GMA is the only state organization that represents municipal governments in Georgia. Based in Atlanta, GMA is a voluntary, nonprofit organization that provides legislative advocacy, education, and employee benefit and technical consulting services to its members. GMA is a grassroots lobbying network that includes all regions of the state and more than 485 municipal governments.

GMA's membership accounts for more than 99 percent of the state's municipal population. A 56-member board of directors, composed of city officials, governs GMA. Program implementation is charged to the executive director and a staff of 60 to 70 full-time employees.

GMA's strength lies in its membership. Through its policy process, GMA studies issues that affect municipal governments across the state. To determine its legislative agenda, issues are assigned to one of GMA's six standing committees: community development, environment and natural resources, public safety, municipal government, revenue and finance, or transportation. By participating in committee meetings, municipal officials are able to personally participate and influence GMA's legislative agenda and, in doing so, play a part in establishing statewide policy.

After each standing committee has determined its legislative policy platform, the policies are presented to the entire GMA membership for approval. The issues may be discussed and debated again before being voted on. Each GMA member city, regardless of size or the activity level, has one vote. Only after a majority of the membership approves the policy agenda items do they become a part of GMA's official legislative policy agenda.

National League of Cities

Membership in NLC can provide a significant resource to a city. The NLC can give local elected officials insight into the federal legislative and rule-making process and the ability of local elected officials to be strong advocates for their cities.

NLC describes itself as follows:

> The National League of Cities is the oldest and largest national organization representing municipal governments throughout the United States. Its mission is to strengthen and promote cities as centers of opportunity, leadership, and governance.
>
> Working in partnership with 49 state municipal leagues, NLC serves as a national resource to and an advocate for the more than 18,000 cities, villages, and towns it represents. NLC was founded in December 1924 by 10 state municipal leagues that saw the need for a national organization to strengthen local government through research, information sharing, and advocacy on behalf of hometown America. It was initially an organization of state municipal

leagues. In the 1960s and 1970s, membership was gradually opened to cities of all sizes giving local elected leaders a more direct opportunity to shape the priorities, policies, and advocacy positions of the organization.

Today, the unique partnership among NLC, the 49 state municipal leagues, and the elected leaders of the 1,700 member cities and 18,000 state league cities provides a powerful network for information sharing and for speaking on behalf of America's cities in Washington, D.C. and all state capitols.[4]

RELATIONS WITH STATE GOVERNMENT

The Legislative Branch

The Georgia General Assembly is composed of 180 members of the house of representatives and 56 senators. It convenes annually on the second Monday in January for its nonconsecutive 40-day legislative session. The purposes of the legislative session are to adopt the state budget for the next fiscal year and to address legislation and resolutions passed each session. State legislators are elected to two-year terms of office. Legislative matters introduced during the first year of a legislative term (odd-numbered years) may be carried over and addressed during the second year of the term. Any business pending at the end of the second year must be reintroduced during the next legislative cycle (biennium) in order to be considered again. Should an important matter need to be addressed between regular sessions, the governor may convene a special session, for which the General Assembly will address only those issues called by the governor. In recent years, special sessions have been convened primarily to address reapportionment.

Legislation introduced in the General Assembly is presented in the form of a bill or a resolution. A bill is proposed legislation. A resolution is similar to a bill but may not have the force of law. However, all constitutional amendments are introduced in the form of resolutions. A bill becomes a law once it has passed both the house of representatives and the senate in identical form and is signed by the governor, becomes law without the governor's signature, or is passed despite the governor's veto. (see Figure 31-1)[5]

Unless otherwise stated, the typical date on which a bill becomes law is the following July 1. However, some general bills will become effective upon the date of their approval by the governor or upon becoming law without such approval.[6]

Many bills that are introduced would have an impact on municipal governments. These bills often carry unfunded mandates, which require a city to provide services without compensating the city for the cost of those services. Other bills reduce the sales or property tax bases from which municipalities generate the majority of the revenue needed to provide basic services. Because general legislation can significantly affect cities, it is important for elected city officials to contact their legislators regarding the potential effects of legislation and to be aware of the policy positions taken by GMA members. Likewise, certain general legislation may greatly benefit cities. It is equally important to contact legislators in support of beneficial legislation.

Often, legislation is introduced as the result of a specific concern of a legislator's constituents. City officials are among a legislator's most influential constituents because they themselves represent the same constituency. Whether a city's interests at the state level are legislative or financial, city officials should never underestimate the importance of communication with their state representatives. Although GMA does represent municipal interests at the state level, it is also essential for legislators to hear directly from voters in their home districts, especially from other elected officials. Elected officials should be able to clearly articulate their position on an issue to increase the likelihood of getting legislation introduced, adopted, or—if it would negatively affect cities—stopped. Advocacy is especially effective when city officials have developed and maintained good relationships with their legislators.

During each session, the General Assembly addresses many bills that are referred to as local legislation. Local legislation applies only to the city, county, or special district named in the legislation. Such legislation is typically used to incorporate new cities, change city boundaries, otherwise amend city charters, alter forms of government, create local authorities or special districts, or make other changes that apply only to the political subdivision named in the legislation.[7]

One of the most important functions of the General Assembly is to determine the budget for the following fiscal year. In so doing, the legislature authorizes funding for all state agencies and state programs. It is therefore important for local elected officials to communicate with their legislators about programs funded through the state budget. Although local governments in Georgia do not receive a great deal of outside assistance from the state government, the state budget does help significantly to fund local transportation projects and provides important low-interest loans to help cities finance environmental projects and downtown development projects. Furthermore, the state budget may contain funding for

Figure 31-1. *How a Bill Becomes Law in Georgia*

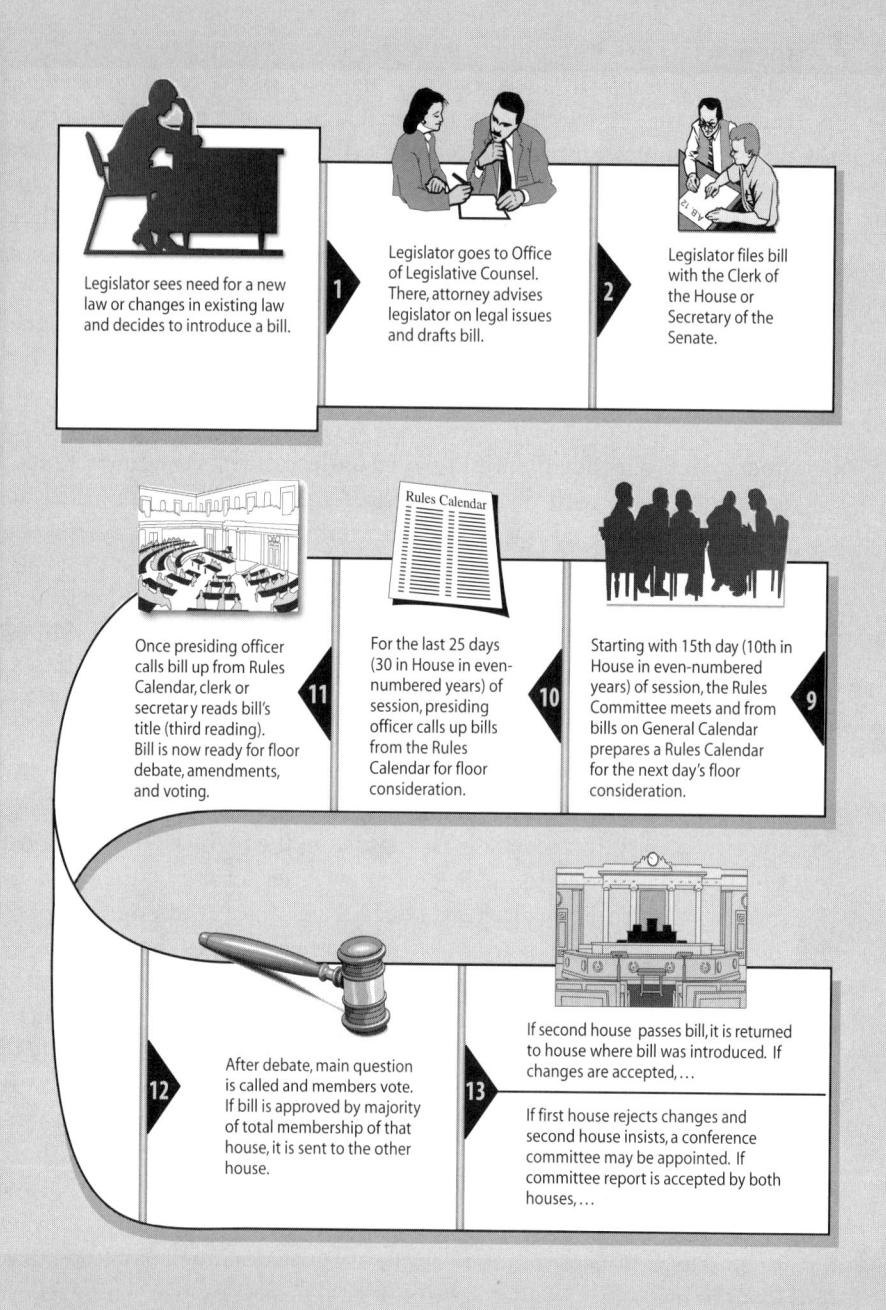

1 Legislator sees need for a new law or changes in existing law and decides to introduce a bill.

2 Legislator goes to Office of Legislative Counsel. There, attorney advises legislator on legal issues and drafts bill.

Legislator files bill with the Clerk of the House or Secretary of the Senate.

11 Once presiding officer calls bill up from Rules Calendar, clerk or secretary reads bill's title (third reading). Bill is now ready for floor debate, amendments, and voting.

10 For the last 25 days (30 in House in even-numbered years) of session, presiding officer calls up bills from the Rules Calendar for floor consideration.

9 Starting with 15th day (10th in House in even-numbered years) of session, the Rules Committee meets and from bills on General Calendar prepares a Rules Calendar for the next day's floor consideration.

12 After debate, main question is called and members vote. If bill is approved by majority of total membership of that house, it is sent to the other house.

13 If second house passes bill, it is returned to house where bill was introduced. If changes are accepted,...

If first house rejects changes and second house insists, a conference committee may be appointed. If committee report is accepted by both houses,...

479

3 On legislative day after filing, bill is formally introduced. In chamber, bill's title is read during period of first readings.

4 Immediately after first reading, presiding officer assigns bill to a standing committee.

5 In the House only, on next legislative day, clerk reads bill's title (second reading) in chamber, although actual bill is now in committee. In Senate, second reading comes after bill is reported favorably from committee.

8 Clerk or secretary prepares a General Calendar of bills favorably reported from committee. For first 15 days (10 in House in even-numbered years) of session, presiding officer calls up bills from this calendar for floor action.

7 Bill is reported favorably by committee and returned to clerk or secretary.

6 Bill is considered by the committee. Author and other legislators may testify. If controversial, public hearings may be held.

14 Bill is enrolled and sent to the governor (if requested). Otherwise, all enrolled bills are sent to governor following adjournment *sine die*.

15 Governor may sign bill or do nothing, and bill becomes law. Governor may veto bill, which requires two-thirds of members of each house to override.

16 Acts and other laws enacted at the session are printed in the *Georgia Laws* series. Also, act is incorporated into the Official Code of Georgia Annotated.

Act becomes effective the following July 1, unless a different effective date is provided in act.

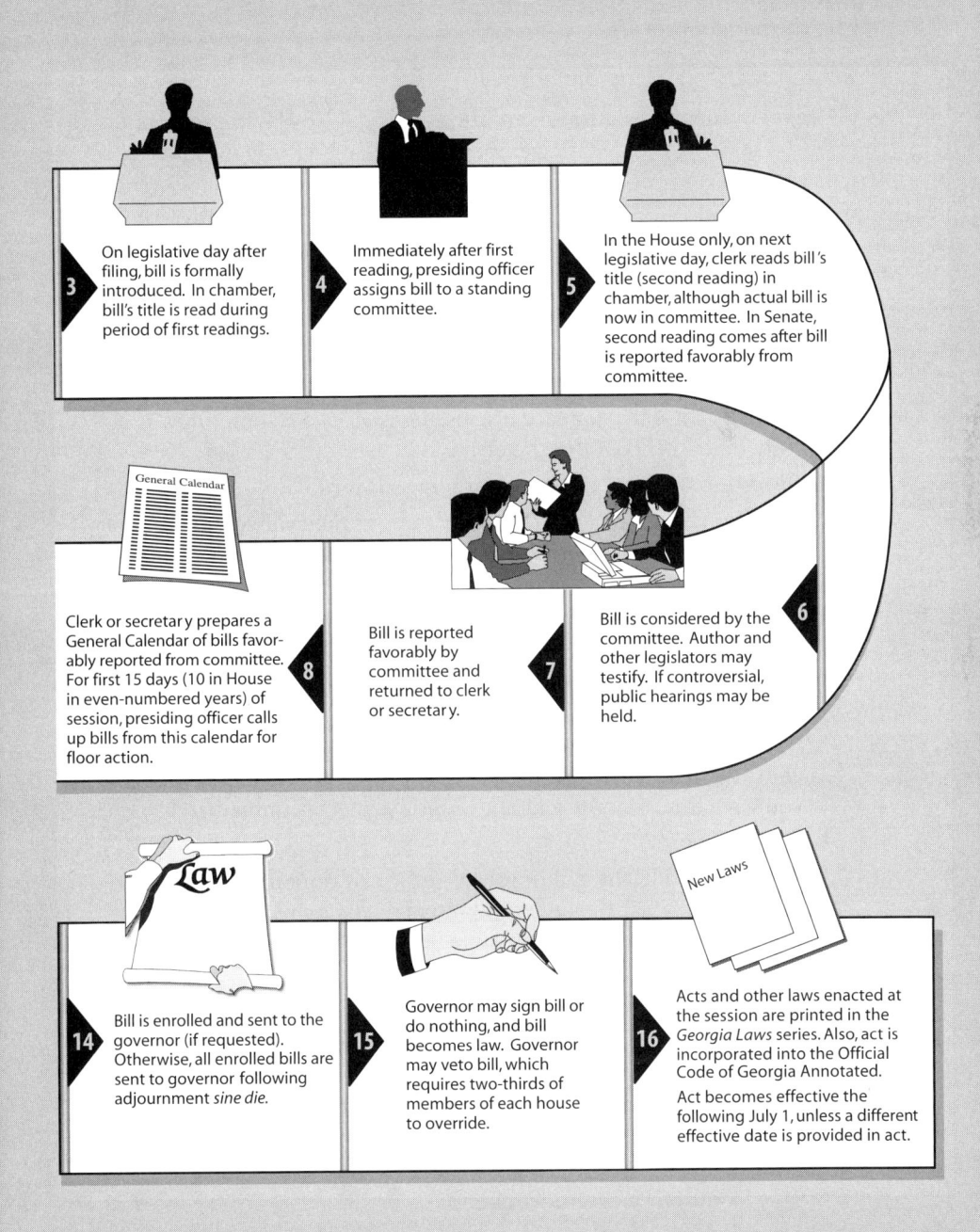

special local projects. Legislators should be contacted regularly regarding a city's financial needs or concerns so that they may be addressed during the budget process.

Effective Lobbying at the State Level

GMA's governmental relations staff are a city's day-to-day representatives at the state capitol. Staff members meet daily with legislators to articulate GMA's position and to brief them on pending bills that GMA supports or opposes. However, the most effective voice is that of the local official. To help prepare city leaders for effective lobbying, the following tips are offered:

1. **Know how to reach your legislator(s).**

   Be sure to obtain your legislators' telephone and fax numbers, mailing addresses, and e-mail addresses. Double check the information in early January because legislators are sometimes assigned new offices after the election.

2. **Find out the best time to reach legislators.**

   Ask them when they're most likely to be in their office. It will, of course, depend on their committee assignments. As a rule, early morning and late afternoons are the best times to catch a legislator in his or her office. But also keep in mind that their schedules are less predictable in the final weeks of the session.

3. **Remember that calls or faxes are better than letters.**

   The legislative process is very fast paced. Legislation can be introduced and voted on in committee within 24 hours. If you want your legislators to know how you feel about a bill, don't assume you have time to write a letter. Call or send a fax immediately.

4. **Be specific.**

   Always provide the bill number, author of the bill, and a brief summary of what the bill is about when you contact a legislator. In addition, to the extent possible, let them know how the legislation will impact your city.

5. **Be concise.**

   Remember, legislators are inundated with letters, faxes, and phone calls from lobbyists and constituents. Your message, whether it's communicated orally or in writing, should be brief and to the point. Try to keep anything you write to no more than one page.

6. **Stay in touch over the weekend.**

   Away from the hustle and bustle of the capitol, legislators won't be as pressed for time and will be able to listen more attentively.

7. **Don't expect them to be an expert on every bill.**

    Each session, more than 1,000 bills and resolutions are introduced. If your legislator is not familiar with the bill you are referring to, don't be surprised or offended. It may be the first time they've heard about it.

8. **Don't burn your bridges.**

    It's natural to be disappointed if your legislator doesn't vote the way you ask him or her to, but don't let one vote destroy your relationship. Remember, you're going to need his or her support on many other issues.

9. **Avoid personal attacks in the newspaper.**

    Calling a legislator's character into question serves no purpose other than to create controversy and sell newspapers. If you feel it's necessary to air your grievances publicly, stick to the issues. You'll accomplish more in the long run.

10. **Don't forget to say "thank you."**

    Legislators, like mayors and councilmembers, appreciate positive feedback, so look for opportunities to give them a pat on the back, especially publicly.

The Executive Branch

Communications with Georgia's regulatory agencies, which are part of the executive branch, are critical to city officials and their staff. It is essential to understand how these agencies and their boards operate. Boards typically meet monthly to create policies, promulgate rules, and take action that can affect cities. City officials and city staff must know who appropriate state agency personnel and board members are and communicate with them.

Administrative and regulatory agencies exist to address specific issues and areas, such as the environment, transportation, planning, and community development. Their charge is to implement laws passed by the legislature. The legislature may delegate rule-making power to agencies. However, rules that exceed an agency's rule-making authority may be challenged in court or changed by the General Assembly.

State agencies, such as the Department of Transportation, the Department of Natural Resources, and the Department of Community Affairs often take regulatory actions that have the force of law and that significantly affect local governments. Each agency's board of directors oversees this process. Most agency board members are political appointees who do not answer directly to a voting constituency. They are nevertheless responsive to input from interested parties. Municipal officials and staff should keep state agency board members informed regarding issues that may affect municipalities. Most state boards have at least one representative from each of the state's 13 congressional districts.

RELATIONS WITH THE FEDERAL GOVERNMENT

Unfunded Mandates and Devolution

Over the past two decades, reductions in federal program assistance for local governments have negatively affected relationships among federal, state, and local governments. Also eroding intergovernmental relationships are the adoption of new unfunded federal mandates, the establishment of devolution as a federal policy, and the increased federal preemption of home rule.

Unfunded mandates are directives from one level of government, usually the federal or state governments, to another level of government, typically local governments. Local governments began to experience the full impact of these mandates when federal revenue sharing and other federal grant-in-aid programs were either eliminated or drastically cut. A national initiative was undertaken in the early 1990s to curtail adoption of new unfunded mandates. This initiative culminated in the approval of the Unfunded Mandates Reform Act of 1995.[8] This law has required closer scrutiny of the fiscal impacts of proposed federal legislation and regulations by federal agencies.

Over the past decade, responsibility for public programs that were federally mandated and federally funded has increasingly been delegated to state and local governments. This process is known as federal government devolution. In principle, devolution signified a return to the original spirit and intent of the U.S Constitution, returning responsibility for public programs to states and communities—the level of government closest to the people. In practice, however, devolution has resulted in passing the responsibility for operating and funding public programs to local governments. Although home rule is vital to local governments, it is difficult for cities and counties to assume additional financial responsibilities for programs devolved from higher levels of government. Local governments have worked to mitigate the problems associated with local responsibility for programs that are not adequately funded.

The federal government is actively involved in the passage of legislation that affects local governments. Moreover, local governments may be eligible for annual federal appropriations assistance. It is therefore important for local officials to communicate effectively with their congressional representatives, even though it may be more difficult to maintain the same level of communication with congressional members and those in the federal executive branch than it is with state government officials. Utilizing the advocacy service of NLC is one method of keeping apprised of the issues under consideration by Congress. Whether visiting members of Congress in their district offices or in Washington, D.C., elected officials should follow certain guidelines (see Table 31-1).

Federal Appropriations

Each year, Congress passes and the president signs 13 appropriations bills that make up the federal budget. Through the federal appropriations process, Congress directs funding to numerous city and county governments for a wide variety of projects. The following is a listing of several opportunities that local governments may pursue.

VA, HUD, and Independent Agencies

Several accounts in the Veterans Administration–Housing and Urban Development (VA-HUD) appropriations bill are important to local governments. These accounts include funds for wastewater, storm water, the Federal Emergency Management Agency, the Environmental Protection Agency, and Economic Development Initiative grants. Each year the VA-HUD appropriations bill has included funding for wastewater and storm water infrastructure needs in the State and Tribal Assistance Grant (STAG) account. The EDI account in the VA-HUD bill includes funding for projects such as parks, roads, community centers, and museums.

Transportation

Each year, Congress approves a transportation appropriations bill that funds the activities of federal transportation agencies as well as investments in local transportation structure that includes buses, intelligent transportation systems, ferryboats, airports, and railways. Local governments may use this funding to offset local funding currently obligated for this purpose. Securing an individual line item for your project in the appropriations bill under this account would certainly complement any grant application pending at the U.S. Department of Transportation. Also included in the transportation appropriations bill is funding for streetscapes programs. These grants have been used by many Georgia cities as a means to finance downtown street beautification projects.

Table 31-1. *How to Communicate with Congressional Offices*

Before meeting with your U.S. senator, representative, or his or her staff, it is important to have a thorough understanding of the major aspects of any issue, project, or financial request for which you are seeking assistance. If possible, bring background material and a brief white paper outlining the request. Prepare answers to potential questions if you are seeking financial assistance. Be prepared to explain the alternatives that have been examined, the level of support the project enjoys, and the resources the city will contribute. If you are instead communicating a specific position about an issue that needs a federal legislative remedy, you should thoroughly understand the issue in order to be able to communicate what the local impact will be if your position is (or is not) supported at the federal government level.

Understanding how a congressional office functions and having strong relationships with key staff is vital. Generally, the Washington, D.C., office has legislative staff, and the district and state offices have staff who focus on constituent services, such as helping with federal benefits and assistance with federal agencies.

For purposes of acquiring federal appropriations, city officials should interact with the Washington, D.C., staff. The Washington office of a House member typically includes 8 to 10 people, and a senator's office can have as many as 30 staff members, depending on the size of the state. The Washington staff typically consists of a chief of staff, legislative director, several legislative assistants, legislative correspondent, press secretary, scheduler, and staff assistant. The chief of staff oversees both the administrative and political operations of the office. The legislative director monitors the legislative schedule and works to implement the member's overall agenda. Legislative assistants each focus on a set of specific policy issues (e.g., health care, defense, environment, etc.). Legislative correspondents respond to constituent inquiries on policy matters. The press secretary oversees communication between the member and the media and public. The scheduler prepares a daily minute-by-minute schedule for the member and establishes the travel arrangements. The staff assistant performs general support duties.

Maintaining contact with the district offices of congressional members is also beneficial. These offices maintain daily contact with the Washington, D.C., office and are the local "eyes and ears" for members of Congress. The district offices typically concentrate on specific constituent services that members of Congress can assist with at the federal level, such as tracking down missing federal assistance payments—like Social Security checks for example. In addition, the offices maintain staff members who regularly attend policy issue meetings within the member's district. These staff members are very close to their congressional member and typically accompany him or her on travels within the district.

When meeting in Washington, D.C., be flexible. Every effort will be made to arrange a meeting between a city official and the particular member of Congress or the Senate. Unfortunately, due to the unpredictable congressional schedule, you may find yourself meeting with staff only—and sometimes in a hallway—but take advantage of the opportunity. Meeting with staff can, in many cases, be as important as meeting with your U.S. senator or representative. The representative or senator will be fully apprised of your visit and issues of concern. Congressional staff members play a vital role in the process, and members are heavily dependent upon them for input and advice.

After the meeting, follow up with a brief note. In the note, review the topics discussed and outline next steps. Also use the note as an opportunity to answer any questions that were left unanswered during the meeting. Finally, thank the legislator and staff for their time and attention.

Energy and Water

Funding for the Army Corps of Engineers is included in the Energy and Water appropriations bill. These funds are typically directed toward the maintenance of water systems and waterways. The corps is involved in many projects, including harbor deepening, seawall construction and restoration, ecosystem restoration, and shore protection. As with other federal programs, the corps requires specific congressional authorization to proceed on such projects. A corps project generally takes two years to initiate: one to secure congressional authorization and a second to secure funding.

Commerce, Justice, State, and the Judiciary

This broad-based bill funds many different federal departments and agencies. Some sections that apply to local governments are the Department of Justice accounts covering areas such as violent crime reduction, community-oriented policing services (COPS), and juvenile justice. Competition for these funds is fierce and often requires an innovative approach to reducing violent crime. The COPS program has traditionally helped communities meet their law enforcement needs by providing law enforcement equipment, mobile emergency communication systems, 911 infrastructure, and public safety programs. Any funds secured through this account would supplement funds secured through the discretionary grant process.

CONCLUSION

Maintaining strong relationships with other local officials and state and federal officials is important to the success of any city. Whether seeking local cooperation with respect to service provision or to foster economic development or pursuing state or federal legislative or regulatory solutions or financial assistance, city officials must always strive to work with other local, state, and federal governments. In fact, the more a city works with other local governments, including counties and school boards, for a common purpose, the easier it will be for everyone to achieve their objectives and better serve their constituents. GMA at the state level and NLC at the federal level are available to assist local officials in forming and maintaining these relationships. Remember, however, that the local elected official is a city's most influential advocate.

NOTES

1. Ga. Const. art. IX, §II, ¶III.
2. Official Code of Georgia Annotated (O.C.G.A.) tit. 36, ch. 69. *See also* O.C.G.A. §§38-3-29 and 38-3-30 concerning mutual aid agreements.
3. *See* O.C.G.A. §§ 15-7-80–15-7-85 regarding the provision of municipal court services by counties.
4. *See* http://www.nlc.org.
5. Edwin L. Jackson, Mary E. Stakes, and Paul T. Hardy, *Handbook for Georgia Legislators*, 12th ed. (Athens: Carl Vinson Institute of Government, University of Georgia, 2001), 101.
6. Ibid., 193–94.
7. Ibid., 109.
8. 2 United States Code Annotated (U.S.C.A.) §1501 et seq., Pub. L. 104-4.

Index

Note: The notations showing *n*, *t*, or *f* refer to notes, tables, or figures on the respective page.

–A–

Absolute immunity, 72
Abuse of office, 82–84
  bribery, 82–83, 86
  campaign finance disclosure violations, 84
  extortion, 83, 86
  false or fraudulent claims, 87–88
  negligence of duties or malpractice, 84
  oath of office violations, 83
  political coercion, 166–67, 181*n*49
  sale of property, 81–82
  tampering with public records or documents, 83
Accident reports, 106
Accounting
  financial policy samples, 383*t*
  policy issues raised, 379*t*
Accounts, budgetary, 418
Accrual basis of accounting, 371
  described, 372–73
ADA. *See* Americans with Disabilities Act
Administration, of revenues, 405–6
Administrative agencies (state government), 480–81
Administrative fees, 396
Administrative powers, 41, 42, 44
Administrative Procedures Act (Georgia), 311
Administrative staff, financial policy considerations, 380
Advisory groups, 47
Advocacy
  role of, 470
  state and federal, 474–76
Age discrimination, 169, 172
Age Discrimination in Employment Act, 169

Agency funds, 369
Agenda, 7, 97, 102, 122–24
  discussion on agenda, 123–24
  sample agenda, 123
Agricultural property assessments, 388
Air pollution, 241
Airport authority, 55–56
Air quality, 240, 253–54
  sources of information, 263
Air Quality Act (Georgia), 253
Alcoholic beverage excise taxes, 395
Alcoholic beverage licenses, 399
Amendment 19. *See* Supplementary Powers provision
Amendments. *See under* Constitution (U.S.); Georgia Constitution
American Bar Association (ABA), police department functions, 330–31
American Public Works Association (APWA), 291
Americans with Disabilities Act (ADA), 154, 169–70
Animal control, 341–42
  licensing and registration, 342
  pet ownership programs, 341–42
  rabies control, 341
Annexation, 231–35
  Georgia General Assembly actions, 233
  100 percent method, 232–33
  purpose, 231–32
  relationship with counties, 234
  resolution and referendum method, 233
  service delivery strategy and, 234
  60 percent method, 233

of unincorporated islands, 233
Annual operating budget, 363
Annual reports ("state of the city"), 7, 15
Appellate courts, 63
Appointed officials
  characteristics of successful, 4
  communication, 7
  operating cities as a business, 8–9
  planning, 8
  roles of, 3–9
  teamwork, 6–7
  trust and confidence, 5–6
  understanding and acceptance of roles, 4–5
Appropriations, 418
  encumbrances, 425–26
  federal, 483, 485
Arbitration, 151*t*, 152*f*
Army Corps of Engineers, 485
Arrests, 64
Association County Commissioners of Georgia (ACCG), 334
Atlanta Regional Commission (ARC), 58, 59
Attorney-client privilege, 98–99, 105
Audits, 45
  annual financial reports, 362
  budgetary process, 419
  citizen compliance, 406
  efficiency audits, 419
  financial and compliance audits, 365
  financial audits, 419
  financial policy samples, 383*t*
  GASB recommendations, 365
  independent, 364–65
  benefits of, 365
  operations budget, 410, 411–12

488 INDEX

management budget, 413
performance audits, 419
policy issues raised, 379t
preaudit function, 418
program audits, 419
single, 366
types of, 365–66
Authorities, dependent and independent, 473–74
Authority bonds, 442
Automated mapping/facilities mapping (AM/FM), 269

—B—

Balanced budget requirements, 410, 424
Balance sheets, 362
Banks, occupational license tax on, 396
Basis of accounting, 371–74
Benefits. *See also* Compensation
  compensation and, 27, 43, 167–69, 173, 177
  deferred compensation benefits, 173
  leave benefits, 177
  Social security benefits, 173
Bidding on contracts
  disclosure, 105
  "lowest reliable bidder," 194
  municipal road contracts, 188–89
  prequalification, 190
  public works contracts, 190–91
  sealed bids and proposals, 191
  successful bidder, 194–95
Bills (state government), 476–77, 478f–79f
Board of Community Affairs, 311
Board of Education, 56, 57
Board of Tax Assessors, 95
Board of Tax Equalization, 95
Boards, 47
  open meetings requirement, 95
Boards of directors, 52–53

Bond issues, voting, 442
Bond rating, CIP value in, 431
Bond requirements
  bid bonds, 193
  payment bonds, 193
  performance bonds, 193
  public works construction, 192–93
Bonds
  classification
    by issuer, 442
    by maturity, 442
  described, 441
  general obligation, 45, 51, 298, 441–42
  local amendment, 447n2
  marketing, 446–47
  revenue, 45, 51, 298, 442, 444
Bottom-line concept, 363
BREP. *See* Business Retention and Expansion Process
Bribery, 82–83, 86
Brownfields Economic Redevelopment Initiative, 259
Budget adoption, 416–17
Budgetary accounts, 418
Budgetary operating statements, 362
Budget calendar, 413, 413–14, 414t
Budget document
  detailed requests, 416
  message, 416
  summary, 416
Budget execution, 417–18
Budget expenditure request form, 415
Budget formats, 420–23
  line-item budgets, 420–21, 421t
Budget message, 416
Budget officer, 413
Budget preparation, 413–16
  budget document, 416
  budget request forms, 415
  guidelines, 415
  suggested calendar, 413–14, 414t
Budget proposal, 410
  public review of, 411

Budget-related policies, 423–26
Budget requests, 413, 415
  detailed, 416
  types of forms, 415
Budget resolution or ordinance, 417
Budgets
  purpose of, 45
  state government, 477, 480
Budget summary, 416
Budget values, 420–23
Building codes, 307–16. *See also* Uniform Codes Act (Georgia)
  administrative code procedures, 309, 311–12
  code enforcement, 307
    advantages to city enforcement, 308–9
    local code enforcement programs, 313
    permit or regulatory fees, 314, 315t
    permits and inspections, 313–14
    training, 314
  DCA Web site, 314
  fire prevention program and, 338
  information and assistance, 314, 316
  purposes of, 308
  state advisory committee, 310–11
  state minimum standard codes, 307, 309–10
    amendments or modifications, 311, 312–13
    base code, 309
    local code amendment requirements, 312–13
    mandatory codes, 309, 310t
    permissive or optional codes, 309, 310, 311t
Business and occupation tax, 396
Business Retention and Expansion Process (BREP), 226

—C—

Cable television, 304–5
Campaign financial disclosure, 84

Capital assets
  accrual basis vs. modified accrual basis, 374
  borrowing instruments, 402–3
  financial reporting, 371
  project requests and proposals, 436–37
  replacement of, 430, 432
  special purpose revenue sources, 391–93
  uses compared, 362
Capital asset threshold, 433
Capital budgets
  CIP related, 430
  operating budget resources allocated, 435–36
  operating budgets compared, 429
Capital budget year, 438
Capital Improvements Program (CIP)
  annual reviews, 434
  benefits of, 430–31
  capital asset threshold, 433
  capital budget related, 430
  data-gathering forms, 436
  described, 429
  evaluation criteria, 434–35
  financial policy samples, 383t
  issues raised, 378t
  length of program, 433–34
  planning, 429–39
  policies for councilmembers
    allocating operating budget resources, 435–36
    criteria for prioritizing, 434–35
    defining capital projects, 433
    length of CIP, 433–34
    prioritizing, criteria for, 434–35
  process, 432–39
    calendar, 432
    leader to coordinate, 432
  policies, establishment of, 433–36
  project requests and proposals, 436–37
  sample general fund allocations, 439t
  timing projects, 431
Capital projects
  education, 394
  examples of, 392–93
  funding, 429, 438
  funds, 369
  project budgets, 410–11
Carl Vinson Institute of Government, University of Georgia, 229
  financial policy training, 382
Carpooling records, 106
Cash basis of accounting, 372
Cash (reserves)
  cash flow for fund balances, 425
  policy issues raised, 379t
  sample financial policies, 383t
Certified City of Ethics program, 85–86
Certified Public Accountants (CPAs), audits, 364, 366
Charter. See Municipal charters
Charter commission, 461
Chief administrative officer (CAO), planning process, 220
CIP. See Capital Improvements Program
Citations, 64
Citizen participation
  budget, 409, 411, 417
  CIP process, 431, 438
  financial policies, 382
  planning, 222–23
  taxation issues, 270
City attorneys, 125
City clerks
  budget preparation, 413
  recordkeeper at meetings, 125
City council. See Councilmembers
City-county relations, 451–66
  alternative methods of interaction, 471–73
  extraterritorial powers, 451–52
  merger of governmental functions
    functional consolidation, 460
    governmental consolidation, 460–66
  revenue agreements, 471
  service delivery agreements, 452–59, 470–71
City managers
  budget preparation, 413
  participation at meetings, 125
  powers and duties of, 41, 42
  responsibilities of, 15–16
Civil rights, 71–72
Civil Rights Act of 1866, 71
Civil Rights Act of 1964, 167, 173
Civil Rights Act of 1991, 167, 173
Clean Air Act, 253–54
Clean Water Act, 245–48
Clerks, of municipal courts, 66
Coastal management, 237, 242–43
Coastal Management Act (Georgia), 243
Coastal Marshlands Protection Act, 242
Code of ethics for government service, 80
Codes, construction. See Building codes
Codification of ordinances, 33
Collaboratives, 151t, 153–54, 155f
Commission form of government, 3, 12, 16–17
  executive roles, 42
  organization chart, 19f
Commission on Accreditation for Law Enforcement Agencies (CALEA), 333
Commissions, 47
  open meetings requirement, 95

490   INDEX

Common law, 78
Communication, debate and dialogue comparison, 155*t*
Communications, 7, 9. *See also* Media; Public relations
  newsletters, 141
  telephone habits, 134
Community development, 346–47
Community Development Block Grant (CDBG) program, 226
Community facilities and services, comprehensive planning, 207
Community indicators report, 366–67
Community oriented policing (COP), 330–31
  federal appropriations, 485
Community service, 68
Compensation. *See also* Salaries
  compensatory time, 167–69
  for elected officials, 27
  equal pay laws, 169
  garnishment of wages, 172
  for mayor and councilmembers, 43
  minimum wage requirement, 167
  normal workweek, 167
  overtime pay requirements, 167–69
  pay-for-performance systems, 178, 183*n*106
  for public employees, 27
  workers' compensation, 173
Compliance audits, 365
Composting, 302
Comprehensive plan
  community facilities, 207, 241
  economic development, 206, 241
  elements of, 206–8, 241
  housing, 206, 241
  intergovernmental coordination, 207
  land use, 207, 241

natural and cultural/historic resources, 206–7, 241
  population/demographics, 206, 241
  transportation, 207–8
Comprehensive planning
  comprehensive plan, 205–7, 241
  DCA approval function, 237
  environmental planning criteria, 242
  other components, 209–14
  vital areas, 241–42
Comprehensive Solid Waste Management Act of 1990 (Georgia), 211–12, 256–58, 300
Computer-aided drafting (CAD), 269
Computer programs or software, 106
Condemnation. *See* Eminent Domain clause
Confidentiality
  accident reports, 106
  attorney-client privilege, 98–99, 105
  carpooling records, 106
  fire alarms and security systems records, 106
  identity theft and, 104
  medical records, 104
  public records, 104
  of tax matters, 99, 104
Conflict of interest, 78, 79–80, 186–87
  in zoning actions, 84–85, 216–17
Conflict resolution, 145–58
  acknowledging conflict, 157*n*2
  arbitration, 151*t*, 152*f*
  avoidance, 148, 149, 157*n*5
  capitulation, 148
  collaboration and competition, 151*t*
  collaboratives, 151*t*, 153–54, 155*f*
  culture diversity and, 158*n*9
  debate and dialogue comparison, 156*t*

disputes with constituents, 153–56
  facilitation, 151*t*
  factors for dealing with conflict, 148–49
  function of, 146
  in government, 146–47
  intragovernmental and intergovernmental disputes, 155–56
  litigation, 152*f*
  management of conflict, 148, 157*n*5
  mediation, 150, 151*t*
  negotiation, 151*t*
  policy dialogues, 151*t*, 153
  reactive and proactive responses, 149–50
  strategies, 150
  supervisors role, 150
  suppression, 148, 157*n*5
  value disputes, 158*n*9
  waiting, 149
Congressional representatives, 483
  how to communicate with, 484*t*
Connectivity, 285–86
Consolidated governments 406–7*n*28
  advantages, 461, 466
  disadvantages, 466
  functional, 460
  governmental consolidation, 460–66, 474
  structure comparisons given, 462–63*t*
  types of service districts, 461
  in the United States
    by date, 465*t*
    map, 464*f*
Constitutional amendments. *See under* Constitution (U.S.); Georgia Constitution
Constitution (Georgia). *See* Georgia Constitution
Constitution (U.S.)
  First Amendment rights (free speech and freedom of religion), 36, 165–67
  Fourteenth Amendment (due process and equal protection), 36

Index   491

Fourth Amendment (drug testing as search), 171
public employee rights, 161–67
Supremacy Clause, 36
Thirteenth, Fourteenth, and Fifteenth Amendments (civil rights), 71–72
Construction contracts
  municipal roads construction, 187–89
  public works construction, 189–93
Construction management (CM) methods, 192
  agency construction management, 192
  program/project management, 192
Construction project delivery methods, 191–92
  construction management at-risk method, 192
  design-bid-build method, 192
  design-build method, 192
Contingency funds, 425
Contraband property, forfeiture of, 400
Contracts and contracting, 45–46, 185–95
  bids and proposals disclosure, 105
  breach of contract liability, 69
  conflict of interest, 79–80, 186–87
  contractor's oath, 193
  contracts for professional services, 186
  illegal contracts, 185–86
  intergovernmental contracts, 193–94
  municipal road contracts, 187–89
  penalties, 193
  public works contracts, 189–93
  successful bidder, 194–95
  types of, 187
  void contracts, 186, 198–99n10
Contracts for services, 473

Controlled substances, forfeiture of assets, 400
Cooperation, informal, 472
COP. *See* Community oriented policing
Corrupt act statutes, 86
Council-manager form of government, 3, 13–16
  city manager's powers and duties, 42
  executive role, 17t
  ICMA recognized cities, 21t
  organization chart, 19f
  policymaking role, 17t
  primary features of, 14
  pros vs. cons, 17t
Councilmembers
  budget
    adoption, 416
    issues raised, 423–24
    legal level of budgetary control, 412
  budgets, capital budget, 430–31
  capital improvement policy making, 433–36
  capital projects evaluation, 437
  characteristics of successful, 4
  financial policies and, 364
  financial policy considerations, 380–81
  intergovernmental relations, 469
    city and county, 469–74
    federal government, 482–85
    state and federal advocacy, 474–76
    state government, 476–82
  mayor pro tem, 42
  meeting participation, 124–25
  planning process and, 220
  policy-making responsibilities, 12, 14
  powers and duties of, 43
  relationships with boards and commissions, 46–47
  roles of, 3–9
  vacancies, 43

Counties. *See also* City-county relations
  debt limitations, 442–43
  service delivery agreements, 470–71
County school districts, 394
Courts. *See* Municipal courts
Criminal action statutes, 81–85, 86
Criminal activities in office. *See also* Conflict of interest
  bribery, 82–83, 86
  campaign finance disclosure violations, 84
  extortion, 83, 86
  false or fraudulent claims, 87–88
  federal legislation and, 86–88
  negligence or malpractice, 84
  oath of office violations, 83
  suspension and removal from office, 88
  tampering with public records or documents, 83
Criminal Code of Georgia, conflict of interest provisions, 186–87
Criminal justice system. *See* Municipal courts
Current financial resources measurement focus, 372

—D—

Debt
  financial policy samples, 383t
  policy issues raised, 378t
Debt instruments, types of, 441–42
Debt limitations, 442–43
  exceptions to, 443–46
    development authority debt, 444
    multiyear installment purchases and leases, 444–46
    revenue bonds, 444
Debt service funds, 369
  financial reporting, 374

Debt structure
  economic considerations, 441
  financial analysis of CIP process, 437–38
  legal restraints and exceptions, 442–46
    debt limitations, 442–43, 443–46
    special district debt, 443
    temporary loans, 443
Department heads, budget preparation, 415
Department of Community Affairs (DCA), 50, 59
  Coastal Resources Division, 237, 242–43
  community indicators report, 366–67
  comprehensive plans reviews, 204–5, 237
  economic development opportunities training, 348
  financial reporting, 410
  leave benefits data, 177
  Main Street and Better Hometown Programs, 226, 349–52
  Office of Downtown Development, 354
  PlanBuilder Web site, 224, 225
  Planning and Environmental Management Division, 311
  Quality Growth Assistance Program, 226
  recreation and parks/leisure services, 317
  regional offices, 355
  salary survey of municipal employees, 175
  service delivery strategy, 452, 457–58
  solid waste reduction goals, 212, 257
  state codes advisory committee, 310–11
  state minimum standard codes
    administrative procedures, 311–12
    local code amendment requirements, 313
    uniform chart of accounts, 361, 366
  Web site, 314
Department of Economic Development (DED), 349–50
  Business Retention and Expansion Process (BREP), 226
  regional advisory council and, 59
  salary survey of manufacturing jobs, 176
  tourism industry, 357
Department of Human Resources, on-site sewage management program, 237
Department of Industry, Trade, and Tourism (DITT), 357. *See also under its later name* Department of Economic Development (DED)
Department of Justice (U.S.), 485
Department of Natural Resources (DNR)
  Environmental Protection Division, 237
  grant and loan funds, 205
  Greenspace program, 243–44, 322
  Historic Preservation Division, 356
  Pollution Prevention Assistance Division, 258
  vital areas, 241–42
  water supply system classification, 298
Department of Transportation (DOT)
  downtown traffic management, 357
  Local Assistance Road Program (LARP), 294
  maps of city's street system, 224
  subdivision regulations and, 218, 294
  traffic management, 357
Dependent and independent authorities, 473–74
Depreciation, accrual accounting, 373
Design-bid-build method, for public works construction, 192
Design-bid method, for public works construction, 192
Detention facilities. *See* Jails
Development. *See also* Downtown development; Economic development
  grant programs, 226
  impact fees, 213–14, 218
  sources of help, 354–57
Development authorities debt, 444
Development impact fees, 399–400
Development of Regional Impact (DRI), 209–10, 211, 212, 228
Development rights, transfer of, 219
Devolution, 482
Dillon's Rule, 25
Disabled people. *See also* Americans with Disabilities Act (ADA)
  access to services disputes, 154–55
  curb ramp construction, 295
  discrimination by employers prohibitions, 169–70
Disaster preparedness, 142–43
Disaster relief assistance, 340
Discretionary action, 71
Dispute resolution. *See* Conflict resolution
Distilled spirits local excise taxes, 395
DNR. *See* Department of Natural Resources
DOT. *See* Department of Transportation
Downtown development, 348–53
  assistance to non–Main Street and Better Hometown cities, 354
  consistent support for, 353
  development conference, 354
  downtown revitalization, 349

Main Street and Better Hometown Programs, 226, 349–52
  public participation, 353
  public-private partnerships, 353
  research resources, 354
  sources of help, 354–57
Downtown Development Authority (DDA), 53–54, 95, 353
Downtown Development Office, 353
Downtown Development Revolving Loan Fund, 226, 355
Drinking water, 238, 299
Driver safety courses, 68
Driving under the influence (DUI), 64
Drug testing, of city employees, 171–72
Due process, 36, 64, 164–65, 180n27
Duplication of service delivery, 455

—E—

Economic development, 345–57
  as a process, not an event, 347–48
  business development, 347
  business recruitment, 347
  business retention and expansion, 347
  comprehensive plan, 206, 345
  development essentials
    community development, 346–47
    economic development, 347
    leadership, 346
  downtown development, 348–53
  economic development strategy, 345
  entrepreneur development, 347
  grant programs, 226
  knowledge needed for, 346–47
  small business development, 347
  sources of help, 354–57
  training, 348
Economic resources measurement focus, 372
Education, sales taxes funding, 393–94
Effectiveness of program operations, 419
Efficiency audits, 419
Elected officials
  characteristics of successful, 4
  communication, 7
  compensation and salary adjustments, 43
  executive role, 11
  operating cities as a business, 8–9
  planning, 8
  policy-making role, 11
  recall election, 43, 88
  suspension and removal from office, 88
  teamwork, 6–7
  trust and confidence, 5–6
  understanding and acceptance of roles, 4–5
Election districts, reapportionment, 27
Election recalls, 43
Electricity and natural gas, 302–3
Electronic governance, 283–87
  citizen and employee access, 284–85
  connectivity, 285–86
  e-commerce, 286–87
  electronic signatures, 283, 284, 289n14
  impact on municipal revenues, 286–87
  intellectual property rights, 285, 286
  network architecture, 285
  privacy issues, 285, 286
Electronic government, 279–82
  in-house technical staff training, 281
  intra-Internet strategy development, 280–81
  outsourcing technical services, 281
  planning and implementation, 280
  Web databases, 281
Electronic mail (E-mail), 134–35
Electronic network infrastructure, 282–83
Electronic Signature Act (Georgia), 283
Electronic Signatures in Global and National Commerce Act, 284
Emergency management, 339–41
  directors' qualifications and performance standards, 341
  disaster relief assistance, 340
  government role, 339
  operations plan, 340
  organizations and agencies, 339–40
  program functions, 340–41
Emergency Management Act of 1981 (Georgia), 98
Emergency medical services, 335
Emergency meetings, 96–97, 97–98
Emergency notifications, 7
Eminent Domain clause, 26, 28, 29
  extraterritorial, 452
Employees
  age discrimination, 169, 172
  compensation and benefits, 27, 43, 167–69, 173, 177
  discharging or demoting, 163–64, 166–67, 181n39
  discrimination, 167, 169–70, 172
  dispute resolution, 150, 152–53
  drug testing, 171–72
  duties and rights, 161–73
  employer relations, 133, 161
  employment at will, 162, 163
  equal pay laws, 169, 172
  family and medical leave policy, 170–71
  First Amendment rights, 165–67

Index   493

freedom of association, 166
freedom of speech, 166
garnishment of wages, 172
labor union rights, 166
leave benefits, 177
liberty rights, 163–64, 179n16
overtime pay exemptions, 168–69, 182n68
performance appraisal, 177–78
personnel policies and procedures, 178
political belief and association, 166–67, 181n49
posttermination hearing, 164
pretermination hearing, 164, 165
probationary period, 162
procedural due process, 164–65
property rights, 162–63, 180n20
recruitment and selection, 174, 183n99
social security benefits, 173
training and development, 177
voting rights, 172
Employees Retirement System of Georgia, 173
Endangered Species Act (ESA), 259t
Energy use and conservation, 254–55
  federal appropriations, 485
  sources of information, 263–64
Engineering
  for public works projects, 292–93
  selecting a professional engineer, 293
Enterprise funds, 369
  as revenue source, 385
Environmental advisory committee, 260
Environmental courts, 260
Environmental ethic, 319
Environmental management, 237–64

air quality, 240, 253–54, 263
coastal management, 242–43
energy use and conservation, 254–55, 263–64
erosion and sediment control, 245–46
greenspace, 243–44
hazardous waste, 258–60, 264
land use, 240–41, 263
local government impact, 237–38
local government stewardship role, 319
multijurisdictional and regional efforts, 239–40
safe drinking water, 249–50
solid waste management, 212–14, 237–38, 255–58, 264
sources of information, 263
storm water system, 247–48
wastewater systems, 246–47
water quality, 246–50
water quantity, 250–53
Environmental preservation, 203
Environmental Protection Agency (EPA)
  Brownfields Economic Redevelopment Initiative, 259
  sanitary sewer collection, 300
  water supply security assessment, 299
Environmental Protection Division (EPD)
  erosion and sediment control, 245
  hazardous waste regulation, 258, 259
  sanitary sewer collection, 300
  wastewater regulation, 247
Environmental quality
  land use and, 239
  quality of life and, 239
Equal Pay Act, 169
Equity issues, with revenue burden, 404
Equity reserves

issues raised, 378t
sample policies, 383t
Erosion and Sedimentation Act of 1975, 245
Erosion and sediment control, 237, 245–46
  ordinances, 237
ESPLOST (sales tax for capital projects for education), 391–93
Ethical principles, 78–81, 89
  Certified City of Ethics program, 85–86
  in charters and ordinances, 85–86
  code of ethics, 80
  conflicts of interest, 78, 79–80, 84–85
  incompatible offices, 80–81
  model ordinance, 86
Ethics in Government Act, 84
Excise tax
  alcoholic beverage excise taxes, 395
  hotel-motel tax, 397
  rental motor vehicles, 397–98
  revenues, 386t, 386, 387t
Executive branch (state government), 481–82
Executive role, 11, 20
Executive sessions, 98–102, 118
  for appointments or dismissal of employees or officials, 99
  for condemnation of real estate, 99
  exemptions from open meetings requirement, 98
  for potential/pending lawsuits, 98–99
  procedures for conducting, 100–101
Extortion, 83, 86
Extraterritorial powers, 451–52

—F—

Facilitation, 151t
Factor Evaluation System (FES), 175

Fair Labor Standards Act (FLSA), 167–69
False Claims Act (FCA), 87–88
Family and Medical Leave Act of 1993 (FMLA), 170–71, 182n84
Federal appropriations, 483, 485
Federal courts, 63
Federal Emergency Management Agency (FEMA), 339
Federal funds, 401
Federal government devolution, 482
Federal government relations, 474–76, 482–85
Federal Insecticide, Fungicide and Rodenticide Act (FIFRA), 259t
Federal legislation
    criminal action statutes, 86
    liability laws, 71–73
    absolute immunity, 72
    qualified immunity, 72–73
Federal mandates, unfunded, 482
Fermented beverages, excise taxes on, 395
Fiduciary fund types, 367–68, 369
    agency funds, 369
    pension trust funds, 369
    private purpose trust funds, 369
Fiduciary responsibilities, 77
Finance director, and budget preparation, 413
Financial Accounting Standards Board, 364
Financial audits, 419. *See also* Audits
Financial institutions business license tax, 396
Financial Management Standards Act (FMSA), 410
Financial plans, long term, 381
    CIP process related, 431
Financial policies, 377–83
    based on precedent, 379
    concept of, 377
    considerations, 380–81
    continuity, 380–81
    how to develop, 381–82
    obstacles to overcome, 381
    policy book for, 382
    questions and issues raised, 378
    sample policies, 382, 383t
Financial reporting, 361–62
    account classifications, 366
    accounting and financial reporting rules, 364
    annual operating budget, 363
    annual reports, 362
    basis of accounting, 371–74
    budget execution, 419
    financial policy samples, 383t
    fund accounting, 367–69
    governmentwide
        after GASB Statement 34, 370–71
        benefits, 371
    hotel-motel tax revenue schedule, 397
    interim reports, 362
    legal requirements, 363
    letter from auditor, 419
    municipal versus business finances, 362–63
    policy issues raised, 379t
    statement of net assets, 371
    types of statements, 362
    uniform chart of accounts, 361, 366–67
Financial statements, 362
Fines and fees, of municipal courts, 67, 398
Fire alarms and security systems, 106
Fire departments
    emergency communications, 337
    employment and training standards, 337–38
    equipment and facilities, 337
    fire prevention program, 338
    functions and responsibilities of, 337
    insurance ratings, 231, 338–39
    master plan, 337
    minimum requirements and standards, 336
    mission and authority, 336–37
    water supply, 339
Firefighters
    employment and training standards, 337–38
    incompatible offices and, 81
    overtime pay, 168–69
Fire hydrant inspections and maintenance, 339
Fire protection, 335–39
Fire safety education, 338
Fire sprinkler systems, 338
Fiscal emergencies, 381
Fiscal year
    appropriations encumbrances, 425–26
    establishing, 410
Flood control, 296, 298
    storm water utilities, 296, 298
Floodplains, 240, 243
Flow of funds, 372
FLSA. *See* Fair Labor Standards Act
FMLA. *See* Family and Medical Leave Act
Formal agreements among governments, 472–73
Forms of government. *See also* Consolidated governments
    changing a city's, 22
    commission, 3, 12, 16–17
    council-manager, 3, 12, 13–16, 17
    mayor-council ("strong" mayor), 3, 12, 17t, 18f
    mayor-council ("weak" mayor), 3, 12, 13, 17t, 18f
Franchise fees, 399
Fund accounting, 367–69
    after GASB Statement 34, 370
    budget execution, 417–18
    generic fund types, 367–69
Fund balances, 372

contingency funds, 425
how much, 424–25
Funding sources, service delivery, 454

—G—

GAAP. *See* Generally accepted accounting principles
GASB. *See* Governmental Accounting Standards Board
GASB Statement 34, 370–71. *See also* Governmental Accounting Standards Board
General Assembly
described, 476–81
exclusive rights of, 27–28
General fund, 368
capital funding, 436
sample allocations, 412*t*
Generally accepted accounting principles (GAAP), 364
authoritative statement, 427*n*10
generic fund types, 367
recognizing taxes and grants, 373
General obligation bonds, 45, 51, 298
described, 402, 441–42
General obligation debt
education capital outlay projects, 394
financial reporting, 371
SPLOST projects, 393
General revenues, four major sources, 386, 387*t*
General service district, 461
Geographic information systems (GIS), 265–76, 280
benefits and costs, 271–75
concept of, 266–68
coordinate system, 266*f*, 266
database standards, 274
data issues, 273–75
implementation, 272–73
multiagency model, 274*f*, 273

multidepartment model, 273
single department model, 273
local government applications, 267, 269–71
map overlay potential, 268*f*
questions users can ask, 265
related technologies, 268–69
resources, 275
suggested literature, 276
Georgia Academy of Economic Development (GAED), 348
Georgia Air Quality Act, 253
Georgia Association of Chiefs of Police, 334
Georgia Association of Zoning Administrators, 229
Georgia Business Retention and Expansion Process (BREP), 226
Georgia Cities Foundation, 355
Georgia Cities Revolving Loan Fund, 226
Georgia Coastal Management Act, 242
Georgia Code, administrative powers, 44
Georgia Code of Judicial Conduct, 65
Georgia Code of Public Transportation, 294
Georgia Comprehensive Solid Waste Management Act, 211–12, 256–58, 300
Georgia Constitution
community improvement districts, 324
Eminent Domain clause, 26, 28, 29
general constitutional amendments, 31–32
Gratuities clause, 26, 30–31
Home Rule provisions, 26–28, 44, 201
Intergovernmental Contracts provision, 26, 29

local constitutional amendments, 31–32
local legislation, 32
municipal self-government (1954), 25
Planning and Zoning provisions, 26, 28–29, 35
population acts, 32
Special District clause, 26, 29–30
Supplementary Powers provision, 26, 28
taxation and spending, 35–36
Georgia Court of Appeals, 63
Georgia departments. *See under the name of the department*
Georgia Development Impact Fee, 213–14, 218
act, 218
Georgia Downtown Association (GDA), 354, 356
Georgia Downtown Development Conference, 354
Georgia Electric Membership Cooperatives (EMCs), 356
Georgia Emergency Management Act of 1981, 98
Georgia Emergency Management Agency (GEMA), 339, 340
Georgia Environmental Facilities Authority (GEFA)
grant and loan funds, 205, 237
revolving fund for wastewater systems, 246
safe drinking water, 249
Georgia Environmental Policy Act, 259*t*
Georgia Fair Cable Competition Act, 304
Georgia Firefighters Standards and Training Council, 336, 337
Georgia Forestry Commission (GFC), 205
Georgia Future Communities Commission (1995), 452
Georgia Greenspace Act, 243

Georgia Greenspace Commission, 243, 322
Georgia Hazardous Site Reuse and Redevelopment Act, 259
Georgia Hazardous Waste Management Act of 1979, 258
Georgia Interlocal Risk Management Agency program, 73
Georgia Local Government Public Works Construction Law, 189, 193
Georgia Main Street Association (GMSA), 349
Georgia Municipal Association (GMA)
  cable television regulation, 304
  described, 474–75
  electricity and natural gas franchises, 302
  law enforcement certification program, 334
  lobbying at state level, 480–81
  membership, 475
  multiyear purchases, 446
  municipal officials training, 347
  radon gas abatement, 258
  source of help, 228
  standing committees, 475
  telecommunications franchises, 303, 304
Georgia Peace Officer Standards and Training Act, 332
Georgia Peace Officer Standards and Training Council, 334
Georgia Planning Act of 1989, 204–9, 227–28, 241–42
Georgia Planning Association, 229
Georgia Police Accreditation Coalition, 334
Georgia Ports Authority, 194
Georgia Power, 356
Georgia Public Defender Standards Council, 66
Georgia Public Service Commission, 28, 303

Georgia Regional Transportation Authority (GRTA), 210
Georgia Revenue Bond Act, 444
Georgia Rural Water Association, 247
Georgia Safe Drinking Water Act, 246
Georgia Sheriffs' Association, 334
Georgia Soil and Water Conservation Commission, 237, 245
Georgia Supreme Court, 63
Georgia Technology Authority, 284
Georgia Territorial Electric Service Act, 303
Georgia Trust for Historic Preservation, 356
Georgia Water and Pollution Control Association, 247
Georgia Water Quality Control Act, 246
GFOA. *See* Government Finance Officers Association
Gifts to public officials, 82
GIS. *See* Geographic information systems
Global positioning system (GPS), 269
GMA. *See* Georgia Municipal Association
Governing body, powers and duties of, 43–46
Governmental Accounting Standards Board (GASB)
  audit recommendations, 364, 365
  business-type accounting, 363, 364
  capital asset thresholds, 433
  described, 364
  fund types, 367–69, 418
  GASB Statement 34, 370–71
Governmental fund types, 367–68
  budgets, 411
Government Auditing Standards, 45

Government Finance Officers Association (GFOA), 365
Grant programs, 401–2
Gratuities clause, 26, 30–31
Greenspace, 322–23
  government responsibility, 317
  map of, 244*f*
Greenspace Act (Georgia), 243
Greenspace Commission, 243, 322
Greenspace programs, 238, 243–44, 322
Greenspace Trust Fund, 243, 322
Griffies, Audrey T., 131–44
Griggs v. Duke Power Co., 174
Groundwater, 241
Guhl v. Holcomb Bridge Road Corporation, 215

—H—

Hazardous Site Inventory, 258
Hazardous Site Reuse and Redevelopment Act (Georgia), 259
Hazardous waste management, 258–60
  sources of information, 264
Hazardous Waste Management Act of 1979, 258
Hazardous wastes, fire department response to emergencies, 335
Historic and cultural resources, 203, 210–11
Hobbs Act, 86–87
Homeland security. *See* Public safety
Home Rule Act of 1962 (Georgia), 25, 26
Home Rule Act of 1965 (Georgia), 25, 26–27
Home Rule provisions, 26–28, 44, 201
Honest services statutes, 86, 87
Horizontal equity, 404

498 INDEX

Hospital Authority, 52, 54, 95
Hotel-motel tax, 397
Housing, comprehensive planning, 206
Housing Authority, 52, 54, 95
Human resource administration, 173–78. *See also* Compensation; Employees; Personnel management
 employee benefits, 177
 employee recruitment and selection, 174, 183*n*99
 Factor Evaluation System (FES), 175
 pay plan, 176
 performance appraisal, 177–78, 183*n*102
 personnel policies and procedures, 178
 position classification, 174–75
 salary administration, 175–76
 training of municipal employees, 177

—I—

ICMA. *See* International City/County Management Association
Identity theft, 104
Impact fees, 213–14, 218
Incarceration, 68
Income tax
 equity issues, 404
 local option, 398
Incompatible offices, 80–81
Independent authorities, 473–74
Independent school districts, 394
Industrial Development Authority, 53, 95
Information Technology Outreach Services (ITOS), 275
Insurance premium taxes, 395
Insurance Services Office (ISO), fire department ratings, 231, 338–39

Intangible personal property tax, 389–90
Intellectual property rights, 285, 286
Intergovernmental contracts (agreements), 193–94, 472–73
 provision, 26, 29
Intergovernmental coordination
 comprehensive planning, 207, 227–28
 dependent and independent authorities, 473–74
Intergovernmental relations, 469–85
Intergovernmental revenues, 385, 386*t*
 sources of, 400–401
Interlocal risk management agency, 70, 73
Internal service funds, 368
International Association of Chiefs of Police (IAP), 333
International City/County Management Association (ICMA)
 council-manager form of government, 16
 professional management recognition, 21*t*, 21–22, 22*t*
 salary surveys, 176
International Municipal Lawyers Association (IMLA), 86
Investments
 nontax revenues, 398–99
 policy issues raised, 379*t*
 sample financial policies, 383*t*

—J—

Jails, 334–35
 standards and training, 335
Jail time, 68
Joint service agreements, 472–73
Judges, 65–66
Judicial Qualification Commission (JQC), 65
Junkyards, 295

—K—

Knowledge management privacy issues, 285–86

—L—

Labor unions, 166
Land information system (LIS), 268
Land use
 decision making, 240–41
 disputes, 467*n*8
 and environmental quality, 239
 sources of information, 263
Land-use controls, 214–19
 subdivision regulations, 217–19, 294
 transfer of development rights, 219
 zoning and rezoning actions, 216–17
 zoning ordinance, 214–15
 Zoning Procedures Law, 215–16
Land-use planning, 46, 49
 comprehensive planning, 207
 decision making, 240–41
 zoning ordinance, 214–15
Land-use plans, 456
Law Enforcement Certification Program (Georgia), 334
Law enforcement services. *See also* Police departments
 accreditation process, 333–34
 officers overtime pay, 168–69
 self-evaluation process, 334
Lawsuits, 98–99
Legal compliance, audit testing of, 365
Legislation, state government, 476–80
Legislative branch, state government, 476–81
Legislative budget, 413, 417
Legislative responsibilities, 41

Leisure services, recreation and parks, 317–28
Level of budgetary control, legal, 412
Liabilities, in accrual accounting, 373
Liability, 69–74
  breach of contract, 69
  discretionary functions, 71, 72
  federal legislation, 71–73
  indemnity insurance coverage, 72
  interlocal risk management agency, 70, 73
  ministerial functions, 71, 72–73
  motor vehicle waiver law, 70
  negligence, 71
  nuisance, 71
  official immunity, 70–71
  prevention, 74
  respondeat superior, 69
  sovereign immunity, 69–70
  state legislation, 69–71
  tort actions, 69, 70
Liberty rights of employees, 163–64, 179n16
Life insurance premium taxes, 395
Line-item budgets, 420–21, 421t, 423
Litigation, 152f
Lobbying, 84
  how to communicate with congressional representatives, 484t
  at state legislature, 480–81
Local legislation, 477
Local option income tax, 398
Local option sales tax (LOST), 390–91
  negotiations among governments, 471
  statute, 30
Long-range goals, 8
Long-term debt, financial reporting, 374

—M—

Magistrate courts, 63
Main Street and Better Hometown Programs, 226
  four point approach, 350–51
  history of, 349–50
  performance criteria for successful programs, 352
  principles for downtown revitalization, 351
Management budget, 413
Management's discussion and analysis (MD&A), 371
MARTA, SPLOST (special purpose local option sales tax), 393–94
Mayor-council form of government, 3, 12, 13
  executive role, 17t
  organization chart, 18f
  policy making role, 17t
Mayor pro tem, powers and duties of, 42
Mayors
  administrative duties, 41, 42
  characteristics of successful, 4
  communication, 7
  executive duties, 42
  incompatible offices, 80
  legislative duties, 41, 42
  operating cities as a business, 8–9
  planning, 8
  planning process and, 220
  policy-making responsibilities, 15
  powers and duties of, 41–42
  relationships with boards and commissions, 46–47
  roles of, 3–9
  teamwork, 6–7
  trust and confidence, 5–6
  understanding and acceptance of roles, 4–5
Measurement focus, 371–72
Media. *See also* Public relations
  cable television, 141
  good working relations with the, 135–38
  news media records access, 104
  reporters at meetings, 129
  television reporters, 136
  workbook for open meetings, 103
Mediation, 150, 151t
  complex mediation model, 154f, 154
  debate and dialogue comparison, 156t
  face-to-face, 155–56
  protection for participants, 152
  regional planning projects provisions for, 211–12, 228
  small group model, 152f, 153
  team mediation model, 155f
  two-mediator or co-mediator model, 154
Medical facilities, public, grant programs, 402
Medical records, 104
Meetings
  agenda, 7, 97, 102, 122–23
  closed or executive sessions, 98–102, 118
  how to conduct
    agenda, 122–23
    discussion of agenda, 123–24
    order of business, 122
    rules of procedure, 120–24
  minutes of, 7, 97
  notice of emergency meeting, 96–97
  open meetings requirement, 96
  parliamentary procedure, 120–24, 126–28
    calling the question, 127–28
    tabling or postponing the motion, 127
  participants at meetings
    city attorney counsel, 125
    city clerk as record keeper, 125
    city manager role, 125
    councilmembers role, 124–25
    presiding officer role, 124

public participation,
  126–29
preparing for, 119
public access. *See* Open
  meetings
public hearings, 119, 142
public participation,
  126–92
  encouraging attendance, 128–29
  news media relations,
    129
  public record of, 97
  quorum of members,
    96, 117
  regular meetings, 96, 118
  rules of procedure,
    120–24
  special meetings, 96, 118
  summary of, 97
  types of, 118–19
    executive sessions, 118
    pre-meeting work sessions, 118
    public hearings, 119
    special meetings, 118
    visual aids for presentations, 129
    work sessions, 118
Merger of city-county
  governmental functions,
  460–66, 474
Merit System Board, 95
Minimum wage, 167
Ministerial acts, 71
Misdemeanors, 65
Mission statement, 8
*Model Code of Ethics for
  Georgia City Officials*, 86
Modified accrual basis of
  accounting, described,
  373–74
Monthly reports, 7
Motor vehicle waiver law,
  70
Multiyear installment purchases or leases, 444–45
Municipal authorities,
  50–60
  accountability, 52
  advantages vs. disadvantages of, 51–52
  boards of directors,
    52–53
  funding and support
    for, 52
Municipal bonds, 442

Municipal charters, 25, 32
  amendments
    by initiative and referendum, 27
    by ordinance, 27
  contracting authority,
    185
Municipal court personnel,
  65–67
Municipal courts, 63–68
  appeals, 68
  arrests, 64
  citations, 64
  court fees and costs, 398
  defined, 63
  due process and, 64
  environmental, 260
  fines and fees, 67
  incarceration/jail time,
    68
  jury trials, 64
  misdemeanors, 65
  ordinance violations, 65
  personnel, 65–67
  probation, 67–68
  procedure, 63–64
  public defender standards, 66
  right to counsel, 64
  sentencing, 67
  traffic offenses, 64
  warrants, 64
Municipal Courts Training
  Council, 66
Municipal Electric Authority of Georgia (MEAG),
  303, 356–57
Municipal Gas Authority
  of Georgia (MGAG),
  303
Municipal government
  structure. *See* Forms of
  government
Municipal Home Rule Act.
  See Home Rule Act
Municipal indebtedness.
  See Debt; Debt structure
Municipal legislative enactments, 33–35
Municipal officials. *See* Appointed officials; Elected
  officials; Mayors
Municipal revenues. *See*
  Revenue sources
Municipal road contracts,
  187–89

Municipal solid waste
  (MSW) landfills, 256,
  257
Mutual aid agreements
  among governments, 472

—N—

National Association of
  Counties, line-item budgets, 412
National Center for Geographic Information and
  Analysis, 271
National Civic League, 20
National Commission on
  Accreditation, parks and
  recreation standards,
  320–21
National Environmental
  Policy Act (NEPA), 259*t*
National Fire Protection
  Association, 338
National League of Cities
  (NLC), 475–76, 483
National Organization of
  Black Law Enforcement
  Executives (NOBLE),
  333
National Pollutant Discharge Elimination System (NPDES), 245
National Sheriffs' Association (NSA), 333
National Trust for Historic
  Preservation, 349, 350
Natural resources, comprehensive planning,
  206–7, 210–11
Negligence doctrine, 71
Negotiation, 151*t*
News conferences, 139
Newsletters, 141
News release, 139, 140*f*
NLC. *See* National League
  of Cities
Nontax revenues, 398–403
Nuisance doctrine, 71

—O—

Oath of office, violations
  of, 83
Occupational license taxes,
  396
Office supplies, 196
Official immunity, 70–71

OneGeorgia Authority, 205
One-on-one conversations, 7
Open meetings, 95–103
  compliance during an emergency or disaster, 97–98
  exemptions, 98–99
  materials distribution, 103
  media workbook, 103
  noncompliance, consequences of, 101
  notice of meetings, 96–97, 102
  preventing problems, 101–3
  requirements of the law, 96–97
  space for meetings, 102
  televising, 103
Open records, 103–12
  bureaucratic traps, 112
  city actions for public access, 109–12
  compliance, 103
  confidential records, 104–5
  copying, 110
  credit reporting agencies and, 104
  disclosure, 103
  disclosure exemptions, 103–5
  exemption limits, 110–11
  legal review for requests, 11
  legal technicalities and, 112
  penalties and fines for noncompliance, 108–9
  reimbursement for costs, 111–12
  requests for records, 107–8
  timetable for access to records, 111
  trade secrets and, 104
  written record of oral requests, 111
Open space. *See* Greenspace
Operating budget
  as accountability document, 409
  annual, 409

balanced budgets, 410, 424
budgetary trends, 423
capital budget compared, 429
described, 409
fund balances, 424–25
legal requirements, 410–12
line-item, 420–21, 421*t*, 423
policy issues raised, 378*t*
as political document, 409
public review, 411
results-oriented format, 423
sample financial policies, 383*t*
stages of the process, 412–20
  adoption, 416–17
  auditing, 419–20
  execution, 417–18
  overlap of, 420
  preparation, 413–16
Operating statements, 362
Ordinances
  adoption of documents and maps, 35
  amendment of charters, 27
  annexation of unincorporated islands, 233
  basic elements of, 34–35
  codification of, 33
  criminal offense laws and, 27
  enactment of, 32, 34
  erosion and sediment control, 237
  format, 33–35
    body, 34
    definition section, 34
    effective date, 35
    enactment clause, 34
    preamble, 34
    repealer clause, 34–35
    severability clause, 34
    title, 34
  impact fee, 213–14
  model ethics ordinance, 86
  procedural requirements, 35
  Rules of the Road model ordinance, 297*f*

violations of, 65
zoning ordinances, 35, 214–15, 225
Organizational values, 8
Organization charts
  commission form of government, 19*f*
  council-manager form of government, 19*f*
  mayor-council ("strong" mayor), 18*f*
  mayor-council ("weak" mayor), 18*f*
Oversight, operational, 5
Overtime pay requirement, 167–69

—P—

Parks and recreation. *See* Recreation and parks
Parks and Recreation Boards, 47–48
Partners for Livable Communities, 318
Pay-for-performance systems, 178, 183*n*106
Peace Officer Standards and Training Act (Georgia), 332
Peace Officer Standards and Training (POST) Council, 332
Pension trust funds, 369
Performance appraisal, 177–78, 183*n*102
Performance budgets, 421, 422*t*
Permanent funds, 369
Personal politics, 471
Personal services cost explanation forms, 415
Personnel disputes, 150, 152–53
Personnel management, 161–83. *See also* Compensation; Employees
  conflict management, 148, 157*n*5
  constitutional duties and rights, 161–67
  federal statutory duties and rights, 167–72
  human resource administration, 173–78
  policies and procedures, 178

state statutory duties and rights, 172–73
Personnel Review Board, 95
Physically handicapped persons. *See* Disabled people
PlanBuilder Web site, 224, 225
Planning, 201–30
 citizen participation, 222–23
 comprehensive planning, 202–4
 comprehensive plan, 205–7, 241
 DCA approval function, 237
 other components, 209–14
 documents for planning, 225
 economic benefits, 203–4
 environmental preservation, 203
 goals statement, 208
 historic and cultural preservation, 203
 impact fees, 213–14
 implementation program, 209
 intergovernmental coordination, 207, 227–28
 land-use controls, 214–19
 long-range planning, 203
 as management tool, 8
 mediation and conflict resolution, 211–12, 228
 participants in planning process, 219–22
  board of zoning appeals, 222
  chief administrative officer (CAO), 220
  mayor and council, 220
  planning commission, 220–21
  professional planner, 221
  zoning administrator, 221–22
 public benefits, 202–3
 public hearings, 222
 regional development centers (RDCs), 58–59, 204–5, 210–11, 212, 227, 275

regional development impact, DRI review, 209–10, 211, 212, 228
 regionally important resource (RIR), 210–12, 228
 retreat for planners, 8
 solid waste management plan, 213–14, 237
 sources of help, 228–29
 task forces, 223
 vision statement, 208
 workshops for citizens, 223
Planning activities, 223–26
 basic documents, 225
 information collection, 224–25
 plan implementation, 225–26
 planning responsibilities, 223–24
 sources of maps, 224–25
Planning and zoning provisions, 26, 28–29, 35, 49
Planning commission, 46, 49, 95
 role in planning process, 220–21
Planning documents, 225
Police departments. *See also* Law enforcement services
 community oriented policing (COP), 330–31
 functions of, 330–31
 jails or detention facilities, 334–35
 litigation issues, 329
 management, 329–30
 organizational structure, 331*t*, 331–32
 role in community, 330
Police Executive Research Forum (PERF), 333
Police officers
 conduct, 72
 employment and training standards, 332–33
 overtime pay, 168–69
Policy dialogues, 151*t*, 153
Policy-making responsibilities, 12, 14
Policy-making role, 11
Pollution Prevention Assistance Division, 258

Population
 comprehensive planning, 206
 growth (1990–2000), 238*f*
 growth patterns, 239
Population acts, 32
Preaudit function, 418
Privacy issues, electronic governance and, 285, 286
Private purpose trust funds, 369
Probate courts, 63
Probation, 67–68
Professional engineer, 292
Professional management
 ICMA recognition, 21*t*, 21–22, 22*t*
 responsibilities in municipal government, 20–22
 theory of, 21
Professional managers. *See* City managers
Professional planner, 221
Profit objectives, 363
Program audits, 419
Program budgets, 421, 422*t*, 423*t*
Program Fraud Statute, 86–87
Progressive tax, 404
Property, public
 acquisition for public road or transportation purposes, 295
 criminal law provisions, 81–82
 future purchase or condemnation of, 99
 land acquisition records, 105
 management and disposition of, 45–46, 77
 sale of city-owned utilities, 198
 sale of municipal property, 197
 sale of real property, 81–82
Property assessments, 388
Property rights of employees, 162–63, 180*n*20
Property tax
 administrative costs, 405
 ad valorem, 388

Index   503

equity issues, 404
forecasting revenues, 414
revenues, 386t, 386, 387t
  as revenue source, 386–89
  rollback rate, 389
  tangible property tax, 386–89
  tax (millage) rates, 44–45, 389
Proportional tax, 404
Proposals and requests for CIP funding, 436–37
Proprietary fund types, 367–68
  budget execution, 418
  enterprise funds, 368
  internal service funds, 368
Prosecutors/solicitors, 66–67
Public defenders, 66
Public employees. *See* Employees
Public health, grant programs, 402
Public hearings, 119, 142. *See also* Citizen participation
  comprehensive plan, 222
Public information officer, 131, 143–44
Public input. *See* Citizen participation
Public records. *See also* Open records
  confidentiality, 104–5
  file inventory, 111
  of meetings, 97
  minutes of meetings, 97
  open records request, 107–8
  stealing or altering, 83
  timetable for access, 111
Public relations, 131–44. *See also* Media
  appearance of offices and facilities, 134
  broadcast media, 139–40, 140f
  cable television, 141
  CIP value in, 431
  day-by-day contact with the public, 132–33
  direct mail with utility bills, 142

electronic mail, 134–35
employee relations, 133
face-to-face contact, 133–34
news conferences, 139
newsletters, 141
news releases, 139, 140f
personal appearance of employees, 134
reporting to the public, 138
role in disaster preparedness, 142–43
speakers' bureau, 142
telephone contacts, 134
Web sites, 134
written communications, 134
Public safety, 329–43
  animal control, 341–42
  emergency management, 339–41
  federal appropriations bills, 485
  fire protection, 335–39
  police and law enforcement services, 329–35
Public Safety Training Center (Forsyth, Georgia), 335
Public Service Commission (Georgia), 28, 303
Public utilities
  direct mail advertising for the city, 142
  electricity and natural gas, 302–3
  rates, reserves, and transfer policies, 305
  relocation, 295
  sale of city-owned, 198
Public works
  defined, 291
  engineering, 292–93
  flood control, 296, 298
  funding, 444
  selection process for architects, engineers, and technical consultants, 293
  sewerage, 300
  solid waste collection, 300–301
  streets, 293, 294–95
  traffic control, 295–96
  water supply system, 298–99

Public works contracts, 189–93
  advertising requirements, 190
  bidders prequalification, 190
  bond requirements, 192–93
  competitive sealed bids and proposals, 191
  construction management methods, 192
  construction project delivery methods, 191–92
  exemptions, 189
Purchasing, 195–97
  evaluating purchasing practices, 196–97
  invoice processing, 197
  receiving reports and practices, 197
  sample financial policies, 383t

—Q—

Qualified immunity, 72–73
Qualified local government (QLG)
  certification, 205
  environmental planning criteria, 242
  loss of certification status, 205, 211
Quality Growth Assistance Program, 226
Quality of life, 239, 318, 319

—R—

Rabies control, 341
Real estate notes, taxes on, 389–90
Real estate transfer taxes, 390
Reapportionment, 27
Recall Act of 1989 (Georgia), 88
Recall election, 43, 88
Recommendations on issues, 7
Recreation and parks, 317–28. *See also* Greenspace; Greenspace programs
  accreditation standards, 320–21

benefits to municipality, 318–19
community relations, 324
Georgia historical perspective, 317
grant programs, 401
local government responsibility, 317, 319
management
  budgeting, 326–27
  financial management, 323
  personnel, 326
  policy development, 326
open space, 321–22
operations responsibility, 322–24
  organizational structures, 322–23
  recreation and park authorities, 324
  Recreation and Park Policy Board, 323–24
performance evaluation, 324
policy making, 323, 326
program planning, 323
public opinion surveys, 324–25
quality of life, 318, 319
Recreation Enabling Law, 319–20
resources
  expansion and development, 326
  facilities, 325–26
  programs, 325
strategic plan, 325
structure and organization, 321
Recreation Enabling Law, 319–20
Recycling programs, 238, 256, 301–2
Regional Advisory Councils (RACs), 59–60
Regional Development Centers (RDCs), 58–59, 204–5, 210–11, 212, 227, 275
  CIP coordination, 432
Regionally important resource (RIR), 210–12, 228
Regressive tax, 404

Regular meetings, 96, 118
Regulatory agencies, state, 481–82
Regulatory fees, 396
Remote sensing, 269
Rental motor vehicles, excise taxes on, 397–98
Rescue and ambulance service personnel, 168, 182n68
Resolutions, enactment of, 32
Resolutions (state government), 476
Resource Conservation and Recovery Act, 255, 258
Results-oriented budget formats, 423
Revenue
  authority to raise, 385
  availability of, accounting approaches, 373
  balanced flows, 405
  ease of administration, 405–6
  fair share issues, 403
  statutory population formula, 401
Revenue agreements, service delivery related, 471
Revenue bonds
  described, 402, 442
  nature of debt, 444
Revenue patterns, 385–86
Revenue resolution or ordinance, 417
Revenue sources, 385–406
  estimating amounts, 414
  evaluative criteria, 403–6
    ability-to-pay approach, 403
    benefits-received approach, 403
  financial policy samples, 383t
  nontax revenue, 398–403
    alcoholic beverages licenses, 399
    borrowed revenue, 402–3
    compliance costs, 405–6
    controlled substances forfeitures, 400
    development impact fees, 399–400

  fines, forfeitures, and court fees and costs, 398
  franchise fees, 399
  grants to municipalities (and counties), 401–2
  intergovernmental revenues, 400–401
  investments, 398–99
  other revenues, 403
  sale of contraband property, 400
  unauthorized sewage dumping forfeiture, 400
  user charges, 399
  weapons forfeiture, 400
  policy issues raised, 378t
  yields, 1996 and 2001, 386t
Risk management. *See under* Liability
Robert's Rules of Order, 120–22
Roles of mayors, councilmembers, and appointed officials, 3–9

—S—

Safe Drinking Water Act, 246, 249, 298
Salaries. *See also* Compensation
  adjustments, 43
  administration, 175–76
  annual or cost-of-living increases, 176
  merit increases, 176
  salary surveys, 175–76
Sales taxes
  joint sales and use taxes, 391
  local sales tax limits, 390–95
Sales tax revenues, 386t, 386, 387t
School boards, 56–58
School districts
  debt limitations, 442–43
  sales taxes funding, 393–94
School Superintendent, 58
Sentencing, 67
Separation of powers, 11, 12, 14
Service charge revenues, 386t, 386, 387t

Index   505

Service Delivery Strategy, 452–59
  adoption, 457
  agreements, 452–59
    negotiating, 470–71
  annexation and, 234
  components, 453–54
  comprehensive planning and, 227
  criteria, 454–57
  DCA approval function, 237
  Department of Community Affairs and, 452, 457–58
  described, 452
  dispute resolution, 457
  sanctions for noncompliance, 458
  state service delivery regions, 458–59, 459f
  updates, 458
Service Delivery Strategy Act, 239, 452, 467n9
Sewage dumping (unauthorized), penalties for, 400
Sewage management program, 237
  components of, 248t, 248
Sewerage system, 300
Shore Protection Act, 242–43
Short-term goals, 8
Social security benefits, 173
Solicitors/prosecutors, 66–67
Solid Waste Disposal Act of 1965, 255
Solid waste management, 255, 256–58
  collection, 300–301
  composting, 302
  grant programs, 401
  incineration, 256
  landfills, 256, 257
  plan, 212–14, 237–38, 301
  recycling, 238, 256, 301–2
  sources of information, 264
  sustainable practices, 238
  transfer stations, 301
  waste reduction goals, 212, 257–58

Solid Waste Management Authority, 53
Sovereign immunity, 69–70
Speakers' bureau, 142
Special District clause, 26, 29–30
Special district debt, 443
Special district taxes, 390, 391
Special meetings, 96, 118
Special reports, 7
Special revenue funds, 368
Special use tax revenues, 386t, 386, 387t
SPLOST (special purpose local option sales tax), 320, 393–94, 471
State agencies, 480–81
State and Tribal Assistance Grant (STAG), 483
State courts, 63
State government relations
  advocacy, 474–76
  executive branch, 481–82
  legislative branch, 476–81
State liability laws
  nuisance, 71
  official immunity, 70–71
  sovereign immunity, 69–70
Statement of net assets, 371
"State of the city" report, 7, 15
State service delivery regions, 458–59, 459f
Storm water management, 247–48
Storm water utilities, 296, 298
Streets, 293, 294–95
Sunshine laws. *See* Open meetings; Open records
Superior courts, 63
Supplementary Powers provision, 26, 28

—T—

Tangible property tax revenue, 386–89
Taxation
  citizen participation, 270
  confidentiality of tax matters, 99, 104

double taxation for service delivery, 455–56
redistribution of burden, 403, 404
and spending, 35–36, 44–45
Taxpayer bill of rights, 389
Taxpayer revolt (1980s), 386–87
Tax rates
  calculating, 389
  nominal (statutory) vs. effective, 404
Tax revenue, 28
  electronic governance impact on, 286–87
  of Internet sales, 286–87, 289n22
  local option sales tax (LOST), 30, 390–91, 471
  special local option sales tax (SPLOST), 320, 393–94, 471
Teamwork, 6–7, 9
Telecommunications, 304
Telecommunications Act, 304
Telephone habits, 134
Television reporters, 136
Timber land assessments, 388
Tort, 69
Tourism. *See* Downtown development
Tourism, convention, and trade-show promotion, 397
Toxic Substance Control Act (TSCA), 259t
Traffic control, 295–96
  devices and signs, 295
  Georgia Uniform Rules of the Road, 295–96, 297f, 398
Traffic offenses, 64–65
  driver safety courses, 68
  driving under the influence (DUI), 64
Training
  code enforcement, 314
  conflict resolution, 150
  economic development opportunities, 348
  firefighters and fire service personnel, 337–38

geographic information systems (GIS), 272
jail operations, 335
municipal court judges, 66
municipal employees, 177
municipal officials, 347
planning commissioners, 49
police and law enforcement officers standards, 332–33
Transfer stations, 301
Transportation
 comprehensive planning, 207–8
 federal appropriations bill, 483
Transportation Enhancement Act, 357
Trial courts, 63
Trust and confidence, 5–6, 77
Trusteeship, of public officials, 77

—U—

Understanding and acceptance of roles, 4–5
Unfunded Mandates Reform Act of 1995, 482
Uniform chart of accounts, 361, 366–67
Uniform Codes Act (Georgia), 308, 309, 312
University of Georgia
 Business Outreach Services, 355
 Carl Vinson Institute of Government, 229
 College of Environment and Design, 356
Urban and Regional Information Systems Association (URISA), 275
Urban Georgia Network, 354
Urban service district, 461
U.S. Department of Agriculture (USDA), Department of Rural Development, 357
User fees, 399
U.S. Single Audit Act of 1984, 1966 amendments to, 366
Utilities. *See* Public utilities

—V—

Vacancies, and councilmembers, 43
VA-HUD appropriations bill, 483
Vertical equity, 404
Veterans Administration–Housing and Urban Development (VA-HUD) appropriations bill, 483
Vision statement, 8
Voting rights, 172

—W—

Warrants, 64
Wastewater management, 238
Wastewater treatment systems, 246–47, 298
Water and sewer
 extraterritorial services, 451
 land-use plans and, 456–57
 municipal sales taxes, 394–95
 rate differentials, city-county, 456
Water and Sewer Authority, 95
Water management, 240
 comprehensive plan, 299
Water pollution, 247
 grant programs, 401
Water quality, 238, 241, 246–50
 public wastewater systems, 246–47
 safe drinking water, 249–50
 storm water system, 247–48
Water Quality Control Act (Georgia), 246
Water quantity, 250–53
 Atlanta metropolitan region, 251
 coastal counties, 251
 groundwater, 250
 groundwater regions map, 250*t*
 river basins, 250
 map, 250*t*
 Southwest Georgia, 251
 water supply components, 252*t*, 252
Water resources, 240
 federal appropriations, 485
Water supply system, 298–99
 classification, 298
 emergency plan, 299
 fire suppression efforts and, 339
 watersheds, 241
Weapons, forfeiture of, 400
Web sites, 134, 281, 288*n*6
Wetlands, 240, 241, 243
Workers' compensation, 173
Workload measures, 419
Work plan for developing financial policies, 382
Workweek, defined, 167

—Z—

Zoning
 conflict of interest, 84–85, 216–17
 constitutional provisions, 26, 28–29, 35, 49
 factors to consider in decision making, 215
 procedures, 215–16
 rezoning issues, 201–2, 216
 special-use permit, 215
Zoning administrator, 221–22
Zoning Board of Appeals and Variances, 48–50, 95, 222
Zoning maps, 35
Zoning ordinances, 35, 201, 225
Zoning Procedures Law, 215–16